The New Security Concept and German-French Approaches to the European 'Pillar of Defence', 1990-2000

von

Siret Hürsoy

Tectum Verlag
Marburg 2002

Hürsoy, Siret:
The New Security Concept and German-French Approaches to the European 'Pillar of
Defence', 1990-2000
/ von Siret Hürsoy
- Marburg : Tectum Verlag, 2002
Zugl: Marburg, Univ. Diss. 2002
ISBN 3-8288-8431-8

Tectum Verlag
Marburg 2002

CONTENTS

Chapter 1: The New Security Concept in Post-Cold War Europe

2

Preface and Acknowledgements

A historic opportunity without precedent is gradually becoming reality in the 21st Century with the chance taken to pave the way in the period 1990-2000 towards the organisation of defence in Europe. The corresponding conditions have been brought about by concrete steps taken at the Masstricht, Amsterdam, Cologne, Helsinki, and Nice European Council meetings. In the end, the EU/WEU is developing into an 'equal' partner to the US by assuming greater responsibility in the security and defence sphere. The French and German bilateral relationship – which is the driving force behind every European integration process – is the historical force behind this development of the ultimate desire to reach a robust European 'Pillar of Defence' through reconfiguration of the transatlantic relationship. This book provides the first comprehensive and up-to-date analysis of German and French approaches to the European 'Pillar of Defence' from the view of 'Europeanisation' emanating from the process of integration.

In the period of the new security environment, Germany and France are confronted with the need to adjust their national strategic security and defence doctrines to each other in order to realise the new security concept together, which has emerged in the early post-Cold War years. Thus, their historically significant national policies, security and defence concepts, and alliance commitments have entered into a significant mutation. Likewise, in view of the UK's formerly strong but currently loosening Atlanticists' policy, France and Germany's European Integrationists' desire for greater European defence autonomy gradually began to gain momentum after 1990. Although they have different and divergent political motives, strategic cultures, security and defence statuses, the period 1990-2000 saw the reinforced meshing of French and German policies and attitudes. Germany's role is evolving in European security and defence through the *Bundeswehr*'s crossing the threshold of *Realpolitik* and taking a step-by-step military role. France's new role and desire in the sphere of European security and defence, formu-

5

lating the EU/WEU as an 'equal' partner to the US within NATO, often compelled French poli-cymakers to trade-off French national independence with the European integration process. The contours and parameters for evaluating the European 'Pillar of Defence' are indeed very much dependant on the future successful transferral of Germany and France's converging internal po-litical demands from the bilateral to the community level by leaning more towards the EU.

The writing of this Philosophy of Doctorate thesis was finished in early 2002. It was a great pleasure for me to do my research on *The New Security Concept and German-French Approaches to the European 'Pillar of Defence'*, which I developed as a rough idea whilst doing my Master of Arts studies at the University of Kent at Canterbury, UK, and then planned while I was working as a Research Assistant in Ege University, Turkey. Finally, the implementation of this plan was fleshed out in Germany. The single difficulty I met during the writing process, albeit I enjoyed obtaining the information from the first source, was translating some German and French texts into English. Therefore, any deficiencies that may emanate from translating some paragraphs from German and French languages into English are my own fault. On the whole, my years in Marburg, Germany are full of delightful memories. This is not only because I have fallen in love with the beauty of the town, but also because of friendships that have de-veloped during my time there.

From the beginning of my thesis in early 2000 until its completion, many people gave morale and financial support to my studies from North Cyprus, Turkey, the UK, and Germany. Among those people, my depth of gratitude goes for my parents, my mum, Aydanur Hürsoy, and my dad, Yusuf Hürsoy, my sisters, İlknur, Gülnur, and their husbands, for my close friend Engin Hussein, and for Nora Dannigkeit who needs to be particularly mentioned here.

I am indebted to Prof. Dr. Dr. h.c. Wilfried von Bredow, who supervised me, and who read and made helpful comments on this manuscript. Without his patience to listen to my sometimes naïve interpretations about German and French foreign and security policies' and to deal periodically with my absurd personal problems bureaucratically, I would have neither found the courage to continue in this research area, nor the nerve to unravel the enduring bureaucracy.

I would also like to acknowledge the financial assistance of the Konrad-Adenauer-Stiftung, which supplied me with research funding throughout my PhD studies by facilitating my stay in Germany, financed my research trip to the UK and providing the publication costs of this book.

Siret Hürsoy

Philipps University in Marburg,

April 9, 2002

Germany

Abbreviations

ABMT	Anti-Ballistic Missile Treaty
AFSOUTH	Allied Forces Southern Europe
ARRF	Allied (Command Europe) Rapid Reaction Force
AWACS	Airborne Warning and Control System
BAe	British Aerospace
BMO	Basic Military Organisation
C3I	Command, control, communication, and intelligence
CD	Common Defence
CDP	Common Defence Policy
CDU	Christlich-Demokratische Union (Christian Democratic Union)
CEEC	Central and Eastern European Countries
CEP	Centre d'Expérimentation du Pacifique
CESDP	Common European Security and Defence Policy
CFSP	Common Foreign and Security Policy
Cimic	Civilian-Military Co-operation
CINCSOUTH	Commander in Chief Allied Forces Southern Europe
CJTF	Combined Joint Task Forces
CNTBT	Comprehensive Nuclear Test Ban Treaty
COFT	Commandement Opérationnel des Forces Terrestres (Land Forces Operational Command)
CRF	Crisis Reaction Forces
CSCE	Conference for Security and Co-operation in Europe
CSU	Christlich-Soziale Union (Christian Social Union)
DASA	DaimlerChrysler Aerospace
DCI	Defence Capabilities Initiative
DGA	Délégation Générale pour l'Armement
DOM-TOMs	Départments d'Outre-Mer and Territories d'Outre-Mer
DPC	Defence Planning Committee
EAA	European Armaments Agency
EADS	European Aeronautic Defence and Space Company
EC	European Community
ECSC	European Coal and Steel Community

EDC	European Defence Community
EDITB	European Defence Industrial and Technological Base
EMU	Economic and Monetary Union
EPC	European Political Cooperation
EPU	European Political Union
ESA	European Space Agency
ESDI	European Security and Defence Identity
ESDP	European Security and Defence Policy
EU	European Union
FAR	Force d'Action Rapide (Rapid Reaction Force)
FAWEU	Forces Answerable to the WEU
FCC	Federal Constitutional Court
FDP	Frei Demokratische Partei (Free Democratic Party)
FRG	Federal Republic of Germany
FLA	Future Large Aircraft
GDP	Gross Domestic Product
GEC	General Electronic Corporation
GIAT	Groupement Industriel des Armements Terrestres
HQ	Headquarter
IFOR	Implementation Force
IGC	Intergovernmental Conference
INF	Intermediate Nuclear Forces
JACS	Joint Armament Cooperation Structure (Organisation Conjoint de Coopération en matière d'Armements (OCCAR))
JHA	Justice and Home Affairs
KFOR	Kosovo Force
KLA	Kosovo Liberation Army
LPM	loi de programmation militaire (Military Programme Law)
MC	Military Committee
MDF	Main Defence Forces
MLF	Multilateral Force
NAC	North Atlantic Council
NACC	North Atlantic Co-operation Council
NADs	National Armaments Directors

NATO	North Atlantic Treaty Organisation
NATO IMS	NATO Integrated Military Structure
NMD	National Missile Defence
NPG	Nuclear Planning Group
NPT	Non-proliferation Treaty
NVA	Nationale Volksarmee (National Peoples Army)
OSCE	Organisation for Security and Co-operation in Europe
PCG	Policy Coordination Group
PfP	Partnership for Peace
PPEWU	Policy Planning and Early Warning Unit
PS	Partie Socialiste (Socialist Party)
QMV	Qualified Majority Voting
R&D	Research and Development
RCV	Radical, Citoyen, et Vert (Radical, Citizen and Green Group)
RF	Readiness Forces
RMA	Revolution in Military Affairs
RPR	Rassemblement pour la République
SACEUR	Supreme Allied Commander Europe
SACLANT	Supreme Allied Commander Atlantic
SDI	Strategic Defence Initiative
SFOR	Stabilisation Force
SHAPE	Supreme Headquarters Allied Powers Europe
SPD	Sozialdemokratische Partei Deutschlands (Social Democratic Party)
TEU	Treaty on European Union (Maastricht Treaty)
ToA	Treaty of Amsterdam
ToN	Treaty of Nice
UDF	Union pour la Democratie Française (French Democratic Union Party)
UN	United Nations
UNPROFOR	UN Protection Force
UNSC	UN Security Council
WEAG	Western European Armaments Group
WEAO	Western European Armaments Organisation
WEU	Western European Union

INTRODUCTION

Foreign, security, and defence policies are national views of the world, a traditional ground for different national interests, as well as the bedrock of rapprochement at the heart of the historical Franco-German partnership in the EC/EU. For almost half a century, since the foundation of the ECSC in 1950, 'military' and 'defence' remained taboo subjects within the European integration process. Even though the necessity of a *real* European military capability was realised before 1989/1990, the momentum for integrating the WEU's operational and military structures into the EU for the creation of a credible *military-diplomatic* ('soft' military) instrument to back up the European foreign policy (diplomatic/political and economic) instruments was originally resuscitated by the Franco-German letter on the Political Union in April 1990 and the Anglo-French St. Mâlo meeting in December 1998, which marked the formal inauguration of a new and permanent set of security and defence institutions through the gradual integration of the WEU into the EU. Later, the Cologne, Helsinki, and Nice European Council meetings brought to fruition the twofold structures of the Common European Security and Defence Policy (CESDP) towards the end of 2000.

The research area of this dissertation is to redefine Germany and France's new roles in the sphere of European security and defence in the post-Cold War new security era by covering the period 1990-2000. While systematically analysing this period, I also refer to historically significant concepts and circumstances, which occurred in the Cold War era, in order to indicate important continuities in the German and French approaches to European security and defence. The years 1989/1990 are historically accepted as the end of the Cold War era with the collapse of the Soviet Union and beginning of the post-Cold War era with the reunification of East and West Germany and the emergence of a complex *new security concept*. This major change in world politics has instigated a process of reconfiguration in the foreign and security policies' of Germany and France individually, in their security and defence relationship bilaterally, and in their relationships with the European security institutions multilaterally, to such an extent that that reconfiguration, the relationship, and the institutional structure in Europe were still not completed or fully balanced by the end of the year 2000.

The year 2000 is chosen because it is the turning-point of the decade, which saw substantial growth and transformation from a Common Market and an Economic and Monetary Union (including the Euro) to a Common Foreign and Security Policy (CFSP) and a Common Security and Defence Policy (CESDP), with the capability provided to the EU/WEU to decide and act autonomously when the need arose with respect to the new twist on traditional Franco-German aspirations, in favour of strengthening the EU/WEU's contribution to NATO by endowing the EU/WEU with the capability to achieve *a common defence policy* and *a common defence*, with the necessary corresponding links to the US/NATO in the form of two more or less equal pillars concept. Hence, realising the metaphor of the 'two pillars' declared by former US President John F. Kennedy (the simultaneous creation of a 'North American Pillar' and a 'European Pillar') during his address at the Independence Day in Philadelphia in 1962 and using this as a subject for my dissertation in the wake of the construction of the European 'Pillar of Defence', became meaningful and more propitious around the year 2000 than at any other time in the post-World War II period. Yet this could be seen as an elusive goal, the process of inventing a new model of crisis prevention, protection, and management techniques that would cause a new and equitable transatlantic bargain based on a more complex military-diplomatic model appropriate to the new security concept and 'soft' military conflicts of the 21st Century, instead of traditional military interventionism alone, has just begun for the Europeans.

In addition to the new complex military-diplomatic model, which the EU will take on through implementation of the CESDP, maintaining the collective defence clause (Art.V) of the WEU's modified Brussels Treaty with the intention of integrating it into the EU still remains one of the main Franco-German desires. In this context, closer Franco-German military partnership in Europe will continue to matter and foreign and security policies' will continue to converge into the EU's constitutive policies, perhaps even more than ever before, as far as European security and defence integration represents the most important challenge to their future security and defence role in Europe and in the world. For analysing this research area, I formulated a central hypothesis, which is theorised and tested by empirical studies: *Although German and French have different and divergent political motives, strategic cultures, security and defence statuses, the period 1990-2000 also saw a partial convergence of Franco-German policies and attitudes towards the elusive notion of a European 'Pillar of Defence' under the challenge of 'Europeanisation' in the new security era.*

The *theoretical section* of this dissertation pins down a set of concepts, which are central in comprehending the process of partial convergence between Germany and France in the sphere of security and defence, through building a set of ideal-type way of thinking. The *new security concept*, which legitimises 'soft' military missions, compels France and Germany to make the EU assume its own military-diplomatic responsibilities in world politics and, thus, to embark on formulating a European security and defence policy equipped with the necessary military capability for enabling the EU to act independently in crisis prevention and management situations. While contributing the EU with the security and defence policy, France and Germany are confining themselves into regional institutionalisation (or *communitarisation*) through social constructivist temptations, which is enthused by similar expectations among a societal group of states and, accordingly, creates a sense to the concept of 'Europeanisation'. The concept of 'Europeanisation' is not only a means for France to control

14

Germany and for Germany to control itself through converging their political motives, strategic cultures, security and defence statuses into the EU, but also a major desire for the Franco-German partnership to control the international economic competition through the Euro (monetary) block and, finally, to form a European defence 'pillar' within NATO before the finalisation of the European integration process.

The vantage of the end of the Cold War, however, did not help much to forge the creation of the contentious concept of the European 'Pillar of Defence' between France and Germany, with the possible joining of the UK, in the early 1990s. The failure of creating it put France and Germany into a camp called the *European Integrationists*, who are in favour of a total incorporation of the WEU – including Art.V of the modified Brussels treaty – into the EU, with the UK and its supporters' in an opposition camp called the *Atlanticists*, who are in favour of the EU not having a defence role competitive with NATO and the collective defence clause not being integrated into the EU. The noose of dilemma later developed around the perception that if the Europeans' dependence upon the US/NATO is taken for granted, then it would be foolish to strive for a European 'Pillar of Defence' within NATO; and, if the Europeans' were wary about the US military commitment to 'soft' military conflicts in and at the European periphery, then it would be meaningful to ask for more security and defence responsibility sharing through the creation of a European 'Pillar of Defence' separable from NATO. This stagnation in the period 1990-1997 was finally broken in the period 1998-2000 and the differences between the two camps of the spectrum became narrower with the surprise appearance of the UK as a leading proponent of European defence on the side of the European Atlanticisits at St. Mâlo. However, prospects for the creation of a European 'Pillar of Defence' depends on the ability of the European Integrationists and the Atlanticists to act in concert on the future evolution of the two pillars structure of the transatlantic relationship. One should also bear in mind that co-ordination and integration of national defence programmes are urgently needed further consolidation of Europe's defence industry for collective new force structures and procurement programmes if a robust European 'Pillar of Defence' will be created. Moreover, the proponents of the European 'Pillar of Defence' concept – France and Germany – must continue making their *political motives, strategic cultures, security and defence statuses converge*, which has been aspired to during the last decade, but in fact more needs to be done to achieve this.

I predominantly believe that historically significant political cultures and circumstances, which had their roots into the Cold War era, have a determinant constructive role in the analysis of the post-Cold War era foreign and security policies' of Germany and France. In Germany, these policies are conceptualised around the *Policy of Multilateralism, Verantwortungspolitik (policy of responsibility)*, and the *Policy of 'Zivilmacht' (civilian power)* and, in France, these policies are conceptualised parallel to the German foreign and security policies', albeit having an opposite implication, around the *Policy of National Independence, Universalist Policy*, and the *Policy of Power Projection*. Although these foreign and security policy areas are encompassing national, European and international dimensions, this research is constrained to analyse – but not exclusively – the first two domains only.

Germany with the end of the East-West conflict found itself (with population, strategic position, and economics, the strongest power in the middle of Europe) under a greater international responsibility for endowing the entire EU with a security and defence responsibility of its own. It is obvious that, theoretically, Germany has to assume a greater military duty in various multilateral institutions if it wants to contribute to the CESDP. It has been theorised that Germany has to gradually transform its security and defence position in military-diplomatic affairs from 'passive multilateralism' to 'active multilateralism' through contributing to structuring and determining the goals of multilateral organisations in order to forge its

Verantwortungspolitik in the frame of *Moralpolitik* without significantly deviating from the *Policy of Zivilmacht*. The following questions are analysed: Which security and defence roles can or shall Germany undertake in the framework of the European security structure? Is the time for overhauling the transatlantic security and defence relationship approaching in favour of the European defence 'pillar'? What would be the exact German contribution to it?

France, on the other hand, demonstrated a greater willingness to keep its *Policy of National Independence* intact after the end of the East-West conflict, but often compromised with a trade-off between its national sovereignty and the European integration process in order not only to pull Germany into the French aim of balancing power between 'Europe' and the US/NATO, but also to use the EU as a platform for exercising French leadership. French politicians consider that France has been accredited an exceptional role – historical responsibility – in shaping the future European system as a part of its global responsibility. This is legitimised by *Universalist Policy*, which is related to French universal responsibilities, interests, and duties that are directly related to France's unique role in international relations. Thus, France customarily used to translate its interior politics to exterior through its *Policy of Power Projection*, but, since the beginning of the 1990s, France has had to compromise with a trade-off between national power projection and the European defence 'pillar' for the sake of strengthening its own national military leadership role in Europe. The following questions are analysed: What are the basic motives behind the French national interest in the reorganization of a European security structure? Which conditions should be fulfilled for the French to realise the aim of overhauling the transatlantic security and defence relationship in order to create a European defence 'pillar' within – but separable from – NATO for a realistic commitment to European autonomy? Is France, in the beginning of the 21st Century, more ready and willing to sacrifice its traditional Gaullist concepts for a 'genuine' European defence than in the 20th Century?

To contrast German and French traditional security and defence cultures and claim that they are divergent, simply by ignoring the obvious pressure of 'Europeanisation' on exposing German and French foreign and security policies' to the trade-off option with each other in the EU, would indeed be a shortsighted posture. For historically deep-seated reasons and because of their dissimilar understanding of the notions of 'state' and 'nation', while Germany conceives the diffusion of its national power into the EU compatible with further institutionalisation (meaning integration) of the concept of 'Europeanisation' in a federal Europe, France conceives the diffusion of its national power into the EU as a serious encroachment and hardly compatible with an often painful institutionalisation process (meaning intergovernmentalism) so that the concept of 'Europeanisation' could only be brought further if it would lead to a European confederation made up of nation-states. However, this dissertation argues that despite Germany and France being confronted by the transformation of their different political cultures into correlated political objectives, there has never been a serious disagreement on the need to keep the partnership robust and effective. Thus, they have so far been successful in controlling and pushing ahead with the European integration process bilaterally towards the following political objective: To legitimise their power aggregation, steering and projecting European economic, political, and military power collectively, which would individually be impossible to do, as a part of the growing weight of their converging national foreign and security policies for bringing about and employing the 'soft' military and foreign policy instruments for the sake of European responsibility in a globalised world.

The theoretical foundations of the traditional security and defence cultures of Germany and France are further based in each relevant section separately on concepts of US/NATO politics, EU/WEU politics, military strategy and armed forces. Although the relationship between the EU's CESDP and NATO's ESDI is considered by German policymakers to be in favour of *integration* and campaigned for by French policymakers in favour of European *autonomy*, both sides are aware of the fact that full autonomy of the EU/WEU from the US/NATO is neither desirable nor possible in the foreseeable future. This elusive goal is bound to the rapprochement between the Germans' tolerance of the French sensitivities that a strategically autonomous EU/WEU separable from US/NATO is necessary in certain circumstances and the French tolerance of the German sensitivities that building such a strategic entity within a 'Europeanised' NATO in which France would participate permanently is required. In terms of military strategy and armed forces, both countries have already taken a big stride in restructuring, modernising, and professionalising their armed forces through reorienting them from the national to the European level in order to harmonise and increase their crisis-reaction and force projection capabilities in 'soft' military issues.

The *empirical section* of this dissertation supports the findings of theoretical facts through applying and illustrating the relevance of conceptual foundations by relaying on a difficult task of reasoning by analogy. While the Franco-German security and defence partnership is at the core of the European 'Pillar of Defence' discussions, a genuine European defence entity should ideally include the third biggest country in the EU, the UK, if it is to offer reliable insight. Even though London, under Tony Blair, has turned the Franco-German bilateral partnership into a tripartite partnership since 1998, which led to the inclusion of the UK security role in relevant sections, it is obvious that tight security co-operation between Paris and Berlin is indispensable with regard to the Franco-German institutionalised negotiating process. The empirical analysis of this dissertation will particularly focus on close collaboration, special problems relating to the Franco-German bilateral partnership as well as on their individual national foreign and security policies' and interactions with international security institutions. It should also to be noted that drawing firm conclusions from the empirical part of this study would unavoidably lead to some speculation. As far as my hypothesis permitted me, I avoided speculations by arguing that France and Germany, instead of transcending the *Realpolitik*, began to modify their positions to each other in a significant way throughout the 1990s under the supranational pressure of 'Europeanisation'. It also systematically examines the French and German security and defence roles in Europe after the collapse of the Soviet Union, which has spawned to the new security concept and shifted the power balance in favour of Germany, with the end of the division of East and West Germany, and set off a reconfiguration of their traditional and contemporary strategic postures in the future development of transatlantic security relations and European security and defence integration. France and Germany found themselves in an uncomfortable post-Cold War environment, but from the Maastricht European Council meeting in the early 1990s until the Nice European Council meeting on the eve of 2000, they successfully managed to shape the European security order through converging their foreign and security policies to the concept of 'Europeanisation' under the challenge of deepening the EC/EU's integration process.

The German policy-makers in the post-Cold War era found themselves overtaken by 'soft' military issues and thus compelled to become more dynamic in leading a Europe that is more responsible and committed in European and global security affairs. In light of Germany's size and economic-diplomatic influence, which forms one-third of the Euro-zone's GDP, Germans can not simply ignore their own responsibility when a crisis situation necessitates preventive 'soft' military missions in stabilising Europe. Germany, under Helmut Kohl, gradually altered its '*die Kultur der Zurückhaltung*' (the culture of reticence) posture and began diplomatically and militarily to participate, albeit cautiously and step-by-step, in peacekeeping and peace management operations in the 1990s. This is a sign of the 'normalisation' of the German foreign and security policy without being 'normal'. In addition, the SPD-Greens/Alliance'90 government's decision to send German troops to Kosovo, not only indicated a continuation of previous CDU/CSU-FDP government's security policy, but also the *Bundeswehr*'s participation in such a conflict situation, which is not overtly mandated by a UN Security Council resolution, was regarded as a quite revolution in German politics. Nevertheless, it seems the process of 'normality' will never really end and, therefore, every military-diplomatic step will be carefully calculated, analysed, and discussed in Germany.

The superior French political, diplomatic, military, and nuclear position over the financially and economically strong Germans lost its value in the post-Cold War era and the new security environment subsequently challenged the French national independence and autonomous defence doctrine. France, under François Mitterand, tried to contain the reunified Germany by binding it firmly into Western European security structures, notably into the EU and NATO, but continually resisted to be drawn by Germany into a total transfer of its security and defence policy into an integrated Europe. Under President Chirac's new policy style, the French became more aware of the limited capability of the nation-state in a globalised world and gradually began adapting their foreign and security policy conceptions more into a European format – being fully conscious that French leadership could only be realised within a deeply integrated EU – instead of pursuing an independent leadership course. However, without fully participating into, France's NATO *rapprochement*, where Germany has always demanded a clarification of this for its full commitment to the creation of European 'Pillar of Defence', used by French policymakers as a strategy not only to balance German-US/NATO relations, but also to bolstering the French conventional forces' weakness by working together with US's NATO forces in conflict situations and to attempt reforming NATO from *within*, rather than insisting for separate formations *outside* it.

This dissertation also looks at the precise nature of the crucial Anglo-French defence convergence, which took place at St. Mâlo towards the end of 2000. Indeed, for the first time in the history of European security and defence integration, the UK backed a security role for the EU. The British backing of a CESDP for the EU is a historical watershed that would most likely spillover into the common defence realm. The seeds of a genuine European defence 'pillar' have been planted into the Anglo-French Joint Declaration on European Defence at St. Mâlo on December 4, 1998, with the following words: 'the EU will also need to have recourse to suitable military means (European capabilities pre-designated within NATO's European pillar or national or multilateral European means *outside* the NATO framework).' After the creation of CESDP, France seems prepared to put the EU into a major global actor rank in every domain, which would still retain a sort of close transatlantic partnership with the US through NATO, but would resist the US's tendency of snubbing international rules and norms in certain situations through unilateral temptations. On the other hand, the UK and, particularly, Germany conceives the CESDP with a more limited regional role dealing only with EU/WEU's Petersberg Tasks-type collective security missions in and around Europe. All three agree that strengthening the EU/WEU militarily, thus making it a more functional partner for the US, would make negotiating the new transatlantic relationship easier by building the EU/WEU up, instead of pulling NATO down, in a fluctuating global context.

Europe has entered a fundamentally new stage of integration at the end of the year 2000. The Economic and Monetary Union, with the Euro, became reality, but it would not make sense if Europe remains crippled in guaranteeing peace and freedom for itself and for neighbouring regions in the sphere of security and defence. Hence, St. Mâlo became the first step towards a common European defence before a single political will – a European Political Union – emerges. However, there are differences between Germany and France as to what this political union should look like. The institutional reforms, which were promised in the Maastricht Summit in 1991/1992, postponed in the Amsterdam Summit in 1996/1997, and laid on the table in the Nice Summit in 2000, became a major stumbling block in shaping the EU by the year 2005. The main concern is not that the Franco-German couple is heading towards divorce, but how deepening interests and interdependencies would be restructured. The following questions within the vast and diverse Nice Summit agenda are analysed in the epilogue: How will the future of CESDP be effectively and functionally settled in complex structural and institutional nexus? What are the prospects for the creation of a core group of leading military powers in the form of enhanced co-operations in the realm of CESDP? Even though the aftermath of the Nice Summit seems to be irritating both sides, 'an indefinable mystique' of the relationship is that France and Germany appears to be ready to make a serious effort to ensure that their special partnership remains intact.

Although certain developments in the period 1990-2000 are indispensable for the European security and defence integration process, the realisation of convergence in the German-French approaches to the European 'Pillar of Defence' still remains a question of 'if' circumstances compel them into that course. Until Germany becomes comfortable in the use of military power comparable to a 'normal' state and France begins integrating its foreign and security policy wholeheartedly into the EU, it will remain a question of 'how'. A rational reply to the questions above is of course becoming a question of 'when'.

1 THE NEW SECURITY CONCEPT IN POST-COLD WAR EUROPE

'Only the dead have seen the end of war.'

--Plato[1]

'The EU must confess and fulfil its [security and defence] role and responsibility in Europe and in the world.'

--Mathias Jopp,

3rd *German-French Dialogue, Saarbrücken Declaration*[2]

Introduction

The emergence of Western Europe from the Cold War as a 'pluralistic security community' – defined by *Karl Deutsch*[3] as a 'zone of peace' where the war between Western European countries is almost unthinkable – is not a new concept. The concept of 'security through integration' in the Cold War era, which was a by-product of the shared perception of the Marxist-Leninist threat, became an intuitive European integrationism and transnationalism in economic, social, foreign, security and defence spheres in the post-Cold War era.

---

[1] Plato quoted in Mark Helprin, 'Europe Hasn't Seen the End of War', *The Wall Street Journal*, (May 31,1991).
[2] See Jopp's remarks in the final session of the 3rd German-French Dialogue, '3. Deutsch- Französischen Dialog', *Saarbrücker Erklärung*, (Saarbrücken: 31 Mai-01 Juni, 2001); 'Die NATO bleibt Sicherheits-Pfeiler – Europa soll sich zu seiner globalen Verantwortung bekennen', *Saarbrücker Zeitung*, (Juni 2-4, 2001).
[3] Deutsch, K. (et. al.), *Political Community and the North Atlantic Area: International Organisation in the Light of Historical Experience*, (New Jersey: Princeton University Press, 1957).

Since the end of the Cold War, there has been a widespread discourse that 'Europe' is on its own, and that the EC/EU[4] – in addition to economy – should take over its own foreign, security, and defence policy responsibilities. The necessity for further integrationism, transnationalism, and even internationalism in these EU policy areas has been pointed out in *The Economist*, 'the EC's illusion of privacy within the international system, of living in a charmed circle bounded entirely by its own problems and pre-occupations can no longer hold'.[5] Although there is an absence of explicit security guaranty in the EU, the objective of Political Union suggests that there is an implicit commitment to security and defence assistances between the EU members.[6] Nonetheless, the EU states share common values, interests, and expectations and they remain committed to democracy, human rights, freedom, and justice in their own 'European security zone'.[7]

Although the US armed forces were reduced from 300,000 to 100,000 between 1990 and 1997, some US politicians were discussing much deeper cuts. US citizens have also been losing their willingness to accept an extensive US military involvement in Europe. However, this only partly reflects the reality of the situation. Europe has never been alone, as both sides of the Atlantic are sustaining the security culture derived from their common shared experiences. Even so, in the present day few would dispute that new security arrangements between the Americans and Europeans are now necessary, but deciding on what those arrangements should be and how to put them into practice is only one of the difficulties in the transatlantic security relationship. Another difficulty is the US complaint regarding the European culture of depend-

---

[4] Since the ratification of the Maastricht Treaty (or the Treaty on European Union (TEU)) on February 7, 1992, the European Community (EC) replaced its name with the European Union (EU).
[5] 'United in Rivalry', *The Economist*, (July 11, 1992), p.S27.
[6] 'Challenges and Instruments of Foreign and Security Policy', *The EU in a Changing World*, (Bruxelles: European Commission, September19-20, 1996), p.230.
[7] See Karl Kaiser, 'Challenges and contingencies for European defence policy' in Martin, L., Roper, J. (eds.), *Towards a Common Defence Policy*, (Paris: Institute for Security Studies of WEU, 1995), pp.29-36.

ence on US leadership, whist insisting in the same breath that it has to continue. Moreover, every European step towards greater European security and defence integration is considered by the US not only as a danger to the Europeans themselves, but also a danger to US interests. This danger to US interests is clearly defined by Zbigniew Brzezinski as '...a wider but weaker EU to expand the range of American influence without simultaneously creating a Europe so politically integrated that it could challenge the US on matters of geopolitical importance, particularly in the Middle East'.[8] As a result, Europeans and Americans are growing resentful of each other and this becomes difficult to reverse into a balanced relationship.

The question of how future developments in the European security and defence sphere would affect the US involvement in Europe is still a challenge to the EU-US relationship. Although the American politicians will make decisions regarding the degree of US involvement in Europe, the Americans decisions will also be influenced by European behaviour. This is a game of politics that would determine the fate of the EU-US relationship: '...[a] game of hide-and-seek with their real intentions and pulling rabbits out of their hats every now and then when the other party seems to have found a clear move'.[9] However, the end of the Cold War left an intellectual and strategic vacuum in the new security environment so that setting the new rules for the game of hide-and-seek became not only difficult but also extremely complex.

The security environment[10] in the world and regionally in Western Europe has changed. Although the foremost change has been that the prospect of a major inter-state war in Europe

---

[8] Wallace, W. & Zielonka, J., 'Misunderstanding Europe', *Foreign Affairs,* (Vol.77, No.6, November/December 1998), p.66.
[9] WEU Council Report, Rapporteur Mr. Marshall, 'European Security Policy', *Document 1370,* (Brussels: WEU Council, May 24, 1993), p.17.
[10] The security environment has a broad definition. In this study, it will cover *new security thinking* and *military-diplomatic* factors ('soft' military issues) of security. For a detailed study of the concept of the new security environment see, next section and part *(2.1) Understanding The New Security Concept* below.

has been considerably decreased with the fall of the Berlin Wall, if not removed, the underlying assumption for the new security environment is that *Plato* was right: the world will remain a dangerous place. As a result of new forms of global security threats (political, social and economic anarchy), the pacification of international politics is not on the horizon. Post-Cold War Europe is indeed in a strategic vacuum, which is causing a structural crisis, and thus necessitating a change in the organisation of European security in order to meet new security threats. Alas, the post-Cold War period could not entirely eradicate Europe's deeply rooted cultural, political, and historical landscape. For example, the French Gaullism; British Atlanticism; and the lingering fear of Germany's neighbours about the Germans' pre-Cold War impact on European security, and their fear of what the impact of a united Germany on the future course of European security arrangements would be, are all still perceptible. Structural crisis in and between European security institutions carry a high risk, but staying inactive and rejecting security and defence co-operation in the EU would run even higher risks. Washington made it clear that it could not and would not be involved in every trouble spot worldwide, and would rely more on local powers' crisis management capabilities.[11] Even though the US decided to keep its involvement in Europe, it would follow the 'pick and choose' strategy and assume less responsibility for security issues unless they were vital to US national interests. Thus, attitudes, foreign policies, and strategic understandings of the three major EU powers – France, Germany, and the UK – are expected to be different than those of the Cold War period. For the purpose of this study, the focus will be on the first two countries' understanding of post-Cold War European security developments. European integration will mainly be stirred by the Franco-German partnership and exert a major impact on European diplomacy and the overall European security structure.

---

[11] Nye, Joseph S., 'Conflicts after the Cold War', *Washington Quarterly*, (Vol.19, No.1 Winter 1996), p.20.

France and Germany had been Europe's political and economic leaders throughout the Cold War. Since then, they remain the 'motor' of the European integration process and are more inclined to bind themselves and their hinterland into the EU politics. For example, they have been a catalyst in the Common Foreign and Security Policy (CFSP) and the Economic and Monetary Union (EMU) during the Treaty on European Union (TEU) – also known as the Maastricht Treaty. Former State Secretary in the German Defence Ministry, Lothar Rühl, argued that '...the psychology and political ramifications of German unification and opening of the East [as well as] the global impact of what happens outside Europe ... and the US in the next century will define its interests in a different, [more self-centred] way ... if the EU essentially remains [only] a conglomeration of European countries, that conglomeration will not produce a structure.... The Western ties cannot be strengthened unless you have Western European integration'.[12] France is also enthusiastic about the European integration process through far-reaching ties within the EU. It took important steps together with Germany not only in the area of CFSP and the EMU, but also working together with Germany in the area of Political Union. It is the Franco-German 'alliance within the alliance' that the French leaders carefully nurtured, when they had faced difficulties with the Germans. One of the EU ambassadors stated that, 'the political will is there on the German and French side'.[13] This statement will be an essential discourse for the European security analysis throughout this chapter.

In order to conceptualise European security, not only security threats derived from a wide range of directions will be specified, but their diverse natures will also be analysed in section one. The primary European institutions, EU, WEU (Western European Union), and NATO

---

[12] Interview with Lothar Rühl in Bonn, September 1996, in Pond, E., 'Letter from Bonn: Visions of the European Dream', *Washington Quarterly*, (Vol.20, No.3, Summer 1997), p.54.
[13] *Ibid*, p.63.

(North Atlantic Treaty Organisation), which came forward to meet those security challenges are the institutions struggling to shape themselves into a new European security structure. Therefore, this section will be an analysis of the interplay between the EU, WEU, and NATO and how they have been shaped by the development of instruments like the European Security and Defence Identity (ESDI) and the Combined Joint Task Forces (CJTF) in the first half of the 1990s. In Europe, there is scope for different degrees and types of security, different degrees and types of unity and co-operation, and different degrees and types of institutional involvement. This will form the theme of the first section of Chapter One.

Section two will provide the analysis of *Communitarisation of Foreign and Security Policies Under the Impact of the New Security Concept*. This section will be analysed from the perspective of post-Cold War, globalisation, and their consequent impact on the complex new security thinking. The EU, which is economically integrated but not politically, is unlikely to acquire the capability of acting as an effective military-diplomatic entity in non-economic spheres. Therefore, this understanding reopened the debate on communitarisation of foreign and security policies during the TEU discussions. Later, the Amsterdam Treaty will be analysed with regard to the impact of French and German reform initiatives upon the CFSP. The discussion of security issues in this chapter will provide the necessary background for the in-depth analysis and identification of new developments occurring in the European defence sphere. Correspondingly, the conceptualisation of the European 'Pillar of Defence' and European defence developments occurred in the last decade from the TEU to the Helsinki European Council Declaration will be the subject of the next chapter and relevant 'substantive amendments' upon some of the CFSP Amsterdam Treaty provisions, which are amended with the Treaty of Nice, held on December 11, 2000, will be re-evaluated in the Epilogue.

(1) The New Security Environment In Post-Cold War Europe

(1.1) An Overview of European Security

In specialised foreign, security and defence policy think tanks, in academic circles, and in diplomatic meetings on both sides of the Atlantic, there is an ongoing debate about how the new European security arrangements will be shaped. Indeed, the loss of the Warsaw Pact threat meant the loss of NATO's main raison d'être. Former US ambassador to NATO, Robert E. Hunter, said, 'we are turning this great super-tanker of an alliance 180 degrees from its former focus on the single challenge of the old Soviet threat'.[14] This development has brought Europe into the new strategic environment and seriously complicated its long-term future with regards to security. Although progress has been made in the re-organisation of European security institutions, some fluidity remains following the dissolution of Cold War rigidities and nobody knows how and when a new system will freeze into place. This fluidity in Europe, which demands institutional flexibility, nowadays is in the form of instability and uncertainty and can only be managed by a new organisational structure, inter-institutional co-ordination, and flexible security networks.

As a result of the Soviet menace and the difficulty of building consensus within NATO,[15] US officials tended to view other European security and defence alliances, multinational organisations and institutions as a potential threat and rival to NATO. These 'threats' were for example, the Franco-German alliance and the WEU. In the autumn of 1993, R. D., Asmus, R. L. Kugler and, S. F. Larrabee proposed an ambitious program for reorganising NATO to manage

---

[14] Quoted in Kitfield,J., 'NATO's New Horizons', *National Journal,* (Vol.28, No.37, September 14, 1996), p.20
[15] Helmut Sonnenfeld said in July 1996, 'People seem to think that because of the Soviet threat, everything went smoothly within NATO. In reality, every decision was the result of a compromise, and every adaptation was agony. You always had to balance the attitudes and interests of the member states.' Quoted in Kitfield, J., 'NATO's New Horizons', p.23; Kaiser, K., 'Reforming NATO', *Foreign Policy*, (No.103, Summer 1996).

the new security environment. They argued that, in order to build a new Europe, the US should pursue the following strategy: *Firstly*, the priorities of the US should be to share burdens and responsibilities with the Europeans through 'a more balanced and equal relationship.' *Secondly*, NATO should be 'Europeanised' through Washington's explicit commitment to support a stronger European identity in security affairs and to work for strengthening ties with Paris. *Thirdly*, the US should help Germany to strategically emancipate itself and in turn, the German participation in out-of-area operations, including combat missions, would contribute to the Alliance reform. *Fourthly*, the EC and NATO membership should be open to Visegrad countries and the option of their participation to the WEU should be considered.[16] Some political analysts argued that unless the Western European allies were allowed to share burdens and responsibilities in the new strategic environment, the US would not be able to maintain its leadership role in NATO. However, sceptics expressed an opinion that such a new transatlantic bargain could endure.[17] Whether it was for this reason that the US accepted the French and Germans' – and a number of other European states' – initiatives of developing a new ESDI at NATO's Brussels Summit in January 1994 or not, it was obvious that there was a strengthening of will amongst French and German officials toward possessing more weight in the area of security and defence.

Some commentators however argued that the US does not aim to offer a balanced and equal relationship, but to perpetuate America's own supremacy. Schwarz and Layne stressed that, 'American policy-makers seem not to understand that while hegemons love themselves other states inevitably fear them and therefore form alliances to balance against them'.[18] French

---

[16] Asmus, R. D., Kugler, R. L. & Larrabee, S. F., 'Building a New NATO', *Foreign Affairs*, (Vol.72, No.4, September/October 1993), pp.28-40.
[17] Exponents of this view are Huntington, S. P., 'America's Changing Strategic Interests', *Survival*, (Vol.33, No.1, January/February 1991), pp. 3-17; Tucker, R. W., 'Realism and the New Consensus', *The National Interest*, (Winter 1992/1993), pp.33-36.
[18] Schwarz, B. & Layne, C., 'NATO: At 50, It's Time to Quit',*Nation*, (Vol.268, No.17, October 5, 1999), p.18.

leaders are the traditional opponents of the American 'hegemony'. Jacques Chirac, the French President, complained about the US's 'unilateral temptations'. Likewise, Hubert Védrine, French Foreign Minister, said that 'the entire foreign policy of France ... is aimed at making the world of tomorrow composed of several poles, not just a single one ... what is required is not just strengthening the 'several but weakening the one'.'[19] Although France is a stiff opponent of the American 'hegemony' and the one most outspoken, it is not alone in its complaints. There is a German term similar to the French term 'hegemony'. This is the 'McWorld'. This term means that Americans are behaving as if they have a 'blank cheque' in their 'McWorld'. Chancellor Gerhard Schröder, like Chirac, has pointed out the danger of US unilateralism.[20] However, the majority of Europeans' desire to keep the US engaged in Europe and to share security responsibilities between Europe and North America more equally. While the US grabs the responsibility in major strategic confrontations, Europe will be responsible for dealing with less tense prolonged European conflicts. Although such a flexible solution could be seen as weakening the US 'hegemony' in Europe, it will endow the EU with a degree of political will to act alone.

France would like to see the US engaged in Europe only if Washington more actively supports responsibility sharing and allows the Europeans to take some military actions independently. Xavier Magne clearly stated that, 'if Europeans take a more active role on their own continent, that won't stop them from acting in concert with the US when a situation, in Europe or else-

---

[19] The term hegemony is also described as 'connoting menace'. Védrine and other French leaders have given another name to the US: 'hyperpower'. This term in French, as in English, means excessive, needing to be diminished. For similar critics see, Muravchik, J., 'How to Wreck NATO', *Commentary*, (Vol.107, No.4, April 1, 1999), pp.29-34.
[20] There is also a difference between French and German attempts in weakening the hyperpower. While French politicians are explicitly trying to pull Americans down, Germans are trying to do this implicitly. The authors of 'How to Wreck NATO' explained this difference between German and France policies through 'abstraction' and 'not abstraction'. *Ibid*, p.32.

where, warrants it.'[21] Another French think tank deputy director, Dominique Moïsi, stated the benefits of US commitment to Europe as: 'A European force is a plus for the US, because it means you won't have to do the dirty work alone'.[22] Germany, traditionally being a strong proponent of NATO and the EU, considers all type of multinational institutions a vehicle for its own defence and economic fortunes. Under these circumstances the Germans' support for the idea of responsibility sharing, which is significant for the EU security and defence sphere, should not be surprise. Former German State Secretary in the *Auswärtigen Amt* (Federal Foreign Office), Wolfgang Ischinger, said: 'In Europe we have more soldiers than the US. However, their suitability for the kinds of missions now required leaves something to be desired. This problem can only be solved by constructive approaches based on integration'.[23] He also stressed that Europeans have a long way to go to achieve equitable burden and responsibility sharing. The problems in European security and defence initiatives lie in putting principles into practice,[24] and managing these initiatives requires both strategic vision and political will.

Fundamental structural security changes in Europe are influencing the responsibilities of both the US and EU to such a degree that a transformation of the old transatlantic bargain into a new partnership needs to be accomplished. However, without knowing what these new security threats in the European periphery are, one cannot define the process of developing a new security and defence structure for the EU. Thus, it is important to review the new potential threats or risks in the periphery of Europe and analyse later how the EU, WEU, and NATO could respond to them.

---

[21] Xavier Magne is a French captain see, Dahlbung, T-J., 'Plan for Europe Strike Force Worries US', *The Los Angeles Times*, (Dec 6, 1999), p.3.
[22] *Ibid.*
[23] Interview with Wolfgang Ischinger conducted by Peter Hintereder and Michael Zipf. See 'Contours of a New German Foreign Policy', *Deutschland*, (No.4, August/September 1999), pp.18-21.

(1.1.1) Post-Cold War Security Threats: Europe's Periphery

Europe's periphery encompasses a broad range of multi-facet risks. In other words, conflicts occur in and/or emanate from, which later gives rise to cross border (spillover) threats, in geo-graphically proximate neighbouring regions of Europe. The current European security arrangement represents neither a bipolar formation of the two alliances (NATO and the EU/WEU[25]) nor a pan-European order of collective security (OSCE) for a wide range of responses to multi-facet risks. Furthermore, zones of security today divide Europe into two. One of the security zones is the EU – a security zone that has been stirred by the preponderant Franco-German partnership as the core of a central consensual formation (or a 'regional order'). The integration process brought the EU into an improved position in economic, political, and even military spheres (currently with the help of the US). The other security zone is Europe's periphery – a security zone that includes the European eastern and southern arcs and remained inferior in economic, political, and in military spheres. In contrast to the classical imperial influence, 'regional orders' emerge from a consensual bargain, not from coercion. Kupchan explained the 'regional order' as the '[centre] engages in self-restraint and agrees to subject the exercise of its preponderant power to a set of rules and norms arrived at through multilateral negotiations'.[26] In turn, the EU's eastern arc, as far as the applicant Central and Eastern European Countries (CEECs) are concerned, enters willingly into the EU's zone of influence.

The key challenges in Europe's periphery are so diverse, that the EU often does not know how to react and finds itself hesitant and troubled. Raymond Aron described the Cold War era as

---

[24] Dale, R., 'Defending Europe: The problems lie in putting principles into practice', *Europe*, (Washington, No.351, November 1995).
[25] It has been agreed among the members of the EC in the TEU discussions that, in principle, the WEU is the defence arm of the EU and since Cologne European Council decision on June 4, 1999, the WEU partly combined with the EU. For more information, see the second section of this Chapter and Chapter 2.
[26] Kupchan, A. C., 'After Pax Americana', *International Security*, (Vol.23, No.2, Fall 1998), pp.42.

'peace impossible, war improbable'. Hassner explained this phrase as 'neither peace nor war' and further explained the post-Cold War situation as 'both peace and war'.[27] While the idea of settling any kind of dispute by military means in the centre of Europe would be considered improbable, this is not the case for Europe's periphery. The challenges and difficulties the EU faces are extremely complex, because we are living both in the era of peace and war.

The EU's southern arc, from North Africa, Middle East to Central Asia, is potentially a troublesome region that threatens the EU's security. Islamic radical movements in some countries, for instance in Algeria, Libya, Sudan, Syria and Iraq, might require military intervention to bring peace and stability, evacuation of EU citizens, or protection of civilians. Demographic and economic pressures might lead to a flood of immigrants into the EU. Last, but not least, tensions on sharing natural resources, for example, beggar-thy-neighbour policies for water and oil, might cause regional wars. The EU in all these cases may find itself in a position of intervening militarily in order to protect its economic, social, and political interests, to protect cities and citizens, or prevent the proliferation of weapons of mass destruction.

The EU's eastern arc is quite different from its southern arc. The CEECs' Europeanness and their potential EU membership process separate the eastern arc noticeably from the southern arc. The eastern arc has not only been the source of instability (inter-state ethnic conflict, resurgence of nationalism, border disputes, regional wars, fragile economic performance, illegal drugs' trade, religious extremism and migration) that increases the tension of insecurity, but

---

[27]'Peace was impossible as a result of the ideological confrontation of the two blocks and war was improbable because of their state of equilibrium, which was fixed by their nuclear weapons. In the post-Cold War period, on the other hand, peace has become a little less impossible thanks to the disappearance of the ideological schism but war was become a little less improbable because of the combination of political and economic anarchy and nuclear proliferation.' Hassner, P., 'An Overview of Problem' in Gnesotto, N. (ed), 'War and Peace: European Conflict Prevention', *Challiot Paper 11*, (Paris: Institute for Security Studies, WEU, October 1993), p.4.

also has twice been the catalyst in a global confrontation. Henry Kissinger observed that, 'the

principal cause of European conflicts [...] has been the existence of a no man's land between

the German and Russian people'.[28] However, withdrawal of Russians from the region left the

regional countries as the 'orphans' of the Cold War by creating a 'security vacuum' or 'secu-

rity limbo' and unleashed long-term suppressed national animosities.[29] Josef Joffe

paraphrased Thomas Hobbes: 'In the East, history returned in the guise of long-suppressed

nationalities. ..."nasty, brutish and prolonged"' and; Goldstein and Lanzo argued that,

'...Europe is unstable and torn by hyper-nationalism and ethnic conflict that could potentially

explode into a continent-wide conflagration ... although ... a conflict beginning there [in

Eastern Europe] and engulfing Western Europe is highly unlikely'.[30] The instability has

returned to Europe's eastern and southern arcs.

However, the different security threats are causing different security concerns among the EU

countries from south to north and from east to west.[31] These diverse threats are towards the

EU and should be repelled at the European Community level collectively. However, in the

present situation there is no 'clear and present danger' in the form of an 'identifiable enemy',

stated Borislaw Geremek, and further argued, 'it was easier to see the enemy, but it is not easy

to see dangers.'[32] Such diverse insecurity and uncertainty in the periphery of the EU not only

---

[28] Henry Kissinger quoted in Price, A. H., *The International Politics of East Central Europe*, (UK: Manchester University Press, 1996), p.223.
[29] Martin Wight presented a very good explanation to 'power vacuum'. He argued that 'power vacuum' is also a 'buffer zone', '[a] region occupied by one or more weaker powers between two or more strong powers' in Price, -H.A., p.225; For the 'orphans' of the Cold War, see Zielonka, J. 'Security in Central Europe', *Adelphi Paper 272*, (London: IISS, 1992).
[30] Joffe, J. 'The New Europe: Yesterday's Ghosts', *Foreign Affairs*, (Vol.72, No.1, 1992), p.39; Goldstein, L. & Lanzo, D., 'Negotiating New Terrain', *Harvard International Review*, (Vol.15, No.2, Winter 1993), p.46.
[31] While southern and western EU member states are concerned about developments in the Mediterranean region, eastern and northern EU members are concerned about developments in the Central and Eastern Europe and Russia. For example, Helmut Kohl stated that 'the West's frontier must no longer be Germany's eastern border' in Dale, R., 'Defending Europe: The problems lie in putting principles into practice'. France, on the other side, launched a dialogue with southern European countries at Barcelona in November 1995.
[32] Borislaw Geremek, 'Post Communist Challenges' in Clesse, A., Cooper, R. & Sakamato, Y. (eds.), *The International System After the Collapse of the East-West Order*, (Dotdrecht Martinus Nijhoff, 1994), pp.356-61

requires planning a formal structure against possible conflict scenarios, but also requires military preparation. However, divergence of security threats, such as who the enemy is, decreases the confidence in any sort of scenarios.

In this new security environment, enormous changes in the EU's periphery influenced immediate institutional changes in the West. NATO, a primary security institution dominated by the US, is now faced with an uncertain future. It is clear that NATO was geared to a massive land war in Europe and not to deal with post-Cold War security threats in the new European security environment. Other European institutions are arguably better suited to address the new security problems, notably the EU and the WEU. Despite the redefinition of NATO during the January 1994 Brussels summit,[33] its enlargement plans towards the East and out-of-area missions met with French opposition. One of the main reasons for NATO's enlargement towards the East was to fill the 'security vacuum' in Europe between Germany and Russia and bring about economic and political reform. However, the French political elite argued that the crisis in Europe would be more appropriately addressed by the EU/WEU. Hubert Védrine criticised NATO's expansion, saying it would be a 'Trojan horse' for Washington to keep Europe under the US hegemony.[34] On the other hand, the German political elite considered NATO's expansion differently than the French. Volker Rühe's statement is still finding resonance among German policymakers:

> *'On both sides of the Atlantic it must be made clear why we still need the US*
>
> *commitment to Europe.... Europe still has a long way to go before it can act on the*
>
> *basis of a really unified power. The political evolution in Europe is not yet*
>
> *finished. Although Europe is no longer suffers from a military threat that could*

---

[33] See *Partnership for Peace (PfP) Invitation*, (Brussels: NATO Office of Information and Press, January 10-11, 1994); *Declaration of the Heads of State and Government Participating in the Meeting of the North Atlantic Council Held at NATO Headquarters*, (Brussels: NATO Office of Information and Press, January 10-11, 1994).
[34] Kitfield, J. 'NATO's New Horizons', *National Journal*, (Vol.28, No.37, September 14, 1996), p.22.

> *lead to a devastating war, it is now plagued by a number of local crisis and*
>
> *regional conflicts that had previously been suppressed under the concrete layer of*
>
> *the communist dictatorship'.*[35]

Ironically, although the Americans proposals to renew NATO have been received negatively by some European countries, this should be balanced by a co-operative effort between the Europeans and Americans through addressing it to new security challenges. The co-operation for burden and responsibility sharing will be understood better through the following two scenarios. According to the first scenario, advanced military threats ('hard' military issues) from outside the EU might require a complex defence. The second scenario is the occurrence of chaos, inter-state ethnic conflict, nationalism, or regional war threats ('soft' military issues) in Southern and Eastern Europe, which might necessitate a limited military intervention, peace-keeping and policing response.[36] A military structure designed for the first differs for a military structure designed from the second. In the former scenario, the EU needs the US leadership both militarily and politically. In the latter scenario, the EU/WEU should be able to increase their capability for taking on some 'soft' military responsibilities. Europeans understood well that in an increasingly interdependent world, they must be prepared to go to the crisis' source, rather than waiting it to grow up and reach to them. However, the two wars in the Balkans and the Europeans' obvious military shortcoming in the Kosovo operation had proved once again that they are still dependent on the military capability of the US for handling trouble spots in their own continent. Indeed, the multiplicity of potential roles in different scenarios today can only be met by preserving the flexibility, burden, and responsibility sharing among security institutions, notably between the EU/WEU and NATO.

---

[35] Volker Rühe quoted in Conry, B., 'The WEU as NATO's Successor', *Policy Analysis*, (Cato Institute: No.239, September 18, 1995), p.6.
[36] 'Soft' military issues and 'hard' military issues are also known as 'low-intensity' conflicts and 'high-intensity' conflicts. For an excellent description of 'soft' and 'hard' military issues see, Paul Latawski, 'Central Europe and

(1.1.2) Fine Balancing the Western Institutions: EU/WEU and NATO

Books, journals, and newspaper articles are continuously circulating proposals for new European security arrangements. Political analysts are continually arguing over the vague European security arrangements, which have emerged from the rubble of the post-Cold War security environment. In broad terms, some propose the reformation of existing institutions, some interlocking of institutions and others, a very few, offer the creation of new institutions. Following 'hard' and 'soft' military issues from the previous section, this section will contain and analyse to give those diverse scenarios form.

Today no state in the world, not even a superpower, is powerful enough to manage global 'hard' and 'soft' military issues alone. Therefore, the US can only manage to continue to be a superpower by 'enabling' and 'mobilising' coalitions. A leading official from the former Clinton Administration described the US pivotal role in the world as, 'leading and shifting coalitions of friends and allies to address shared security concerns'.[37] In order to make such coalitions, interoperability of equipment and common rules of engagement viable, burden and responsibility sharing arrangements need to be agreed.

Since the London Declaration of 1990, the US is supporting the development of the ESDI through every high-level NATO document in order to enhance the contribution of Europe to the Alliance *within* NATO and create options for military response to situations where the US decides not to act.[38] It was agreed during NATO's Brussels Summit of 1994 that the US would commit to assist militarily in strengthening European states' defence capabilities for

---

European Security', in Park, W. & Rees, W. (ed.), *Rethinking Security in Post-Cold War Europe*, (New York: Addison Wesley Longman Limited, 1998), pp.82-95.
[37] Nye, S.J., 'Conflicts after the Cold War', *Washington Quarterly*, p.20.
[38] 'London Declaration on Transformed North Atlantic Alliance', *North Atlantic Council Heads of State and Government Meeting*, (Brussels: NATO Office of Information and Press, July 5-6, 1990); also see Cox, M. *US Foreign Policy after the Cold War*, (London: Royal Institute of International Affairs (RIIA), 1995).

European operations.[39] This was later endorsed in NATO's Berlin agreement in 1996. The

Berlin agreement on the CJTF concept made the EU/WEU-led military missions possible

under the leadership of the 'coalitions of the willing'. The CJTF concept is based on a 'single

multinational command structure,' 'separable but not separate' capabilities, assets,

headquarters and command positions.[40] In other words, some NATO members could use

NATO structures to fulfil certain tasks with non-NATO countries' participation where the US

decided not to act. This means that the EU/WEU could have a diplomatic-military leadership

capability through forces and staff acquired from within NATO and supplemented by those of

the WEU states that are not represented in NATO.[41] The CJTF is also a milestone for the

EU/WEU in that it can execute its policies through a military force with the invitation of

NATO forces and staff to conduct military missions, for example, for peacekeeping and

conflict management.

Although Europeans gained some responsibility within NATO through the ESDI and the

CJTF, the US is in fact intolerant of any notion that would put NATO into a secondary posi-

tion. Van Mierlo was considered the CJTF '...not only decisive for a credible operational role

for the WEU and NATO itself, but also a test case for NATO-WEU relations.'[42] However, the

interoperability is not yet tested in reality and thus there are important questions awaiting an-

swers. The difficulties for the EU/WEU in use of the operational capability of the CJTF are

---

[39] NATO North Atlantic Declaration, July 10-11, 1994. *Berlin North Atlantic Council Ministerial Meeting*, (Brussels: NATO Office of Information and Press, M-NAC1(96)63, June 3, 1996). Former US President Bill Clinton said in June 17, 1994, that, 'we want Europe to be strong. That's why America supports Europe's own steps so far towards greater unity in the EU, the WEU and the development of a European security identity.' *The Financial Times*, (July 17, 1994).

[40] Berlin North Atlantic Council, July 3, 1996, paragraph 3 and 5. The CJTF stands for deploying conventional, multinational (combined) flexible, inter-service (joint) force combination (task forces) across the full range of contingencies. It should be noted that, although the CJTF is established between NATO and the EU/WEU, it is technically under the NAC/NATO auspices. For detailed analysis of the CJTF, see Barry, C., 'NATO's Combined Joint Task Forces in Theory and Practice', *Survival*, (Vol.38, No.1, Spring 1996), pp.81-97.

[41] Schake, K., Laine, A. B. & Grant, C., 'Building a European Defence Capability', *Survival*, (Vol.41, No.1, Spring 1999), p.23.

[42] Van Mierlo, H., 'The WEU and NATO: Prospects for a more balanced relationship', *NATO Review*, (No.2, March 1995), p.9.

several. Firstly, assets assigned to the CJTF are primarily national. This first problem generates the second difficulty: keeping the principle of unity in a single multinational command structure for the EU/WEU-led operations will not be an easy task. Thirdly, although the US agreed in principle to make its national assets available to its European allies for military operations that itself would not involve, this does not mean that the US is offering them a signed 'blank cheque' for unknown future circumstances.[43] This dependency of the EU/WEU and the CJTF upon the US/NATO support, led Simon Duke to argue that, 'the possibility of a *de facto* US veto over non-NATO area uses of WEU use of the CJTF therefore still exists'.[44] It can be deduced from these three main difficulties that potential EU/WEU-led operations will not only remain small in scope for the foreseeable future, but also that the US would decide on the use of its assets on a case-by-case basis. Robert Hunter defined NATO's new burden and responsibility sharing between the Americans and Europeans as:

> *'[The Europeans] will need to support defence budgets; NATO will continue to be*
> *an additional multinational institution through which Germany expresses its*
> *future; it reassures Europeans that they have the capacity to conduct operations if*
> *for some reason the US doesn't want to participate; and it convinced France that*
> *instead of trying to create a military capacity outside of, and in competition with,*
> *NATO, it would create something within NATO. So we are at an extraordinary*
> *moment in NATO, when on the central issues we are all singing the same sheet of*
> *music'.*[45]

---

[43] Cottey, A., 'NATO Transformed: the Atlantic Alliance in a new era', in Park, W. & Rees, W., (ed.), *Rethinking Security in Post-Cold War Europe*, pp.43-60. Also see Bowen, W. N. & Dunn, D. H. *American Security Policy in the 1990s: beyond containment*, (US: Dartmouth Publishing Company Ltd., 1996), pp.68-72.
[44] Duke, S., 'The Second Death (or the Second Coming?) of the WEU', *Journal of Common Market Studies*, (Vol.34, No.2, June 1996), p.179.
[45] Kitfield, J., 'NATO's New Horizons,' *National Journal*, (Vol.28, No.37, September 14, 1996), p.30.

Nevertheless, as a result of the difficulties before the EU/WEU use of the CJTF, many American officials do not – want to – understand that some steps have also been taken to enhance the operational capability of the EU/WEU. The analysis conducted by the RAND Corporation stressed that, 'American resistance to the formation of an EU identity within NATO will only rekindle European interests in an eventual EU military alliance outside NATO'.[46] It seems after all, German and French approaches to the recent new security and defence arrangements are imperative in determining the fate of these arrangements.

Since Konrad Adenauer, Germany not only firmly became embedded in the European political and economic integration, but also committed itself to support NATO in Europe for security and political reasons. Therefore, Germany is supporting the subordination of the ESDI to NATO. With the unification of Germany, withdrawal of Soviet troops and reduction of US troops in Europe in 1990, Germany also pressed for deeper European security and defence integration. It is partly because of the German traditional loyalty to multilateral institutions and partly because of its strong commitment to the European integration process, that Germany with the end of the Cold War is more in favour of the WEU than during the Cold War. Former Chancellor of Germany, Helmut Kohl, observed that NATO is evolving into a looser structure and therefore he considered the WEU as a viable European security organisation in the long-term.[47] Germany today is taking new diplomatic and economic initiatives in Eastern Europe, Russia and the Balkans, and is strengthening its military ties with France and stabilising the former Soviet Union, Southern Europe, and the Middle East. These initiatives demonstrate that Germany will be an active leader in the new Europe if the German political consciousness decides to integrate German security and foreign policies within a wider European framework. German Chancellor Gerhard Schröder said that, 'the

---

[46] Wallace, W. & Zielonka, J., 'Misunderstanding Europe', *Foreign Affairs*, p.80.

conflicts in Bosnia-Herzegovina and Kosovo have shown in a dramatic way that Europe must be able to act in a crisis. The EU must get political and military decision-making structures, and the ability of crisis awareness and crisis management'.[48] It is obvious that diplomatic and economic spheres of security are insufficient to preserve the European order, and in the military sphere, Germany is primarily dependent on its West European neighbours and notably to the US. However, the US military deployment in Europe cannot endure. As German Defence Minister Rudolf Scharping said, 'American politicians, not only in the Senate but in public discussion generally, have to make big efforts to explain to the public why they should be engaged in Kosovo with billions of dollars and thousands of soldiers even though their vital interests are not in the least involved'.[49] This is not to say that transatlantic relationship is no longer needed or Germany is turning against the US. On the contrary, Germany and France are together demanding more European responsibilities for managing European conflicts and decreasing the burden from the American shoulders (see Chapter 4).

On the other hand, under Chirac's presidency, French-NATO relations have gained a new orientation for the first time since France left NATO's integrated military structure in 1966 under the presidency of Charles de Gaulle. However, it should be noted that French-NATO relations has never been at ease. During the CJTF discussions, France argued that the CJTF should be kept outside the existing NATO structure. France was seeking the possibility of independent operations conducted by the EU/WEU, which would draw on some NATO military capabilities through the CJTF, but would not fall under the NATO command. Wyn Rees explained the French frustration as, '...the idea of a US officer having a veto over a military operation that would be predominantly European in nature, was a bone that stuck in French

---

[47] *Ibid.*
[48] Gerhard Schröder quoted in Dahlbung, T.T., *The Los Angeles Times*, (December 6, 1999), p.2
[49] Rudolf Scharping quoted in Whitney, R. C., 'US and NATO Allies Divided Over Defence Needs', *New York Times*, (December 3, 1999), p.20.

throats'.[50] Nevertheless, the decision to build the ESDI, within rather than outside NATO, and the concept of the CJTF became radical steps for closer co-operation between France and NATO's integrated military command. For example, France accepted the subordination of French troops in the Eurocorps to NATO's Supreme Allied Commander in Europe (SACEUR) through the CJTF if a crisis in Europe necessitates this. Enhancement of the WEU's operational capability through the ESDI and the CJTF brought French military forces closer to NATO's military planning. In other words, all forces assigned to the possible employment of the WEU are also assigned to NATO's integrated military command. Therefore, any possible EU-led operation not only requires co-ordination between the WEU and NATO, but also requires co-operation between France and NATO. Moreover, by December 1995, French executives made their new pragmatism official by fully joining into the NATO Military Committee and announcing the French Defence Minister's further participation – but not joining – in NATO's integrated military command.

The new French approach towards NATO reflects the French intention of influencing NATO's reform process. Former French Foreign Minister, Hervè de Charette, argued that Americans were willing to oblige to give NATO a European defence identity, partly because they wanted talks on NATO's enlargement and he stressed at that time that France could have blocked this unless the new European military structure reflected the desired European identity.[51] France's main aim has been to influence the US/NATO and to develop an autonomous EU/WEU capability for intervening in regional crisis where European interests are at stake. Ironically, the war in Bosnia and in Kosovo forced French policymakers to accept that US help for European security problems is still needed. However, the interesting thing is that France supports the US role in European security, not NATO's role. According to France,

---

[50] Rees, W. G., *The Western European Union at the Crossroads*, (US: Westview Press, 1998), p.86.

the US should become a bilateral partner to the EU in the security sphere.[52] However, the

continuous US doggedness in NATO is endangering the healthy transatlantic relationship

between the EU and US. After all, it seems French-NATO convergence will work better in

theory than in practice (see Chapter 5).

Germany and France are the two major dominant states in the new Europe and, thus, it is natu-

ral for them to expand their military co-operation in order to meet their mutual security inter-

ests. According to the Germans, France is a necessary security partner and the US will stil!

remain an important security partner but in a diminished form.[53] On the other side, French and

Americans are the two extreme thinkers about the European security debate at a level of gen-

erality that is either too high or too low. For France, the US troops at a low level would stay in

Europe with little regard to what these forces will really do; and, at a high level, a reformed

EU/WEU backed by the Franco-German 'motor' that will not subordinate to NATO. For the

US, at a low level, the French idea of searching for an *ideal* post-Cold War European security

structure between the two equal pillars – US/NATO and the EU/WEU – will be kept as rheto-

ric; and, at a high level, a reformed and dominant NATO in Europe will not tolerate taking a

back seat to the EU/WEU.

France and the US[54] are also at the extremities in the European security and defence debate in

a positive sense. France has begun to accept that NATO will likely remain the guarantor of

European security and defence in the foreseeable future. The US, on the other hand, has begun

to encourage the growth of the EU/WEU force and to transfer some security responsibilities to

---

[51] 'NATO Acquires a European Identity', *The Economist*, (8-14 June, 1996), pp.43-44.
[52] Schmidt, P., 'Germany, France and NATO', *Report presented in Stiftung Wissenschaft und Politik in Ebenhausen*, summarised by Rapporteur Maria R. Alongi, (Ebenhausen: June 1994), pp.1-8.
[53] Bracken, P.&Johnson, S., 'Beyond NATO:Complementary Militaries',*Orbis*, (No.5, Spring 1993),pp.205-221
[54] The UK, a traditional *Atlanticist*, has always backed the US/NATO involvement in European security. Therefore, the UK is also an extremist on the side of the US. The UK has never considered European security to be a purely self-serving process that might harm NATO's role in European security.

the Europeans for stabilising Europe's periphery. Therefore, the better approach to the EU-US military relationship is to be aware of the 'spirit' of co-operation and work for a better division of military labour in transatlantic relations. The Franco-German security and defence co-operation is essential for deepening economic and defence integration in the EU and the US, instead of seeking a confrontation with France and Germany, should plan various strategic possibilities both for itself and for the Europeans. In other words, there are enough security threats in Europe's periphery both for NATO and for the EU/WEU.

(1.2) Prescription: Pragmatism and Flexibility Instead of Institutional Uniformity

The diverse and broad security concerns in post-Cold War Europe do not allow planning any conflict prevention scenarios in advance. The pragmatic solution of these diverse and broad security concerns will be to promote a differentiated integration framework while keeping European security indivisible.[55] According to Guido Lenzi, European security demand is two-fold: Firstly, it is about reintegration after years of forced integration. Secondly, it is also about participation in a 'brave new world'.[56] It is true that after the East-West confrontation Europe has an increased responsibility for global security, a responsibility that can be fulfilled militarily in addition to financial and economic initiatives. The 'European Security Agenda', written by former NATO Secretary-General Javier Solana, is basically about stability and predictability in Europe in that European security is affecting every nation, irrespective of whether or not that nation is a full member of any security institutions. Solana made his analysis entirely on the institutional interlocking (synergies rather than hierarchies) between NATO and the EU/WEU.[57]

[55] Crisis in any part of the continent affects whole Europe, see WEU Council of Ministers, *Noordwijk Declaration*, (Noordwijk, November 14, 1994), Section I, parag.8.
[56] Lenzi, G., 'Defining the European Security Policy', *EUI Working Papers*, (Florence: European University Institute, RSC, December 1997), pp.1-17.
[57] Solana,J.,'European Security Agenda',*NATO Review*, (Vol.43, No.6,November 1995),pp.11-14; Bailes,A. J.K, 'European Defence and Security–The Role of NATO, WEU and EU', *Security Dialogue*, (Vol.27, No.1, 1996).

Ideally, NATO and the EU/WEU, in a complementary fashion, must defend the *Deutschian* 'European security zone' against *Plato*'s events as they have actually unfolded in the form of regional conflicts. The prescription should not be abstract uniformity of institutions, but should be the diversification of tasks between institutions and flexibility of actual institutional commitments as they might be demanded by situations. While trying to do this, the relevant institutions should keep their commitment to complementarity and transparency, and they must avoid competition and duplication. The European security institutions must improve their interlocking relationships and they should be aware of the strength of flexibility and borrowing formulas that would be applicable to each other's managerial endeavours. Some analysts, like Dominique Moïsi, Michael Mertes and David Morrison, criticised these interlocking institutions as being an 'alphabet soup' and even causing more 'mess' through their lack of targeted missions, 'a mishmash of universalist slogans' instead of working proposals.[58] Philip Zelikow also argued that the main aim is to unscramble rather than interlock the existing institutions, and obtain a pluralized and multi-layered framework, which would involve the most appropriate mixture of preventive, reactive, and proactive responses.[59] Their ideas can easily be refuted by the following argument: NATO and the EU/WEU relationship, which is sustained by consensus, legitimacy, credibility, and complementarity through improving 'functional inter-linkage', rather than seeking a strict hierarchical subordination of institutions to one another, might diminish the very nature of pragmatism and flexibility.

NATO should facilitate politico-military transatlantic co-operation and might constitute an essential European common denominator, at least until the EU/WEU develops a sustainable

---

[58] Moïsi, D.,& Mertes, M.,'Europe's map, compass, and horizon', *Foreign Affairs*, (Vol.74, No.1, January 1995), pp.12-21; Morrison, D. C., 'Tattered Partnership', *National Journal*, (Vol.26, No.1, January 1, 1994), pp.11-21.
[59] Philip Zelikow 'The Masque of Institutions' in Gordon, H. P. (ed.), *NATO's Transformation*, (US: Rowman and Littlefield Publishers, Inc., 1997), pp.77-89.

and credible political and military structure. The EU would provide the coherence and sense of 'integrated community' supplemented by the CFSP. The WEU – defence arm of the EU and European 'pillar' of NATO – is transferring its functions into the EU and will act as an instrument for the implementation of the EU's politico-military plans, possibly with the participation of non-NATO countries. Even France, which has been enthusiastic about demonising NATO and strengthening European defence co-operation, is closer in the present day to NATO than in the Cold War era. Germany, which was 'more NATO' than NATO itself in the Cold War era, is today more assertive for task sharing, convergence and linkage between NATO and the EU/WEU. Former German Foreign Minister, Klaus Kinkel, called for 'a coherent division of labour among radically reformed multilateral organisations.'[60] Since the Clinton Administration, the US has also changed its attitude to the EU/WEU. This is concerned not to subject the US allies' to unilateral decisions or commitments that would bind them to the US decisions only. The concept of the CJTF demonstrates that US itself intends to diversify and choose between different formulas designed for addressing hybrid situations through creating a link between the EU/WEU and NATO.

In present strategic circumstances, with the declining defence budgets of the European nations in mind, none of the EU states will object to the US military presence in Europe. However, defining which circumstances the US will act militarily in European armed conflicts' is still a significant question, as is the question of when Europeans will undertake military responsibilities. Unless a major attack on a NATO member state occurs, the Americans and Europeans will likely follow the strategy of selective engagement in crisis situations where conditions for action would not be clearly specified in advance and the full consensus would be less certain. Therefore, the complexity of European security does not only derive from the existing inter-

---

[60] Kinkel, K. quoted in *International Herald Tribune*, (December 24-25, 1996).

locking institutional structure, but also derives from a more delicate inter-state issue: the *political choice* and *will* of undertaking risks and burdens through joint actions.[61] The US does not trust that the EU will conduct its own foreign, security and defence policy obligations' properly and thus fears it will be dragged into conflicts only after they have been knotted due to the Europeans' lack of skill and/or political will. US foreign policy has been guided by the idea that it will be wiser to work independently in Europe rather than waiting for trouble to develop into a complicated situation. However, the crucial notion is that the Europeans and Americans should continue revising their old bargain by replacing it with a new partnership. They will continue sharing important and far-reaching common economic, political and security interests, because in the new security environment neither party would be able to achieve its principal objectives separately. Indeed, this will require analysing transatlantic relations through military-diplomatic responsibility rather than financial burden sharing only.[62]

Americans and Europeans should understand two things very well. *Firstly*, in and around Europe an uncertain period lies ahead. The threat of confrontation between the East and West, which was the central factor in European security questions, has taken second place, while threats on Europe's periphery ('soft' military issues) is a priority since the collapse of the Soviet Union. *Secondly*, instead of seeking concessions from the US, the Europeans should strengthen their own foreign, security and defence policies through a strong communal political will and establish their political decision-making mechanisms and operational

---

[61] Kelleher, M. C., 'A renewed security partnership?', *The Brookings Review*, (Vol.11, No.4, Fall 1993), pp.30-41. This delicate issue is given an emphasis in the WEU Council Report that, 'in many ways Europe's new security structure is an empty vessel. Institutions have been revised and mechanisms elaborated, but the will to utilise these regimes often seems lacking.' WEU Council Report, Mr. Marshall, *Document 1370*, p.46.
[62] *Burden sharing* described by Jenonne Walker 'that others should pay more -- in money, men and political risks -- to help implement Washington's policies.' Walker, J., *Europe*, (Washington: January/February 1991). On the contrary, *responsibility sharing* is including liability, such as good credit or position. The liability for Europeans is to take an action, including military, for preventing European conflicts.

capabilities parallel to the ESDI and the CJTF. In order to bring their power into balance with the US, the Europeans should build themselves up, not pull the Americans down. Only then will the EU/WEU be strong enough to access necessary assets from NATO under the principle of 'separable but not separate,' if NATO decides not to deal with the issue itself. The US on the other hand should help strengthen Europe's 'core' by dealing with France and Germany collectively rather than individually. The US should encourage greater Franco-German co-operation and activism in managing European security.

It is impossible to figure out the new security environment in post-Cold War Europe without looking in depth at the new security concept and analysing what had happened in the TEU and in the Amsterdam Treaty. Therefore, a better understanding of the first section of this Chapter and the rest of this study, necessitates not only an analysis of the European security environment through new security concept, but also requires defining the institutional links between the EU and the WEU.

(2) Communitarisation of Foreign And Security Policies Under the Impact of the New Security Concept

(2.1) Understanding The New Security Concept

(2.1.1) The New Security Concept

Economic issues today dominate the world more than at any other time in history. This is the result of growing economic interdependence between states, with less emphasis on military force and more on comprehensive armaments reduction. Even if military power is required, it will be exercised as a last resort through peacekeeping, crisis prevention and management, and will indeed be secondary to conflict resolution, mediation, and cease-fire initiatives. In all democratic countries, economic values replaced military values and intensified the interdependence between the market-oriented societies. The growth of a comprehensive network of interdependence increased the transnational obligations on economic activities and thus resulted in globalisation.[63] On the other hand, 'cyberworld' conditions ruined the existing barriers between the security studies and international political economics, which brought the geopolitics into the study of regionalism. This is the identification of 'glocalism' (a mixture of globalism and localism), where 'the functions of the nation-state are diminished, eroded as they are from above by global communications and financial flow as much as from below by renewed aspirations to communitarianism and self-determination of the most varied kind.'[64] Although a nation-state structure remained the gatekeeper of states' international relations, vital national interests are protected by inexorable multilateral structures and cross-national interactions.[65] Buzan described states' relationship in a new security environment as a 'mature anarchy':

> *'A system of strong states (in terms of high levels of socio-political cohesion),*
>
> *embedded in a well-developed international society (a dense network of mutually*

---

[63]Nicole Gnesotto argued that, rules of economic and military interplay are deeply disrupted by the growing intrusion of non-state factors. E.g. international organisations, gangs, or networks in various sense of the world. The influence of the audio-visual media is also radically changing the concept of diplomacy; instantaneous communications are affecting monetary speculation, but equally make it difficult to control or isolate societies. Gnesotto, N., 'Introduction' in Gnesotto, N. (ed.), 'War and Peace: European Conflict Prevention', p.13; see Von Bredow, W. & Kümmel, G., 'Das Militär und die Herausforderung globaler Sicherheit – Der Spagat zwischen traditonalen und nicht-traditionalen Rollen', *SOWI Arbeitspapier Nr119*, (Strausberg: September 1999), pp.4-13.
[64] Lenzi, G., 'Europeanising Security' in Lankowski, C. and Serfaty, S. 'Europeanising Security? NATO and an Integrating Europe', *AICGS Research Paper*, (US: The Johns Hopkins University, American Institute for Contemporary German Studies (AICGS) Research Report, No. 9, 1999), pp.118-132; also see Gretschmann, K., 'Traum oder Alptraum? Politikgestaltung im Spannungsfeld von Nationalstaat und Europäischer Union', *Aus Politik und Zeitgeschichte*, (Beilage zur Wochenzeitung, Das Parlament, B5, Januar 26, 2001), pp.25-32.
[65] Simonis stated that, 'it is not "state formations" (at the EU level), but "state decomposition" that seems to be the appropriate concept for defining the direction in which the change processes which are currently evident in the administrative structures of Western European societies are moving.' Simonis, J. B. D., 'European Integration and the Erosion of the Nation-state', *International Journal of Social Economics*, (Vol.22, No.7, 1995), pp.1-11.

> *agreed norms, rules and institutions...). It keeps states as the basic unit, but*
>
> *contains the security dilemma within a liberal-inspired 'non-violent conflict''.*[66]

In contrast to the definition of stability in Cold War international relations, which was the military balance of power, present day stability in international relations means progress towards pluralistic democracy, human rights, market economy, and the Western level of development.[67] This understanding occupied the minds of the American and European policymakers' as a *new security concept (or thinking)* – manifestation of the new security environment – with the end of the ideological tension between the East and West.

Before an analysis of the impact of new security thinking on Europe, it will be fruitful to consider the nature of security. In today's interdependent world, security has become an amorphous concept and therefore encompasses a broad range of issues. The concept of security in the Cold War era was primarily understood in terms of military and defence aspects of security.[68] However, military and defence aspects are only two factors shaping the concept of security. Adam Rotfeld argued that, 'reducing the [security] process to military security alone was a mistake in the past; in today's realities this would mean ignoring its essence'.[69] It is apparent that security under new security thinking, in addition to military and defence factors, embraces a range of non-military factors. These are political (e.g. refugee influx), economic (e.g. restricted market access), social (e.g. cultural/religious conflict), and environmental fac-

[66] Buzan, B., 'Security, the State, the "World Order," and Beyond' in Lipschutz, R. (ed.), *On Security*, (New York: Columbia University Press, 1995), p.205.
[67] Van Eekelen, W., *The Security Agenda for 1996 – Background and prospects*, (Brussels: Centre for European Policy Studies (CEPS), Paper No. 64, 1995), pp.1-5.
[68] The concept of defence interpreted by many foreign and security policy analysts as a matter related to actual and potential deployment of military forces. See Duke, S., pp.174-175; Hurd, D., 'Developing the CFSP', *International Affairs*, (Vol.70, No.3, 1994), p.426; Jannuzzi, G., p.16.
[69] Adam Rotfeld quoted in Marauhn, T., *Building a European Security and Defence Identity*, (Bochum: UVB – Universitätsverlag, 1996), p.66.

tors (e.g. trans-border disaster) that their transnationalisation resulted in global effects.[70] These four main non-military factors have gained an importance in the post-Cold War era and, in the current form, continue to gain considerable importance. Therefore, to say that there is nothing at the moment that would threaten the transition from totalitarian to free-market economics, to assert that possible threats are unlikely, to claim that any conceivable threat could be handled in time of its appearance, is to miss a key feature of international relations.

In the new security environment, partly because of new security thinking and partly because of the current importance of non-military factors of security, the threat of using military force or the use of military force in the resolution of new security risks is limited.[71] However, P. Bracken and S. Johnson stated:

> 'The developed states have to lean against certain doors, even though no one is
> trying to open them. For if the developed states stop leaning against those doors,
> because it appears safe to do so or because they are confident they can rush back
> if needed, then they are neglecting the single most important role for military
> forces in the new order [new security concept]: policing the international system
> so to insure that vital interests are not violated'.[72]

It became shockingly visible that differences between new security thinking and military security factors are extremely complex. The disappearance of the Soviet empire reduced the possibility of any direct military confrontation between the US and the Russia; however, it unleashed ethnic conflicts, resurgence of nationalism and as a consequence broadened the concept of security. It is apparent that ignoring the importance of these challenges to new

[70] Non-military factors are aptly explained by Paul Latawski 'Central Europe and European Security' in Park, W. & Rees, W., pp.82-95. For his detailed study about non-military factors, see next page – Table 1.1.
[71] Duff, A., *Reforming the EU*, (UK: Federal Trust, 1997), pp.74-98.
[72] Bracken, P. & Johnson, S., 'Beyond NATO: Complementary Militaries', *Orbis*, p.220

Table 1.1: Central European security complex: threats/vulnerabilities

Level	Military-diplomatic sector	Political sector	Economic sector	Societal sector	Environmental sector
System (Europe)	Renationalisation policy Limitations on sovereignty (involuntary) Hegemony	External limits Domestic politics Ideological menace	Restricted market access Low investment Migration Organised crime	Global culture Migration Organised crime	Ecosystem crisis Energy crisis Trans-border disasters Food and health problems Migration
Sub-system (sub-region)	Frontier disputes Minority problems State disintegration	Instability in neighbours Refugee influx	Restricted market access Migration Organised crime Transit restrictions	Cultural/religious conflict	Ecosystem crisis Energy crisis Trans-border disasters Food and health problems Migration
Unit (state)	Lack of policy consensus Weak defence forces Technology gap	*Failure Reform:* Weak political system Political fragmentation Problems civil-military relations Minority separatism	*Weak Reform:* Slow privatisation Weak merketisation Weak banking and financial system Slow reform law and regulation Protectionism Crime/corruption	Weak civil society Corruption Organised crime Weak human rights regime Archaic class structure Minority discrimination	Crumbling infrastructure Ecosystem crisis Energy crisis Trans-border disasters Food and health problems Migration
Sub-unit (internal state)	Internal collapse Regional separatism	Political extremism Extreme polarisation Massive protests/strikes	Unemployment Recession/depression Organised Crime Corruption	Human rights violations Organised crime Corruption Xenophobic nationalism	Crumbling infrastructure Ecosystem crisis Energy crisis Trans-border disasters Food and health problems Migration

security thinking would be a vital mistake for the Europeans. Moreover, there is another aspect of security somewhere in between the *military* ('hard' military issues, e.g. inter-state war cases) and *non-military* (e.g. trans-border disasters) aspects of security. In view of the interdependence and globalisation of security, and the diversity of crises from military to non-military factors, the *military-diplomatic* factor ('soft' military issues, e.g. the initial state disintegration – like the ones in former Yugoslavia (i.e. Bosnia, Kosovo), and Albania – that have to be prevented before escalating into a full-scale armed conflicts),[73] is also extremely important.

Although the non-military factor of security is considered to be separate from 'soft' military issues, they will herein be analysed under 'soft' military issues. P. Latawski, S. Landgren, and J. Zielonka argued that most of these non-military threat factors are 'soft' rather than 'hard' cases.[74] In order to understand the current international relations of European security and the inter-play between the EU, WEU, and NATO, ways of meeting these 'soft' military issues will be analysed in detail in this Chapter under the title of the *Commnitarisation of Security Policy*.

(2.1.2) The EU Dimension

There are inherent links in the EU between the economic field, where the EC has been successful, and the security field, where economic interdependence and globalisation exerts a further pressure for its integration into the EU. In the field of security, threats and risks

---

[73] NATO Secretary-General, George Robertson, has said in an interview on the *BBC World* that the war in Kosovo was a '*military exercise* not a full-scale war where the nuclear power threat had been involved.' *BBC World*, interview on TV with NATO Secretary-General George Robertson at 11:30 a.m. (GMT), October 10, 2000. The in-depth analysis of his statement is not the focus of this paper, but could be a topic for another study.
[74] Paul Latawski, 'Central Europe and European Security' in Park, W. & Rees, W., (ed.), *Rethinking Security in Post-Cold War Europe*, p.88; Landgren, S., 'Post-Soviet Threats to Security' in *SIPRI Yearbook 1992: World Armaments and Disarmament*, (Oxford: SIPRI Oxford University Press, 1992), pp.531-557; Zielonka, J. 'Security in Central Europe', *Adelphi Paper 272*, (London: IISS, 1992).

emanating from multiple directions can no longer be managed at the national level. Mathias

Jopp has argued, 'as many conflicts and tensions are rooted in political, social and economic

instabilities, the Union is much better equipped than any other international organisation to

address related problems'.[75] The EU addresses these insecurities economically, socially, and

technically rather than simply militarily. Therefore, this strengthens the position of the EU

since the concept of security has always been broader than the military dimension. The fact is

that greater efforts must be made for taking concrete steps and enabling the EU to reconstruct

its role for the preservation of security in the European continent, either economically or

militarily.

The early reconstruction attempts came with the EC's TEU in December 1991 and the EC's

plan to launch two conferences, first an IGC on Economic and Monetary Union (EMU) and

second, an IGC on European Political Union (EPU). The aim was to give the EC greater po-

litical power in the area of foreign and security policy in order to match its growing economic

might. At the same time, there were external and internal pressures on the EC that forced its

member states to launch these two IGCs. The agreement on EMU is one of the issues covered

by the TEU that was mainly the result of external economic pressures. The EMU is a competi-

tive response by the EC's member states to tackle global economic developments.[76] The

discussions on the EPU that included foreign, security and defence issues, was the other

explanation of the TEU. The EPU was a response to internal (re-unification of Germany) and

external (end of the Cold-War) pressures rather than simply the outcome of political will

within the Western Europe. However, the reluctance of the EC member states to sacrifice their

political interests and the impenetrability of their national sovereignties led to the inclusion of

---

[75] Jopp, M., 'The Strategic Implications of European Integration', *Adelphi Paper*, (London: Brassey's Publications, No.290, 1994), p.67.
[76] For an excellent study on the EMU see, Helleiner, E., 'One Nation, One Money – Territorial Currencies and the Nation-State', *ARENA Working Papers*, (Oslo: No.17, 1997).

the CFSP – but not the defence policy – into the TEU.[77] Although the TEU has its roots in economic and institutional developments of the EC prior to the 1990s, it was primarily a political response by the EC countries to the end of the Cold War and German unification. Crucially, it represented a political bargain between the EC's two most important members, Germany and France, that they viewed the agreement as a means of securing their own vital national interests. While France was inspired by the desire to bind the newly unified Germany into the strengthened European framework through the EMU, Germany was inspired by the desire to press for the EPU to be added to the EMU.

It was not until the end of the Cold War that the idea of incorporating the defence dimension into the EC framework was seriously discussed. In the new security environment, the EC and the WEU were confronted with the issue of merging into a single structure, adding a defence dimension to the EC. The WEU, albeit to a lesser extent than the EC, has also been structured to meet broader security issues. Flockhart and Rees argued, 'because of the ill-defined role in the past, the WEU has proved to be flexible enough to undertake missions that are either quasi-military or civilian in nature.'[78] An organic relationship developed between the EU and the WEU through the EU's TEU and the WEU's Maastricht Declarations in December 1991. Thus, *in principle*, the WEU began to be called the defence arm of the EU.[79] However, the EU member states could not develop a military dimension within the EU and, therefore, the question of common defence policy was developed outside the EU, within the WEU and NATO. Instead, the CFSP was established for strengthening the EU's economic, social, and environ-

---

[77] The TEU led the EU's so-called three-pillar structure. In addition to the existing formal communal structure (Treaty of Rome procedures – First Pillar) on economic matters (European Coal and Steal Community (ECSC), European Atomic and Energy Community (EAEC), European Economic Community (EEC)), another institutional structure, namely an intergovernmental structure, was chosen for non-economic matters. It is chosen particularly for those concerning traditional tasks of the state, such as for the determination of foreign, security (CFSP – Second Pillar), and domestic and legal policy (Justice and Home Affairs (JHA) – Third Pillar) areas.
[78] Flockhart, T. & Rees, W. G., 'A Core Europe? The EU and the WEU' in Park, W. & Rees, W., p.73.

mental aspects of security. Although its competences are economic, nobody denies that the military dimension of the EU is still under intense discussions. The European security policy cannot be completed without a robust defence policy. However, a defence policy demands a considerable investment to sustain it over a period of time. As Wæver suggested, perhaps the evaluation of the institutions of the EU and the WEU should be taken into account not so much in terms of what *has* happened in Europe since the end of the Cold War, but rather in terms of what has *not* yet happened.[80]

Since the failure of the European Defence Community (EDC) in 1954, it is assumed that economic integration has to be achieved – at least to a certain degree – in order to manage integration in foreign and security policy areas. Placing the economic aspect of security in the centre of European integration was a deliberate strategy of the Commission. It was based on the idea that the engine of economic integration will pull the EPU behind it. This has been supported by recent developments in the EMU. The Euro, as the EU's single currency, is the final stage of the EMU and the first step to the EPU.[81] French Foreign Affairs Minister Hubert Védrine argued that, 'it is the real unifying European project ... it will create a new dynamic whose consequences are far from being appreciated', and German authorities expressed a similar idea when Klaus Kinkel asserted that the Euro 'was a question of destiny for Europe'.[82] Although French and German approaches are clashing over the *means* of Euro, both are critical about the global hegemony of the US dollar. Jean Boissonat put forward French aims clearly by stating, 'we are developing the Euro partly in order to put into question the privilege of the [US] dollar...' on the contrary, former head of the *Bundesbank*, Karl Otto

---

[79] WEU's *Maastricht Declarations*, (Maastricht: 10 December 1991) in Bloed, A. & Wessel, R. A. (ed.), *The Changing Functions of the WEU – Introduction and Basic Documents*, (Utrecht: Martinus Nijhoff Publishers, August 1994), pp.131-135.
[80] Ole Wæver quoted in Park, W. & Rees, W., p.76.
[81] Jean Boissonat, economist and the member of the Bank of France, quoted in Boyer, Y., 'Whither Core Europe? France and the European Construction: Issues and Choices' in Lankowski, C. & Serfaty, S., p.24.

Pöhl, stated, 'Paris sees the Euro as an instrument to break the hegemony of the US dollar and

possibly create a new reserve currency. This is in contrast to the German conception of the

Euro as a means to put an end to monetary fragmentation within the single market space.'[83]

Nevertheless, Joschka Fischer (leader of the Greens) declared in August 1997, before he

formed a government with the SPD (Social Democratic Party), that he would give support for

the EMU and added, '… if the Euro does not come, the US will define the development of a

globalised economy in the 21st century'.[84]

In fact, Franco-German propositions seem to be stirred more by the semi-presidential French

system than by the German federalism.[85] Thus, as they differ over the means of the EMU, they

also differ over the means of the CFSP. While the Germans favour a *supranational model*, the

French favour an *intergovernmental model* in the governance of the CFSP. However, these

obvious differences between Germany and France over the *means* of the EMU and the CFSP

do not hamper the ongoing collaboration between them. Instead, a trade-off occurred between

the German CFSP aims and the French EMU objectives. Concisely, neither country can

achieve its aims without the other. The French, who are in favour of the communitarisation of

the EMU, were delighted by the German support for communitarisation of economic and

monetary policies and the Germans, who are in favour of the deeper integration in the area of

---

[82] *Ibid.* pp. 24-25.

[83] 'The Germans want the planned stability pact to discipline the budget deficits of national governments by rules that are fixed and automatic; the French want rules that allow for political judgement. For the Germans monetary stability is an absolute priority; but the French want something like an economic government for Europe which would promote stability and growth.' *Ibid.*

[84] *Ibid.* pp.25-26.

[85] Germany is in favour of transferring state powers gradually to Brussels as integration deepens. This functionalist view stresses that some degree of authority is necessary in governing the transferred power and socialising common views and interests at the 'Community' level. Hence, functionalists' emphasis is on the *supranationality*. However, France is in favour of protecting its national interest, national foreign policy power and unwilling to compromise its core national interests. Therefore, France puts emphasis on the lowest-common denominator – *intergovernmentalism*. This was also confirmed by the fact that, as in French foreign policy, the European Parliament was not given much of a role in the Mitterrand-Kohl letter of December 1990. Rummel, R., 'Germany's Role in the CFSP. 'Normalität' or 'Sonderweg'?' in Hill, C. (ed.), *The Actors in Europe's Foreign Policy*, (UK: Routledge, 1996), p.50; Pappas, S. A. & Vanhoonacker, S., *The EU's CFSP – The Challenges of the Future*, (The Netherlands: European Institute of Public Administration, 1996), p.9.

the CFSP, were delighted by the French support for communitarisation of foreign and security policies. However, according to the TEU, the CFSP will be considered in one communitarian body, the Council of Ministers.

The Franco-German couple, which has been successful in ensuring the European economic integration process since the inception of the Treaty of Rome, will also fully realise the need for fulfilling diplomatic-military initiatives. To obtain a better understanding of what the TEU entails in the area of the CFSP, the following section will analyse the foreign and security policies separately.

(2.2) Maastricht, European Foreign and Security Integration, and Beyond

(2.2.1) The Communitarisation of Foreign Policy

The demand for a more coherent and invigorated European foreign policy has been discussed for many years throughout the European Political Cooperation (EPC). However, pressures from the new security environment for a single European voice and a desire to meet new security thinking through a comprehensive political co-operation led to a more promising intergovernmental structure within the CFSP.

In addition to security and defence policies, the foreign policy itself is another element of 'high politics'. In broad terms, an effective foreign policy defined by Hill and Wallace as, '[it] rests upon a shared sense of national identity, of a nation-state's place in the world, its friends and enemies, its interests and aspirations. These underlying assumptions are embedded in national history and myth, changing slowly over time as political leaders reinterpret them and external and internal developments reshape them'.[86] Foreign policy reaches to the very centre

of national identity and sovereignty, both of which are known as 'taboo' areas of a nation-

state. Wallace argued that '[the] foreign policy is about national identity itself: about the core

elements of sovereignty it seeks to defend, the values it stands for and seeks to promote

abroad'.[87] 'Institutionalisation' of the national identity occurs through various forms of politi-

cal socialisation. Therefore, it tends to make identity constructions relatively resistant to

change. It explains and legitimises particular identities, practices, and rules associated with the

identity construction.[88]

The interesting question is how deep the sense of 'institutionalisation', 'socialisation', 'iden-

tity,' and 'community' is and how it may be affecting the foreign policy perceptions at EU

level. The social constructivist understanding of Aggestam is that institutions generate a sense

for a community once its actors consistently adopt a particular role conception and modify

their behaviours according to each other's roles, behaviours, and expectations.[89] This is a dis-

tinct re-framing of foreign policy by communitarised actors. In fact, the concepts like

intergovernmentalism and sovereignty have *de facto* been weakened by the intensification of

interdependence. Hill and Wallace argued that, '[the CFSP] have moved the conduct of

national foreign policy away from the old nation-state national sovereignty model towards a

collective endeavour, a form of high-level networking with transformationalist effects'.[90] The

above argument – a depiction of the communitarisation of foreign policy – is a manifestation

of the functionalist theory.

---

[86] Hill, C. & Wallace, W., 'Introduction: Actors and Actions' in Hill, C. (ed.), *The Actors in Europe's Foreign Policy*, p.8.
[87] Wallace, W.,'Foreign Policy and National Identity in the UK',*International Affairs*, (Vol.67, No.1, 1991), p.65
[88] March, J. G. & Olsen, J. P., 'The Institutional Dynamics of International Political Order', *ARENA Working Papers*, (Oslo: No.5, 1998), p.7.
[89] Aggestam, L. 'Role Conceptions and the Politics of Identity in Foreign Policy', *ARENA Working Papers*, (Oslo: No.8, 1999).
[90] Hill, C. & Wallace, W., 'Introduction: Actors and Actions' in Hill, C. (ed.), *The Actors in Europe's Foreign Policy*, p.6

Contrary to the functionalist theory, the intergovernmentalist theory describes the nature of the CFSP as a potential and useful instrument for member states' in achieving their own national foreign policy goals. Rummel and Wiedemann argued that the EU's foreign policy is a careful 'balance of interest' among the member states, and if member states' national interests do not coincide with the EU's foreign policy they have other – national – options, they do not need to wait for the EU mechanisms' for coordinating actions.[91] Furthermore, Hill considers the EU 'as a system of external relations', which has a mismatch between its capabilities and expectations. By this, he means that, the EU represents a subsystem of an international system and is a system (i.e. not a single actor) which generates international relations – collectively, individually, economically, politically – rather than a clear cut 'European foreign policy' as such. This system is essentially decentralised and consists of three decision-making procedures: national foreign policy, CFSP, and external relations of the EU.[92] Another intergovernmental critic has concentrated on the gap between economic issues (concerned with external relations of the supranational EC) and political issues (concerned with the previous intergovernmental EPC). Although economic and political issues of foreign relations have moved closer to each other, distinction between them has remained: external relations of the EC are still governed by the supranational structure, whereas the CFSP has been baffled with the intergovernmental structure in the new EU system.[93] Michael Smith criticised that the EU has not been very successful in translating its economic potential into economic and

---

[91] Rummel, R. & Wiedemann, J., 'Identifying Institutional Paradoxes of CFSP', *EUI Working Papers*, (Italy: European University Institute, RSC, No.97/67, December1997), pp.10-12.

[92] Hill, C., 'The Capability-Expectations Gap, or Conceptualising Europe's International Role', *Journal of Common Market Studies*, (Vol.31, No.3, September 1993), pp.305-325.

[93] The Council, rather than the Commission, is responsible for the CFSP. Morgan, R., 'How Common Will Foreign and Security Policies be?' in Dehousse, R. (ed.), *Europe After Maastricht – An Ever Closer Union?*, (Munich: C.H. Beck'sche Verlagsbuchhandlung, 1994), pp.189-199. Art.J.1(4) of the *Treaty on European Union (TEU)/Maastricht Treaty*. <http://www.altairiv.demon.co.uk/ maastricht/title5.html> (Visited on: September 05, 1997). Jacques Delors has also drawn the distinction between the *single* and the *common* foreign policy. The *single foreign policy* would be like a directive defining both means and ends. The *common foreign policy* would draw a consensus with regard to ends only. Each state would decide separately which means to take upon. See Delors, J., 'European Integration and Security', *Survival*, (Vol.33, No.2, March/April 1991), pp.99-109.

political effects.[94] While the member states of the EU began to discuss the option of a European central bank many years ago, the option of 'European foreign ministry' was not even considered. On the other hand, Hill also asserted that a truly European presence in the world requires collective policies in all major areas by bringing economics and politics closer to each other as well as rationalising the decision-making process.[95]

By and large, the TEU brought the economic and political issues closer to each other. Political issues are dependent on economics and economic issues are dependent on the Community's political instruments. Duff argued that, in order to improve 'consistency', member states have tried to strengthen the CFSP through 'common positions' and 'joint actions.'[96] Although Jannuzzi found the communitarised foreign policy largely incomplete, he emphasised that the CFSP has preserved and consolidated a fundamental procedure of the EPC: the interrelationship between political objectives and economic instruments.[97] The economic, political, and diplomatic instruments of the EU and the mode of their operation are similar to that of the nation-state. Hazel Smith also stated that, there is no reason not to consider the EU as a foreign policy actor that has many attributes comparable to that of the nation-state.[98] The EU's communitarised foreign policy not only includes traditional state-type foreign policy instruments, but also includes its own *sui generis* foreign policy instruments. David Baldwin described foreign policy instruments as, 'used by policy-makers in their attempts to get another

---

[94] Smith, M., 'The EU, foreign economic policy and the changing world arena', *Journal of Common Market Studies*, (Vol.1, No.2, Autumn 1994), p.285.

[95] Hill, C., 'The Capability-Expectations Gap, or Conceptualising Europe's International Role', pp.322-324.

[96] Duff, A., *Reforming the EU*, (UK: Federal Trust, 1997), p.78; 'Common positions' (Art.J.2) are an effective continuation of the EPC practice. Although they are not legally binding (CFSP and JHA are not subject to the European Court of Justice (ECJ)), they are designed to enable the EU to speak with one voice. 'Joint actions' (Art.J.3) are under the liability of the Council and designed to develop the EU into a single (purposive) actor. Once a unanimous approval obtained in the Council (Art.J.3(2)), 'Joint actions' could be implemented by qualified majority voting (QMV). See Art.J.4(3) of the TEU.

[97] Jannuzzi also stressed that 'in economic sector, however, the dynamics of market forces can be counted upon to promote increased integration, regardless of – and even despite – the political will. This is not self-evident in the case of foreign policy, where integration requires the convergence of determined political wills, against the forces of deeply-rooted customs, traditions, and interests.' Jannuzzi, G., 'The EU's CFSP and Its Contribution to Global Security', *NATO Review*, (Vol.42, No.1, January 1995), pp.13-16.

international actor to do what they would not otherwise do.'[99] Karen Smith focused on the two main foreign policy instruments: diplomatic/political (sanctions, recognitions, offering peace proposals, sponsoring peace conferences, etc.) and economic instruments (providing/suspending economic aids, tariff reduction/increase, quota increase/decrease, concluding trade agreement or applying embargo, etc). She argued that, although the CFSP includes 'common positions' and 'joint actions', they are not *instruments* per se.[100] She defined them as mechanisms for making decisions to use diplomatic/political instruments. It should also be noted that instead of using the technique of 'sticks' (threatening or using force), the EU prefers using economic strength for political purposes as a technique of 'carrots' (offering/granting rewards).

Although France and Germany were the prominent supporters of the CFSP in the TEU discussions, their philosophical differences over future European political development was undeniable. Although France is firmly embedded into the EU, unlike Germany and the UK, its traditional political and economic philosophies are at odds with the US. For France any convergence in the European foreign policy area should mean European emancipation from the US.[101] With the end of the Cold War and German unification, France found itself in the dilemma of a 'German Europe' or a 'European Europe'. France became convinced that the EC's foreign policy process had to be strengthened in order to tie Germany in a 'European Europe' for an effective French struggle against the US hegemony in Europe. De la Serra argued:

---

[98] Smith, H., *The EU Foreign Policy and Central America*, (UK: Macmillan, 1995), pp.44-45.
[99] David Baldwin quoted in Smith, K. E., 'The Instruments of EU Foreign Policy', *EUI Working Papers*, (Italy: European University Institute, RSC No.97/68, December 1997), p.2.
[100] Diplomatic/political instruments require the decision to be either 'common positions' or 'joint actions' for their employment. *Ibid*, p.3.
[101] 'OTAN, les Européens tentent de s'émanciper de la tutelle américaine', *Libération*, (June 4, 1996); Guyomarch, A., Machin, H. & Ritchie, E., *France and the EU*, (US: St. Martin's Press, Inc., 1998), pp.104-128. For similar arguments also see Guéhenno, J-M., 'A Foreign Policy in Search of a Polity', *EUI Working Papers*, (Italy: European University Institute, RSC No. 97/65, December 1997).

> *'Tensions exist between the declared priority of Europeanising [communitarising]*
>
> *foreign policy, which binds Germany to the Union but limits France's margins for*
>
> *manoeuvre, and the desire to maintain France's 'ranking' as a world power, a*
>
> *desire asserted all the more stridently as this status has been shaken by changes*
>
> *within Europe'.*[102]

However, the communitarisation of foreign policy through granting the Commission a significant role was strongly opposed by France. The reason behind this decision is that France favours the intergovernmental authority of the Council and thus signalled its opposition to any
further convergence of the French national sovereignty within the EU.[103] French foreign
policy is deeply rooted in de Gaulle's philosophy of independent, distinctive, and 'superior'
foreign policy concepts where subordination to any supranational policymaking body seems
intolerable.[104]

Unlike de Gaulle's philosophy, for historical reasons the Germans found themselves
supporting multilateral internationalism and thus are ardent supporters of the European
integration process. The fully sovereign Germany in the post-Cold War era is developing an
independent outward-looking foreign policy. However, in order to soothe its neighbours'
pessimistic claims, Germany decided to push even harder for communitarisation the CFSP
than it had done so far.[105] Since Adenauer, Germany's economic and political philosophies
have been in favour of European integration through multilateralism and strengthening the

---

[102] De La Serra, F., 'France – The Impact of François Mitterand' in Hill, C. (ed.), *The Actors in Europe's Foreign Policy*, p.35.
[103] *Ibid.*
[104] Guyomarch, A., Machin, H. & Ritchie, E., *France and the EU*, p.104. For a detailed study of de Gaulle's philosophy see, Chapter 5 – *France's new roles and desires in the sphere of European security and defence*.
[105] Rummel, R., 'Germany's Role in the CFSP. 'Normalität' or 'Sonderweg'?' in Hill, C. (ed.), *The Actors in Europe's Foreign Policy*, pp.40-67.

EU-US relations through transatlanticism. Germany indeed committed itself to the supranational approach and for that reason supports an increase in the power of the European Commission and Parliament for a communitarised foreign policy. Furthermore, the German elite is in favour of a move to the QMV on CFSP matters in the Council of Ministers.[106] The communitarisation of foreign policy is the prime target of German philosophy. Therefore, Paris sometime finds conversation easier with London than with Berlin.

Although European foreign policy contains a national scope, it actually stands in between the national autonomy and the communitarisation of foreign policy. Foreign policy decision-making within the CFSP is a dynamic process and, consequently, the gradual accumulation of shared norms and rules within the CFSP could lead to 'rational' bargaining among the EU's member states. The question of how to identify national interests and reconcile different na-tional foreign policy traditions will be a challenge for the communitarised foreign policy. In order to understand this better, one needs to pay closer attention to the dynamic political inter-action between national and European levels. This interaction between these levels would boost the process of 'complex social learning' and states would accordingly be forced to re-adapt their fundamental beliefs and values. Norms, which stem from a 'complex social learn-ing' process though transparency, consultation, and compromise, are galvanising the funda-mental features of the political solidarity within the CFSP.[107] Helene Sjursen argued that, 'we do not know the end station of this process and we must reflect on the possibility that *it may never lead to one single European foreign policy in the traditional sense of the word*'[108]

[106] Cameron, F., Ginsberg, R., Janning, J., 'The EU's CFSP: Central Issues … Key Players', *Strategic Outreach Roundtable and Conference Report*, summarised by Stuart Mackintosh, (US: May 10, 1995). <http://carlisle-www.army.mil/usassi/ssipubs/pubs95/union/unionss.htm> (Visited on: September 19, 1999), p.8. For a detailed study see, Chapter 4 – *Germany's evolving European security and defence role.*
[107] Checkel, J., 'Social Construction and Integration', *ARENA Working Papers*, (Oslo: No.14, 1998); Hill, C., 'Convergence, Divergence & Dialectics: National Foreign Policies & the CFSP', *EUI Working Papers*, (Italy: European University Institute, RSC No.97/66, December 1997).For the *solidarity clause*, see J.1(4) of the TEU.
[108] Sjursen, H., 'Enlargement and the CFSP: Transforming the EU's External Policy?', *ARENA Working Papers*, (Oslo: No.18, 1998).

(emphasis added). Moreover, more communitarisation of foreign policy means foreign policy is becoming more formally institutionalised within the EU.

However, it will be misleading to believe that there could be an effective communitarised foreign policy without a credible security dimension. Therefore, the following section will analyse the communitarisation of security policy through the EU-WEU connection.

(2.2.2) The Communitarisation of Security Policy

The notion of the 'civilian power' role of Europe was developed under the threat of the US-USSR nuclear confrontation by François Duchêne and occupied the minds of Europeans even after the fall of the Iron Curtain.[109] Under Cold War pressure, the EPC dealt with the economic aspects of security, while the CFSP in the post-Cold War era includes all aspects of security.[110] Security here includes the relationship between economic and security aspects of politics, for example, disarmament and arms control. However, while the TEU strengthened the EU-WEU ties, it kept the defence concept in the WEU and NATO spheres.

In order to respond effectively to security challenges and detect crisis situations, unlike military alliances, the CFSP is constructed on the human rights dimension under the impact of new security thinking.[111] The EU must protect its citizens against various types of hostile

---

[109] According to Duchêne, the 'civilian power' concept rests upon the banishment of war from the Western Europe and, therefore, it will be irrational to develop a militarily equipped European federation. See Juliet Lodge, 'From Civilian Power to Speaking with a Common Voice: The Transition to a CFSP' in Lodge, J. (ed.), *The EC and the Challenge of the Future*, (London: Pinter, 1993).

[110] Art.J.4(1) of the TEU.

[111] 'Joint actions' of the CFSP defined in the Lisbon Report (26-27 June 1992) and in the Art.J.1(2) of the TEU that: strengthening democratic principles and institutions, respect for human and minority rights; promoting regional political stability and regional cooperation; contributing to the prevention and settlement of conflicts; contributing international efforts to deal with emergency situations; strengthening existing cooperation against arms proliferation, terrorism, traffic in illicit drugs, and supporting good government. For a good account on the CFSP see, Fink-Hooijer, F., 'The CFSP of the EU', *European Journal of International Law*, (Vol.5, No.2). Available at: <http://www.ejil.org/journal/Vol5/No2/art2.html> (Visited on: October 20, 1999).

infiltration and should ensure stability in its periphery. While the basic norms and values of human rights were severely violated in the former Yugoslavia, the Europeans understood well that it was the violation of norms and values which were widely accepted to be the basis of any common European ethics.[112] The protection of values and norms of the Europeans lay in 'soft' military issues and the protection of EU interests' may require military operations as a complement to preventive – political and economic – instruments or a military operation alone if the latter fails. However, the role of the military in the new security environment is different to and more complex than its previous collective defence role. Thus, the communitarisation of security policy is gradually emerging from the Cold War glacier not in the form of an old collective defence alliance, but in a new form – conflict resolution, military peacekeeping, humanitarian interventions, and crisis prevention and management. These new forms are also known as 'soft' military issues and explicitly defined in the WEU's Petersberg Declaration as Petersberg Tasks.[113]

The post-Cold War role of the EU, which falls somewhere between security and defence issues, is explained in a new form – quasi-military missions or 'soft' military missions.[114] At best, 'soft' military missions can only be tackled by the reconfiguration of existing defence institutions into quasi-military (or civilian in nature) organisations. The WEU is one of the best examples of this. The EU countries have therefore begun establishing an organic link between the EU and the WEU with the TEU and opened the door to the communitarisation of security (quasi-military) policy. In comparison to 'hard' military missions that are purely defensive missions under the responsibility of NATO-only, the following table at the same

---

[112] Chilton, P., 'A European Security Regime: Integration and Cooperation in the Search for CFSP', *Journal of European Integration*, (Vol.19, No.'s 2-3, Winter/Spring 1996), pp.239-240.

[113] The WEU, 'together with the EU, is ready to play a full part in building Europe's security architecture' (Title I, paragraph 1-3). Petersberg Declaration, WEU Council of Ministers, (Bonn: June 19, 1992) in Bloed, A. & Wessel, R.A (eds.), pp.137-148; also see Martin, L. & Roper, J. (eds.) *Towards a Common Defence Policy*.

time illustrates 'soft' military missions, quasi-military missions, under the responsibility of

NATO and the EU/WEU.

Table 1.2

'HARD' MILITARY MISSIONS (NATO-ONLY)	'SOFT' MILITARY MISSIONS[115] (NATO AND EU/WEU)
Alliance and territorial defence (nuclear and conventional) Peace Enforcement Peace-making	Crisis prevention and management (Peacekeeping, humanitarian interventions, evacuation operations, de-mining operations, police-type operations, monitoring embargoes, protection of humanitarian corridors, containment, enforcement of sanctions)

'Soft' military missions are designed for the non-Art.V/5 situations of the WEU/NATO.[116]

Having mentioned this distinction, the WEU is not needed as a *collective defence alliance* in

the presence of NATO. Arguably, even though the WEU is founded as a collective defence

alliance, it has no such a capability today either. Furthermore, although NATO is still holding

this as its foremost responsibility, it has also shifted significantly from the collective defence

---

[114] Westendorp Report on the progress of the Reflection Group's work, Brussels, December 15, 1995 in 'WEU, Security and Defence', *European Parliament*, (Brussels: Briefing No.11, March 21st, 1997).
[115] For more explanations see, WEU Assembly Report, Rapporteur Sir Keith Speed, *Document 1415*, (Paris: WEU Assembly, May 10, 1994), pp.7-8; Sperling, J. & Kirchner, E. *Recasting the European Order*, (UK: Manchester University Press, 1997), pp.37-38.
[116] Art.V of the WEU's founding treaty, *Protocol Modifying and Completing the Brussels Treaty* (October 23, 1954), states that: 'If any High Contracting Parties should be the object of an armed attack in Europe, the other High Contracting Parties will, in accordance with the provisions of Article 51 of the United Nation, afford the Party so attacked all the military and other aid and assistance in their power.' Bloed, A. & Wessel, R. A., p.3; It is crucial to make a distinction between the *peacekeeping* intervention and *military* intervention. Peacekeeping forces traditionally require the consent of both parties' and are not heavily armed. The military intervention is a last resort and many conditions have to be fulfilled, including peacekeeping, in order to be considered as a 'just' intervention. See WEU Council Report, Rapporteur Mr. Marshall, 'European Security Policy', p.12.

alliance model to a 'soft' military model through NATO's Oslo Communiqué of 1992 and the CJTF concept of 1996.[117] Therefore, NATO's 'soft' military missions have also become as well known as its 'hard' military missions. Even so, what is needed and is going to be implemented is for the EU to accept for 'soft' military issues by allowing the CFSP to exploit the WEU's operational capability fully and thus resorting less to the US dominated NATO. The EU, while trying to impose a peace agreement and cease-fire on the conflicting parties', might need a bigger force than the sum of the conflicting forces' in order to stop the deterioration of the conflict. In such a situation, after a feasibility study on the possibility of a military operation and with the mandate of the United Nations (UN), the EU will be able to use the operational capability of the WEU as a 'soft' military mechanism to stop fighting. The EU/WEU military forces should be ready for deployment between the conflicting parties' for *military operations* and not for *fighting wars*. Crucially, in order to enhance the capability of 'soft' military missions, as in every armed conflict, priority should be given to *early warning* and *action*.

The member states of the EC have been very busy in the TEU, discussing how to build up a military capacity for fulfilling 'soft' military missions. However, the search for increasing the potential military capability of the EU through the WEU does not mean that 'soft' military missions are given priority over the EU's diplomatic/political and economic instruments. The idea behind the development of 'soft' military missions within the purview of the EU is to strengthen the CFSP and turn it into a *proactive, forward planning mechanism*, instead of a *reactive* one. For this purpose, the WEU is considered as a potential military arm of the EU, and this was reflected in Art.J.4(2) of the TEU. According to Art.J.4(2), the EU could request

---

[117] NAC Oslo Communiqué of 4-5 June 1992; Gärtner, H., 'European Security, NATO and the Transatlantic Link: Crisis Management', *Austrian Institute for International Affairs*, (US: International Studies Association, 40th Annual Convention, February 16-20, 1999). Available at:

the WEU – being an integral part of the EU integration process – to elaborate and implement decisions and actions, which have defence implications.[118] In other words, the EU Council must mandate the EU/WEU for particular 'soft' military missions. On the other hand, it is stated in the WEU's Maastricht Declarations that, 'the WEU will be developed as the *defence component of the EU* and as the means to strengthen the *European pillar of the Atlantic Alliance*'[119] (emphasis added). The WEU is declared as the military arm of the CFSP and the 'bridge' between the EU and NATO. It is noteworthy to mention that, the CFSP is bound to unanimity and governed through intergovernmentalism.

Peacekeeping is on the agenda of every EU member state and will continue to be so in the future. While Germany has recently displayed some interests in the use of military force in Kosovo, France and the UK are particularly well experienced in peacekeeping doctrines. The Germans are enthusiastic in empowering the CFSP through more communitarisation, more multilateral actions, more institutional flexibility, and more initiatives that are parliamentary. This is one of the main reasons why Germany is supporting the strengthening of the CFSP through mutually reinforcing institutions, a concept that suggests better coordination of the UN, NATO, WEU, OSCE, and the Council of Europe in the area of conflict prevention and crisis management.[120] The major development in Germany was the Federal Constitutional Court's Karlsruhe decision of July 1994 that, in addition to the use of the *Bundeswehr* (federal army) for the defence of NATO territory, German forces would also be sent on WEU, OSCE, and UN peacekeeping missions under a UN mandate. Thus, the gradual strengthening of the relationship between the CFSP and the WEU would allow more political and military options

---

<http://alhan.cc.columbia.edu/sec/dlc/ciao/isa/gah01/> (Visited on: June 12, 1999); Drew, Nelson S., 'NATO From Berlin to Bosnia, "The Bonfire of the Certainties".', *McNair Paper 35*, (US: National War College,1995).
[118] See Art.J.4(2) of the TEU.
[119] *Maastricht Declarations*, Maastricht, December 10, 1991 (title I, paragraph 2) in Bloed, A. & Wessel, R. A. (eds.), p.131.
[120] Rummel, R., 'Germany's Role in the CFSP. 'Normalität' or 'Sonderweg'?' in Hill, C. (ed.), *The Actors in Europe's Foreign Policy*, p.56.

for Germany in multilateral partnerships with the other EU states in the course of 'soft' military missions.

On the other hand, it was not surprising that the intergovernmentalist French and British officials were rejecting the Germans supranational/integrationist idea of the communitarisation of security policy. Historically, the French desire was not to develop a communitarised security policy in the EPC agenda and therefore not to develop it in the CFSP, but the revival of the WEU had been the main French strive.[121] However, a strengthened European security and defence policy through the WEU had been politically unacceptable for the UK, in that it would threaten the defence and security links with the US/NATO. The only concession France obtained at that time was the inclusion of the Art.J.4(5) that, 'the provisions of this Article shall not prevent the development of the closer cooperation between two or more Member States on a bilateral level…' In this context, the French desire has clearly been the development of Franco-German military cooperation. However, the French struggle for an independent WEU was watered down by multilateral conditions in favour of German and American proposals. This article stipulates that bilateral cooperation should take place '…in the framework of the WEU and the Atlantic Alliance, provided such cooperation does not run counter to or impede that provided for this Title [Title V of the TEU].'

France, Germany and, particularly the UK are still looking to the communitarisation of security policy through different lenses. However, the main responsibility of these three powerful EU states is to reach an agreement on balancing the military and non military action that would enable them to carry out 'soft' military missions. France and Germany have understood very well that the main forces behind the CFSP and the WEU are too loose for effective action. The lack of consensus, failure of the identification of common interests, and the lack of clarified priorities in the CFSP became an obstacle to a 'joint action' and paralysed the WEU whilst acting on behalf of the EU. As a result of the continual pooling of sovereignties in security, defence, and foreign policy areas, concentration on non-collective defence aspects of military co-operation seems preferable. Sooner or later, the quasi-military capability of the WEU will be a touchstone for effective EU/WEU conflict prevention or conflict management.

Since the CFSP is still developing, the future will show whether it will be able to effectively embrace the communitarisation of security policy comparable to its economic might. French and German arguments of a *complete* merger between the EU and the WEU – with its Art.V competencies – into a single body are not yet persuasive;[122] instead, *meshing* between them today is found to be a plausible option (see Chapter 2). After all, the fundamental concepts of the meshing are evolving on the way to the communitarisation of security policy. The Amsterdam Summit was opened not only with the debate on the 'constructive abstention', but also the 'enhanced co-operations'. These aspects of the Treaty of Amsterdam (ToA) will be analysed from the standpoint of France and Germany in the following section.

(2.3) The Franco-German Tandem: Embracing the Amsterdam Treaty Together or Separately?

(2.3.1) Reforming the CFSP

The complexity of issues in the TEU demanded their renegotiation in a new IGC in 1996. The renegotiation of the TEU did not provide for direct communitarisation of the CFSP. The ToA,

---

[121] De La Serra, F., 'France – The Impact of François Mitterand' in Hill, C. (ed.), *The Actors in Europe's Foreign Policy*, p.22.

[122] See the respective German and French positions in favour of the EU-WEU merger, including the defence alliance clause of the WEU, for the aim of undertaking greater share of responsibility in NATO tasks. *German White Paper on the 1996 Intergovernmental Conference.* Available at: <http://www.europa.eu.int/en/agenda/igc-

however, summoned a more coherent political expression of common interests and priorities, structural networks and a clearer 'political solidarity'. The apparent result of a clearer political solidarity has been the concept of *constructive abstention*. The ToA reasserted once again that the decision-making mechanism would remain intergovernmental and thus the essence of national sovereignties would be kept intact. However, the appointment of a representative to enhance the EU's position abroad and the creation of a European planning section were the issues weakening national sovereignties to a certain degree. Another significant issue, *enhanced co-operations*, was explicitly cut off from the other ToA issues. The aim behind this issue was a Franco-German statement for the deepening and enlargement of the EU. According to the enhanced co-operations, either group of core states, which are willing and able to agree on a closer military cooperation, or coalition of changing states could agree on joint defence operations on an *ad hoc* basis.

The IGC of 1996/1997 discussed various proposals for upgrading the EU's ability to respond to crisis situations through 'soft' military missions. It was once again confirmed that collective defence is NATO's primary responsibility, but the ToA was designed under Franco-German pressure for a merger between the EU and the WEU. This was the main idea of the WEU Reflection Group while they were presenting their report to the IGC on the merger between the EU and WEU in 1995.[123] The UK argued against the merger between the EU and the WEU, even more strongly than five years previously, also against any possible political subordination of the WEU to the EU. The proposals aiming at a merger between the WEU and the

---

home/ms-doc/state-de/pos.htm>; *French White Paper on the 1996 Intergovernmental Conference*. Available at: <http://www.europa.eu.int/en/agenda/igc-home/ms-doc/state-fr/pos.htm> (Visited on: June 14, 1999).
[123] Options for the EU-WEU relations were stated in the work of the Reflection Group as follows: (1) some members advocated maintaining the full autonomy of the WEU in the foreseeable future, but keeping the EU-WEU 'reinforced partnership' should still be the ground for cooperation; (2) other countries advocated a greater role for the Union in the Petersberg Tasks while preserving the WEU as a separate defence organisation; (3) the majority of representatives supported the integration of the WEU into the EU. See the Westendorp Report on the progress of the Reflection Group's work.

EU had become a victim of the UK in the end, but a number of provisions were agreed in strengthening their links. Art.J.4(1) of the TEU worded provisions on the CFSP as '...including the *eventual* framing of the common defence policy ... which might *in turn* lead to a common defence' (emphasis added). The ToA modified this phrase into a new Art.17(1) (ex Art.J.7(1)) as '...including the *progressive* framing of a common defence policy ... which *might* lead to a common defence, *should the European Council so decide*'[124] (emphasis added). Although the word 'might' kept its own volatile character in the Article, it was the first time that the integration of the WEU – with its Art.V provisions – into the EU through a common defence has been mentioned: '*the possibility of the integration of the WEU into the Union,* should the European Council so decide' (same Article as above, emphasis added).

Art.17(2) (ex Art.J.7(2)) of the ToA related to the scope of possible uses of the WEU's operational capability in 'humanitarian and rescue tasks, peacekeeping tasks and tasks of combat forces in crisis management, including peacemaking.' With this provision, the so-called Petersberg Tasks were included into Title V of the ToA. Although any uses of the WEU military forces need a unanimous decision in the Council, this was a key step forward for the EU's 'soft' military capability. Furthermore, the former TEU Art.J.4(2), which was replaced with the Art.17(3) (ex Art.J.7(3)) of the ToA, also replaced the term 'the Union *request* the WEU' with 'the Union *avail* itself of the WEU.' For Jorg Monar, this was the first sign of the *de facto* merger of the EU with the WEU's crisis management capabilities.[125] However, one of the significant stumbling blocks in front of the full merger between the EU and the WEU is their asymmetrical membership structure. For example, the role and position of associate members of the WEU will be an obstacle in any possible Petersberg Tasks operation.

---

[124] *Treaty of Amsterdam (ToA)*, 'Draft Treaty of Amsterdam – Chp.12, the CFSP', (Brussels: Secretary General Parliament European, Task Force CIG/96, June 19, 1997), pp.EN99-EN114. Consolidated version of the TEU is also available at: <http://europa.eu.int/eur-lex/> (Visited on: July 14, 2000).

Although the ToA disappointed those who had advocated the EU-WEU merger at that time, the EU continued expanding its military capabilities and the issue of European common defence still remained on the agenda.[126]

German delegates wanted the CFSP to be capable of planning and acting in advance as a whole in any potential crisis situation and to be able to call on the WEU more easily to fulfil the required operations on behalf of the EU. German officials were also aware of the fact that this could only be attained if the EU member states managed to circumvent the hurdle of unanimous voting in the CFSP decision-making mechanisms. Initially, French delegates were reluctant to agree to the German idea of watering down the unanimous voting. However, after the ministerial meeting in Freiburg on February 27, 1996, German Foreign Minister Klaus Kinkel and French Foreign Minister Hervé de Charette agreed on a joint proposal declaring the 'constructive abstention.'[127] By this, it was aimed to avoid the double veto in the TEU on 'Joint Actions'. The double veto was the method of a first vote on the nature of the action and then a second vote on whether it could be implemented by the QMV. Duff criticised the double vote aptly, 'if you have to decide unanimously to vote by QMV, then you are going to vote unanimously anyway.'[128] Art.23 (ex Art.J.13(1)) of the ToA states that when the European Council adopts a decision, a state may abstain (unanimity minus one), in the spirit of solidarity through '[constructive abstention] shall not be obliged to apply the decision...[but] the Member State concerned shall refrain from any action likely to conflict with or impede Union action based on that decision....'[129] Moreover, if the number of

---

[125] Monar, J., 'The EU's Foreign Affairs System after the Treaty of Amsterdam: A 'Strengthened Capacity for External Action'?', *European Foreign Affairs Review*, (Vol.2, 1997), p.430.

[126] For detailed analysis of the European Common Defence Policy (CDP) and Common Defence (CD) and their delimitation see Chapter 2 - *(1.2) Contours of the CDP and CD.*

[127] See 'Guidelines adopted at the Franco-German Seminar of Ministers of Foreign Affairs', *Speeches and Statements – France/Germany/IGC/CFSP*, (Freiburg im Breisgau, February 27, 1996). Available at: <http://www.info-france-usa.org/fsearch.htm> (Visited on: September 8, 1999).

[128] Duff, A., *Reforming the EU*, (UK: Federal Trust, 1997), pp.79-80.

member states abstaining represents more than one-third of the QMV then the decision automatically will drop. Decisions of the EU, which have defence implications, are not subject to this procedure. All decisions related to defence must be passed by unanimous voting. Chris Patten, who is in charge of the EU's External Relations, considered these changes in the decision-making process as innovations and stated that extending the QMV fully into CFSP matters is not necessary and 'warned', '...implementing what was agreed under the Amsterdam Treaty and at the Cologne summit would be "a considerable enterprise".'[130]

Although French and German governments put forward a joint proposal in support of the EU-WEU merger and 'constructive abstention', France obviously diverged from its ally with regard to institutional arrangements for policymaking. France, as it was in the IGC of 1992, found itself closer to the UK with regard to the intergovernmental implementation of the CFSP arrangements in the IGC of 1997. The negotiations on who shall be bound to speak on behalf of the EU focused on French, German, and British proposals. It was indeed difficult to ensure consistency in the EU while the leadership was rotating every six months. The succeeding presidencies were so occupied with their own separate security concerns that third parties were often confused as to what the principal EU policy was. Therefore, the EU member states decided to appoint a senior figure in charge of CFSP affairs under the authority of the European Council. While France desired the appointee to be a senior politician, Germany insisted the appointee should be a bureaucratic personage and the UK wanted the appointee to be a civil servant. Germany was concerned that a political post could not only

---

[129] *Treaty of Amsterdam (ToA)*, p.EN108; For detailed information on 'common position' and 'joint actions' see Whitman, R. G., 'Creating a Foreign Policy for Europe? Implementing the CFSP from Maastricht to Amsterdam', *Australian Journal of International Affairs*, (Vol.52, No.2, July 1998).
[130] It will be informative to note that Chris Patten is a British citizen and was the governor of the UK's former colony, Hong Kong! See *European Voice*, (September 9-15, 1999), p.6.

overlap with the work of the European Commission, but could also widen the gap between the EU's first and second pillars. The Germans argued that as a result of this gap the political personality would be separated from the EU institutions.[131] Germany and the UK, though for different reasons, were in harmony on this issue. Member states in the end agreed on a watered down version of the French proposal. The post, to be known as the High Representative of the CFSP, would be filled with a diplomat instead of a senior politician.[132]

In the aftermath of the unsuccessful Yugoslav experience, it was also agreed that the CFSP failed in its analysis and planning function. Therefore, the *Policy Planning and Early Warning Unit* (PPEWU) was established and placed under the responsibility of the High Representative. Duff considered the PPEWU as a *think-tank*, it should think the unthinkable and stimulate the imagination. Above all, he also argued that the CFSP should simply improve the habit of thinking the thinkable through sharing a wide range of information and political intelligence among the EU member states.[133] The EU's new High Representative of the CFSP and the Secretary-General of the Council and the WEU, Javier Solana, declared his plans in the *European Voice* one month before he took his post on October 18, 1999. He said that he would concentrate on boosting the EU's ability for dealing with humanitarian emergencies like the turmoil that was happening in East Timor at that time. One official said, previous conflicts such as those in Kosovo and in Bosnia had shown that wherever the EU tried to

---

[131] Duff, A., 'Ratification' in Duff, A., Pinder, J. & Pryce, R., (eds.), *Maastricht and Beyond: Building the EU*, (London: Routledge, Federal Trust, 1994), p.18.
[132] Art. 26 of the ToA states that, 'the Secretary-General of the Council, High Representative of the CFSP, shall assist the Council in matters coming within the scope of the CFSP, in particular through contributing to the formulation, preparation and implementation of policy decisions, and, when appropriate and acting on behalf of the Council at the request of the Presidency, through conducting political dialogue with third parties'.
[133] Duff, A., *Reforming the EU*, p.86; The ToA Declaration to the Final Act on the establishment of a PPEWU sets the objectives of the unit as follows: (a) monitoring and analysing developments in areas relevant to the CFSP; (b) providing assessments of the Union's foreign and security policy interests and identifying areas where the CFSP could focus in future; (c) providing timely assessments and early warning of events, situations and potential political crisis that may have significant repercussions on the CFSP; (d) producing, at the request of either the Council or the Presidency, or on its own initiative, policy option papers to the Council, which may contain analysis, recommendations and strategies for the CFSP. p.EN114; For detailed information on the PPEWU, also see Monar, J., 'The EU's Foreign Affairs System after the Treaty of Amsterdam:', pp.416-418.

provide humanitarian relief, it had to work very closely with the military to be effective. Solana has underlined his determination to use military action for humanitarian aims if necessary. He also demonstrated his strong dedication to his new post by appointing previous NATO press officer, Christina Gallach, to work in the PPEWU, and 20 other NATO staff. [134]

(2.3.2) The Franco-German Joint Letter: 'Enhanced Co-operations'

There are lots of terms in the EU's terminology that are difficult to identify or to differentiate from each other. The first group of terms in the ToA, used particularly in academic literature, range from 'differentiation' and 'flexibility' (used by the Westendorp group) to 'enhanced co-operations'. The second group of terms are 'multi-speed', 'variable geometry', 'à la carte', 'hard core', and 'concentric circles'. The second group of terms, if compared to the former one, are narrow in scope and they are a sub-group of the former. The diversity of social, political, and economic interests in an enlarging and deepening EU is making the everyday use of these various integration and co-ordination techniques a common strategy in the EU chambers. [135] The focus in this section will be put on 'enhanced co-operations' from the first group and on 'hard core', 'concentric circles' and 'à la carte' from the second group. Other terms will briefly be mentioned throughout this section for the clearer analysis of these chosen terms.

The European integration process has always contended with the search for a way out of the difficulty between the 'slow members' and 'fast members'. Throughout the European integra-

---

[134] Taylor, S., 'Solana to boost EU's humanitarian role', *European Voice*, (September 16-22, 1999), p.6.
[135] Simonis captivatingly observed that, 'in addition to the conception of a strong nation-state and of the supranational European state, no light is thrown on a third possibility, namely the development of a new, and hitherto unknown, *polycentric* administrative structure. This would mean a multi-level administrative structure, presently not seen as an independent model, but perhaps representing an administrative structure *sui generis*!' (Emphasis added). Simonis, J. B. D., 'European Integration and the Erosion of the Nation-state', p.2; for discussions on integration and co-ordination techniques, which were prepared the way to the Treaty of Nice, held on December 11, 2000, see Chapter 3 - *(3) The Necessity for the Franco-German Tandem's Continuance: Recent Developments and Future Strategic Choices, 1998-2000* and *Epilogue.*

tion process the various group of 'fast members' are allowed to progress with closer integration and coordination, while 'slow members' remained uninvolved. Indeed, this technique of differentiated integration *within* the EU has always been widely applied as a remedy. The EMU (the UK and Denmark opted-out) and the European Social Chapter (the UK opted-out) of the TEU are in turn time-limited and non-time-limited examples of this 'multi-speed' Europe respectively.[136] Ehlermann has also found that in some respects the term 'multi-speed' overlaps with the term 'variable geometry'. The different positions of states are no longer subject to differences in time factor, but subject to states' different views on the substance.[137] The UK's rejection of the European Social Chapter, even of its principles, is a good example for the term 'variable geometry'.

The difficulties in the area of defence among the 'fast members' have resulted in different structural processes *outside* the EU framework. This can be illustrated by the example of the WEU, Eurocorps, Eurofor, Euromarfor, and Bosnian Contact Group. The execution of 'soft' military missions (Petersberg Tasks) for non-Art.V cases through *coalitions of the willing* (or *ad hoc coalitions*) is allowed outside the EU or the WEU framework.[138]

This 'differentiation' became a popular politico-diplomatic item in the European integration process with the Lamers-Schäuble paper of 1994.[139] The Lamers-Schäuble document started a storm, shaped the Westendorp Group, and marked the ToA. This document suggested that core states, which belong to the economic/monetary (EMU) and political (CFSP) 'hard cores',

---

[136] Ehlermann wrote that, 'one or several member states are allowed, either in the Treaty or in Regulations, Directives or Decisions, temporarily not to apply a norm valid in principle for all member states.' Ehlermann, C. D., 'Differentiation, Flexibility, Closer Cooperation: The New Provisions of the Amsterdam Treaty', translated by Iain Fraser, *European University Institute*, (Italy: RSC Publication, March 1998).
[137] *Ibid.*
[138] Silversti, S., Gnesotto, N. & Vasconcelos, A., 'Decision-Making and Institutions' in Martin, L. & Roper, J. (eds.) *Towards a Common Defence Policy*, pp.51-68.
[139] *CDU/CSU Bundestag Paper*, ' Überlegungen zur europäischen Politik (Reflections on European Policy)', (Bonn: September 1, 1994).

should move ahead in integration across an additional range of issues. Furthermore, they ar-

gued that the political and economic 'hard cores' would be institutionalised to include defence

capabilities. The Lamers-Schäuble paper was proposing a 'quasi-constitutional document'

based on the model of a 'federal state' encompassing of France, Germany, and the Benelux

countries, with organs fulfilling functions similar to those performed in democratic countries

by parliament and government. Wolfgang Schäuble even went further and claimed the

communitarisation of defence – a *Gemeinschaftsaufgabe*.[140] The document also reflected the

German official interests' in achieving a Political Union through the strengthened European

Commission and Parliament. Charles Kupchan, one of the prominent supporters of the

'Atlantic Union', argued that EMU will help to reach the two main objectives: *Firstly*, it will

lock the Franco-German coalition into the EU by transferring authority in the monetary policy

from the national to the supranational level and will abolish one of the most powerful symbols

of sovereignty – national currencies. *Secondly*, it is expected to create an inner core (hard

core) and act as a magnet for the EU's other smaller states.[141] Kupchan also emphasised the

side effects of this model. The participation to the inner core would provide benefits, but it

could definitely create divisions between the core and the periphery. This might also trigger

competition and raise old and new rivalries among peripheral states for the aim of attaining

entry into the inner circle.[142]

France, Germany's usual workmate, strongly opposed the 'hard core' idea by proclaiming its

traditional preferences on the side of intergovernmental procedures. Former French Prime

Minister Edouard Balladur proposed an alternative proposal for facilitating the development

---

[140] *Ibid.*

[141] Kupchan's model is similar to the Lamers-Schäuble's 'hard core' model. Unlike the Lamers-Schäuble's model, Kupchan's model focuses only on France and Germany by stating that they will guide the EU without appearing to dominate it. Kupchan, C. A., 'From the EU to the Atlantic Union', *EUI Working Papers*, (Italy: European University Institute, RSC No.97/73, December 1997), p.7.

[142] *Ibid.* pp.8-9.

of several core states on specific issues. For example, defence core states, and foreign and security core states which would be created in a form of 'concentric circles' (overlapping circles of co-operation). Indeed, the French model was not the federalist type integration and suggested a large number of speeds, more than two 'concentric circles' that would allow members to join into their preferred circles and stay out of others. Thus, several 'hard cores' would be formed rather than a single one.[143] Balladur's proposal contained the elements of institutionalisation, so that the 'hard core' members would have some power to decide on which countries could join in or not.

The UK, on the other hand, declared its own idea with the former Prime Minister John Major's September 1994 speech in Leydan. He argued that the EU is no more than a simple 'association of European nations', and therefore the better option is 'à la carte' – countries should be free to cooperate with any partner on any project. 'À la carte' marked by the total absence of institutionalisation.[144] Le Gloannec argued that, 'hard cores' and 'à la carte' models later influenced the French 'concentric circles'; while Balladur's successor Alain Juppé envisaged a version of shifting configurations around the Franco-German core, President Chirac leaned more on the UK side. Former French Prime Minister Alain Juppé stated that:

> *'Let us have the courage to state that tomorrow's Union will be composed of*
> *distinct levels: a common law or de jure Union, with its present fifteen states plus*
> *those who will join us; in the core of this Union, of this first circle, there will be a*
> *second one, more limited but adaptable, with a small number of states working*

---

[143] Silversti, S., Gnesotto, N. & Vasconcelos, A., 'Decision-Making and Institutions' in Martin, L. & Roper, J. (eds.), *Towards a Common Defence Policy*, pp.58-60.
[144] *Ibid.* p.59; Ehlermann wrote that boundaries between 'à la carte' and 'variable geometry' are blurring. They have different positions, but the differentiation for 'variable geometry' is possible only in marginal areas, whereas in 'à la carte' differentiation is possible almost in all areas. In other words, the 'variable geometry' is implicitly based on a plan. Whereas, 'à la carte' based on absolutely free choices. Ehlermann, C. D., p.3.

> *with France and Germany, ready to go further or faster than the others, in areas*
> *such as money or defence'.*[145]

However, President Chirac initially chose the middle way between Germany and the UK and searched for a way to strengthen Franco-British ties, as he thought the intergovernmentalist tendencies of the British policymakers would serve the French national interests better than the federalist tendencies of the German policymakers.[146]

The Lamers-Schäuble document underlined an ongoing dangerous divergence of interests within the EU and that the existing European institutions were proven not to be functioning properly. The authors of the document also claimed that the EU would be unsustainable once the EMU and enlargement was completed. They claimed that in order to guarantee the uniformity of the EU, reunified Germany should remain firmly anchored in Europe and supranationalism should be extended in practice. Under the impact of these notions, two Franco-German joint letters were presented. One of them presented by Kohl and Chirac on December 6, 1995, and the other one presented by former Foreign Ministers Klaus Kinkel and Hervè de Charette on October 17, 1996. Despite their opposing views on the 'hard core' and 'concentric circles' concepts, France and Germany chose to work together on these letters. France and Germany called for a new flexibility in the functioning of the EU in order to allow the EU members to deepen their collaborations without risking a veto from reluctant partners. This new flexibility brought forth the development of 'enhanced co-operations' within the EU. De

---

[145] Alain Juppé quoted in De Areilza, Jose M., 'Enhanced Co-operations in the Treaty of Amsterdam: Some Critical Remarks', *Conference Organised by the Copenhagen Research Project on European Integration*, Conference on 'Rethinking Constitutionalism in the EU', (Copenhagen: March 19-20, 1998). Available at: <http://www.law.harward.edu/programs/JeanMonnet/papers/98/98-13.html> (Visited on: September 16, 1999).
[146] Le Gloannec, Anne-Marie, 'Germany and Europe's Foreign and Security Policy: Embracing the "British" Vision' in 'Break Out, Break Down or Break In? Germany and the EU After Amsterdam', *AICGS Research Report*, (US: The Johns Hopkins University, AICGS Research Report No.8, 1998), p.25.

Arezila argued that the ToA's 'enhanced co-operations' provided member states with 'a power to initiate "enhanced co-operations legislation" and to control its adoption in this inner circle more tightly than in normal Community situations.'[147] French and German officials continuously declared their support for the 'enhanced co-operations'. Kinkel stated that, 'the French and Germans are closing ranks and we hope that our Franco-German tandem will be a stimulus for further European integration.'[148] On the other side, Chirac declared that, 'France proposes that the states that have the will and the capacity be allowed to develop close co-operation among themselves.... Once approved by the Council, their projects would be considered as those of the Union, and backed as such. Flexibility and consistency would be then conciliated'.[149]

France and Germany were particularly enthusiastic on extending 'enhanced co-operations' into common defence and armaments policies creation.[150] Predictably, the UK firmly rejected the idea of flexibility in 'enhanced co-operations' to be applied to defence. British diplomats repeatedly argued at that time that the ten WEU full member states were already a *de facto* core group on defence and this would be undermined if a group of states advances separately. The UK, therefore, demanded unanimous voting for launching 'enhanced co-operations'. In the end, a compromise was found, in that only 'institutional practice' would show whether the veto could be applied in 'enhanced co-operations'.[151]

---

[147] De Areilza, Jose M., 'Enhanced Co-operations in the Treaty of Amsterdam: Some Critical Remarks'; Kupchan also defined similar views in detail. He defined core states as 'power-constraint devices' in two forms: Firstly, core states erect internal rules and institutions that check their external power. Secondly, core states erect external rules and institutions that bind themselves to other states. For a more detailed study on 'power-constraint devices' see, Kupchan, C., 'After Pax Americana', p.46.

[148] Klaus Kinkel quoted in Boyer, Y., 'Whither Core Europe? France and the European Construction: Issues and Choices' in Lankowski, C. and Serfaty, S., pp.19-34.

[149] Jacques Chirac quoted in de Areilza, Jose M., 'Enhanced Co-operations in the Treaty of Amsterdam:' p.10.

[150] 'Enhanced co-operations' concept was inserted into the WEU Maastricht Declarations and attached to the Maastricht Treaty on December 10, 1991. Section C, parag.5: 'enhanced co-operation in the field of armaments with the aim of creating a European armaments agency.' See WEU's *Maastricht Declarations* in Bloed, A. & Wessel, R. A. (ed.), pp.131-135.

[151] After the Commission gave its affirmative opinion on that the proposed 'enhanced co-operations' concept is consistent with the EU policies, qualified majority voting will be applied later. However, any individual member

Against the background of French and German philosophies, the 'enhanced co-operations' proposal is not surprising. France no longer has the capacity to be a leading political actor since the East and West Germans unification. On the other hand, Germany with its multilateralist tendency will continue to support all future advances in the European integration process. Hence, France and Germany are convinced that the CFSP, defence, and JHA offers more opportunity for 'enhanced co-operations' than the Treaty of Rome procedures. However, as a result of strong resistance from the UK, the European Council excluded 'enhanced co-operations' from the CFSP and defence spheres during the Amsterdam Treaty negotiations. In no other sphere has 'enhanced co-operations' been *de rigueur* as it is in the CFSP and defence spheres. However, provisions on 'enhanced co-operations' were written only into the Treaty of Rome and JHA pillars at that time. Therefore, member states sought to exercise 'enhanced co-operations' in security and defence spheres outside the EU through Art.J.4(5) of the TEU, revised Art.17(4) of the ToA (see above), until the Treaty of Nice amendments were endorsed by the EU Council on December 11, 2000, to implement 'enhanced co-operations' in the CFSP, but not in the defence sphere, (see Epilogue).

(3) Conclusions

Durable peace in Europe can only be attained if it relates to principles of freedom, human rights, democracy and co-operation, but at the same time law and justice must also be guaranteed. France and Germany understand very well that without a robust common European security and defence policy (CESDP) under the CFSP, the EU would be seen as a divided actor and thus could not develop a capability for shaping international politics in accordance with the principles mentioned above. The EU should embrace its *conflict prevention function* and

---

state can veto the decision. This veto has to be explained to the Council of Ministers. If the explanation is convincing, the Council by qualified majority voting will ask the European Council to take the decision by unanimous voting. For more information see, ToA – Title VII (ex Title VIa) – Provisions on Closer Co-operation.

military crisis management responsibility, through pursuing an active stabilisation policy in its periphery, which together form the 'soft' military pillar of the CFSP/CESDP. In short, the EU should equally be both a civilian and a military power for the robust pursuit of any peace operation.[152]

Concomitantly, the EU/WEU must build an equal partnership with the US and as a precondition for this, should develop an 'autonomous' EU/WEU pillar in parallel to the 'North American Pillar' of NATO. The EU/WEU forces must be, up to a certain extent, separable from NATO structures in order to be able to assume 'soft' military missions (Petersberg Tasks) and guarantee stability, through their own efforts, in the European periphery, where NATO as a whole cannot or does not want to become involved. However, a *fully* autonomous European security and defence policy is neither desirable nor attainable and, thus, its construction must be realised within NATO. At this point, flexibility and pragmatism, interlocking and dependencies should not be diluted, instead they should thrive among the EU/WEU, US, and NATO in order to reduce the US's unilateral and hegemonic tendencies through constructing a symmetrical European 'Pillar of Defence' structure.

Paradoxically, it has been shown in many cases that decision and co-ordination problems among the EU states – largely between European Integrationists (headed by France and Germany) and Atlanticists (headed by the UK) – paralysed the common European security and defence policymaking. The question of transferring national sovereignties into a CESDP has always brought to the fore by Germany, but in addition to the dissident UK, France also explicitly refrained to fully compromise its national sovereignty. The transfer of national sovereignties into the EU was discussed and agreed through the 'constructive abstention' and 'en-

---

[152] '3. Deutsch-Französischen Dialog – Mit Sicherheit in die europäische Zukunft: Deutsch-französische

hanced co-operations' without distorting the veto powers of the member states during the ToA. Since the QMV in the area of security and defence would not directly be applicable in the foreseeable future, putting 'constructive abstention' and 'enhanced co-operations' into effect seems not much problematic. Nicole Gnesotto argued that even Germany, who advocates European federalism, admits that intergovernmentalism would remain the rule in foreseeable future. She further asks, 'can a military 'hard core' be built in the same way as a monetary one, when Germany remains reluctant to get deeply involved in military crisis management and when, without the UK, a European defence would be like a duck without feet?'[153] At the same time, she emphasised that there would not be any significant security and defence policy initiatives in the absence of agreement among the 'core states' – France, Germany, and the UK – and expects no serious discussion among them since the 'core group model' is compatible with the 'constructive abstention'.[154]

In order to construct an effective European defence policy, divergent national interests should be focused and targets must be found for the clear identification of a CESDP. Furthermore, realising civilian and military crisis management not only requires the effective restructuring of the European Defence Industrial and Technological Base (EDITB) through the EU member states' systematic financial investments in military resources, but this is also recognised as one of the principal conditions for a robust CESDP. Otherwise, the EU/WEU will lose its credibility before the US and potential conflicting parties in future situations. In the meantime, there has been significant developments in the relationship between the European Integrationists and Atlanticists' since the Anglo-French Joint Declaration on European Defence at St. Mâlo

---

Perspectiven einer gemeinsamen Sicherheits – und Verteidigungspolitik', *Diskussionsbericht*, (Saarbrücken: 31 Mai-01 Juni, 2001), p.10.
[153] Gnesotto, N., 'Common European Defence and Transatlantic Relations', *Survival*, (Vol.38, No.1, Spring 1996), p.22.
[154] See '3. Deutsch-Französischen Dialog – Mit Sicherheit in die europäische Zukunft: Deutsch-französische Perspectiven einer gemeinsamen Sicherheits – und Verteidigungspolitik', *Diskussionsbericht*, pp.23-24.

on December 4, 1998, which led to the declaration of the CESDP at Cologne on June 4, 1999, and the creation of a European Rapid Reaction Force by 2003, announced in the Helsinki European Council meeting on December 10-11, 1999. Is the European defence venture after all a duck without feet in the way as Gnesotto argues? The next Chapter will be analysed by opening the *Pandora's box* of European Defence Dilemma.

2

RESOLUTION OF EU's DEFENCE DILEMMA
RATCHETS UP
THE EUROPEAN 'PILLAR OF DEFENCE'

'Same bed different dreams: This is an ancient Chinese description of any marriage of flesh,

politics or ideologies. Today it is also the best way to describe the defence policies of the

nations that won the Cold War. The problems created by their joint success encourage them

to retreat into self-reliance and individuality. The US, Western Europe and Japan still live

and work together in history's most successful trilateral alliance. But they look nervously into

each other's eyes every morning to see what new things their partners have been imagining

on their own time'.

--Jim Hoagland[1]

Introduction

While the allocation of 'soft' military missions to the EU/WEU and 'hard' military missions
to the US/NATO seems a feasible (though not very easy) solution for the Europeans and
Americans, the way ahead for 'hard' military missions is perhaps less clear than it was in the
Cold War era, which may impair this successful allocation. In order to underline the significance of 'soft' military missions (or quasi-military missions), the overall aim of this chapter
will be to highlight the significance of defence (or military-diplomatic) aspects of European
security and to look at the developments, which have occurred in this area. Undeniably, 'soft'
military issues whether national or regional conflicts, are horrific enough due to the death and
destruction involved. However, 'soft' military issues are not the only concerns that could

---

[1] Hoagland, J., 'Nervous Looks Among Allies', *The Washington Post*, (December 19, 1999), p.B07.

cause instability in Europe. 'Hard' military issues, such as proliferation of ballistic missile technology and the spread of nuclear, chemical or biological weapons, are other significant areas that would affect 'soft' military missions as threats to all humanity.

Firstly, a rogue governments'[2] missile attack might threaten crisis intervention troops, as was experienced in the Gulf War. The EU/WEU's 'soft' military intervention might therefore require missile defence against missile attack. In this case, 'hard' military backing from the US/NATO is necessary. In relation to the first reason, secondly, the re-emergence of the US scheme to develop a protective shield against ballistic nuclear missiles is seriously agitating its European allies.

The long-standing US ballistic missile defence projects of the Cold War, designed to place space based autonomous interceptors which are capable of destroying attacking missiles early in their flight path, regained prominence in the post-Cold War era through the national missile defence (NMD) plan of the Clinton Administration.[3] President Clinton therefore hoped to persuade Moscow to modify the Anti-Ballistic Missile Treaty (ABMT) of 1972. However, building a US missile defence shield was firmly rejected by Russians on the basis that any

---

[2] The WEU's Assembly suggested that the term 'rogue states' should not be used, since it does not distinguish between government and population. For this reason, the term 'rogue government(s)' is found more appropriate. WEU Assembly, 'WEU Assembly seeks common position on US missile defence', *Press Releases*, (Paris: Plenary Session 5-8 June 2000, June 06, 2000).

[3] The ballistic missile defence discourse has its roots in the US President Ronald Reagan's famous Strategic Defence Initiative (SDI), which let to the coining of the phrase 'Star Wars' in March 1983. The SDI was created in the Cold War period and referred to nuclear standoff, Mutual Assured Destruction (MAD), between the US and the USSR. After the collapse of the USSR, a device called Brilliant Pebbles, a comprehensive suite of weapons circling the globe, was tailored and a new architecture in 1990 called Global Protection Against Limited Strikes (GPALS) discussed for destroying missiles that could be launched accidentally by the Soviets or more limited missile attack (unauthorised launch) that could be mounted by another nation. The US Congress had rejected the GPALS and none of the US ally accepted co-operation on such a project. See Fox, E. & Orman, S., 'The Vital Role of Policy: Or "what happened to ballistic missile defence?"', *The Journal of Social, Political, and Economic Studies*, (Vol.21, No.3, Fall 1996), pp.243-252. Also see, 'Current state of industrial studies on anti-missile systems in Europe', WEU Assembly, *Anti-Missile Defence for Europe – Symposium 20-21 April 1993*, (Rome: Second Sitting, April 20, 1993).

unilateral abrogation of the ABM Treaty by the US would provoke a new arms race.[4] Like-

wise, the then US Defence Secretary William S. Cohen tried to convince sceptical Europeans

that not only the US, but also Europe would face a real threat to its security in coming years if

North Korea, Iran, Iraq, Libya or other nations continue developing or acquiring interconti-

nental nuclear missiles.[5] The US Senate's rejection of the Comprehensive Nuclear Test Ban

Treaty (CNTBT) was severely criticised by European governments. They declared that the

US is exploiting its global military and economic power to lock itself into strategic superiority

and make itself immune to future challenges from the rest of the world. They also claimed

that the US missile shield could weaken political and military links between the US and

Europe and might also trigger a dangerous arms race with Russia and China. William

Drozdiak wrote in *The Washington Post* that, 'European governments have stepped up their

warnings that such a system could destroy the concept of shared risk that for decades has been

the foundation of NATO security doctrine'.[6]

In addition to the risk of antagonising the Russians, European governments were drawing at-

tention to another risk that the US and China might face with a new confrontation over bal-

listic missile defences in Asia. French President Chirac said that, 'we must avoid questioning

of the ABMT that could lead to disruption of strategic equilibria and a new nuclear arms

race'.[7] At the same time, German Foreign Minister Joschka Fischer said, 'Germany's commit-

ment to be non-nuclear was always based on our trust that the US would protect our interests,

---

[4] Drozdiak, W., 'Possible US Missile Shield Alarms Europe; Allies Fear Arms Race, Diminished Security Ties', *The Washington Post*, (November 6, 1999), p.A01.
[5] Pentagon officials are warning that a three-stage missile, Taepo Dong-2, which North Korea is still developing, but has agreed not to test in exchange for American economic aid, could destroy all targets in the US and most of Europe with a nuclear payload. Whitney, C. R., 'US and NATO Allies Divided Over Defence Needs', *New York Times*, (December 3, 1999), p.20.
[6] Drozdiak, W., 'Possible US Missile Shield Alarms Europe…', p.A01.
[7] Whitney, C. R., 'US and NATO Allies Divided Over Defence Needs', p.20; During Jacques Chirac-Jiang Zemin (Chinese President) meeting in China in May 1997, they expressed their worries about the installation of a sea-based US missile defence system that would protect Taiwan and Japan. Drozdiak, W., 'Possible US Missile Shield Alarms Europe…', p.A01; Clinton was also planned to modify the Navy's Aegis fleet with the air defence system in order to make it an effective worldwide ballistic missile-killer. See Gaffney, Frank J. (Jr.), 'The Newest 'Isolationist'', *Washington Times*, (November 9, 1999), p.A17.

that the US, as the leading nuclear power, would guarantee some sort of power' and added, 'a drive by the US to built its own missile defence would erode that confidence by effectively putting European cities at greater risk of nuclear missile than those in America. Wouldn't that be a legacy for Bill Clinton – converting the Greens into advocates of a 'German bomb'.'[8] He also said that this would 'split the security standards within the NATO alliance'.[9] Even the closest ally of the US, British Prime Minister Tony Blair, said that they had serious reservations about the US plans on ballistic missile defence and their support 'would be critical, because of the need for the US to upgrade its tracking stations there in order to shoot down missiles before they strike North America'.[10]

In the face of all criticisms raised by the European and other governments, Democrats and Republicans in the US Senate 'alike understand that – in a world increasingly awash with ballistic missile threats – effective anti-missile systems are becoming an essential ingredient to the US's engagement internationally as well as its security at home'.[11] Moreover, the US Undersecretary of Defence, Walter Slocombe, made a striking comment that the US could withdraw from the ABMT if Russia rejected modifications, and added, 'we will not permit any other country to have a veto on actions that may be needed for the defence of our nation'.[12] William Drozdiak quoted a senior European diplomat at NATO headquarters in Brussels: 'This issue [NMD] could end up driving a stake through the heart of the alliance. First, there is the danger that it will cause the Russians and the Chinese to ratchet up the arms race by finding ways to beat missile defences. But, there is also the fear that if the system

---

[8] Gaffney, Frank J. (Jr.), 'The Newest 'Isolationist'', p.A17; Chairman of the Committee on EU Affairs and member of the *Bundestag*, Friedbert Pflüger (CDU), argued that he would not be against the US plans with regard to NMD. However, he emphasised 'the need to engage all partners into the process in order to avoid slowing down the disarmament discussions.' See 'Discussion with Mr. Friedbert Pflüger', *An American Institute for Contemporary German Studies*, (Washington: February 2, 2000). Available at:
<http://www.aicgs.org/cgibin/aicgs/events/ search_engine.cgi> (Visited on: June 20, 2000).
[9] Drozdiak, W., 'Possible US Missile Shield Alarms Europe...', p.A01.
[10] *Ibid.*
[11] Gaffney, Frank J. (Jr.), 'The Newest 'Isolationist'', p.A17.
[12] *Ibid.*

works, American and European security interests will no longer be bound by exposure to the same threats'.[13] Drozdiak also aptly commented:

> *'[NATO's] strategic doctrine held that the US would be willing to share the same*
> *exposure to nuclear attacks by placing its own cities at risk in the defence of the*
> *European allies. But if the US develops a missile shield on its own, it would no*
> *longer be subject to the same constraints. In the view of the allies, such a dramatic*
> *change in the US strategic environment would soon lead Washington to abandon*
> *its commitments under NATO's nuclear doctrine'.[14]*

Jim Hoagland argued that, 'the US has a dream: a [NMD] system that would protect American territory from being hit by ballistic rockets from rogue [governments]. The gathering debate in Congress on this big idea adds to European fears about *the US going its own way on defence in the future, or establishing different zones of security within the alliance'*[15] (emphasis added).

While state policies were written for the Cold War's bipolar world, technology was brought into the multipolar world with the end of the East-West conflict. However, the European policymakers are slow in understanding the necessity of their own partially detached defence needs from the US. John Lloyd argued, '[f]orget the peace dividend. Under the impact of above developments, the US and Europeans might find themselves diverged in encapsulating the new world conditions. If we [Europeans] want to follow our ideals and protect human rights, we must spend far, far more on defence and aid'.[16] In addition to this, two wars in the Balkans, particularly the one in Kosovo, indicated to the Europeans that the EU urgently needed a Common European Security and Defence Policy (CESDP).

---

[13] Drozdiak, W., 'Possible US Missile Shield Alarms Europe…', p.A01.
[14] *Ibid.*
[15] Hoagland, J., 'Nervous Looks Among Allies', p.B07.
[16] Lloyd, J., 'Prepare For a Brave New World', *New Statesman*, (Vol.128, No.4432, April 19, 1999), p.8.

In the first section of this chapter, the period 1990-1997 will be analysed in order to summarise discussions on the inclusion of the defence concept into the EU. The murky concept of the European 'Pillar of Defence' will be explored as a core dilemma centring on the Atlanticists (headed by the UK) and the European Integrationists (headed by France and Germany). The UK pledged vigorously for the *status quo*, that the EU should not have a defence role competitive with NATO, thus the maintenance of an autonomous WEU was the UK's desire. On the other side, being the 'hard core' of the European 'Pillar of Defence', the Franco-German partnership committed itself to advocating a phased merger between the EU and the WEU that would ultimately empower the EU to develop a Common Defence Policy (CDP) and a Common Defence (CD) respectively. This section will mainly focus on the confusion over the Europeans' complicated defence dilemma.

The second section will focus on an analysis of the European defence industry. The concept of the EU's security-economics will be analysed from the perspective of spillover into the defence sphere. The analysis of restructuring and rationalising the European defence industry will be the primary motive of this section to which all EU governments should pay particular attention. Even the Atlanticist UK finally decided to be the part of the European Armaments Agency (EAA). Therefore, if Europeans wants to catch up with the US in precision-guided weapons technology, battlefield intelligence, command-and-control systems, heavy-lift air transport and other high-technology assets that they found vital in the Kosovo operation, they have to show more political will and collaborate to give European defence industries more financial support.

The last section of this chapter will address developments, which occurred in the sphere of European security and defence from the year 1998 until the year 2000. The following topics will be examined: Firstly, the long lasting French desire to rely less on the US has taken a qualitative leap forward with the Anglo-French Joint Declaration on European Defence at St. Mâlo on December 4, 1998. Thus, Paris managed to persuade the US's closest friend and the strongest Atlanticist – the UK – to a certain degree to come on its side and pushed the EU to create its own military intervention force. Secondly, the Common European Security and Defence Policy (CESDP) issued at Cologne on June 4, 1999, will be evaluated. Thirdly, Germany's support for the Anglo-French initiative of creating a 60,000-member rapid reaction force by 2003, made official in the Helsinki European Council meeting on December 10-11, 1999, will be analysed. Although the UK has repeatedly assured the US that NATO will not be undermined with these recent developments, it is obvious that in comparison to the period 1990-1997 the UK is becoming less vocal in its opposition to assigning the EU a defence dimension. Nonetheless, the following question will find a reply in the future: Is the European Integrationists' path becoming a ratchet?

(1) The European Sisyphus (1990-1997): The Franco-German Desire, Common Defence Policy (CDP), and Common Defence (CD)

(1.1) The Murky European 'Pillar of Defence'

There are several reasons for choosing the title European 'Pillar of Defence' instead of the 'North American Pillar' of NATO. *Firstly*, the 'European Pillar' ambition of European Integrationists' is necessary for rebalancing the power relationship against the dominant Atlanticists' view in the EU and NATO. Instead of an 'Anglo-Saxon' dominated NATO, the creation of two equal military pillars ('European' and 'North American' Pillars) would contribute to a balanced and objective Atlantic Alliance. This reconfiguration plan for NATO has been the major Franco-German desire.[17] *Secondly*, relying on formerly 'strong' and currently 'loosen-ing' Atlanticists' views and passing over the European Integrationists' desire for a greater European defence autonomy will probably be a naïve and shortsighted posture. However, no matter what happens to NATO in the future, it seems the transatlantic security ties will remain the building block of the European 'Pillar of Defence'. *Thirdly*, France and Germany are the strongest founding fathers of the EC and the 'motor' of every European integration process including the Franco-German initiative for a European 'Pillar of Defence'.[18] Without the Franco-German cooperation – bearing in minds the two countries' pre-1945 hostility and divi-sion – any step towards the goal of a European 'Pillar of Defence' will be futile. Ideally, one should also keep in mind that a robust European 'Pillar of Defence' would be incomplete if France and Germany were to harmonise their strategic doctrines and defence policies without including the other major European power, the UK. *Fourthly*, as a result of the former reason, since the Anglo-French St. Mâlo Declaration the concept of a Common European Defence Policy has turn into a commonly accepted topic in EU circles.

It is always easy to argue that in comparison to previous years the forthcoming year(s) will symbolize significant changes or improvements in European defence integration. In order to

---

[17] See '3. Deutsch-Französischen Dialog – Mit Sicherheit in die europäische Zukunft: Deutsch-französische Perspectiven einer gemeinsamen Sicherheits – und Verteidigungspolitik', *Diskussionsbericht*, (Saarbrücken: 31 Mai-01 Juni, 2001), p.18; Although Kennedy was the first US President who pledged in 1962 to a variant of the 'two pillars' concept, with a 'North American Pillar' and a 'European Pillar' in his Independence Day speech in Philadelphia, this equal two pillars concept has never been realised. See Haglund, D. G., *Alliance Within the Alliance? Franco-German Military Cooperation and the European Pillar of Defence*, (US: Westview Press, 1991), pp.1-7; The 'two pillars' structure is also the basic Gaullist thesis and will be analysed more in Chapter 5. The term 'Atlanticist', which is the inheritor of the term 'atlantist', reminds French politicians the unfair creation of the 'Atlantic Charter' between the US (Franklin Roosevelt) and the UK (Winston Churchill) on August 14, 1941, by excluding de Gaulle's *Free French Regime* at that time. He considered the US an historical extension of the UK and an Anglo-Saxon country. See Cogan, Charles G., *Oldest Allies, Guarded Friends – The United States and France Since 1940*, pp.2-3, 15; Also see Howorth, J., 'European integration and defence: the ultimate challenge?', *Chaillot Paper 43*, (Paris: Institute for Security Studies, WEU, November 2000), p.10; Guyomarch, A., Machin, H. & Ritchie, E., *France and the EU*, (US: St. Martin's Press, Inc., 1998), p.108; also see, Speech by François Bujon De L'Estang, French Ambassador to the US, on 'France, Europe and the Transatlantic Partnership', (US: Cornell University, September 29, 1997). Available at: <http://www.info-france-usa.org/fnews.htm> (Visited on: January 28, 2000).

[18] France and Germany proposed the creation of a new pillar to the Union through the WEU and European intervention force, Eurocorps. *Hochrangige Expertengruppe für die GASP*, 'Die Voraussetzungen für eine glaubwürdige GASP im Jahr 2000', (Brussel: den 19 Dezember 1994), p.13.

find convincing reasons that past patterns will change or improve the future, one has to under-

stand what has happened in the past between France, Germany, and the UK. France and the

UK have always been on opposite sides of the European defence integration process with re-

gard to the transatlantic security relationship, whereas Germany often found itself torn be-

tween them. Philip H. Gordon's definition of French and British attitudes to the US is a hall-

mark in understanding their opposing attitudes to European defence integration. He argued

that, 'after the disaster of the 1956 Suez Crisis, when the US undermined a joint British-

French invasion of Egypt, the British concluded "never again be on the wrong side from the

Americans," whereas the French concluded "never again depend on them."'[19]

In order to adapt itself to the changed strategic environment NATO underwent a transforma-

tion in the post-Cold War era. NATO's London Summit in July 1990 laid down the founda-

tion for the ESDI and tried to strengthen the EC's CFSP and the WEU's defence aspects with

greater shared responsibility and a more balanced role between the EU, WEU, and NATO.

France was an ardent supporter of the ESDI for the purpose of pushing the EU/WEU to obtain

its own independent defence arrangements. According to the French government, the creation

of European defence policy is important for the reasons that: *First*, the idea of European

autonomy in the sphere of defence, which would boost either the revitalisation of the WEU or

its integration into the EU, should set the EU free from US/NATO through establishing loose

transatlantic security ties between the EU and the US. *Second*, it should enhance the goal of

European integration in the area of a European 'Pillar of Defence' that would be more or less

equal to the 'North American Pillar'. *Third*, it should tie the unified Germany firmly into the

European 'Pillar of Defence' through the EC.[20] David Haglund, in his book called the

Alliance Within the Alliance, defined French aims on the European 'Pillar of Defence' as: '[It

---

[19] Gordon, P. H., 'Does the WEU Have a Role?', *Washington Quarterly*, (Vol.20, No.1, Winter 1997), p.134.
[20] Haglund, D. G., *Alliance Within the Alliance?* p.17. He emphasised that defence ministers of both France and Federal Republic of Germany have called for the construction of a European Pillar as the best means of integrating unified Germany into a Western security framework.

is] a construction that, while implying greater Euro-autonomy in defence and security than

now exists, at the same time is predicted upon the continuation of some form of transatlantic

security ties'.[21]

Germany not only supported French aims of creating foreign, security, and defence compo-

nent within the EC, but also supported a strong NATO under US leadership to reassure the

UK and Germany's other allies. Germany also found the EC as a vital actor for its own inter-

est in projecting stability into Central and Eastern Europe. Hence, policy divergences have

existed between France and Germany. Germany rejected the expansion of the EC's compe-

tencies at the expense of NATO and supported deepening and enlargement of the EC at the

same time. In other words, Germany pursued a dual strategy of European integration and

transatlantic enlargement. On the other hand, France wanted a merger between the EU and the

WEU to emancipate Europe from NATO and supported deepening, albeit for different rea-

sons, but not enlargement of the European integration process.[22] However, the Franco-

German partnership, 'in the form of strategies and recognition of mutual interests, has under-

pinned much of the EC's economic and political development and has become a necessary, if

not a sufficient, condition for any major initiative in the integration process'.[23] Rummel wrote

that, 'traditionally, the German debate on *Europapolitik* has focused on, monetary and finan-

cial issues and less on questions on foreign policy, security and defence. [...] During the

1980s this attitude started to change. Bonn together with Paris, felt that the West Europeans

needed a stronger security and defence identity, at first in order to deal with American initia-

tives such as the SDI, later in order to constructively meet Gorbachev's policy of liberalisa-

tion and transformation of Eastern Europe. Like other members, Germany therefore supported

---

[21] *Ibid*, p.4.
[22] As far as the EC's deepening is concerned, the German government vigorously supported a strong European integration process for reaching Political Union and empowering institutions, particularly the Commission and Parliament, whereas the French government supported a weaker European integration process and rejected strengthening the Commission and Parliament in order to keep its national sovereignty intact.
[23] Guyomarch, A., Machin, H. & Ritchie, E., *France in the EU*, (US: St. Martin's Press, Inc., 1998), pp.104-128.

initiatives to extend West European cooperation and integration into security matters and eventually into defence'.[24]

The UK opposed the inclusion of the defence aspect into the EC and supported the WEU's strengthening within the framework of NATO. The UK, in order to derail French aims (which were backed by Germany) of inserting the defence policy into the EC, used the WEU strata-gem. Therefore, the WEU was revived and fashioned into the ESDI within NATO. The UK was the main opponent of the Franco-German ambitions and opposed both the tight European integration process and the reactivation of the WEU as a political form.[25]

With this rhetoric in mind, the Franco-German letter launched the Intergovernmental Confer-ence (IGC) on the Political Union in April 1990. Although France and Germany were ardent supporters of the Political Union and common foreign, security and defence policies' inclu-sion into the EC, the UK was sceptical and unhappy with that letter. Germany particularly supported the Political Union together with its security and defence dimension in order to 'in-crease its influence in Europe as well as to develop a genuine community of nations'.[26] Germany and France submitted a proposal to the Luxembourg EC Presidency and to the Ex-traordinary Meeting of the WEU Council in February 1991.[27] The Franco-German proposal highlighted the significance of the WEU's development as an integral part of the European integration process and its core function in the development phase of the common defence policy. Therefore, France and Germany sought to exploit the WEU by merging it into (or subordinating it to) the EC. The Franco-German proposal was also supported by Belgium,

---

[24] Rummel, R., 'Germany's Role in the CFSP – 'Normalität' or 'Sonderweg'?' in Hill, C. (ed.), *The Actors in Europe's Foreign Policy*, (UK: Routledge, 1996), p.47.
[25] The UK wanted to use the WEU as a 'security' forum, not a 'political' one. See Brenner, M., 'Multilateralism and European Security', *Survival*, (Vol.35, No.2, Summer 1993), p.144.
[26] Rees, W. G., *The Western European Union at the Crossroads*, (US: Westview Press, 1998), p.47.
[27] See Franco-German proposals in Rummel, R. (ed.), *Toward Political Union – Planning a CFSP in the EC*, (Germany: Baden-Baden Nomos Verlagsgesellschaft, 1992), pp.350-357.

Luxembourg and Spain. The proponents of this proposal are called the *European Integrationists* and their main philosophy is to develop the WEU as the 'defence arm of the EC'[28] or a component of the future European 'Pillar of Defence'.

Even though the UK and Italy had different stances, the opposite argument to the WEU's future European defence role was put forward by a surprise Anglo-Italian letter in October 4, 1991.[29] British officials argued that the WEU should be a link between the EC and NATO, and should stay as an autonomous defence organisation. On the other hand, Italy was aiming to play the role of arbiter between the UK, France and Germany. The UK opposed any tight security structure and strongly rejected the inclusion of a defence concept into the EC on the basis that it would empty NATO of its meaning and thereby cause the US to depart. The UK signalled acceptance of a European defence policy in the long-term, only if it continued to adhere to and be compatible with NATO. In order to maintain the balance in favour of the 'North American Pillar', the UK also raised the idea of an Allied Rapid Reaction Force (ARRF). The UK took the permanent command of the ARRF and made it available to both the WEU and NATO. The former WEU Secretary-General Willem van Eekelen argued that such a force after the experience of the 1990-1991 Gulf War had been needed.[30] The UK's basic WEU stratagem was to strengthen the WEU's operational capability as an alternative to the Franco-German defence initiatives within the EC. In an interview, as one of the high-level officials in the British Ministry of Defence in 1992 put it, '...we felt that unless we would contemplate some mechanism for a greater European security role, we would find it taken over by European political union enthusiasts. The WEU was the obvious institution to go for,

---

[28] Myers, J. A., *The WEU: Pillar of NATO or Defence Arm of the EC?*, (London: Published by Brassey's for the Centre for Defence Studies, March 1993), pp.22-32.
[29] 'An Anglo-Italian Declaration on European Security and Defence', December 5, 1991, reproduced in Rummel, R. (ed.), *Toward Political Union*, pp.353-354.
[30] Van Eekelen, W.,'WEU and the Gulf Crisis', *Survival*, (Vol.32, No.6, November/December 1990), pp.519-532.

but not with enthusiasm'.[31] Robert Art defined at that time the UK's WEU stratagem through three main points: First, the WEU was not part of the EC and therefore could not be automatically controlled nor easily absorbed by it. Second, the WEU has an organic relation with NATO agreed by treaty. Third, because of this organic relationship there are legal and institutional barriers for developing the WEU into something that could rival NATO.[32] The Anglo-Italian proposal was supported by Denmark, the Netherlands, and Portugal. The proponents of this proposal are called the *Atlanticists* and their main philosophy was to keep the WEU as either an autonomous defence organisation or to integrate it into NATO.

As a reaction to the Anglo-Italian proposal, France and Germany issued another proposal on October 11, 1991.[33] This proposal emphasised four main aspects: First, the creation of a strong CFSP; second, to work for a CDP and ultimately for a CD; third, building a European Armaments Agency (EAA); and fourth, in order to give operational strength to the WEU the Franco-German brigade, which was established in 1987, would be converted into the Eurocorps and would operate under instructions from the EC.

The Franco-German and Anglo-Italian proposals created a dilemma for the other EC states, who found themselves torn between the two. Van Eekelen emphasised: 'The two poles of the ... negotiations concerning the precise arrangements for the WEU's relations with the European institutions and the Atlantic Alliance'.[34] The dilemma was a choice between two unwelcome alternatives in the form of an *action* (Franco-German proposal) – *reaction* (Anglo-

[31] Art, R. J., 'Why Western Europe needs the US and NATO?', *Political Science Quarterly*, (Vol.111, No.1, Spring1996), p.26.
[32] Art, R. J., p.27. Article IV of the 'Protocol Modifying and Completing the Brussels Treaty' delimits the WEU: 'In the execution of the Treaty, the High Contracting Parties and any Organs established by Them under the Treaty shall work in close cooperation with the NATO. Recognising the undesirability of duplicating the military staffs of NATO, the Council and its Agency will rely on the appropriate military authorities of NATO for information and advice on military matters.' See Bloed, A. & Wessel, R. A. (ed.), *The Changing Functions of the WEU – Introduction and Basic Documents*, (Utrecht: Martinus Nijhoff Publishers, August 1994), pp.1-6.
[33] Rummel, R. (ed.), *Toward Political Union*, pp.355-357.
[34] Van Eekelen, W., 'WEU's Post-Maastricht Agenda', *NATO Review*, (Vol.40, No.2, April 1992), p.14.

Italian proposal) quandary. Therefore, the EC states found themselves locked in increasing

their interests' against each another. If a state (or a group of states) tries to change the balance

of power (or interests), then another state (or a group of states) thereby experiences dimin-

ished power (or interests). The latter group must then act to counter the balance or has to ac-

cept diminished interests.[35] After the TEU negotiations, both side claimed that the TEU fa-

voured the victory of their own philosophies.[36] The dilemma appeared once again with the

two poles' relative (not absolute) arguments. The French side perceived that the TEU ar-

rangements meant the WEU is an integral part of the EU – 'defence arm of the EC'.[37] The

British side insisted that the TEU negotiations meant any European defence initiative would

be within the Alliance – the WEU is drawn more towards NATO.[38] As a consequence of their

respective preferences, France supported the Political Union with a strengthened defence di-

mension in it through either the WEU or the Eurocorps; the UK pushed for NATO through

subordinating the WEU to NATO and keeping it outside the Political Union; and, Germany

supported all of the above except keeping the WEU outside the Political Union.

In the end, a compromise was found between the Atlanticists and European Integrationists

and the noose of the dilemma was loosened to a certain degree. On December 10, 1991, it was

stated in the WEU's Maastricht Declarations that the WEU would be the 'defence arm' of the

EU and an 'organic' part of NATO; thereby, becoming a 'bridge' ('crossroad' organisation)

between these two organisations.[39] For this reason, unless the major European states' commit-

---

[35] This is the basic concept of the Realist school of thought. Art, R. J., pp.8-10.

[36] 'The Deal is Done', *The Economist*, (November 14, 1991), p.56.

[37] Bonvincini, G., Cremasco, M., Rummel, R. & Schmidt, P. (eds.), *A Renewed Partnership for Europe – Tackling European Security Challenges by EU-NATO Interaction*, (Baden-Baden: Nomos Verlagsgesellschaft, 1995/1996), p.174.

[38] For more British view on the WEU see Deighton, A., 'On the Cups: Britain, Maastricht and European Security', *EUI Working Papers*, (Italy: European University Institute, RSC No.97/59, October 1997); Heathcoat-Amory, D., 'The next step for the WEU: a British view', *The World Today*, (July 1994), pp.133-136; Goulden, J., 'The WEU's role in the new strategic environment', *NATO Review*, (Vol.44, No.3, May 1996).

[39] 'WEU will be developed as *the defence component of the EU and as a means to strengthen the European pillar of the Alliance*' (emphasis added). WEU Maastricht Declarations – I. Declaration, parag. 1, Maastricht, December 10, 1991 in Bloed, A. & Wessel, R. A. (ed.), pp.131-135; Wyn Rees' book *'The Western European*

ments to defence are fully integrated into the EU with Art.V (collective defence) competencies, the WEU will likely stay as a bridge between the aspirations of Atlanticism and European Integrationism. As far as the CFSP is concerned, it was accepted by the UK as a separate pillar beside the Community pillar and eventually agreed to include the defence aspect into the EC. The UK also accepted the establishment of links between NATO and the Political Union. France in turn accepted the primary responsibility of NATO in the defence of Western Europe and envisaged the gradual expansion of the ESDI's responsibility. Germany was happy to see the continuation of NATO's commitment in Europe with its nuclear guarantee. However, keeping the CFSP outside the Community pillar and intergovernmental, leaving the defence sphere outside the EU in the framework of the WEU and NATO, and maintaining a limited role for the Commission and Parliament frustrated the Germans.

Five years later, the TEU files were again on the table as part of an effort to improve the functioning of decisions in the Amsterdam Summit of June 1997. The question of the WEU's future and the development of the European security and defence policy were discussed once again. The Amsterdam Summit became the renaissance of expectations for bringing the WEU into the EU after the tragic lesson of the Bosnian crisis. The lesson learnt was that the Europeans were unable to undertake coordinated military action to ensure the security of their own continent. The Atlanticists realised that in certain crisis situations, where the US is not willing to intervene, autonomous European action might be necessary. On the other hand, the European Integrationists realised that an independent European security and defence capability is not yet a realistic option without the NATO military hardware and integrated military command structure. Therefore, the European Integrationists, headed by the Franco-German partnership and supported by Italy, Spain, Belgium, Luxembourg, and Greece, put forward a

---

Union at the Crossroads' is a comprehensive study of the WEU's 'crossroad' function. See Rees, W. G., (US: Westview Press, 1998); Also, see Julia A. Myers' analysis on the WEU's 'bridge' function, *'the WEU as a 'Bridge' between the EC and NATO.'* in Myers, J. A., pp.36-41.

timetable for the gradual merger of the EU and the WEU, strengthening the transatlantic alliance by consolidating the European pillar through this merger, and consequently integrating the common defence policy (CDP) and common defence (CD) into the EU's CFSP.[40]

The UK was once again strongly opposed the merger of the two organisations for several reasons. Firstly, British officials argued that members of these two organisations are different. Secondly, the EU-WEU merger would make extending the EU membership to Eastern Europe more difficult. Few in the EU had been willing to offer the Eastern European countries the EU membership and the EU defence guarantee at the same time. Thirdly, moving defence and security issues from the defence expertise organisation, NATO, to the organisation that had no defence experience, the WEU, would have been a foolish decision. Finally, a merger would result in the EU institutions (Commission, Parliament, and European Court of Justice) intruding in security and defence matters. The UK was strongly opposed to this and aimed to keep them purely intergovernmental.[41] Therefore, the UK had always been for military cooperation and opposed to supranational military integration. Former Prime Minister of the UK, John Major, pointed out that, 'our security does not always come from the barrel of a gun, EU has its own formidable armoury of political and economic instruments with which to build security and reunite our continent'.[42]

Although the Atlanticists disagreed with the European Integrationists' ambitions for the inclusion of a defence component into the EU, a number of key steps have been taken during the development of the CFSP. The EU member states signalled their intention of moving beyond

---

[40] *German White Paper on the 1996 Intergovernmental Conference.* Available at: <http://www.europa.eu.int/en/agenda/igc-home/ms-doc/state-de/pos.htm>; *French White Paper on the 1996 Intergovernmental Conference.* <http://www.europa.eu.int/en/agenda/igc-home/ms-doc/state-fr/pos.htm> (Visited on: June 14, 1999); Gordon, P. H., 'Europe's Uncommon Foreign Policy', *International Security,* (Vol.22, No.3, Winter 97/98), p.88.
[41] Gordon, P. H., 'Does the WEU Have a Role?', p.136.
[42] Major quoted in Rogers, M., 'The IGC: committed to creating a common foreign capability', *Jane's Defence Weekly,* (March 27, 1996), p.18.

the civilian power Europe and developing a defence dimension. The CFSP unleashed the defence discussions on a far greater scale than before. Therefore, defence is no longer a taboo area for the Council of Ministers. After all, the EU empowered the WEU with the competence of developing a CDP through the Treaty of Amsterdam.[43]

(1.2) Contours of the CDP and CD

In order to comprehend the CDP and CD, careful attention to both external (new security environment and military cooperation with NATO) and internal (CFSP, Petersberg Tasks of the EU/WEU and the process of developing a Political Union) aspects of security will briefly be recalled from Chapter 1. However, this section is not for the verification or formulation of the European 'Pillar of Defence'. Nor is it intended to demonstrate that the European 'Pillar of Defence' is axiomatic. Instead, possible approaches and solutions to the EU's Defence Dilemma will be analysed for a more viable European 'Pillar of Defence'.

Rene van Beveren defined the focus of 'defence' as '... to assure, at all times, in all circumstances and against all forms of aggression, the security and integrity of national territory, as well as the life of the population'.[44] The governments of states' are responsible for structuring a defence policy. Therefore, the state's sovereignty is central in the defence sphere. Van Beveren also aptly classified two types of alliance between the two types of organisations. The first type of alliance has 'a *limited goal* of collective self-defence *against any direct attack* on the territory of their members' (emphasis added). He termed such an alliance as a 'self-defence alliance' and presented NATO as an example. The other type of alliance is '*not limited to self-defence accords or operations but have wider military objectives,* including

---

[43] Art.17(3) of the ToA authorised the WEU to develop, 'elaborate and implement decisions and actions of the Union which have defence implications.'

[44] Van Beveren, R., 'Military Cooperation: What Structure for the Future?', *Chaillot Paper 6*, (Paris: Institute for Security Studies, WEU, January 1993), p.3.

military activities beyond the borders of their member countries'[45] (emphasis added). He termed this type of alliance as a 'general defence alliance' and presented the EU/WEU as an example of this type of alliance.

NATO, as a self-defence alliance, has a responsibility to Europe. However, sudden changes in the strategic environment triggered the following question: Would self-defence alliances still be necessary? Even before the collapse of the Soviet Union, some analysts started to talk about the disappearance of NATO, whilst others emphasised the autonomy of Europe. Chief of Staff of the disintegrated Warsaw Treaty Organisation, General Lobov, rang a death knell for NATO by saying that the new military situation in Europe would, soon or later, lead to the elimination of its military structures.[46] France, being a strong exponent for European auton-omy, started to point out the differences between the Europeans and Americans. Haglund pointed out that the aim is not to eradicate, but to alter the transatlantic security relationship, 'this seems to be what the current momentum for a European Pillar of Defence represents'.[47]

Defence cannot easily be argued as a 'motor' for European Integration, because it not only lies at the heart of the federalists (German preference) – intergovernmentalists (French prefer-ence) division, but is also central to the Political Union debates and federal union ambitions.[48] The following argument can be put forward as a reaction to the former: The EC did not emerge after discussions upon the transfer of financial sovereignty, but with discussions over coordinating coal, steel, and atomic energy. Finally, industrial goods and services were in-cluded. It was after all these successful initiatives that the EMU and Political Union were

---

[45] *Ibid.*
[46] Stephanie Anderson, 'Maastricht: Negotiating a Security Agreement without an Enemy' in Williams, A. J. (ed.), *Reorganising Eastern Europe*, (UK: Dartmouth Ltd., 1994), p.4.
[47] Haglund, D. G., *Alliance Within the Alliance?* p.24.
[48] Smith, C. J., 'Conflict in the Balkans and the Possibility of a EU CFSP', *International Relations*, (Vol.13, No.2, August 1996), pp.1-21.

even considered.[49] Jean Monnet, the father of European integration, used to say that the EC is

the expression of shared values. The responsibility of the European 'community' is to defend

those values where they were threatened and to promote them where they did not exist. Any

Community issue will be the outcome of successive crisis: Europe will be the final product of

these successive crises.[50] Former French President François Mitterrand noted, '[i]f we want to

build Europe, we must realise that this Europe needs its own defence. If it simply remains de-

pendent on outside powers, it will not be itself'.[51]

Although the WEU effectively became answerable to the European Council through the TEU,

Cologne and Helsinki European Council meetings in June and December 1999, where both

meetings declared that the WEU's decision-making framework would be integrated into the

EU by making the arrangement of the EU to *avail* itself of the WEU obsolete, the most sensi-

tive debate in the EU is still whether and how to extend the EU states' cooperation into the

common defence sphere. The CFSP covers all areas of security including the safeguarding of

common values and fundamental interests. Moreover, Art.17(1) of the ToA declares that,

'[t]he common foreign and security policy shall include all questions relating to the security

of the Union, including the progressive framing of a *common defence policy*, which might

lead to a *common defence*, should the European Council so decide'. Patricia Chilton argued

that a European integration model based on intergovernmental political cooperation (CFSP)

would lead to the creation of a supranational political institution (CDP) and, in turn, provide

---

[49] Richard Dale quoted by Barbara Conry: 'Condemning the EC for not behaving like the United States of Europe is like setting the high jump bar at twenty feet and criticizing a five-foot athlete for failing to clear it…. It is worth remembering that when the US was at the age of the Community, it was in the middle of the War of 1812 with Britain. That was half a century before the Civil War and nearly a century before the US dollar became the nation's single official currency.' Conry, B., 'The WEU as NATO's Successor', *Policy Analysis*, (Cato Institute: No.239, September 18, 1995), p.18.

[50] Delors, J., 'European Integration and Security', *Survival*, (Vol.33, No.2, March/April 1991), p.99.

[51] Conry, B., p.14; Likewise, US President Eisenhower in 1955 emphasised that: 'Europe must, as a whole, provide in the long run for its own defence. The US can move in and, by its psychological, intellectual and material leadership, help to produce arms, units and the confidence that will allow Europe to solve its problems. In the long run, it is not possible – and most certainly not desirable – that Europe should be an occupied (sic) territory defended by legions brought in from abroad, somewhat in the fashion that Rome's territories vainly sought security many hundred years ago.' Van Beveren, R., p.24.

the way for supranational security institutions (CD) with implications of a sovereign super-

state.[52] The CDP and CD are not defined by the EU's *l'acquis communautaire* and, therefore,

their meaning is left open-ended. For this reason, the following interpretations are not binding

for the EU or for the WEU. John Roper defined the CDP as:

> *"A common policy with respect to the use of the armed forces of the member*
>
> *states of the EU' and will aim at developing concepts as to how the necessary*
>
> *means for the pursuit of the EU's objectives in the field of defence can be*
>
> *constituted and employed'.*[53]

Roper's definition of the CDP is more than a definition of policy coordination in a 'collective

self-defence alliance'. This definition of the CDP also includes some conceptual framework

for the evolution of CD. He stressed that the agreement among parties on the use of armed

forces not only encompasses the assessment of military staff and feasibility of upgrading

equipment, personnel, and financial resources, but also encompasses working on operational

plans and organisational aspects of armed forces, including their training to meet different

military operations through different contingencies (or *ad hoc* arrangements).

On the other hand, Roper defined CD in broad terms and for practical reasons he decided to

divide CD into two versions. He explained CD and its two versions as:

> *'CD means more than a closer integration of the armed forces of the EU's/WEU's*
>
> *member states for collective self-defence, which would be implied by a narrow*
>
> *interpretation of Common Defence; It will cover the whole range of the functions*
>
> *of armed forces. [...] 'A stronger version would be the organisation of the armed*

[52] Chilton, P., 'A European Security Regime: Integration and Cooperation in the Search for CFSP', *Journal of European Integration*, (Vol.19, No.'s 2-3, Winter/Spring 1996), p.222.
[53] Roper, J., 'Defining a common defence policy and common defence' in Martin, L. & Roper, J. (eds.) *Towards a Common Defence Policy*, (Paris: Institute for Security Studies, WEU, 1995), pp.8-9.

forces of the members states in common', and a weaker one 'the organisation of

the activities of the armed forces of the members states in common'.[54]

The stronger version of CD refers to a centralised military structure commanding armed forces equipped by the common procurement of defence equipment, common budget, logistics, training, common communications infrastructure and intelligence. The weaker version of CD, on the other hand, is the common organisation of certain activities of different nation's armed forces. Roper connects the weaker version of CD with the WEU through "ready and willing' form coalitions."[55] The definition of the WEU's 'soft' military role in section two of Chapter 1 (*Communitarisation of Security Policy*), highlights many features, which are complimentary to the weaker version of CD.

The amalgamation of stronger and weaker versions of CD will result in 'general defence alliances'. Since the WEU's Petersberg Declaration on June 19, 1992, the 'general defence alliances' function of the WEU has been instigated. In addition to the WEU's 'self-defence alliance' function (Art.V – collective defence alliance), the Petersberg Declaration has been formulated so that member states could make their military units available for the following types of non-Article V tasks: 'Apart from contributing to the *common defence* in accordance with Article 5 of the Washington Treaty and Article V of the modified Brussels Treaty respectively, military units of WEU member states, acting under the authority of the WEU, could be employed for: Humanitarian and rescue tasks; peacekeeping tasks; tasks of combat forces in crisis management, including peacemaking'[56] (emphasis added). Instead of using the

---

[54] *Ibid.*
[55] *Ibid.* p.10
[56] WEU Council of Ministers, Petersberg Declaration, 19 June 1992, Bonn, (Part II, parag. 4). Paragraph 2 also reinforces the paragraph 4: 'WEU member States declare that they are prepared to make available military units from the whole spectrum of their conventional armed forces for military tasks conducted under the authority of WEU'. See Bloed, A. & Wessel, R. A. (ed.), pp.137-146; The 'collective defence' commitment of Art.V of the Brussels Treaty is even offering more straightforward guarantee through 'an armed attack in Europe...will give

phrase 'collective defence', authors used 'common defence' in the Declaration. John Roper

defined the distinction between them as: *'a common defence provides forces for collective*

defence and for other military activities. In 'common defence' a broad definition of 'defence'

is employed, whereas in 'collective defence' it is the narrow definition'.[57] Therefore, the

WEU documents, through the phrase of 'common defence', offer WEU members a more

straightforward defence guarantee than NATO's 'collective defence'.

It is unrealistic to think of a European CDP without planning to build up the military capa-

bilities and resources of the WEU. In the WEU's Petersberg Declaration in June 1992, the

concept of Forces Answerable to the WEU (FAWEU) was launched by its member states in

order to make military units available to the WEU during crisis situations.[58] Moreover, the

Planning Cell in Brussels was established and made operational in April 1993.[59] This enabled

the WEU with its own planning capability to prepare strategies for a wide range of situations.

The Planning Cell was also fortified in June 1996 with a Situation Centre and provides a

twenty-four hours monitoring facility for regional crises. An Intelligence Section and a Mili-

tary Committee came into being in May 1997 to improve the military decision-making and

planning capabilities of the operational and organisational aspects of armed forces within the

WEU. However, the WEU's command capabilities remained extremely small in comparison

to NATO's Integrated Military Structure. Therefore, during a crisis, the WEU plays a negligi-

ble role in the transfer of military inputs. On such decisions, the WEU heavily depends on the

---

assistance and support with all military and other means within their power' (emphasis added) than Art.5 of the North Atlantic Treaty, which it does only require allies' 'assistance'.

[57] Roper, J., 'Defining a common defence policy and common defence' in Martin, L. & Roper, J. (eds.), p.8.

[58] In addition to the Franco-German's Eurocorps, including Belgium, Spain and Luxembourg, Anglo-Dutch Amphibious Force, Multinational Division (Belgium, Germany, The Netherlands and the UK), Eurofor (Rapid Deployment Force), and Euromarfor (naval amphibious capabilities and naval air support units of France, Italy, Portugal and Spain), German-Dutch Combined Corps, Spanish-Italian Amphibious Force, and Anglo-French Euro Air Group have been established. *WEU Today*, (Brussels: Secretariat-General, March 1998), p.14.

[59] Planning Cell is responsible for: (1) carrying out contingency plans for a possible operation; (2) keeping updated list of units and combination arrangement which might be allocated to WEU for specify operations; (3) preparing recommendations for the necessary command, control and communication arrangements for each operation. *WEU Today*, pp.44-45.

individual member states. Thus, it is obvious that in certain types of operations, individual states would take on responsibility for managing a task and the EU/WEU would only be used as a platform for coordinating their operational capacities. However, the military planning is based much less than before on concrete geographic areas and more on flexible planning of specific military capabilities. This will allow the EU/WEU to develop a potential independent planning capacity without engaging in major military integration or a strong version of CD.[60] Van Beveren described four possible ways, which are still holding a light to the current evolution of the European military structure, of achieving the weaker version of CD in 1993[61]:

First, units can be placed under the *command of a pilot nation*. The past has proved that political consensus for such a solution is difficult, but several national headquarters (HQs), like the French army corps-level *Force d'Action Rapide* HQ, could be used for command and control of a peacekeeping mission. Second, units might be assigned to an *existing integrated structure*. HQs of the Eurocorps would be an obvious solution. He suggested the ACE Rapid Reaction Corps' (ARRC)[62] HQs as another solution. Third, a *permanent command structure* for general defence missions could be created. This idea was also put forward in an Anglo-Italian Declaration on October 4, 1991. Fourth, the creation of an *ad hoc command structure* could be a solution. If, for example, six states provided brigade each, HQs could be created at both division and corps level. Each level of command could have its own organic support units – such as artillery, engineers and combat helicopters – as well as logistics support.

---

[60] Peter Schmidt in Sergei Medvedev, 'The WEU after Maastricht: Trends and Perspectives' in Bonvincini, G., Cremasco, M., Rummel, R. & Schmidt, P. (eds.), p.187.
[61] Van Beveren, R., 'Military Cooperation: What Structure for the Future?', pp.29-30.
[62] ARRC is the land component of the ACE Rapid Reaction Forces. Its role is to be prepared for employment throughout Allied Command Europe (ACE) to augment or reinforce local forces in a NATO country whenever necessary. It allows a rapid response to a wide range of eventualities. Headquarters of the ARRC is multinational. *NATO Handbook*, (Brussels: NATO Office of Information and Press, October 1995), pp.174-175.

For the time being, the EU countries are not yet politically willing or seriously thinking of cutting off Europe from NATO. Instead, they prefer a transatlantic relationship based on necessary transparency and complementarity between the EU/WEU and NATO. The EU/WEU will develop its role as the 'European politico-military body for crisis management, contributing to the progressive framing of a common defence policy and carry forward its concrete implementation through the further development of its own operational role'.[63]

Another significant factor affecting the integrated structural capability of the Europeans is the nuclear deterrent. If the EU members want to progress towards CD, particularly the stronger version, they have to make far-reaching decisions regarding the pooling of their national sovereignty in order to establish a nuclear guarantee. Apparently, such an issue would be of serious concern to the only two European nuclear powers, France and the UK, but this issue is certainly a concern to all continental states. France, being an ardent supporter of an independent European CD, has shown interest in the concept of a European nuclear force on the way to achieve CD. France had also set up regular meetings with the UK, in which they decided to launch a 'Common Nuclear Concept' in 1990, and agreed that it should be offered to other EU states later.[64] In 1993, the two countries founded the 'Anglo-French Joint Commission on Nuclear Policy and Doctrine' for deepening the 'Common Nuclear Concept' discussions.

A discussion on the 'Common Nuclear Concept' presents several problems for CD. First, there are serious disagreements between the nuclear and non-nuclear states. France would have to change its rigid stance on nuclear weapons, so that they would no longer be seen as a

---

[63] WEU Council Declaration on 'The role of the WEU and its relations with the EU and the Atlantic Alliance', (Brussels: WEU Council, October 1997); For more information on the WEU's operational capability see 'The EU's CFSP and the ESDI', Vanhoonacker, S., 'CFSP: Can History be Overcome?', *European Institute of Public Administration*, (Maastricht: Paper Prepared for ECSA Conference, Seattle, May 1997).

[64] Yost, D., 'France's nuclear dilemmas', *Foreign Affairs*, (Vol.75, No.1, January/February 1996). Franco-German bilateral discussions on extension of the French nuclear deterrence over the German territory will be analysed in the next chapter, see Chapter 3 – *(2.2) The Franco-German 'Common Strategic Concept'*. The French use of nuclear weapons as a foreign policy instrument will be analysed in Chapter 5 – *France's New Roles and Desires in the Sphere of European Security and Defence*.

sanctuary for its national sovereignty; the UK would have to renegotiate its special bilateral relationship with the US on this concept; a non-nuclear Germany would have to sacrifice the strong nuclear guarantee provided by the US for a much weaker one provided by the UK and France; and, finally, including the nuclear concept into the EU's CD discussions would most likely be condemned by neutral members.

Second, even if nuclear capable countries in the EU decide to go for a nuclear capable EU, they might need to violate the Non-proliferation Treaty (NPT) by developing a nuclear guarantee text within CD. None of the EU countries are yet ready to sacrifice their national sovereignties for a far-reaching nuclear capable CD. However, as it stated in the introduction, the US Senate's rejection of the Comprehensive Nuclear Test Ban Treaty (CTBT) for setting free the NMD plans irritated the European governments. If the political cleavage and resentment between the Americans and Europeans continues, the Europeans might enter into serious debate on having an independent nuclear deterrence for the EU.

Not until the WEU Noordwijk Declaration, was a conceptual document on a CDP presented for discussions. At Noordwijk, the WEU endorsed the formulation of a document outlining objectives, scope and means of the Common European Defence Policy (CEDP) on November 14, 1994.[65] Hans van Mierlo commented on this document that it seeks to provide the basis of future work in shaping a CDP and 'enumerates a number of elements of a CEDP – the *acquis*

---

[65] Some important points from the Document are: (1) the study of possible harmonisation of national practices under the light of the CFSP's competence in the area of arms export controls; (2) the identification of conditions and measures that could improve market conditions for a more competitive approach to the European (or intra-European) procurement; (3) the creation of conditions for an integrated, rationalised and competitive European defence industry; (4) the reduction of duplicative national research, development and production costs; (5) the improvement of the inter-operability of armed forces through inter alia the promotion of harmonised requirements and standardised equipment; (6) the role of armaments cooperation in strengthening the European Defence Identity. WEU Council of Ministers, *Noordwijk Declaration*, Noordwijk, (November 14, 1994), pp.1-9; also see Van Eekelen, W., *The Security Agenda for 1996 – Background and prospects*, (Brussels: Centre for European Policy Studies (CEPS), Paper No. 64, 1995), p.102.

as it were – which have already been developed in the WEU, in the EU and in NATO'.[66]

Richard Whitman argued that, with this document 'the Union, through the WEU, has, although tentatively, created a defence force and an embryonic defence policy. These are intended to be compatible with the Atlantic Alliance and to strengthen its European pillar based upon the principle of separable, but not separate, military capabilities'.[67] The Noordwijk Declaration dealt extensively with upgrading the operational role of the WEU.[68] The Declaration also became a light to the Reflection Group and a mirror to the EU's Westendorp Reflection Group in the IGC of 1996.

It needs to be mentioned that for all efforts to develop the CDP and CD and to strengthen the WEU's operational role, Europeans are still militarily dependent on NATO. Yet, command, control, communications, long-range heavy transport aircraft, air-refuelling capabilities, satellite intelligence systems, and principally, an Integrated Military Structure, like that of NATO, all remain crucial problems for the WEU. Although the vision of CD is implicitly stated in the EU documents, the EU/WEU is far from being defined as a stronger version of CD. Above all, the stronger version of the EU/WEU, CD (collective self-defence alliance), is not feasible in the existence of NATO's current collective self-defence alliance role. It was also proven at the IGC in 1997 that including the Petersberg Tasks into the CFSP was relatively uncontroversial, but the inclusion of territorial defence commitments were proved to be more problematic. Unless an agreement on the building blocks of the CDP and CD addresses more complex and deeper issues within the EU/WEU, the EU/WEU would be preferable as a weaker version of CD.

---

[66] Van Mierlo, H., 'The WEU and NATO: prospects for a more balanced relationship', *NATO Review*, (Vol.43, No.2, March 1995), pp.7-10; WEU Council of Ministers, *Noordwijk Declaration*.

[67] Whitman, R. G., 'The EU's CFSP – Achievements and Prospects', *Centre for the Study of Democracy*, (London: Research Paper, No.11, Published by University of Westminster, Winter 1996), p.27-28.

[68] For more information see *Noordwijk Declaration*, particularly Title VII and section *(2.1.3) The Path From the WEAG/WEAO to the European Armaments Agency (EAA)* in this Chapter.

Nevertheless, the EU's current military capabilities are insufficient, but there is no doubt its 'potential' military and economic capacity is more than adequate to meet its defence needs.[69] The Europeans should continue developing military hardware to enhance their operational capabilities through competition with, but not in open contradiction to the US. In Jan Geert Siccama's prickly words, the 'construction of a European Pillar of Defence must, in some cases, be an "anti-American" act....'[70] Thus, the Armaments Procurement Policy is important for the concept of CDP, but Article 223 of the Treaty of Rome is a serious stumbling block in developing common policies for arms procurement and integrating the arms markets into the EU trade laws. Although significant progress has been achieved, there are still many obstacles before the European defence dilemma can be resolved to ratchet up the European 'Pillar of Defence'. The prophecy, made by Jacques Santer in November 1995, came to be reality: The EU was left with 'feet of clay' to face future crises.[71] The following section will analyse the achievements and obstacles the European Defence Industry faces.

(2) Overhauling the European Defence Industrial and Technological Base

(2.1) Recent Discourses

(2.1.1) Post-Cold War Pressure on European Defence Industries

While the EU has benefited from economic integration, the European Defence Industrial and Technological Base (EDITB) – necessary for the evolution of a robust European 'Pillar of Defence' – tended to remain somewhat fragmented and functions along national lines. Until

---

[69] Jeffrey Gedmin at the same time pointed out that the problem of European defence is the concentration on building 'institutions' instead of 'capabilities'. Gedmin, J., 'A Yawning Gap on Defence: We Should Care About Europe's Weapons', *Washington Times*, (December 8, 1999), p.A15.

[70] Jan Geert Siccama quoted in Haglund, D. G., *Alliance Within the Alliance?* p.5.

[71] Santer, J., 'The EU's security and defence policy. How to avoid missing the 1996 rendezvous', *NATO Review*, (Vol.43, No.6, November 1995), p.9.

1989, the fragmented defence industry was characterised by a special market embedded in national sovereignty, national prestige, and thus heavy political control detached the defence market from the free market industries'.[72] Although the post-Cold War world remains a dangerous place where security still dependent on military capabilities, the political support for defence budgets fell dramatically with the demise of the Soviet Union. There is no doubt that the EDITB found itself under pressure of globalisation from spiralling unit costs, production overcapacity and declining exports before the evaporation of the Warsaw Pact. The post-Cold War era subsequently added other pressures like shrinking defence budgets and intensifying complex industrial interdependence in the presence of new defence uncertainties. The EDITB is also faced with stiff competition in the global market and has been forced to adjust its overall structure. Because France, Germany, and the UK are the major countries dominating the EDITB and the European defence market, they will be predominantly referred to throughout this section.

The EDITB is under pressure from three main challenges. *Firstly*, a decline of domestic demand for defence equipment, which is associated with the decrease of East-West tension, forced all European countries to cut their national defence budgets and expenditures considerably. France, Germany, and the UK have undergone significant military force and defence spending reductions. The following table compares these three countries' decreased military personnel size and defence spending in 1989 and in 1999/2000.

---

[72] Politi, A., 'On the Necessity of a European Defence Industry' in von Bredow, W., Jäger, T. & Kümmel, G., *European Security*, (UK: Macmillan Press Ltd., 1997), p.102.

Table 2.1

France, Germany, and the UK's Military Personnel and Defence Spending[73]

COUNTRY	MILITARY PERSONEL		DEFENCE SPENDING AS % OF GDP	
	1989	1999/2000	1989	1999/2000
France	466,000	317,300	3.8	2.8
Germany	494,000*	338,000	2.0*	1.5
UK	311,650	212,400	4.5	2.6

*West Germany figures. Military personnel numbered 173,000 in East Germany at the time the Berlin Wall fell.

The Europeans are aware that they should do more to defend themselves and their interests. However, the above statistics prove that the Europeans are not yet ready to do more to meet this need. The continuous rise in the price of sophisticated technological defence equipment puts the three country's defence budgets under pressure. The EU's foreign policy spokesman Javier Solana said that, European defence budgets will have to rise, but there is no sign of this happening.[74] Discourses upon the professional army and revolutionary developments in electronic technology also confirm that the Europeans must spend far more on defence.

Secondly, a huge debate is going on in most of the EU countries about rethinking and restructuring their national military policies or ending conscription and establishing professional armies in the new security environment.[75] The British, French, and Germans have unilaterally

---

[73] Data compiled from *The Military Balance 1999/2000*, (UK: International Institute for Strategic Studies, Oxford University Press, 2000); also see *Seely*, R., 'With the Cold War a Memory, Europe's Defence Industries Fight for Life', *The Los Angeles Times*, (October 24, 1999) and Cullen, K. 'In European Force, US Fears a Loss of Power', *Boston Globe*, (December 21, 1999), p.A4.

[74] Solana also asks: Is anyone really waiting for a shaky Red-Green coalition in Berlin to spend less on health, education and the environment so that it can spend more on high-tech weapons? NATO's European members currently spend some 12 times as much on social welfare as they do on defence. See Gedmin, J., 'A Yawning Gap on Defence', *Washington Times*, (December 8, 1999), p.A15; Secretary-General of NATO, George Robertson, said that: 'You cannot buy security on the cheap'. Whitney, C. R., 'US and NATO Allies Divided Over Defence Needs', *New York Times*, (December 3, 1999).

[75] William Pfaff wrote that, '[European] forces still are mainly developed and equipped for central European tank battles, rather than the mobile missions necessary today. The countries that have depended on national service for military manpower are still in the course of professionalising their armies'. Pfaff, W., 'Europeans are marching to different drummer', *The Sun*, (November 29, 1999).

undertaken some form of defence review by initiating some reforms in respective military force structures and forward equipment planning. Karl Haltiner explains the new trend in reconstructing the national armies as follows:

> *'The enormous economic productivity and the high living standards in*
>
> *industrialised modern societies are based on a continuously increasing degree of*
>
> *functional division of labour and professional specialisation. The driving forces of*
>
> *this process are technological progress and market penetration into all spheres of*
>
> *life and society, which imply an increasing degree of individualisation and*
>
> *normative pluralisation as well as the decreasing importance of traditional values*
>
> *and an erosion of the normative norm of compulsory military service. [...] The*
>
> *more the internal military division of labour grows, the higher the tendency*
>
> *becomes to rely on well-trained professional soldiers'.*[76]

In order to attain operational success, professional military forces need sophisticated and innovative electronic weapons. However, the military capability gap between the EU and US is growing. This gap is undermining the hopes of European politicians' of participating in 'soft' military missions on an equal footing with the US. Technological developments also blurred the distinction between civilian and military technologies. Cliffort Beal stated that, 'market forces and geopolitics are now moving faster than national policy wills in Europe. Governments must accept that the times are changing rapidly and some degree of integration in both industrial and military capabilities is the only way forward to a robust and credible European

---

[76] Karl W. Haltiner also stated that, '[t]he multi-polar and global conflict scenario compels modern armed forces of the late twentieth century to comply with multiple tasks that are independent of a given threat scenario. Smaller, faster, more mobile, and functionally and technologically more flexible military organisations, which may be integrated into multinational armed forces as well, meet these requirements much better than armies of the *levée en masse* type.' Haltiner K. W., 'The Definite End of the Mass Army in Western Europe?', *Armed Forces and Society*, (Vol.25, No.1, Fall 1998), pp.7-36. Von Bredow, W. & Kümmel, G., 'Das Militär und die Herausforderung globaler Sicherheit – Der Spagat zwischen traditonalen und nicht-traditionalen Rollen', *SOWI Arbeitspapier Nr.119*, (Strausberg: September 1999), pp.13-15. German and French defence reviews and changes in their military force structure will be analysed in more detail at Chapter 4 and 5 respectively.

defence'.[77] Intelligence is tied to modern precision weapons, such as surveillance, target at-

tack, radar, digital communication systems, information technology, optical and electronic

sensors, satellites, anti-ballistic missile defence, and accurate stealth systems for supporting

command, control, communication, and intelligence (C3I). The development of electronic

weaponry is not specifically military in nature, so they will be maintained primarily in the

civil sector. However, the actual trend is dual-use (civil and military) technologies. Katia

Vlachos argued that, since the technology for innovative electronic weapons' markets are in-

ternational by nature, 'the trends towards commercialisation will mean drawing upon interna-

tional supplier resources and/or seeking international cooperation'.[78] These technologies have

also increasingly become necessary for the success of Western military operations in peace-

keeping and peacemaking with fewer casualties.[79] In comparison to the US defence industry,

the European defence industry is weaker, because not only fewer resources have been devoted

to developing C3I, but also the US has a considerable advantage in 'commercial information

technologies' over Europe.[80]

Thirdly, the international demand for defence equipments is either shrinking or stagnating –

with the exception of East Asia – and competition for international sales from 'America to-

day, Asia tomorrow' is intensifying.[81] In response to changing market conditions, US defence

firms have consolidated themselves considerably through a series of mergers and acquisitions.

[77] Beal, C., 'Be Rational, Europe', *Jane's International Defence Review*, (August 1, 1996).
[78] Vlachos, K., 'Safeguarding European Competitiveness – Strategies for the Future European Arms Production and Procurement', *Occasional Papers 4*, (Paris: Institute for Security Studies, WEU, January 1998), p.14.
[79] Klaus Naumann, retired senior NATO officer, said that in Kosovo air campaign only the US had enough sophisticated fighters ('stealth' F-117) and fighter-bombers (B-2) to win the war without ground troops. Most European planes have to fly more or less over the targets, which is the most stupid thing you can do, since you expose yourself to the enemy air defence. See Gedmin, J., 'A Yawning Gap on Defence', p.A15; Holger Mey asks: 'will all [technological developments] lead to "war without warriors," "war of the machines," "bloodless war," "cyberwar?".' See Mey, H. H., 'The Revolution in Military Affairs: A German Perspective', *Comparative Strategy*, (No.17, 1998), pp.309-319.
[80] Deutch, J., Kanter, A. & Scowcroft, B., 'Saving NATO's Foundation', *Foreign Affairs*, (Vol.78, No.6, November/December 1999), p.62.
[81] Vlachos stated that East and South-East Asia is particularly emerging as a major arms market, accounting for a bit less than a quarter (23%) of global arms purchases. Defence spending in East Asian countries has increased by more than a third since 1985 and almost a quarter since 1992. Vlachos, K., p.16; 'A French Projection', *Economist*, (Vol.338, No.7955, March 2, 1996), p.46.

This resulted in the emergence of giant US defence companies' and their domination of the world market. In order to match the competitiveness of the US defence firms, to create a 'two-way street'[82] in arms purchases between the EU and the US and to change the practice of a 'buy American' principle, European governments and defence firms all agreed in principle that the EDITB has too many factories and must reorganise itself into larger, more coherent companies – fewer companies, bigger market – so that they can begin to compete with the US giants. Although many politicians believe the defence sector is too important to be left to free market forces, national defence budgets of the EU member states came under even more free market pressures due to the EMU convergence criteria and the need to share rising military research and development (R&D) costs. European defence industries and governments have responded to the globalisation of defence markets through capacity reductions, mergers, market nicheing, lay-offs, plant closures, rationalisation through downsizing or organic diversification through acquisition of civilian activities, and conversion (switching defence plants to civilian production).[83] International economic and technological competitiveness is pushing the EDITB towards a greater reform of the industrial structure of the defence market and in procurement systems and programmes management. Moreover, the armaments production through 'competitive interdependence' at the European level would reduce the 'divisive competition', wasteful internal competition and overproduction.[84] Alessandro Politi stated that, 'in terms of political decision, it is essential to have truly transnational European groups, capable of making profit and of retaining strategic capabilities. Intra-European competition should be

---

[82] Hayward resembled the past transatlantic weapons trade to a 'west-east one way highway'. Hayward, K., 'Towards a European Weapons Procurement Process', *Chaillot Paper 27*, (Paris: Institute for Security Studies, WEU, June 1997), p.44.

[83] Kenny, B., 'Change and Cross-Border Activity in the European Defence Industry', *European Business Review*, (Vol.99, No.2, 1999); Bishop, P. 'Strategic Change in the European Defence Industry', *European Business Review*, (Vol.97, No.4, 1997).

[84] Edgar, A. D., 'A New European Defence Market: Cooperation, Competitive Interdependence, or Divisive Competition?' in Haglund, D., *From Euphoria to Hysteria – Western European Security After the Cold War*, (US: Westview Press Inc., 1993), pp.255-274.

regarded as a complementarity means, but the real competition is global, with US industry being the benchmark'.[85]

The role of the EC in defence industry matters has traditionally been problematic. However, Katia Vlachos argued that 'Maastricht budgetary pressure may favour consolidation, by forcing nations to form joint ventures and collaborative efforts to afford major new systems, but also by encouraging the armaments cooperation'.[86] Although the EC rules and procedures are significant obstacle for the protectionism in civil markets, the defence sector lacks this kind of straitjacket. National security considerations, sustaining the intra-Europe technological and competitive advantage, employment protection, and differences in national defence structures have collectively been less than conducive to developing a single European defence policy. For these reasons, Article 223 of the EC is still seen as a safeguard for member states' national defence industries.

(2.1.2) The EC's Article 223: Leeway for Member States

The direct relationship between arms procurement and national sovereignty is compelling the European defence industry to be under national control through the Rome Treaty's golden rule of Art.223. Art.223(b) reads as follows: 'Any member state may take such measures as it considers necessary for the protection of the essential interests of its security which are connected with the production or trade in arms, munitions and war material...'[87] Rolf Hallerbach argued that Art.223 represents 'the last bastion' permitting EU members to exempt part of their economies from the common discipline and competition. If there is to be a truly inte-

---

[85] Politi, A., 'On the Necessity of a European Defence Industry', pp.108-109.

[86] She tried to strengthen her argument by the Title V-Article 17 of the Treaty of Amsterdam: Cooperation among the Member States in the field of armaments is a step towards achieving the ultimate goal of a common European defence policy. See Vlachos, K., 'Safeguarding European Competitiveness...', p.16.

[87] Art.223 in the Treaty Establishing the EEC quoted in Trevor Taylor, 'Arms Procurement' in Howorth, J. & Menon, A. (ed.), *The EU and National Defence Policy*, (London: Routledge, 1997), p.122.

grated armaments market, the bastion must fall.[88] While Art.223 favours member states' direct control over arms production and trade through intergovernmentalism, it does not undermine the EU involvement in defence industry matters. Economic integration in the EU, as functionalist theory predicts, sooner or later will spillover into the security sphere.[89] For the time being, the spillover is limited to the 'grey area' between economics and security, but revolutionary technological developments are having an impact on military affairs. Jürg M. Gabriel defined this 'grey area' as 'security-economics'.[90] Likewise, Pierre De Vestel explained the 'grey area' between economics and defence as 'defence economy.'[91]

Recent economic, technological, and military considerations placed significant pressures on keeping defence procurement isolated from the EU agenda. Guay argued that, 'most European defence firms produce for the civilian and military [dual-use production] markets, and as the civilian side of their operations adapted to the pressures unleashed by economic integration, it has become increasingly difficult to keep the defence side separate'.[92] The European Commission put forward proposals in the 1990 TEU discussions for fundamental reform of the defence market and called for the abolition of Art.223 with the intention of rationalising the defence industry at the European level and introducing rules for competition.[93] The TEU did not change the position of Art.223 in the Treaty of Rome, but the Commission gained some powers. *Firstly*, the Commission gained a right to veto large mergers and acquisitions within the

---

[88] Rolf Hallerbach quoted in Gabriel, J. M., 'The Integration of European Security: A Functionalist Analysis', *Aussenwirtschaft*, (Heft I, April 1995), pp.153-154.
[89] For theoretical explanations of the European defence industry see, Guay, T. R., 'Integration and Europe's defence industry: A "reactive spillover" approach', *Policy Studies Journal*, (Vol.24, No.3, Autumn 1996).
[90] According to Jürg M. Gabriel 'security-economics' should not be mistaken by 'economic security'. 'Economic security' covers broad issues such as autarchy, protectionism or mercantilism, whereas 'security-economics' refers to much narrower issues concerning *arms* (arms production, arms procurement, arms transfer etc.). See Gabriel, J. M., 'The Integration of European Security: A Functionalist Analysis', p.143.
[91] 'Defence economy' covers all economic aspects of defence: industrial, technological, budgetary and employment aspects, and transactions between buyers and producers. The differences between defence production and civilian production became invisible due to the pace of internationalisation of the defence sector. This is also changing the traditional relationship between buyer and producer. De Vestel, P., 'Defence Markets and Industries in Europe: Time for Political Decisions?', *Chaillot Paper 21*, (Paris: ISS, WEU, November 1995).
[92] Guay, T.R., *At Arm's Length – The EU and Europe's Defence Industry*, (UK: Macmillan Press Ltd, 1998), p.46
[93] *Commission of the European Communities*, COM(90) 600 final, (Brussels: October 23, 1990), p.5.

EC, even if the merger has a defence dimension. *Secondly*, after discussions between individual governments and the Commission in December 1994, a list of dual-use exports were agreed and a licence-free regime introduced for defence goods within the EU.[94] *Thirdly*, as a result of the defence industries rationalisation, the Commission has given some funds to alleviate unemployment in defence areas (e.g. Konver programme). *Fourthly*, the Commission has also been given the power to administer the EU's R&D programmes, such as ESPRIT (European Strategic Program for Research in Information Technology), BRITE (Basic Research in Industrial Technologies in Europe), and RACE (Research in Advanced Communications Technology for Europe). All of these programmes are used for civilian and military markets. Guay wrote that, 'more technology spin-offs today are flowing from the civilian side to the military side of a company's business, and dual-use products are making up an ever-larger proportion of military equipment'.[95]

However, the construction of a single defence market in the EU is not a simple task. This requires circumventing at least three hurdles. *Firstly*, technical (the Commission's competition policy needs to be empowered); *secondly*, strategic (how and under which conditions the single defence market could be opened to competition with the US defence industries);[96] and, *thirdly*, political (the difficult question of eliminating Art.223 and giving the EU more competence to deal with armaments production and sales including procurement, R&D, industrial policy and common arms export policy). Although Art.233 is still based on intergovernmental practice and therefore keeps the Commission at bay, this does not mean that defence pro-

---

[94] The Commission asked to prepare a report on 'The cost of non-Europe regarding defence equipments' in 1992 (made public in 1994). *Official Journal of the European Communities*, L367(37), (Brussels: December 31, 1994)
[95] Guay also informing that the Commission has a 'don't ask, don't tell' policy with regard to defence industry benefits from EU-sponsored R&D funds! See Guay, Terrence R., *At Arm's Length...* pp.57.
[96] Hendersen has observed that a single defence market can mean quite two different things: Either a market with common rules of competition for those inside it, but protected against the rest of the world; or, one that is open to global multilateral competition on same terms throughout the region. Hendersen quoted in Walker, W. & Gummett, P., 'Nationalism, Internationalism and the European Defence Market', *Chaillot Paper 9*, (Paris: Institute for Security Studies, WEU, September 1993), p.43.

curement has been left entirely in national hands. The European governments are instead continuing to develop their cooperative efforts outside the EU, particularly in the WEU.

(2.1.3) The Franco-German Enthusiasm: The Path From the WEAG/WEAO to the

European Armaments Agency (EAA)

In 1991, French and German governments pressed for the creation of an EAA by proposing
cooperation in the manufacture of armaments, administered by a WEU agency. Instead, an
Independent European Programme Group (IEPG) was created and incorporated into the WEU
in September 1992. A year later, it was renamed as the Western European Armaments Group
(WEAG) and formed the future basis of the EAA as a principal policy forum for European
armaments cooperation. WEU defence ministers form the administrative and National Armaments Directors (NADs) form the WEAG's operational core. The main aims of the WEAG
are to increase the harmonisation of European weapons procurement, opening-up national defence markets to cross-border competition, strengthening the EDITB, and enhancing cooperation in R&D (i.e. European Cooperative Long-Term Initiative for Defence (EUCLID) programme).[97] Thus, some of the EU countries aim to Europeanise the armaments market. For
this reason, Guay argued that the restructuring of the European defence industries might soon
be the primary task of the EU/WEU.[98] However, the WEAG's function is constrained by the
inevitable divergence of national interests and procedures and with technical administrative
matters. Thus, the Germans' initiative of establishing the EAA through the WEAG at
Noordwijk in 1994 was refused by other states on the basis that conditions for pooling national sovereignties into European defence integration were not yet in existence. During the
WEAG's NADs meeting, the creation of the Western European Armaments Organisation
(WEAO) was agreed, instead of the EAA, in November 1996. The WEAO, as an executive

---

[97] *WEU Today*, p.47. Belgium, Denmark, France, Germany, Greece, Italy, Luxembourg, the Netherlands,
Norway, Portugal, Spain, Turkey and the UK are the members of WEAG. The EUCLID programme has not
been successful as expected for. De Vestel, P., 'Defence Markets and Industries in Europe ...', p.71.
[98] Guay, Terrence R., *At Arm's Length...* p.47.

organ of the WEAG and the subsidiary body of the WEU, is the first European armaments body.[99] This decision was taken in order to press ahead with cooperation in the area of armaments until the EAA could be established. The Board of Directors of the WEAO consists of WEAG NADs or their delegated representatives. The responsibility of the WEAO is to manage the WEAG's research and technology programme activities and to support WEAG's efforts to promote the Common European Armaments Policy as a part of the CEDP.[100] Thus, the WEAO's main objective is to improve the commonality and interoperability of its member states' military equipment.

The aim of the WEAG/WEAO is to integrate the European defence markets, so enhancing the EU's supranational mechanisms for managing these markets on the way to European military 'autonomy', and to restructure and rationalise the EDITB that would improve its ties with the CFSP. The WEAG/WEAO could play an effective role in generating binding agreements under which its members would open their national defence markets to WEU/WEAG-wide competition. Moreover, the WEAG/WEAO could also fulfil procurement management functions and improve the interoperability of European military equipment between its members by serving as a buying agency or by encouraging standardisation, common development methods and means of production for collectively required EU/WEU defence material. The WEAG/WEAO has, for instance, begun to systematically evaluating the anti-tactical ballistic missile defence system. Hence, the coordination between WEAG/WEAO's NADs and NATO's Conference of National Armaments Directors (CNADs) became essential.[101] The Satellite Centre in Torrejon, which was founded in April 1993 as a component of the WEU in Spain, could also serve as a first step in a collective EU/WEU/WEAG/WEAO effort to estab-

[99] WEU Council of Ministers, *Ostend Declaration*, (November 19, 1996).
[100] European Armaments Policy is initiated by Germany in the WEU Council of Ministers' Noordwijk Summit. 13 members of the WEAG are participating on an equal footing in WEAO activities. The WEAG is responsible to NADs and operates at a higher decision-making level than the WEAO.
[101] The CNAD is for coordinating political, economic and technical aspects of NATO forces' arms procurement. It also supervises cooperative ventures designed as 'NATO Projects' through specialised committees.

lish space and ground-based facilities for global surveillance, early-warning and data proc-

essing.[102] France and Germany share the idea that Europe needs its own military satellites.

Former German State Secretary of Defence Jörg Schönbohm argued that building European

military satellites would not only help to create a strong CFSP and European defence identity,

but would also help to maintain the technological capabilities of the European defence indus-

try.[103] Likewise, when French officials talk of a European defence identity, they insist it must

have a space based industrial component.[104]

Ludwig and Hess argued that, 'Europe has a wide range of technical and methodological

competence, a record of outstanding scientific results, and its own access to space (through

the [European Space Agency's (ESA)] ARIANE launcher system). All these make it one of

the leading space powers on the globe. However, *it does not yet use this power politically!*'[105]

Germany and France took a significant step forward by merging space sectors of Daimler-

Chrysler Aerospace (DASA) and Matra-Marconi Space to form Alcatel Space and Astrium.[106]

France and Germany are eager to set up an autonomous European intelligence satellite sys-

tem, whereas the political sensitivity of any move to establish a capability independent of the

US is still a major obstacle. The UK, which enjoys privileged access to US satellite intelli-

gence, is keeping itself aloof from the Franco-German enthusiasm. Hence, while financial

contributions to the ESA by France and Germany are the most significant and almost equal to

---

[102] Satellite Centre is operating for the verification of arms control agreements, monitoring crisis and risks affecting European security. WEU Council of Ministers approved in May 1997 that this Centre would use the Franco-Italian-Spanish Hélios I defence observation satellite. See *WEU Today*, pp.45-46.

[103] 'Pie in the Sky', *The Economist*, (Vol.335, No.7915, May 20, 1995), p.61-62.

[104] 'It cannot be Done Alone', *The Economist*, (Vol.334, No.7903, February 25, 1995), pp.19-21.

[105] Space technology is becoming a means to control economic and foreign affairs. The ESA founded in 1973 as a civil development organisation for scientific purposes with no specific mandate on industrial policies. Its 12 members out of 14 are EU members, except Norway and Switzerland, and Canada are associate members. Since summer 1999, the European Commission began financing large-scale space projects like the Galileo. Ludwig, K. P. & Hess, S., 'Toward a European Space Policy', *Internationale Politik*, (Vol.1, Summer Issue, July 14, 2000). Available at: <http://www.dgap.org/english/tip/tip2/eurospace.html> (Visited on: July 14, 2000).

[106] France, Germany, and Italy are the major nations where the major European space companies are located. The *Deutsche Luft- und Raumfahrt* in Germany, the *Centre Nationale d'etudes Spatiales* in France, and the *Agenzia Spaziale Italiana* in Italy have given the EU a growing supranational role in space through the ESA.

each other, the UK is on the fourth rank behind Italy with a huge financial gap in comparison to the top two financial contributors (see Graph 2.1).

Graph 2.1

Space Budgets of the ESA Member States, 1999[107]

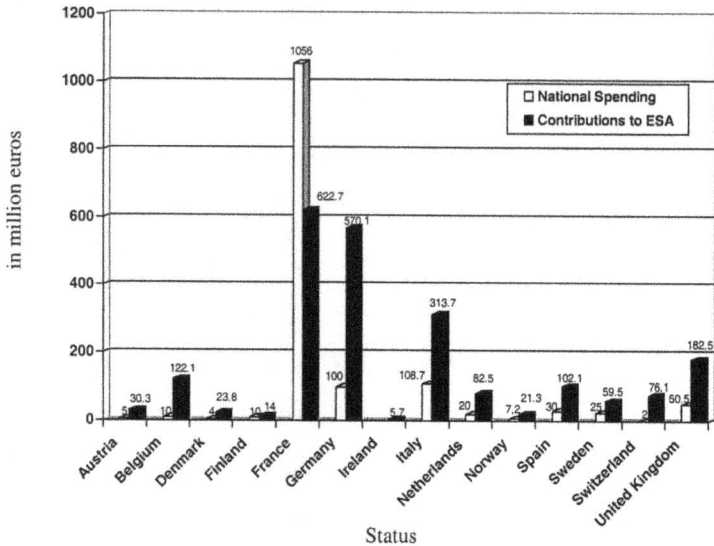

Another major obstacle, which is the most unfortunate one, is that EU member states are not focusing on common specific goals and for this reason they devote marginal financial support to the European intelligence satellite system. It was suggested in *The Economist* in February 1995, that the WEU might obtain 'a complete family of satellites, including one for communications, which would cost $19 billion over 25 years. Even this would probably not give Europe a command-and-control system as good as America has now'.[108] De Vestel argued

---

[107] Ludwig, K. P. & Hess, S., 'Toward a European Space Policy', *Internationale Politik*, (Vol.1, Summer Issue, July 14, 2000).
[108] 'It cannot be Done Alone', *The Economist*, pp.19-21.

that because of the ESA's interactions with defence forces on such questions as industry, technology and state involvement, the ESA is a good comparison to the EAA.[109]

In theory, as the structure of the WEAG/WEAO evolves, production of armaments would begin to be harmonised amongst its member states, eventually making the *de jure* creation of the EAA unavoidable. The EAA would also be looking to open the arms market in all NATO countries to competition and concentrating on creating a common European defence arms market. Co-operation in defence procurement also means that governments will loose their ability to control the defence contracts. However, it is difficult to see how the three big European countries – France, Germany, and the UK – would manage to bring their different defence philosophies together. The next section will analyse these three different philosophies and the Franco-German's attempt in going one step further in the realisation of the EAA.

(2.2) Defence Philosophies of France, Germany, and the UK

(2.2.1) The 'Big Three's' Defence Philosophies

With regard to military forces, innovative capabilities, defence budgets, and armament industries, France, Germany, and the UK overwhelmingly dominate the European defence sector (80% of defence production and 90% of defence R&D expenditure in the EU)[110]. According to their historical, economic and political background, the 'big three' countries' defence companies and state-industry relations differ substantially from each other. Of the major defence companies in France, Aérospatiale and Dassault, concentrated on aircraft production, Matra and Aérospatiale specialised in missile, Thomson-CSF and Matra produce defence electronics, and *Groupement Industriel des Armements Terrestres* (GIAT) makes tanks, artillery, and

---

[109] De Vestel, P., 'Defence Markets and Industries in Europe…', p.78.
[110] *Ibid*, p.71.

munitions; in Germany, DASA is producing aircraft and missile, and Siemens was the pri-

mary electronics firm; British Aerospace (BAe) is the main British aircraft and missile firm,

and General Electronic Corporation (GEC) is the major military electronic supplier.[111]

The most powerful armaments agency in Europe, *Délégation Générale pour l'Armement*

(DGA), and the closest link between state and industry is based in France. Defence autonomy

and national procurement, the struggle against American competition, and strong export ori-

entation strategies are the basics of the French defence philosophy. The collapse of the Soviet

empire, unification of Germany, and the consequent sharp fall of the world arms export mar-

ket share of France, altered the political and economic aspects of French defence philosophy.

Although Germany and the UK, with the end of the Cold War, followed the course of reduc-

ing their defence budgets sharply and restructuring their defence industry gradually, France

began to realise the necessity of these changes in the mid-1990s. Since the mid-1990s, France

has aspired to reach a *préférence européenne* (European preference) by creating European

defence firms big enough to match and resolve trade imbalances with the US through aug-

menting EU defence competences and defending the special needs of the European defence

industrial base.[112] With the 'European preference', France also aims to create a pan-European

defence industrial base that would inevitably force the EU governments to buy as much Euro-

pean weapons as possible. This has been a significant U-turn from the previous French 'na-

tional preference' policy, which left France torn between the desires of national independence

and privatisation, merger, cooperation, and combined European export efforts in the post-

Cold War era.[113] France wants to lead the EU states into a Europe-wide joint defence

---

[111] Siemens sold its defence electronics business to BAe and DASA in October 1997. See Guay, Terrence R., *At Arm's Length...* pp.27-28. The French government is also trying to merge Aérospatiale, Dassault and Matra, and the UK already merged the defence components of BAe and GEC to form the BAE systems.

[112] Walker, W. & Gummett, P., 'Nationalism, Internationalism and the European Defence Market', p.44-45; Taylor, T., 'West European security and defence cooperation: Maastricht and beyond', *International Affairs*, (Vol.70, No.1, 1994), p.14.

[113] 'National preference' means purchasing arms from national industries as much as possible. For this reason, France involved in developing the *Rafale* fighter aircraft rather than entering into four-nation (Germany, the UK,

organization through the Europeanisation of their security and defence policies on an inter-governmental basis.

In order to achieve its aims and to bring French firms into a competitive position, France is pressing for French 'champions' and looking for profitable and internationally competitive European alliances. For this reason, French President Chirac announced the French defence restructuring proposal in 1996 and pressed for the privatisation of Thomson-CSF and merger between Dassault and Aérospatiale.[114] After protracted negotiations, which had taken almost three years, BAe and Matra merged their missile businesses in order to create Europe's largest missile company in May 1996. Russel G. Chaddock argued that, 'this is the result of French political moves to unify Europe's defence and lessen its dependence on the US. On the indus-trial front, this effort means creating defence giants that can compete with American compa-nies such as Lockheed Martin.'[115] The French government has also attempted to integrate French defence companies by merging Thomson-CSF with Dassault and Aérospatiale to cre-ate Alcatel Althsom. Brian Kenny argued that, 'this may be a forerunner to creating a "single company" in Europe, as, for example, both in the UK (BAe) and Germany (DASA) have, along with France, supported the idea of a unified aerospace industry'.[116]

Italy, and Spain) *Eurofighter* programme. Even so, many analysts and industrialists see a single next-generation combat aircraft programme the most likely outcome. Barrie, D., 'Launching a joint offensive', *International Management*, (Vol.49, No.7, September 1994), p.26. The controversy between national and European options written in the French military programme as: 'Pour ces deux projets, l'objectif est le maintein du capital industriel, technologique et humain, la préservation des intérêts de la défense nationale, l'ouverture de nouvelles perspectives de développment, enfin, la poursuite et le renforcement de la politique d'alliance et de concentration à l'échelle européenne.' 'Projet De Loi – relatif à la programmation militaire pour les années 1997 à 2002', *Assemblée Nationale No.2766*, (Paris: Sté Nouvelle des Librairies, May 20, 1996), p.48

[114] One of the main reasons of privatisation attempts and defence budget cuts in France was to catch up the EMU eligibility criteria. Guay also observed that France is very slow in the privatisation. 80% of the French defence industry can still be considered as public sector. Guay, Terrence R., *At Arm's Length...* pp.31-32.

[115] Chaddock, G. R., 'France Hits Snags on Path to a Euro-Defence', *Christian Science Monitor*, (Vol.88, No.120, May 16, 1996), p.5; Seely, R., 'With the Cold War a Memory, Europe's Defence Industries Fight for Life', *The Los Angeles Times*, (October 24, 1999); DASA's chairman Manfred Bischoff declared his intention by joining Matra and BAe. He said: Europe needs a single missile maker to compete effectively with the Americans. 'Getting together', *The Economist*, (August 10, 1996), p.46.

[116] Kenny, B., 'Change and Cross-Border Activity in the European Defence Industry', p.3; 'Business: Puffs of white Gaulouise smoke', *The Economist*, (November 7, 1998), pp.66-71.

However, France is still unwilling to become involved in cooperative programmes with its European partners unless French firms play the leading role and rationalisation of cooperative programmes maintain their self-sufficiency in the arms production. France actually wants a common European defence, but on its own terms. Nonetheless, the French government began to realise that other countries would not accept the French 'European preference' model if it favoured French prerequisites only. Thus, the success of French plans in the EU is very much dependant on Germany and the UK, and their political, industrial and financial collaborations with each other.

Unlike the strong national autonomy status of French defence industries, defence industries in Germany are private and there is a special kind of relationship between the German govern-ment and defence industries. This special relationship was defined by Monier as a 'secret cir-cle' that exists within a private body called the *Rüstungswirtschaftlicher Arbeitskreis* (Rü-AK) and periodically brings together senior officials from the defence ministry and chief executives of major arms firms.[117] Therefore, without the consent of the German government, defence industries rarely act on their own. The German government's military requirements plan, known as the '*Bundeswehr* plan', is the major plan that determines the production agenda of the defence industries. Katia Vlachos named the German government as a 'reliable partner' and its business with defence industries defined by one of the executives in the German Federal Ministry of Defence as 'a good business relationship; a customer-supplier relationship'.[118] Another significant feature of German defence industries is that almost none of them are purely defence-oriented. Therefore, the government and defence industry officials always underline the importance of civil-military dual-use technology.

---

[117] In Walker, W. & Gummett, P., 'Nationalism, Internationalism and the European Defence Market', p.26.
[118] Vlachos, K., 'Safeguarding European Competitiveness...', p.20 & 60.

On the other hand, Germany's strict arms export regulations are a significant obstacle to European defence industries' integration. Germany's unilateral adherence to a more restrictive arms export policy not only restricts German participation in European defence industrial restructuring programmes, but also paralyses the ability of German companies' to participate in competitive joint ventures and industrial alliances on an equal footing with other European firms. In order to loosen tight arms export regulations, the German government passed regulations in 1994. Guay wrote that, 'if German industry supplies less than 20% of the manufactured product, then [Berlin] will waive its right to decide whether the export will be issued a license'.[119]

In order to circumvent legal restrictions, German officials support EU-wide regulations. Therefore, Germany refused the French version of 'European preference' on the basis that it would amount to national protectionism and would perpetuate the division of the European defence market along national lines. The German officials aim is to create a genuine European defence market – a defence industry 'Big Bang' – by abolishing Art.223 for political and economic reasons.[120] The political reason of aiming German defence industries' integration into the European defence industrial evolution is shaped by Germany's historical role in World War II, and the economic reason has three main facets: *First*, Germany will work together with other EU member states for harmonising its arms export policies in the EU/WEU framework. *Second*, economic progress in the EU will encourage collaborative armaments projects, will strengthen ties among European defence firms, and finally would promote defence integration in the EU.[121] *Third*, strengthened EU competencies' in the European defence industry sphere would also empower the position of the EU institutions in international arms

---

[119] Guay, Terrence R., *At Arm's Length...* p.110.
[120] Walker, W. & Gummett, P., 'Nationalism, Internationalism and the European Defence Market', p.45.
[121] German defence firms currently produces 75% of its weapons through cooperative programs together with other countries. This is 15% for France and 10.5% for the UK. See Vlachos, K., 'Safeguarding European Competitiveness...', p.20.

trade negotiations and could make transatlantic relations truly a 'two-way street'.[122] Although Germany reassessed its defence industrial relations with the US in parallel to the reduction of defence budgets on both sides of the Atlantic, Germany is still considering itself a pivot between French and American ambitions. German officials state that 'strengthening the European pillar and adding it to the American pillar' is our primary policy goal, and therefore 'no priority is given to either relationship in general; it depends on the specific project'.[123]

German and French defence philosophies in theory are based on their different national preferences. Unlike the French intergovernmentalism, the Germans favour supranational structure through empowering the European Commission and Parliament. Furthermore, the German officials found the Commission too weak in dealing with mergers and supervising the state role in defence matters. Therefore, Germans even press for a 'European Competition Office', which is free from national prerogatives, in the defence sphere.[124] On the other hand, French officials found the Commission too tough on mergers and its supervising role extremely rigid on national defence matters. They complained that conditions are too difficult for European firms to compete internationally and, therefore, their claim is for more independence and more regulations that are flexible. Nevertheless, both countries have a shared interest in building a common European defence dimension, so they want to open the Commission to third parties (such as to competitors) in order to minimise the friction between the Commission and member states.

The UK is, on the other hand, traditionally less enthusiastic than France and Germany in giving the EU a role in defence industrial matters. The important concept for the UK is to attain a clearer national policy in the defence industry area. Therefore, the UK strongly opposes Euro-

---

[122] Guay, Terrence R., *At Arm's Length...* pp.112-113.
[123] Vlachos, K., 'Safeguarding European Competitiveness...', p.20.
[124] Guay, Terrence R., *At Arm's Length...*p.55.

pean defence industrial integration and instead advocates coordination. British officials favour

free intra-European competition, but the British defence philosophy, as the French defence

philosophy, rejects sacrificing any national prerogatives to Brussels through the abolition of

Art.223. However, unlike the French DGA, a non-centralised body called the *Procurement*

Executive of the Ministry of Defence, which includes technical-civilian officials and military

officers, administers arms procurement in the UK.[125] Moreover, the defence industry is

mainly in private hands. The armaments procurement policy of the UK is also traditionally

characterised by 'value for money' – decisions for ordering weapons are open to any domestic

or foreign defence firm on the basis of competitive cost and quality based bidding.[126] The

'value for money' policy of the UK is often strongly criticised by European governments

(particularly by the French) and defence firms in that it results in arms contracts' being won

by strong US defence firms. Unlike the UK, France and Germany are struggling for a Euro-

pean defence market in order to strengthen the European defence integration process through

regulating intra-EU competition and making the European 'Pillar of Defence' viable by cre-

ating a robust 'two-way street' between the EU and the US.

The UK's special strategic relationship with the US in the military technology field is another

distinct feature of the British defence philosophy. While Germany enjoys maintaining its po-

sition between France and the US, the UK does the same thing between Europe and the

America. The main target of British diplomacy is to avoid a situation that would force the UK

to choose the side of one's. Guay put it, 'British defence firms seem to want to have it both

ways as well: access to leading-edge technologies in the US as well as the option of partici-

---

[125] Walker, W. & Gummett, P., 'Nationalism, Internationalism and the European Defence Market', p.20.
[126] Guay, Terrence R., *At Arm's Length*...pp.114-115; The privatised British national 'champions', which are operating through competition and strict price control measures, do not enjoy the similar financial and political support of the government as has their French and German counterparts.

pating in European collaboration'.[127] The UK's 'value for money' procurement strategy and its US preference have long been counterproductive to the creation of a unified EDITB and particularly irritated the French politicians.

Vlachos summarised the national defence industry philosophies' of the 'big three' as, the British industries are private and highly rationalised, German industries are private, but still in the process of rationalisation, and French industries are fragmented, substantially state-controlled, experiencing privatisation and heavy rationalisation at the same time.[128] However, with joining the Franco-German Joint Armament Cooperation Structure (JACS), the UK has hinted that it might, in the future, commit to the development of a strong EDITB. The following section will demonstrate that significant convergence is taking place between the 'big three's' defence philosophies.

(2.2.2) The 'Big Three's' Defence Philosophies are Converging: The Franco-German's Joint Armament Cooperation Structure (JACS) Initiative

In the absence of a single European defence market, the lack of governments' free hand over cross-border mergers and their interest in maintaining their domestic production capabilities, collaborative projects inevitably emerged to meet the European defence industrial cooperative needs. However, most of the collaborative projects involved parcelling out the work among members of a particular consortium through *juste retour* rather than rationalising the production capacity.[129] Instead of making private industrial co-operations among two or more

---

[127] The British participation in the EU-wide collaborative projects is sometimes constrained by its special relationship with the US. Guay warned that, while British defence firms may gain access to more advanced technologies in comparison to its European competitors, they may also be excluded from the continental defence collaborations. Even if British defence firms collaborate with another European defence firm, they do not accept it to be in the expense of the 'value for money' principle. The condition for collaboration should be competition for an agreed specification. Guay, Terrence R., *At Arm's Length*...p.114-122, 142-146.

[128] Vlachos, K., 'Safeguarding European Competitiveness...', p.8.

[129] *Juste retour* (or fair-return) is an old principle applied to collaborative projects. It is an industrial and technological compensation proportional to the share in orders. In a typical collaborative project, work shares for each participating country are apportioned according to how much of the final product each nation intends to

companies easier, collaborative projects are usually influenced by national political strate-gies.[130] Thus, collaborative projects have often become an ineffective and time-consuming process due to protracted national *beggar-my-neighbour* strategies. Another negative impact of *juste retour* on the European defence market is the difficulty of industrial co-operation among European defence manufacturers with a European arms procurement agency, which results in the production of low quality high cost weapons and so channels most European countries to buy high quality low cost weapons from the US.

As talks upon the EAA were postponed within the WEU, France and Germany pressed for creating a bilateral agency in their Franco-German Summit at Bonn in December 1993. French and German governments repeatedly complained about the lack of progress in the WEAG and urged the formation of a common procurement system through a bilateral initia-tive, while keeping it open for other states' participation. It was decided that this system would eliminate the *juste retour* by creating common procurement practices, giving greater cost-effectiveness through rationalisation of procurement procedures, improving industrial competitiveness among the member states, and developing a multi-programme approach through joint programme offices based along functional lines. During the WEU Noordwijk meeting on November 14, 1994, it was decided that the Franco-German common procurement initiative be institutionalised through the Joint Armaments Cooperation Structure – as a sub-sidiary body under the modified Brussels Treaty – in order to accomplish the above targets.[131] From the outset, the British government was unwilling to join its European partners in such a structure with the aim of building cross-border industrial ties through rationalising European

purchase. See Guay, Terrence R., *At Arm's Length...*pp.37-38. Increased collaboration in the post-Cold War era has two main impulses for meeting defence budget cuts and high-technology costs: Firstly, firms share risks and costs; secondly, they acquire the chance of buying costly 'complementary assets' produced by their competitors.
[130] Although industrial cooperation has grown as a reaction to ineffective political cooperation, one should keep in mind that the creation of the EAA would require sufficient political integration in order to enable the defence market to be treated like a single free European market!
[131] WEU Council of Ministers, *Noordwijk Declaration*, Title VIII, p.9. The JACS will also establish a common set of procedures for contracting intellectual property rights that would prevent duplicating the work carried out by other national bodies. Hayward, K., 'Towards a European Weapons Procurement Process', p.28.

defence industries. However, the UK could not reject the Franco-German's JACS initiative. The main reason of the UK's participation in JACS was to prevent the 'Franco-German Agency' that would have set the terms and rules of the future European procurement collaboration. The Italians followed the British by joining the Franco-German structure in 1996. These four countries formally founded JACS in January 1997 with the aim of empowering it to act as a programme office, providing a framework for the future EAA and promoting coordination, complementarity, and increased capability in the military area.[132] JACS comprises four NADs and representatives of chiefs of staffs of the four member countries. Initially they have taken over the management of Franco-German collaborative programmes.[133]

However, JACS has several problems. The first problem is that the incompatible national defence philosophies of the UK and France continue to cause a lot friction in JACS. The UK advocates an open competitive procurement system that would best help to procure weapons it needs cost-effectively through worldwide commitments. On the other hand, France – backed by Germany – favours a well-defined and pre-determined procurement system.[134] France also strongly favours the idea of partial duplications and extra costs, so that autonomous European defence industries could compete effectively, and only then cooperate with the US industry. While the German state policy is to take a middle path between the US and the European defence structures, German defence industries are more in favour of duplicating the US. Hayward argued that, 'Germans were prepared to concede a degree of competition at

---

[132] France, Germany, the UK, and Italy are the founders of JACS (or OCCAR – *Organisation Conjoint de Coopération en matière d'Armements*). Spain, Belgium, and the Netherlands have also interested to become the member of the JACS. JACS has freedom of action only in the field of research, but, as de Puig argued, it is currently gaining a considerable significance and efficiency. De Puig, L. M., 'The European Sea and Defence Identity Within NATO', *NATO Review*, (No.2, Summer 1998), p.9.

[133] Franco-German *Milan* and *Hot* anti-tank missile programs, *Tiger* attack helicopter project, *MRAV* (Multi-Role Armoured Vehicle) and possibly satellite projects will follow.

[134] France warned the UK several times that unless it adheres to JACS's pro-European principles, the UK's application to JACS will be suspended. *C-130* and *Apache* attack helicopter purchases of the UK from the US irritated French officials, who were trying to marshal support for the proposed multilateral *Future Large Aircraft (FLA)* – on which Britain is a partner – and Eurocopter's Franco-German *Tiger* attack helicopter. Muradian, V., 'UK-France Dispute Over Procurement Could Impact US Firms', *Defense Daily*, (September 24, 1996).

the design stage between two international consortiums, with guaranteed industrial participation at the production stage'.[135] Theoretically, in future all European and transatlantic programmes could come under the aegis of JACS. Therefore, JACS will bind its member states' procurement policies, especially the UK's unpredictable 'value for money' policy, more into the EU/WEU framework.

The second problem is that, if JACS is to be developed further, it needs a legal status in order to authorise and administer industrial contracts. This legal status could be provided through the integration of JACS into the WEU as a subsidiary body and probably with the further integration into the WEAG/WEAO framework. European NADs advised that this could be possible only if JACS absorbs all members of the WEU. However, providing a possible legal status to JACS politically seems a difficult task.[136]

The second problem generates the third problem. If France, Germany, and Britain harmonise their armed forces, differences between JACS participants and non-participants will inevitably be created. The 'big three' states are vying for control of the JACS's overall direction. This might bring the idea of 'variable geometry' into the prospective EAA picture as well, but the answer to the question of how their smaller partners will react to the evolution of JACS is still unknown.

Consequently, even the persistent Britain has come to understand one thing clearer that no country can go it alone to develop the defence capabilities it need. Therefore, it can be argued

---

[135] Hayward, K., 'Towards a European Weapons Procurement Process', pp.29-30; Manfred Bischoff, Chairman of DASA, said: 'Why are there no incentives to create optional restructuring in Europe? At the least, we should duplicate in Europe the US government's 'Buy American' policy... Why not a European missile company?... Why not common export rules in the defence sector? I don't care if they are German, French or Italian, as long as there is a harmonised approach. If we do not coordinate our industries and policies soon we will grow weaker.' Manfred Bischoff quoted in Guay, Terrence R., *At Arm's Length*...p.137.

[136] For more information see WEU Assembly, 'WEAG, the course to be followed', *Document 1483*, (Paris: WEU Assembly, November 6, 1995).

that the UK is becoming agreeable to the idea of the 'European preference'. Former British

Defence Secretary, George Robertson, argued that:

> *'As a customer, I need to have a strong industrial base in Europe. In the face of*
>
> *the ever-rising cost of defence equipment, I need sources of supply in Europe*
>
> *which can compete with the concentrated might of the major US contractors. I*
>
> *don't want to face monopoly suppliers in the US. [...] If we [Europeans] go into*
>
> *the next century with a multitude of competing national companies and industries*
>
> *attempting to find a place in a global market dominated by giant American*
>
> *companies then the result will be industrial suicide'.*[137]

Indeed, centralisation between the leading defence contractors in the 'big three' countries is

occurring. The 'European preference' will be tested by the interaction of various structures

(EU/WEU/WEAG/WEAO/JACS) and perhaps these would someday lead to the creation of

an EAA. There is also an ambiguous proposal put forward in July 2000 for the creation of a

single European Aeronautic Defence and Space Company (EADS) between 'Fortress Europe'

and 'Fortress America'.[138] The construction of the EDITB has obviously been set off by

French and German initiatives, which are widely accepted to be amongst the essential condi-

tions for realising the Franco-German desire for a European 'Pillar of Defence'.

---

[137] Speech by the Defence Secretary, Mr George Robertson, *Annual Dinner of the Society of British Aerospace Companies*, (June 17, 1998). <http://www.fco.gov.uk/news/speechtext.asp?1183> (Visited on: August 1, 2000).
[138] EADS comprises Aérospatiale, BAe, DASA, Spain's aerospace company *Construcciones Aeronáuticas S. A.* (CASA), Sweden's *Saab*, and Italy's *Finmeccanica-Alenia* and aims to produce military aircraft, helicopters, space systems, guided weapons, and other defence systems. Markusen, A., 'The Rise of World Weapons', *Foreign Policy*, (No.114, Spring 1999), pp.40-51; 'Sécurité commune: l'Europe doit changer de cap', *Les Dernières Nouvelles d'Alsace*, (June 2, 2001). For more information see: <http://www.eads.net>

(3) Breaking the European Sisyphus (1998-2000): The Heyday of the European Defence Force

Not until 1998 did the UK significantly change its stance on the provision of the necessary competencies to the EU in the sphere of defence. France and Germany have long argued that adding a defence dimension to the EU – through a merger between the EU and the WEU – would render the CFSP more effective. On the opposite side, the UK has always proved to be a stumbling block in front of Franco-German ambitions. However, in autumn 1998, Prime Minister of the UK, Tony Blair, began to change the traditional British foreign policy on assigning Europe a defence dimension. As a result of this, the Anglo-French St. Mâlo Declaration on an *autonomous* EU defence capacity triggered a series of meetings culminating in the Cologne European Council Declaration in June 1999 and the Helsinki European Council Declaration in December 1999. In the first part of this section, the period from the Anglo-French St. Mâlo Declaration, including the Cologne European Council Declaration on 'strengthening the Common European Policy on Security and Defence (CEPSD)',[139] until the Helsinki European Council Declaration will be analysed. The second part will only be devoted to the Helsinki European Council Declaration.

(3.1) The Road from the Joint Anglo-French St. Mâlo Declaration to the Cologne European Council Declaration

The sudden changes to British foreign policy in the defence sphere vis-à-vis the EU have not occurred by chance. There were several combined challenges that triggered the possible marginalisation of the UK from the EU's two powerful members – France and Germany: *Firstly*, NATO member states' decision to launch an air campaign against Serbia in autumn 1998 and then having to watch this operation later in early 1999, which was almost entirely conduced

---

[139] For practical reasons, from this page onwards the Common European Security and Defence Policy (CESDP) will replace the CEPSD throughout the study. *Cologne European Council Declaration* on 'Strengthening the Common European Policy on Security and Defence', (SN 150/99 EN ANNEX, CAB 33-42, June 3&4, 1999). Available at: <http://europa.eu.int/council/off/conclu/June99/June99_en.pdf> (Visited on: June 20, 2000).

by US's technologically advanced fighter planes, urged Blair to realise the need for a robust

European defence capability. Since British and French troops worked harmoniously together

in Bosnia and Kosovo, the UK began to accept that there are times when it makes sense for

European armies to act together through the EU/WEU.[140] *Secondly*, British diplomats have

accepted that if the UK continues to ignore the European defence dimension, the Franco-

German couple would find no alternative but to act on their own. Then, as has happened so

often in Europe before (e.g. JACS, see above), the UK will be left to play the role of catch-up.

Thus, the UK, for the sake of its standing in the world, wanted to maintain its leading role in

Europe together with France and Germany.[141] *Thirdly*, the end of the Cold War has loosened

the bonds that tied the US to its European allies. This loosening has also changed the opinion

of the UK's Atlanticist friends. Therefore, the UK's loneliness forced it either to jump on to

the EU defence train or stay out and become marginalized.[142]

These changes in British thinking marked the Anglo-French Declaration at St. Mâlo, which

was signed between Tony Blair of the UK and Jacques Chirac of France on December 3-4,

1998. The Anglo-French Declaration was very much along the same lines as the statements

written in the Franco-German Declaration two days before at the Potsdam Summit on

December 1, 1998, between the French President Chirac and Prime Minister Lionel Jospin

---

[140] Firstly, former Prime Minister John Major displeased with the US air attacks in Bosnia while French and British troops were on the ground; and secondly, Tony Blair exasperated with the Clinton administration over its unwillingness to deploy ground troops in Kosovo resulted in the British irritation against the US's European policies. Thus, the UK recognised the necessity of more healthy and independent European defence capability. Rees, W. & Monar, J., 'Force for Europe', *The World Today*, (June 2000), pp.14-16.

[141] Lindley-F., J., 'Time to Bite the Eurobullet', *New Statesman*, (Vol.127, No.4391, June 26, 1998).

[142] Bruno & Guglielmo Carchedi associated the UK's reluctance in a common European defence force creation to the UK's opt-out status in the EMU. They argued that, 'the reluctance of the UK to proceed towards greater political and military integration is being eroded by economic forces and might come to an end sooner than one might expect. For example, the awareness is growing that no single European stock market (including London) is sufficiently large to compete with other, much greater, stock exchanges... This would be an important factor pushing for the introduction of the Euro in the UK. For similar reasons, the UK will sooner or later have to join the EMU. At this point its attitude towards a common military force might change.' Carchedi, B. & Carchedi, G., 'Contradictions of European Integration', *Capital & Class*, (No.67, Spring 1999), pp.119-154.

and the German Chancellor Gerhard Schröder.[143] The St. Mâlo Declaration visualized the

creation of a Common European Security and Defence Policy (CESDP) with means and

mechanisms to allow the EU to act 'autonomously' – backed by credible military forces –

where NATO as a whole is not willing to engage (parag.2&3); to endow the EU to play its

full role on the international stage through progressively framing the CDP on the basis of in-

tergovernmental decision (parag.1); to ensure the maintenance of collective defence commit-

ments of NATO and the WEU (parag.2); to give the EU an appropriate structure and a capac-

ity for analysing situations, sources of intelligence and relevant strategic planning without un-

necessary duplication, and taking into account the existing assets of the WEU and the evolu-

tion of its relations with the EU (parag.3); to strengthen European armed forces that can react

rapidly to new risks, which will be supported by a strong and competitive European defence

industry and technology (parag.4).[144]

It is obvious that the UK took a great leap forward in the development of the CESDP.

However, this is both comforting and displeasing to the US. It is comforting because the US

trusts British diplomacy, which is based on strong transatlantic cooperation, and it is dis-

pleasing because of the fear that the UK might gradually move towards the French thinking

and might sacrifice something from the privileged US-UK transatlantic relationship in order

to consolidate its leading role in Europe. Therefore, the St. Mâlo Declaration was actually a

delicate compromise between the French wish for boosting the EU profile, through keeping

the option of an autonomous European military capability potent and putting pressure on

Washington to cooperate more in the development of ESDI within NATO, and the UK's in-

sistence that any upgrading of European defence should be kept firmly under NATO's

---

[143] *Franco-German Potsdam Declaration*, (Potsdam: Franco-German Summit, December 1, 1998). Available at: <http://www.ofaj.org/reseau/decoff/sommaire/potsdam.html> (Visited on: June 20, 2000).
[144] *St. Mâlo Declaration*, (France: Anglo-French Summit, December 4, 1998) in Missiroli, A., 'CFSP, Defence and Flexibility', *Chaillot Paper 38*, (Paris: Institute for Security Studies, WEU, February 2000), Annexe C.

aegis.[145] The US Administration's final reaction to the Anglo-French initiative took the form

of a 'yes, but' approach. The US Secretary of State, Madeleine Albright, emphasised that

European allies should not cause the 'three D's', decoupling, discrimination, and not to dupli-

cate what NATO already effectively does.[146] This was the typical US reaction similar to the

former Bush Administration's warning during the Franco-German's Eurocorps creation.

Almost a week before the European Council's Cologne meeting, the Toulouse Declaration

was announced by the Franco-German Defence and Security Council on May 29, 1999. The

opportunity the Franco-German couple found to persuade the UK to agree to integrate the

WEU into the EU came for the first time with the St. Mâlo Declaration, echoed in the

Toulouse Declaration, and galvanised the European Council meeting in Cologne. The Franco-

German Defence and Security Council stated that, '[o]ur two countries reaffirm their determi-

nation to put their full weight behind the effort to secure for the EU the necessary autonomous

assets it needs to be able to decide and act in the face of crises. [...] The WEU's integration

into the EU will also further these aims'.[147] The Council, 'with the same aim in mind', also

consolidated one of the basic steps of the European 'Pillar of Defence' through the following

statement: '...we are convinced that the new strategic environment has to lead us, with our

three other Eurocorps partners, to adapt this major multinational unit, and first and foremost

its headquarters, so that in future it becomes a European rapid reaction corps'.[148]

---

[145] 'Leaders: Defending Europe', *The Economist*, (December 4, 1999), p.18; 'Count Your NATOs', *The Economist*, (April 24, 1999), p.9-11.
[146] NATO allies, who are not the EU members, Turkey, Norway, Iceland, the Czech Republic, Hungary, Poland, as well as Canada and the US, should not be discriminated. However, as a result of complaints from the EU side the NATO's new Secretary-General, George Robertson, replaced the negative connotation of 'three D's' with the positive 'three I's: *Improvement* in European defence capabilities; *inclusiveness* and transparency for all Allies; and, the *indivisibility* of transatlantic security, based on shared values.' Robertson, G., 'NATO in the New Millenium', *NATO Review*, (No.4, 1999), p.6; Finn, P., 'Six in NATO Upset Over EU Corps Plan', *The Washington Post*, (April 9, 2000); Sloan, S. R., 'The US and European Defence', *Chaillot Paper* 39, (Paris: Institute for Security Studies, WEU, February 2000), p.22; Heisbourg, F., 'European Defence Takes a Leap Forward', *NATO Review*, (Vol.48, No.1, Spring/Summer 2000), pp.8-11.
[147] *Franco-German Summit –Defence and Security Council – Toulouse Declaration*, (Toulouse: May 29, 1999). Available at: <http://www.ambafrance.org.uk/cgi-bin/htsearch> (Visited on: June 20, 2000).
[148] *Ibid.*

As a result of the TEU decision on the creation of a CDP within the framework of the CFSP, the possible integration of the WEU into the EU – should this be agreed by the European Council – in the Treaty of Amsterdam (ToA) and the creation of autonomous EU actions backed by credible military forces in St. Mâlo, the European Council invited the German Presidency to work on the above debates and agreed examining the existing questions at the European Council in Cologne (June 3-4, 1999). The EU member states declared their intentions in Cologne to supply the EU with a whole range of military as well as political and economic capabilities in order to form an effective decision-making mechanism for crisis management operations within the range of the Petersberg Tasks.[149] Therefore, the EU would contribute to international peace and security in accordance with the principles of the UN Charter through building up more effective European military capabilities based on the existing national, bi-national and multinational capabilities (parag.1&2). This means that either the EU as an association of states, a 'core' group or the 'coalition of the willing' states could undertake the military action. For effective functioning of the CESDP, the sustainability of a military action in the field of intelligence, strategic transport, command and control is also essential. Therefore, the Cologne Declaration emphasised the importance of strengthening the EDITB through restructuring the European defence industries into a competitive, dynamic and effective industrial collaboration and searching for a better harmonisation of military requirements among the member states (parag.2).

The dilemma is whether the autonomous CESDP really needs the EU/WEU's costly 'European' weapons production or occasionally borrowing them from the US/NATO through the CJTF, so partially being dependent on the US, would be a satisfactory solution. Whether the 'European preference' is the priority of Europeans or not one thing is very clear, if Europeans are aiming to reach CD in the future then the EU must develop its own robust EDITB.

---

[149] *Cologne European Council Declaration*, see CAB37, '2. Guiding Principles.'

Therefore, the EU should take a step forward in regulating the defence industries cooperative efforts through a joint procurement and European armaments budget together with binding rules, authorisations and export controls so that standardisation and interoperability among the European forces, as well as between the European and US forces in NATO, will provide crisis management operations sustainability, flexibility, mobility and effective fire power.[150] The Cologne Declaration also laid down two forms of EU-led operations: *First*, EU-led operations using NATO assets and capabilities through the Berlin agreement of 1996 (CJTF) and the Washington NATO Summit decision of April 1999.[151] *Second*, EU-led autonomous operations through 'either national command structures providing multinational representation in headquarters or drawing on existing command structures within multinational forces'.[152] However, if one reads the St. Mâlo and Cologne texts carefully it is not difficult to discover that the second form of autonomous EU-led operations is not the preferred choice and will be conditional on the following provisions: (a) the EU will take decisions and approve military actions where NATO is not engaged (parag.3 of St. Mâlo Declaration); (b) the EU will take autonomous military actions without prejudicing NATO actions (parag.1 of Cologne Declaration).

As far as the definition of the operations' 'modality' is concerned, the Council stated that the inclusion of WEU functions and tasks into the EU will allow it to fulfil new responsibilities in the domain of Petersberg Tasks and '[t]he WEU as an organisation would have completed its

---

[150] In order to achieve sustainability, mobility and flexibility in crisis management operations, the following decisions were also adopted: 'Regular (or *ad hoc*) meetings of the General Affairs Council, as appropriate including Defence Ministries; a permanent body in Brussels (Political and Security Committee) consisting of representatives with political/military expertise; an EU Military Committee consisting of Military Representatives making recommendations to the Political and Security Committee; an EU Military Staff including a Situation Centre; other sources such as a Satellite Centre, Institute for Security Studies.' *Cologne European Council Declaration*, see CAB39, '3. Decision Making.'

[151] In addition to the development of an effective mutual consultation, cooperation, and transparency between the EU and NATO, which were adopted in the *Cologne European Council Declaration* (parag.3), the Defence Capabilities Initiative (DCI) was also adopted at the NATO Washington Summit in order to help the Europeans to catch up the US Revolution in Military Affairs (RMA). NATO *Washington Summit Communiqué* (April 24, 1999). Available at: <http://www.nato.int> (Visited on: September 02, 2000).

[152] *Cologne European Council Declaration*, see CAB40, '4. Implementation'; also see Van Beveren's four possible ways of achieving the weak version of CD in section *(1.2) Contours of the CDP and CD.*

purpose' (parag.5). It is also stated in the same paragraph that, the different status of the EU member states with respect to collective defence guarantees will not be affected and the WEU-NATO connection will remain the foundation for the collective defence of its member states. Moreover, Wolfgang Ischinger, the German Ambassador to US, said that '[t]he CESDP is, at present, an institutional project... Some steps forward are in the interest of states like Ireland, Austria, Sweden or Finland who are now taking part in thinking of a harmonised development of the military forces. One year ago they stood outside, now we sign papers commonly'.[153] So far, no non-allied states have been asked to sign 'collective defence' clauses (Art.5/V of NATO/WEU), therefore the achievement of Petersberg missions under the CESDP principles do not seem very problematic. Lothar Rühl argued that paragraph 5 of the Cologne Declaration 'means that for the purpose of a common "European defence policy", membership in NATO is not a criterion and politically not even relevant'.[154] It is worth mentioning that although Art.V of the WEU Treaty is stronger than Art.5 of the North Atlantic Treaty and although the EU began absorbing most of the WEU functions in accordance with the CESDP, the EU's CESDP is kept distinct from the 'collective defence' clauses. The 'collective defence' function of the WEU is not absorbed into the EU and perhaps will not be absorbed until the creation of CD.

---

[153] 'A Discussion with Dr. Wolfgang Ischinger', *An American Institute for Contemporary German Studies Seminar*, (Washington: July 13, 2000) <http://www.aicgs.org/events/2000/ischinger_summary.html> (Visited on: August 1, 2000)

[154] Rühl, L., 'Conditions and options for an autonomous 'Common European Policy on Security and Defence' in and by the EU in the post-Amsterdam perspective opened at Cologne in June 1999', *Centre for European Integration Studies (ZEI)*, (Bonn:Rheinische Friedrich-Wilhelms-Universität, Discussion Paper, C54, 1999), p.8. It is stated in the 'modalities of participation and cooperation' that successful creation of the CESDP is, however, based on three principles: '(1) the possibility of all EU Member States, including non-allied members [Austria, Ireland, Finland and Sweden], to participate fully and on an equal footing in EU operations; (2) satisfactory arrangements for European NATO members who are not EU Member States [Turkey and Norway] to ensure their fullest possible involvement in EU-led operations, building on existing consultation arrangements within WEU; (3) arrangements to ensure that all participants in an EU-led operation will have equal rights in respect of the conduct of that operation, without prejudice to the principle of the EU's decision-making autonomy, notably the right of the Council to discuss and decide matters of principle and policy.' *Cologne European Council Declaration*, see CAB41, '5. Modalities of participation and cooperation.'

(3.2) The Helsinki Declaration and Beyond

Before the Helsinki European Council meeting two important incidents occurred. First, Javier Solana was appointed to the posts of EU High Representative for CFSP, Secretary-General of the Council and WEU in order to pave the way towards the implementation of decisions taken at Cologne regarding the WEU's 'friendly take-over' by the EU and to participate, at that time, in the upcoming Helsinki European Council Summit.[155] Second, in order to discuss the details and prepare a more attractive text for the Helsinki European Council's meeting, the Anglo-French Summit on European defence was held in London on November 25, 1999.[156] Most of the decisions taken in this summit were later inserted into the Helsinki European Council's (HEC) CEPSD Declaration and approved by the EU Member States. Hence, those Anglo-French Summit (AFS) articles, which were approved later on December 10-11, 1999, at the HEC Summit, will be given in the same reference together with the Helsinki European Council Summit articles.

During the period from the Anglo-French Summit held in London until the HEC Summit, the EU governments declared their expectations continuously. France aimed with the HEC to create the 'core of Euro-army'. French Defence Minister Alain Richard said, 'the emergence of a true European defence pillar will help make the alliance better able to adapt to the requirements of new missions – and make it stronger, because it is more balanced', whereas the UK rejected such an evolution.[157] German Defence Minister Rudolf Scharping said that, the crea-

---

[155] Duties of Javier Solana written into the Helsinki Declaration as follows: '(i) assist the Presidency in coordinating work in the Council to ensure coherence on the various aspects of the Union's external relations; (ii) contribute to preparing policy decisions and formulating options for the Council on foreign and security policy matters, so that it constantly focuses on the major political issues requiring an operational decision or political guidance; (iii) contribute to the implementation of foreign and security policy decisions in close coordination with the Commission, Member States and other authorities responsible for effective application on the ground. *Helsinki European Council Declaration*, (Helsinki: SN 300/99 EN, December 10-11, 1999), 'B. External Relations' <http://europa.eu.int/council/off/conclu/dec99/dec99_en.pdf> (Visited on: June 20, 1999).
[156] *Anglo-French Summit – Joint declaration by the British and French governments on European defence*, (London: November 25, 1999) <http://www.ambafrance.org.uk/cgi-bin/htsearch> (Visited on: June 20, 1999).
[157] Bering, H., 'The peskiest ally put an end to transatlantic squabbles', *Washington Times*, (November 24, 1999), p.A17.

tion of a European rapid reaction corps would strengthen the European contribution to NATO and added, 'in the transatlantic alliance, we don't have too much America, we have too little Europe.'[158] Tony Blair, four days before the HEC Summit, declared his intention by arguing, '[l]et me make one thing quite clear: This is not about creating a single European army under single command; it is not an attempt in any shape or form to supplant or compete with NATO.'[159] British Defence Secretary Geoff Hoon also said, 'I accept that different countries have different views, but what Britain will do is to negotiate effectively to ensure, first of all, that European nations can pull their weight within NATO military operations but at the same time preserve the essential link with NATO'.[160]

The Helsinki decision not only went beyond the previous CESDP statements, but also beyond the Europeans' previous transatlantic commitments. The HEC took a decisive step forward in the development of an autonomous capacity and the necessary means and mechanisms for taking decisions for launching and conducting EU-led military operations as a response to international crisis where NATO as a whole is not willing to engage. These developments are conditional on avoiding any unnecessary duplication and do not imply the creation of a European army (HEC-Art.27; AFS-Art.3). In addition to the Cologne Declaration guidelines, the HEC also agreed on the following principles:

- Cooperating voluntarily in EU-led operations for rapid deployment within 60 days (within this period also providing smaller rapid response elements available and deployable at very high readiness) and sustain for at least 1 year combat forces which are militarily self sufficient up to Corps level (50,000-60,000 men) with the necessary command, control and intelligence capabilities, logistics, combat support and other

---

[158] Whitney, C. R., 'Europe Offers Military', *New York Times*, (December 2, 1999).
[159] Dahlbung, J. –T., 'Plan for Europe Strike Force Worries US', *The Los Angeles Times*, (December 6, 1999).
[160] Whitney, C. R., 'Europeans Envisioning Strike Force Without US', *New York Times*, (November 26, 1999).

service support and appropriate naval and air combat elements capable of the full

range of Petersberg Tasks by 2003 (HEC-Art.28 (1) and EN22; AFS-Art.5 (a and b));

- Setting out new political and military bodies and structures to enable the Council to

  run EU-led military operations, ensuring the necessary political guidance and strategic

  direction for such operations and, to this end, a standing Political and Security

  Committee (PSC), Military Committee (MC), and Military Staff (MS) will be estab-

  lished within the Council, while respecting the single institutional framework (HEC-

  Art.28 (2) and EN24 (a, b and c); AFS-Art.7 (a)), (see Graph 2.2);[161]

- Developing modalities for full consultation, cooperation and transparency between the

  EU and NATO and taking into account the needs of all EU Member States (HEC-

  Art.28 (3); AFS-Art.7(c));

- Defining appropriate arrangements that would allow – while respecting the EU's

  decision-making autonomy – non-EU European NATO members and other interested

  States to contribute to the EU military crisis management tasks (HEC-Art.2(4); AFS-

  Art.7(b));

- Establishing a non-military crisis management mechanism for coordinating and mak-

  ing various civilian means and resources more effective complementary to military

  ones within the scope of the EU and Member States (HEC-Art.28 (5)).

---

[161] Duties of political and military bodies are written in the Helsinki Declaration as follows: (a) The PSC in Brussels will compose of national representatives at senior/ambassadorial level. The PSC will deal with all aspects of the CFSP, including the CESDP, in accordance with the provisions of the EU Treaty. In case of a military crisis management operation, the PSC will exercise under the authority of the Council and politically control the strategic direction of the operation. The PSC will also forward guidelines to the MC. (b) The MC will compose the Chiefs of Defence and military delegates. This MC will give military advice and make recommendations to the PSC, as well as provide military direction to the MS. (c) The MS, within the Council structure, provides military expertise and support to the CESDP, including the conduct of EU-led military crisis management operations. The MS will also perform early warning, situation assessment and strategic planning for Petersberg tasks including the identification of European national and multinational forces. *Helsinki European Council Declaration*, EN24.

Graph 2.2

EU Crisis Management Command Chain

European Council
↓
General Affairs Council
↓
COROPER
↓
——————————— PSC ———————————

Secretary-General/
High Representative
(Javier Solana)
↓
Policy Unit
↓
Situation Centre

EU Military Committee
|
↓
EU Military Staff

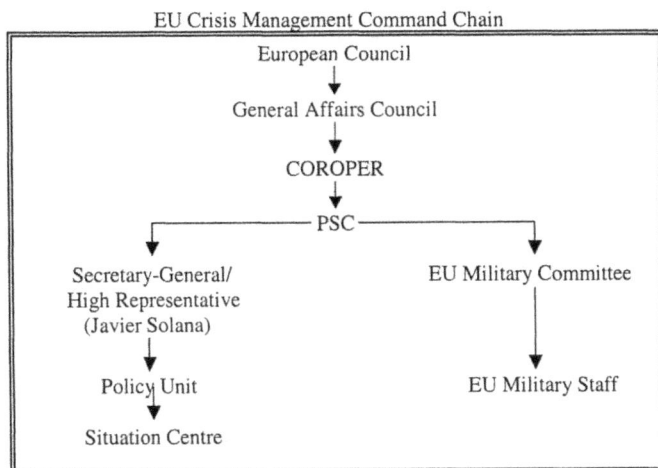

Chirac welcomed the Helsinki agreement on the CESDP for the reason that it also corresponded with the 'Action Plan' drawn up by France and Germany at Potsdam in December 1998. The 'Action Plan' indicates the steps the EU has to take for developing a rapid reaction force capability by using non-military instruments in the field of crisis management.[162] Thus, there is no doubt that creating an autonomous and combined European capacity for military action through the CESDP would substantially change the balance and dynamics of the transatlantic relations in favour of French aims. The St. Mâlo initiative and subsequent developments at Cologne and Helsinki gave more emphasis on 'autonomy' than the US Administration would have liked. However, promoters of the European rapid reaction force, France, Germany and the UK, have reassured the US through the Anglo-French Summit and Helsinki European Council Summit that NATO is the bedrock of their collective defence (AFS-Art.4;

---

[162] It is stated in the *Helsinki European Council Declaration*, EN27 – Action Plan, that the EU should have the ability to deploy at short notice and sustain for a defined period a set number of civilian police as a contribution to *civpol* (civilian police) missions and a combined search and rescue capability up to 200 people within 24 hours. Also see 'Helsinki European Council: Big Decisions Made – But Big Problems Still to Solve', *European Report*, (Brussels: December 15, 1999).

HEC-EN19). Dahlbung quoted one of the EU official, '[w]e know Americans – summing up what is widely perceived in Europe as a schizophrenic US reaction – they want the Europeans to do more in defence matters, but on the other hand, they are worried about something being done behind their back'.[163]

In theory, there are differences between the ESDI (which means something happening within NATO) and CESDP (which takes place autonomously and separable from the Alliance, something happening within the EU/CFSP).[164] However, the division of labour between the ESDI and CESDP is not as easy as it seems. Schmidt argued that according to the April 1999 Washington Summit, NATO's regional crisis management would take place only on a *case-by-case* basis.[165] On the other hand, the crisis management for the EU/WEU in Europe will be a *permanent* function. This means that in order to not duplicate the investments in structures, forces, efforts and assets of NATO, the CESDP is oriented towards the WEU's Petersberg missions with all the means and mechanisms in the EU/WEU. Rühl argued that the question of suitable division of labour between the EU/WEU and NATO still falls into the intermediate 'grey area' contingencies. He also stated that, until the ambiguity of 'interlocking' versus 'overlapping' between the EU/WEU and NATO is precisely addressed, what the 'strength-ened' CESDP can and will achieve by its own military means, with or without NATO assets, will stay before the Europeans as a potential challenge.[166]

---

[163] Dahlbung, J. –T., 'Plan for Europe Strike Force Worries US', *The Los Angeles Times*, (December 6, 1999); 'US Is the Enabler to Europe's Dependency', *The Los Angeles Times*, (December 20, 1999).

[164] Schmidt, P., 'The Contours of the ESDI and the Transatlantic Connection' in 'Franco-German Relations and European Integration: A Transatlantic Dialogue – Challenges for German and American Foreign Policy', *AICGS Conference Report*, (US: The Johns Hopkins University, December 16, 1999), p.29.

[165] Such a division of labour between the EU/WEU and NATO would relegate NATO to collective defence only, while leaving crisis management to the EU. However, this carries the risk of marginalisation of NATO and its non-EU members. Schmidt, P., 'ESDI: "Separable but not separate"?', *NATO Review*, (Vol.48, No.1, Spring/Summer 2000), pp.12-15.

[166] Rühl presented the Balkans as an example to the 'grey area'. Rühl, L., 'Conditions and options...', pp.12-13.

The first-ever WEU-NATO Joint Crisis Management Exercise CMX/CRISEX 2000 was held on February 17-23, 2000. The exercise became an important test of ESDI-related concepts and arrangements (such as the WEU-NATO consultation arrangements and framework documents), which were developed since NATO's 1996 Berlin decision, on the use of the CJTF for handling the WEU-led operations using NATO assets and capabilities. At the same time, the inclusion of the WEU into the EU, evaluated in the WEU Council of Ministers' Porto Declaration on May 15-16, 2000, as: '...for whatever use the EU may consider appropriate, of a package of WEU politico-military concepts. This package reflects part of the legacy of a decade of experience, which the WEU is able to transmit to the EU in the field of crisis management'.[167] Furthermore, the EOLO 2000 Exercise also successfully tested a Peace Support Operation under the control of a combined joint HQ by deploying significant air, sea and land forces (over 12,000 troops) from the four EUROFOR/EUROMARFOR countries, including Greece and Turkey for the naval part, aiming at improving operational readiness, interoperability of systems and procedures.

The Porto Declaration has also called for the improvement of measures adopted by the five Eurocorps members during the European Council Cologne meeting in order to carry out the so-called crisis management operations on behalf of the WEU. This can be read in the Porto Declaration as follows: 'to adapt the Eurocorps, and in particular its HQs, to the new strategic environment and to develop it into a European rapid reaction corps available for actions by the EU and NATO. Ministers welcomed the possibility offered to their European partners by the five Eurocorps nations to take part in Eurocorps activities and possible operations, and also to place liaison officers in the Eurocorps HQs at Strasbourg'.[168] According to the Anglo-French London Declaration, the UK – its traditional opposition to the Eurocorps in mind – agreed to the transformation of the Eurocorps into a rapid reaction corps, which will contrib-

---

[167] WEU Council of Ministers, *Porto Declaration*, (Porto: May 15-16, 2000), parag.5 and 12.
[168] *Ibid.*, parag.13.

ute to giving the EU a 'big stick' with which to undertake crisis management tasks, in par-

ticular by providing it with HQs. Astonishingly, the UK not only declared the availability of

its Permanent Joint HQs along with France's *Centre Opérationnel Interarmées* to command

EU-led operations, but also declared its willingness to provide British forces to the Eurocorps

HQ for specific operations (AFS-Art.5(c.i-iii)). It is written in *The Economist* that, '[t]he EU

corps, it seems, would have a less permanent structure than the mainly French and German

Eurocorps, which has hitherto been the main standard-bearer of European-only defence; but,

once assembled, the new EU force would presumably be much more mobile than the

Eurocorps, which would have to borrow transport aircraft from America (or rent them from

Ukraine), if it ever wanted to bring its unwieldy tanks to a war zone in a hurry. But this mo-

bility would come at a price: an expeditionary corps without any tanks would not be able to

fight much of a war'.[169] As a step forward towards a credible European defence mission, the

Eurocorps members asked the Supreme Allied Commander in Europe, General Wesley K.

Clark, to consider allowing the Eurocorps in Strasbourg to take command of peacekeeping

operations in Kosovo. The WEU Council of Ministers in Porto welcomed such a commitment

from this large multinational unit, as a nucleus for the KFOR (Kosovo Force) III HQs, and

Ministers further stated that, this commitment demonstrates that implementation of the deci-

sions taken by the EU at Cologne and Helsinki, with regard to the strengthening of European

defence capabilities, is contributing to the capability of the CESDP and the vitality of NATO.

As far as the WEU's 'collective defence' clause is concerned, although the Helsinki

Declaration rejected the incorporation of 'collective defence' through stating that the creation

of an autonomous capacity 'does not imply the creation of a European army' (HEC-Art.27),

discourses on 'friendly take-over' of the WEU functions into the EU is still keeping the door

open to the incorporation of the 'collective defence' clause into the EU. However, the pro-

---

[169] 'Europe: The EU Turns its Attention from Ploughshares to Swords', *The Economist*, (November 20, 1999), pp.51-52; Whitney, C. R., 'Europe to Form Its First Military Force', *New York Times*, (June 4, 1999), p.A6.

spective merger of the WEU and the EU left some potential problems unsolved amongst the EU, WEU, and NATO. Will the 'collective defence' clause in the WEU Treaty be eventually incorporated into the EU's *l'acquis communautaire*? What will happen to the WEU agencies and treaty legislation?

Following the Lisbon initiative (March 21, 2000) on 'European security and defence: the parliamentary dimension', the WEU Assembly President Klaus Bühler (German) – successor of Luis Maria de Puig (Spanish) – began to work on the transference of the WEU functions into the EU and to transform the WEU Assembly into a European Security and Defence Assembly (ESDA).[170] Bühler stressed the need for a wholly European parliamentary assembly that would not exclude any country in Europe. Therefore, he proposed the formula of '15+15' in order to consider the group of EU applicant countries with a view to an enlarged ESDA. In the WEU Assembly's plenary session on June 5-8, 2000, he also said that it would be a serious mistake to endorse the idea of leaving ESDA in the hands of the European Parliament and NATO's Parliamentary Assembly. He emphasised the fact that, 'the European Parliament cannot speak for the EU applicant countries or the non-EU European NATO member states which participate in the ESDA. And, the NATO Parliamentary Assembly is not an appropriate forum to scrutinise what is a specifically European security and defence policy'.[171] Bühler further added, the WEU's 'valuable legacy' would not be lost and that is why the Assembly urged the EU to give associate and associate partner countries at least the same participation rights that they already enjoy in the WEU. On the other side, de Puig was urgently called on the WEU Council to clarify what would happen to those WEU responsibilities, which would not be transferred into the EU, and their resultant consequences on the organisation once the ESDA was created. The WEU parliamentarians also urged the Council to ensure that the col-

---

[170] WEU Assembly, 'The Lisbon Initiative on "European security and defence: the parliamentary dimension"', *Press Release*, (Paris: April 7, 2000).

[171] WEU Assembly, 'WEU Assembly to agree on transformation into ESDA', *Press Release*, (Paris: Plenary Session June 5-8, 2000).

lective defence commitment provided in Article V of the modified Brussels Treaty should effectively be maintained.[172]

Javier Solana, speaking as the WEU Secretary-General, told the WEU Assembly that he
would strive for 'an open and honest dialogue' with the 15 EU countries on maintaining the
'parliamentary dimension' of European security and defence aspects after the WEU's responsibilities transferred into the EU. He stated that, 'I can assure this Assembly that I will continue to work for open and honest dialogue between the Council and Assembly over the
coming months as consideration is given to the future role of the Assembly and its relations
with the Council.' He further added:

> *'The WEU has indeed made a significant contribution over the past six months to*
> *European security and defence. As the Union comes closer to completing the work*
> *needed for it to fulfil its crisis management responsibilities, the WEU must start to*
> *plan its own structural configuration. It will gradually lose the function it has in*
> *relation to the Petersberg missions, and the goal will then be to provide the*
> *smoothest handover to the EU in the operational field'.* [173]

On the last day of the WEU Assembly's plenary session on June 7, 2000, the WEU Assembly
agreed to transform itself into the 'Assembly of WEU – the Interim European Security and
Defence Assembly' and created a steering committee to ease the way. According to the
Lisbon initiative of March 21, 2000, the new Assembly will be responsible for 'monitoring
the development of the CESDP in a wider European Security and Defence Framework'.[174] On

[172] *Ibid.*
[173] *Ibid.*
[174] Steering Committee of the ESDA comprises the WEU Assembly President, leaders of 28 national delegations
to the WEU, and the chairman of political groups. Representative of the European Parliament will be invited to
participate as an observer. Steering Committee will also draw up proposals on a draft charter for ESDA based on
the remit and legal foundation, size and composition, and the status of participating countries. These will include
EU member states, candidate states, and non-EU members of NATO. *Ibid.*

the next day, on 8 June, the report of the Assembly of WEU (the Interim European Security and Defence Assembly) on '[t]he persistent instability and insecurity in Kosovo a year after the end of Operation Allied Force' was urged European governments to support the EU Corps HQs role in commanding KFOR in the province.[175]

(4) Concluding Remarks

After the two crises in the Balkans, the French, German, and British leaders all saw how far Europe still has to go in order to be taken seriously as a military power. Neither in Bosnia nor in Kosovo, were European countries, whose total armed forces exceed the US armed forces in size, able to project military power convincingly enough to stop military crisis. In his speech at Strasbourg, Chirac said, '[t]he military manpower of the 15 is quantitatively superior to that of the US. But, the Europeans would today be unable to conduct combined operations, including fielding an army corps and backing it up with significant air strike and naval capacities. It is incredible, but that's the way it is!'[176] Although NATO's EU members showed their willingness to fight for human rights, but not yet to die for them, almost all analysts emphasise the serious shortcomings of the EU/WEU. These shortcomings are stated in the *European Report* as: collective capability (as regard to strategic information acquisition, planning and crisis assessment capacity), forces (forming operation HQs, inter-armed and deployable multinational forces), and operational and technical capabilities (deployability of forces, air and sea strategic mobility of forces, transport assets and capabilities (e.g. 'Eurolift force'), strate-

---

[175] WEU Assembly – The Interim European Security and Defence Assembly, 'WEU-ESDA urges Europe to step up policing in Kosovo', *Press Release*, (Paris: Plenary Session June 8, 2000).
[176] Speech by French President Jacques Chirac on 'A Responsible Europe in a Renewed Atlantic Alliance' before the Assembly of Atlantic Societies on October 19, 1999, in Strasbourg, France in *Internationale Politik*, (Vol.1, July 14, 2000) <http://www.dgap.org/english/tip/tip2/chirac191099.html> (Visited on: July 14, 2000).

gic and tactical communication information systems, electronic warfare (e.g. precision-guided munitions)), and civil-military cooperation.[177]

In addition to the above shortcomings, there are many WEU reports repeatedly emphasising the following EU/WEU difficulties: (a) the heterogeneous nature of the military assets do not provide a suitable level of interaction between multinational forces; (b) the national forces (the level of land, sea and air troops), which are coming under the WEU and made available for crisis management missions, are largely insufficient to cover the range of Petersberg operations. These operational shortcomings and difficulties will definitely limit the autonomous capabilities of the EU/WEU in any large-scale conflict. However, replicating the WEU-NATO military exercises, such as CMX/CRISEX 2000 or EOLO 2000, by borrowing the US/NATO assets and buying strategic military weapons according to experiences gained within these military exercises will help to overcome these shortcomings and difficulties. French Defence Minister, Alain Richard, drew attentions to another important point by saying that, 'I think it's not realistic for Europeans to say we are spending enough and that all we need to do is to create more synergy and achieve more efficient cooperation,' and another French defence official supported Richard by arguing, 'France will press its European partners to set spending targets for buying the new satellite-based navigation and guidance systems, fighter planes and transport aircraft that will be needed to make a European fighting force ready to be deployed within 60 days, the target set by the Helsinki plan.'[178] To this end, the British government spent $100 million to upgrade its seven Airborne Warning and Control System (AWACS) aircraft.[179]

---

[177] 'CFSP: Defence Policy Given Institutional Setting', *European Report*, (November 17, 1999); also see 'Who'll Carry Kosovo', *The Economist*, (May 1, 1999), pp.17-18.
[178] Whitney, C. R., 'Military Posture of Europe to Turn More Independent', *New York Times*, (December 13, 1999).
[179] Cullen, K., 'In European Force, US Fears a Loss of Power', *Boston Globe*, (December 12, 1999), p.A4.

Richard Eichenberg, who did research at Tufts University on public support of the single defence policy, argued that, it is still unclear whether the European public is willing to pay for a defence structure that would make Europeans less dependent on NATO. The public support for that is still low, but it has been growing in recent years.[180] Although French leaders are saying that NATO is an essential element of European 'collective defence', they are not missing any opportunities to say explicitly that the need for an autonomous European pillar in the security and defence sphere is necessary for a more dynamic and balanced alliance. British leaders are explicit about safeguarding NATO's integrity and keeping it as a bedrock to European security. However, the UK's support for the EU's CESDP is considered as indirect US approval of the CESDP and a direct input to help avoid negative effects in the transatlantic link. Germany is caught in the middle of French and British assertions. German leaders are arguing that the Europe of the future must be able to defend its interests and values effectively and it should be done through closer cooperation with the US/NATO, not unnecessary competition against it. Above all, the CESDP is based on intergovernmental clauses. Hence, there are no treaty-based binding agreements between the CESDP signatory states that would force them to transfer their national sovereignties into a supranational body. This is in the spirit of harmonising the defence spheres of the 15 EU states where their national prerogatives are kept intact.[181] The EU's CESDP will struggle for a time to develop its security and defence institutions under intergovernmental practice. Only the future will tell whether the European 'Pillar of Defence' will become a ratchet or not; perhaps, it will not become one until the creation of a European Political Union. Undeniably, Franco-German collaboration in the future will be even more strategic than before.

---

[180] *Ibid.*

[181] The intergovernmental character of the CESDP allows no role to the European Commission or the European Parliament. Any decision to deploy military forces to crisis spots would require in practice the consent of all 15-member states. Only then, a military action would be planned and carried out by bigger countries. In effect, this system will work like NATO's key organs. See Fitchett, J., 'EU Takes Steps to Create a Military Force, Without Treading on NATO', *International Herald Tribune*, (March 1, 2000).

The fact is that France has become a bit more Atlanticist, Germany has started to consider it-self a more 'normal' military power, and the UK has become more European. There is no doubt that they will act differently in the Europe of the future. Although the EU still needs US support in military operations, some concrete steps have also been taken to shape the future of the European 'Pillar of Defence'. In the end, the Franco-German couple's growing partner-ship and cooperation became a magnet for the Anglo-French initiative for an autonomous EU Corps. However, there is no doubt that Franco-German partnership and cooperation needs to grow more in order to draw the UK closer to the Franco-German's European 'Pillar of Defence' enthusiasm. In order to encapsulate Franco-German approaches to the European 'Pillar of Defence' and the dynamics behind European security and defence developments, the next chapter will analyse the Franco-German partnership from the perspective of past and possible future developments.

3 LINCHPIN TO THE EUROPEAN 'PILLAR OF DEFENCE': THE FRANCO-GERMAN SECURITY AND DEFENCE PARTNERSHIP

'When German soldiers of the Eurocorps drove down the Champs Elysées in armoured cars on July 14th last year, the average Frenchman liked what he saw. It is not clear that German soldiers marching down Whitehall would have the same effect in Britain'.

--Jean-Marie Guéhenno[1]

Introduction

The prevalent thinking in the EU is that words like 'linchpin', 'core', 'locomotive', 'motor', or 'engine' implies the Franco-German partnership. The proof of this is that when Paris and Bonn/Berlin are working together on a European integration policy it may (or may not) reach a feasible point in every single initiative they take on, but nothing will reach the point of feasibility if both parties refuse it. In order to understand this better and refute the ideas of those who have been pessimistic in the current and future value of the Franco-German partnership, its origin and development needs to be known. The Franco-German security and defence partnership lies at the centre of a fundamental as well as a broad political target: to move from *Erbfeindschaft* (hereditary enmity) into reconciliation[2] for the construction of social, cultural, economic, military and political ties at the bilateral and European level. The Franco-German security and defence partnership was born out of a historical necessity, so it did not develop

---

[1] Jean-Marie Guéhenno quoted in *The Economist*, (February 25, 1995), p.19.
[2] Reconciliation explained by Alice Ackerman as a peace-building strategy: A process by which countries can establish structures and procedures for establishing durable peace with their adversaries once they have entered a post-settlement or post-conflict phase. Ackerman, A., 'Reconciliation as a Peace-Building Process in Post War Europe', *Peace & Change*, (Vol. 19, No.3, July 1994), p.229.

spontaneously where one might sense there is simply a special relationship, but emerged gradually and painstakingly.

The Federal Republic of Germany's (FRG) post-World War II experience has been associated with the dangers of possessing excess military power, catastrophe, defeat, and dependence. Thus, the FRG's reconciliation with France has grown out from the need of rehabilitation, both politically and morally, providing room for political manoeuvring, rebuilding trust by anchoring the FRG firmly into the Western community with the aim of reflexive multilateralism, and constructing a European political community on the Franco-German pillar. On the other hand, France's post-World War II experience has been associated with the necessity of possessing strong military forces backed by *force de frappe* (nuclear force), victory, glory, and independence.[3] Therefore, reconciliation for France was to keep Bonn under control within the framework of European construction and, thus, enhancing French national security. Although France and Germany have different and divergent political motives, 'strategic cultures', security and defence status, it has been amazing how they sustained constant reconciliation for their common political commitment, which is European economic integration and cooperation on security and defence. To echo General de Gaulle's words: 'France and Germany, like two exhausted wrestlers, had no other choice than to lean against each other'.[4] Amaya Bloch-Lainé explains this amazing reconciliation as a 'permanent back and forward movement between the bilateral dynamics and the broader European picture', and in turn, this process is reflected in the following statement:

---

[3] Until the reunification of East and West Germany, Germany would mean the Federal Republic of Germany (FRG). After reunification, Germany will refer to reunified East and West Germany's continuation under the FRG. For more information about post-World War II experiences of Germany and France see Gordon, P. H., *France, Germany, and the Western Alliance*, (US: Westview Press, Inc., 1995), p.11; also see Philip Gordon, 'The Franco-German Security Partnership' in McCarthy, P. (ed.), *France-Germany 1983-1993. The Struggle to Cooperate*, (New York: Martin's Press, 1993), pp.139-160.
[4] De Gaulle quoted in Bujon de l'Estang, F., speech of French Ambassador to the US on 'The French-German Relations, Europe and the Transatlantic Partnership', Joint Conference with the French and German Ambassadors, (US: University of Berkeley, February 26, 1998, and University of Stanford, February 27, 1998). Available at: <http://www.info-france-usa.org/fsearch.htm> (Visited on: August 30, 2000).

'Indeed, failures to organise security and defence co-operation at the European

level have been most of the time followed by the strengthening of bilateral co-

operation. In turn, there are numerous examples of France and Germany having

tried to transpose their model of the bilateral co-operation on to the European

Communities and later the EU'.[5]

There is no doubt that the Franco-German partnership has always been extremely resilient, but what makes it so special? What are the basics of it? Both first post-World War II leaders in France, President Charles de Gaulle, and in Germany, Chancellor Konrad Adenauer, understood that destinies of the two countries are irrevocably linked to each other. The signature of the Franco-German initiative of the Rome Treaty in 1957, the talks between de Gaulle and Adenauer on military affairs in 1958 and the failure of the Fouchet Plan to create a European Political Union in 1962, formed the basis for institutionalising Franco-German reconciliation bilaterally through the *Elysée Treaty* on January 22, 1963. The obligation of consultation on foreign affairs 'prior to any decision, on all important questions of foreign policy, and in the first place on questions of common interest, with a view to arriving, insofar as possible, at a similar position', and the obligation of harmonising their security and defence policies 'with a view to arriving at mutual concepts' and 'doctrines' are significant convergences.[6] However, differences between France and Germany became totally blatant after the signature of the Treaty. France's insistence on an independent national defence policy, or at least the formation of West European defence independence through the Franco-German security and defence pillar separately from NATO and the US, was at odds with Germany's political and military reliance on the US and NATO's multinational defence structure. Furthermore, the

---

[5] Bloch-Lainé, A., 'Franco-German Co-operation in Foreign Affairs, Security and Defence – A Case Study' in Webber, D. (ed.), *The Franco-German Relationship in the EU*, (UK: Routledge, 1999), p.150.
[6] Apart from arranging regular meetings between foreign and defence ministers, the Elysée Treaty touched every human activity from the spectrum of political, economic, cultural to scientific events. See *Treaty Between the Republic of France and the Federal Republic of Germany on French-German Co-operation*, (Paris: January 22, 1963) <http://info-france-usa.org/news/statmnts/germany/fglink.htm> (Visited on: August 30, 2000).

---

attachment of a preamble to the Treaty in the *Bundestag* confirming the German reliance on the US and NATO, and, later on, the disagreement between Paris and Bonn on the creation of the Multilateral Force (MLF) project ruined the Franco-German security and defence partnership attempts. In addition, the deterioration of the French-US/NATO relationship upon NATO's basic structure ended up with France quitting the integrated military structure of NATO in 1966 (see Chapter 5). De Gaulle had later considered the Elysée Treaty's *raison d'être* destroyed and the Franco-German security and defence partnership moribund.

It was not until the leadership of Valéry Giscard d'Estaing (from the centre-right party – *Union pour la Democratie Française* (UDF)) in France and Helmut Schmidt (from the *Sozialdemokratische Partei Deutschland* (SPD)) in Germany that the Franco-German security and defence partnership found a new impetus. They came to power in the mid-1970s and stayed in office until the early 1980s. Giscard and Schmidt were like-minded strong supporters of the Franco-German partnership in almost every policy area. Both had less faith in US President Jimmy Carter's policies and both struggled for *détente* between East and West. Kocs even argued that, 'Schmidt had sought to use the Franco-German partnership as a basis for greater European self-assertion vis-à-vis the US'.[7] The Franco-German relationship had developed so well that Giscard thought about extending French nuclear deterrence, which is the eternal symbol of the French national sovereignty, to Germany. Their most successful bilateral cooperation had been in the economic and financial area (European Monetary System). Nevertheless, the periodic attempts to form a Franco-German security and defence partnership in the Giscard-Schmidt period had been realised after Giscard was defeated in French elections a year later. François Mitterand (*Partie Socialiste* (PS)) replaced Giscard in 1981 and agreed in February 1982 to pursue deeper consultations on security and defence with Germany. Likewise, Schmidt's agreement on conditions for a Franco-German security and

---
[7] Kocs, Stephen A., *Autonomy or Power – The Franco-German Relationship and Europe's Strategic Choices, 1955-1995*, (US: Praeger Publishers, 1995), p.188.

defence protocol was signed after he lost German elections against Helmut Kohl (*Christlich Demokratische Union* (CDU)) in 1982. In October 1982, Kohl and Mitterrand put the 'Franco-German Commission for Security and Defence' into force. The decision was given to deepen co-ordination in foreign and security spheres through regular meetings between French and German foreign and defence ministers. This was the reinforcement of co-operative linkages, which were already mandated in 1963.

It was generally accepted that socialist Mitterand and conservative Kohl initiated far stronger and convergent co-operative ties than previous leaders. Philip H. Gordon illustrates three sets of factors why Franco-German co-operation after 1982 was more imperative than after 1962. First, the Soviet threat was pervasive and the US permanent existence in Europe was vague. The second factor was attributed to internal political developments in Germany. The SPD was following a pacifist and anti-nuclear policy in Germany at that time. Therefore, they were against the US intermediate nuclear forces (INF) deployment in Germany, which was calculated to counter the growing Soviet conventional force in Europe. On the other hand, the CDU was putting emphasis on Western defence co-operation through European (principally around the Franco-German core) and Atlantic Alliances so on the INF deployment. French leaders were terrified with the thought of the SPD leading Germany into the neutralists' flank that would have then left France on the 'front line' in the East-West tension. Mitterand's willingness to call for the German acceptance of the INF deployment on German land, forced Mitterand to support the CDU side in the German electoral campaign. During the commemoration of the Elysée Treaty's twentieth anniversary, Mitterand gave his famous speech in the *Bundestag* on January 20, 1983, and expressed the necessity of the INF deployment on the German soil. Steven P. Kramer argued that, after the victory of the CDU, CDU/*Christlich Soziale Union* (CSU)-*Freie Demokratische Partei* (FDP) coalition, the SPD and PS became *frères énemis* (brother enemies) to each other, but the PS's co-operation with the Kohl government had became very good indeed.[8] Third, after the bad economic experience of 1981,

France decided to stay in strong economic partnership with Germany and, in turn, France be-

came closer to Germany through a strong Franco-German security partnership.[9] The Franco-

German relationship was characterised during this period by complementary factors: The

overwhelming economic strength of Germany counterbalanced by France's international role

through the permanent UN Security Council membership and military strength, namely by

possessing nuclear power.

However, the picture drawn above should not hide the realities. Kocs argued convincingly

that, 'the impetus for co-operation came from the desire by one side to limit the real or poten-

tial damage to its security caused by the policies of the other'.[10] In fact, Mitterand – one of the

followers of Gaullist foreign policy – was a staunch supporter of France's foreign policy in-

dependence and had shown no serious willingness to sacrifice French sovereignty for multi-

national formations; considered *force de frappe* as sanctuary only for France and refrained

from extending the French nuclear protective umbrella over German soil; felt uncomfortable

due to the German officials' continued dedication to the East-West *détente* and *Ostpolitik*;

and, although he was at ease with NATO in comparison to former French leaders, his aim was

the creation of an autonomous European 'Pillar of Defence' separable from NATO. On the

other hand, Kohl had shown strong willingness to sacrifice German sovereignty and military

capability in various multinational formations in order to keep Germany embedded in multi-

lateral forms; was interested in gaining influence over the French *force de frappe* in order to

ensure the French strategic commitment to deterrence against the Warsaw Pact; occupied

more with the *Ostpolitik*, East Germany, and the US than with France; kept Germany's strong

ties to NATO and tried to pull France into a closer strategic alignment with NATO; and,

---

[8] Kramer, Steven P., 'France and the New Germany', *AICGS German Issues 11*, (US: The Johns Hopkins University, 1993), p.14.
[9] Philip Gordon, 'The Franco-German Security Partnership' in McCarthy, P. (ed.), pp.146-147.
[10] Kocs, Stephen A., *Autonomy or Power*, p.255.

showed no serious desire to use the Franco-German defence co-operation as a springboard for a *fully* autonomous European 'Pillar of Defence' separately from NATO.

Indeed, the Franco-German security and defence interaction was cemented into the dynamics of East-West affairs. Although Kohl's government had demonstrated its immediate loyalty to the US government during Reagan's Presidency and pushed its relations with Paris into a secondary position, developments between the two superpowers culminated in a strategic *rapprochement* between Germany and France. This, subsequently, proved once again the resilience of the Franco-German partnership. The Reykjavik Summit between the US President Reagan and USSR President Gorbachev in October 1986 deeply undermined the Europeans confidence to the US. Reagan accepted the bargaining away of all ballistic missiles and demonstrated his willingness to further bargain away the intermediate range nuclear forces treaty (INF) without seriously consulting its European partners in 1987. France and in particular, Germany was seriously concerned about the US budget deficits and inevitable cutbacks and under-funding of the US strategic commitments abroad; degradation of the US-initiated Strategic Defence Identity (SDI) that could undermine the basis of their own nuclear deterrence force; and, the US 'decoupling'. Mitterand was dismayed that *force de frappe* might have also been drawn in an arms control agreements and the US decoupling in the absence of an autonomous European defence system might have forced Germany to guarantee its own security, most probably, through leaning towards neutralism. On the other hand, in Germany, Kohl was disappointed by Reagan's action in the same way as Schmidt had criticised Carter. Both Mitterand and Kohl observed that the US met its own needs, but ignored sensitive West German needs. Therefore, they agreed that reliance on NATO should be counterbalanced by a strong Franco-German partnership. Germans began seriously considering the Franco-German security and defence partnership as a step towards an autonomous European military role and a possible long-term alternative to NATO (see Chapter 4). In Kocs' pungent words:

'The traditional West German view, which had regarded Franco-German defence ties as useful only insofar as they could pull the French back into NATO's orbit, began giving way to a new premise that intra-European defence relationships were valuable in themselves given American unreliability'.[11]

The bilateral Franco-German relationship reached an unmatchable level of intensity in a much broader area of security co-operation than ever before and the full implementation of the Elysée Treaty was realised. In February 1986, Mitterand and Kohl declared the beginning of a broad and intense co-operation on the use of a French conventional force – the 47,000-strong *Force d'Action Rapide* (FAR) – against a possible Soviet conventional force invasion of the German territory, a telephone crisis 'hotline' between Paris and Bonn was established and, for the first time, Mitterand made a commitment to Kohl that France would consult with Germany before using the French nuclear weapons on German territory. Moreover, with the signature of the Franco-German Defence and Security Council protocol to the Elysée Treaty on January 22, 1988, the intense co-operation between France and Germany was reinforced. In addition to the overseeing function of this Council upon the Franco-German Commission for Security and Defence, it also created a framework for the Franco-German Finance and Economic Council.

One of the primary aspirations of French and German leaders' was to reduce the effort of any US diplomatic ploy upon their national policies. This has been the main motivation of French European policies and was the reason for both Giscard and Schmidt's hard-working on the harmonisation of French and German foreign policies, the reason for Kohl's turning to the robust Franco-German security and defence partnership, and was even the main reason for the UK's (though the most reliable and loyal partner of the US in Europe) embracing the French

---

[11] *Ibid*, pp.201-202.

and German European 'Pillar of Defence' ambition during the Anglo-French St. Mâlo Declaration on December 3-4, 1998, as a result of its dissatisfaction with the US policies in Kosovo. As a matter of fact, France, Germany, and ultimately the UK, recognised that if the Europeans want to act as they wish, they must have a European defence identity in addition to their economic might.

This brief historical overview of the relationship between France and Germany at the bilateral and European level not only epitomizes the resilience of their partnership, but also verifies the central role they have played in the systematic definition and institutionalisation of the European security and defence policy and bolsters the idea of true progress in the European 'Pillar of Defence'. Against this background, this chapter will focus on the resilience (divergences and convergences) and on the possible future evolution of the Franco-German security and defence relationship in the period 1989-2000.

The first section of this chapter will examine the period 1989-1995. Although the Franco-German partnership became a tradition in the Cold War era, the first five post-Cold War years seriously tested the Franco-German resilient relationship. After the sudden disappearance of the common threat (i.e. Soviet Union), those who prophesied a divergence in the Franco-German partnership had been disillusioned. However, the Franco-German partnership had to pass through a period of scepticism and irritation during Mitterand and Kohl presidencies. This section will analyse power balancing efforts between France and Germany from the end of 1989 until the end of 1991 and the evolution of the Franco-German Eurocorps from early 1992 until the end of Mitterand's presidency in May 1995.

The second section will focus on the dynamic factors of the period 1995-1998. This period is marked by the election of Jacques Chirac (leader of the French Right – Gaullist –

Rassemblement pour la République (RPR)) as the new President of France in May 1995 and the defeat of Kohl in the German elections on October 27, 1998. Chirac's coming to power initiated a tougher period to the Franco-German relationship. Chirac, in the beginning, gave the impression that he would deviate neither from the autonomous French national defence policy nor from the Gaullist tradition. Moreover, French military reforms and the abolition of the conscript army prior to consulting with German officials soured the Franco-German partnership. However, the French rapprochement with the US/NATO and the Franco-German nuclear force discussions brought a new dimension to the partnership. These issues will be analysed in this section under the title of *'Half-Baked' Franco-German Security and Defence Balance.*

The last section will analyse recent developments, and future strategic choices from the perspective of the necessary endurance of the Franco-German tandem. The election of Gerhard Schröder (SPD) as a new Chancellor of Germany on October 27, 1998, developments regarding giving the EU an autonomous defence capability, and the German Foreign Minister Joschka Fischer's (The Greens) 'federal' Europe discourse have activated the Franco-German 'motor' once again. Some flesh and muscles are yet missing on the Franco-German bones, but it will be foolish to wedge on the old rhetoric and say that the Franco-German tandem is collapsing. The main theme of this section will be to prove the permanent need for the Franco-German partnership by considering another major player beside them: the UK. The triangular interaction between France-Germany-UK seems determinant, but French and German officials still have to work together more carefully for the true European 'Pillar of Defence'.

(1) Finding the Franco-German Balance Back in the Post-Cold War Era, 1989-1995

(1.1) Initial Strategic Hurdles and Re-adaptations in the Post-Cold War Franco-German Relationship

By the end of the 1980s, the Franco-German partnership was indeed at its zenith. However, the reunification of Germany had shifted the heretofore graciously accepted myth of the Franco-German centre of gravity: the analogy of political, diplomatic, military and nuclear French 'rider' of the economic and financial German 'horse' lost its value (sometimes this analogy was presented as 'bomb' versus 'D-Mark') and, therefore, altered the leading French role in the Franco-German partnership. Michael Baun observed this alteration as a 'shift from a security order, dominated by military power and concerns, to one based on economics favoured the German civilian power over the French nuclear state'.[12] The realist thinking asserts that, 'in neither phase of Europe's integration can economic considerations alone explain elite motivations', so the desire for security and relative power vis-à-vis one another, as it was in the late 1940s and early 1950s, has been a significant factor for *re-adapting* the Western European states policies' to each other in the first half of the 1990s.[13] On the contrary, according to idealist thinking, for a variety of deep-rooted reasons (common institutions, practices, policies, personal commitments, and inevitability of interdependence), *re-adaptation* has been realised through the 'marriage of interests between the two countries' – the turbulence once again led the two countries to realise once and for all that neither Bonn nor Paris had any credible political alternative but to deepen their partnership.[14]

---

[12] Baun, M. J., 'The Maastricht Treaty as High Politics: Germany, France, and European Integration', *Political Science Quarterly*, (Vol.110, No.4, Winter 1995/1996), p.611.
[13] Art, R. J., 'Why Western Europe needs the US and NATO?', *Political Science Quarterly*, (Vol.111, No.1, Spring1996), p.1.
[14] Yves Boyer 'France and Germany' in Heurlin, B. (ed.), *Germany in Europe in the Nineties*, (UK: Macmillan Press Ltd., 1996), p.242.

The initial shock waves emanating from the German unification was met by fear, confusion, and by extreme 'concerns' in France. The anxieties of the French government like those for the devaluation of Franco-German security and defence partnership, vanishing of the *raison d'être* of the French commitment to the forward defence and nuclear deterrence, the German policy of *détente* with Moscow on the one side and the possible neutralisation or 'renationalisation' of the German security and defence policy in the future on the extreme side, culminated in serious fluctuations in the Mitterand-Kohl relationship. Furthermore, Kohl's announcement of the Ten-Point Plan on German unity – without consulting his French counterpart – on November 28, 1989, and the agreement of a ceiling on the future size of the *Bundeswehr* (370,000-man) and the German membership in NATO – agreed directly between Kohl and Soviet President Mikhail Gorbachev – in July 1990, aggravated a series of policy responses from the French side at that time. Mitterand's attempt to prevent or at least to delay the reunification process came during his Kiev and East Berlin visits in December 1989 and his agitation was later demonstrated by his rebuffing Kohl's invitation to the official opening of the *Brandenburger Tor*. Both these visits were signs of upset against Kohl's '*Alleingang*'.

Kohl also achieved a bilateral solution together with Gorbachev about a united Germany's remaining as a NATO member in July 1990 and emphasized repeatedly that neutrality or departure from NATO was not a price he would have paid for the reunification. Former German Foreign Minister Hans-Dietrich Genscher declared to his EC partners that 'if they were worried about growing German power, their best strategy was not to isolate Germany into some *Sonderweg* [an autonomous foreign policy] that the Germans did not want anyway, but rather to tie up Germany in a deepened, thickened and more federalised European Community, which the Germans would happily accept because it had been their proposal all long'.[15] French and German policymakers' resentment of each other was finally hatched during the

---

[15] Tiersky, R., 'France in the New Europe', *Foreign Affairs*, (Vol.71, No.2, Spring 1992), p.132.

Franco-German Summit in Munich in September 1990, and in Gordon's words, '[it was] one of the least amicable ever'.[16] The French agitation and upset was met by German delegations' bitterness to the French attempts at hindering the reunification process. Gordon perceptively quoted Mitterand's speech in the aftermath of the Franco-German Summit as, 'there will be no lack of conflicts, rivalries and misunderstandings... Indeed, I don't know why I speak in the future tense'.[17]

As it became increasingly apparent that reunification was inevitable, Paris moved quickly to tie Bonn firmly into Europe through the process of economic, political, and security integration and into NATO through making German reunification conditional to Germany's full membership and commitment to the North Atlantic Treaty principles. France declared at that time that it would only recognise the German reunification under the following four conditions: (1) a united Germany would be in both the EC and NATO; (2) it would permanently renounce nuclear, chemical and biological weapons; (3) it would make clear its permanent acceptance of existing frontiers, including the Polish-German Oder-Neisse border; (4) free elections would be held in East and West Germany.[18] Kohl's immediate response to these conditions was positive and declared the German reunification and the unification of Europe as two sides of the same coin.[19] However, France, which had an interest in deepening the EC, but not for enlargement, was concerned that Germany was still paying more attention to the *Ostpolitik* than to the Franco-German relationship in the post-Cold War era.

Genscher aptly extracted Germany's new *Ostpolitik* from the following reasons: The challenges from East to West Europe in the post-Cold War era are more diverse than the previous

---

[16] Philip Gordon, 'The Franco-German Security Partnership' in McCarthy, P. (ed.), p.151.
[17] *Ibid.*
[18] Yost, D., 'France in the New Europe', *Foreign Affairs*, (Vol.69, No.5, Winter 1990/1991), p.113.
[19] Schmidt, P., 'The Special Franco-German Security Relationship in the 1990s', *Challiot Paper 8*, (Paris: Institute for Security Studies, WEU, June 1993), p.11.

direct Soviet threat. It is true that Germany is freed from its military 'front line' status by the withdrawal of Soviet troops from East Germany in 1994, but it is still at the 'front line' which is threatened by a new security environment – 'soft' military issues based on economic, political and social instabilities in Central, Eastern, and South-Eastern Europe.[20] Genscher grasped this 'new line of thinking', in other words the *new security concept*, from the point of view of 'shaping' (*Gestaltung*) and indicated a wide range of parallel solutions to the old dilemma of Cold War *détente* from crisis management to complex interdependence (*Verflechtung*).[21] In addition to old French fears (for example, the German-Russian entente or possible German neutralisation), a wide range of new security threats, such as the emergence of a 'security vacuum' (militarily uncontrolled weak and potentially unstable zone) between France and Russia, is another major reason why French politicians were concerned about the direction of German foreign policy. Although the question of guaranteeing stable political, social and economic development in Central and Eastern Europe is a higher political priority for Germany than a threat emanating from North Africa, a whole new array of security threats are challenging Germany and France collectively. Therefore, there is a basic assumption that the perpetuation of the Franco-German security and defence partnership remained in the deepest interest of whole Europe. Yves Boyer commented on such an assumption that 'there is obviously the feeling on both sides of the Rhine that European stability can no longer be guaranteed if basic agreement is not maintained between France and Germany. Without such agreement, Western Europe may return to a balance-of-power game ... [this] in the longer run, is synonymous with collective suicide'.[22]

As a result of the Germans' desire to calm French fears, Germany was pulled towards France. This German policy refuted the ideas of those who believed that reunification had destroyed

---

[20] For detailed information on the *new security concept* and 'soft' military issues see Chapter 1 sections *(1.1.1) Post-Cold War Security Threats: Europe's Periphery,* and *(2.1) Understanding The New Security Concept.*
[21] Gutjahr, L., *German Foreign and Defence Policy after Unification,* (UK: St. Martin's Press Inc., 1994), p.82.
[22] Yves Boyer, 'France and Germany' in Heurlin, B. (ed.), p.249.

the pre-existing balance of power and undermined the very foundation of the Franco-German relationship. Kohl was well aware that Germany's new national economic, political, and military posture in the EC had to be legitimised by France. While the Franco-German security and defence partnership was finding a new balance within the EC, the first serious external impact on the European security and defence discussions came with the Gulf crisis (Iraq's invasion of Kuwait in August 2, 1990). At that time, security and defence discussions were neither settled between France and Germany nor within the EC framework. Therefore, it was not a surprise to conclude later that the Franco-German partnership played no significant role in the Gulf crisis. Schmidt pointed out that Franco-German security talks about the Gulf crisis 'frequently appeared less as dialogues than 'collective monologues'.'[23] While France, which assumes a 'global role' and occupies a permanent seat in the UN Security Council, realised from experiences that its power projection capabilities were inadequate, Germany realised from experiences that the dominating political perception of the *Grundgesetz* (German Basic Law) was excluding Germany from taking on the leading military role in international relations, even after it gained full sovereignty by the ratification of the Two-Plus-Four Treaty on September 12, 1990. Germany also understood well that potential security threats to Europe are emanating not only in the Central and Eastern European periphery, but could also emanate from further afield. After all, France and Germany experienced how distant they really were with regard to being strong security and defence partners to each other and, therefore, they decided during the Maastricht Treaty preparations that a common European security and defence policy must be built.

As a result of the eventual Franco-German trade-off on monetary and political union within the EC in December 1990, the Franco-German 'motor' started functioning once again. France was strongly committed to the monetary union, but accepted to bargain its foreign and de-

---

[23] Schmidt, P., 'The Special Franco-German Security Relationship in the 1990s', p.15.

fence affairs – albeit reluctantly – with the sole aim of tying Germany more tightly into a comprehensive European integration process. Robert Art observed that, in monetary affairs, 'France had favoured integration because it was dealing from a position of weakness. More integration in monetary affairs, the French believed, would strengthen France's hand on the German mark. [In foreign and defence affairs], however, France had been dealing from a position of strength. More integration in foreign and defence matters could well strengthen the German hand on France's much valued autonomy in foreign and defence affairs. Integration would thus likely have different results for France, depending upon whether it was relatively weak or strong in a give realm.'[24] On the other hand, Germany was profoundly committed to both monetary and foreign and defence policies, but also understood that strong French backing is required in order to realise European Political Union. In fact, the Franco-German proposals on foreign and security matters during the Maastricht Treaty discussions described a process by which Europe would develop a robust security policy that would ultimately lead to a common defence. Moreover, the Kohl-Mitterand statement of October 14, 1991, enhanced the position of the WEU as a platform for a European security system, tied to but autonomous from NATO, for an eventual replacement of NATO. In all these cases, the Franco-German accord was the bedrock of the entire negotiation process; in its absence, the failure was inevitable.

The disintegration of Yugoslavia in 1991 was the second serious external impact on the Franco-German security and defence discussions, which were going on within the EU's CFSP framework. As in the Gulf crisis, the Franco-German partnership was far from taking a joint action in the Yugoslav crisis. The two Franco-German military proposals, the first issued in September 1991 and the second in April 1992, were even contradicted by their own national foreign policies and finally found to be unfeasible. The Germans' historical pro-Croatian and

---

[24] Art, R. J., 'Why Western Europe needs the US and NATO?', p.20; Patrick McCarthy, 'France Looks at Germany, or How to Become German (and European) while Remaining French' in McCarthy, P. (ed.), pp.57-63.

pro-Slovenian policy contradicted with the French historical pro-Serbian policy and anti-German responses. The situation was even later aggravated by the Germans' early recognition of Croatia and Slovenia. The legal constraints on the German use of military force in NATO 'out-of-area' operations were another obstacle to the joint Franco-German military action where its deployment was envisaged by a Franco-German military proposal within the framework of a WEU-led peacekeeping force. The failure of deploying an intervention force under the auspices of the WEU led France to play its prominent national role in the UN Security Council and led it to intensify the search for a way to boost the European military component. On the other hand, Germany began demonstrating greater willingness for taking more international security responsibility in the military aspects of peacekeeping, embargo and humanitarian interventions.[25] In the end, instead of a Franco-German peacekeeping force, the Anglo-French ground troops were deployed in Bosnia. As in the Gulf crisis, the Yugoslav crisis proved that the absence of a Franco-German military force structure and the lack of harmony in security and defence areas not only humiliated the EU/WEU, but also once again required the US and UK's interventions in managing the trouble spots.

There is no doubt that the Gulf and Yugoslav wars urged the Franco-German couple, and to a certain extent the other EC members, to improve their defence capabilities through the CFSP, the WEU, and the operational creation of the future nucleus of the EU force in October 1991 – the Franco-German army corps (Eurocorps).

---

[25] For more information on French and German roles in the Yugoslav crisis see Gordon, P. H., *France, Germany, and the Western Alliance*, pp.53-81. Current international security and defence responsibilities and recent developments in Germany and France are analysed in Chapter 4 for Germany and Chapter 5 for France.

(1.2) Nucleus of the EU Force: The Conventional Franco-German Eurocorps

(1.2.1) A Historical Path to the Eurocorps: Tentative Franco-German Joint Military Exercises

Since the early 1980s, the Franco-German security and defence partnership has grown closer.

France wanted military *rapprochement* with Germany in order to integrate it in a fairly tight

Western politico-military framework and Germany wanted to gain the French confidence and

legitimisation for German European politico-economic policies. Meanwhile, developments in

the military area, based on joint Franco-German studies, were an important practical break-

through. After they revitalised the military clauses of the Elysée Treaty in 1982, they per-

formed a small bilateral joint military exercise (3,100 German and 1,500 French troops)

called *The Alliance* in June 1985.[26] Given France's continued absence from the integrated

NATO command, joint military exercises were a significant instrument for the employment of

French armed forces in an allied defence of Germany. However, the first major bilateral mili-

tary exercise, named the *Fränkischer Schild* (Franconian Shield), took place in September

1986 near Würzburg, Germany. Although this was a bilateral military exercise, some 50,000

German, French, and even a US contingent were involved in manoeuvres in southern

Germany outside the NATO framework. Kocs notified that 3,500 French troops, which took

part in this military exercise, represented the largest French military participation in such ex-

ercises in German territory since the French departure from the integrated NATO command in

1966.[27]

A year later, in September 1987, the second major military exercise – even larger and more

significant than before – *Kecker Spatz/Moineau Hardi* (Bold Sparrow) took place beyond the

normal geographical zone of the French forces in Bavaria and Baden-Württemberg. This was

[26] Philip Gordon, 'The Franco-German Security Partnership' in McCarthy, P. (ed.), p.164.
[27] Kocs, Stephen A., *Autonomy or Power*, p.199.

the first in which the units of FAR crossed the Rhine and came under the command of a German corps. In this exercise, some 20,000 French (nearly half of the FAR's total strength) and 50,000 German troops (troops that were not assigned to NATO) became an important symbol of the Franco-German security and defence partnership. This exercise was not only the true measure of French willingness to contribute to a forward defence in Central Europe, but also demonstrated the French decisiveness in keeping its troops outside the NATO command. However, the French rejection of including the nuclear force in this exercise disappointed the Germans, who were trying to gain the nuclear guarantee of French *force de frappe* over German soil throughout the Cold War era. Moreover, France's insistence to keep NATO forces outside this bilateral exercise, which resulted in the French rejection of NATO's SACEUR invitation, frustrated the German desire of transforming the solidarity that occurred between France and Germany into a comparable solidarity between France and its other NATO allies.

In comparison to the second military exercise, the third military exercise *Champagne 89* (5,000 German and 25,000 French troops) became less significant in terms of its size, but illustrated a historic significance. As a result of the Franco-German bilateral agreement, the *Bundeswehr* for the first time came under the command of French army corps in an exercise performed on the World War I battlefield of Marne, France, in September 1989. Almost a year after this military exercise, the Franco-German Brigade (4,200-men) was created in October 1990.

Chancellor Kohl construed in the end of 1986 that allocation of a sufficient amount of money for US forces in Europe would be unlikely in the aftermath of the US-Russia Reykjavik Summit. Therefore, he dedicated his efforts to the creation of a European conventional force. The idea of a joint brigade first proposed by Kohl in 1987 and later accepted by Mitterand with the aim of checking what many in France were scared was Germany's drift into neutral-ism.[28] While Kohl considered the joint brigade as a 'nucleus' of the 'European army',[29] Mitterand considered it as a 'laboratory' or 'educational brigade' to test joint training, exer-cises, and future tactical and operational principles instead of considering it as the 'embryo' of a mixed, or even European, army.[30] Former Defence Minister of France André Giraud pointed out that the Franco-German Brigade must stay outside the integrated NATO com-mand structure, but should be covered by France's independent nuclear umbrella. He said, 'the question now is how to use the unit, because we can not envisage putting French soldiers in a position where they would not be covered by France's nuclear umbrella'.[31] Giraud was implying that the French and German troops would be under French nuclear protection, which was a long desired German foreign and defence policy. Initially, French officials wanted to keep the troops outside NATO, whereas Germans wanted the opposite, but they later agreed to use the Brigade within the Alliance framework as well.

(1.2.2) The Eurocorps Initiative

Prior to the Maastricht agreement, Mitterand and Kohl announced another Franco-German joint initiative in October 1991. The Brigade would be replaced by a corps-size unit (nucleus of a European army) – composed of French and German forces and kept open to other WEU members – in order to give the WEU an operational capability. Boyer argued at that time that, 'the Eurocorps gives WEU real operational capabilities, based on impressive capacities. It possesses, for example, more heavy tanks than the whole British army'.[32] Robert Art pru-dently quoted the following paragraph, which was from a text provided by the US Department of State on October 18, 1991:

---

[28] Wetterqvist, F., *French Security and Defence Policy – Current Developments and Future Prospects*, (Diane Publishing Company, 1993), p.67.
[29] Schmidt, P., 'The Special Franco-German Security Relationship in the 1990s', p.27.
[30] Wetterqvist, F., *French Security and Defence Policy...* p.67.
[31] André Giraud quoted in Wetterqvist, F., *French Security and Defence Policy*, p.68.
[32] Yves Boyer 'France and Germany' in Heurlin, B. (ed.), p.244.

'*The German-French military co-operation will be strengthened beyond the*

currently existing brigade. These enhanced German-French units could therefore

become the core of a European Corps, in which the armed forces of other WEU

member states could be absorbed. This new structure could in turn become the

model for closer military co-operation between all WEU member states'. [33]

With the Mitterand-Kohl announcement on May 22, 1992, in La Rochelle, France, the

Eurocorps initiative was made official in order to reinforce the April 1991 Kohl-Mitterand

call for the creation of a common European Defence Identity (EDI) and to make the idea of a

European 'Pillar of Defence' – comparable to the 'North American Pillar' of NATO – more

credible.[34] They restated that the WEU would become a true platform for the Common Euro-

pean Security and Defence Policy. The announcement of the Eurocorps initiative seemed to

be motivated not only by US President George Bush's approval of the further withdrawal of

US troops from Europe in 1991, but also by the creation of an autonomous European military

capacity, long desired by French policymakers, and drawing out of this a serious discussion

about European Political Union, as well as fulfilling the German desire to prevent the com-

plete departure of French troops from the German territory.[35] Eurocorps was given

responsibility for three major missions: (a) action within the joint defence framework of allies

in accordance with the Article 5/V of NATO/WEU Treaties; (b) action aimed at preserving

peace (peacekeeping and peacemaking either in or outside of Europe, possibly – but not

necessarily – under UN command); (c) action aimed at providing humanitarian assistance.[36]

---

[33] This paragraph quoted from the footnote 52 in Art, R. J., 'Why Western Europe needs the US and NATO?'
[34] Communiqué, *La Rochelle*, Franco-German Council, (France: May 22, 1992).
[35] Kocs argued that the Eurocorps arrangement exhibited an interesting resemblance to the Franco-German troop stationing agreement of 1966. In both cases, France announced its intention of withdrawing its troops from German territory, but Germany responded by proposing a new arrangement that would – even if they were for symbolic reasons – keep French troops in Germany. Kocs, Stephen A., *Autonomy or Power*, p.222.
[36] Clarke, J. G., 'The Eurocorps: A Fresh Start in Europe', *Foreign Policy Briefing No.21*, (US: CATO Institute, December 28, 1992), pp.2-3.

While the Eurocorps was later regarded by French policymakers as the kernel of a European army outside American influence, for German policymakers, it was an insurance of both the EDI and NATO, as well as planned to bring French armed forces closer into NATO. A British official from the Foreign Office unveiled the French and German officials' contradictory position with regard to the EDI and NATO as follows:

> *The Germans told us not to take this [Eurocorps initiative] seriously; we are bringing the French closer into NATO, they said. The French told us something different. In the permanent representatives meeting of the EC in Paris, we asked whether these forces would be assigned to NATO and whether they would be for use outside the NATO area. The German representative promptly said "yes" and "no". His French colleague said "no" and "yes." This was a day after they had launched this proposal. It was born in an atmosphere of confusion'.*[37]

The Bush Administration reacted sharply to the Franco-German corps initiative and the President made his famous speech at NATO's Rome Summit in November 8, 1991. He said, 'if, my friends, your ultimate aim is to provide independently for your own defence, the time to tell us is today.'[38] Even though Bonn contradicted Paris in the definition of the EDI, it never came to consider NATO and the EDI incompatible. Germans found themselves in a thorny position between the French and the Anglo-Americans. Hans von Plötz, at that time was the German ambassador to NATO, said in an interview: 'Germany's arms were twisted to choose between France and the US, but we never did choose. We resisted the choice'.[39] The Anglo-Americans treated the Germans role in the Franco-German initiative with a great deal of suspicion. Kramer argued that, 'although the French and Germans asserted that it was

---

[37] Art, R. J., 'Why Western Europe needs the US and NATO?', p.34.
[38] Bush quoted in Gordon, P. H., *France, Germany, and the Western Alliance*, p.42.
[39] Art, R. J., 'Why Western Europe needs the US and NATO?', p.34.

compatible with NATO, the Bush administration had doubts about the good faith of the former and the good sense of the latter'.[40]

German officials had serious difficulties in explaining that the Eurocorps would not stay outside NATO and the *Bundeswehr* in this unit would be 'double-hatted' to NATO and the
Eurocorps command. Moreover, the German Defence Minister Volker Rühe repeatedly explained that the creation of a European army was a 'long-term proposal' and reminded that the
US had frequently urged its European partners to take greater responsibility in situations in
which NATO would be 'neither willing nor able to intervene'.[41] Other European members of
NATO also became upset about the Franco-German bilateral initiative, no one else participated in the unit until the problems between the Eurocorps and NATO had been solved.[42]

In fact no one, the French very much included, seriously wanted to see the US military departure from Europe. Tiersky commented on the former French Defence Minister Pierre
Joxe's announcement that, 'the French, without joining NATO's integrated command, are
going to increase their participation in NATO's military affairs by attending the meetings of
the Military Committee and the Defence Planning Committee. This French step forward – a
quid pro quo for the American acceptance of a WEU attached to the EC – indicates that everyone's goal is to create compatible NATO/WEU structures'.[43] Although French officials
never opposed the idea of the Eurocorps' coming under the NATO command, they asserted
that they would have objected to it if the following three conditions of the Franco-German
accord had not been accepted by NATO: if the Eurocorps would be placed under the NATO

---

[40] Kramer, Steven P., 'France and the New Germany', p.19; Stein, G., 'The Eurocorps and Future European
Security Architecture', *European Security*, (Vol.2, No.2, Summer 1993), p.200.
[41] Volker Rühe quoted in Clarke, J. G., 'The Eurocorps: A Fresh Start in Europe', p.3.
[42] Italy, for example, was reacted angrily at what it perceived as a Franco-German bid for leadership in Europe
and concerned at the prospect of its own exclusion. See Rees, W. G. *The Western European Union at the
Crossroads*, (US: Westview Press, 1998), p.63.
[43] Tiersky, R., 'France in the New Europe', p.141.

command, it should not be broken into constituent parts – it should remain 'as a unit'; the re-

lationship between the Eurocorps and NATO should be based on an 'operational control' (for

a specific and predetermined mission and time), not on permanent peacetime integration; and

that the units in Eurocorps, while 'double-hatted', would be loyal first to the Eurocorps and

only secondarily to NATO if the corps' political leaders decide so.[44] The Franco-German ac-

cord makes clear that, although the Eurocorps could be under NATO command, its primary

task is in the WEU framework. The main problem was the different statuses of the troops in-

volved in the Eurocorps: French troops have not been the part of the integrated NATO com-

mand, but German troops have remained part of it. However, even if NATO asks the

Eurocorps to come under the NATO command in an emergency situation in which the French

does not want its Eurocorps forces to be involved, the German ones would be available as

they have always been under the NATO command.[45]

Not until January 21, 1993, was the nature of the EDI, the WEU's exact relation to NATO,

and the relationship between the Eurocorps and NATO worked out. The agreement, which

was aptly negotiated between France, Germany, and NATO's SACEUR, made it possible for

the Eurocorps to be used in a time of emergency under the operational command of NATO.

However, this is made conditional on the three preliminary conditions: (a) preauthorisation

must be acquired from France and Germany; (b) according to a plan, which was approved by

France and Germany, the Corps must operate for a preliminarily defined mission 'as a unit';

(c) the Corps must operate as such and can only be split up with the agreement of the Franco-

German Security Council.[46] For explicitly linking the Eurocorps to the EDI, a similar agree-

ment was signed at the WEU Council of Ministers' Luxembourg meeting on November 22,

---

[44] Gordon, P. H., *France, Germany, and the Western Alliance*, p.43.
[45] See 'Qu'est-ce qu'on fait? Ich weiss nicht', *The Economist*, (May 23, 1992), p.51.
[46] WEU Council Report, Rapporteur Mr. Marshall, 'European Security Policy', *Document 1370*, (Brussels: WEU Council, May 24, 1993), p.26. The WEU's relation to NATO is analysed in detail in previous chapter.

1993, between the EC and the WEU.[47] Assignment of military units to the WEU (Forces Answerable to WEU), including the Eurocorps, were made available for performing specific tasks, which are explicitly defined in the Petersberg Declaration since June 19, 1992. The Eurocorps is a permanent unit for various tasks, not only for the WEU and NATO's Art.V/5 obligations, but also for peacekeeping, humanitarian and rescue, airborne and maritime tasks.

The venture began in 1988 with the creation of a Franco-German Brigade (Command level) and then expanded in 1993 into the Eurocorps (HQs level) based in Strasbourg. It became operational in 1995 and consists of approximately 45,000 soldiers from France, Germany, Belgium, Luxembourg and Spain. Chilton argued that the Eurocorps provides ready-made permanent command structures for 'a potentially wider European land army'.[48] The striking result with respect to the French attitude was that French troops were for the first time placed permanently under an integrated Eurocorps command. France had previously rejected taking this step of pooling French military sovereignty with another European force or a larger pooling of sovereignty in the EU. France accepted bringing its Eurocorps troops under NATO command not only for the defence of Europe, but also for peacekeeping missions; French policymakers hitherto had rejected putting them in NATO's scope. France accepted the concept of multinational military integration, which was rejecting since 1958, by allowing for the first time a permanent stationing of German soldiers in France and provided a means for the

---

[47] The Luxembourg Declaration was the completion of what the WEU Council of Ministers was agreed in Rome on May 19, 1993. The WEU Council of Ministers in Rome welcomed the Franco German Memorandum: 'The States participating in the European Corps recall the terms of the Franco-German Memorandum of 30 November 1992, of which the Council has taken note, to the effect that they consider that the European Corps forms part of units designated as 'forces answerable to WEU''. WEU Council of Ministers, *Rome Communiqué*, (Rome: May 19, 1993) in Bloed, A. & Wessel, R. A. (ed.), *The Changing Functions of the WEU – Introduction and Basic Documents*, (Utrecht: Martinus Nijhoff Publishers, August 1994), pp.171-177. Part I, parg.4 of the Luxembourg Declaration states that: 'Ministers warmly welcomed and endorsed the adaptation of the Joint Declaration setting the conditions for the use of the European Corps in the framework of the WEU and the understandings in this regard.' WEU Council of Ministers, *Luxembourg Declaration*, (Luxembourg: 22 November 1993), in Bloed, A. & Wessel, R. A. (ed.), *The Changing Functions of the WEU*, pp.183-190.

[48] Chilton, P., 'A European Security Regime: Integration and Cooperation in the Search for CFSP', *Journal of European Integration*, (Vol.19, No.'s 2-3, Winter/Spring 1996), p.229.

continued presence of French soldiers in Germany.[49] The striking effect on the German side was, Gordon wrote, 'the acceptance of a military unit with international peacekeeping and peacemaking as a declared mission represents a new commitment to play an international security role and, importantly, to do so in a multilateral European context'.[50] Ironically, the Eurocorps initiative had the effect of bringing France closer to NATO, and Germany closer to use of its armed forces, if necessary, even outside the traditional NATO area.

In the post-Cold War era, the concept of static defence has been replaced by concepts of mobile and flexible units. NATO solved this difficulty with the ACE Rapid Reaction Corps. However, the Eurocorps is inflexible for operations requiring a rapid reaction capability. Thus, the US officials note that the Eurocorps cannot do much in the absence of sea- and airlift, air defence and refuelling capabilities, and C3I. Gordon aptly put it that 'the very capabilities the Europeans need but do not have, NATO does not "have" either', the US has.[51] The French desire for an autonomous Eurocorps capability was rebutted by one of the American officials as: 'The French have a second-rate nuclear deterrent, a third-rate real time intelligence capability, and a third-rate conventional army'.[52] On the ground level, French military co-operation with British forces (e.g. in the former Yugoslavia) is often much easier than co-operation with the German forces and, at the operational level, the Franco-German partnership suffers political difficulties – such as German public criticisms with regard to the *Bundeswehr*'s participation in military operations.

The new security thinking and German reunification inevitably raised the issue of a need for new international status with a more active military-diplomatic German involvement in Euro-

---

[49] The last small French division in Germany pulled into the Eurocorps HQs in mid-1998 and a significant French military presence therefore ceased to exist on German territory.
[50] Gordon, P. H., *France, Germany, and the Western Alliance*, p.45.
[51] See Gordon, P. H., 'Does the WEU Have a Role?', *Washington Quarterly*, (Vol.20, No.1, Winter 1997); Gordon, P. H., 'Europe's Uncommon Foreign Policy', *International Security*, (Vol.22, No.3, Winter 97/98).
[52] Quoted in Clarke, J. G., 'The Eurocorps: A Fresh Start in Europe', pp.4-5.

pean security and defence spheres. France has been gradually adapting itself to the new security environment, but Germany was stuck with the view that the *Grundgesetz* had outlawed German armed forces' operation outside the NATO area. Although the German Constitutional Court in Karlsruhe declared that Article 87(a) (Germany's armed forces are for defence purpose) and Article 24 (which explicitly permits Germany's adherence to a collective security system) are not an obstacle to German participation in the UN, WEU and NATO military operations outside the NATO area, there are still political and public reservations. Nevertheless, novel thinking in *The Economist* indicates that the German military forces 'participation in the Franco-German corps might help speed a change in German attitudes'.[53]

From late 1993 until the late 1994 saw a major breakthrough in building a genuine EDI around the Franco-German partnership. Kocs argued that, 'in some ways, in fact, official French and German strategic concepts were more compatible in 1994 than at any time since the creation of the Fifth Republic in 1958'.[54] At the zenith of the Franco-German partnership, Alfred Grosser wrote, 'when on July 14, 1994, President Mitterand invited German-European units to march down the Champs Elyseés on France's national holiday, the event had a double significance. On the one hand, it was intended to show that France was powerful only within the framework of the community, and on the other hand, Germany was supposed to recognise that it would be accepted as a full member of Europe only when it accepted all its European responsibilities, including the military ones. The presence of German soldiers in Bosnia is a sign that this acceptance has taken place'.[55] Boyer also informed that, '[i]t was the first time since 1945 that foreign troops had marched on the Champs Elyseé'.[56]

---

[53] 'Qu'est-ce qu'on fait? Ich weiss nicht', *The Economist*, (May 23, 1992), p.51. The *Grundgesetz* restricts German troops to missions of collective security. This outlaws the possibility of German unilateral military operations and strengthens the probability that Germany could act within the framework of NATO, the WEU, and the Eurocorps. This is analysed in more detail in Chapter 4 – *(1.2) Perceptions Before and After the Decision of the Federal Constitutional Court (FCC): Germany Crossed the Rubikon.*
[54] Kocs, Stephen A., *Autonomy or Power*, p.223.
[55] Alfred Grosser 'Deutschlands Weg Nach Europa' in *Deutschland*, (No.6/98, December/January 1998), p.13.
[56] Yves Boyer 'France and Germany' in Heurlin, B. (ed.), p.243.

Even so, it is difficult to say that the Germans in the 1990s considered the Franco-German relationship in the same way as they did in the 1980s. In the 1980s, close political, economic, and military relations with France were considered as *sine qua non* for the German foreign and security policy. After all, Germany in the post-Cold War era became less willing than in the past to bargain its own direct interests simply in order to keep good relations with France. After Kohl and Mitterand's successful co-operation, the next generation of politicians became more critical and less receptive to the Franco-German partnership. The replacement of Francophile' Hans-Dietrich Genscher in the German Foreign Office by 'Atlanticist' oriented Klaus Kinkel, who also reaffirmed German priorities by arguing that 'the Eurocorps might turn out to be a final fling in a relationship', was only one of the signs of a change in the partnership.[57] He also made a stiff remark in 1993 against the French officials threat to veto the GATT farm deal by saying: 'We reached a point where our conception no longer coincides with that of France'.[58] Otto G. Lambsdorff (former FDP leader) said, '[t]he German economy is more important than the quality of our relations with France'.[59] It was also stated in *The Economist* that former German Defence Minister Volker Rühe leaned more towards Britain than to France.[60] On the other hand, although Jacques Chirac (the leader of neo-Gaullists (RPR)) declared before he became the new president of France in 1995 that the Franco-German relationship to be of 'primordial' importance for France, it should be borne in mind that he and other anti-Maastricht Gaullists campaigned against the ratification of the Maastricht Treaty.[61] A bold reaction to French policymakers' anti-Maastricht thoughts came at that time with the Schäuble-Lamers Paper of 1994: if France did not begin acting on its

---

[57] 'Qu'est-ce qu'on fait? Ich weiss nicht', *The Economist*, (May 23, 1992), p.51.
[58] 'Chauvin was a Frenchman', *The Economist*, (March 20, 1993), p.53.
[59] *Ibid.*
[60] 'Qu'est-ce qu'on fait? Ich weiss nicht', *The Economist*, (May 23, 1992), p.51.
[61] 'Chauvin was a Frenchman', *The Economist*, (March 20, 1993), p.53.

pro-European rhetoric, Germany still had enough 'actions room' for an independent national movement.[62]

On the whole, the fact is that the two old enemies together have taken a big stride in the new strategic environment towards a degree of convergence in joint decision-making structures and multilateral formations, with both began restructuring their armed forces in order to place greater emphasis on rapid reaction forces planned for joint actions outside the Central European zone. As has happened so often before through Schengen, Maastricht, and JACS, France and Germany decided to set off the Eurocorps process bilaterally in order to go forward more rapidly without outflanking the rest, but hoping one day to draw their other European partners into the Franco-German Eurocorps initiative.[63] Clarke wrote that, even the UK (the most 'Atlanticist' country in Europe), while refusing to participate in the Eurocorps, had been forced to moderate their opposition and to find a way to wrap the Eurocorps in a 'NATO-friendly' WEU embrace.[64] Furthermore, noticeable differences from the previous years were, France became willing to discuss the 'Europeanisation' of its *force de frappe*, Germany began showing interest in restructuring its armed forces, and French and German policymakers promised to complement the CFSP through the Eurocorps/WEU.[65]

In the following section, the Franco-German partnership will be analysed from May 7, 1995, until October 27, 1998. The former marked the election of neo-Gaullist Jacques Chirac as a

---

[62] The key sentence is: 'Nach der Wiedervereinigung Deutschlands und – was in diesem Zusammenhang noch wichtiger ist – nachdem der Osten als Aktionsraum für die deutsche Außenpolitik zurückgekehrt ist und der Bewegungsspielraum für Deutschland derselbe ist wie für alle seine westlichen Partner...' in *CDU/CSU Bundestag Paper*, ' Überlegungen zur europäischen Politik (Reflections on European Policy)', (Bonn: September 1, 1994), p.9.

[63] Gabriel, J. M., 'The Integration of European Security: A Functionalist Analysis', *Aussenwirtschaft*, (Heft I, April 1995), p.152.

[64] Clarke, J. G., 'The Eurocorps: A Fresh Start in Europe', pp.6-7.

[65] The French willingness of considering the 'Europeanisation' of nuclear doctrine was first signalled by Mitterand on January 10, 1992, but the discussions remained limited at that time. For a detailed study on this subject, see Chapter 5 on France.

new president of France by replacing Mitterand and the latter marked the election of the SPD leader Gerhard Schröder as a new Chancellor of Germany by replacing Kohl.

(2) The 'Half-Baked' Franco-German Security and Defence Balance, 1995-1998

Reconciliation between France and Germany has been the cornerstone of partnership from de Gaulle and Adenauer to Mitterand and Kohl. However, the victory of Jacques Chirac in the French presidential elections on May 7, 1995, led to a brief disruption in the Franco-German partnership. In fact, Kohl and Chirac did not have the same close personal relationship as Mitterand and Kohl once had. Neither President Jacques Chirac nor the socialist Prime Minister Lionel Jospin shared Kohl's vision of a politically integrated Europe. Therefore, it has to be mentioned here that reconciliation does not mean that there will never be conflict, it is just providing the necessary procedural arrangements and structures that can function as an essential communication tool for preventing conflicts in times of crisis. Undeniably, the French and German relationship became resilient after the reconciliation due to working together: The French say it is difficult to work with the Germans and the Germans say it is difficult to work with the French, but eventually they manage together to bring things about.[66] Therefore, returning to the normal course of the Franco-German dialogue, which remained 'half-baked', did not take much time. This section will be analysed to understand the 'half-baked' Chirac-Kohl period by going over the following topics: The Franco-German dialogue on European security and NATO; the suddenly announced French army reforms, the end of French conscription, and the reduction of French forces in Germany; the resumption of French nuclear tests; and, the Franco-German 'Common Strategic Concept'.

---

[66] Le Gloannec, A. M., 'The Future of the Franco-German Relationship', *US-CREST's Franco-American Seminar Series*, (April 16, 1998). Available at: <http://www.adetocqueville.com> (Visited on: January 1, 1999).

(2.1) Causes of the Rocky Kohl-Chirac Security and Defence Dialogue

Despite profound doubts about Chirac's commitment to lean more towards 'Europeanisation',

the German policymakers saw that Chirac had given a priority to meet the Maastricht criteria

through cutting the budget deficit in order to keep France in the EMU.[67] However, the devil is

always in the detail. In reality, the Franco-German partnership was proven to be shakier

throughout Chirac's Presidency. Chirac had to lean on the construction of European monetary

institutions in order to strengthen its political control over the Euro, but, in fact, had no other

credible choice than to follow the dominant economic and monetary power – Germany – in

order to gain German monetary support for relieving the deteriorating French economy.[68]

Chirac was also seriously concerned about the German persistence in seeking to forge the EU

into a 'United States of Europe', where France and the UK were not happy with such an anal-

ogy, and in order to bring this German idea into balance, he called the Franco-German part-

nership 'necessary, but not sufficient' and proclaimed 'no Europe without Britain'.[69] On the

other side, the Germans considered political integration and the 'Federal Europe' concepts

more seriously.

The main challenges to the Franco-German security relationship came from neo-Gaullist

Chirac's commitment to France's grandeur and independent military role, independent for-

eign and security policy, desire for a greater leadership role in the CFSP and NATO, con-

tinuation of the French national influence in Africa and Middle East, and the resumption of

nuclear tests in June 1995, while positioning himself pro-European and pro-Atlanticist. The

French policymakers have been concerned that adapting NATO to the post-Cold War new

---

[67] Yves Boyer 'Whither Core Europe? France and the European Construction: Issues and Choices' in
Lankowski, C. and Serfaty, S. 'Europeanising Security? NATO and an Integrating Europe', *AICGS Research
Report*, (US: The Johns Hopkins University, American Institute for Contemporary German Studies (AICGS)
Research Report No. 9, 1999), pp.20-21.
[68] Yves Boyer 'France and Germany' in Heurlin, B. (ed.), p.250. The biggest challenge in front of Chirac at that
time was adjusting conservative monetary and salary policies, which France had pursued since 1983 and
perceived to be the primary reason of 12% unemployment.
[69] 'Ever Closer, More Tactfully', *The Economist*, (June 17, 1995), p.57.

security environment might perpetuate US domination of Europe indefinitely. France wanted to realise the Franco-German proposal of a merger between the EU and the WEU in order to curtail NATO's domination of Europe, but was disappointed by the US hindrance. On the other hand, the Kohl government tried to include France into the reform process of NATO and tried to convince the US that the Franco-German Eurocorps would not exist at the expense of NATO.[70] German policymakers were also pleased to see that Chirac was taking France closer to NATO and Clinton came to accept the notion of the ESDI. There were several factors that pushed France closer to the US and NATO: The inability of the EU states to take common action in the Yugoslavian war; the undeniable political and military might of the US/NATO; severe budgetary constraints in France, especially in the field of defence; and, the aim of exploiting the military capacities of NATO through the concept of ESDI. In December 1995, President Chirac announced that France would fully join the NATO Military Committee and the French Defence Minister would participate – but not join – in NATO's integrated military command, which it left in 1966. This was a conditional participation to NATO's military organs that NATO, on the other side, would reform itself in order to make the ESDI more viable (see Chapter 5). Germany, however, at that time had serious budgetary constrains due to the cost of reunification, focused on the new economic, security, and ethnic conflict problems in Eastern Europe, and supported the Central and Eastern European countries' participation into European and Atlantic security frameworks through EU and NATO enlargements. France was extremely reluctant about the EU and NATO enlargements and therefore preferred to keep a smaller Europe with the Franco-German partnership at its core.

None of the above strains were new. However, the suddenly announced French defence reforms on February 22, 1996, infuriated policymakers in Germany. Whether the French army reforms were outside the Franco-German dialogue or the German Defence Ministry was in-

---

[70] The Germans proximity to NATO defined by Karl Lamers in *The Economist*: 'NATO is Heimat… Germany grew up feeling it in the bones.' 'The Helmut and Jacques Show', *The Economist*, (April 6, 1996), p.49.

formed about it or not, Chirac's announcement troubled the former German Defence Minister

Volker Rühe. The consequences of these French defence reforms on Germany, such as the

end of conscription and the withdrawal of French troops from German soil, were not even se-

riously considered in France. French defence reforms are targeted to make French military

forces ready for rapidly intervening in regional crises, such as for crisis prevention and crisis

management operations ('soft' military missions). The German army at that time was still

primarily organised for territorial and the collective defence of NATO countries. These two

different armies' orientations were also the basis for the ongoing discussions about where the

Eurocorps could be employed. While France prefers projecting the Eurocorps for military in-

tervention in regional crises as an overseas and Europe-only force, Germany prefers keeping

it as a land force serving only for collective defence purposes within the framework of

NATO. Rühe argued that, 'the potential transformation of the Eurocorps into an expeditionary

force, suggests that Europe would be deserted by troops sent overseas'.[71] While the French

policymakers are trying to modernise and professionalise their army with the abolition of con-

scription since the beginning of 1996, the German policymakers just managed to complete the

reform of the *Bundeswehr* through the absorption of the former NVA (*Nationale Volksarmee*

of the GDR) and the creation of the *Krisenreaktionskräfte* (Crisis Reaction Forces). Le

Gloannec pointed out that, 'abolition of conscription [in France] opened up a debate unwel-

comed by the German government... The debate was ill-timed, as integration of young East

Germans in the *Bundeswehr* was as desirable as a means of anchoring them in a democracy as

it was difficult to achieve, because of extreme right elements among them'.[72] Therefore,

Germany, partly because of this reason and partly because of historical, economic, and politi-

cal reasons, hesitated to enter into a serious debate on the abolition of conscription until mid-

1998 (see Chapter 4).

---

[71] Volker Rühe in Anne-Marie Le Gloannec 'Germany and Europe's Foreign and Security Policy: Embracing the "British" Vision' in 'Break Out, Break Down or Break In? Germany and the EU After Amsterdam', *AICGS Research Report*, (US: The Johns Hopkins University, AICGS Research Report No.8, 1998), p.27.
[72] *Ibid*, pp.27-28.

Amaya Bloch-Lainé put forward two main arguments why Chirac announced French defence reforms prior to consultation with Bonn: The *first* argument was for domestic reasons. Chirac had to prove that decisions on important national matters, such as on security and defence, are still taken independently without 'consulting'/'asking' for the approval or even the advice of other foreign countries including the closest friend, Germany. The *second* argument was for compelling Germany to follow France. Chirac might have thought that if France first begins reforming the French army, Germany would be forced to catch up the French agenda. Bloch-Lainé clarified the second argument by stating that, 'such moves are usually aimed at sending signals to the other party to modify its own position'.[73]

Joint Franco-German defence projects were also influenced after Chirac became president in France. Although France rejected a reduction in its defence spending after the end of the Cold War, Chirac announced the French defence budget for 1997-2002 in 1996 within the French defence reform framework: The defence budget reduced spending by 30% to $37 billion a year, including cuts in a number of joint ventures with its European partners. French Defence Minister Charles Millon argued that, 'this defence budget will give France a professional army by the year 2002 and anchor our national defence in Europe'.[74] The sharpest criticism of the French defence budget cuts did not come from the nationalist opposition politicians in the French parliament, but Germany, France's closest European partner, alarmed that the proposed budget cuts would jeopardise joint projects. With almost all Franco-German defence projects, except *Tiger* and *NH90* helicopters, frozen after the budget cuts in France. The French decision to cancel its participation in the Future Large Aircraft (FLA) military transport, a concept initially proposed by French officials, irritated France's European industrial partners. Even before the plan was announced, the head of DASA warned that French cuts

[73] Bloch-Lainé, A., 'Franco-German Co-operation in Foreign Affairs, Security and Defence...', pp.153.
[74] Chaddock, G. R., 'France Hits Snags on Path to a Euro-Defence', *Christian Science Monitor*, (Vol.88, No.120, May 16, 1996), p.5

could jeopardise the other Franco-German joint ventures, such as the joint satellite program.[75] In short, not until the signature of the Franco-German 'Common Strategic Concept' at Nuremberg, was an independent strategic intelligence capability even discussed seriously. After all, the Franco-German 'Common Strategic Concept' was touching on a sensitive issue: A Franco-German dialogue upon the nuclear deterrence within the context of the European defence policy. The next section will go into an in-depth analysis of this highly sensitive issue.

(2.2) Franco-German Nuclear Force Discussions

(2.2.1) Harnessing the pre-1996 Discourses

Chirac's offer for a dialogue upon nuclear deterrence in Nuremberg within the framework of European defence policy was not a surprise for Kohl. Since de Gaulle's presidency, the nuclear deterrence issue was always a debate for the Franco-German couple with a core dilemma of how to build a Western European defence structure, which would include nuclear protection for Germany.

France has always considered nuclear deterrence a primary prerequisite to its national foreign policy independence and the most reliable means of war-prevention. However, it was almost comparably important to provide nuclear protection to Germany against Soviet nuclear coercion during the Cold War era. This also had another dimension in that not only the US, but also France was standing beside the Germans' political and psychological war against the Soviets. Simultaneously, the Franco-German dialogue upon French tactical nuclear weapons

---

[75] *Ibid. Helios II* and *Horus* radar observation satellite programmes.

was also primarily developed around the possible US withdrawal of nuclear forces due to an uncertain future role of the US in Europe.

The Franco-German couple tackled the following nuclear concepts in the Cold War era: *Firstly*, the former German Defence Minister Franz-Josef Strauss proposed to his French counterpart François Chaban-Delmas in 1957 that the Germans wished to finance French research on the nuclear warheads production and, in turn, Germany would have access to ballistic missiles in France during a crisis situation. *Secondly*, the Franco-German secret bilateral agreement of 1958 on 'Common Research and Utilisation of Nuclear Energy for Military Purposes', which would have made possible the German production of weapon-grade uranium at a gaseous diffusion enrichment plant at Pierrelatte, had been discussed.[76] *Thirdly*, the French production of the *Pluton* missile in the 1970s was planned as a symbol of French independent national foreign and security policy, as a contribution to 'European deterrence' and for an advantage in the Franco-German bargain. However, this was met by great German suspicion.[77] *Fourthly*, the former German Chancellor Helmut Schmidt proposed to former French President Giscard d'Estaing in Paris in 1987 the formation of a joint Franco-German defence budget with Germany supplying money for conventional forces and nuclear programs and, in turn, France would provide nuclear protection not only for itself, but also for the entire continental Western Europe. This would have been the realisation of the European 'Pillar of Defence' on the Franco-German columns through the autonomous West European defence system at that time.[78]

---

[76] This information is obtained from Burkhard Schmitt in Hibbs, M., 'Tomorrow, A Eurobomb?', *Bulletin of the Atomic Scientists*, (Vol.52, No.1, January/February 1996), p.16.

[77] If French *Pluton* missiles were fired from French soil, they would not have reached beyond the FRG's borders. Therefore, majority of German politicians were considered them as 'German-range nuclear missiles.'

[78] Schmidt had proposed that the FRG's non-nuclear forces along with those of Belgium, the Netherlands, and Luxembourg should be integrated into a single force constituting more than one million soldiers. This number would have been reached to two million soldiers ready for combat only after five days if France and Germany had mobilised their soldiers. The FRG with its strong economy and large conscript army would have been responsible for the enlargement of conventional forces and France would have covered both countries with its nuclear umbrella. Nuclear forces would still have had a French commander and the decision of using them

However, in order to protect France's international status of military independence and its national consensus on defence, President Mitterand persistently rejected the idea of Franco-German co-operation in building a joint nuclear force and explicitly refrained from providing a French nuclear guarantee to Germany. In fact, German policymakers have never really considered French *force de frappe* as an alternative, but they conceived it as additional to the US nuclear forces.[79] They found the French nuclear capability not only unreliable, but also insufficient to protect German soil. Therefore, Germany's reliance on the US nuclear capability within the integrated NATO structure has always been considered as stronger guarantee than just the French nuclear guarantee.

However, not until the US decision to partially eliminate American nuclear weapons in Europe in 1986, did French politicians think to consult to Germans in the event of the need to use nuclear weapons. Furthermore, Mitterand declared in 1988 that the 'French nuclear policy was a policy of deterrence and "non-war," and that France's "final nuclear warning" would not be delivered on German territory'.[80] A new political situation in Europe had changed the *raison d'être* of the use of nuclear weapons in the aftermath of a significant amount of Soviet tactical nuclear weapons withdrawal after the disintegration of the USSR. For this reason, the French nuclear capability was faced with *'déflation nucléaire'*. On the other hand, the US nuclear umbrella, which according to France had prevented the development of a European nuclear deterrence policy, was no longer the first policy priority for the Europeans in the after-

---

would have remained with France. Schmidt had also proposed that the existing NATO structure should be replaced by a West European defence system, which would be led by a French Supreme Commander. This was an interesting proposal and was similar to what de Gaulle had apparently envisaged with the Fouchet Plan and Elysée Treaty: An autonomous European defence system would have been headed by nuclear France and non-nuclear Germany would have provided large part of the manpower and funding. Kocs, Stephen A., *Autonomy or Power*, pp.187-211; Wetterqvist, F., *French Security and Defence Policy...*pp.63-66.

[79] Former German State Secretary for Defence Lothar Rühl stated at that time that Bonn would welcome 'if the French nuclear forces were to extend their protection to include the Federal Republic in addition to the protection offered by the American nuclear forces and NATO's own nuclear weapons in Europe. However, only as an addition, not as an alternative.' See David Yost, 'Franco-German Defence Co-operation' in Szabo, S. F. (ed.), *The Bundeswehr and Western Security*, (UK: Macmillan Press Ltd., 1990), pp.241 & 243.

[80] Mitterand quoted in Philip Gordon, 'The Franco-German Security Partnership' in McCarthy, P. (ed.), p.149.

math of the Cold War. In this new strategic environment, French policymakers had thought to put their nuclear weapons in an advantageous position by transferring them from the national to the European level. Schmidt argued that, ''Europeanisation' would take on the task of guaranteeing the continued existence of French nuclear policy, while simultaneously preserving the difference between those states which have nuclear weapons and those who 'have-not,' in as much as this can still be achieved'.[81] French leadership in a nuclear capable Europe has always been the goal of the French foreign and security policy.[82]

Former French Defence Minister Jean-Pierre Chevènement argued in July 1990 that as US protection is becoming even less certain after the Cold War, the French contribution to Germany's defence became more imperative.[83] Although some French commentators expressed their concern that the July 16, 1990, Kohl-Gorbachev agreement could be understood as banning any German participation in a joint West European nuclear deterrence agreement, former French Foreign Minister Roland Dumas argued that the Kohl-Gorbachev agreement did not indicate Germany's denuclearisation in the meaning as forbidding the presence of foreign nuclear weapons on the German territory.[84] French speculations that Germany might someday find itself in the possession of nuclear arms as a 'logical' consequence of the fall of the Berlin Wall were repeatedly rejected by Kinkel, who reiterated that, Germany's non-nuclear vows has been 'unambiguous and forever'.[85] In fact, there are serious obstacles before Germany could possess nuclear weapons: *Firstly*, Germany is a signatory of the Nuclear Non-Proliferation Treaty (NPT) since July 1, 1968. *Secondly*, maintaining Germany's non-nuclear

---

[81] Schmidt, P., 'The Special Franco-German Security Relationship in the 1990s', p.32.
[82] Former French Defence Minister Andre Giraud expressed, in March 1990, the reason behind the French nuclear protection of Germany as: 'To assure deterrence in Europe and protect Germany from a conventional attack, nuclear weapons must be stationed in Germany, which, by their mobility and range, assure its sanctuarisation in satisfactory conditions. To be sure, these nuclear weapons cannot be German. They can be American and/or European. But it would be normal for Germans to have a veto right regarding their employment... It is in the solution to this problem that there resides the decisive key to the construction of a European defence.' in Yost, D., 'France in the New Europe', pp.120-121.
[83] *Ibid.*
[84] *Ibid*, p.121.
[85] Hibbs, M., 'Tomorrow, A Eurobomb?', p.17.

weapons status was also a condition for reunification in the Two-Plus-Four Treaty, which was agreed between Kohl and Gorbachev in July 16, 1990.[86] *Thirdly*, it was one of the French conditions of accepting the German reunification. Germany would renounce nuclear, chemical and biological weapons permanently. *Fourthly*, the German public reactions against nuclear weapons are extremely negative.

Mark Hibbs quoted a senior US government official who was responsible for NATO affairs: 'Germany is locked into a fabric of international treaties and obligations that should reassure sceptics who are worried about a reassertive Germany going for bomb. There are no grounds to challenge [Germans'] statements that [Germany's non-nuclear] commitments are for real. Nevertheless, nothing is forever, particularly in a situation where we haven't defined what the role of nuclear weapons will be, say, 20 to 30 years'.[87] This indicates that questioning the course of European defence would soon or later open a discussion about transferring the nuclear deterrence concept into the EU sphere. President Mitterand first declared on January 10, 1992, the abandonment of long-range *Hadès* missiles,[88] placed a conditioned moratorium on nuclear tests and, later, hinted that the doctrine and strategy for *force de frappe* could be reassessed: 'The beginnings of a common defence raises problems that have not yet been resolved and which will have to be resolved. I am thinking in particular of nuclear weapons. [France and the UK] have a clear doctrine for their national defence. Is it possible to imagine a Euro-

---

[86] According to Article 3(1) of the Two-Plus-Four Treaty (*"Zwei-plus-Vier"-Vertrag*): 'Die Regierungen der Bundesrepublik Deutschland und der Deutschen Demokratischen Republik bekräftigten ihren Verzicht auf Herstellung und Besitz von und auf Verfügungsgewalt über atomare, biologische und chemische Waffen. Sie erklären, daß auch das vereinte Deutschland sich an diese Verpflichtungen halten wird. Insbesondere gelten die Rechte und Verpflictungen aus dem Vertrag über die Nichtverbreitung von Kernwaffen vom 1. Juli 1968 für das vereinte Deutschland fort.' 'Vertrag über die abschließende Regelung in bezug auf Deutschland ("Zwei-plus-Vier"-Vertrag) vom 12.09.1990' in *Deutsche Aussenpolitik Nach Der Einheit 1990-1993 – Eine Dokumentation*, (Bonn: Auswärtiges Amt, Dezember 1993), p.40.
[87] Hibbs, M., 'Tomorrow, A Eurobomb?', p.17.
[88] François Heisbourg claimed that if Bonn had requested the *Hadès*, it could have been based in the FRG so the missile could have reached targets beyond East Germany. This proposal became unnecessary after the development of a long-range *Hadès* or 'strategic' systems for the 'prestrategic' mission of ultimate warning. Later, Mitterand abandoned *Hadès* and placed a conditioned moratorium on nuclear tests on January 10, 1992. For more information on nuclear weapons discussion between France and Germany prior to the 1990s, see David Yost 'Franco-German Defence Co-operation' in Szabo, S. F. (ed.), p.217-258.

pean doctrine? That question will very quickly become one of the major issues in the con-

struction of a European defence'.[89] The main target of France is to extend the French nuclear

umbrella, which would still be in the hands of France, over the entire EU. However, in the

absence of a European Political Union to develop a comprehensive political nuclear concept

in the EU, justification of the 'Europeanisation' of French nuclear weapons seems more rheto-

ric than reality.

A prudent discourse upon the 'Europeanisation' of French and British nuclear forces has been

set forth in Germany. The German nuclear forces policy has been developed around the in-

definite extension of the NPT. Hibbs pointed out the German defence ministry officials' ar-

guments skilfully in that, 'if the NPT were to be indefinitely extended, Germany would be

legally blocked from equal partnership in a future nuclear-armed EU'.[90] He also informed that

the experts in the German defence ministry agreed to support an indefinite NPT extension

only after a legal analysis suggested that an indefinite extension would *not* prevent Germany

from acquiring nuclear weapons if it seeks to do so in the future.[91] Therefore, there is still an

option for Germany to participate in the French plan of establishing a 'Western European

Nuclear Council' within the framework of the WEU. According to the WEU's Petersberg

Declaration of June 1992, Germany agreed that states seeking to join the WEU should not

only sign the WEU Treaty, but also all WEU Declarations since the Rome Treaty of 1984.[92]

Schmidt pointed out that, in doing so, Germany accepts all that the so-called platform of

---

[89] Tiersky, R., 'France in the New Europe', p.142; See Chapter 5-*(3.2) A Common European Nuclear Deterrent?*
[90] Hibbs, M., 'Tomorrow, A Eurobomb?', p.17.
[91] According to Article 10 of the NPT, member states are free to abandon the treaty if it bound that its 'supreme interests' are in jeopardy. Experts also pointed out that the NPT had originally been formulated to allow the possibility of a European nuclear defence option. Bonn stated that it signed the NPT, because officials 'convinced that no stipulation in the Treaty can be construed to hinder the future development of European unification, especially the creation of a European Union with appropriate capabilities.' *Ibid.*
[92] See WEU Council of Ministers, *Petersberg Declaration*, (Bonn: June 19, 1992), Title III (B) in Bloed, A. & Wessel, R. A. (ed.), *The Changing Functions of the WEU...* pp.143-146.

European security interests of the WEU's Hague Platform of October 1987, including the statements relating to nuclear deterrence as part of Western defence.[93]

It is stated in another WEU document on May 19, 1994, that no European country, including Germany, could be prevented from acquiring nuclear weapons if its security deteriorates significantly.[94] Alfred Dregger argued during a *Bundestag* debate on the eve of extending the NPT that 'the permanent members of the Security Council, the nuclear weapon states, have failed to keep their bargain and move forward the process of disarmament and non-proliferation ... we must get rid of the notion that states have a privileged role to play in world politics just because they have nuclear weapons'.[95] After stormy debates in May 1995, the NPT was extended unconditionally for 25 years. However, Chirac's decision to break the moratorium on nuclear testing in the aftermath of the NPT discussions in Germany and before he signed the Comprehensive Test Ban Treaty (CTBT) in 1996, raised mix feelings among Germans. Whilst the German public, European, and other world leaders sharply criticised Chirac's decision, government officials in Germany – particularly Kohl and Kinkel – were noticeably silent as if they were supporting the efforts to indemnify a future role in Europe's nuclear defence attempt. The chairman of the CDU parliamentary group, Wolfgang Schäuble, outlined the discreet official German position as, 'the announcement of a new campaign of nuclear tests complicates the debate on a common foreign and security policy in Europe ...

---

[93] Title II(2) of The Hague Platform states that: 'In the present circumstances as far as we can see, there is no alternative to the Western strategy for the prevention of war, which has ensured peace in freedom for an unprecedented period of European history. To be credible and effective, the strategy of deterrence and defence must continue to be based on an adequate mix of appropriate *nuclear and conventional forces, only the nuclear element of which can confront a potential aggressor with an unacceptable risk*' (emphasis added). See *Platform on European Security Interests*, (The Hague: October 27, 1987) in Bloed, A. & Wessel, R. A. (ed.), *The Changing Functions of the WEU...* p.77. Also see Schmidt, P., 'The Special Franco-German Security Relationship in the 1990s', p.32.
[94] WEU Assembly, 'The Role and Future of Nuclear Weapons', *Document 1420*, (Paris: WEU Assembly, May 19, 1994), p.29.
[95] Alfred Dregger quoted in Hibbs, M., 'Tomorrow, A Eurobomb?', p.18.

But, in order to make progress, we have to minimize problems between Paris and Bonn, whose respective positions on that topic are so different'.[96]

However, the French concerns that Germans might 'go it alone' in providing a defence option of its own still urges France to insure that a reunified Germany needs to be solidly anchored into the EU with a European defence identity provided with credible nuclear deterrence. It is obvious that Mitterand prepared the ground for 'Europeanising' French nuclear weapons and Chirac later in Nuremberg offered the Germans a consultative role in nuclear strategy, planning and targeting in 1996.

(2.2.2) The Franco-German 'Common Strategic Concept'

On August 31, 1996, President Chirac announced that France might eventually offer its nuclear weapons for the creation of common European defence. A week later, former Prime Minister Alain Juppé hinted that France might invite Germany to join together with Britain into future discussions on concerted nuclear deterrence (*dissuasion concertée*) in Europe independently from NATO. German Foreign Minister Klaus Kinkel replied publicly that he found the proposal 'very interesting', but another official from the foreign ministry went one step further and said that Germany did not seek to 'co-possess' nuclear weapons in any way, 'not even through the back door'.[97] However, the CDU/CSU disarmament spokesman Friedbert Pflüger boldly argued that, since rogue governments and Russian nationalists – like Vladimir Zhirinovsky – who could come to power might get the nuclear weapons, Germany should press for 'Europeanisation' of those nuclear weapons now in French and British hands. He further said that, 'the weapons are there, no pacifist or well-intentioned idealist on this planet

---

[96] Yves Boyer 'France and Germany' in Heurlin, B. (ed.), p.250; The two main reasons for this silence defined by Hibbs: *Firstly*, 'Germany is held back by its past and present reliance on nuclear weapons in the hands of others'; *secondly*, Germany saw the 'special relationship' with Paris as a building block in creating a federal Europe. Therefore, Bonn has 'steered away from taking any step that would provoke Chirac to down-grade the Franco-German special relationship in Europe.' Hibbs, M., 'Tomorrow, A Eurobomb?', p.21.

[97] Hibbs, M., 'Tomorrow, A Eurobomb?', p.16.

is going to convince me that in five, or may be in two or three years, some dictator won't rule in the Kremlin who is holding 25,000 nuclear weapons. Nobody wants that, but who can exclude it?'[98] The strongest reaction to the Chirac-Juppé announcement came from the SPD and the Greens in Germany. Although leading SPD leaders are in favour of Franco-German defence co-operation, as well as a diminished European dependence on the US, anti-nuclear sentiments in the party spilled over the French nuclear tests. The foreign policy spokesman of the SPD Karsten Voigt said that, given NATO's dominant role in the defence of Germany and Western Europe, French leaders should 'join the Nuclear Planning Group (NPG) in NATO', instead of attempting to 'Europeanise' their nuclear deterrence.[99] The Greens, on the other hand, demanded the demilitarisation of the Franco-German relations, elimination of nuclear power plants and dismantling the French *force de frappe.*

Although Germany later agreed at the Franco-German Nuremberg Summit on December 9, 1996, to conduct with France a 'dialogue on the role of nuclear deterrence, in the framework of the European defence policy', this was far from dismissing the significance of US nuclear protection of Europe.[100] By this they meant, French nuclear weapons – possibly complemented by British nuclear weapons – would be available to the WEU. In the Franco-German 'common strategic concept' paper, both countries committed themselves to creating a European defence identity and a balanced 'European' engagement with the US/NATO.[101] Originally, France pursued the idea of an independent European defence construction with the

[98] *Ibid.* p.21.
[99] *Ibid.* p.17.
[100] *Franco-German Common Security and Defence*, (Nuremberg: December 9, 1996, made public in Paris on January 30, 1997), Title III, parag.1. The Franco-German concept was kept under wraps nearly for two months and published only after it was leaked. According to *The Economist*, German insiders reckon this was because Chirac suspected that it would cause ructions at home – though French officials say the Germans wanted time to discuss the paper with the Americans before releasing it. 'Otanising', *The Economist*, (February 8, 1997), p.53.
[101] Title II parag. 2(2): '...permanent partnership with the USA, and in order to ensure the establishment of the European defence and security identity and *the Europeans' ability to act on a mutually supportive and independent basis*. We intend to promote the establishment, under the European Council's aegis, of a *common European defence policy... This is why we are committing ourselves to the future defence policy set out in the Treaty on European Union.* In this respect, we both share the objective of WEU's eventual integration into the EU' (emphasis added). *Franco-German Common Security and Defence*, (Nuremberg: December 9, 1996).

'Europeanisation' of French nuclear weapons, but France could not find a partner. The CDU foreign policy spokesman Karl Lamers said that, 'the question of a German finger on the 'nuclear trigger' did not even come to the fore. It has always been difficult in German circles to [explain] the rationality of the tasks of nuclear weapons as part of a political-military means to preserve peace... If the EU is to develop into a security community that is able to act, considerations about the inclusion of a nuclear component in available military potentials are inevitable. But this does not mean that Germany is automatically a nuclear power. Logic should tell critics that Germany would then also have been a nuclear power in the framework of NATO'.[102] Harald Müller, a specialist from the *Peace Research Institute* in Frankfurt, and Kurt Kister, an editorial in *Süddeutsche Zeitung*, argued that, in the interest of Bonn and NATO, it must be the aim of the announced dialogue to link French nuclear power with the Alliance or getting France involved in nuclear arms control.[103]

The Franco-German security and defence concept also constitutes a framework for the ongoing bilateral relations between France and Germany. In essence, the concept has the following components: (1) the definitions of common objectives for common security and defence policies; (2) a common analysis of security environment and framework; (3) a common approach on the strategy and missions of the armed forces; (4) common guidelines on military cooperation and armaments policy, including the foundation of the assembly of common military capabilities.[104] In the light of the above four main objectives, they decided to reinforce their common intervention capabilities in crisis prevention and management through cooperation in the fields of airlift capacities, intelligence, logistics, interoperability, and command resources.[105] Nevertheless, there is a strong paradox in the Franco-German security and

---

[102] Moniac, R., 'No German Finger On the Trigger', *Die Welt*, (January 29, 1997).
[103] Harald Müller in Hibbs, M., 'Tomorrow, A Eurobomb?', pp.21-22; Kister, K., 'Only Within NATO', *Süddeutsche Zeitung*, (January 28, 1997).
[104] *Franco-German Common Security and Defence*, (Nuremberg: December 9, 1996).
[105] *Ibid.* Title III, parag. 3(2).

defence partnership that complicates bilateral interactions. Practically of all the ingredients are present for a genuine and extensive security and defence partnership, there are close and intense interactions for a common policy in military relations, and there are bilateral agreements, protocols, and treaties. However, there are serious disagreements in their bilateral relationships with NATO.

The unusual statement that Kohl and Chirac agreed on in the Franco-German 'common strategic concept' was referring to the European strategic defence that must be guaranteed by NATO and above all by the US. The French nuclear deterrent, similar to the British one, was assumed as supplementary to the US nuclear forces and to the Allies' overall deterrent capability that Germany pledged for the first time to discuss with France regarding the role of nuclear forces in such a frame.[106] Former German Defence Minister Volker Rühe, however, hurt French pride by making a comment that France has for the first time accepted the prime role of the US nuclear weapons in NATO. Rühe's comment seemed designed to assure the public that the German government is not planning any European defence separate from NATO and the US, but aiming to push France in 'Natoisation.' The Franco-German 'common strategic concept' declaration and Rühe's comment provoked extensive criticism in the French press and among the French elite. The familiar band of anti-Europeanists – the National Front, the Communists, and traditional Gaullists – attacked the 'Otanisation' (OTAN being NATO in French) of France. It is stated in *The Economist* that Lionel Jospin, the Socialist Prime Minister, warned against the American 'hegemony' and urged France not to rethink relations with NATO before it had set the base for a European defence.[107] According to some

---

[106] Title II, parag 2(2): 'The Alliance remains an essential guarantee of Europe's stability and security...We intend to reform the Alliance so that it remains an effective military tool in the new strategic context, so that the transatlantic partnership is maintained on the basis of a permanent partnership with the USA...' Title III, parag. 3(1): 'The *ultimate guarantee* of the Allies' security *is provided by the Alliance's strategic nuclear forces, particularly those of the US; the independent nuclear forces of the UK and France,* which fulfil their own deterrent roles, *contribute to the Allies' overall deterrent capacity and security*' (emphasis added). *Franco-German Common Security and Defence*, (Nuremberg: December 9, 1996).
[107] 'Otanising', *The Economist*, (February 8, 1997), p.53.

commentators, the document was the result of a compromise in which France confirmed its willingness to get closer to NATO, while Germany was inclined to give up some of its past taboos with regard to the 'Europeanisation' of the French nuclear deterrence and the unwillingness of the German force projection, particularly, in the Mediterranean area.[108] As a matter of fact, the Franco-German 'common strategic concept' is another good example of both a resilient relationship – a contract guiding perceptible deepening of their defence interactions – and a 'half-baked' relationship – a mechanised way of thinking, a policy of bending backwards and forwards in order to pull their partner eventually on their own side.

France is still trying to play a leadership role, albeit in a diminished form, in the post-Cold War era yet continues to be an influential actor in Europe. French strategic experts claim that failure to resolve nuclear security issues in the EU, might not only soon direct Germany to look for its own nuclear capability, but also the situation might get worse and be overtaken by events. On the other hand, Germany today is more secure than during the period of the Cold War. Thus, the 'Europeanisation' of nuclear issue will not be in the interest of Germany in the foreseeable future. German strategic experts today believe that nuclear weapons are more a liability than an asset, particularly in the presence of US nuclear protection of Europe. However, if the new American administration changes its European nuclear policy and seeks to protect only itself through the use of national missile defence (NMD) shield, then France and the UK have no other choice but to form a common 'European' missile defence shield of their own. The subject of linking nuclear weapons to the EU's CFSP/CESDP will persist as long as the EU unreservedly moves forward in the direction of crisis management ('soft' military issues). 'Europeanisation' of nuclear issue remains problematic in the Franco-German agenda. Ultimately, the nuclear issue is a question beyond the Franco-German dialogue and must include the UK, which has recently started to consider the Franco-British nu-

---

[108] Yves Boyer 'Whither Core Europe? France and the European Construction: Issues and Choices' in Lankowski, C. and Serfaty, S., p.22.

clear dialogue more seriously. As long as nuclear policy divergences between France and Germany continue, realisation of a robust European 'Pillar of Defence' will not be possible.

There is no doubt that with the formation of the SPD-the Green/Alliance'90 coalition on October 27, 1998, Germany has been led further by this Red-Green government to underplay its role in the fabric of 'Europeanisation' of nuclear forces. The next section will be analysed from the view of the new relationship between Chancellor Gerhard Schröder and President Jacques Chirac.

(3) The Necessity for the Franco-German Tandem's Continuance: Recent Developments and Future Strategic Choices, 1998-2000

The period 1995-1998 was marked by a significant number of *faux pas* and differences of opinion that was barely saved by the declarations of friendship, which were signed between Kohl and Chirac. However, the arrival of the SPD and the Greens/Alliance'90 in power in Germany on October 27, 1998, has once again put the Franco-German relations under strain. Although Chirac and Jospin in France and Schröder and Fischer in Germany declared their desire for breathing new life into the two countries' bilateral relationships, there were as many storm clouds on the French side as there were on the German side when Chirac came to power.[109] Most French politicians came with an idea that Germany is shedding many of its former 'complexes' and becoming more self-assured and assertive.

Of the two leading newspapers in France *Le Monde*, announced 'the breakdown of the Franco-German motor', and *Le Figaro*, proclaimed 'France and Germany at daggers

---

[109] There are debates about the generational change in France (e.g. Chirac, Jospin) and Germany (e.g. Schröder, Fischer). This new generation of leaders were born after the World War II and they have different ideas on the necessity for the Franco-German reconciliation. I do not want to go to the in-depth of this issue, because it does not only leads much further, but also its scope is outside of this study.

down!'[110] France's European-affairs minister, Pierre Moscovici, declared bitterly that it is

'time for Germany to put its presidency of the European Union above its own national inter-

ests'.[111] Philippe Delmas, a senior civil servant and former speechwriter for the French for-

eign minister, Roland Dumas, argued that '[the French] idyllic image of Germany as eco-

nomic giant but political dwarf, consenting apparently forever to France's political and mili-

tary leadership in Europe, had always been an illusion ... France had to forge a 'common

power' with Germany... It might take 20 years to achieve, but it was the only way: The one

without the other today is the one against the other tomorrow.'[112] Furthermore, French offi-

cials were upset by Schröder's suggestion in the German election campaign that their hitherto

exclusive partnership with Britain should be broadened and added to the Franco-German tan-

dem. However, when Schröder made his first foreign visit to Paris, he repeatedly assured the

French that any improvement in German relations with Britain would not be at the expense of

the Franco-German partnership.[113] This incident was similar to when Kohl had been upset

with Chirac's declaration of the Franco-German partnership as 'necessary, but not sufficient'

and proclaimed his proximity to Britain in the aftermath of French presidential elections.[114]

However, the necessary continuation of the Franco-German partnership received backing by

the SPD-the Green/Alliance'90 coalition agreement that the Franco-German friendship will

be given a 'new impetus' and the co-operation will be based on a 'broad political situation'.[115]

Ulrike Guerot argued that, 'the focus should not be on whether or not Schröder will try to

counterbalance the special Franco-German friendship with a more triangular relationship

among Berlin, Paris and London, but rather on which conditions need to be met to ensure a

---

[110] *Le Monde* and *Le Figaro* newspapers are quoted in 'French Unease Over the New Germany', *The Economist*, (March 6, 1999), p.48.
[111] *Ibid.*
[112] *Ibid.*
[113] For a comprehensive analysis on Schröder's leaning towards the UK see, 'Welcome, Whoever You Are', *The Economist*, (October 3, 1998).
[114] 'Britain, France and Germany: The return of triangular diplomacy', *The Economist*, (November 4, 1995), p.55.
[115] See 'Kapitel XI. Europäische Einigung, internationale Partnerschaft, Sicherheit und Frieden' in *Aufbruch und Erneuerung –Deutschlands Weg ins 21st Jahrhundert – Koalitionsvereinbarung zwischen der Sozialdemokratischen Partei Deutschlands und Bündnis 90/Die Grünen*, (Bonn: Oktober 20, 1998).

new era for Franco-German relations – and how likely such a new beginning is'.[116] French

Foreign Minister Hubert Védrine said that it is 'neither shocking nor worrying', the Franco-

German marriage had merely entered a franker 'post-reconciliation' phase, and he pointed

out, 'if only because if we cannot get on, the whole construction of Europe will be para-

lysed'.[117] The Franco-German relationship is still necessary for getting things done in Europe.

In its absence, the EU cannot sustain itself.

In this section, firstly, Franco-German attempts to strengthen the EU in matters of security

and defence will be searched out. The Franco-German partnership will remain the basic

'pillar' of European defence and shape the future of the transatlantic relationship. Secondly,

the (dis)agreement between France and Germany upon the comprehensive vision for the EU

of twenty-five or more member states will be analysed. The SPD and the Greens have made it

clear that the eastward enlargement of the EU could not be met, unless the inner-EU institu-

tional reforms are being seriously discussed.

The Franco-German partnership is a critical component of the efforts to fabricate a more ca-

pable European defence. Germany's Foreign Minister Joschka Fischer said that one of the

reasons Germany wants to further develop the EU's common defence and security policy is to

convince the US to renounce the possible 'first use' of NATO's nuclear weapons and to

counterbalance the unilateral approaches the US is increasingly taking up in the world.[118] In

addition to this, German policymakers have well understood that Germany's non-participation

---

[116] Guerot, U., 'Prospects for Franco-German Relations after the German Elections: The New Look or New Deal?', (US: Paul H. Nitze School for Advanced International Studies, The Johns Hopkins University). Available at: <http://www.aicgs.org/After_the_1998_Election/guerot2.htm> (Visited on: August 18, 2000); The necessary continuation of the Franco-German partnership was emphasised in *The Economist* as, 'talk of a possible new Paris-Bonn-London triangle in Europe is nothing new: every time, over the past decade, that a new president or prime minister has taken over in France, he briefly – and in the end unsatisfactorily – flirts with the Eurosceptical British, only to fall back in relief on the old liaison with Germany.' 'Germany: Where is it going?', *The Economist*, (December 5, 1998), pp.21-23.

[117] 'French Unease Over the New Germany', *The Economist*, (March 6, 1999), p.49.

[118] 'Germany: Where is it going?', *The Economist*, (December 5, 1998), p.22.

in crisis spots – first, to the Gulf crisis in August 1990 and, second, the Yugoslav crisis in fall 1991 – were lessons of humiliation for the Franco-German couple. The Franco-German couple were also faced with the third serious crisis before the fall of 2000: the crisis in Kosovo. Joint Franco-German initiatives searched for a solution to the Kosovo tragedy politically towards the end of 1997 until no other political/diplomatic choice was left other than participating in the US military air campaign, which was launched at the beginning of 1999. In November 1997, Foreign Ministers of Germany and France, Klaus Kinkel and Hubert Védrine, launched a joint proposal for the peaceful resolution of the escalating crisis in Kosovo. This followed the Franco-German Foreign Ministers' joint visit to Zagreb and Belgrade in March 1998 and the Rambouillet negotiations then took place between the conflicting parties in France. The Stability Pact, a product of French and German efforts, particularly the product of Joschka Fischer's personal creativity, gained the other EU countries' support in April 1999.[119] In November 1999, Foreign Minister of Germany, Joschka Fisher, and his French counterpart, Hubert Védrine, took a trip to Pristina together.

Gordon argued that Kosovo actually brought the French and German perspectives with regard to military policy closer to each other in a number of ways: *Firstly*, while France has proven its willingness for deploying military force abroad and Germany was reluctant to do so because of its *Grundgesetz* or its past, Kosovo saw both countries directly involved in a major military campaign together. Although Germany's participation with 15 *Tornados* in *Operation Allied Force* was not very significant in comparison to France's second highest number of combat flight missions, the significant point was that they were flying together. If one compares it with Bosnia, where German AWACS pilots had to take the symbolic duty of detecting targets on radar screens, this was a great event. *Secondly*, Germany's participation in combat missions made it look more like France, while France's participation in a NATO-led

[119] For detailed information see Oschiles, W., 'A Fresh Start: The Stability Pact for the Balkans', *Deutschland*, (August/September 1999), pp.22-25.

'out-of-area' mission made it more look like Germany. *Thirdly*, France and Germany's justi-

fications for military interventions had also converged: 'Germany tended to emphasise the

legitimacy of the operation derived from European agreements like the 1975 Helsinki Final

Act and 1990 Charter of Paris while France tended more to justify it on humanitarian basis

alone, but the effect was the same. Both governments were saying that there were cases in

Europe when military intervention was justified even in the absence of an explicit UN

Security Council Resolution'.[120]

All these were signs of the French and German willingness to put their own national interests

behind them – given that, unlike in Bosnia, they did not have a considerable national interest

other than a common concern for crimes against humanity in Kosovo – and to take joint con-

structive steps in re-building disintegrated states. Michael Foucher argued that, 'for all of its

virtues, especially as a potential template in conflict-ridden regions, the historic model of

Franco-German reconciliation is just that: historic evidence turned into fact. The Franco-

German relation has graduated from a mutually beneficial endeavour – each country being the

other's most important partner, including in the economy – to one that is able to find its points

of application in third parties'.[121]

While the conflict in Kosovo was going on throughout 1998, a significant initiative has been

launched towards the development of a common European security and defence policy

(CESDP). Given that France had been considered as one of the main promoters of the ESDP,

the UK – not Germany – surprisingly changed its course to became the second promoter to

French ambitions for discussing defence matters in a European framework outside of NATO

---

[120] Gordon, P. H., 'Franco-German Security Co-operation in a Changing Context' in 'Franco-German Relations and European Integration: A Transatlantic Dialogue – Challenges for German and American Foreign Policy', *AICGS Conference Report*, (US: The Johns Hopkins University, December 16, 1999), p.72.
[121] Foucher, M., 'The Definition of the Nature of the Franco-German Relationship and its Role for the European Integration' in 'Franco-German Relations and European Integration: A Transatlantic Dialogue…', pp.57-58.

in September 1998. While Germany was at that time focusing more on its internal affairs –

absorbing the costs of reunification and cutting defence budget for the sake of streamlining its

economy – than on the project of developing a European defence policy, the UK Prime

Minister Tony Blair together with Jacques Chirac signed the 'Declaration on European Secu-

rity' at an Anglo-French Summit in St. Mâlo, France, in December 1998. The Anglo-French

Declaration became a milestone in the creation of an 'autonomous' capacity for action,

backed by a credible military force. Even though the Franco-German Defence and Security

Council agreed on the principles of the ESDP at Toulouse in May 1999 and later Germany

successfully joined the St. Mâlo initiative during its EU Presidency at Cologne in June 1999,

François Heisbourg argued that Germany took the role of a *Trittbrettfahrer* within the future

evolution of the ESDP.[122] Philip Gordon perceptively put it, 'the Germans (unlike the Ameri-

cans) had no significant objections to the final outcome, but it must have been a new feeling

for them not to be the ones at the table during the discussions with France of an important

communiqué'.[123] It is true that Franco-German tandem is not always sufficient to get things

done in the EU, however they usually set a general structure for a policy and push it forward

by their combined weight towards greater European integration.

Although the EU Summit in Helsinki on December 10-11, 1999, sets out 'military bodies,

planning and the carrying out of operations led by the EU', the decision-making structures

and military instruments of a possible future European 'Pillar of Defence', which were actu-

ally drafted by the UK, France, Germany and Italy, stand out as serious policy divergences

particularly between France and the UK.[124] The French Defence Minister Alain Richard and

the German Secretary of State Günter Verheugen – responsible for European affairs –insisted

---

[122] Heisbourg, F. 'Trittbrettfahrer? Keine europäische Verteidigung ohne Deutschland', *Internationale Politik*, (Nr.4, April 2000).
[123] Gordon, P. H., 'Franco-German Security Co-operation in a Changing Context' in 'Franco-German Relations and European Integration: A Transatlantic Dialogue…', p.71.
[124] For these differences see Chapter 5 – *(4.2.2) Resetting former differences is not yet settled: French and British Perceptions of the EU/WEU's CESDP and NATO's ESDI.*

on bringing Europe's sole current defence arm, the WEU, fully under the control of the EU, whereas the UK wanted to see the WEU abolished and its political functions to be transferred into the EU and military roles to be taken over by NATO.[125] France and the UK are still very different in their industrial and competition policies as well as in the role played by the state in the economy. Claire Rosemberg pointed out that this makes for a rocky road when the time comes for industrial choices to be made jointly.[126] The French defence industries and technological base is much closer to the Germans' than to the British defence industrial and technological base.

Less than two weeks before the EU Helsinki Summit, the Franco-German security and defence partnership provided fresh momentum to the European defence policy with a declaration issued at their 74th Franco-German Summit on November 30, 1999, in Paris. The Franco-German couple declared its desire once again that a reasonable 'military pillar' to the EU's security policy needs to be urgently built. Schröder set forth the basic argument of his speech by saying: 'Without agreement between France and Germany, there would not be any solution to a major European homework', and he added, 'Europe is counting on Germany and France'.[127] They also declared their intention to complete the conversion of the nucleus of the EU force, Eurocorps, into a Rapid Intervention Force within the framework of the creation of the EU-Corps by the end of 2000. Meanwhile, the Franco-German declaration also stressed the need for both France and Germany to revive their efforts and harmonise their future military equipment needs. Thus, they proposed the creation of a European military air transport

---

[125] Richard also said that, 'there is still a long way to go towards a genuine European defence. We must not forget that it [took] 10 years to create the Euro. It would be reasonable for the moment to be content with a realistic, pragmatic initiative, taken step by step: first find a way to manage together all the crisis on our continent.' in 'Calls For Common European Defence', *Agence France Press*, transcript, (The Tocqueville Connection, US-CREST, March 12, 1999). Available at: <http://www.ttc.org> (Visited on: August 14, 1999).
[126] Rosemberg, C., 'Euro-Defence Coming of Age', *Agence France Press*, transcript, (The Tocqueville Connection, US-CREST, December 4, 1998). Available at: <http://www.ttc.org> (Visited on: August 14, 1999). For the French and Germans' defence industrial co-operation see Chapter 2 – *(2) Overhauling the European Defence Industries and Technological Base.*
[127] 'Kanzler sagt Paris Kontinuität zu', *Frankfurter Rundschau*, (December 1, 1999), p.1.

command for the joint management of European military air transport operations and co-ordination of the use of civil resources. They also signalled their willingness at that time to produce a common European transport aircraft through the European Aeronautic, Defence, and Space Company (EADS).[128] The 75th Franco-German Summit on June 16, 2000, in Mainz, focused on the military equipment programmes for reinforcing the ESDP and on the discourse upon Fischer's future EU model. In this Summit, Schröder and Chirac declared their willingness to work 'Hand-in-Hand' for solving their problems.[129] As far as the procure-ment of military air transport and observation satellites are concerned, some progress has been made on the *Airbus A400M* transport aircraft issue after Germany decided to buy 75 and France 50; inserting into orbit a European military reconnaissance satellite through the ESA's *Galileo* programme; and sharing the French optical reconnaissance satellite (*Helios*) and the radar-satellite SAR magnificent glass (*Syracuse III*) with Germany. The ESA's *Galileo* pro-gramme is fully backed by France and Germany and became a significant sign of the Franco-German intent to realise future 'autonomous' EU/WEU 'soft' military missions.[130]

At this point, the historic speech of Germany's Foreign Minister, Joschka Fischer, on May 12, 2000, at the Humboldt University in Berlin once again brought the long desired Franco-German common target of building a political Europe into the agenda, notably through the EMU on the one side and security and defence on the other side. Fischer outlined his vision of a 'Federal Europe' under the three major headings:

---

[128] The EADS was found to replace the *Hercules C-130* and *Transall C-160* of seven countries (France, the UK, Germany, Italy, Spain, Belgium and Turkey) by 228 aircraft at a cost € 22.8 billion. Initially Germany pressed for purchasing a Russian-Ukrainian made *Antanov 70*, whereas France pressed for the establishment of Airbus consortium. In the end, they decided to produce a new transport aircraft through the Airbus consortium. 'Defence: Franco-German European Defence Declaration', *European Report*, (December 4, 1999), p.1; 'Allies Mull Franco-German Draft Accord on EU Defence', *Agence France Press*, transcript, (The Tocqueville Connection, US-CREST, December 5, 1999). Available at: <http://www.ttc.org> (Visited on: August 14, 1999).
[129] 'Berlin und Paris demonstrieren Einigkeit', *Frankfurter Rundschau*, (June 17, 2000), p.1.
[130] *Ibid.* The first *Airbus A400M* will be delivered to *Bundeswehr* in 2008. See 'Monopolist zieht die Zügel an', *Focus*, (Nr.44, October 30, 2000), p.13; For an excellent study see, Hagen, R. & Scheffran, J., 'Europas hochfliegende Weltraumpläne mit militärischem Anstrich', *Frankfurter Rundschau*, (Juli 10, 2001), p.7. For more detail also see Chapter 2 – *(2.1.3) The Franco-German Enthusiasm: The Path From the WEAG/WEAO to the European Armaments Agency (EAA).*

- The architecture of already existing teamwork between states must be strengthened and co-operation should be tightened in following areas: the Euro-11 will be developed further into a politico-economic Union, tighter co-operation for better environmental protection, fighting against crime collectively, and further developing the CFSP as well as the Common Defence Policy.

- Completion of political union. As an intermediate step, a 'centre of gravity' will be developed. The 'centre of gravity', including the avant-garde states, will be kept open to the EU's prospective member states.

- Completion of integration into 'European Federation'. The creation of 'European Government' (e.g. a Council with 30 head of governments) and 'two-chamber' European Parliament (one chamber for legislative delegates and another for national parliaments) will ultimately be realised.[131]

Fischer's speech instigated widespread debate in France and Germany and, consequently, extended over the Franco-German 'Governments Seminar' on May 18, 2000, in Rambouillet.[132] Former French Interior Minister Jean-Pierre Chevènement construed that Fischer's speech implies a nationalistic motive through the notion of a new *Heiliges Römisches Reich Deutscher Nation* (Saint Romanian Empire of German Nation) and Fischer's French colleague Hubert Védrine made a more moderate comment to *Le Monde* on June 11-12, 2000, that he prefers talking about a federation made up from the nation-states.[133] During Chirac's

---

[131] Fischer, J., *Vom Staatenverbund zur Föderation – Gedanken über die Finalität der europäischen Integration*, (Germany: Suhrkamp Verlag Frankfurt am Main, 2000); Senk, D., 'Europäische Reaktionen auf die Rede von Joschka Fischer zur Zukunft Europas', *Welt-Report*, (Bonn: Sankt Augustin, Berichte aus den Auslandsbüros der Konrad-Adenauer-Stiftung, August 2000), pp.12-15.

[132] Meng, R. & Bremer, H-H., 'Auf der Suche nach Europas Zukunft – Kanzler Schröder und Außenminister Fischer reisen zu Mini-Gipfel nach Rambouillet', *Frankfurter Rundschau*, (May 19, 2000), p.7.

[133] Some German Catholic politicians consider European integration as the continuation of 'Saint Roman Empire of German Nation'. For a good account see, 'Chevènement, Fischer Discuss EU's Future', *Le Monde*, (internet version, FBIS-WEU (Foreign Broadcast Information Service/Western Europe)-2000-0622, June 21, 2000), pp.15-17. Available at:<wnc.fedworld.gov> Hereafter referred to as FBIS-WEU; Védrine's comments are in Bremer, H-H, 'Unverhohlen rüffelt Paris den Berliner "Flötenspieler"', *Frankfurter Rundschau*, (November 24, 2000), p.2; Senk, D., 'Europäische Reaktionen auf die Rede von Joschka Fischer zur Zukunft Europas', p.13.

visit to Berlin on June 26, 2000, President of the Federal Republic of Germany, Johannes Rau, said that the EU might develop an 'identity' but it should not be subjected to a forced uniform rule and, he added, a 'Federal Europe' can and must not mean that the member states' constitutions could be replaced by a 'uniform model'.[134]

Chirac's response to Fischer came on June 28, 2000, during his direct speech in front of the members of the *Bundesrat* in Berlin. As a respond to Fischer's idea of an 'avant-garde group', Chirac proposed that 'groups' according to their self-will could proceed separately in different political fields: (1) deepened politico-economy; (2) strengthened common defence and security policy; (3) effective fighting against criminality.[135] Chirac chose a limited middle-term vision for Europe's future by setting up a 'pioneer group' of community countries that would move forward at an accelerated pace through 'enhanced co-operation' on three such areas. Given the traditional French reticence about federalist schemes, the old French notion of the 'pioneer group' in European 'concentric circles' form would have its own secretariat and be open to any EU country that wants to join in.[136] President of the *Bundestag* Wolfgang Thierse argued that Chirac's vision of Europe needs more clarification on matters like demarcation and authority definition between the different European levels.[137] Chirac also proclaimed his desire for preparing the first 'European constitution', then the establishment of a 'European government' and, in the end, the creation of a 'European nation'. Chirac later emphasised that his European perception does not contradict with the continuation of existing nation-states, as they have already successfully pulled some of their sovereignties collectively into the EU.[138]

---

[134] Rau's original speech is 'Bei der europäischen Einigung dürfen gewachsene Identitäten ... nicht den Zwängen einheitlicher Regelungen unterworfen... Ein föderales Europa kann und darf nicht bedeuten, die bewährten Verfassungen seiner Mitgliedstaaten durch ein einheitliches Modell zu ersetzen' in 'Rau beschwört neues, starkes Europa', *Frankfurter Rundschau*, (June 27, 2000).
[135] Meng, R., 'Chirac regt EU-Pioniergruppe an', *Frankfurter Rundschau*, (June 28, 2000).
[136] For more information on 'concentric circles' see Chapter 1-(2.3.2) *The Franco-German Joint Letter: 'Enhanced Co-operations'*.
[137] Meng, R., 'Chirac regt EU-Pioniergruppe an', *Frankfurter Rundschau*, (June 28, 2000).
[138] '...wäre genauso absurd wie zu leugnen, dass sie bereits einen Teil ihrer Souveränitätsrechte gemeinsam wahrnehmen und dies auch weiterhin tun werden, weil dies in ihrem Interesse liegt. Ja, die Europäische Zentral-

In fact, Chirac is wary that, in a tight 'Federal Europe', France would be unable to check and balance Germany. Interestingly, Chirac's vision of Europe's future democratic structure, the 'two-chamber' European Parliament, is similar to Fischer's proposal.[139] Fischer argued that the substantial questions regarding European politics are validating the necessity of unity between Berlin and Paris. The foreign policy spokesman of the CDU/CSU-Fraction Karl Lamers said that Chirac's speech upon the creation of a 'European constitution' is 'revolutionary thinking for French European-thoughts'.[140]

At first sight, it also seemed that Chirac was putting forward a federalist agenda. However, after closer inspection, it could be seen that Chirac and Fischer's speeches are contradicting each other in some respects. John Vinocur argued in the *International Herald Tribune* that Chirac, in his speech in Berlin, proposed 'no blueprint of a final model of government and sovereignty for the EU. [He] was meant to set down the French position on Europe's institutional future ... a plan that traced the middle ground while carefully avoiding a delineated concept for the horizon. There was no mention of a future pan-European government or a European president-to-be or a European Parliament assembled by direct vote.'[141] Chirac might have said that in the future 'the governments, then the peoples, would be called to have their say on a text that we could consider as the first European constitution', but this does not mean that he wants more power for Brussels. Julie Smith stated, 'in fact quite the reverse; a

---

bank, der Luxemburger Gerichtshof oder die Beschlussfassung mit qualifizierter Mehrheit sind bereits Elemente einer gemeinsamen Souveränität. Indem wir diese gemeinsame Wahrnehmung von Souveränitätsrechten akzeptieren, werden wir eine neue Stärke und eine größere Ausstrahlung erlangen.' Chirac's full speech is in 'Die Europäische Union muss demokratischer werden', *Frankfurter Rundschau*, (June 28, 2000), p.5.

[139] 'Die Demokratie in Europa muss – insbesondere durch das Europäische Parlament und die einzelstaatlichen Parlamente – mit mehr Leben erfüllt werden.' *Ibid.*

[140] Fischer and Lamers are quoted in Meng, R., 'Chirac regt EU-Pioniergruppe an', *Frankfurter Rundschau*, (June 28, 2000); The CDU/ CSU *Bundestagsfraktion* paper, written by the CDU Chairman Dr. Wolfgang Schäuble and foreign policy speaker Karl Lamers on May 3, 1999, reflects the similar vision of Chirac's 'concentric circles'. 'Heute mehr noch als vor vier Jahren sind wir von der Richtigkeit der Idee eines festen – nicht harten – Kerns überzeugt. [...] Auch unsere Feststellung, daß Deutschland und Frankreich "der Kern des Kerns" seien...' in *CDU/CSU Bundestag Paper*, 'Überlegungen zur europäischen Politik II (Reflections on European Policy II) – zum Fortgang des europäischen Einigungsprozesses', (Bonn: May 3, 1999), p.22.

[141] The French presidential election of 2002 in his mind, Chirac surely saw no gain at that time in defining how should sovereignty be parcelled out in an enlarged and changing Europe. Vinocur, J., 'Chirac Offers Just a Sketch of New Europe', *International Herald Tribune*, (June 28, 2000).

clearly defined constitutional order can be used to ensure that powers remain at a national level. Nor was the neo-Gaullist President speaking to the French government'.[142] Furthermore, Chirac pointed out that neither Germany nor France wants a 'European super-state' that would substitute nation-states; nation-states will not disappear.[143]

In the end, there is no doubt that the European integration process portrays the same image to France as it does to Germany. While the European deepening and enlargement discussions are going on within the framework of Fischer's model of 'centre of gravity' and Chirac's model of 'pioneer group', one thing is very clear for both sides: They need to show some bilateral effort for an immediate institutional reform in order to pave the way for the next EU enlargement. The models of Fischer and Chirac presage that only few states would be in the Franco-German core and the rest will try to catch up with them. The anxiety among some EU states, which are staying outside of the Franco-German future European model discussions, is exacerbated by a feeling that the Franco-German 'motor' is at work setting the direction of integration. Smith argued that the concept of flexibility – first introduced in the Treaty of Amsterdam – is intended to allow states, which are willing and able to go ahead of the rest in some policy areas, now offers a way to make Fischer and Chirac's models effective.[144]

The political and institutional Franco-German relationship in the EU is once again encountering rocky dialogue, but one should think that it is only a matter of time before the Franco-German partnership works out its differences and removes the ambiguities in the bilateral co-

---

[142] Smith, J., 'Destination Unknown', *The World Today*, (Vol.56, No.10, RIIA, October 2000), p.21.

[143] 'Zu behaupten, es stünden sich diejenigen, die die nationale Souveränität verteidigen, und diejenigen, die deren Ausverkauf betreiben, gegenüber, käme einer Verfälschung der Wahrheit gleich. Weder Sie Deutsche noch wir Franzosen wollen einen europäischen Superstaat, der an die Stelle unserer Nationalstaaten treten und deren Ende als Akteure auf der internationalen Bühne markieren würde.' in Meng, R., 'Chirac regt EU-Pioniergruppe an', p.5; This future European vision of Chirac is also comparable to the CDU/CSU paper. 'So würde sich zeigen, daß die Begriffe wie "Superstaat Europa" oder "Bundesstaadt Europa" oder "Vereinigte Staaten von Europa" **unangemessen** sind, um das Neuartige der europäischen Rechtskonstruktion zu erfassen.' *CDU/CSU Bundestag Paper*, ' Überlegungen zur europäischen Politik II, pp.8-9.

[144] Smith, J., 'Destination Unknown', *The World Today*, (Vol.56, No.10, RIIA, October 2000), p.21.

operation. As far as defence and security matters are concerned, they occupy a significant place in both Fischer and Chirac's future European model discussions. The 'centre of gravity' and 'pioneer group' models offer various options for some states, which are continuously disappointed by the obstructionist states, to co-operate more effectively on security and defence issues in the EU. A careful investigation of both proposals will not only reveal the significance of European Security and Defence Policy (ESDP), but will also verify the long-term interests of France and Germany in the 'Europeanisation' of their state identities in areas such as the EMU and the ESDP, which are grounded in a system of diffusion of their sovereign powers. The creation of collective European identity needs strong architects and the Franco-German partnership usually appears as a well-known collective identity maker in the EU. Both French and Germans are well aware that if they want to reach a coherent policy on the Common European Defence Policy area, an overarching agreement on the concept of European Political Union must be reached. Therefore, it is not surprising that there have been tensions and misunderstandings in such areas that touch on the sovereign building blocks of a nation state, but rather what is surprising is that the overall Franco-German partnership has up to now held up so well. However, in the end, success (or failure) in achieving a European 'Pillar of Defence' has been attributed to an external (continuation of a US commitment, albeit diminished, to European security) and an internal factor (greater political will in France and Germany to work more on the ultimate aim of Common European Defence). Due to the UK's obstructionist policies in the past, failure to make progress in the area of defence led the Franco-German couple to co-operate outside the EU. Progress was made possible within the EU only after Tony Blair's surprise lift of the UK's veto block on the way of the Franco-German ultimate aim of constructing a European 'Pillar of Defence' in 1998. Evidently, in the absence of the necessary continuation of the Franco-German tandem, there will not be any 'Pillar of Defence' for the EU.

(4) Conclusions

The existence of the Franco-German alliance has contributed to a widespread understanding

that France and Germany are needed as co-leaders of the EC/EU. It is not just that neither side

could be in a leadership position alone, but hitherto there has not been a real substitute for the

Franco-German partnership. France and Germany occupy a central position on the European

continent, they are neighbours to each other, and they naturally have vital interests in main-

taining their inevitable historic and geographic partnership. Charles de Gaulle 40 years ago

said that:

> *'You have only to look at a map to see the interdependence between Germany and*
>
> *France, on which depends any hope of uniting Europe in the political field as also*
>
> *in the defence or economic fields. So on that interdependence depends the destiny*
>
> *of Europe as a whole'.*[145]

Instead of remaining as stagnant or despair, the two countries' capability for effective bilateral

conflict management has certainly developed through the increased tendency towards recon-

ciliation since the foundation of the EC. Although the end of the Cold War raised fears in

France that Germany might translate its economic power into political power in the EU and

could dominate Central and Eastern Europe, French and German policymakers are aware that

these sort of problems could only be solved by strengthened partnership, not by returning

back to rivalry. This certainly explains why the Franco-German partnership did not function

well in the beginning of the 1990s. Although new generation politicians in France (President

Jacques Chirac and Prime Minister Lionel Jospin) and Germany (Chancellor Gerhard

Schröder and Foreign Minister Joschka Fischer) are more critical of the Franco-German rela-

tionship in particular and the EU integration process in general, they never rebutted the sig-

nificance of the necessary continuation of the Franco-German partnership or the deepening of

---

[145] See 'Qu'est-ce qu'on fait? Ich weiss nicht', *The Economist*, (May 23, 1992), p.52.

the European integration process. In turn, the EU integration process, to a certain degree, constrains or locks Germany and France into interaction and negotiation with each other in a conflict resolution pattern.

Boyer explained that the Franco-German *'marriage de raison* has created envy, if not suspicion and even anxiety, elsewhere in Europe, particularly in the UK. At the beginning of the Franco-German *rapprochement*, London did not believe it could work very long. When this diagnosis turned out be wrong, London has since tried either to insert a wedge between the two partners or to join them'.[146] It seems that the recent British willingness to build a EU defence component replaced the Franco-German 'motor' with the Anglo-French partnership after the St. Mâlo Declaration on European Security in December 1998. Yet, France and the UK carry 'big power' nostalgia, share common defence interests such as nuclear power and power projection capabilities, and are reluctant to abandon their national sovereignty. In view of this, the Franco-German 'motor' is no longer an exclusive one. On the contrary, a range of issues on which France and the UK are getting closer to each other are relatively narrow in comparison to what still unites France and Germany: Nothing of significance can really be achieved unless both Paris and Berlin are part of it. The recent growing convergence and striking similarities between France and Germany is summarised by Deubner, a researcher at the CDU-oriented think-tank *Stiftung Wissenschaft und Politik*, as a constant Franco-German reconciliation and rapprochement through reciprocal influences, the Germans tend to become more 'French' and the French more 'German'.[147]

Firstly, the Germans became more 'French' by upgrading their countries' political status into an equal power through gaining full sovereignty among the big European countries after the

---

[146] Yves Boyer 'France and Germany' in Heurlin, B. (ed.), p.251.
[147] Christian Deubner 'Food for Thought in 'Leftovers': France, Germany and the Coming IGC on Institutional Reform' in 'Franco-German Relations and European Integration: A Transatlantic Dialogue...', pp.9-11.

reunification of East and West Germany in the aftermath of the Cold War. This major change

in Germany's status has provided German policymakers with more power and room for po-

litical manoeuvring, and the chance of grounding Germany's relationship with France more

on objective interests and less on status aspects. Deubner also added that this has not made the

bilateral relationship easier, but can make it healthier in the long run.[148] Germany domesti-

cally began demonstrating some similarities to France by becoming more state-oriented,

thereby reducing structural inequality between Germany and other Western European coun-

tries. Deubner pointed out that if this is a positive aspect for more balanced inner-EU negotia-

tions, the negative aspect is that Germany became more critical of its net contribution to the

EU budget.[149] Germany is also becoming comparable to France in military terms.

'Europeanisation' of the German security policy through the CFSP and the ESDP, seeking for

more political progress towards meeting new security challenges, and taking a great leap for-

ward in reforming its armed forces, all demonstrate that German policymakers are willing to

undertake some security responsibilities including military action abroad (Germany became

more 'French', see Chapter 4).

Secondly, the French became more 'German' by adapting liberal economic (*laissez-faire*)

policies on foreign trade and investment, privatising state-owned companies, as well as rais-

ing the state's hand over *La Banque de France*, which all paved the way for France's joining

the EMU. The domestic policy of France, which was sacrosanct, has also gradually been

adapted and reoriented towards a more consistent system through adjusting it to uniform rules

and policies within the EU context. While France was formerly the most sensitive country

with regard to its autonomous national foreign, security and defence policies, and often con-

fronted the US in NATO, at the end of 20th Century, it appeared as one of the proponents of

more restrictive EU institutional procedures, including the CFSP and the ESDP, and favours

---

[148] *Ibid.* p.9.
[149] *Ibid.* p.10.

some convergence in its relations with NATO (France became more 'German', see Chapter

5).

Unlike the French public, who doubts Germany's structural capability in fulfilling the

Helsinki Summit's 'Headline Goals', French policymakers recognise that its 'political ca-

pacities' have progressed enormously during the Kosovo conflict and, therefore, step by step

led German armed forces into sharing a culture of power projection together with France in

humanitarian actions.[150] In addition to this, as far as Germany's ability to participate in

Petersberg-type operations ('soft' military missions) and the general orientation of its defence

budget is concerned, French military analysts initially doubted the operational capability of

the *Bundeswehr*. However, hefty doctrinal shifts began in Berlin due to the *Bundeswehr*'s

participation in Kosovo Force (KFOR) after Secretary-General of NATO, Lord Robertson,

instrumentally pushed the Eurocorps to take command in Kosovo.[151] Defence experts in

Germany are well aware that German military force structure is an anachronism in the new

security environment. Thus, since the beginning of 1999, they have begun demonstrating a

strong willingness to restructure the *Bundeswehr* in order to cope with new 'soft' military

missions.

French Foreign Minister Hubert Védrine was asked a question on March 15, 1999, about how

he would describe the relationship between France and Germany. The quotation of questions

and his reply will be imperative: 'What is the Franco-German relationship? It has been at the

core of European integration for the past 40 years and *will certainly continue to be deter-*

---

[150] Froehly, J-P., 'The French Perspective: France's Position Towards ESDI and ESDP', *Internationale Politik*, (July 2000) <http://www.dgap.org/english/text/france_esdi.html> (Visited on: September 8, 2000), p.1.
[151] Joseph Fitchett, editor in the *International Herald Tribune*, made a remarkable comment on the delicacy of balance relationship between the EU/WEU and US/NATO. He wrote that, 'Lord Robertson, Britain's defence minister last year during the Kosovo conflict, in which Mr. Solana's leadership was widely praised, embodied London's new tilt towards EU defence. The shift has opened the way to rapid changes that do not always gratify Washington.' Fitchett, J., 'EU Takes Steps to Create a Military Force, Without Trading on NATO', *International Herald Tribune*, (March 1, 2000).

mining factor in its progress. Just why a good understanding between France and Germany is necessary to Europe? The challenges that the 'new Europe' will have to face in the months and years ahead can only be met provided the two countries understand each other'.[152] The Franco-German security and defence partnership in the near future will not only be a central factor in managing trouble spots on the continental, but will also control both direction and speed of a closer political union. Gordon pointed out that during the Cold War, Germany has always refused to make clear-cut choices between French and American models with regard to European defence and, later commented, 'if it is forced to choose now and goes along with a French model that emphasises autonomy, the result could be a leading role for the Franco-German couple'.[153]

This chapter analysed the perspectives of how French and German policymakers developed a bilateral security and defence partnership and which direction the new Franco-German part-nership headed into in their ultimate aim of achieving the European 'Pillar of Defence'. In short, in order to realise the European 'Pillar of Defence', France – at least for the time being – must accept that a credible ESDP needs the US/NATO, and Germany must speed up re-forming its armed forces. In the following two chapters, Germany and France will be analysed separately – Germany being the first – by going over the following subjects: traditional secu-rity and defence political culture, US/NATO politics, EU/WEU politics, military strategy and armed forces.

---

[152] De l'Estang, F. B., *France, Germany and the New Europe*, remarks by François Bujon de l'Estang, Ambassador of France to the US with German Ambassador Chrobog, (Washington: Meridian International Centre, March 16, 1999).
[153] Gordon, P. H., 'Franco-German Security Co-operation in a Changing Context' in 'Franco-German Relations and European Integration: A Transatlantic Dialogue…', p.78.

4

GERMANY'S EVOLVING EUROPEAN SECURITY AND DEFENCE ROLE: BACKGROUND, NEW VISIONS AND REALITIES

'Germany cannot and does not want to follow a unique path. We reached our [national]

adulthood ... in Alliance. We want to remain just like that. We are therefore ready today,

without ifs and buts, to take over responsibilities as a 'normal' ally – whether

in the EU or in NATO'.

--*Gerhard Schröder,*

Chancellor[1]

Introduction

At the beginning of the last decade, it was almost impossible to envisage that the newly reuni-fied Germany would have taken such a big stride towards a military-diplomatic role in the settlement of Kosovo-type crisis by the end of the 20th Century. This evolution was not planned deliberately, but rather Germany was compelled to modify some of its mutually in-compatible and irreconcilable core values in order to tackle the post-Cold War 'new security environment'. Those core values of Germany were moulded by the deep-seated traumatic ex-periences of World War II to when Hitler's Germany was subsequently divided between the two powerful opposing hegemonic countries (USSR and US) at that time. West Germans, on the one hand, strongly rejected the militaristic, authoritarian or totalitarian cultures and their erstwhile nation-state formations (Wilhelminian, Weimar, and Nazi) and, on the other hand,

---

[1] Quoted in Jeffrey, C. & Handl, V., 'Germany and Europe After Kohl: Between Social Democracy and Normalisation?', *Institute for German Studies Discussion Papers Series No. 99/11*, (UK: University of Birmingham, November 1999), p.33.

they fully embraced pro-Western orientation, pro-democratic values, and multilateralism (integration into Western structures like NATO, WEU and the EU) and kept national and nation-state profile low. Thus, West Germany has been strictly restrained by various formal institutional structures and its security and defence largely remained under the shadow of US Cold War strategic regulations. The *Bundeswehr* (federal army) was even formed in 1955 after the US was convinced that the German land force contribution to NATO had become a high priority in order to deter Soviet conventional forces in Europe due to the communists' attempt of capturing the whole Korean peninsula in the 1950s. As a reaction to NATO and the formation of the Bundeswehr, the USSR founded the Warsaw Pact and signed a treaty with the East German regime, which granted it the prerogatives of a State, and included the GDR's army (*Nationale Volksarmee*) into the Pact in the fall of 1955. In order to shield an immediate military attack from the Warsaw Pact forces, the Bundeswehr was commanded by the NATO Commander of Allied Land Forces Central Europe. The international reticence and absolute multilateralism of West Germany was the product of its semi-sovereignty, structured by the physical, as well as moral, destruction and division of the country due to the ugly Nazi legacy.

However, after the removal of the East-West antagonism, Germany was suddenly faced with tectonic changes in its geo-strategic situation even in a more fundamental way than the changes that occurred in France, Britain, and the US. The massive threat of a tank and nuclear battle over German soil no longer exists and the Russian army moved one thousand kilometres away from Germany's Eastern border. Germany is now united, free, a fully sovereign state, and seemingly as 'normal' as any other nation-state in the international system. As Josef Joffe pointed out, '*never before in history has Germany, in whatever political guise, enjoyed such a benign strategic setting*'.[2] Germany with its extended capabilities and improved geo-

---

[2] Josef Joffe, 'No Threats, No Temptations: German Grand Strategy After the Cold War' in Heurlin, B. (ed.), *Germany in Europe in the Nineties*, (UK: Macmillan Press Ltd., 1996), p.264. Ten years after the fall of the Berlin Wall, the Weizsäcker Commission Report stated the similar fact on 23 May 2000 in Berlin: 'For the first

strategic political and economic position is now standing astride the centre of the continent.

Yet, Germany shows no desire to depart from its previous core values that were inserted in

the political, economic, and social evolution of the post-World War II institutions since

Konrad Adenauer. Instead, subsequent German governments insisted for apparent continuity

in multilateralism, strengthened their commitment to maintain the US's involvement and

NATO's existence in Europe, and proposed far-reaching integration plans in the EC (devel-

opment of the CFSP and eventual creation of the European Common Defence). However, the

international system has been left in flux. As Mary McKenzie argued, 'the multilateral world

order itself is changing. Federal Republic is thus compelled to redefine its policies toward

these institutions; in other words, it is compelled to redefine its multilateralism and to re-ex-

amine the principles upon which it is based'.[3] The changed international strategic environ-

ment from bipolarity to multi-polarity has forced Germany to reconsider its relations to the

new perceptions of military security requirements: taking an active role in shaping the course

of international institutions on the one hand and reviewing new roles and responsibilities of

the Bundeswehr on the other.

Germany's future is inextricably bound to that of politically, economically and socially less

stable adjacent nations more than any other country in Europe. While 'hard' military matters

lost some importance with the end of the East-West conflict, the new security environment in

Europe began to be primarily characterised by a large range of 'soft' military matters. These

new type of security threats provide not only the base of Germany's new security and defence

policies, but also compels the Bundeswehr to undertake a more active international military

time in its history, Germany is surrounded on all sides solely by allies and integration partners and faces no threat to its territory from neighbours. This new basis of German security is not of a transitory nature, but will remain valid for the foreseeable future.' 'A Fundamental Renewal', *Common Security and the Future of the Bundeswehr*, (Germany: Report of the Commission to the Federal Government, 23 May 2000).
[3] McKenzie, M. M., 'Germany and the Institutions of Collective Security in Europe', *Peace Research Institute Frankfurt*, (Frankfurt: PRIF Reports No.36, November 1994), p.1.

role.[4] So far, international relations analysts have debated a lot about the Bundeswehr's international military role. Some critics say that Germany do not take on enough of a military-diplomatic international role, particularly in the area of peacekeeping and peacemaking, while others express their concern over what they see – memories of Nazi aggression in mind – as increased German assertiveness in the international arena. Therefore, German policymakers often hesitate to formulate a more active military-diplomatic role for Germany at the international level. Assuming that Germany in the post-Cold War era is 'normal' and claiming that it has to develop a military-diplomatic capability comparable to its politico-economic might, it will actually be encountering a complex German political culture. As Heurlin pointed out, 'Germany is now formally a normal state and at the same time is not behaving like one, nor is it considering itself one. Germany is talking normality and no-normality at the same time'.[5] Since it would be naïve to believe that the international community would permit Germany to turn fully within itself or to shy away from stabilising turbulent regions in the new security environment, primarily for recovering its own economic difficulties due to reunification, the definition of a clearer military-diplomatic role became imperative in addition to its politico-economic might (the third largest economy in the world and the second most active exporter in Europe). The new Europe, if it is to be well organised in the 21st Century, needs Germany not only economically, but also politically and militarily in order to overcome instabilities in the new security environment.

Although the most intricate theme is that Germany should utilize its military role for defending the rule of law in military-diplomatic operations is vaguely defined, one thing is very

---

[4] The first detailed official attempt to outline the spectre of new security environment from the German Defence Ministry perspective was undertaken by the *Weißbuch 1994*. See 'Weißbuch zur Sicherheit der Bundesrepublik Deutschland und zur Lage und Zukunft der Bundeswehr', *Weißbuch 1994*, (Bonn: Bundesministerium der Verteidigung, April 5, 1994), pp.23-39.
[5] Bertel Heurlin 'The International Position and the National Interest of Germany in the Nineties' in Heurlin, B. (ed.), p.45.

clear: Germany must give priority to such 'soft' military matters and related non-military instruments without 'ifs' and 'buts', because Germany cannot simply ignore the strategic potential, which derives from its population, economic strength, national interest, and responsibilities to those trouble spots in and beyond Europe. Nor can it ignore the fact that Germany's
military role today is inescapable. Joschka Fischer, Federal Minister of Foreign Affairs, made
a significant remark on this point by saying: 'To deny that unification has enhanced
Germany's opt out [from its strategic potential] would be both foolish and dishonest, showing
mistrust rather than trust. The question is therefore not whether a united Germany has more
power and influence than before but how it can and should exercise that power and influence
as wisely and responsibly as possible'.[6] As a result of the new amorphous risks and challenges
inside and outside of Europe and in response to its allies' new demands, Germany has steadily
changed and is changing (though not all) its foreign and security policy patterns. The Iraqi
invasion of Kuwait (Second Gulf War) became the first serious pressure on Germany's political establishment where the Bundeswehr's global military role was the key issue concerning
debates about military responsibilities. The culture of self-restraint that has been followed
since 1949 will not make the process of gradual normalisation in military affairs an easy task.
However, it is clear that post-Cold War German governments have made a strong commitment to German military affairs' normalisation as far as domestic political and social conditions permitted. After all, Germans do not desire to deal with security problems in the new
security environment alone and always assert that security of Europe is indivisible and thus
calls for comprehensive multilateral insurance.[7]

---

[6] Speech by Joschka Fischer at the general meeting of the German Society for Foreign Affairs, *German Information Centre*, (Berlin: November 24, 1999).
[7] See 'The Bundeswehr – Advancing Steadily into the 21st Century', *Cornerstones of a Fundamental Renewal*, (Berlin: The Federal Ministry of Defence, June 14, 2000), parag.2(7).

Any attempt to present a fair perspective on Germany's European security and defence role[8]

needs the inclusion of a normative dimension if it is to offer reliable insights. As Anderson

and Goodman argued, 'institutions restructured and ultimately remoulded German interests,

so that, in the eyes of German political elite, institutional memberships were not merely in-

struments of policy but also normative frameworks for policy-making'.[9] A judgement that ig-

nores taking into account the institutions and norms of the German political elite conception,[10]

and focuses merely on debating different interpretations of the meaning of the past (asserting

for 'national interest' or 'cultural restraint' on the country's future policy) is likely to be

lacking credibility and explanatory power. With these caveats in mind, in order to give struc-

ture and perceive the security and defence role of Germany at home and abroad, the following

three policies will be examined in the first part of section one:

1. *Policy of Multilateralism*: never again a *Sonderweg* (unique path), but always join on

   the bandwagon with a company of friends.

2. *Verantwortungspolitik (policy of responsibility)*: always proceed attentively, gradu-

   ally, and responsibly.

3. *Policy of 'Zivilmacht' (civilian power)*: do not be boastful and look for non-military

   solutions for conflicts; truly be a *Handelsstaat* (trading state).

The next part will be about how the German government has succeeded in bringing the

Bundeswehr deployment step-by-step into out-of-area missions, since the debate begun with

the Gulf War in 1991 and reached its peek with the Constitutional Court's decision in

---

[8] Aggestam defined 'role' in international relations theory as a general concept denoting 'role-expectations' within a system of balance of power. Aggestam, L. 'Role Conceptions and the Politics of Identity in Foreign Policy', *ARENA Working Papers*, (Oslo: No.8, 1999).

[9] Jeffrey J. Anderson & John B. Goodman 'Mars and Minerva? A United Germany in a Post-Cold War Europe' in Keohane, R. O., Nye, J. S. & Hoffman, S., *After the Cold War – International Institutions and State Strategies in Europe, 1989-1991*, (US: Harvard University Press, 1993), pp.23-24.

[10] The German political elite conception includes different groups of policymakers' definitions of the general kinds of decisions, commitments, rules, and actions suitable for their state, and of the functions, if any, their state should perform on a continuing basis in the international system or in subordinate regional systems. Aggestam, L., 'Role Conceptions and the Politics of Identity in Foreign Policy', *ARENA Working Papers*.

Karlsruhe on July 12, 1994. Although restructuring military forces has at least nominally en-

abled Germany to develop a more robust crisis intervention capability in international conflict

management and peacekeeping operations in addition to the territorial defence function of the

Bundeswehr, it would be a mistake to conclude that there is broad consensus regarding the

future roles and missions of the Bundeswehr. How will Germany, while embracing anti-

militaristic attitudes, continue to shoulder its future responsibilities, international roles and

missions? Are there any boundaries for the Bundeswehr's out-of-area missions? Or, will deci-

sions simply be given on a case-by-case basis? This part will be analysed from the political,

legal, and institutional spectrum. The last part of section one will address how new leaders,

Chancellor Gerhard Schröder and Foreign Affairs Minister Joschka Fischer, presented a new

set of structures, challenges, and responses to the German foreign and security policy. The

SPD-The Greens/Alliance'90 coalition announced their intention to 'develop further the

guidelines of the previous German foreign policy'.[11] This expression exhibits continuity as

Schröder declared his support to the previous government's target of making the WEU the

defence arm of the EU.[12] Ignoring his party's former policy position of withdrawing Germany

from NATO, Fischer gave strong support to the German military participation in NATO's

Kosovo operation. This is a continuity of former CDU Defence Minister Volker Rühe's pol-

icy of using military force for humanitarian and peace-making operations. The last section

will be an overview of the Red-Green government's foreign and security policy where details

will be analysed in each relevant section separately.

---

[11] 'Die neue Bundesregierung wird die Grundlinien bisheriger deutscher Außenpolitik weiterentwickeln' in Kapitel XI - Europäische Einigung, internationale Partnerschaft, Sicherheit und Frieden – 1. Ziele und Werte. See *Aufbruch und Erneuerung –Deutschlands Weg ins 21st Jahrhundert – Koalitionsvereinbarung zwischen der Sozialdemokratischen Partei Deutschlands und Bündnis 90/Die Grünen,* (Bonn: Oktober 20, 1998). Hereafter *Koalitionsvereinbarung.*
[12] See '3. Europäische Außen und Sicherheitspolitik', *Koalitionsvereinbarung.* For an overview, see a survey on Germany in 'A Less Frightening World And an Unfrightening Germany', *The Economist,* (February 6, 1999), pp.15-18.

Although US/NATO, EU/WEU, UN (United Nations), and OSCE (Organisation for Security and Co-operation in Europe) are perceived to be indispensable and inherently complementary to Germany's comprehensive multilateral security needs, section two – for the purpose of this study – will focus on Germany's multilateralism in the first two organisations in order to contemplate the values and principles underlying the redefinition of Germany's European defence role. During the East-West conflict, the German-American alliance within NATO gave both nations the utmost sense of security that they could not have had with any other partner. However, the most risky moment in any relationship is when a mutually approved balance of power between partners is challenged by drastic events. The end of the East-West conflict and the reunification of Germany brought about such a drastic and unexpected challenge to the German-American relationship, which has still not yet fully adjusted. The reunified Germany is no longer exclusively dependent on the US/NATO for its security. Nowadays, Germany backs a strong European pillar in NATO and supports a European security and defence policy in the EU in accordance with the TEU, Amsterdam, and Nice Treaties. This does not, however, suggest that NATO is no longer wanted in Germany. While German policymakers amicably support NATO with regard to strengthening the ESDI, they are at the same time frankly advocating the need for developing a European 'Pillar of Defence'. The analysis will focus on the continuation of a strong German-US/NATO relationship on the one hand, and changes in the parameters of Germany's European defence role on the other hand.

The second part of section two will examine the crucial posture of Germany in the EU/WEU. The preliminary agreement of integrating the WEU into the EU was reached between France and Germany and endorsed by EU member states during the Helsinki European Council meeting in December 1999. Whilst remaining in close partnership with the US/NATO, this part will analyse Germany's inclination in favour of a genuine European 'Pillar of Defence' through assuming a bigger share of responsibility in the EU/WEU.

Finally, the first part of section three will examine the military reform initiatives of the Bundeswehr. As a result of the new security environment, NATO's Defence Capabilities Initiative (DCI), and the Helsinki European Council 'Headline Goals' of creating an autonomous European corps, the German government was forced to adapt the structure of the Bundeswehr for NATO and the EU/WEU's future international conflict management roles.[13] In the last part of section three, the impact of the Kosovo crisis on the German security and defence policy in Europe is examined.

On March 24, 1999, when NATO forces began a military operation in Kosovo, it became an exceptional case for German military units. If one disregards the German *Luftwaffe* reconnaissance participation in Bosnia military operation of 1994 as an offensive action, the Bundeswehr in Kosovo for the first time since 1945 participated in a serious offensive military action even in the absence of a UN-mandate. Although Fischer repeatedly reiterated that in light of the country's past, as well as its current economic and political weight, Germany has special responsibility to preserve peace and stop human rights violations in Kosovo, there was a deep-seated unease among the Greens members' about the Bundeswehr's military role. They even accused the government of being the tool of US in its quest for 'hegemony'.[14] However, the German political elite has learnt well from the Kosovo crisis, which was more than just a police-operation and less than a conventional military operation, that Europe must have a strong security and defence identity beside its governmental and non-governmental diplomatic, foreign, and economic instruments.[15] Hence, the Red-Green government faces tough choices, which may force Germany to undertake military responsibilities in a rapidly

---

[13] 'The capability profile derived from the changed security environment, the international commitments, the mission laid down in the constitution, the [NATO's] Defence Capabilities Initiative and the European Headline Goal set the priorities for the issue of material and for acquisition.' 'The Bundeswehr Advancing Steadily into the 21st Century', parag.47.
[14] Fischer, J., 'Berlin's Foreign Policy', paper presented to the annual meeting of the German Council on Foreign Relations, (Frankfurt: Frankfurter Societäts, 2000).
[15] See Chapter 1 - *(2.2) Maastricht, European Foreign and Security Integration, and Beyond.*

changing military-diplomatic arena. This also includes taking peace research seriously, civilising international relations through an effective development of conflict prevention and
peaceful conflict settlement, and strengthening international law and human rights, which are
utilised slightly better under the Red-Green government than under its conservative predeces-
sor.[16]

Profound domestic political changes took place over the last ten years in Germany. Although
Germans reluctantly support their country's involvement in a military role, profound changes
took place gradually from a policy of 'without us' to a policy of 'we are willing to accept a
greater share of responsibility'.[17] In the last ten years, political leaders of Germany have stum-
bled along the way, but it seems they more or less found the way to deal with military-
diplomatic operations. However, few seem to have more than a vague idea where they might
be going in the 21st Century. With this difficulty in mind, this chapter will examine
Germany's basic security and defence policies through *background*, new organisational relationships through *new visions*, and army reforms and effects of military operations through
realities.

(1) Background to the Contemporary German Foreign and *Sicherheitspolitik*: Insight, Perceptions and Reflections

(1.1) Insight to the German Foreign and *Sicherheitspolitik*

Post-World War II German foreign and security policy has been principally characterised by
the *policy of multilateralism*. Chancellor Konrad Adenauer's commitment to characterise the

[16] 'German Commentary Notes Lack of Discussion of Security Policy in Bundeswehr Reform', *Frankfurter Rundschau*, (internet version, FBIS-WEU-2000-1117, November 18, 2000).

German foreign and security policy with principles of multilateralism and *Westbindung* (integration into the West) in various multilateral institutions, became so reflexive that all succeeding German governments categorically embraced them. Evidently, this was written into the *Grundgesetz* (German Constitution) as 'Germany may transfer its sovereign rights to international institutions by means of law'.[18] In the post-World War II period, the policy of multilateralism became remarkably effective in West Germany's 'rehabilitation' and facilitated regaining its sovereignty through participation in a web of interlocking network of institutions, particularly in the EC and NATO. Anderson and Goodman stated that, 'because the Federal Republic was a semi-sovereign state operating within a bipolar system, the country was forced to rely almost entirely on international institutions to achieve its objectives'.[19] West Germany embraced broad inter-state interaction and co-operation beyond its traditional boundaries by drawing national sovereignty into international institutions.

In order to gain international reliability, obtain a place in the Western democratic community and remove the fears of its neighbours, Germany pooled its sovereignty into multilateral institutions in the pursuit of what Arnold Wolfers called 'policies of self-abnegation'.[20] Therefore, Germany willingly institutionalised its military power into NATO and economic power into the EC in the post-World War II era. Gutjahr stated that, 'the tradition of multilateral approaches must be seen as an expression of the country's broken traditions of *realpolitik*'.[21] Peter Katzenstein perceptively explained the 'institutionalisation of power' with the following words:

---

[17] May, B., 'Domestic Political Chance and Foreign Policy: One Year "red-green" foreign policy in Germany' lecture at Norfolk University, (US: September 1999).
[18] 'Der Bund kann durch Gesetz Hoheitsrechte auf zwischenstaatliche Einrichtungen übertragen.' Art.24, Titel: 'Kollektives Sicherheitssystem' in Sartorius, C., *Verfassungs- und Verwaltungsgesetze der Bundesrepublik Deutschland – Band I*, (München: C.H. Beck'sche Verlagsbuchhandlung, Februar 15, 1999), p.18.
[19] Jeffrey J. Anderson & John B. Goodman 'Mars and Minerva?', p.24.
[20] Wolfers quoted in James Sperling, 'Less Than Meets the Eye: A Reconsideration of German Hegemony' in Hampton, M. N. & Søe, C. (ed.), *Between Bonn and Berlin –German Politics Adrift?*, (US: Rowman & Littlefield Publishers, Inc., 1999), p.267.
[21] Gutjahr, L., *German Foreign and Defence Policy after Unification*, (UK: St. Martin's Press Inc., 1994), p.85.

'The institutionalisation of power matters because it takes the hard edges off

power relations. Over time, institutions constitute actors rather than merely

constraining their preferences. They do so within particular norms (collective

expectations for the proper behaviour of actors with a given identity) or for

specific collective identities (varying constructions of statehood). Norms and

identities typically have two effects. They constitute actors and thus shape their

interests. And they constrain actor preferences'.[22]

The 'institutionalisation of power' through the *Selbstbindung* (self-binding or self-restriction), which is deeply ingrained in societal attitudes, has profoundly restricted the policies of military power projection in Germany. This form of strong commitment associated with Germany is what Jeffrey Anderson called 'exaggerated multilateralism'.[23]

Throughout the Cold War, West Germany's manoeuvring in a network of multilateral institutions had been very successful in bringing peace, stability and prosperity in Europe so that, at the end of the Cold War, Germany had embedded itself more firmly than before into multilateral frameworks in order to contribute to stable and peaceful relations with its neighbours and gain their accreditation for a reunified Germany. In institutional terms, the collective identities of the German nation, in contrast to the strong national identities in France and the UK, are formulated within European supranational institutions and became identical to the 'Europeanisation' process. Hence, German foreign and security policymaking in the post-Cold War period is strongly interconnected with the EU/CFSP, Council of Europe, WEU, NATO, and OSCE. Ulf Hedetoft pointed out, 'Germany serves its own interests and visions of itself and its future best by embedding its political actions and discourses in the framework

---

[22] Katzenstein, P. J., *Tamed Power – Germany in Europe*, (US: Cornell University Press, 1997), p.3.
[23] Anderson, J., 'Hard Interests, Soft Power, and Germany's Changing Role in Europe' in Katzenstein, P.J, p.85.

of Europe. For the same reason, Germany can come across and represent itself as a relatively insignificant country, shying away from political and military leadership, paying its moral dues etc., but in very real terms still being an extremely influential country with great political and economic clout'.[24] The process of 'Europeanisation', which is located in the centre of multilateralism, requires partners. It should be emphasised here that the Franco-German partnership remains the core of Germany's political, economic and military power legitimisation in Europe (see Chapter 3).

Arguing that Germany has always been shy and pursued multilateralism in the conduct of its foreign policy would be a rejection of historical facts. Foreign policymaking in Germany is hardly explicit on this aspect, but there have always been German 'national interests' during and after the East-West conflict. This was attributed to the termination of Germany's division and various international questions during and after the Cold War respectively.[25] Former Chancellor Helmut Kohl conceived the unification of East and West Germany as an outcome of Adenauer's *Westbindung* policy: a way of returning to 'normality' and pursuing integrationist policies through the *Westbindung* are two sides of the same coin. Although the question of whether Germany is 'normal', 'not normal' or becoming 'normal' is completely another topic, one thing that is very clear is that multilateralism, which is deeply ingrained in the German political elite, will continue to be the bedrock of Germany's foreign and security

---

[24] Ulf Hedetoft 'Germany's National and European Identity: Normalisation by Other Means' in 'Break Out, Break Down or Break In? Germany and the EU After Amsterdam', *AICGS Research Report*, (US: The Johns Hopkins University, AICGS Research Report No.8, 1998), p.3.
[25] Morgan argued before reunification that 'every aspect of foreign relations was linked more or less directly to *the great national objective* of overcoming or ending Germany's division: *Europapolitik*, alliance or *Bündnispolitik*, *Westpolitik*, *Ostpolitik*, and development aid or *Entwicklungspolitik*, were all conceived and executed in relation to *Deutschlandspolitik*.' Roger Morgan, 'German Foreign Policy and Domestic Politics' in Heurlin, B. (ed.), p.158. With the end of the Cold War, German interests in various international questions could be summarised as: Reunification process, early recognition of Slovenia and Croatia, demand for an additional seat in the European Parliament, push for a permanent seat in the UN Security Council with full veto rights, the German insistence on a command position in NATO's Rapid Reaction Corps, German insistence that the European Monetary Institute to be located in Frankfurt, and the German decision not to abide by EU trade sanctions on telecommunications dispute with the US.

policy.[26] However, a striking change for post-Cold War Germany would be in responding to

significant changes, which are occurring in a 'multilateral world', through transformation

from a *passive multilateralist* position (participant, but more shy, more vulnerable and less

critical to other countries' proposals) to an *active multilateralist* position (growing German

influence in structuring and determining goals of multilateral organisations through collective

decision-making and collective action). Schlör argued that, 'multilateral organisations are be-

coming increasingly associated with military commitments' in a changing multilateral

world.[27] Germany is, therefore, expected to be an *active multilateralist* in the military-

diplomatic sphere of multilateral organisations. When Hans-Dietrich Genscher demanded

worldwide responsibilities of Europe (Germany being at its centre) in 1991, it was for a mix-

ture of reasons: the preservation of 'national interest' as well as *management of international*

system through multilateral institutions.[28] That is, Germany needs to be an *active*

multilateralist. This argument brings us to the second feature of the post-Cold War German

foreign and security policy: the *Verantwortungspolitik* (policy of responsibility).

The *policy of responsibility* had first been developed in the German liberal party (FDP) long

before the 1980s and, later, expressed by former Foreign Minister Hans-Dietrich Genscher in

1987. Létourneau and Räkel defined the reason for preferring the term 'responsibility' in the

country's foreign policy (instead of the word 'role') as an avoidance from reawakening pain-

ful memories: the political elite in Germany much prefers to talk in terms of 'responsibilities'

and defines it through using more forceful words such as *Pflicht* (duty) and *Verpflichtung*

---

[26] Prof. Dr. Dr. hc. Wilfried von Bredow from the Philipps-Universität Marburg argued in a conversation with me on April 24, 2001, that ''normality' or 'normalcy' seems would not be possible to Germans for at least one more generational change'. I thank Prof. von Bredow for his helpful remarks on this matter.
[27] Schlör, W., 'German Security Policy', *Adelphi Paper 277*, (London: IISS, 1993), p.65.
[28] Gutjahr, L., *German Foreign and Defence Policy after Unification*, p.87.

(commitment) – concepts suggesting ethical and altruistic behaviour – rather than in terms of interest or power.[29]

Germany's foreign and defence policy has been shaped by Genscher through the values of liberty, democracy, human rights, justice, ethical and moral principles. He said that, 'we Germans recognise our responsibility for World War II, we realise that it is our duty to work towards a better world; a world of peace, democracy, and solidarity between peoples, a world of freedom and human rights, a world at peace with nature'.[30] The German foreign policy priorities' should be the protection of the above values at home and in the international arena, promotion of international law, and prevention of war through non-military efforts. The policy of responsibility also means *Moralpolitik* – being responsible for peace (*Friedensverantwortung*). The use of military force is just one of the options, which is under mandate of international law, and could be applied in accordance with the UN Charter if the conflict is diplomatically inevitable. The policy of responsibility means taking into account diplomatic, political, economic, and humanitarian efforts for the purpose of early identification and resolution of conflicts, trans-national cooperation, disarmament, and arms control, rather than just classical power politics. Indeed, Genscher developed a new version of *realpolitik*: 'It appeared to be demilitarised but it was still founded on Germany's economic might'.[31]

Although Genscher left a deep impact on German foreign and security policy in the last two decades of the Cold War, his objection to Germany's taking on military responsibilities in two post-Cold War crisis, the Second Gulf War (1991) and the war in Yugoslavia (1992), put internal and external pressures on Genscher for redefining Germany's new status and foreign

---

[29] Paul Létourneau & Marie-Elisabeth Räkel, 'Germany: To Be or Not to Be Normal?' in Le Prestre, P.G., *Role Quests in the Post-Cold War Era – Foreign Policies in Transition*, (Canada: McGrill-Queen's University Press, 1997), pp.115 & 118.
[30] *Ibid*, p.117.
[31] Gutjahr, L., *German Foreign and Defence Policy after Unification*, p.85.

policy priorities within the newly created international order. Helga Haftendorn pointed out that, 'Germany's allies and partners encourage it to assume larger international responsibilities and to accept a leadership role in international affairs. Fulfilling those expectations and combining them with its traditional multilateral style is indeed the biggest foreign policy challenge Germany has faced since reunification'.[32] The reunification of East and West Germany and the consequent rise of Germany power in the middle of Europe led its partners' to conclude that it must be assigned a 'new international role' and should become a reliable security exporter. To be more precise, Germany should not stay as a *passive multilateralist*, but should be an *active multilateralist* with a 'new international role' or a 'new international responsibility' assigned to it.

The 'new international role' for Germany is more than Genscher's 'responsibility' rhetoric. However, the self-restrictive character of the policy of responsibility in Germany would not fit its 'new role' that it should have to take on. Genscher's policy of responsibility was losing credibility both inside and outside the country. Haftendorn stated that, 'it will only be able to overcome those elements of self-restraint which are clearly out of step with today's challenges if its government's ability to combine foreign policy demands with domestic needs is strengthened. Thus, the links between foreign and domestic policy should be increased in strength and number'.[33] The 'new international role' of Germany does not only mean assuming *new political responsibilities* (taking an active role in formulating the international politics), but also *new military responsibilities* (taking an active role in out-of-area operations). The growing perception among policymakers in Germany is that political responsibility inevitably necessitates the use of military force. Whenever political discussions about the of use military force to protect human rights and enforcing of international law as a legitimate in-

[32] Helga Haftendorn, 'Gulliver in the Centre of Europe: International Involvement and National Capabilities for Action' in Heurlin, B. (ed.), p.113.
[33] *Ibid*, p.115.

strument of foreign policy comes up, it signals the coming of a big pain that German policy-makers would often have to face.

With the arrival of two younger and more dynamic new ministers in foreign and defence ministries, Klaus Kinkel (FDP) and Volker Rühe (CDU) respectively in 1992, the policies of Genscher were questioned. In fact, Germany's moving towards shouldering new international responsibilities or questioning Genscher's policies do not mean that there have been funda-mental changes to all previous foreign and security policy norms and values. Thomas Berger argued that, 'while political cultural orientations can change in response to new conditions, they tend to change slowly and in an incremental fashion, discarding more peripheral, instru-mental beliefs rather than revising core norms and values'.[34] Although the subject of whether Germany had fundamentally changed or revised its core norms and values is a deadlock within itself, one thing is very clear that Germany is practicing 'new style diplomacy' after Genscher.

In the early 1990s, debate upon whether the use of military force is a legitimate instrument of foreign policy or not divided the political parties in Germany into two camps. On the one side, the CDU/CSU and a group within the FDP supported the use of power – the military option should be attentively employed. On the other side, the SPD, a group within the FDP, and the Greens accepted the responsibilities of the united Germany and put an emphasis on the burden of German history and the mission of home defence, which was explicitly authorised by the *Grundgesetz*. Genscher's successor Kinkel stressed the moral component of the German for-eign policy, but at the same time pointed out 'his embarrassment at NATO and WEU meet-ings when he is unable to offer a contribution to military peace-keeping or peace-making op-erations and critics that Germany has the "only constitution in the world" – except for Japan –

that prohibits the country from using its armed forces even for the most noble or humanitarian of causes'.[35] Similarly, it is stated in *The Economist* that, Rühe defined 'the new German approach' as '*it can be immoral not to use force*' (emphasis added).[36] This debate calls for the third feature of the German foreign and security policy: Is the policy of civilian power still applicable in Germany or not?

German policymakers' self-restraint understanding and their focus on Genscher's non-military security matters only, characterised the German foreign and security policy with the conscious avoidance of being boastful, the elimination of high profile and classical power politics ('hard-power'). The resultant foreign policy role concept has been cultivated by Hans Maull and described Germany as a 'civilian power' (in other words, in a 'soft-power' style).[37] He argued that, "'civilian power' represents a foreign policy role concept – a complex bundle of norms, beliefs, attitudes and perceptions – which tells a state (or, more precisely, its decision makers) how to behave'.[38] After the Second World War, Maull argued, the West German foreign and security policy was embedded into a civilian power paradigm. The major norms and beliefs of the ideal type civilian power were summarised by Maull in three dimensions:

- Willingness to take initiatives and assuming responsibilities in non-military spheres, primarily political (diplomatic bargaining) and economic (chequebook diplomacy), for shaping events.

---

[34] Berger, T., 'Unsheathing the Sword?', *World Affairs*, (Vol.158, No.4, Spring 1996), p.180.
[35] Gordon, P. H., 'Berlin's Difficulties. The Normalisation of German Foreign Policy', *Orbis*, (Vol.38, Spring 1994), pp.234-235.
[36] 'No Longer Shy About Being German', *The Economist*, (November 9, 1996), p.58.
[37] Maull, H. W., 'Germany and Japan: The New Civilian Powers,' *Foreign Affairs*, (Vol.69, No.5, Winter 1990/1991), pp.91-106; Maull, H. W., 'Zivilmacht Bundesrepublik Deutschland,' *Europa Archiv*, (May 10, 1992), pp.269-79. Reimund Seidelmann defined 'hard' and 'soft-power' as: 'Hard-power' is concerned with the pursuit of national interests and the maintenance of international order through the projection of power resources (in particular military power); 'soft-power' is the search for global justice and peace by way of compromise, co-operation, and consensus using primarily non-military means. Quoted in Prince, K. M., 'Under Construction: The Berlin Republic', *Washington Quarterly*, (Vol.22, No.3, Summer 1999), p.133.
[38] Maull, H. W., 'German Foreign Policy, Post-Kosovo: Still a 'Civilian Power'?', *German Politics*, (Vol.9, No.2, August 2000), p.14.

- Strong emphasis on institution-building, promotion of rule of law, democracy, economic liberalisation in international affairs and transfer of sovereignty through axiomatic multilateralism, supra-nationalism, co-operation, interdependence (*Verflechtung*) and integration.

- Use of military power for the implementation of international norms and decisions left as residual and subject to the authorisation of international law. Pursuing a value-based foreign policy (anchored in certain norms) – even if there are no significant immediate material interests at stake – should be given special priority. E.g. interventions in humanitarian situations, crisis management and prevention.[39]

Maull and Gordon argued that Germany has developed a foreign policy style which corresponds to its vocation as a *Handelsstaat* (trading state) during the Cold War: 'The Federal Republic conducts its foreign policy predominantly – but not exclusively – in the role and style of a merchant.'[40] Therefore, the main concern of German governments is securing their interests through unrestricted trade and stability in international regimes. Garton Ash argued that economically Germany diffuses its power in two distinct ways: 'First, economic instruments and incentives have been liberally and skilfully used by the German government to achieve its foreign policy goals. Second, the Bundesbank's single-minded pursuit of domestic monetary and fiscal policy objectives has had a direct impact on the economies of Germany's neighbours and trading partners, and hence on the country's foreign relations. The Bundesbank has, as it were, made foreign policy by not making foreign policy'.[41] Likewise, as Patricia Davis put it:

---

[39] With an additional information from Maull's other articles, this three dimensions mainly follows Maull, H. W., 'German Foreign Policy, Post-Kosovo: Still a 'Civilian Power?', pp.16-17; also see '3. Deutsch-Französischen Dialog – Mit Sicherheit in die europäische Zukunft: Deutsch-französische Perspectiven einer gemeinsamen Sicherheits – und Verteidigungspolitik', *Diskussionsbericht*, (Saarbrücken: 31Mai-01 Juni, 2001).
[40] Gutjahr, L., *German Foreign and Defence Policy after Unification*, p.84.
[41] Timothy Garton Ash, 'Germany's Choice' in Mertes, M., Müller, S. & Winkler, H. A. (eds.), *In Search of Germany*, (US: Transactions Publications, 1996), p.82.

'The foundation of Germany's "new patriotism" lay in its citizens' admiration for

German social and economic achievements, [in which] a majority of Germans

clearly [think] their nation superior to others...'[42]

Keeping this 'civilianised' power image and Genscher's low-profile diplomacy at the begin-

ning of the tragedy in the former Yugoslavia (1991) in mind, a significant historical record

will be overlooked if one leaves out the German premature recognition of Croatia and

Slovenia. Although German officials justified their action through basing their recognition on

self-determination rights and the inability of multilateral initiatives to stop the massive blood-

shed, the German recognition could be seen as an assertive foreign and security policy feature

of the German diplomacy. The decision of Genscher certainly generated a great deal of criti-

cism not only abroad, but also within Germany. Robert Dorff argued that as a result of that

reaction the Kohl government consciously adopted a 'lower key' approach in later years.[43]

Kohl also said on a television programme in 1995 that, 'United Germany is number one in

Europe, but we ought not to advertise it and better not talk too much about it'.[44] However, for

some German politicians, particularly those on the conservative flank, optimal Germany in

the post-Cold War era ought to have a more assertive foreign policy than Germany in the

Cold War era – Germany should be more like 'the other' nation-states. They believe that the

changed context of the European security order has already ended the viability of Germany's

---

[42] Quoted in Prince, K. M., 'Under Construction: The Berlin Republic', p.131; The opinion poll conducted by *Le Figaro/SOFRES* among French and Germans indicated the superiority of Germany in economic matters. The French response to the question: Which country is more economically powerful? It was 19% for France and 73% for Germany. The German response to the same question was 8% for France and 80% for Germany. 'French Unease Over the New Germany', *The Economist*, (March 6, 1999), pp.48-52.

[43] Dorff also quoted Lefebvre and Lombardi's interpretations: 'International criticism that that action [the recognition] had exacerbated the situation in the former Yugoslavia and, moreover, the charge that it was "throwing its weight around" within the EU, led the Federal Republic to alter its approach. During the subsequent four years, it adopted the role of "helpful fixer," operating behind the scenes in the pursuit of a negotiated peace settlement.' Dorff, R. H., 'Germany and the Future of European Security,' *World Affairs*, (Vol.161, No.2, Fall 1998), pp.59-68.

[44] Kohl quoted in Edinger, L. J. & Nacos, B. L., *From Bonn to Berlin – German Politics in Transition*, (New York: Columbia University Press, 1998), p.243.

role as a civilian power and they demanded a permanent seat for Germany in the UN Security Council and active participation in international peacekeeping and peacemaking missions. While, for others, particularly those on the left and part of the liberal flank, optimal Germany might be expected to focus more on co-operative, trans-national values and should stay re-strained – Germany should be more like a model for 'the other' nation-states. Sperling argued that, the last group usually 'equate Germany's status as a civilian power with the status of an incomplete power'.[45] Moreover, Wilds pointed out: 'the experience of National Socialism represented a profound obstacle to the cultivation of conventional patriotism as it clearly dis-rupts the perception of organic historical continuity and acted to discredit indigenous national traditions'.[46] Germany's foreign and security dilemma is actually expressed more vividly by Maull and Gordon as:

> *'If Germany is to remain a civilian power, it will have to convince others to be*
> *'more like Germany' and to convince them that compromise, multilateralism and*
> *civilian solutions are always best. That will be no easy task and if it does not work,*
> *Germany may be forced to become more like them!'*[47]

Although the military-diplomatic missions of Germany are currently incremental, the pre-vailing feature of German security policy is to avoid any accusations of military activism. Moreover, it has to be emphasised that anti-militaristic sentiments in Germany remain intact. Therefore, apart from core missions such as territorial defence, German officials consider military-diplomatic missions primarily within a multilateral framework.

---

[45] James Sperling, 'Less Than Meets the Eye: A Reconsideration of German Hegemony' in Hampton, M. N. & Søe, C. (ed.), p.259; For an excellent review article on this subject also see McAdams, J., 'Germany After Unification – Normal at Last?', *World Politics*, (Vol.49, January 1997), pp.282-308.
[46] Wilds, K., 'Identity Creation and the Culture of Contrition: Recasting 'Normality' in the Berlin Republic', *German Politics*, (Vol.9, No.1, April 2000), p.86.
[47] Quoted in William Paterson 'Beyond Bipolarity: German Foreign Policy in a Post-Cold-War World' in Smith, G., Paterson, W. E. & Padgett, S. (eds.), *Developments in German Politics 2*, (UK: Macmillan, 1996), p.141.

(1.2)   Perceptions Before and After the Decision of the Federal Constitutional Court

(FCC): Germany Crossed the *Rubikon*

The question of an active German involvement in international crisis for preserving world

peace and security goes back to the creation and integration of the Bundeswehr in NATO in

1955. Following this rubric, although the military policy of Germany was principally confined

to homeland defence and alliance deterrence only, the NATO out-of-area rhetoric was actu-

ally rooted in the Cold War era.[48] Moreover, Germany's participation in the UN in 1973 pre-

sented another serious problem, that of defining it a new international military role regarding

the deployment of the Bundeswehr in UN peacekeeping missions. As a result of the high in-

ternational demand for German participation in international crisis, the Federal Security

Council interpreted during the SPD-FDP government in 1982 and confirmed later by the

CDU/CSU-FDP government that the *Grundgesetz* was prohibiting any German participation

in out-of-area missions. This non-military foreign policy stance is formally identified as a

'security-political consensus'.[49] However, the German government's rejection of the US re-

quest to support sweeping the Persian Gulf of mines, laid during the Iran-Iraq War in 1987,

and the UN request for Germany's participating in various peacekeeping efforts triggered a

protracted debate among the German political elite.

Not until the Iraqi invasion of Kuwait in 1991 and consequent sharp criticisms from the US

and other Allies against Germany's reluctance to assume any direct military operations in the

liberation of Kuwait, did the German government considered revising legal and political con-

---

[48] In the Cold War period, the out-of-area issue rose with the US demand of German military support during the Vietnam War (Germany rejected, and sent a floating hospital instead); international demand to stop the Greek Cypriots organized brutal military attacks against the Turkish Cypriots in Cyprus (Germany decided to provide a German component for an eventual UN intervention in 1964, but it did not take place); the Arab-Israeli War in 1967 (Germany accepted to participate in an eventual multilateral force to open the Egyptian blockade of the Gulf of Aqaba); and, again, within the context of Middle East in the 1980s. See Maull, H. W., 'Germany and the Use of Force: Still a 'Civilian Power'?', *Survival*, (Vol.42, No.2, Summer 2000), pp.67-68.
[49] According to the Federal Security Council, the Bundeswehr would not be used as a foreign policy instrument outside the East-West conflict and Germany's participation in UN operations would be restricted to the conflict

straints upon the Bundeswehr. German policymakers rejection of the Allies' call for military

assistance, based on the insufficient legal justification for out-of-area activities, left Germany

with no choice but to play the secondary role of financial contributor.[50] This was a role that

did not fit German policymaker's previous promises with regard to sharing greater responsi-

bilities in maintaining international peace and security. The CDU's Kohl announced at the

Bundestag in 1991: 'There is for us Germans no niche in world politics, and there can be no

flight from responsibilities; we intend to make a contribution to the world of peace, freedom,

and justice'.[51] In order to be seen as an active and responsible member of the international

community, Kohl committed to revise the German Constitution for the Bundeswehr's UN-

mandated out-of-area peacekeeping and peacemaking missions and supported the interna-

tional mine-clearing action in the Persian Gulf (UN resolution 678). The deployment of mine-

sweepers in the Persian Gulf indicated the beginning of an effective 'salami tactic' (step-by-

step approach from 1991 to 1994) of the Defence Minister Volker Rühe. The 'salami tactic'

has proved its effectiveness through the Bundeswehr's commitment in various UN peace-

keeping missions with the aim of accustoming the German public and the army to out-of-area

deployments without a prior interpretation of the *Grundgesetz*.[52]

As far as the main opposition party SPD is concerned, although the pacifists (SPD-left and

anti-NATO wing) had secured victory over the pragmatists and portrayed themselves as pro-

moters of fundamental reforms in the European and international system since the resignation

of Chancellor Helmut Schmidt in 1982, the SPD has always had some intra-party difficulties

prevention. See Hoffman, A., 'Germany and the Role of the Bundeswehr: A New Consensus,' *Institute for German Studies Discussion Papers Series No. 98/9*, (UK: University of Birmingham, September 1998), pp.4-5.
[50] When the Second Gulf War began, Germany was in the middle of the Two-Plus-Four negotiations. Therefore, Karl Kaiser argued that there were good reasons for the German government not to sent troops to the Gulf. Kaiser, K., 'Forty Years of German Membership in NATO', *NATO Review*, (Vol.43, No.4, July 1995), pp.3-8.
[51] Kohl quoted in Jeffrey J. Anderson & John B. Goodman 'Mars and Minerva?', p.47.
[52] Germany also provided air support for UNSCOM (UN Special Commission) in Iraq (UN resolution 687) and supplied food, shelter and field hospitals to Kurdish refugees in Turkey and Iran (UN resolution 688). As a result of the Turkish request for protection against an Iraqi attack, Germany also deployed in January 1991 an air wing

in making a coherent and clear foreign and security policy. As a result of the strong pacifist

wing in the party, the SPD has never had an easy time in defining an appropriate military role

in foreign policy.[53] The debate between pacifists and pragmatists escalated after the issue of

Bundeswehr participation in out-of-area operations came into view with the Iraqi invasion of

Kuwait in 1991. The pacifists wanted Germany, except for self-defence, to contribute to non-

violent means of conflict prevention and strongly rejected the Bundeswehr's participation in

out-of-area operations. On the other side, the pragmatists were more willing to use the

Bundeswehr in UN-mandated actions. The dispute was somehow resolved in 1993 and the

SPD foreign and security policy was modified for the use of the Bundeswehr in UN 'blue

helmet' peacekeeping operations abroad, but not in peacemaking, and not in NATO opera-

tions without a UN or CSCE mandate. On the other side, the Greens strongly rejected the de-

ployment of the Bundeswehr to out-of-area during the Second Gulf War in 1991 and advo-

cated purely civilian peace politics. The Greens demand the dismantling of the Bundeswehr

and discarding or substituting NATO with the CSCE or the UN.

Although the consensus between the government and opposition was reached on the basis of

'purely humanitarian' missions from the Persian Gulf to peacekeeping (medical corps) mis-

sion in Cambodia in 1992, the consensus was broken when German warships and surveillance

aircrafts participated in the NATO-WEU co-ordinated maritime operation in the Adriatic Sea

on April 2, 1993, to help monitor the embargo against Serbia on the basis of UN Resolutions

713 and 757. This new mission of the Bundeswehr under NATO and the WEU banner, other

than using it for UN humanitarian missions or as a foreign policy instrument for self-defence,

caused severe protests from the opposition parties in the *Bundestag.* Even though the foreign

---

to NATO ally Turkey within the framework of the collective defence principle. Even that deployment became a
serious debate between the government and opposition parties at that time.
[53] Giessmann, H. J., 'The "Cocooned Giant": Germany and European Security', *Hamburger Beiträge zur
Friedensforschung und Sicherheitspolitik,* (Hamburg: Institut für Friedensforschung und Sicherheitspolitik an
der Universität Hamburg, No.116, September 1999), p.17.

policy spokesman of the SPD, Karsten Voigt, from the pragmatists tried to assert that the distinction between peacekeeping and peacemaking is impossible, the pacifists (Heidi Wieczorek-Zeul, Oskar Lafontaine and Gerhard Schröder) rejected such a claim and challenged the German presence in the Adriatic due to the absence of a UN-mandate.[54] The logic behind the SPD MPs criticism was that NATO is not a regional organisation appropriate for collective security under Chapter VIII of the UN Charter.[55]

On the other hand, the Greens party, which merged with the Eastern German party Alliance'90 in June 1993, is deeply rooted in pacifist and non-militaristic principles, thereby strictly rejected any form of military as a political instrument. The Greens/Alliance'90, was divided even more bitterly than the SPD over the issue of military force use. The Greens, much like the SPD, has been divided into two distinct wings: the *Realo faction*, gathered around Joschka Fischer, who advocates the idea that the party should be flexible and reform itself according to given realities; and, the *Fundi faction*, left wing, like former party member Jutta Ditfurth, who are entrenched in the principal ideas like pacifism, anti-militarism, basic democracy into the Greens political identity and advocate the general rejection of the existing socio-economic order in favour of a radical political and social overhaul.[56] In fact, the main debate between the two factions derives from Germany's past. The *Fundi faction* believes that Germany is under moral as well as political burden and bears the responsibility for World War II. German military force use is therefore unacceptable. On the other hand, the *Realo faction* argues that this is the primary reason why Germany has to support military actions aimed at preventing aggressions similar to those Hitler brought about.

---

[54] Harald Müller 'Military Intervention For European Security' in Freedman, L. (ed.), *Military Intervention in European Conflicts*, (UK: The Political Quarterly Publishing Co. Ltd., 1994), pp.134-136.
[55] Art.52 of the UN Charter-Chapter VIII, which is about regional arrangements or agencies that their activities should be consistent with *Purposes* and *Principles* of the UN, considered by some of the SPD MPs as incompatible with NATO military operations.
[56] Prince, K. M., 'Under Construction: The Berlin Republic', p.122.

The SPD MPs and the government's coalition partner FDP MPs argued that the Bundeswehr participation to NATO and WEU operations is not *collective security*, but a *collective defence* matter, and this requires a substantive legal judgement. On the other hand, the CDU/CSU MPs argued that action is taken in order to show the reliability of Germany to its allies and this matter requires a constitutional judgement, which would be based on political not on legal grounds. Müller described the differences between the CDU and the FDP as, 'while the CDU did not see a contradiction between power and responsibility, the FDP wanted Germany to choose responsibility over power'.[57] The SPD demonstrated its historical scepticism towards NATO and firmly rejected the out-of-area operations of the Bundeswehr. It insisted that the Bundeswehr could just serve as peacekeepers in UN operations, not only under non-combat but also ceasefire conditions like the one in Cambodia. Although the FDP followed a similar path to the SPD, it moved to the CDU side after the Second Gulf War and claimed that the Bundeswehr's role should be more than just peacekeeping.[58] On the other hand, the CDU was prepared to dispatch the Bundeswehr not only for peacekeeping, but also for peacemaking operations (UN Chapter VII missions) – except for direct military combat missions – in which active military engagements might take place. In addition to the UN missions, the CDU was also planning to put the Bundeswehr under UN-mandated NATO out-of-area operations or similar missions conducted under the aegis of the WEU. Moreover, the *Weißbuch* of 1994, in addition to the *Hauptverteidigungskräfte* (Main Defence Force), for the first time had stated the creation of an highly mobile *Krisenreaktionskräfte* (Crisis Reaction Force) and a supreme command for the purpose of enabling the Bundeswehr to participate effectively in UN conflict prevention missions, as well as in NATO out-of-area and WEU multilateral crisis-

---

[57] Harald Müller 'German Foreign Policy After Unification' in Stares, P. B., *The New Germany and the New Europe*, (US: The Brookings Institution, 1992), p.134. For a similar argument from Defence Minister Volker Rühe (CDU) see Janning, J., 'A German Europe – a European Germany? On the Debate Over Germany's Foreign Policy', *International Affairs*, (Vol.72, No.1, 1996), p.39.

[58] Harald Müller 'German Foreign Policy After Unification' in Stares, P. B., pp.140-141. Gutjahr argued that, as with other issues, the FDP officially adapted a middle course between the CDU's *realpolitik* and the SPD's *idealism*. See Gutjahr, L., *German Foreign and Defence Policy after Unification*, p.100.

management operations.[59] The ambitious goal of Kohl was to eliminate all obstacles in front of the Bundeswehr's participation in a common European defence structure. A broad interpretation and application of law was already made *politically* by the CDU before the matter was transferred to the FCC. This redefinition of Bundeswehr missions was challenged by the SPD and the FDP and the case was brought before the FCC questioning what the correct interpretation of relevant articles in the *Grundgesetz* was.

While leaving many details unanswered, the FCC in Karlsruhe clarified the controversy centred at the Bundeswehr's out-of-area role on July 12, 1994. The FCC had focused on the interpretation of two problematic articles (Art.87(a)(2) and Art.24(2)) separately and jointly.[60] It is clear that Art.87(a)(2) permits the maintenance and use of armed forces for self-defence only and Art.24(2) empowers the Federation to participate in systems of collective security. For this reason, Art.24(2) authorises the participation of the Bundeswehr into activities performed according to the rules of collective security systems. Apart from the self-defence function of the Bundeswehr, the FCC considers the authorisation of the Bundeswehr's involvement in collective security systems as *lex specialis* (special law).[61] The core dilemma was actually the interpretation of the 'collective security system'.

According to international law, collective security is for deterring any illegal resort to force use among the member states of a particular organisation, e.g. the UN system. In view of this, the Bundeswehr's participation in NATO operations could not be considered as an Art.24(2) case, because NATO is entirely a collective defence system, which guarantees mutual assis-

---

[59] *Weißbuch 1994*, No.510, 519.
[60] Art.87(a)(2) says:'Apart from defence, the armed forces may only be used to an extent explicitly permitted by the *Grundgesetz.*' Art.24(2) stands for: 'The Federation may enter into a system of mutual collective security for the maintenance of peace; in doing so, it will consent to such limitations upon its rights of sovereignty as will bring about and secure a peaceful and lasting order in Europe and among the nations of the world.' Sartorius, C., *Verfassungs- und Verwaltungsgesetze der Bundesrepublik Deutschland*. Hereafter: Sartorius.
[61] The FCC does not explicitly interpret Art.87(a)(2). See Zöckler, M., 'Germany in Collective Security Systems – Anything Goes?', *European Journal of International Law*, (Vol.16, No.2, 1998).

tance and protection of Alliance members against attacks from a non-member. Until 1994, nobody in the FCC had attempted to interpret the 'collective security system' as it might also cover the defence alliances. The FCC construed that this concept might not be limited to collective security in the classical sense. The FCC finally found some leeway in this dilemma through Art.51 of the UN Charter as collective security and defence alliances are *not mutually exclusive* but *supplement each other.*[62] With such an interpretation, one can easily predict that not only the UN, but also NATO and the WEU could qualify as organisations establishing a 'collective security system.' Hence, the FCC supported the CDU side and approved the participation of German warships and surveillance aircraft in the NATO-WEU co-ordinated maritime operation in the Adriatic Sea as constitutional on the basis that NATO-WEU operations were implementing the UN Security Council resolutions and somehow were integrated into the collective security system.[63]

On the other hand, the FCC also decided in favour of the SPD claims that the Bundeswehr is not a power tool of the executive branch, but a *Parlamentsheer* (also called 'Parliamentary Army'). In other words, the *Bundestag* guarantees integration of the Bundeswehr into a democratic order under the rule of law and scrutinises its functioning. Former FDP Foreign Minister Klaus Kinkel strongly opposed any 'militarisation' attempts of the German foreign policy, and divisions between him and former CDU Defence Minister Volker Rühe later

---

[62] Although the UN reacts to an act of aggression through diplomatic and economic sanctions (Art.41), collective security system's last sanction is military (Art.51), Chapter VII. Art.41 of the UN Charter stands for: 'The Security Council may decide what measures not involving the use of armed forces are to be employed to give effect to its decisions, and it may call upon the UN to apply such measures. These may include complete or partial interruption of economic relations and of rail, sea, air, postal, telegraphic, radio, and other means of communication, and the severance of diplomatic relations.' Art.51 refers to: 'Nothing in the present Charter shall impair the inherent right of collective self-defence if an armed attack occurs against a Member of the UN, until the Security Council has taken measures necessary to maintain international peace and security....'

[63] The NATO-WEU operation was related to the fulfilment of Art.41 and Art.48 of the UN Charter. Art.48 refers to: 'The action required to carry out the decisions of the Security Council for the maintenance of international peace and security shall be taken by the Members of the UN or by some of them, as the Security Council may determine.' The UN Charter is available at <http://www.un.org>

turned into conflicting claims to leadership in the government's foreign and security policy.[64]

The insistence of the SPD and the FDP turned the employment of the Bundeswehr into a puzzling process. The FCC pronounced a new constitutional principle that the employment of the Bundeswehr requires the prior approval of the *Bundestag* by simple majority voting in each single case.[65] In addition to the requirement of a positive vote in the *Bundestag*, the following conditions, which were outlined by the Foreign Minister in October 1994, have to be met before the Bundeswehr's participation in UN, WEU, or NATO operations:

- Specified operations must have some foundations in the constitution of respective organisations;

- They must be carried out within the framework and according to the rules of the collective security system and international law;

- The government has to 'prove' that risk of death for participant Bundeswehr soldiers would be low;

- The Bundeswehr's participation should be part of the solution in post-conflict peace operations, not before, and must not exacerbate the conflict. This could be the case particularly in areas invaded by Hitler's army during World War II, where some people still might be living and feeling strong animosity;

- They must be carried out with other partners or allies and an institutional context is also necessary for multilateral action.[66]

[64] Werner A. Perger argued that foreign minister can be said to be guilty of trespassing responsibilities of defence minister, the latter in turn has been accused of touring the world like a foreign minister, making foreign policy speeches on his travels to America and elsewhere. Perger in Roger Morgan 'German Foreign Policy and Domestic Politics' in Heurlin, B. (ed.), p.165-166.
[65] See *Sartorius*, Art.42(2) of the *Grundgesetz*, p.24.
[66] Kinkel, K., 'Peace-keeping Missions: Germany Can Now Play Its Role', *NATO Review*, (Vol.42, No.5, October 1994), pp.3-7; Maull, H. W., 'Germany and the Use of Force: Still a 'Civilian Power'?', p.71; The third condition is leading to somewhat an absurd consequence that the government will be in a position of judging in between operations pertaining to high-risk or low-risk! Harald Müller 'Military Intervention For European Security: The German Debate' in Freedman, L. (ed.), p.130.

It is almost impossible in the new security environment to make distinction between 'armed' and 'purely humanitarian' operations. Nevertheless, the entire spectrum of possible missions ranging from modern guerrilla warfare to Second Gulf War-style combat missions were made possible with the creation of the *Krisenreaktionskräfte*.[67] In parallel to this, the FCC empowered the *Bundestag* to decide on whether to send the Bundeswehr on all kinds of peacekeeping operations authorised by the Security Council, irrespective whether if these forces are empowered to apply coercive measures under Chapter VII of the UN Charter.

Since the FCC decision in July 1994, public and party support for Germany's participation in politically and diplomatically inevitable multinational military peacekeeping operations of the WEU, NATO, and the UN, have been tremendously boosted.[68] This public and party support has been demonstrated during the successful participation of the Bundeswehr in UN-mandated NATO aerial attacks against Serbia in 1994. This was the first time that Germany assigned *combat units* to a UN mission. Participation of the Bundeswehr in these operations began with the IFOR (Implementation Force, NATO-led evacuation of the UNPROFOR (UN Protection Force)) in December 1995 and continued with the SFOR (Stabilisation Force), which replaced the IFOR in December 1996. These successful German military actions led Rühe to conclude: 'In only a few years, a new consensus about the central tasks of German security policy, the mission and role of the armed forces, has developed'.[69]

The FCC clarified *legal* questions with regard to the Bundeswehr's participation in out-of-area operations, but left many questions of detail to painful *political* interpretation in the

---

[67] *Weißbuch 1994*, No.538.
[68] Those who agreed on future peacekeeping and peace-enforcement tasks of the Bundeswehr in West Germany: 63% agree, 35% disagree in 1994 and 86% agree, 11% disagree in 1999. East Germany: 52% agree, 47% disagree in 1994 and 82% agree, 14% disagree in 1999. For more statistical detail see, Hoffmann, H.-V., "New Tasks of the Bundeswehr in Communication Processes Between Society and the Military", *Akademie der Bundeswehr für Information und Kommunikation*, (Germany: AIK-Texte, June 1999).
[69] Rühe quoted in Johannes Bohnen 'Germany' in Howorth, J. & Menon, A. (ed.), *The EU and National Defence Policy*, (London: Routledge, 1997), p.55.

Bundestag. Which specific decisions are left to the political process? What kind of collective security operations does the *Grundgesetz* approve? Should Bundeswehr deployments be confined to the European theatre (Rühe's preference) or should the mandate be a global one (Kinkel's preference)? Neither *Weißbuch* nor the FCC had indicated the difference between the various forms of crisis management missions, such as peacekeeping, peacemaking, or combat missions. The fuzziness of the FCC's decision was criticised by Zöckler as, even in classical peacekeeping (or purely humanitarian) operations the use of force might be needed for self-defence, or, initially peaceful operations might escalate and quickly reach to a level where outright military force is used.[70] Nor did the FCC clarify whether the Bundeswehr could also be used in out-of-area operations without a UN Security Council (UNSC) mandate.

Germany has undergone profound changes in its foreign policy from strictly refusing the use of any sort of military power, except self-defence, to one of participating in multinational combat operations and accepting the probability of casualties. No one can deny that Germany crossed the *Rubikon* and is coming to see its international roles and responsibilities in different terms than it did prior to the FCC's decision.

(1.3) Reflections from the SPD-the Greens/Alliance'90 Government

Since the beginning of rules 'salami tactics' of Rühe in 1991 and the subsequent decision of the FCC in July 1994, discussions about active German involvement in international peacekeeping operations took place amongst all groups of the political spectrum, particularly more fervently in the SPD and the Greens/Alliance'90 than in the CDU/CSU and the FDP. Crisis management and intervention missions, as new key missions for the Bundeswehr, have cate-

---

[70] Zöckler, M., 'Germany in Collective Security Systems – Anything Goes?'

gorically been added to collective defence.[71] The SPD-the Greens/Alliance'90 government's support for the Bundeswehr's participation to the Kosovo military operation verifies that Germany is increasingly undertaking these new key missions as part of its policy of responsibility. This section will analyse the government's foreign and security policy commitments.

Since public opinion in Germany has steadily changed with the brutal images of atrocities in Bosnia in 1993, the FCC's decision in 1994, and the Serbian aggression again in Kosovo in 1999, so did the non-military foreign and security policy of the SPD. The initial strict non-military humanitarian policy of the SPD, changed later to the approval of peacekeeping missions under a UN-mandate in 1993, and finally transformed its foreign and security policy – primarily through the efforts of Rudolf Scharping, Günter Verheugen and Karsten Voigt – to the Bundeswehr participation in peace-enforcement and peacekeeping missions both for political and moral reasons under the authority of the UN Charter (Chapter VII) and *Grundgesetz* (Art.24(2)).[72]

The first sign of change in the coalition partner's (the Greens party) attitude towards the use of force came in 1994 when the party's Regional Council voted for the UN military intervention in Bosnia and German military participation in the UN system of collective security on the basis of humanitarian principles. The Greens support for NATO military operations were conditional on a clear UN-mandate. Although this stance was seen as strengthening the *Realo faction* in the intra-party balance, the *Realo faction* was overruled by the *Fundi faction*, who want to abolish NATO and the Bundeswehr, civilising international politics, and end of power politics, at the Magdeburg Party Congress in March 1998. Although Joschka Fischer came

[71] Walter Schilling quoted in Szabo, S. F., 'Germany: Strategy and Defence at a Turning Point', *AICGS Academic Advisory Council Brief*, (US: Johns Hopkins University). <http://www.aicgs.org/IssueBriefs/szabo.html> (Visited on: August 18, 2000).
[72] Maull, H. W., 'German Foreign Policy, Post-Kosovo: Still a 'Civilian Power?'', p.6; Giessmann, H. J., 'The "Cocooned Giant"', p.17.

forward with the idea that he use of military force at certain times and under certain situations is needed, his redefinition of the Greens foreign policy principles does not compromise the party's mainstream policy. The Green's federal election programme in September 1998, *Grün ist der Wechsel* (Green is the Change), virtually kept the basics of the Greens foreign and security policy – *Entmilitarisierung und Zivilisierung: die Schlüssel der Friedenspolitik.*[73]

Fischer became well aware of various security threats in the new security environment and plans to thwart them with his 'soft-power' understanding comparable with the new German international responsibility in multilateral institutions. In his speech before the German Society for Foreign Affairs in Berlin on June 8, 1998, he said: '*Classic and military power politics will continue to play an important role for quite some time, but it will not really be able to contribute to the solution of urgent global problems...*' Later, Fischer continued his argument by referring to the principles of 'soft power': 'Globalisation is thus not only an economic question, but it entails taking the responsibility for the solution of global problems.... To find answers here will not be possible, I believe, in the framework of classic European nation states, but only in the framework of a strengthened international structure, with a power transfer to international organisations, with the UN on top'.[74]

Having mentioned all this, it should also be kept in mind that the Red-Green government made a strong commitment in September 1998 towards multilateralism, 'Europeanised' national identity and deeper European integration, which was motivated by multifaceted circumstances in a web of international institutions in order to achieve German interests and strate-

---

[73] Demilitarisation and Civilisation: A key to the policy for peace. See *Grün ist der Wechsel*, Bündnis 90/Die Grünen, Programm zur Bundestagswahl 1998, pp.141-142.
[74] He also said, '[Germany] will follow a policy of self-restraint, in other words a constrained foreign policy which no longer directly pursues national interest politics and which includes a clear rejection of any power-state politics.' Fischer, J., address to the German Society for Foreign Affairs, 'The Self-Restrained of Power Must be Maintained: Germany's Role and Objective in the Globalised World of the 21st Century', (Berlin: June 8, 1998).

gies. Chancellor Gerhard Schröder gave support to the previous government's foreign policy

and made a strong commitment for Euro and European integration. Rubinstein argued that

Schröder would follow tactical rather than principled policies and thus European integration

will proceed further, but will likely proceed at a much slower speed and stop more frequently

in response to local and national interest.[75] It will be fair to argue that Germany is now using a

new tone in its foreign policy: 'normality' without being 'normal'. Schröder has hinted his

support to the main three foreign and security policy areas (see above) and added that his gen-

eration is less shy in formulating German national interests: 'My generation and those fol-

lowing are Europeans because we want to be not because we have to be. [...] I am convinced

that our European partners want to have a self-confident German partner which is more cal-

culable than a German partner with an inferiority complex'.[76]

The appointment of Joschka Fischer to the position of Foreign Affairs Minister seemed to be

a radical change in the *Auswärtigen Amt* (Foreign Ministry). However, being the leader of the

Realo faction of the Green party, and in contrast to mainstream party policy, he continued

giving support to the integration of Germany into the EU/WEU and NATO and strongly

backed German military participation in the Balkans. In one of his first statements as Foreign

Minister, Fischer stated that his foreign policy '*would not be a Green foreign policy, but a

German foreign policy*' (emphasis added).[77] He often calls for what former President Roman

Herzog said in 1995, 'globalisation of the economy inevitably means also the globalisation of

foreign policy', and argues that in order to thwart 'soft' military threats in the new security

environment, the German foreign policy urgently needs to be globalised, though not with a

---

[75] Rubinstein, A. Z., 'Germans On Their Future', *Orbis*, (Vol.43, No.1, Winter 1999), p.143.
[76] Schröder quoted in Jeffrey, C. & Handl, V., 'Germany and Europe After Kohl:', p.19.
[77] Quoted in Szabo, S. F., 'Germany: Strategy and Defence at a Turning Point.'

'radical overhaul', but with 'recalibration.'[78] Fischer's vow is for *foreign policy realism*, but at the same time strictly advocates a future for Germany as a 'civilian power' abstaining from any form of 'hard power' projection.[79]

The previous CDU/CSU-FDP government formulated the *Krisenreaktionskräfte* in 1994 with the purpose of 'true' crisis management. However, Schröder, Fischer and Scharping presented their own crisis management strategies differently under the lofty title: *Deutsche Außenpolitik ist Friedenspolitik* (German foreign policy is policy for peace). The 'targets and values' of the foreign and security policy of the Red-Green coalition agreement highlighted the underlying differences of their policies from the previous government with *non-military* and *civilian* strategies of crisis management.[80] They also emphasised that the government would dedicate its efforts to strengthening the UN and facilitating increased participation of the Bundeswehr as peacekeepers (stand-by-forces) in UN-mandated missions in order to contribute to world peace and international security within the limits of *Grundgesetz* and international law.[81] Although they accepted NATO in its present form and empathised its importance for European security and stability, they opposed any NATO military action that would not be mandated by the UN.

---

[78] He underlined conflict prevention aspects as promoting universal respect for human rights and democracy, which are the key conditions for peace both within and between countries, enhancing the rule of law in international relations, making progress on disarmament and limiting arms exports, improving peacekeeping and peace-building mechanisms. Speech by Joschka Fischer at the general meeting of the German Society for Foreign Affairs, *German Information Centre*, (Berlin: November 24, 1999). Also, see the Greens/Alliance'90 party programme *Grün ist der Wechsel*, pp.148-149.
[79] Janning, J., 'A German Europe – a European Germany? On the Debate Over Germany's Foreign Policy', p.38
[80] 'Sie [Außen- und Sicherheitspolitik] wird sich mit aller Kraft um die Entwicklung und Anwendung von wirksamen Strategien und Instrumenten der Krisenprävention und der friedlichen Konfliktregelung bemühen. Sie wird sich dabei von der Verpflichtung zur weiteren **Zivilisierung** und **Verrechtlichung** der internatzionalen Beziehungen, zur Rüstungsbegrenzung und Abrüstung...' '1. Ziele und Werte' in *Koalitionsvereinbarung*.
[81] See Kapitel-VII 'Vereinte Nationen' in *Koalitionsvereinbarung*. Defence Minister Rudolf Scharping visited UN Secretary-General Kofi Annan in November 2000 and promised to provide more support to the UN from soldiers to logistic equipment. 'Demnächst deutsche Blauhelme', *Kölner Stadt-Anzeiger*, (November 3, 2000), p.6. For a good overview also see Hogrefe, J. & Szandar, A., 'Deutschland und die Globalisierung', *Der Spiegel*, (Nr.47, November 20, 2000), pp.40-42.

With these promises of the Red-Green government in mind, most of the opposition party members argued that concentrating on peace-oriented, civilian, conflict-prevention, non-military techniques would not lead to the government's effective participation in military crisis management operations. At this point, if one does not scrutinise the Bundeswehr's participation in the Kosovo operation under the Red-Green government, the first main foreign and military policy experience of the government will not only be overlooked, but also will not be seriously assessed. What were the conditions at the time that led the Red-Green government to break their promises and commitments by joining a NATO intervention force even in the absence of a UN-mandate? Before looking in-depth at the Kosovo operation and the Bundeswehr's historic participation in such a unique war, it is essential to know the relationship between Germany and the US/NATO and the EU/WEU. In which direction today the German foreign and security policy leaned? What are the pros and cons of Germany's relation to this two organisation? These questions will be analysed in the following section.

(2) New Visions: Rediscovering Germany in the European Defence Framework

(2.1) Continuities and Changes in the German-US/NATO Relationship

The German-US forward defence military strategy through NATO in the East-West conflict era was so immensely vital that West German governments always had to adjust, except in financial areas, their foreign and security policies to the American foreign and security policies in order to keep continuity in American-German common strategic interests. However, the disintegration of the Soviet Union and the achievement of Adenauer's primary foreign policy objective (unification of East and West Germany) in 1989/1990, have transformed NATO, West Germany, and the international security environment in Europe. From a semi-sovereign partner, Germany has suddenly upgraded to a full sovereign partner position and the four occupation powers pulled their forces back from Berlin. Smyser argued that, 'a no from united Germany is stronger, more credible, more important, and more sustainable than a West German no. It can be affirmed even under pressure. It will be more widely felt. It can and will shape the world'.[82]

Before the German unification, the Reagan Administration identified German-American relationship as a 'mature partnership', and later President Bush singled out Germany as the US's key strategic partner in Europe while he was offering Kohl the 'partnership in leadership' in Mainz in May 1989. The US urged West Germany to undertake more than just economic responsibilities and to engage in NATO out-of-area operations in order to be an active partner to the US in defending Western values politically and militarily in the world. This was the main American expectation that backing German reunification would in turn bring the US Germany's global partnership. Furthermore, this would have kept the US in Europe (militarily and economically) and Europe in NATO (the 'autonomous' European defence plan should not undermine NATO).

In the beginning of the 1990s, the German government did not want to play a global role or even a European one, which might have contradicted the foundations of the German foreign and security policy, neither alone nor with its closest ally, and thus it tried to avoid any commitment in that direction in order to keep German-American relations intact. For almost half a century, there had been some serious irritations on particular aspects of policies pursued by the US in NATO, but there was a little disagreement on the need to keep the partnership robust and NATO effective. The survival of NATO in the post-Cold War era was explained by Pond as: '[NATO] is a real community and not just a frontier alliance against the wolves. The trans-Atlantic community is in its own way already post-national ... that has made NATO the

---

[82] Smyser, W.R., *Germany and America – New Identities, Fateful Rift?*, (US: Westview Press, Inc., 1993), p.124.

longest-lived alliance in history'.[83] There are several reasons why the German government

remained so resolutely committed to NATO even after the end of the East-West conflict:

- It is an invaluable security balance where the US nuclear power is needed against a

  potential resurgent Russia[84] and offers an effective security mechanism to tackle a

  wide spectrum of problems in Central and Eastern Europe (CEE).

- Its integrated command structure is still an important platform for multilateral security

  and defence co-operation.

- It is an organisation founded on democratic Western values – 'a real community' –

  that could reliably bring security and stability to the entire European continent.

The German support for NATO should be understood from the perspective of reshaping it ac-

cording to the realities of the new Europe. German officials are aware of Germany's increased

strength in Europe as well as its weakness against stabilising the Central and Eastern

European turmoil. German officials are also aware that Germany needs US support to stabi-

lise CEE and the Americans are aware that the US needs German support to reshape and keep

NATO involved in Europe. Therefore, the German government was the prime mover behind

NATO's London Declaration of July 1990. This was the German push towards a complex

network of bilateral diplomatic and political co-operation between NATO and former Soviet

Union's Eastern European satellites. Former US Secretary of State James Baker and former

German Foreign Minister Hans-Dietrich Genscher expanded the scope of the London

Declaration in October 1991, when they presented the 'Euro-Atlantic Community' as

---

[83] Pond, E., 'Germany in the New Europe', *Foreign Affairs*, (Vol.71, No.2, Spring 1992), p.128.

[84] The Russian sheer size with regard to its military strength (conventional and nuclear) is still the biggest uncertainty in the 21st century. Russia's ambiguous 'near abroad' doctrine, the war in Chechnya and the Western reaction to Russian military operations for suppressing nationalist problems on Russia's southern flank have been the major signal of differences between the West and Russia. See Krautscheid, A. (MdB), 'Contemporary German Security Policy', *Institute for German Studies Discussion Papers Series No. 97/8*, (UK: University of Birmingham, August 1997), pp.12-14. For the 'near abroad' concept see Wyllie, James H. *European Security in the New Political Environment*, (New York: Addison Wesley Longman Limited, 1997), pp.69-70.

stretching from Vancouver to Vladivostok, and further formulated the North Atlantic Co-operation Council (NACC) during NATO's Rome Summit in November 1991. These were no doubt very much in the interest of Germany not only for primarily ending its status as a front-line state, but also for having access to the CEE market and cheap labour through financial-industrial penetration. In the same Summit, Germany also prodded for the adaptation of NATO's 'New Strategic Concept', which grew out of the Alliance strategy announced in July 1990, backed the formulation of a smaller, more flexible and mobile multilateral corps (ACE Rapid Reaction Corps). NATO countries also declared their intention to co-operate with non-NATO countries and to curtail the Alliance's military functions.[85]

In relation to German traditional political and strategic policies, while Rühe put forward the proposal for NATO's enlargement in 1993 to include Poland, Hungary, the Czech Republic, and Slovakia, Kinkel rejected this and instead insisted on keeping close ties with Russia.[86] Nevertheless, the US push for NATO enlargement and the Partnership for Peace (PfP) initia-tive, which were planned with the aim of inviting the NACC partner countries and CSCE states to join NATO's Brussels Summit on January 10-11, 1994, forced Kinkel to take a step back. Only seven months later, former US President Clinton offered Bonn a 'unique partner-ship' with Washington on July 1, 1994, in the aftermath of the FCC's affirmative decision in favour of the Bundeswehr's participation to out-of-area missions. Whilst German motives for NATO enlargement were strategic and political, the Clinton Administration's policy was based on promoting democracy and free market economy in the CEE. There was no serious resistance to NATO's enlargement amongst Western European countries and no one doubted that democracy and the free market economy would bring stability to the region. However,

---

[85] For more information: 'London Declaration on Transformed North Atlantic Alliance', *North Atlantic Council Heads of State and Government Meeting*, (Brussels: NATO Office of Information and Press, July 5-6, 1990).
[86] See Kinkel's arguments in Michael Meimeth, 'Germany' in Brenner, M. (ed.), *NATO and Collective Security*, (UK: Macmillan Press Ltd., 1998), p.91; Rubinstein, A. Z., 'Germans On Their Future', p.134.

the two US stratagem struck them: *Firstly*, the strategy of finding a *raison d'être* to retain NATO and consolidating the US hegemonic position in Europe through NATO's out-of-area operations (peacekeeping and peace-enforcement) and developing the ESDI and the CJTF in order to bypass the French aims of creating an 'autonomous' European 'Pillar of Defence'. *Secondly*, while sharing burdens and responsibilities in Europe through the ESDI and the CJTF, the US found the chance of concentrating on other regions, where it holds strong interest in the Middle East, Central Asia, Central and Latin America and in the Pacific Rim, and using Germany as an overseas depot for the deployment of its European-based soldiers for global interventions.[87] The US has therefore been more ready than Germany's continental partners to encourage it to participate in global military interventions. However, united Germany rejected undertaking wide-ranging global responsibilities during the Second Gulf War and diluted the US administration's expectations. Even though this picture began to change after the tragic events in the former Yugoslavia, Germany prefers to deal with universal challenges in multilateral forums.

Meanwhile, Czech Republic, Poland and Hungary were invited to join NATO in July 1997 at NATO's Madrid Summit and enlargement was eventually implemented in April 1999 at NATO's Washington Summit. The PfP was upgraded and the NACC was renamed as Euro-Atlantic Partnership Council.[88] In view of this, if Germany manages to stabilise the CEE politically and economically through integrating it into Western Europe around the Franco-German core economically (Euro), politically (Political Union), and militarily (European 'Pillar of Defence'), then the German dream of sitting in the middle of stability and prosperity

---

[87] During the Second Gulf War and operations in Somalia and former Yugoslavia, the US used Germany as a military depot. Smyser argued that, without the American bases in Germany, America would lose a key link in its chain of bases around the globe. The US cannot claim to be a superpower if it gives up its German connection and its bases.... Smyser, W. R., 'Dateline Berlin: Germany's New Vision', *Foreign Policy*, (No.97, Winter 1994-95), p.154.

[88] *Madrid Declaration on Euro-Atlantic Security and Cooperation*, (North Atlantic Council in Madrid, Official Texts Part I, July 8, 1997), paragraph 6; *Washington Summit Communiqué*, April 1999. Available at: <http://www.nato.int> (Visited on: September 02, 2000).

will become reality. Plausibly, this is more attractive than being the continental sword of the

US for global military interventions. In the Cold War, US governments in one way or another

used to settle their different policy interests with German governments along the lines of

American interests. In the post-Cold War era, US governments do not expect German gov-

ernments to align their national interests to those of the US as previously, but they want the

Germans to be one of the most loyal partners of the Americans in Europe. For this reason, US

officials were upset with German leaders during the creation of the Eurocorps. No French de-

sire for an 'autonomous' European 'Pillar of Defence' could be realised without the German

approval. In fact, Germany does not want the US/NATO departure from Europe, but in the

post-Cold War era it needs to work towards a genuine European security and defence capa-

bility within the framework of NATO. Even the SPD and the Greens/Alliance'90 MPs are not

denying NATO's importance to European security, nor has the value of a constructive rela-

tionship between NATO and Russia has been underestimated.[89]

After a severe internal debate, the SPD and the Greens/Alliance'90 endorsed NATO's east-

ward expansion. Yet, a large segment in both parties advocates the evolution of the OSCE as

an alternative platform to NATO. Fischer, in one of his speeches, said: '... a 'Yes' to the

Eastern expansion of NATO also means a 'Yes' to changes towards a pan-European security

system, including Russia in the long-run. I deliberately used the word security system and not

military system. It will be decisive to see whether it is possible to develop, out of this military

system, out of this military alliance, a pan-European security architecture in which the mili-

tary components will play less and less of a role'.[90] Although opponents in both parties argue

---

[89] Giessmann, H. J., 'The "Cocooned Giant": Germany and European Security', pp.25-28.
[90] Fischer, J., address to the German Society for Foreign Affairs, 'The Self-Restrained of Power Must be
Maintained: Germany's Role and Objective in the Globalised World of the 21st Century', (Berlin: June 8, 1998).
This can also be read in the *Grün ist der Wechsel*, Bündnis 90/Die Grünen, Programm zur Bundestagswahl 1998,
as: 'Stärkung und Ausbau der OSZE sind entscheidende Ausgangspunkte für die Schaffung eines neuen
gesamteuropäischen Sicherheitssysteme. Bündnis 90/ Die Grünen unterstützen die Entwicklung eines
gemeinsamen und umfassenden Sicherheitsmodells für Europa, das die schrittweise Überführung
nationalstaatlicher Souveränität in die Verantwortung der internationalen Rechtsgemeinschaft ermöglicht.'

that NATO enlargement would undermine the OSCE as an alternative security model and create a rift in European security, supporters believe that this would eventually lead to a pan-European security system and not only Germany would play a civilian power role at the centre of this security system, but also Russia would be given an effective voice in it.[91]

The majority of party members in the SPD and the Greens/Alliance'90, including the CDU/CSU and the FDP, agree on the following three foreign and security policies: *Firstly*, the expansion of the East-West dialogue in a wider spectrum across Europe in order to create an unprecedented trans-continental European security order. *Secondly*, strengthening security ties within the EU through a common European security and defence policy while enlarging the EU to the East. *Thirdly*, keeping the trans-Atlantic link and maintaining the American presence in Europe must somehow be achieved through the creation of two equal defence pillars ('European' and 'North American') within NATO in order to balance the trans-continental European security order. Hence, with the beginning of discussions for adding the 'trans-continental European security order' to the 'trans-Atlantic security order', Germany has already begun influencing the global security order.

The SPD and the Greens/Alliance'90 declared in their coalition agreement that, 'close and friendly relationship with the US is based on common values and interests. This remains an essential component for German foreign policy', and the Atlantic Alliance is an 'indispensa-

---

However, on the same page, Fischer's argument on NATO enlargement is condemned: 'Da durch den falschen, nun aber zur politischen Tatsache werdenden Schritt der NATO-Erweiterung die bisherigen Chancen auf eine gesamteuropäische Sicherheitsordnung verspielt und Gefahren neuer Risse in Europa heraufbeschworen wurden...', p.144; The SPD's party programme is also reflecting the similar perception: 'Unser ziel ist es, die Militärbündnisse durch eine Friedensordnung abzulösen. Bis dahin findet die Bundesrepublik Deutschland das ihr erreichbare Maß an Sicherheit im Atlantischen Bündnis, vorausgesetzt, sie kann ihre eigenen Sicherheits interessen dort einbringen und durchsetzen, auch ihr Interesse an gemeinsamer Sicherheit'. *Grundsatzprogramm der Sozialdemokratischen Partei Deutschlands*, (am 20. Dezember 1989 in Berlin geändert auf dem Parteitag in Leipzig am 17.04.1998), pp.15-16.

[91] Mary N. Hampton, 'German Security at the Crossroads: Mixed Signals Still Point to NATO' in Hampton, M. N. & Søe, C. (ed.), p.240.

ble instrument for stability and security in Europe and for establishing a durable European Peace Order. Co-operation with the USA, guaranteed through the Alliance, and its presence in Europe is still a precondition for security on the Continent'.[92] The Red-Green government had to prove to the international community that Germany is a reliable partner in Western alliances and the German *Sonderweg* is a completely damned idea.[93] Although German officials are officially advocating a strong European 'Pillar of Defence', the majority of German public opinion backs the official German position to NATO. West Germans public support for NATO membership was 59% in 1991 and 72% in 1999.[94]

Although the above picture demonstrated a promising continuity of Germany's US/NATO policy, a number of factors would push the Red-Green government to change Germany's policy towards the US/NATO. *Firstly*, due to Germany's growing global responsibilities, its international role would evolve according to German interests rather than US interests. The continuity of a good German-US working relationship would therefore depend on the German influence of US interests by encouraging American policymakers to contribute more economically and diplomatically to the UN and OSCE. According to the SPD and the Greens/Alliance'90, influencing US interests need a substantial transition period. Commitment to this policy is highlighted in the coalition agreement as: 'Within the framework of working towards the NATO-reform, the new government will tie the tasks of NATO beyond the Alliance's defence to the *norms* and *standards* of the UN and OSCE'.[95]

---

[92] See Kapitel XI – 4. NATO/Atlantische Partnerschaft in *Koalitionsvereinbarung*.
[93] An interesting statement in the *Grün ist der Wechsel* is striking: 'Ein einseitiger Austritt Deutschlands aus der NATO ist abzulehnen: Er würde den internationalen Dialog zerstören und – historisch begründete – Ängste vor einem deutschen Sonderweg schüren. Doch ein souveränes Deutschland darf und muß eigene Vorschläge und einseitige Vorleistungen zur Entmilitarisierung und Zivilisierung der Außenpolitik machen.' *Grün ist der Wechsel*, p.144.
[94] Maull, H. W., 'German Foreign Policy, Post-Kosovo: Still a 'Civilian Power?', p.9.
[95] 'Die neue Bundesregierung wird im Rahmen der anstehenden NATO-Reform darauf hinwirken, die Aufgaben der NATO jenseits der Bündnisverteidigung an die Normen und Standards von VN und OSZE zu binden.'

Secondly, the Red-Green coalition and the *Bundestag* passed a resolution in November 1998 for sending the Bundeswehr to military intervention in Kosovo under the auspices of the OSCE and NATO.[96] Although this demonstrated continuity with the previous government's foreign and security policy, the Greens/Alliance'90 MPs voted affirmative only for the reason that NATO role was in aid of the OSCE.[97] However, this change came with ambiguity. This was an exceptional situation and it seems the Red-Green government would in certain 'emergency cases' accept these exceptions in accordance with the rules of the UN Charter. After all, for such 'emergency cases' it is very ambiguous what these criteria would be.[98]

Thirdly, the SPD's former *Ostpolitik* is not yet resolved in the post-Cold War era, so this might pose a significant change in the Red-Green government's policies with regard to how Russia will respond to NATO's intervention and enlargement policies in the future.[99] The Red-Green government rejected US policy demands of reviving NATO into an instrument for diffusing Western values worldwide that might one day not only pull Germany into new global military adventures, but might also rekindle Russian animosities.[100]

Fourthly, perhaps the most open dispute between the US and Germany, the Red-Green coalition agreement explicitly stated the government's commitment 'towards the renunciation of first-use of nuclear weapons'.[101] The US intention to adopt a gigantic National Missile

---

Kapitel XI – 4. NATO/Atlantische Partnerschaft in *Koalitionsvereinbarung*. Also see the SPD MPs critics on Art.52 of the Chapter VIII, UN Charter, which I analysed above in relation to NATO.
[96] 'Antrag der Bundesregierung – Deutsche Beteiligung an der militärischen Umsetzung eines Rambouillet-Abkommens für den Kosovo sowie an NATO-Operationen im Rahmen der Notfalltruppe (Extraction Force). *BT-Drucksache 14/397 (22.02.1999) und 14/414 (25.02.1999)*, (Bonn: Deutsche Bundestag).
[97] Richard Meng quoted in Mary N. Hampton, 'German Security at the Crossroads' in Hampton, M. N. & Søe, C. (ed.), p.251.
[98] Giessmann, H. J., 'The "Cocooned Giant": Germany and European Security', p.30.
[99] Mary N. Hampton, 'German Security at the Crossroads' in Hampton, M. N. & Søe, C. (ed.), p.251.
[100] It is stated in the *Weißbuch* that Germany has worldwide commitment in the UN, No.319. It is also emphasised in the *Grün ist der Wechsel*: 'Bündnis 90/Die Grünen akzeptieren nicht, daß die NATO ihre Rolle zu Lasten der UNO und der OSZE ausweitet, um ihre eigene militärische Dominanz durchzusetzen.', p.142.
[101] The coalition agreement also stresses on the 'nuclear free-zone', which is going back to the former Egon Bahr's (SPD) idea of withdrawing nuclear weapons from all states in 1982. See *Koalitionsvereinbarung*; For more information about the SPD and the Greens/Alliance'90 policies on this topic see *Grün ist der Wechsel*,

Defence (NMD) system does not coincide with the Red-Green coalition government's declaration. Moreover, if one evokes the memories of the US deployment of Cruise and Pershing Missiles, which led to large protests and demonstrations throughout West Germany (including the participation of the Red-Green government's leaders) in the 1980s, the seriousness of the disagreement can be understood better. The German government does not agree with the US analysis that long-range missiles from Iran, Iraq, North Korea, or from any other rogue government will soon threaten the Western world. Instead of isolating those states through economic and diplomatic embargoes or threatening them through huge armament programmes, the inherent German foreign policy is to pursue a 'critical dialogue', 'change through rapprochement,' as it had once applied to communist East Germany. Chancellor Schröder echoed this concern in a conference held in Munich by warning that too much emphasis on the military dimension of peace making overlooks the possibilities of a multi-dimensional approach to conflicts.[102]

Fifthly, in addition to the OSCE and NATO, Germany's foreign and security policy has been built on the third European security and defence organisation: the WEU. Although each political party in Germany pays more attention to a particular organisation, the CDU/CSU to NATO and the SPD-the Greens/Alliance'90 to the OSCE, all these parties in principle consider the WEU an indispensable part of the European integration process. Germany's special partnerships with the US through NATO, with France through the WEU, and with other countries on the continent through the OSCE, are satisfying the complex network of German foreign and defence policy needs. However, the current process of merging the WEU into the EU and creation of the CESDP is showing that the Europeans may have a special target

---

pp.145-146 and *Grundsatzprogramm der Sozialdemokratischen Partei Deutschlands*, pp.15-16; For a detailed information also see Chapter 2 – *Introduction*.
[102] Schröder in Janes, J., 'Back to the Future: The German-American Dialogue on Defence', *AICGS Issue Report*. Available at: <http://www.aicgs.org/at_issue/ai_defense.shtml> (Visited on: February 26, 2001); Edinger, L. J. & Nacos, B. L., *From Bonn to Berlin – German Politics in Transition*, p.249.

within the 'European security zone' that may not always be compatible with American inter-

est. They are actually locked into a vicious circle in such a manner that the Americans are re-

peatedly condemning the creation of the CESDP as if it is a potential threat to NATO, but

promoting the NMD as something good for both the Europeans and Americans, and the

Europeans are repeatedly condemning the NMD as if it is a potential threat to the global secu-

rity, but promoting the CESDP as something good for both the Americans and Europeans.

The German-US/NATO relationship is rooted firmly in the past, but realism says that it might

not matter that much to German foreign and defence policy in the future. In fact, Germany

would not be an enemy of the US if NATO fails to survive in the future,[103] but would be a

strong competitor and a critical power within the Franco-German core that may prevent the

US from adopting any unilateral American policies globally. Although the Red-Green gov-

ernment has promised continuity of the previous government's security and defence policy

with regard to the Atlantic Alliance, there is a common understanding on the European side

that the US has shifted its focus from Atlantic to Pacific and Central Asia by leaving more

security responsibilities to the Europeans on the continent. If this is the reality, then Germany

must indeed lean more on the EU/WEU security arrangements in order to contribute to a bal-

anced NATO by facilitating the creation of a European 'Pillar of Defence' comparable to the

'North Atlantic Pillar' together with their French partner.

Europe is currently becoming a military-diplomatic power through the EU/WEU's CESDP

within the scope of the Petersberg Tasks in order to develop robust crisis prevention and man-

---

[103] In a conversation with William S. Cohen (US Secretary of Defence), Josef Joffe said that 'alliances die when they win. The threat is gone, therefore what is the use of NATO?' Cohen's reply was one I mentioned above. See Speech by Secretary of Defence William S. Cohen, 'European Security and Defence Identity' at the 36th Munich Conference on Security Policy, 5 February 2000 in *Stichworte zur Sicherheitspolitik*, (Berlin: Presse- und Informationsamt der Bundesregierung, Nr.02, Februar 2000). For more critics on the German-US/NATO relationship see William Pfaff, 'Germany's Special Relationship with US is Ending Badly', *International Herald Tribune*, (March 29, 2000).

agement capabilities. Germany's interest is indeed European integration and that integration

includes security and defence. Thus, since the Cologne European Council Declaration of June

1999, German policymakers have stopped discussing behind the US/NATO what they cannot

do and began discussing more stridently what they can do in the EU/WEU framework to con-

tribute to the security of the entire European continent in areas where the US might not have

an interest in activating NATO.

(2.2) Leaning Towards the European 'Pillar of Defence': Germany's Role in the

EU/WEU

If the German-US/NATO dimension forms one side of the coin, the German-EU/WEU di-

mension is forming the other. Since the foundation of the Federal Republic of Germany on

May 23, 1949, German policymakers has demonstrated their willingness to 'Europeanise'

German national security and defence policy through the European and Atlantic structures.[104]

The German foreign policy towards the WEU in the Cold War period can be outlined as fol-

lows: In the 1960s and 1970s, one of the core duties of the WEU was no more than an institu-

tional framework for controlling German armaments. In the 1980s, subsequent to the failure

of the Genscher-Colombo Initiative (1981) to include security into the EC, Germany realised

it with the Single European Act (1986) and discovered the WEU as a complementary military

and defence mechanism to the EC's European Political Co-operation, which was encompass-

ing only political and economic aspects of security.[105] The WEU has also been the main plat-

---

[104] Johannes Bohnen, 'Germany' in Howorth, J. & Menon, A. (ed.), *The EU and National Defence Policy*, p.49.
[105] Anderson and Goodman argued that, in any event, if the WEU had not been founded in 1954, it would have been created in the 1980s simply to complete the Single European Act package in order to meet the German policymaker's needs. While remaining in harmony with the Atlantic Alliance, the German policymakers were arguing with conviction that the WEU could be adapted to the defence requirements of the EC. Jeffrey J. Anderson & John B. Goodman 'Mars and Minerva?', p.44. Furthermore, it has to be mentioned that the reactivation of the WEU in 1984 was due to the US President Ronald Reagan's strong anti-communist stance, the ambiguous SDI programme, and the French fear of increasing pacifist and neutralist movements in Germany. Later, in 1986, an additional incentive for revitalising the WEU came with Reagan's acceptance to bargain away all ballistic missiles at the superpowers' bilateral summit in Reykjavik.

form for the Franco-German axis in that the legitimisation of Germany's European security and defence policy was only possible with French approval.

In the post-Cold War era, German policymakers rediscovered the WEU as an instrument for European security and defence integration. Therefore, during the Maastricht Treaty process Kohl not only advocated a European Political Union and a Common European Security and Defence Policy (CESDP), but also played a significant role in the formulation of a treaty-based link between the EU/CFSP, which 'may in time include defence', and the WEU.[106] For the German government, the WEU is a strategic pivot connecting the EU and NATO in order not only to strengthen the EU's 'soft-power' initiative, CFSP (and its supplement CESDP), through the WEU's 'hard-power', where the eventual combination of 'soft-' and 'hard-power' would form the 'real' European 'Pillar of Defence', but would also serve as a second pillar of NATO together with the EU. Moreover, German policymakers understood the Americans' concern about an 'autonomous' European defence creation very well, so they consider the WEU as a halfway house for transferring security and defence into the EU in the long run in order not to undermine NATO in the foreseeable future.[107]

There has been a broad consensus in Germany – as there is in France – that while the EU/WEU needs to be strengthened further in a multi-polar world, the US/NATO must be 'Europeanised' in parallel to the evolution of the EU/WEU. Therefore, as it was agreed in the Maastricht Treaty, the Petersberg Declaration was signed in June 1992 in order to strengthen the operational development of the WEU under the WEU Presidency of Germany and endow it with broader competencies in the sphere of crisis management. As Jopp perceptively put it,

[106] See Chapter 1 – *(2) Communitarisation of Foreign And Security Policies Under the Impact of New Security Concept* and Chapter 2 – *(1) The European Sisyphus (1990-1997): The Franco-German Desire, CDP, and CD.*
[107] Mathias Jopp, 'Germany and the Western European Union' in Lankowski, C. and Serfaty, S., 'Europeanizing Security? NATO and an Integrating Europe', *AICGS Research Report*, (US: The Johns Hopkins University, AICGS Research Report No. 9, 1999), pp.35-52.

it is somewhat interesting that Germany, 'a country which neither had any interventionist tradition nor any preparedness at that time to seriously contribute to peacekeeping and task of combat forces in crisis management, including peace-making', committed itself to such a clause even under its own presidency.[108] On the other side, all NATO allies agreed on the ESDI in the January 1994 NATO Summit in Brussels and later endorsed the CJTF in Berlin (June 1996). Thus, with the ESDI and the CJTF, NATO was 'Europeanised' up to a certain degree with the development of a closer operational links between the WEU and NATO.[109] Nevertheless, although France insists on the vertical deepening of European military structures so that the WEU may develop outside of NATO, Germany is in favour of a horizontal deepening with a healthy web of linkages between the EU, WEU, and NATO, as well as between the WEU and various other multilateral force formations that could be made available to the WEU.[110] Since 1994/1995, this has been a condition of France's moving closer to NATO through horizontal deepening that Germany would move closer to the WEU.

Aside from the fundamental homeland or national defence (*Landesverteidigung*) mission of the Bundeswehr, German policymakers had gone beyond that and accepted the binding clauses of the WEU's Art.V and NATO's Art.5 collective defence clauses within the framework of alliance defence (*Bündnisverteidigung*). Since homeland defence remained the major strategy of the past in the East-West conflict period, the WEU and NATO have been broadening their collective defence commitments into a wide range of missions in the 'soft' military sphere. This reflects the awareness that military intervention must deal with the crisis at

---

[108] *Ibid*, p.40.
[109] For more information see Chapter 1 – *(1.1.2) Fine Balancing the Western Institutions: EU/WEU and NATO* and see particularly next Chapter, *(2) Uneasiness in the Franco-US/NATO Relationship: 'Europeanising' NATO*.
[110] Germany finds European and Atlantic multilateral forces useful for gaining legitimacy to its out-of-area operations through the ACE Rapid Reaction Corps stationed in Mönchengladbach, Eurocorps in Strasbourg (France), US-German Corps in Heidelberg, German-US Corps in Ulm, Dutch-German Corps in Münster and German-Danish-Polish Corps in Stettin (Poland). For a good account on this topic see Paul Klein & Gerhard Kümmel, 'The Internationalisation of Military Life. Necessary, Problems and Prospects of Multinational Armed Forces' in Kümmel, G. & Prüfert, A. D. (eds.), *Military Sociology – The Richness of a Discipline*, (Baden-

its source and any early action would certainly prevent the crises' blowing up and someday reaching the homeland. As a result of this demand in the new strategic environment, both the WEU (Petersberg Declaration) and NATO (North Atlantic Council Oslo Communiqué) declared their readiness to support, on a case-by-case basis, the UN Security Council or the OSCE peacekeeping and peace-enforcement rulings without making any amendments in their respective treaties.[111] The WEU is not just considered subject to Chapter VIII of the UN Charter (regional arrangements), but addressed the UN Charter Art.48 (appropriate international agency) as well. Accordingly, a dilemma arose as to whether the Bundeswehr's participation in these new WEU and NATO developments has created additional obligations to the existing treaties and, of course, to the Bundeswehr with respect to Art.59(2) of the *Grundgesetz*. Zöckler observed that, 'all judges agreed on the definition of an international treaty, on the concept of a "political treaty", and also that, in general, Art.59(2) covers alterations of existing obligations or creation of new obligations in "political treaties"', however, judges disagreed whether the same article covers the 'soft-law' creation, which judicially defines the new developments (not the constitutional part of the basic treaties) in the WEU and NATO.[112] The interpretation of Art.59(2) divided the FCC's judges 4 to 4.

One group of judges argued that various consultations and declarations of the WEU and NATO do not yet require any alterations in their respective treaties, but they considered that new developments are surreptitiously leading to a 'soft-law'. Thus, the final constitutional shape of this process might bind Germany to these new international legal obligations. This

Baden: Nomos Verlagsgesellschaft, 2000), pp.311-328. The remaining ground-mobile division, German 4th Corps at Potsdam, and air-mobile divisions are under national command.
[111] See the Petersberg Declaration of 19 June 1992 and the NAC Oslo Communiqué of 4-5 June 1992.
[112] Art.59(2) reads as follows: 'Treaties which regulate the political relations of the Federation or relate to matters of federal legislation shall require the consent or participation, in the form of a federal law, of the bodies competent in any specific case for such federal legislation....'. *Sartorius*, p.29. Zöckler argued that, 'law-making through soft-law is such a flexible, unpredictable and fuzzy process that governments, parliaments (and constitutional courts) will have great difficulties in determining whether such a process exists, when it begins or which specific acts will actually contribute to the formation of soft-law.' Zöckler, M., 'Germany in Collective Security Systems – Anything Goes?'

group of judges advocate the extensive interpretation of the Art.59(2) and demand the *Bundestag*'s participation in all soft-law processes that might eventually result in an alteration of accepted treaty obligations. However, the *Bundestag*'s role is restricted to the creation of international law in the area of treaty law, because the *Bundestag*'s role in the international political process is after all executive, not legislative.

The other group of judges argued that the Art.59(2) should be extended to the soft-law process, which might eventually result in a change of accepted treaty obligations. However, this group of judges could not decide whether various declarations of the WEU and NATO indicate clear intention on the part of participating governments to formulate new legal obligations or new treaty norms which would modify the existing WEU and NATO treaties. According to them, since the WEU and NATO are still shaping themselves to the new strategic environment, their declarations and communiqués pronounce merely political intentions. Under these circumstances, governments would not accept declarations and communiqués as binding obligations, and thus there would not be treaty modifications. Furthermore, even if there is a treaty change, it is subject to dynamic interpretations and, therefore, no Parliamentary consent is required. The *Bundestag* must approve only those changes of the content of a treaty that would result from modifying a treaty.

In the end, neither side went beyond the legally non-binding features of declarations and communiqués, which provide the basis of the WEU and NATO implementation of the UNSC resolutions. The FCC left the last verdict to the *Bundestag*'s case-by-case decision with regard to the German military participation to the WEU, UN, or NATO operations.

Another substantial attempt at creating the European 'Pillar of Defence' came with the IGC on June 16-17, 1997, which led to the Amsterdam Treaty. In a bid to build more concrete de-

fence implications into the Treaty on the European Union (TEU), the German government
proposed four main targets with respect to the WEU: (a) incorporating the Petersberg Tasks
into the EU; (b) limiting the WEU's decision-making autonomy by binding it to the guidelines of the European Council and strengthening the Commission's role in the defence sphere;
(c) progressing the merger of the EU and WEU would also spill over into defence industrial
matters where common arms market would be established; (d) inserting into the treaty a
timetable for step-by-step integration of the WEU into the EU.[113] These three main targets
were also supplemented by the German foreign ministry's three-phase model: In the first
phase, enhancing the co-operation between the EU and the WEU; in the second phase, transferring the activities and bodies of the WEU into the EU; and, in the final phase, the aim is the
inclusion of Art.V commitments of the WEU into the revised TEU, or a defence protocol attached to the Treaty.[114] Former Defence Minister Volker Rühe made a remark in Brussels on
June 8, 1995, that 'European foreign and security policy could no longer remain separate from
the defence policy dimension and its military instruments'.[115] Such an attempt of the German
foreign ministry in creating a continental defence through the European 'Pillar of Defence'
found immediate support from the French government. In addition, Germany and France
agreed that there might be a veto right in the defence policy field, but a minority should not
block taking decisions by majority voting through 'enhanced co-operations'.[116] Schäuble said,
'[i]t should be our goal to integrate the WEU into the EU – if required, step-by-step and
through increased structural integration – and thereby to create a European army'.[117]
Although there was no agreement among the EU members neither on the inclusion of defence

---

[113] See *German White Paper on the 1996 Intergovernmental Conference*. Available at:
<http://www.europa.eu.int/en/agenda/igc-home/ms-doc/state-de/pos.htm> (Visited on: June 14, 1999); Guay,
Terrence R., *At Arm's Length...*, (UK: Macmillan Press Ltd., 1998), p.182.
[114] *German White Paper on the 1996 Intergovernmental Conference*; Mathias Jopp, 'Germany and the Western
European Union' in Lankowski, C. and Serfaty, S., p.41.
[115] See *German White Paper on the 1996 Intergovernmental Conference*.
[116] See Chapter 1 – *(2.3.2) The Franco-German Joint Letter: 'Enhanced Co-operations'*. For recent
developments upon 'enhanced co-operations' see, Epilogue – *(2) A Way Ahead: What Does the EU's Nice
Summit Offer to the Future European Defence Pillar?*
[117] Quoted in Guay, Terrence R., *At Arm's Length...*, (UK: Macmillan Press Ltd., 1998), p.113.

into 'enhanced co-operations' nor on the three-phased model, it is interesting to note that since the Cologne European Council Declaration on the CESDP (June 1999) the EU-WEU merger is indicating the implementation of the second phase anyway.

The German way of thinking and the rationale behind the merger of the EU and the WEU can be summarised in four main points: *Firstly*, in the long run the German government wants to include the concept of common defence policy into the EU with the intention of one day reaching common defence, ending the present double track system (separate EU and WEU decision-making processes), and to prevent the members' playing one institution to another.[118] *Secondly*, in addition to the EU's foreign policy instruments (see Chapter 1), the EU-WEU merger would enable the EU to develop a truly European 'Pillar of Defence' with a significant German military role in order to respond effectively to the 'soft' military issues (see Table 1.1) in the new security environment. *Thirdly*, the main desire of the German elite is to complete the federal construction of Europe in order to avoid the creation of different zones of security within an enlarged EU. This should also fully cover the common defence field through the EU's treaty-based defence commitment. *Fourthly*, burden and responsibility of the Atlantic Alliance should be shouldered by the EU/WEU and in the long run would become the second pillar of NATO with the European NATO forces, the Eurocorps, and other multinational formations forming the military part of that European 'Pillar of Defence'. Hence, matching the US present weight in Europe would contribute to a healthier transatlantic relationship.

Ulrich Cremer argued that, the two catalysts, first the Amsterdam Treaty and the second, which is the most significant one, NATO's Kosovo operation became the 'father of militaris-

---

[118] Jopp presented the UK's action during the crisis in Africa's Great Lakes region as an example to the blockage of the double track system. The UK first agreed with the EU in asking for the WEU operation and later blocked

ing the EU'.[119] Although Germany was in a secondary position during the Franco-British St.

Mâlo Declaration in December 1998, partly as a result of the failure of the EU's crisis man-

agement methods in Kosovo and partly to catch – if not replace – the UK's diplomatic part-

nership position with France, Germany became instrumental in bringing about a coherent

military-diplomatic project named the CESDP in its own presidency during the Cologne EU

Council meeting in June 1999. These new military-diplomatic initiatives not only paved the

way to the Helsinki EU Council meeting of December 1999, but also triggered the painful de-

fence reform process in Germany. Moreover, the Cologne Summit became decisive in en-

dowing the EU's CFSP with the competences of taking decisions through the CESDP and im-

plementing by the WEU's operational crisis prevention and management capability. Given

that Germany has been instrumental in the creation of the Petersberg Tasks during its WEU

Presidency and pushed hard together with France for its insertion into the EU during the

Amsterdam EU Council meeting, the long-standing German desire of merging the WEU into

the EU has been resuscitated once again during the German EU and WEU Presidencies in the

first half of 1999.[120]

The majority of the political elite in Germany perceives the 'Europeanisation' of national se-

curity and defence policies of the EU states not only as a significant attempt at stabilising the

entire continent through autonomous EU/WEU military means, but also as a 'logical' conse-

quence of European integration and an essential step towards Political Union.[121] Although

---

this through the WEU channel. Mathias Jopp, 'Germany and the Western European Union' in Lankowski, C. and Serfaty, S., p.42. For more information on the CDP and CD see Chapter 2 - *(1.2) Contours of the CDP and CD.*

[119] Ulrich Cremer, 'Militärische Emanzipationsversuche der EU' in Cremer, U. & Lutz, D. S., *Die Bundeswehr in der neuen Weltordnung,* (Hamburg: VSA-Verlag, 2000), p.21; Paul Klein & Gerhard Kümmel, 'The Internationalisation of Military Life. Necessary, Problems and Prospects of Multinational Armed Forces' in Kümmel, G. & Prüfert, A. D. (eds.), p.314.

[120] For details see Chapter 2 – *(3) Breaking the European Sisyphus (1998-2000): The Heyday of the European Defence Force.*

[121] Wolfgang Brauner, 'The German Perspective II: Germany's Europeanised Role in the Development of ESDP' in Maull, H. W., 'Germany and the European Security and Defence Policy: A Time for Reflection?', *German Foreign Policy in Dialogue,* (Vol.1, No.2, July 2000). Available at: <http://www.deutsche-aussenpolitik.de/> (Visited on: February 26, 2001).

many analysts and politicians in Germany have stressed the non-military and civilian dimension (civilian conflict prevention and crisis management) of the CESDP, they are not able to refute the fact that Germany has also initiated a significant 'autonomous' process that could lead to even greater European defence capacity integration. German political analysts often argue that if European security and defence institutions desired to be strengthened, they should be given an 'autonomous' decision-making capability in order to develop an independent European defence pillar within NATO up to a certain degree 'separable' but not trigger US forces departure from Europe or the disintegration of NATO.[122] Furthermore, it has to be mentioned that, for better European stability, almost all politicians and analysts in Germany agree that the CESDP is an important evolution for reforming NATO with regard to giving the EU 'equal' capabilities with that of the US, but at the same time they emphasise that the CESDP should not compete with NATO, but complete and strengthen it.[123] Secretary of Defence Walther Stützle argued that, it should be borne in mind that the future of Europe is in the Euro-Atlantic Community, and the US in this Community wants a strong security partner, not a '*knieweichen*' Europe.[124] German officials, who were caught in between France and the US, are still at pains to explain to the Americans that the CESDP will strengthen, not weaken, NATO.[125]

The Cologne Declaration and all other following developments in the European security and defence sphere – the Franco-German Summits and the Helsinki EU Summit in 1999 – have been instigated during the SPD-the Greens/Alliance'90 coalition government. Therefore, there is a bulk of evidence indicating that the Red-Green government is mainly following the

---

[122] 'Europäische Sicherheitspolitik als eigenständigen Pfeiler innerhalb der Nato etablieren', *Luxemburger Wort*, (June 2, 2001); 'Europäischen Integrationsprozess durch gemeinsame Sicherheits- und Verteidigungspolitik ergänzen und fortführen', *Luxemburger Wort*, (August 4, 2001).
[123] 'Die NATO bleibt Sicherheits-Pfeiler', *Saarbrücker Zeitung*, (June 2, 2001).
[124] '"Knieweiche Europäer" sind nicht erwünscht', *Saarbrücker Zeitung*, (June 1, 2001).
[125] For comprehensive American view on the CESDP see Sloan, S. R., 'The US and European Defence', *Chaillot Paper 39*, (Paris: Institute for Security Studies, WEU, February 2000).

CDU/CSU-FDP government's three-phased model through pressing forward for the implementation of the NATO's ESDI/CJTF concept, inserting the WEU into the EU/CFSP, and eventually bringing the EU/WEU to the European 'Pillar of Defence' posture. The SPD-the Greens/Alliance'90 pointed out the continuation of the former government's foreign and security policies in their coalition agreement by stating that, 'the instruments and mechanisms of the CFSP created in the Amsterdam Treaty will be used by the new government in order to provide a capacity to the EU in the area of international policymaking and press ahead for the common representation of the European interests. The new government will make efforts to develop further the CFSP in the meaning of more 'communitarisation' of the Foreign and Security Policy. Therefore, it will support the implementation of majority voting decisions, more competence in foreign policy, and strengthening the European Security and Defence Identity. The new government will make efforts to further develop the WEU on the basis of the Amsterdam Treaty'.[126] The commitment of the government does not only mean deeper 'Europeanisation' of the German national identities and those of its EU partners' through the transfer of more sovereignty to the common EU institutions, but also implies Germany's willingness to press for more integration in the field of European security and defence (EU-WEU) even in the absence of a clear consensus among EU members. Rummel argued that, '[e]ven those in the political spectrum who traditionally opposed the 'militarisation of the Community', like the left in the Social Democrats and the Greens, are now partly for it. Their argument is that a sovereign Germany needs as many multilateral ties as possible in addition to that with a weakened NATO'.[127]

[126] '3. Europäische Außen und Sicherheitspolitik', *Koalitionsvereinbarung.* Also, see Chapter 1 for more information on 'communitarisation' of foreign and security policies.
[127] Reinhardt Rummel, 'Germany's role in the CFSP 'Normalität' or 'Sonderweg'?' in Hill, C. (ed.), *The Actors in Europe's Foreign Policy*, (UK: Routledge, 1996), p.45.

There should be *two power centres* in the transatlantic community in order to allow the EU/WEU to act 'autonomously' or have recourse to NATO's CJTF through the ESDI in 'soft' military matters, where the US decided not to be involved. An influential party member of the SPD, Egon Bahr, even went one step further and argued a similar opinion with French policymakers that, 'German-French security integration is envisioned as the core of a Europe capable of projecting its own security interests in a multi-polar world. It also raises the possibility of greater competition with the US'.[128] This is indicating that the German national security and defence interests are increasingly becoming internationalised.

However, tones are at play in Red-Greens policies towards the Atlantic and the European perceptions of the CESDP. The Greens/Allaince'90 policies towards the EU's CFSP and the WEU are not well articulated. According to the mainstream party line, which largely forms the policies of the *Fundi faction*, deepened integration, strengthened competencies and capabilities for the CFSP is a key step towards the 'civilian power' Europe. The Green state minister in *Auswärtigen Amt*, Ludger Volmer, presented Germany as a *Friedensmacht* and refuses any form of power politics or national army, and advocates a nuclear free European zone.[129] The *Fundi faction* is also critical that the Amsterdam Treaty embraced common military measures through the WEU and opened the door towards a European military power, instead of strengthening a common civilian foreign policy.[130]

On the other hand, the leader of the *Realo faction*, Foreign Minister Joschka Fischer, is not simply the supporter of majority voting in the EU for a stronger European foreign policy, but

---

[128] Bahr quoted in Mary N. Hampton, 'German Security at the Crossroads: Mixed Signals Still Point to NATO' in Hampton, M. N. & Søe, C. (ed.), p.252. Also, see next chapter for a detailed French view.
[129] Stahl Bernhard, 'Europapolitik I – Umwege oder Abwege?' in Maull, H. W., Neßhöver, C. & Stahl, B., 'Vier Monate rot-grüne Außenpolitik', *Trierer Arbeitspapiere zur Internationalen Politik*, (Lehrstuhl für Außenpolitik und Internationale Beziehungen, Universität Trier, Nr.1, März 1999), p.28.
[130] *Grün ist der Wechsel*, pp.138-139.

also ardently supports 'communitarisation' of it and absorption of the CFSP into the first pillar of the EC.[131] Moreover, Fischer wants Germany to have a global interest through the EU. He said, 'Germany should do everything in its power so that the seats of the nuclear powers [in the UN – France and the UK] will be Europeanised step by step'.[132] According to Fischer, the CESDP and enlargement together forms a major part of the European integration project. Stahl observed that those ideas from Fischer and the *Fundi faction*'s concept of strengthening the CFSP under the control of European Parliament and attempting to use the OSCE in conflict prevention and management missions are partly overlapping with the SPD's party line.[133]

The Social Democrats are in favour of the integration of the WEU into the EU, but refuses a European nuclear power force.[134] Thus, the SPD supports a strong European 'Pillar of Defence' within the Atlantic Alliance and the EU-WEU merger has been envisaged as a first step for it in a federal Europe. In his government policy statement, Chancellor Schröder, emphasised before the *Bundestag* on November 10, 1998, that 'with respect to foreign and security policy, the instruments of the common European foreign and security policy must be enhanced and used to provide Europe with the necessary capacity for action on the international stage'.[135] Although the 'non-allied' contribution to the implementation of the CESDP in the non-military area found widespread resonance in both the SPD and the Greens/Alliance'90 and further the Feira EU Council meeting approved the civilian aspects of crisis management as well as policing, these constructive progresses might be hampered by the SPD Finance Minister Hans Eichel's counter European policies – pursued through national requirements –

[131] Fischer argued that veto rights of the EU members shall only be used as a rule in the European Council for the purpose of treaty changes. Stahl Bernhard, 'Europapolitik I – Umwege oder Abwege?', p.27-28.
[132] Fischer, J., address to the German Society for Foreign Affairs, 'The Self-Restrained of Power Must be Maintained: Germany's Role and Objective in the Globalised World of the 21st Century', (Berlin: June 8, 1998).
[133] Stahl Bernhard, 'Europapolitik I – Umwege oder Abwege?', pp.28-29.
[134] *Grundsatzprogramm der Sozialdemokratischen Partei Deutschlands*, pp.15-19.
[135] Schröder quoted in 'German Security Policy and the Bundeswehr', *Presse- und Informationsamt der Bundesregierung*, (Berlin: November 1999), p.19; Also see Ehrhart, H-G., 'Kontinuität oder Erneuerung? Paris und Bonn/Berlin nach den Machtwechseln', *Internationale Politik*, (No.4, April 1999), pp.50-51.

to Fischer's full EU-WEU integration plans in the area of CESDP.[136] An additional stumbling

block is that, the Social Democrats wonder how opposing groups in the Greens/Alliance'90

will reconcile their party's fundamentalism with respect to the CESDP and continue sharing

power in the coalition.

German policymakers are indeed aware that other EU states will not let Germany be a

Trittbrettfahrer in the development of a common European defence. Germany and its

European partners also recognise that the German contribution to the CESDP is indispensable

and if it hesitates to participate in the implementation of the Petersberg Tasks, this will no

doubt restrict the alternative political choices of its partners.[137] Although the development of

CESDP fundamentally seems incompatible with the 'civilian power' feature of Germany, this

particular left-wing oriented government will push for a deeper European integration in the

sphere of CESDP as long as its partners appreciate that Germany's non-military priorities

come first. There is also significant evidence in the Feira Declaration that Germany's civilian

priorities are given significant attention through '... non-military crisis management [...] as a

first priority, established a database on civilian police capabilities in order to maintain and

share information, to propose capabilities initiatives and to facilitate the definition of concrete

targets for EU Member States collective non-military response'.[138] Paradoxically, the Kosovo

crisis, which will be analysed more in detail in the next section, underlined the fact that in

certain circumstances non-military conflict resolution formulas might not be enough to solve

a crisis situation.

---

[136] *Feira European Council Declaration* 'Presidency Report on Strengthening the Common European Security and Defence Policy' (June 19-20, 2000). Available at: <http:// europa.eu.int/council/> (Visited on: June 20, 2000); Stahl Bernhard, 'Europapolitik I – Umwege oder Abwege?', pp.31; 'Les incertitudes de la coopération militaire', *Le Figaro*, (July 12, 2001); Howorth, J., 'European integration and defence: the ultimate challenge?', *Chaillot Paper 43*, (Paris: WEU, Institute for Security Studies, November 2000), pp.46-47.
[137] Heisbourg, F. 'Trittbrettfahrer? Keine europäische Verteidigung ohne Deutschland', *Internationale Politik*, (Nr.4, April 2000).
[138] Title III – Civilian Aspects of Crisis Management. *Feira European Council Declaration*, parag. 3(b).

Heisbourg summarised the current position of Germany in the European security and defence sphere with three adjectives: 'good' – political capabilities began to allow it to participate in the Petersberg Tasks; 'average' – in view of the currently available permanent units for the fulfilment of these Tasks; 'terrible' – budgetary means concerned.[139] The first adjective was analysed above and the last two adjectives will be analysed below. At the time of the Kosovo crisis, Germany still fielded a large conscript force and was geared for an unlikely Cold War-style territorial defence. Consequently, the radical changes in the military field came with the Bundeswehr reform in Germany.

(3) Realities: The Recent Bundeswehr Reform and the Kosovo Effect

(3.1) The Recent Bundeswehr Reform

A month after the victory of the SPD in the September 1998 elections, Defence Minister Rudolf Scharping in his speech before the Centre for Strategic International Studies, signalled the urgency of the Bundeswehr's adaptation and further synchronisation to the new developments occurring in NATO and in the EU/WEU. The mission and structure of the Bundeswehr have to remain in harmony with the emerging peace order in Europe. It is a peace order that is shifting from a collective defence to a wider spectrum of missions in peacekeeping, peace making, crisis prevention and management operations. He also said that, restructuring of the Bundeswehr would be oriented towards a highly mobile, more flexible, sustainable, rapidly deployable, technologically better equipped force; seemingly a professional army would also be supplied with a streamlined command and control structure in order to improve its interoperability with NATO and the EU/WEU.[140] The former CDU/CSU-FDP government adapted

---

[139] Heisbourg, F. 'Trittbrettfahrer? Keine europäische Verteidigung ohne Deutschland'.
[140] Speech by Rudolf Scharping 'Meeting the Challenges of the Future – Germany's Contribution to Peace and Security in and for Europe', *Centre for Strategic and International Studies*, (Washington: November 23, 1998).

the Bundeswehr to the post-Cold War security environment several times by reducing the overall size, curtailing conscription, creating the *Krisenreaktionskräfte*, and developing a permanent Operational Command Centre in Koblenz.[141] However, the largest military force in Europe is still structured with the Cold War mentality: The bulk of a conscript army is structured for the classical territorial defence.

Instead of abolishing conscription and the territorial defence function of the Bundeswehr, which is still seen as a prudent hedge against the emergence of new threats in the Eastern part of Europe (e.g. instabilities in Russia), Scharping concluded that as long as the core function of NATO remains territorial defence, Germany will pay attention to territorial defence since it is the backbone of Germany's security.[142] The Bundeswehr reform process is caught in the middle of the complex task of finding a reasonable balance between the two following orientations: On the one hand, it has been intended to develop an all-volunteer rapid reaction force for 'soft' military missions and, on the other hand, it is still needed as a relatively large military body with the potential growth of the conscript army. There are also several other reasons why Scharping hesitated to realise the notion of an all-volunteer force for the Bundeswehr. *Firstly*, Scharping did not want to give the impression that the Bundeswehr is switching to an *intervention force* for long-range power projections. *Secondly*, a conscript army is strongly correlated with the internal mechanism of control based on the doctrine of *Innere Führung* (Internal Leadership) – facilitating the Bundeswehr's integration into society. This is in short a mechanism to ensure the protection of German society from an all-powerful military, to find an enduring equilibrium in civil-military relations based on democratic values, where the

---

[141] The Operational Command Centre was established on January 1, 1995, and provides the *Bundeswehr* for the first time since the end of World War II with a *nationales Führungszentrum*. See Feldmeyer, K., 'Bundeswehr erhält Führungszentrum', *Frankfurter Allgemeine Zeitung*, (January 12, 1995).
[142] Franz-Josef Meiers, 'A German Defence Review?' in Wilson, G. (ed.), 'European Force Structures', papers presented at a seminar held in Paris on 27 & 28 May 1999, *Occasional Papers 8*, (Paris: WEU Institute for Security Studies, August 1999), pp.24-25.

Bundeswehr soldiers are *Bürger in Uniform* (citizen in uniform) that would fight for democratic principles out of a personal conviction in the justice of their cause.[143] *Thirdly*, public services in Germany (e.g. hospitals) are highly dependent on the conscript system – conscription objectors who perform their alternative services in the civil service area.[144]

On the other hand, German officials are admitting that the Bundeswehr is too big, ill suited to a wide spectrum of operations, has serious structural problems and thus is no more *bündnisfähig* (Alliance capable). Moreover, the Alliance's Strategic Concept puts emphasis on the fact that NATO is developing a more flexible security understanding from a *collective territorial defence* to a *collective effort in support of its members' common interests*.[145] Therefore, German policymakers urgently felt it necessary to undertake new international responsibilities through becoming an *active multilateralist* and to reorient their defence forces in order to catch up with the US, UK, and France on the rate of intervention force creation for defending the West European interests, values, and ethical dignities.

In addition to the new responsibilities and commitments of Germany in NATO, the Kosovo effect and the Europeans' aspirations to develop a security and defence dimension to the EU have all left a huge impact on the Bundeswehr reform. Scharping established a commission in May 1999 and defined its task as the 'Common Security and the Future of the Bundeswehr' under the chairmanship of former President Richard von Weizäcker. At the same time he

---

[143] The all-volunteer force also recalls the corrosive effect of the *Reichswehr* in Weimar democracy. Kelleher, C. M., 'Fundamentals of German Security: The Creation of the Bundeswehr – Continuity and Change' in Szabo, S. F. (ed.), *The Bundeswehr and Western Security*, (UK: Macmillan Press Ltd., 1990), pp.13-30; Berger, T., 'Unsheathing the Sword?', p.170.

[144] The number of those volunteers, who are doing alternative service, is currently increasing. The number of volunteers was 155,000 in 1997, 171,000 in 1998, and was 174,000 in 1999. See Wiegold, T., 'Der Herr der Zahlen', *Focus* (Nr.44, October 30, 2000); Pauly, J., 'Nun müssen die Politiker Modelle zur Sicherung des Sozialsystems entwickeln', *Frankfurter Rundschau*, (May 19, 2000), p.10.

[145] 'The Alliance embodies the transatlantic link by which the security of North America is permanently tied to the security of Europe. It is the practical expression of *effective collective effort among its members in support of their common interests*' (emphasis added). *Washington Summit Communiqué*, 'The Alliance's Strategic Concept', Press Release, NAC-S(99)65, April 24, 1999.

asked the General Inspector of the Bundeswehr, Hans-Peter von Kirchbach, to prepare an internal study. Additionally, the interrelationship between concepts like international military responsibilities, financial matters, universal conscription and the peacetime strength of the Bundeswehr unleashed a broad national debate on the Bundeswehr planning that has not yet reached national consensus by 2002. The decisive factor for all parties in the *Bundestag* was the question of what sort of capabilities do the armed forces need to fulfil their role as an instrument of German foreign and security policy. The SPD research group on the security question proposed in a paper that the full strength of armed forces should be 280,000, 160,000-*Krisenreaktionskräfte* (CRF), 9-months conscription and 80,000 conscripts. The SPD's coalition partner the Greens' defence spokesperson Angelika Beer worked together with Bundeswehr Colonel Roland Kästner upon the Bundeswehr reform. The Beer/Kästner paper suggested that a smaller, modern, 'intelligent' Bundeswehr could meet the needs of security policy better than an armoured 'dinosaur'. They called for a massive reduction of the Bundeswehr down to 180,000 professional soldiers, also being ready for crisis reaction purposes, without any conscription.[146] Von Weizäcker and von Kirchbach presented their recommendations on strategy, structure and armament of the Bundeswehr in May 2000. The recommendations of both paper were blatant: Overall size of the Bundeswehr needs to be cut down significantly, 240,000 (Weizäcker) and 290,000 (Kirchbach); the CRF should be expanded, 140,000 (Weizäcker) and 157,000 (Kirchbach); and, the conscript period and the number of conscript army should also be reduced, 10-months, 30,000 (Weizäcker) and 9-months, 84,000 (Kirchbach) respectively.[147]

---

[146] For the Greens proposal see 'Zukunft Bundeswehr – Die Entscheidungen zur Reform der Bundeswehr' *IAP-Dienst Sicherheitspolitik – Sonderheft*, (Juli 2000); Tobias Pflüger 'Bundeswehr 2005 – bereit für die nächsten Kriege in aller Welt' in Cremer, U. & Lutz, D. S., *Die Bundeswehr in der neuen Weltordnung*, pp.81-82. The Alliance'90 presented a different paper by proposing the Budeswehr to be 100,000-full strength and no crisis reaction corps or conscription. For party line see the *Grün ist der Wechsel*, pp.146-148; other parties' proposals were, FDP: 260,000-full strength, 150,000-CRF, 5-months conscription, 65,000-conscription size. CDU/CSU: 300,000-full strength, 100,000-CRF, 9-months conscription, 100,000-conscription.

[147] See 'Gemeinsame Sicherheit und Zukunft der Bundeswehr', *Bericht der Komission an die Bundesregierung*, (23. Mai 2000). Tobias Pflüger 'Bundeswehr 2005 – bereit für die nächsten Kriege in aller Welt' in Cremer, U. & Lutz, D. S., pp.83-85.

The subsequent serious disagreement between Scharping and von Kirchbach, the latter argu-

ing that his recommendations had become the victim of political considerations and thus were

paid no attention, led to von Kirchbach's retirement in June. On July 1, 2000, the new

Bundeswehr Inspector General Harald Kujat succeeded von Kirchbach.[148] Scharping's own

paper, *The Bundeswehr – Advancing Steadily into the 21st Century*, presented in the same

month, falls in between the recommendations from von Weizäcker and von Kirchbach. The

Bundeswehr would be reduced step-by-step to a standing force of 255,000, and within this the

MDF and CRF combined to be a Readiness Forces (RF) of 150,000. 80,000 of that force

would be highly operational and the remaining, 70,000, would be augmenting or replacing the

operational forces. A further 105,000-men would form the Basic Military Organisation

(BMO).[149] The basic premise of the paper is that Germany under the EU/WEU and NATO

should be able to deploy and sustain a major operation involving up to 50,000 troops for up to

one year, or multiple medium-size operations involving up to 10,000 troops for several years

as well as a number of minor operations in parallel. The RF would make this possible with its

size almost triple that of the former CRF (see Table 4.1 on the next page).

Conscription would be reduced to 9-months from 2002 onwards and conscripts systematically

from 130,000 to 77,000 by 2013. In addition to this, voluntary military service increased to

23-months in 2001 with better pay and the number of professional soldiers to be increased

from 188,000 to 200,000 by 2010.[150] However, the Greens accepted the Scharping's

---

[148] In view of Germany's international responsibility, Kujat said, 'considerable efforts to optimise the armed forces are unavoidable.' For information about Kujat see 'Bundeswehr Inspector General Profiled', *Süddeutsche Zeitung*, (Internet version, FBIS-WEU-2000-1113, November 14, 2000); 'Scharping Presents Defence Reform Paper to Cabinet', *Süddeutsche Zeitung*, (Internet version, FBIS-WEU-2000-1011, October 12, 2000).
[149] *Cornerstones of a Fundamental Renewal*, parag.54-56.
[150] *IAP-Dienst Sicherheitspolitik – Sonderheft*, (Juli 2000); *Cornerstones of a Fundamental Renewal*, parag.58, 61-63; Wiegold, T., 'Der Herr der Zahlen', *Focus*, (Nr.44, October 30, 2000), pp.86-88.

Bundeswehr reform plan half-heartedly and still argue for the complete abolition of conscription and switching to an all-volunteer force similar to that of the UK.[151]

Table 4.1

The Reform Phases of the Bundeswehr[152]

CATEGORY / YEAR	ARMY		AIR FORCE		NAVY		TOTAL ARMED FORCES	
1990/1991	308,000		106,000		32,000		446,000	
1994/1995	254,300		82,900		30,100		367,300	
1999/2000	MDF	CRF	MDF	CRF	MDF	CRF	MDF	CRF
	196,400	37,000	65,100	12,300	22,900	4,300	284,400	53,600
	Total(MDF+CRF) 233,400		Total(MDF+CRF) 77,400		Total(MDF+CRF) 27,200		Total (MDF+CRF) 338,000	
Targeted Future Reform (Circa 2013)	127,000		60,000		23,000		BMO	RF
							105,000	150,000
							Total (BMO+RF) 255,000*	

*Main Defence Forces (MDF) and Crises Reaction Forces (CRF) will be combined to become *Einsatzkräfte* (Readiness Forces (RF)). This figure is the sum of *Einsatzkräfte* and *Militärische Grundorganisation* (Basic Military Organisation (BMO)). This figure was, however, later increased to 285,000.

In fact, the central argument is not keeping or abolishing conscription, the main debate in Germany is whether the Bundeswehr should be structured as an intervention army or not. The British army has been maintained as a small, but highly professional force, since the 1960s and the French army has been working towards the same end since 1996 in order to obtain a more effective and easily deployable fighting force.[153] Furthermore, the so-called Revolution in Military Affairs (RMA), NATO's Defence Capabilities Initiative (DCI), and the professionalisation of the major European armies have not only made conscript force obsolete, but

---

[151] 'Grüne nennen Scharpings Reform halbherzig', *Süddeutsche Zeitung*, (June 3-4, 2000), p.5; 'Neue Runde im Koalitionsstreit über Wehrpflicht', *Frankfurter Rundschau*, (May 24, 2000), p.8.
[152] Data compiled from *IAP-Dienst Sicherheitspolitik – Sonderheft*, (Juli 2000); *Cornerstones of a Fundamental Renewal*; The Military Balance 1990-1991 and 1994-1995, (UK: IISS, Brassey's Ltd.). At the time of writing this chapter, the data referring to the targeted future reform were still fluctuating since the relevant information from the *Bundesministerium der Verteidigung* was incomplete. The mobilisation strength shall also be reduced from 600,000 to 500,000(?)
[153] For comments on British, French and German defence reforms see Whitney, C. R., 'As the Battlegrounds Shift, the Draft Fades in Europe', *New York Times*, (October 31, 1999), p.3.

also harder to justify legally and constitutionally. In an interview, Willfried Penner, the

Bundestag's commissioner for soldiers' affairs (*der Wehrbeauftragte des Bundestags*) said:

> *'You cannot really say today that the conscript army and the democratically*
>
> *constituted state are mutually dependent. I am firmly convinced that a volunteer*
>
> *army also fits into a democratically constituted state. Would a volunteer army*
>
> *have fit into the developing democratic state of the 1950's? That is a big question.*
>
> *Without the Wehrmacht it would hardly have been possible to build up the*
>
> *Bundeswehr, and the Wehrmacht had its own ideology, but today that is no longer*
>
> *an issue'.*[154]

Until the end of the 20th century, the conscript and rapid intervention forces were running

side-by-side. Even though keeping the conscript army did not prevent the Bundeswehr from

having a crisis reaction capability, increasing international crisis situations demanded new

structural adjustments in favour of rapid intervention army. Formulating a new international

responsibility for Germany in the sphere of 'soft' military missions will not be an easy task

and this will certainly need harmonisation between the changing tasks of the Bundeswehr and

political legitimisation. There is plenty of evidence, not only in Weizäcker and Kirchbach pa-

pers, but also in the Scharping paper that the reform is intended to improve the crisis reaction

and combat ready (*kampfähig*) capability of the Bundeswehr. The Kirchbach paper proposed

the combination of conscription and rapid intervention army and the Weizäcker paper tried to

bring the selected conscript and rapid intervention army under the same roof.[155] Scharping

went down the same road by combining the MDF and the CRF under the roof of RF.

Furthermore, the Scharping's paper put emphasis on the fact that, 'regional conflicts [...]

compelling Germany to also honour its obligation to provide assistance. [...] Armed forces

---

[154] Penner in *Süddeutsche Zeitung*, (Internet version, FBIS-WEU-2000-1027, November 27, 2000).
[155] 'Wehrkommission sucht "europäische Perspective",' *Frankfurter Rundschau*, (May 23, 2000), p.1; Tobias Pflüger 'Bundeswehr 2005 – bereit für die nächsten Kriege in aller Welt', p.87.

capable of being deployed quickly and effectively are therefore an indispensable item among the instruments of security policy', thus 'Germany's armed forces must be mobile, flexible in employment, as well as capable of surviving and sustaining even over lengthy periods of time'.[156] In fact, the Bundeswehr is structured to have a crisis reaction capability, including offensive action. Although nobody in the Ministry of Defence wants directly to call the Bundeswehr an intervention army, the Scharping paper indicated that:

> *'Conflict prevention and crisis management may take on different forms and be*
>
> *comparable to collective defence operations in terms of intensity and complexity.*
>
> *They will mainly be confined to Europe and its periphery and call for national*
>
> *crisis prevention and early crisis detection capabilities. Military assets tailored to*
>
> *be ready in the theatre within a few days and sustainable for up to several*
>
> *years'.*[157]

There is enough evidence in the paragraph above to prove that the Bundeswehr is becoming an intervention army for crisis situations through undertaking different forms of conflict prevention and crisis management operations similar to collective defence and having offensive capabilities through modifying military assets for an eventual intervention to stop military conflicts – like the one in Kosovo. Similarly, a speech given by the new Bundeswehr Inspector General Harald Kujat at a military ceremony in Geltow near Potsdam became the manifestation of this: The new deployable commando plant in Geltow 'will in the future lead all deployable German armed forces in national as well as the international frame. It is the "core for the new leadership structure of the Bundeswehr."'[158] Participation of the

---

[156] *Cornerstones of a Fundamental Renewal*, parag.11, 14 & 28; 'Die Bundeswehr an der Schwelle zum 21st Jahrhundert', *Bestandsaufnahme*, (Bonn: Bundesministerium der Verteidigung, May 3, 1999), pp.164-166.
[157] *Cornerstones of a Fundamental Renewal*, parag.22.
[158] 'Herzstück der neuen Struktur – Einsatzführungskommando der Bundeswehr in Geltow in Dienst gestellt', *Landeszeitung*, (Juli 10, 2001), pp.1 & 2.

Bundeswehr in military operations abroad not only forces it to adjust its structure gradually to an intervention army, but also pushes it to acquire the latest technology weapon systems.

The Bundeswehr urgently needs an improved national command structure and high-tech weapons for power projection. In order to improve strategic deployability of the Bundeswehr, priority areas like building up air and sea transport capabilities, space borne reconnaissance capability, fielding high-performance compatible communication, and command and control facilities are required as a 'pacemakers' for interoperability and for assessing *political* and *military* crisis situations accurately. These requirements have been emphasised in the *Koalitionsvereinbarung, Cornerstones of a Fundamental Renewal,* as well as in the *Bestandsaufnahme.*[159] Federal Ministry of Defence officials are irresolutely informing that the Bundeswehr's targeted future reform plans for the army and procurement of the necessary high-tech weapons systems shall be completed by 2013. Planning for an improved command structure and procurement of high-tech weapon systems are also evidencing once again that the Bundeswehr is becoming an intervention army.

The weapons procurement is however a long-term program and needs a considerable amount of financial investment. Instead of increasing defence expenditure to finance structural re-forms, Scharping agreed with Finance Minister Eichel to balance the Bundeswehr budget through savings from cuts in civilian personnel and the sale of the no longer needed military bases.[160] Although Scharping and Eichel agreed not to make significant changes in to the present low level budget rates, agreed changes were even indicating further financial reduction

---

[159] 'Kapitel XI – 9. Bundeswehr/Rüstungsexporte' in *Koalitionsvereinbarung;* The Acquisition and Operation Company (Gesellschaft für Entwicklung, Beschaffung und Betrieb – GEBB) serves as an executive group of the Federal Ministry of Defence on questions concerning the selection and finalisation of procurement, operation, financing and payment, as well as develops an overall concept for satisfying requirements and running them in the Bundeswehr. *Cornerstones of a Fundamental Renewal,* prg.48-51; *Bestandsaufnahme,* pp.109-113, 167-168; Mey, H. H., 'The Revolution in Military Affairs: A German Perspective', *Comparative Strategy,* (No.17, 1998).
[160] 'Noch sucht Scharping nach auflösbaren Standorten', *Frankfurter Rundschau,* (December 15, 2000), p.4; 'Rüstungsindustrie fürchtet Einschnitte', *Frankfurter Rundschau,* (May 24, 2000), p.8.

for the next three years from 46.80 billion marks in 2001, 46.49 billion marks in 2002 to

45.67 billon marks in 2003, the latter level will be kept beyond 2003.[161] If one keeps in mind

Germany's comprehensive welfare system, Schröder government's promise to reduce the

budget deficit and unemployment in years ahead and the Greens promise for disarmament,

these levels are unlikely to be increased by the Red-Green coalition. Therefore, it seems that

the Bundeswehr reform process will stay at the level of 'average' until the turn of the decade

and the budgetary contributions to it 'terrible' at least until the announcement of the next de-

fence budget and financial plan.

While the EU/WEU was taking a great leap forward through the CESDP on the way to the

European 'Pillar of Defence', budgetary problems of its members remain as a stumbling block

in financing the arms build up for a genuine CESDP. Will the reform of the Bundeswehr be

sufficient to equip Germany with the necessary means to catch the leading European coun-

tries, notably the UK and France? Will the EU countries overall spending on armament be

enough to meet NATO's DCI? Scharping argued that it is impossible to improve the quality

of the Bundeswehr without any significant increases in expenditures, but he misses no op-

portunity to argue that it is not always necessary to spend more money on defence, the

European rapid reaction capability would 'clearly be promoted' with a far-reaching co-

operation (more synergy) in strategic air and naval transportation among the European ar-

mies.[162]

---

[161] See *IAP-Dienst Sicherheitspolitik – Sonderheft*, (Juli 2000), p.14.
[162] After an agreement with his Dutch colleague on joint financing and operation of the new large-capacity
aircraft, Scharping said in Berlin on October 27, 2000, that the door is 'completely open to similar co-operations
with other countries as well' in the EU. The co-operation in this area has already started with the UK and France.
'German Defence Minister Seeking to Expand European Military Co-operation', *Süddeutsche Zeitung*, (Internet
version, FBIS-WEU-2000-0927, September 28, 2000); German State Secretary, Wolfgang Ischinger, also
stressed the similar view in an interview: '[arms build-up] can only be solved by constructive approaches based
on integration. …[I]t's not a matter of an arms build-up, but of readjustment.' Hintereder, P. & Zipf, M.,
'Contours of a New German Foreign Policy', *Deutschland*, (No.4, August/September 1999), pp.18-21;
'Europe's cheap security', *Washington Times*, (December 27, 1999); Speech by Rudolf Scharping at an
American Institute for Contemporary German Studies Seminar, (Washington: September 5, 2000).
<http://www.aicgs.org/events/2000/scharping_summary.html> (Visited on: September 18, 2000).

Even so, the 'non-revolutionary' reform of the Bundeswehr will provide Germany with the necessary flexibility – though it is 'average' – to respond to the operational objectives of the CESDP. In addition to the Bundeswehr reform, a number of significant steps have been taken during the Franco-German Summit that will also augment the role of the Bundeswehr in meeting the CESDP requirements. During the Franco-German Defence and Security Council meeting in Toulouse (May 1999), French and German representatives not only agreed on the principles of the ESDP, but also remodelled the Eurocorps. The German division of the Eurocorps was comprised of both professional soldiers and conscript, thus the NATO out-of-area operation of the Eurocorps was almost impossible since the employment of conscripts were restricted to Art.5 operations (territorial defence) of NATO. However, the Franco-German Toulouse meeting transformed the Eurocorps into a single unit (containing only pro-fessional soldiers) in order to make it compatible with the European Rapid Reaction Corps creation within the framework of the new ESDP.[163] In the June 1999 Cologne European Council meeting, Germany has played a significant role with regard to the development of the EU's defence dimension through the delivery of CESDP during its Presidency. The Helsinki European Council meeting on December 10-11, 1999, agreed on military 'Headline Goals' involving the creation of a European Rapid Reaction Corps (50,000-60,000 men) capable of the full range of Petersberg Tasks by 2003 in addition to reinforcing the CESDP. The creation of the new European Rapid Reaction Corps will be in addition to the Eurocorps and Germany has indeed played a distinctive role in the creation of both units.

The EU/WEU crisis management operations – with its own European Corps – require military leadership structures, headquarters, at the strategic level (Operation Headquarters) and the operational level (Force Headquarters). For such European operations, France and the UK offered their headquarters to the EU/WEU in the Franco-British London Summit on

---

[163] *Franco-German Summit –Defence and Security Council – Toulouse Declaration*, (Toulouse: May 29, 1999).

November 25, 1999. Scharping also said in the 36th Munich Conference on February 5, 2000, that reforms of the Bundeswehr would also make it possible for Germany to offer its own headquarters for EU/WEU operations.[164] However, it has to be stated that the Bundeswehr will be employed within the framework of NATO and the WEU under multinational structures or international command. Scharping stated in his paper that, 'German armed force missions abroad will in the future be planned and conducted by a Joint Operations Command. This command will also be available as an operation headquarters for Petersberg operations mounted on the political responsibility of the EU/WEU'.[165] Even though the Bundeswehr contingents suffered serious structural problems in Kosovo, they made a significant contribution since the headquarters of the Eurocorps in April 2000 served as a core for the KFOR-headquarters. Franz-Josef Meiers argued that, the augmented German force contribution to the KFOR mission might force the German government to move towards an earlier professionalisation of the Bundeswehr than had originally been planned.[166]

Furthermore, Germany became an active participant in military affairs at a conference held in Brussels on November 20, 2000. This conference brought the 15 EU member states together to work on the corresponding Helsinki 'Headline Goals' and organise a 60,000-men rapid reaction force. Germany committed to provide the biggest 13,500-men land forces to the European Rapid Reaction Corps. The UK promised to provide 12,500, France 12,000, Italy and Spain 6,000 each, the Netherlands 5,000, Greece 3,500, Finland and Austria 2,000 each, Sweden 1,500, Belgium, Portugal and Ireland 1,000 each, and Luxembourg 100-men land forces. The sum (around 67,000 troops) only counts land forces with the remaining 30,000

Available at: <http://www.ambafrance.org.uk/cgi-bin/htsearch> (Visited on: June 20, 2000).
[164] Rede des Bundesministers der Verteidigung, Rudolf Scharping, anlässlich der 36. Münchner Konferenz für Sicherheitspolitik am 5. Februar 2000 in *Stichworte zur Sicherheitspolitik*, (Berlin: Presse- und Informationsamt der Bundesregierung, Nr.02, Februar 2000).
[165] *Cornerstones of a Fundamental Renewal*, parag.70; also see *Bestandsaufnahme*, p.24.
[166] Franz-Josef Meiers named the structural problems of the Bundeswehr in Kosovo as 'Kosovo Force Gap' in Franz-Josef Meiers, 'A German Defence Review?' in Wilson, G. (ed.), 'European Force Structures', pp.39-41.

coming from air and naval forces and staffs. Denmark, which has a dispensation from the EU

military creation under the Treaty of Amsterdam, is exempt.[167] These forces are put under the

EU Command Crisis Management Chain (see Graph 2.2) and will be commanded by a

German Lieutenant General, Klaus Schuwirth, with a British Major General, Messervy-

Whiting, as his deputy. German Defence Minister Rudolf Scharping also promised to provide

an additional 6,000-men for the EU air and marine Rapid Reaction Forces until the year

2003.[168] Under these responsibilities and commitments, there is no doubt that the recent

Bundeswehr reform plans will not only strengthen the ESDI within NATO, but also the

CESDP within the EU/WEU as a step towards a robust European 'Pillar of Defence.'

(3.2) The Kosovo Effect

Before Gerhard Schröder was elected as Chancellor, on the flight to Washington in August

1998, he said: 'In the event of a new military intervention in Iraq, Germany should also pro-

vide troops. This is subject to a UN mandate' and 'intervention must try to prevent a second

major war in the Gulf', he added.[169] Of course, he did not expect that his words would have

been judged so soon. Two months later, while the previous CDU/CSU-FDP government was

still in office on October 12, 1998, the case of a possible NATO operation in Kosovo and the

question of whether the Bundeswehr would participate in Allies' air strikes against Serbia or

not surprisingly rose in the *Bundestag*. Although at that time it was already likely that Russia

and China would have vetoed any effective UN-mandated action against Serbia in the UNSC,

nobody in the SPD or in the Greens/Alliance'90 was expecting that the Kosovo crisis would

have been such a unique case for the German foreign and military policy in their own time in

---

[167] See European Council, 'Military Capabilities Commitment Declaration', *Press Release Nr.13427/2/00*, (Brussels: November 20, 2000). Available at: <http://ue.eu.int/pesc/> (Visited on: February 24, 2000).
[168] *Agence France Press*, 'EU Members Pledge 100,000 Troops, 400 Planes to Rapid Reaction Force', transcript, The Tocqueville Connection, US-CREST, November 22, 2000 <http://www.ttc.org> (Visited on: December 27, 2000); 'Deutschalnd stellt 12,000 Mann für die Landstreitkräfte der EU', *Frankfurter Rundschau*, (November 21, 2000).
[169] 'Schröder Promises US Continuity in Foreign Policy', *Süddeutsche Zeitung*, (Internet version, FBIS-WEU-98-218, August 6, 1998), p.1.

the government. Schröder and Fischer, under US pressure, had to decide within a few minutes and get the approval of the *Bundestag* on 16 October for joining the NATO combat operation even in the absence of a UN-mandate. For the first time in history of the *Bundestag*, an affirmative vote had been taken for the Bundeswehr's participation in a NATO combat out-of-area operation in the absence of a UN mandate by a great majority (500 voted in favour, 62 against, 18 abstained).

During the *Bundestag* debate, Klaus Kinkel's statement found immediate support from the upcoming Schröder-Fischer government in that the NATO intervention 'has neither created nor intended to create new legal machinery designed to provide a general authorisation for intervention for NATO. [...] Kosovo case must not be understood as to be a precedent for the weakening of the UNSC's monopoly of force'.[170] Although any military action needs to be supplemented by a UN 'monopoly of force' set as a precondition in the Red-Green coalition agreement of October 20, 1998, this precondition contradicted with the *Bundestag* decision on the Bundeswehr's participation to the NATO military intervention in Kosovo without a UN mandate.[171] However, Foreign Minister Fischer justified the Red-Green government's decision as an exception and tried to base it on 'secure legal basis' by saying:

> *'We must find intermediate ways, but nevertheless stick to the basic decision: yes, we want this UN monopoly on force as a rule. However, if difficult situations arise here, then this discussion will not be concluded. ...[B]ecause in this situation, there was no other way, since a humanitarian catastrophe and threats to peace in the region had to be prevented. However, we also made the decision on the basis of the Security Council resolutions that already existed, although there was no*

---

[170] Kinkel quoted in Giessmann, H. J., 'The "Cocooned Giant": Germany and European Security', p.29.
[171] 'Die Beteiligung deutscher Streitkrafte an Maßnahmen zur Wahrung des Weltfriedens und der internationalen Sicherheit ist an die Beactung des Völkerrechts und des deutschen Verfassungsrechts gebunden. Die neue Bundesregierung wird sich aktiv dafür einsetzen, das Gewaltmonopol der Vereinten Nationen zu bewahren...' Kapitel XI – 7. Vereinte Nationen in *Koalitionsvereinbarung*.

direct authorising resolution of the Security Council. ... [A]nd then turns this

individual case into a strategy has, of course, a problem'.[172]

At the same time, the US envoy, Richard Holbrooke, was searching for a peace agreement between the Serbians and the Kosovars through resuming political dialogue and armistice under OSCE observation, with an additional NATO military force guarantee for securing cease-fire conditions. However, fighting between the Kosovo Liberation Army (KLA) and Serbian security forces was the result of the break down of political dialogue due to the Serbian massacre of Albanian civilians in the village of Racak on January 15, 1999.[173] The last diplomatic/political pressure on Belgrade and the KLA came with the Franco-German initiative during the Rambouillet negotiations in France in February/March 1999, but as it was before, the result was again frustration.

After the failure of all the international diplomatic/political efforts that were urged by the Red-Green government, Germany as a last resort had no other choice but to respond to the conflict in Kosovo on March 24, 1999, by participating in the NATO Operation 'Allied Force' in order to prevent further ethnic cleansing. German politicians and public understood once again that 'soft' military issues in the new strategic environment could not be contained by diplomatic efforts alone, but only with a mixture of *diplomatic skills* and *operational military capabilities*. Chancellor Schröder in a parliamentary debate on March 26, 1999, said: 'Until the very end, the international community endeavoured to stop the killing by diplomatic means [...] – but to no avail. We therefore had no other choice but to carry out together with other allies the threat issued by NATO and to clearly show that the international community is no longer prepared to accept the further systematic violation of human rights in

---

[172] The interview is conducted by Udo Bergdoll and Josef Joffe. 'Fischer on NATO Strategy, France, Turkey', *Süddeutsche Zeitung*, (Internet version, FBIS-WEU-98-331, November 27, 1998), p.9.
[173] Maull, H. W., 'German Foreign Policy, Post-Kosovo: Still a 'Civilian Power'?', p.3.

Kosovo'.[174] While NATO's Kosovo operation was still continuing, public opinion polls conducted on March 26-30, 1999, demonstrated remarkable support for NATO's air strike against Serbia. The public support for NATO air strikes (including 14 German *Tornado* aircraft) was 65% in West Germany, but 48% in East Germany. However, this figure was higher among the younger population from 16 to 20 year old in the East (16-20), 68%. It is also interesting to note that although the government categorically refused to allow the participation of the Bundeswehr's ground forces for peace enforcement, the public support for it was 43% on the West (16-20) and 54% on the East (16-20).[175] During the Kosovo operation, Germany held the Presidencies of both the EU and the G7/8 in the first half of 1999. Therefore, under German leadership, the EU and G7/8 have also played an important role in shaping NATO's Operation 'Allied Force'. Having said this, it will not be wrong to conclude that Germany was one of the important actors behind waging the military operation against Serbia on the following grounds:

Firstly, the main worries of the leading politicians in the Red-Green government was not only the credibility and effectiveness of prominent institutions – notably NATO, the EU, and the UN – that could have been undermined, but also instabilities in Kosovo could spread to a wider area unless the dictator Milošević was stopped in Kosovo. Thus, the leaders of Germany did not want to give up something from their multilateral tradition in order to exert German weight and prestige on the Alliance policies, to maintain peace and security order in the Balkans, and to advocate the international rule of law. Although there was no explicit UN-mandate, Germany – as Fischer argued – acted on the basis of UNSC resolutions that already

---

[174] Schröder quoted in 'German Security Policy and the Bundeswehr', *Presse- und Informationsamt der Bundesregierung*, (Berlin: November 1999), p.93.
[175] Hoffmann, H-V., "New Tasks of the Bundeswehr in Communication Processes Between Society and the Military", *Akademie der Bundeswehr für Information und Kommunikation*, (Germany: AIK-Texte, June 1999).

existed. After all, as it is defined in Art.39 of the UN Charter, the UNSC itself had noted that the situation in Kosovo constituted a threat to international peace.[176]

Secondly, if one is not taking enough time to seek a political solution before using military force, the argument of 'war' against Serbia as a 'just war' will be as wrong as drawing an anti-thesis to it.[177] German policymakers feverishly searched for a diplomatic/political solution to the Kosovo crisis until they came to a conclusion (though diplomatic/political channels were not yet exhausted) that, Milošević was using the Rambouillet negotiations in order to gain some time to defeat the fading resistance of the KLA. Scharping said that, 'I believe the people realise very clearly that this is a turning point in the German foreign policy. ...a turning point certainly in a positive way, in political terms, because for the first time we accepted responsibility in such a fundamental matter... Some people argue: if 10 people drown and I cannot save them all, I do not try to save even one. This would be absurd, inhuman behaviour. ...irresponsible'.[178] Indeed, before participating into an offensive action against Serbia, Germany sought to bring Russia into diplomatic channels and pushed for a UNSC resolution in ensuring a diplomatic/political settlement. Even, in his speech before the *Bundestag* on May 5, 1999, Schröder emphasised the importance of a political strategy in defence of NATO's military operation: 'We had to use a double strategy. One part of this strategy – but only the one part – is military. The other part is political and there has never been a moment where it was useless during military actions. The double strategy here means acting militarily in order to get on politically'.[179] Germany has thus made a distinctive contribution to the

---

[176] Art.39 stands for: 'The Security Council shall determine the existence of any threat to the peace, breach of the peace, or act of aggression and shall make recommendations, or decide what measures shall be taken in accordance with Art.41 and 42, to maintain or restore international peace and security.' NATO's military operation was based on Art.39 and destruction of targets like rail, air, postal, telegraphic, radio, and other means of communication areas were done according to Art.41 and 42 of the UN Charter.

[177] Meyer, B.,'Lehren aus dem Kosovo-Krieg für die Bundeswehr', *Frankfurter Rundschau,*(May 24, 2000), p.8.

[178] Interview with Defence Minister Scharing by Richard Meng in 'Scharping Views Bundeswehr Participation in NATO Strikes', *Frankfurter Rundschau,* (Internet version, FBIS-WEU-1999-0327, March 27, 1999).

[179] Rede Bundeskanzler Gerhard Schröder vor dem Deutschen Bundestag (Auszug), (Bonn: 5. Mai 1999, Presse- und Informationsamt der Bundesregierung, Nr.26, May 6, 1999).

diplomatic/political sphere (preferring to exhaust political channels over the option of military action), as well as to the *military/diplomatic* sphere (which considered effective military crisis prevention, but only as a last resort) by its weight and prestige in Europe and in the world.

Thirdly, Fischer and Scharping reiterated that military intervention had humanitarian justification: stopping atrocities and promoting human rights. In addition to 14 German *Tornado* aircraft participation in the Operation 'Allied Force', Germany also participated in major humanitarian actions in setting up refugee camps in Albania and Macedonia.[180] After the NATO air operation, although the Bundeswehr participation in KFOR raised the UN-mandate question once again in the *Bundestag*, the Red-Green government decided to make military contributions even in the absence of a clear UN-mandate and sent instead a Bundeswehr contingent of 8,500-men to contribute to KFOR in June 1999. One of the Bundeswehr's most important tasks in Kosovo has been the *Cimic* (Civilian-Military Co-operation), post-conflict peace operations. Without military support, civil implementations in complex 'soft' military missions are hardly conceivable. The Bundeswehr had already experienced rebuilding credible political structures through civil implementations in Bosnia-Herzegovina and applied its experiences in the restoration of law and order (court systems), police work, rebuilding infrastructure (schools and hospitals), and establishing new political and economic institutions in Kosovo.[181] The Bundeswehr also deployed in a theatre where the burden of historical memory was condemning such an action. Former commander of KFOR, General Klaus Reinhardt, admitted that anger had existed regarding the deployment of German troops into Croatia in the past, but people in Kosovo – uninfluenced by the Nazi legacy – welcomed KFOR protection, German

---

[180] Göb, S., 'Signs of Hope: Humanitarian Help for Kosovo', *Deutschland*, (No.4, August/September 1999), pp.29-30.
[181] Baumeister, T. & Krizanovic, M., 'KFOR Troops: A Difficult Mission for the Bundeswehr', *Deutschland*, (No.4, August/September 1999), pp.27-28.

or otherwise.[182] The *Cimic* has also contributed to the generation of support from the local community for the stationing of foreign military forces. As Wilds argued, 'the [Nazi] legacy which once acted as a cautionary instance appears to be undergoing transformation into a historically determined moral duty to militarily intervene on the international stage'.[183]

Fourthly, in comparison to other European countries, Germany is the most vulnerable country to instabilities in the Balkans. For instance, Germany received the largest number of refugees of which the great majority were seeking asylum. Germany activated the multilateral channels during the military operation in Kosovo in order to halt the future violence and stabilise the Balkans through a complex network of economic and political initiatives. Thus, until the end of operation on June 3, 1999, the 'Fischer Plan' has been the key to an extensive diplomatic process, which was initiated on April 8, 1999, through forming the basis of the 'general principles' of a political solution to the Kosovo crisis, which was approved by G7/Russia on May 6. This initiative has shaped the 'Stability Pact' by taking the Marshall Plan as a historical model in the NATO Summit on April 25 and, after the Franco-German Summit in May, the 'Stability Pact' was presented as a EU-led project in June 10, 1999.[184]

Since the Gulf War in 1991 and the disintegration of Yugoslavia in 1992 Germany's security and defence role has evolved in a significant way. Particularly shock waves that derived from the disintegration of Yugoslavia with the unspeakable horrors of ethnic clashes have alarmingly reached Germany. The recent phase of those shock waves, the Kosovo crisis during 1998/1999, became an exceptional case in the history of the Bundeswehr since its foundation

---

[182] Reinhardt, K., 'Security and Stability in the Balkans: Germany's Contributions and Capabilities', *An AICGS Seminar*, (Washington: June 21, 2000) <http://www.aicgs.org/events/2000/reinhardt_summary.html> (Visited on: July 3, 2000).

[183] Wilds also argued that, 'the erosion of the constraints imposed upon the German states by the bipolar hegemony of the Cold War appears to have stimulated the impression that the shackles of the German past are gradually breaking and its significance for modern Germany is in a process of transition.' Wilds, K., 'Identity Creation and the Culture of Contrition...', p.96.

[184] Oschiles, W., 'A Fresh Start: The Stability Pact for the Balkans', *Deutschland*, (August/Sept 1999), pp.22-25.

in 1955. The support of the Bundeswehr involvement in military operations with such a high risk of death, from the majority of the electorate, even in the absence of a mandate from the UNSC is certainly a clear move towards the European 'Pillar of Defence' from the German side. As a vindication of this effort, paradoxically, even after the foundation of the Red-Green government in 1998, the Bundeswehr's engagement in military operations abroad quintupled.[185] To be more precise, if Germany did not cross the *Rubicon* in a full manner during the FCC's decision in 1994, Germany undeniably crossed the *Rubicon* with the Bundeswehr's active participation in the military intervention during the Kosovo crisis.

Germany became more like 'the others' by re-appraising the usefulness of armed forces and subsequently realised the fact that the military option might be a necessary part of a range of *diplomatic/political* measures to deal with the evils of ethnic cleansing which can still recur in and around Europe. Maull admitted that, 'Germany has thus modified, though not completely changed, its role concept by integrating the possibility of the use of force under certain circumstances'.[186] However, at the same time, 'the others' have been influenced by Germany in the significant utilization of diplomatic/political channels in every means before using the military force as a last resort. Even the last resort use of military power is conditional to *humanitarian reasons* for getting on *politically*. In Kinkel's words, 'we are moving at present from a prohibition on intervention in the name of state sovereignty to a dictate of intervention in the name of human rights and humanitarian assistance', and similarly German Foreign Affairs Minister Joschka Fischer said, 'national sovereignty must no longer serve as a licence for mass murder and grave violations of human rights'.[187] This was the main logic behind the

---

[185] 'Die überforderte Armee', *Der Spiegel*, (Nr.11, March 11, 2002), pp.172-186.
[186] Maull, H. W., 'German Foreign Policy, Post-Kosovo: Still a 'Civilian Power'?', pp.18; Longhurst, K. & Roper, J., 'Forward March', *The World Today*, (Vol.56, No.10, October 2000), p.25.
[187] Kinkel quoted in Giessmann, H. J., 'The "Cocooned Giant": Germany and European Security', p.31; See Speech by Joschka Fischer at the general meeting of the German Society for Foreign Affairs, *German Information Centre*, (Berlin: November 24, 1999).

German foreign and defence ministry decisions' during the Bundeswehr's participation in the NATO's Kosovo air campaign.

(4) Conclusions

This chapter highlighted the fact that Germany's evolving European security and defence role has already started to take some steps forward and is shaping the future of the European 'Pillar of Defence'. While the German military-diplomatic role is still evolving in response to its 'new international responsibilities', the rate of change from the *passive multilateralist* to an *active multilateralist* position in the military-diplomatic sphere is slow but incremental. The rate of change is of course strongly influenced by the distinctive preferences and patterns of the three post-World War II German foreign and security policies: policy of *multilateralism*, *Verantwortungspolitik*, and the policy of *'Zivilmacht'*. Germany being a 'civilian power' is carefully and sensitively developing its 'new international responsibilities' in co-operation with its allies and partners who committed themselves to free democratic constitutions. Moreover, although German leaders are cautious about any power politics and always prefer diplomatic/political instruments to military/diplomatic instruments, as an 'armed' civilian power Germany is also ready to defend the common values order of the West by rebuffing threats to peace, atrocities and massive human rights violations within the framework of multilateral institutions.

The German political elite has also promised continuity in support of NATO in European security and defence at least until the creation of a robust European 'Pillar of Defence'. Germany will no doubt continue to give full support to strengthen the political and military machinery of the CESDP and reform the Bundeswehr's structure accordingly into a smaller, mobile, and professional intervention army. As Scharping argued, 'the ESDP is part of the

European integration process and they constitute two sides of the same Medal.'[188] The

developments through the CESDP towards the European 'Pillar of Defence' should be con-

ceived as the following lesson to the US and not be the other way round: If the EU/WEU's

CESDP can get useful things done around the Franco-German core and shoulders the respon-

sibilities of NATO that it could not generate on its own, then that policy should be strongly

supported, since it will improve the Atlantic Alliance's overall capability.[189] In the beginning

of the 1990s, the US was expected more but was disappointed during the Second Gulf War,

and the US in the beginning of 21st Century criticise Berlin for cutting Germany's defence

spending about half (1.5%) of what the French (2.8%) and British (2.6%) spend.

Even if the German government at the present time is interested more in the CESDP as a

means towards political ends (Political Union) than as a means towards military ends

(Common Defence Policy), the development of the European 'Pillar of Defence' in the end

seems unavoidable. As Wolfgang Ischinger, German ambassador to US, questioned, 'can we

continue to afford the luxury that 15, 20 or more countries maintain a single currency, co-op-

erate a common trade policy and integrated policies in many other areas, but each one of them

has access to totally different armed forces? [...] I realise that this is still a matter for the fu-

ture, but European security policy will have to move in this direction over the coming years

and decades, to move towards greater integration. In fact, this is the last step towards the

completion of European unification, the only step still missing apart from a European consti-

tution'.[190] Furthermore, the questioning of the Bundeswehr participation in military operations

has become less a matter to 'ifs' and 'buts', but rather a matter to *in which circumstances*,

---

[188] Rede des Bundesministers der Verteidigung, Rudolf Scharping, anlässlich der 36. Münchner Konferenz für Sicherheitspolitik am 5. Februar 2000.
[189] Heisbourg, F., 'While Germany Points the Way to a Strong Self-Sufficiency', *International Herald Tribune*, (May 25, 2000).
[190] Hintereder, P. & Zipf, M., 'Contours of a New German Foreign Policy', p.20; For Ischinger's speech in support of Political Union and the merger of the WEU into the EU see Vortrag 'Perspektiven deutscher Außen- und Sicherheitspolitik' von Staatssekretär Wolfgang Ischinger beim 7. Aktuellen Forum zur Sicherheitspolitik der Bundesakademie für Sicherheitspolitik für Chefredakteure am 27.01.1999, Bad Neuenahr.

what type of conflicts and missions, to which theatre, how distant and *how diplomatic-political and military-diplomatic channels could be fine-tuned for the clear definition of tasks.* The search for a peace settlement in Kosovo became a test case for the fine-tuning of the German diplomatic and military means. The reality in Kosovo once again has shown that a clear separation of diplomatic peace missions and military combat missions is impossible. Hence, Germany's participation in the Kosovo campaign nevertheless raised some serious questions about the future role of the Bundeswehr and the goals of German security policy. Indeed, the SPD-The Greens/Alliance'90 government crossed the threshold of the *realpolitik* by pushing Germany into a military role in Kosovo while successfully maintaining a solid domestic consensus for the international role of the Bundeswehr. However, it will still be interesting to see how the main party line ideologies and fundamental dissents, which rose particularly among the Greens members' when the military operation in Kosovo intensified, will be tailored by the coalition government in order to handle similar crisis in the future.

In the end, nobody should expect a rapid change in the longstanding security and defence policies of Germany. At the same time, nobody was prepared for such unprecedented German active military participation in the Kosovo operation in the absence of a UN-mandate. Nobody should expect from Germany a sudden plunge into the European 'Pillar of Defence'; but, nobody was prepared for such historical British support to the development for the CESDP within the EU and the partial merger of the EU-WEU by keeping the door ajar for French desire of European 'Pillar of Defence' that could one day be fully opened. They all actually acted in response to unexpected events.

5

FRANCE'S NEW ROLES AND DESIRES
IN THE SPHERE OF EUROPEAN SECURITY
AND DEFENCE

'France must play a more active role at the heart of the Atlantic Alliance in order that the

latter can become an Alliance between equals: North America on the one hand, Western

Europe on the other. [...] The Atlantic Alliance should, sooner or later, adjust to the

developments that have taken place [...], characterised by Franco-German reconciliation,

and an irreversible process of European construction. France is in a position to play an

important, and, I hope, central role in the definition of the Alliance of tomorrow'.

--Jacques Chirac,

President[1]

Introduction

The French governments' efforts to redefine France's new roles and desires in the sphere of
European security and defence has been instigated as a result of the end of the East-West tension with the collapse of the Soviet Union in 1989 and the following German reunification in
1990. Since then, France in the 'new security environment' seeks to reorient its security and
defence policy into a new delicate balance between its crumbling national independence in the
EU, persistent pressure for 'Europeanising' NATO, and a growing desire for European
'autonomy'.

---

[1] From Chirac's press conference when he was the Prime Minister of France in 1988. Quoted in Menon, A.,
France, NATO and the Limits of Independence, 1981-1997 – The Politics of Ambivalence, (UK: Macmillan Press
Ltd., 2000), p.122.

In contrast to Germany's foreign and security policy, which is moulded by the deep traumatic experience caused by the Nazi regime, France's overriding foreign and security policy goals have been cemented into the aim of restoring the lost French status and prestige as a result of the German invasion of France during the World War II. Apart from the German defeat of the French army, which resulted in France's humiliation, the emergence of the US and USSR as superpowers also diminished its world power position considerably. Therefore, since Charles de Gaulle (first President of the Fifth Republic), if not from the onset of the post-World War II era, France has been struggling to regain its global role and influence through classic Gaullist imperatives of *grandeur* (greatness) and *rank*, to match the superpower position. Gordon stated that, 'Germany was a great European power, but it never had the global presence of France, and in any case lost any sense of truly global (especially military) ambition after the Second World War'.[2] In view of this, it should not be a surprise that Germany is embedded in a different strategic culture, security and defence status than France, because the French position in international affairs is often defined as *l'exception française*. Alain Peyrefitte aptly explained the French exceptionalism in international affairs:

> *'France stands out from the rest because her vocation is more than disinterested,*
> *and far more universal than that of any other. [...] It is by being fully French that*
> *one is more European and most universal. [...] France has a historical role to*
> *play. That is the reason why she enjoys such a large credit. That is why all the*
> *bells of Latin America were pealing at the Liberation of Paris, because she*
> *pioneered American independence, the abolition of slavery, and the right to self-*

---

[2] He also argued that the UK is better comparison to France than Germany. Given its cultural, linguistic and historical links to the US, the UK possessed an advantage over France: the UK had the option of influencing Washington, 'playing Athens to America's Rome', as Prime Minister Harold Macmillan once put it – an option which is not available to France. Gordon, P. H., 'The French Position', *The National Interest*, (Fall 2000). <http://www.brookings.edu/views/articles/Gordon/2000fall_NI.htm> (Visited on: September 13, 2000).

> *determination, because she now champions the independence of nations, against*
>
> *all forms of domination. Everyone in the world feels it somehow'.*[3]

In this exceptionalism, however, France in the Cold War era chose to work in close partnership with its economically most powerful neighbouring country, the Federal Republic of Germany, in order to gain its support at the European level for attaining the unique Gaullist ambition globally – national *grandeur* and *rank*.[4] The other aspect of this partnership was for attaining Europe's independence from the superpowers in the long run, particularly from the Anglo-Saxon influence, with the help of a robust Franco-German axis. The French politicians, as far as it served their aspirations, have always searched for a French leadership in this axis and stressed 'the *complementarity* between grandeur and European integration'.[5] As a result of this French diplomacy, the Franco-German axis came to be widely accepted as the main driving force within the European integration process (see Chapter 3).

In comparison to Germany, France has consolidated clearer foreign and security policy with its well defined targets during de Gaulle's Presidency between the years of 1958-1969. Particularly, the French withdrawal from NATO integrated military command structures in 1966, but not from the Atlantic Alliance, boosted France's quest for a well articulated foreign and security policy. Menon stated that, 'France succeeded … in defining its own strategy and in appearing as the only state with the ambition and the power to stand up to the superpowers, not least through its attempts to create more European defence structures. The pursuit of

---

[3] Peyrefitte quoted in Charles Thumerelle & Philippe G. Le Prestre, 'France: The Straightjacket of New Freedom' in Le Prestre, P. G., *Role Quests in the Post-Cold War Era – Foreign Policies in Transition*, (Canada: McGrill-Queen's University Press, 1997), p.132.

[4] The first French White Paper of 1972 compartmentalised Gaullist ambitions with 'three circles': The first circle comprises of *national independence*, 'sanctuary', and protected by France's nuclear forces; the second comprises of France's foreign and security policy goals in *Europe*; and, the third circle was to project the French power overseas – the French aim of being to uphold its rank at the *global level* on top of all circles. See *Livre Blanc sur la Défense Nationale*, (Paris: Documentation Française, 1972), pp.6-7.

[5] Jolyon Howorth 'France and European Security 1944-94: Recasting the Gaullist 'Consensus'' in Chafer, A. & Jenkins, B. (eds.), *France From the Cold War to the New World Order*, (London: Macmillan, 1996), p.18.

broad, international goals, therefore, spawned national benefits'.[6] The policies of de Gaulle, nevertheless, appeared to be a source of reference to his successors and captivated their minds. Kramer observed that, 'the great majority of the political class does have the cohesion and will to maintain French international influence and has been generally successful in doing so in recent decades. Perhaps no European country has been so effective in translating its potential into political influence'.[7] The French foreign and security policy, in contrast to the three German traditional policies' (multilateralism, *Verantwortungspolitik*, and *Zivilmacht*), rests on three lofty syntheses of classic Gaullist aspirations for attaining *grandeur* and *rank*:

1. *Policy of National Independence*: strategic political uniqueness, systematic affirmation of French autonomy, national unity, and independent actions.

2. *Universalist Policy*: responsibility for formulating novel and effective worldwide policies, which are originally entrenched in traditional French moral values, for applying them to all members of family of nations.

3. *Policy of Power Projection*: maintaining the value of the use of military force (nuclear and conventional) as a tool of state power, a factor for national prestige, in the service of European and global peace and security.

On the whole, until the end of the Cold War, successors of de Gaulle were in broad agreement over the classic Gaullist synthesis of the French foreign and security policy. There were no major damaging political or social criticisms of the above three Gaullist syntheses amongst the leading French political parties or social strata. None of the politician in the *Assemblée Nationale* proposed French reintegration into NATO, all fervently discussed an effective French foreign policy, and at the same time an agreeable European policy within the Franco-German axis, about developing 'Europe' gradually as an actor in the sphere of security and

---

[6] Menon, A. *France, NATO and the Limits of Independence, 1981-1997 – The Politics of Ambivalence*, pp.32-33.
[7] Kramer, S. P., *Does France Still Count? The French Role in the New Europe*, (Washington: The Centre for Strategic and International Studies, Praeger Publishers, 1994), p.99.

defence through building the European 'Pillar of Defence'. A 'European Pillar' that will come out of NATO's restructuring through developing two equal military pillars ('European' and 'North American' Pillars) by replacing the US's one-sided domination of NATO.[8]

With the new external challenges of 1989/1990 (the end of the Cold War, German reunification, the emergence of a 'new security environment', and increased globalisation), French political leaders found themselves baffled by obsolete domestic Gaullist policies, which became increasingly ineffective in an ever-changing European security environment, and by the need to accustom the French social system to a broader global system. Gordon defines France's initial years in the post-Cold War era, '[w]ithout the Cold War, which ensured stability in Europe, American protection and the division of Germany, France would be a weak and small fish in a big pond, and it could never have pretended to play the leading global and European roles of de Gaulle's dreams'.[9] The entire arrangement of de Gaulle was called into question with the breakdown of the Soviet Union. French Ambassador to the US, François Bujon de l'Estang, said, 'the breakdown throws back into question the actual foundations of our country's foreign policy. France must now re-invent a role for herself'.[10] In such an unprecedented situation, France lost its 'coherent strategic concept' and entered into a significant alteration and redefinition of the classic Gaullist synthesis.[11]

---

[8] De Gaulle was not against NATO, but to the very fact that it was heavily dominated by the US, and that the US would make France and its European partners subject to American decisions that could be in odd with their interests. For the European 'Pillar of Defence' discussions between European Integrationists and Atlanticists in the early 1990s see, Chapter 2 – *(1.1) The Murky European 'Pillar of Defence'*.

[9] Gordon, P. H. (ed.), *A Certain Idea of France. French Security Policy and the Gaullist Legacy*, (US: Princeton University Press, 1993), p.187. For those initial confusing years also see, Frédéric Bozo 'France and Security in the New Europe: Between the Gaullist Legacy and the Search for a New Model' in Flynn, G., *Remarking the Hexagon – The New France in the New Europe*, (US: Westview Press, 1995), pp.213-232.

[10] François Bujon de l'Estang quoted in Charles Thumerelle & Philippe G. Le Prestre, 'France: The Straightjacket of New Freedom', p.133.

[11] Michael Meimeth, 'France and the Organisation of Security in Post-Cold War Europe' in Hodge, C. C. (ed.), *Redefining European Security*, (New York: Contemporary Issues in European Politics: 4, Garland, 1999), p.145.

Firstly, French leaders realised that Gaullist policies, which were based on strengthening France's national power and influence in a divided world, were no longer applicable in the multipolar formation that the world had allegedly been heading into since the end of the East-West conflict. French leaders are forced to change their foreign and security policies from a leadership, as an independent nation-state, into being part of a Europe that needs to be strengthened in a multipolar world. Kramer pointed out that this is '*a recognition that France had to trade sovereignty for influence*. For a country that prided itself so much on its independence, this is a major policy shift. France cannot be a political leader except within Europe'.[12] The end of the division of Germany led to new terms coming into being in the Franco-German foreign and security policy calculation as well. In a world, where the US remained the only superpower, France turned to Europe that the Franco-German leadership in the post-Cold War Europe could led the EU to balance the US's unilateral actions in a world of multipolarity.

Secondly, although France has been enjoying for the first time in its history a peaceful strategic setting in its vicinity since the disappearance of a full-scale war threat on its frontiers in 1989, an array of diverse security threats, which have confronted it in and around the European continent, are the same as those threatening France's allies.[13] French leaders also became aware of their own weaknesses during the Second Gulf War and Yugoslav conflicts in that, in the new security environment, where 'soft' military matters require a rapid intervention capability for missions like peacekeeping, crises prevention and management, rather than 'hard' military missions (e.g. nuclear deterrence), only the US has the capability for conducting both types of mission. The new type of security threats and 'soft' military missions

---

[12] Kramer, S. P., *Does France Still Count? The French Role in the New Europe*, p.101.
[13] This has been acknowledged in the French Defence White Paper as, 'Langfristig kann nicht ausgeschlossen werden, daß, je mehr sich die Interessen der europäischen Nationen einander annähern, die Vorstellung, die Frankreich von seinen vitalen Interessen hat, mit denen seiner Nachbarn zusammenfällt.' *Livre Blanc sur la Défense* (German language edition), (Paris: Ministère de la Défense, March 1994), p.27.

forced France to rearrange its relationships with the mixture of new security structures (EC, WEU, NATO, OSCE, and the UN) as well as restructuring the French military force to the new type operations in military-diplomatic situations.

However, the first serious military and diplomatic attempt by French policymakers to outline the nature of 'soft' military issues, though initially hesitant to evade the priority of 'hard' military issues, came into being with the *Livre Blanc sur la Défense* (Defence White Paper) in 1994 as the first official response of the French Defence Ministry to the end of the Cold War.[14] The publication of *Livre Blanc sur la Défense* at that time did not occur by chance, rather that year was deliberately chosen by Prime Minister Edouard Balladur and Defence Minister François Léotard in order to facilitate a collaboration with German Defence Minister Volker Rühe, who put together the German *Weißbuch 1994*, at that time. Therefore, with a close study, one can easily discover resemblance and synchrony between these two Defence White Papers, because for France, Germany is central (as the former is central to the latter) in determining its foreign and security role in Europe.

In short, partly to emancipate Europe from American domination, and partly due to the French need for tying the reunified Germany into the EC, the 'Gaullist' legacy, based on the eventual creation of an integrated and 'autonomous' European security entity in the service of Europeans (while keeping some degree of US presence in Europe in a restructured NATO), has been resuscitated by making this a paramount aim of the French foreign and security policy. Since the 1990s, this French conception has been the fundamental impulsion for all attempts to construct a European defence 'pillar', integrate the WEU into the EU, develop the EU's CFSP through extending the competence of the EU to include the CESDP (developing it within the EU/CFSP, but 'autonomous' and 'separable' from the Atlantic Alliance).

In the first section of this chapter, while re-encapsulating the significant impact of the three classic Gaullist syntheses on the overall French foreign and security policy, the redundancy of these three syntheses, which resulted with the surfacing of the new security environment in the 1990s and concurrently demanded the further 'Europeanisation' of the French foreign and security policy, will be examined.[15] How has France constructed its foreign and security policy during the Cold War after de Gaulle, and how has that policy been affected by the structural constraints of the post-Cold War new security environment?

Since de Gaulle, French leaders have been the most vocal critics to the US strategy on European security and France became the most conspicuous and dissident ally within NATO. In the post-Cold War era, they tactically initiated a dual strategy for NATO's 'Europeanisation': In the short-term, 'tactical' *rapprochement* with NATO has to be pursued not only for influencing the reorientation of NATO's new organisation, content, and scope, but also for benefiting from the US's overwhelming experience and technical capacity in managing 'soft' military operations. In the long-term, the ESDI should be visible and operational for a full French *co-operation* in NATO's integrated military structure (IMS) and the eventual creation of the European 'Pillar of Defence' as an equal to the 'North American Pillar' a condition for its *return* into the IMS. With this rhetoric in mind, *firstly*, the second section of this chapter will search out the first five years of the last decade with regard to the uneasy Franco-US/NATO *rapprochement* during the Presidency of François Mitterand in the period 1990-1995. With the crumbling bi-polar world structure in the aftermath of the Cold War era, this period saw how would it be politically difficult to retain the old structure of the Atlantic Alliance intact. *Secondly*, this section will move on to analyse the next five years, 1995-2000, in which the Franco-US/NATO relationship entered into a serious *mêlée* with the election of

---

[14] *Ibid*, pp.5, 9, 31-44, 72-73.

Jacques Chirac in May 1995. It is also necessary to examine in detail the Franco-American dispute over NATO's AFSOUTH (Allied Forces Southern Europe) command in order to understand their wedged relationship better in this period. *Finally*, the overall assessment will cover the Franco-US/NATO dialogue, such as the US's NMD, in the end of the period 1990-2000.

The sweeping changes in the nature of security with the emergence of the new security environment, which outdated France's political and military Gaullist doctrines, the French armed forces were forced to cooperate more with national and multinational forces, particularly, under NATO's aegis in order to be able to carry out new type diplomatic-military operations. In order to augment the French military forces' flexibility and capability for co-operation and interoperability with its allies in possible military interventions, French President Jacques Chirac launched radical defence reforms in February 1996, which Balladur had only begun. France began to reform the basic tenets of the French armed forces for the 21st Century by concentrating its efforts particularly on European defence co-operation: Armed forces will dramatically be reduced and conscript army will be abolished by 2002, French defence plans will be harmonised with a European structure, command structures will be streamlined, military equipment will be modernised, the army will be fully professionalised and reoriented towards new roles (crisis *prévention* and power *projection*), which were first presaged in the *Livre Blanc sur la Défense* of 1994.[16] These will be analysed in the first part of section three. The second part will examine new roles and the format of French and British nuclear weapons from the perspective of their co-operation, including the concept of the nuclear forces' 'Europeanisation'.

---

[15] France traditionally pursued both global and European strategies for its foreign and security policy objectives. Although my focus will be on understanding the French interpretation of European security, I will briefly refer to the French universalist policy.
[16] See for details, 'Projet De Loi – relatif à la programmation militaire pour les années 1997 à 2002', *Assemblée Nationale No.2766*, (Paris: Imprimé pour l'Assemblée nationale, May 20, 1996), pp.3-8, 8-9/55.

Finally, no other European nation has as much desire, ambition, or means as France to play a decisive leading role in reorganising European security and defence largely independent of NATO. Since de Gaulle, it recurs like a leitmotiv in all French high official speeches that a European integration process will remain incomplete as long as West Europe fails to develop, up to a certain extent, independent capacities from the US in the sphere of security and defence.[17] Although France tried to gain some 'national' advantage from the German *integrationist* and British *intergovernmentalist* preferences during the process of 'Europeanisation' of their national security and defence policies, French desires usually perished due to the American preference of the UK and counterbalanced by Germany's rejection of choosing between the French and the American options. Since the Anglo-French Joint Declaration on European Defence at St. Mâlo on December 4, 1998, the relationships between these four countries came to a point of re-evaluation. Crucially, desires of French policymakers in the sphere of European security and defence, and indeed in the whole EU process, are still largely connected to the independence versus integration debate within the purview of the Franco-German partnership.

(1) Brief Assessment of the Contemporary French Foreign and Security Policy

(1.1) Three Main Post-World War II French Foreign and Security Policy Syntheses

One of the main reasons for beginning the definition of Gaullist syntheses with the *policy of national independence* is that national independence constitutes an essential factor in the quest for a certain French standing in international politics. In other words, national independence is perceived as the basic feature of 'national personality', promotes to an independent global role that would pave the way to augmenting France's unique objectives of status

---

[17] For a good account see, Yost, D. S., 'France and West European defence identity', *Survival*, (Vol.33, No.4,

and rank, and ultimately would crown France with *grandeur*.[18] Robert Gildea perceptively put

it that, 'to attack the Republic for failing to sustain France's mission of national greatness was

to attack it at its most vulnerable point'.[19] In order to maximise his influence, de Gaulle inter-

mingled the policy of national independence with the foreign policy and the nation-state for-

mation. By doing this, de Gaulle enhanced the consciousness of national identity, and so the

national unity, among French citizens and gained the necessary political legitimacy to utilize

national sovereignty systematically for his foreign and security policy objectives – carrying

France into a great power status.[20] In order to crystallise his position, de Gaulle, with the di-

vided and weak political life and unstable coalition governments of the Fourth Republic[21] in

mind, constitutionalised the presidential and the parliamentary regime into the semi-

presidential regime of the Fifth Republic. Therefore, the President of the Republic was placed

in charge of foreign and defence policies through the 1958 Constitution, which assigns him

the role of 'guarantor of national independence, territorial integrity' (Art.5) and makes him

'commander-in-chief of the armed forces' (Art.15).[22]

In contrast to German policy of *multilateralism*, one of de Gaulle's main assertions was that if

France wants to stay independent and reach great power status, it could do so by 'sustaining a

---

July/August 1991), pp.327-351.

[18] Cogan, Charles G., *Oldest Allies, Guarded Friends – The United States and France Since 1940*, (US: Praeger Publishers, 1994), p.6.

[19] Gildea, R., *The Past in French History*, (UK: Biddles Ltd., 1994), p.124. Also see his Chapter 3 on *grandeur*.

[20] De Gaulle's policies, which were moulded with the concept of 'nation', are deeply rooted in the French history. Thus, the concept of 'state' in France has been the manifestation of 'nation'. National independence, nation-state, national identity and sovereignty concepts are all going back to the Napoleonic period, French Revolution, and Vienna Congress. For these details, see Gildea, R., *The Past in French History*. Although these concepts can easily be formulated as division between unitary and federal states, which Sauder successfully applied in his book between France and Germany respectively, the aim of this chapter is to discover one of the most complicated processes: *convergence* of the French strategic culture towards European supranationalism by *trading-off* some features of the unitary state. For Sauder's thesis, see Sauder, A., *Souveränität und Integration – Französische und deutsche Konzeptionen europäischer Sicherheit nach dem Ende des Kalten Krieges (1990-1993)*, (Germany: Nomos Verlagsgesellschaft, 1995).

[21] At that time, the Fourth Republic had already lost the French colony of Indochina and was dragged into unsuccessful policies upon the Algerian conflict in mid-1950s.

[22] For relevant articles see, *French Constitution of October 4, 1958*, (Paris: Assemblée nationale et Minitère des Affaires étrangères, September 1999). <http://www.assemble-nationale.fr> (Visited on: May 13, 2001).

great quarrel'.[23] The word 'quarrel' later came to be interpreted by Jean Monnet in favour of

European *supranationalism* – any Community issue will be built with successive crisis (quar-

rels): Europe will be the final product of these successive crises (quarrels).[24] For de Gaulle,

'quarrel' meant the gatekeeper of a *nation-state*'s independence. In fact, de Gaulle and

Monnet both strongly believed that Europe could not be an independent actor unless a defence

dimension was integrated into it. As Howorth put it, 'during the passionate debates of 1950-4,

the dichotomy was not between 'European' defence (Monnet/EDC) and 'national' defence

(De Gaulle) *but between two contradictory perceptions of how effectively 'European' the dif-

ferent models would be. Both projects sought to create the greatest possible measure of

European military integration'* (emphasis added).[25] The actual reason for the failure of both

projects was their impracticality in the finalisation of the independent European defence pro-

ject, not whether to have or not to have it. According to de Gaulle, the independent European

defence structure could be vigorous only if it includes the UK and was designed for the target

of Common Defence (CD) around the 'ideal association of nations in a confederation of

states'.[26] He believed that France was positioned best among the European nations for initiat-

ing this intergovernmental process and taking the lead in asserting their interests.

[23] 'To be great is to sustain a great quarrel' (*Etre grant, c'est soutenir une grande querelle*) is written by himself in the foreword of his book *The Edge of the Sword*. Cogan, Charles G., *Oldest Allies, Guarded Friends*, pp.5-7.
[24] Delors, J., 'European Integration and Security', *Survival*, (Vol.33, No.2, March/April 1991), p.99.
[25] For Monnet, de Gaulle's project was offering an unacceptable zero-sum choice: Either the French leadership in multiple national commands or no integrated European army. For de Gaulle, Monnet's project was based on an irrational supranationalism: Brussels-based technocrats would be weak, militarily unsuccessful, and taken permanently over by the hegemonic power (the US). Jolyon Howorth, 'National defence and European security integration – An illusion inside a chimera?' in Howorth, J. & Menon, A. (ed.), *The EU and National Defence Policy*, (London: Routledge, 1997), pp.12-13.
[26] 'Confederal European security system.' De Gaulle said in 1951: 'The confederation would have every reason to ensure that the peoples – including *Germany* – who, together, would guarantee the defence of Europe should adopt joint strategic plans and that every possible means should be pooled [...] in particular infrastructure, airports, ports, communications, deployment of units, types of armaments, procurement of equipment, general staffs etc. ...everything which would allow for the association of peoples in a confederated Europe.' De Gaulle quoted in Jolyon Howorth 'France and European Security 1944-94: Recasting the Gaullist 'Consensus'' in Chafer, A. & Jenkins, B. (eds.), pp.23-24; Jolyon Howorth, 'National defence and European security integration', p.20. For detailed definition of CD, see Chapter 2 - *(1.2) Contours of the CDP and CD*.

The European Defence Community (EDC) initiatives failed, but de Gaulle's insistence on French leadership in any independent European defence entity, which could be built around the conglomeration of nation-states, kept the Gaullist notion that French national independence would still be secured by its leadership claims. French Professor Maurice Vaïsse said that, in the end, independence was the great quarrel of France.[27] Since de Gaulle, national decision-making autonomy of French leaders in political, military, and economic spheres became imperative and the subordination of France to any international body or bipolar world structure, which might limit France's national independent actions to play a leading international role, became unacceptable.

Unsurprisingly, de Gaulle criticised the US more resentfully than before and presented NATO as a net thrown over Europe by the US to form a thinly disguised protectorate for projecting American policies and interests through dominating its European allies. In order to reverse the existing balance of power within NATO and between Europe and America, de Gaulle pursued two main policies. Firstly, de Gaulle, deep mistrust of US global policies in his mind, proposed a 'tridominium' leadership of the US, Britain, and France in a new organisational structure with the 'Memorandum on the Directory' in September 1958 in order to secure the independence of France and obtain a rank in world affairs through managing global (including nuclear) strategy.[28] After the failure of this attempt, secondly, de Gaulle signed the Elysée Treaty with the Germans on January 22, 1963, in order to create a greater continental bloc, 'European Europe', against 'Atlantic Europe', that would rest on intergovernmental practice

---

[27] Maurice Vaïsse quoted in Cogan, Charles G., *Oldest Allies, Guarded Friends*, p.6. After the failure of the EDC, which was envisaged with the Pleven Plan, de Gaulle initiated various other projects in order to empower Europe against America. For example, the famous Fouchet Plan was presented in 1962, but remained fruitless.

[28] De Gaulle's resentment of the US began with Roosevelt's recognition of the *Vichy regime*, rather than de Gaulle's *Free French regime*, as the legitimate government of France. France's exclusion from the Yalta Summit, the US plans to introduce a new French currency without the French consent, the US rejection to support France in Indochina and in Algeria, and the US prevention of the Anglo-French invasion of Suez/Egypt were all reasons to the vitriolic relationship between de Gaulle and US Presidents. See Gordon, P. H., 'The French Position', *The National Interest*, Fall 2000. Available at: <http://www.brookings.edu/views/articles/Gordon/2000fall_NI.htm> (Visited on: September 13, 2000).

and provide France with the resources to resist American economic and cultural domination and to achieve its military-strategic objectives in an eventual independent Europe.[29]

With the snub of de Gaulle's 'tridominium' leadership proposal by the US and the UK, de Gaulle declared that he would neither tolerate French subordination to the Anglo-American dominance in NATO's IMS, where France had no *political* control over its own security related decisions, nor would he tolerate restraints on its own national decision-making autonomy.[30] To maintain French national independence, de Gaulle withdrew France from NATO IMS in 1966, but not from the Atlantic Alliance, and claimed that that was a necessary basis for *grandeur*, which would even render greater independence through an active international role and would allow Paris to form, in a two bloc world, a separate pole of 'nascent multipolarity'.[31] The 'Gaullist' policy was actually placed in between strictly rejecting the subordination of French national independence to unpredictable global American policies and, at the same time, being on the side of Atlantic Alliance when collective western interests were threatened by the Soviet Union.[32]

In a similar vein, the Franco-US/NATO relationship affected French European policies, which were predominantly based upon reconciliation with Germany. De Gaulle's European and US/NATO policies had become a catalyst and an obstacle to the Franco-German recon-

---

[29] Guyomarch, A., Machin, H. & Ritchie, E.,*France and the EU*, (US: St.Martin's Press, Inc., 1998), pp.112-115.
[30] In the IMS of NATO, not only all conventional forces were under the ultimate command of an American officer, but they also directly controlled all nuclear forces in Europe. De Gaulle said: 'This memorandum was only a process of diplomatic pressure. I was seeking at the time a way of leaving NATO and regaining my freedom, which the Fourth Republic had taken away. *So, I asked for the moon. I knew they would not give it to me. The Anglo-Americans would like to use their force as they see fit, and they do not want us involved. What they want is to dominate us*' (emphasis added). Cogan, Charles G., *Forced to Choose: France, the Atlantic Alliance and NATO – Then and Now*, (US: Praeger Press, 1997), pp.123-124.
[31] De Gaulle emphasised that the bipolar world system was diminished independence and sovereignty of European states. See Menon, A., *France, NATO and the Limits of Independence, 1981-1997*, pp.7-33.
[32] Once the situation necessitates French military participation in NATO military operation, French forces would come under the *operational control*, not under the *operational command*, of NATO authorities and French military participation would be based on a pre-planned mission of agreed length and scale. Menon, A., *France, NATO and the Limits of Independence, 1981-1997*, p.21. For theoretical differences between the *operational control* and the *operational command* see the CDP and CD in Chapter 2 - *(1.2) Contours of the CDP and CD*.

ciliation. It became a catalyst because de Gaulle neatly saw that independent French policies for an autonomous Europe, liberated from the American hegemony, could only be realised if they managed to draw diplomatically vulnerable Germans onto their own side. As Haglund put it, 'de Gaulle's leadership was crucial, not because it blazed the path of reconciliation, but because it converted French nationalism from a fundamentally anti-German into a substantively pro-German political phenomenon, if only on the tactical level'.[33] It became an obstacle because French independence and the quest for *grandeur* were reinforced by the relative subordination (or limitation) of other European states' independence to the Anglo-American domination. This provided France with the political advantage of formulating and leading plans, such as creating a new security order in Europe, and trying to dictate them to the economically powerful Germany by forcing reluctant German policymakers to choose France over the US. As Menon wrote, 'assertions of national independence contrasted with the limited sovereignty enjoyed by the Federal Republic of Germany and provided a counterweight to the latter's economic might.'[34]

In fact, the policy of national independence of France is deeply rooted in and inspired by French universal messages. This inspiration brings us to the second distinctive Gaullist synthesis: *Universalist policy*. The universalist policy is ascribed to France's universal responsibilities, interests, and duties that are directly related to its unique role in international relations. It derives from the French national exceptionalism that materialized through the motto: *liberté-égalité-fraternité*. This motto captivated policymakers minds as they shaped French foreign and security policy with the aim of liberating France from the hurdles that abated it from realising its duty and its dignity; matching a rank that should put France into a similar

---

[33] Haglund, D. G., *Alliance Within the Alliance? Franco-German Military Cooperation and the European Pillar of Defence*, (US: Westview Press, 1991), p.80.
[34] Menon, A., 'From independence to co-operation: France, NATO and European Security', *International Affairs*, (Vol.71, No.1, 1995), p.21.

position as those of the great world powers; and, promulgating alliance and friendship for

humanity.[35] The universalist policy also permitted France to fulfil some specific responsibili-

ties regarding the civilising mission (to bring the 'superior' values of the metropole to the

'backward people') in French overseas sovereign territories. The *Francophone* (community of

French speaking nations) is a significant outcome of this civilising mission, 'a way of carry-

ing French culture and values to the people of the colonies. Language was the vessel of the

national genius, and *it was only through it that one could imbibe the universal principles pur-

portedly embodied in French culture itself* (emphasis added), wrote Darrin McMahon.[36]

David Chuter argued that, France was granted by 'history' to be the home of universal human

rights, international law, nation-states (guaranteeing their sovereignty and independence), mi-

nority and self-determination rights, and spread them to the entire world by its army.[37] Robin

Laird stated, 'that gave France the sense that it was itself more than a mere regional power

and, indeed, would come to be virtually the only West European state that saw itself with

global political-military missions'.[38]

Since the establishment of the Fifth Republic under de Gaulle's Presidency, France has advo-

cated that its exceptional universal role – unleashed by historical responsibility – is indispen-

sable in shaping the future European system as a part of its global responsibility. As de Gaulle

said in his meeting with German Chancellor Konrad Adenauer in 1958, 'the French people

had for centuries grown accustomed to think of their country as the mastodon of Europe'.[39]

---

[35] Gildea, R., *The Past in French History*, p.117.
[36] McMahon, D., 'Echoes of a Recent Past: Contemporary French Anti-Americanism in Historical and Cultural Perspective', *Columbia International Affairs Online (Ciao) Working Papers*, (US: International Security Studies, January 1995).
[37] Chuter, D., *Humanity's Soldier – France and International Security 1919-2001*, (US: Berghahn Books, 1996), p.340.
[38] Laird, R., 'French Security Policy in Transition – Dynamics of Continuity and Change', *McNair Paper 38*, (Washington: Institute for National Strategic Studies, National Defence University, March 1995), p.4.
[39] De Gaulle quoted in Cogan, Charles G., *Oldest Allies, Guarded Friends*, p.4; Flynn argued that the contemporary French identity is almost perfectly fit between the content of French identity created by Gaullism and traditional French conceptions of France's uniqueness. The claim of France to an exceptional position in international affairs was considered an entitlement by de Gaulle, given the historic role of French power in

There were abundant indications in those years that de Gaulle wanted to pull Germany – restrained by its own historical responsibility (*Verantwortungspolitik*) – and other West European states closer to France's orbit in order to realise the French-style 'universal model', which epitomizes the world in its own image, and for intensifying direct competition between European and American models. The former Foreign Affairs Minister of France, Claude Cheysson, came to say in an interview in 1981:

> *'There is no foreign policy for a country like France, but a translation to the exterior of its interior politics, an integration of internal demands and priorities into international politics'.*[40]

Since the beginning of the 1950s, there have been serious concerns among the French political and intellectual elite that the paternalistic distinctive French identity and French-style 'universal model' have been confronted with the American identity and American-style 'universal model'. According to French policymakers, the US diffuses its ideological colonisation with the Americans' material culture (cultural standardisation), reduces the prestige of French (corruption of French language) and France on the international scene. McMahon summarised the clash between these two distinctive identities and their 'universal model' images as follows: 'Whereas America is a conformist and homogenous country, seeking to force its values and ideals on dissidents at home and abroad, France is pictured as the defender of pluralism, tolerance, and the right to difference. [...] Riven by cultural fragmentation, the US pays the price of both intolerance and the excess of minority demands. France, by contrast, presents the strength of Gallic liberty chastened by consolidating unity and tradi-

---

Europe. See Gregory Flynn, 'French Identity and Post-Cold War Europe' in Flynn, G., *Remarking the Hexagon – The New France in the New Europe*, pp.233-249.
[40] Caude Cheysson quoted in Françoise de La Serre 'France – The Impact of François Mitterand' in Hill, C. (ed.), *The Actors in Europe's Foreign Policy*, (UK: Routledge, 1996), p.20.

tion'.[41] Nonetheless, as Stanley Hoffmann eloquently pointed out, '...universal models that are seen as models for the rest of the world [by France and the US] ... have trouble distinguishing between what's good for them and what's good for the world. In other words, they act upon the assumption that "if it's good for us, it must be good for the rest of the world."'[42]

The French foreign and security policy in the Cold War era, which was moulded by the policy of national independence and universalist policy, was built on basic Gaullist diplomacy. It also contained the third crucial policy area – France's military stance. Now, what needs to be understood is the French *policy of power projection*. In contrast to Germany's policy of *'Zivilmacht'* (reluctance for military solutions), an autonomous power projection policy of France emphasises the maximisation of the French national military independence for achieving greater French influence through upgrading its military rank and prestige in the European and global security affairs. The priority task of the French military, which typically involves land, air and maritime forces (nuclear and conventional) in close co-operation with each other, is to contribute to the policy of power projection as the basic building block of the first Gaullist synthesis (policy of national independence). The policy of power projection was formulated on political and military reasons: *Firstly*, de Gaulle saw autonomous military strength as a necessary foreign policy priority for reaching a greater power status. The political independence of a nation could only be achieved by an autonomous military capability. *Secondly*, occasional military interventions in defence of French *francophonie* testify the value of the French autonomous military forces and France's claims to attain a world power status.

---

[41] McMahon, D., 'Echoes of a Recent Past: Contemporary French Anti-Americanism in Historical and Cultural Perspective.'
[42] Hoffmann quoted in Gordon, P. H., 'The Eternal French-American Quarrel: An Update', Conference on France and US in a New Century, May 24, 2000, *Centre on the US and France*, (Washington). Available at: <http://www.brookings.org/fp/cusf/events> (Visited on: December 17, 2000).

French leaders are obsessed by national military independence for the reason that France's reliance on others for its own defence would be irrational, as it was twice proven to be disastrous for France in the two World Wars. Therefore, before de Gaulle came to power in 1958, the Fourth Republic leadership was already involved in the process of developing a French nuclear weapons program partly in order to reverse such a French reliance on others. However, it became essentially a Gaullist program: National nuclear weapons and military independence became inseparable components of the policy of national independence.[43] The foreign and security policy status of France was underlined by heavy investments in nuclear arms and conventional forces for power projection. There were two basic reasons for this: *Firstly*, the political target of de Gaulle was to make the national nuclear power (*force de frappe*) one of the basic cornerstones of the French foreign policy (*grandeur* and *rank*) in order to justify his claims to an equal voice in the club of great powers, the UN Security Council. *Secondly*, the nuclear hegemony of France on the continent of Western Europe would subordinate the militarily handicapped Germany to the diplomatically powerful France and facilitate the realisation of the French leadership's desire for a stronger European defence 'pillar'. The military target of de Gaulle was to use national nuclear power as a step towards eventual military self-sufficiency, reinforce national firepower and war-fighting capabilities in order to be able to keep France – if necessary – aloof from any international body, loosen the bipolar world structure by influencing both sides' military calculations, and enjoy decision-making autonomy by carrying out its own military operations. As de Gaulle concluded in his speech at Chambéry in 1960, 'without them [nuclear weapons] we would no longer be a European power, nor a sovereign nation, but simply an integrated satellite'.[44] National nuclear weapons became one of the important symbols, if not the most important, of France's inde-

---

[43] The first French White Paper of 1972 explicitly stated this Gaullist understanding that if the nuclear strategic force is an instrument to nuclear deterrence, it is the will to national independence (the reason for the existence of nuclear strategic forces. *Livre Blanc sur la défense nationale*, (Paris: Documentation Française, 1972), p.14.
[44] Quoted in Axel Sauder, 'France's Security Policy Since the End of the Cold War' in Hodge, C. C. (ed.), *Redefining European Security*, (New York: Contemporary Issues in European Politics: 4, Garland, 1999), p.139.

pendence and national security, and are often conceived as comparable to national sovereignty through *sanctuarisation of the French national territory.*[45]

The years before 1965 saw fierce discussions among NATO countries, particularly between France and the US, about assigning the command of all-European nuclear forces to an American officer (SACEUR) through the scheme of Multilateral Force (MLF). The aim with the MLF was defined by Charles Cogan as, to provide Europeans, 'especially [to] the Germans, a feeling of participation in the operation of NATO's nuclear arsenal and to discourage other European "national" nuclear forces from developing. This meant the French, since the British had already produced a nuclear weapon'.[46] De Gaulle expressed his real intentions, which were to construct a European 'Pillar' and nuclear hegemony under French leadership in parallel to the 'North American Pillar', to the US Secretary of State Dean Rusk on December 14, 1964.[47] On the eve of 1966, de Gaulle concluded that the US were insistent on giving the final decision alone about the MLFs nuclear weapons' employment and was unwilling to share the MLFs control between the two equal 'pillars'. With the production of the first nuclear weapon in 1966, de Gaulle removed France from NATO's integrated military command and reasserted not only the autonomy of French defence policy from NATO, but also sharply criticised American imperialism. The 1966 decision of de Gaulle subsequently increased incongruity between the French solidarity in the Atlantic Alliance and its claims to national military independence.[48] France still continued to benefit indirectly from the positioning of NATO forces in Germany, which were stationed between French and Warsaw Pact forces and supplemented by the US's nuclear deterrent.

---

[45] Jolyon Howorth, 'National defence and European security integration – An illusion inside a chimera?' in Howorth, J. & Menon, A. (ed.), *The EU and National Defence Policy*, (London: Routledge, 1997), p.32.

[46] Cogan, Charles G., *Forced to Choose: France, the Atlantic Alliance and NATO – Then and Now*, p.125.

[47] Cogan, Charles G., *Oldest Allies, Guarded Friends – The United States and France Since 1940*, p.130; Jolyon Howorth 'France and European Security 1944-94...' in Chafer, A. & Jenkins, B. (eds.), p.27.

[48] It is worth to note that, since the 1966 decision of France, a series of agreements signed between France and NATO concerning the French participation (conventional forces participation only) alongside its allies in the

In 1967, General Charles Ailleret developed the French strategic doctrine for nuclear and conventional weapons on an analysis that France would not pursue hostile strategy either side in the East-West conflict. This strategic doctrine is called '*tous-azimuts*' (all-horizons), which is defence against a military attack that could derive from any direction (multi-directional). In this doctrine, 'nuclear neutrality' of France was the basic notion. Additionally, the doctrine of 'proportional deterrence' was declared to the world as the basis of French 'national sanctuary' – not to fight a nuclear war (the opposite was envisaged through NATO's 'flexible response' doctrine in compelling conditions), but to prevent it (*la dissuasion du faible au fort*, which is deterrence of the strong by the weak).[49] This doctrine also indicated that France, even in an emergency situation, could still exclude itself from nuclear co-operation with any other state by utilising nuclear weapons only to ensure its own security.

A national industrial capability, which is essential for military independence or power projection, is a decisive factor for producing military equipment. France seeks technological autarky on the grounds that France could only remain independent if it produced its own armaments. Thus, French leaders continuously avoided the diplomatic entrapment of arms control negotiations as it was once seen to be an instrument of superpower control over third parties. France, being a member of the UN Security Council, has also been willing to take an active part in collective security matters, particularly overseeing them in the *francophonie*. The policy of power projection is imperative not only for the rapid intervention capability of French military forces in humanitarian and peacekeeping actions, which enhance France's claims to great power status, but also necessary for the implementation of French universalist policy,

---

defence of Western Europe: Lemnitzer-Ailleret and Valentin-Feber Accords of 1966-7, Naumann-Laxande-Shalikashvili Agreement of 1993.
[49] The proportional deterrence means that, although France had few nuclear weapons in comparison to superpowers, it could still cause devastation to an aggressor that would outweigh any advantage of invading France. Rodney Balcomb, 'Defence Policy' in Perry, S. (ed.), *Aspects of Contemporary France*, (UK: Routledge, 1997), pp.70-71. Also see Chapter 3 of *Arms Control, Disarmament and Non-Proliferation: French Policy*, (Paris: La Documentation Française, April 2000), pp.36-57.

which stems from France's worldwide responsibility of championing democracy and protecting human rights. Conclusively, none of de Gaulle's successors seriously attempted to challenge these three classic Gaullist syntheses, but they met with some serious repercussions since the relevance of his legacy is far from certain in the new post-Cold War security environment.

(1.2) Pressures for 'Europeanising' the Traditional French Foreign and Security Policy

(1.2.1) Pressure for Change

The *Livre Blanc sur la Défense* of 1972, the first French Defence White Paper, has not only formed the basis of the second *Livre Blanc sur la Défense* of 1994, but also held light to the French military programme of 1996 ('Projet De Loi – relatif à la programmation militaire pour les années 1997 à 2002'). This is particularly true for the 'three circles' doctrine (French *national* interest, continental (*European*) interest, and international (*overseas*) interest) of the *Livre Blanc sur la Défense* of 1972, which still has an undeniable impact on the French foreign and security policy. These 'three circles' are strongly interconnected to each other and characterise the relative French foreign and security policy relationship between national independence, universalist policy, and power projection (nuclear and conventional). Successors of de Gaulle tried to surpass the traditional Gaullist model, which was actually characterised by potential ambivalence through relating France's sacrosanct national independence principle to often far-reaching co-operation with its European allies, with various discreet 'Europeanisation' attempts. However, not until the aftermath of the Cold War did it become increasingly clear that Gaullist policy continuity was not the result of executive traditional bureaucracy, but rather that powerful constraints of the Cold War security order had compelled French bureaucrats to keep his policies intact.

Once the sweeping changes of 1989/1990 removed the bipolar Cold War European security order, which was the bedrock of Gaullist policies, the politico-military status of France began to diminish in the world and in Europe with regard to the rising politico-economic status of Germany. Moreover, a 'new security environment' appeared with an emerging new post-Cold War world – multipolar – structure within amorphous 'soft' military matters (e.g. the growing tension between democratic and totalitarian states, see Table 1.1) and challenged the basics of the Gaullist national security model. Irrespective of France's diminished politico-military status in the post-Cold War era, French leaders also considered this era a chance of freeing the world from the bi-polar constraints that were inhibiting democratic countries struggle against totalitarian regimes, applying traditional French moral values to all members of the family of nations (Universalist Policy) and taking a more active part in military-diplomatic missions.[50] The mutation of the Gaullist synthesis forced the French leadership to re-evaluate France's position in NATO and deepen France's relations with its European allies in the EU's security (CFSP) and economic (EMU) spheres, as well as to promote a substantive European military co-operation (EU/WEU) for re-organising the European security structure.

It is interesting to note that, since the end of the Cold War, all political parties in France, except the National Front and the Communist Party, supported the deepening of the European integration process. Valery Giscard d'Estaing's centre-right (UDF) party called for the EC's evolution into a 'decentralised federation' in 1991.[51] Although socialist governments during Mitterand's Presidency saw some substantial changes in the Gaullist policy, they pursued a quite contradictory policy by demonstrating continuity in the beginning of the post-Cold War

---

[50] Charles Thumerelle & Philippe G. Le Prestre, 'France: The Straightjacket of New Freedom' in Le Prestre, P. G., *Role Quests in the Post-Cold War Era...*, pp.131-160; *Livre Blanc sur la Défense* (German language edition), (Paris: Ministère de la Défense, March 1994), p.28. Although three Gaullist syntheses are inseparable from each other, I will skip the post-Cold War pressures on the 'universalist policy' in this section and focus on policies of national independence and power projection in order to keep this thesis coherent and on its focus.

[51] Yves Boyer 'France and the Security Order in a New Europe' in Schmidt, P. (ed.), *In the Midst of Change: On the Development of West European Security and Defence Co-operation*, (Baden-Baden: Nomos Verlagsgesellschaft, 1992), p.21.

years. In 1993, Prime Minister Edouard Balladur, from the right-wing party (RPR), went one step further by criticising President Mitterand for the lack of adaptation he undertook in French defence policy. Balladur signalled the end of the inherent French 'consensus' on defence and foreign policy and envisaged its 'Europeanisation' through a fundamental reform.[52] He also made his intentions clear in the preamble of the French Defence White Paper in March 1994: 'To be precise, with the coming into effect of the Treaties on European Union, our defence policy must be to contribute to the step-by-step building of the Common European Defence Policy. In the foreseeable future, the political identity of the EU must be expressed and maintained in the area of defence. This option, which should establish a stabilising component of integration and stability, constitutes a strategic priority and a political target'.[53] In line with the French Defence White Paper of 1994, the President of France, Jacques Chirac, announced the French military programme of May 1996. However, Chirac's neo-Gaullist policy, like de Gaulle's own, is characterised by ambivalence: the French goal of national independence inevitably contradicts the French demands of European defence integration. This inconsistency is acknowledged in the French military programme, 'since the beginning of the Fifth Republic, the defence policy of France has combined the preservation of strategic autonomy with solidarity. The upcoming challenge will be giving it a European dimension. [...] Today, less than ever, the defence of France should be conceived as going back on itself: she herself is in a European and an international perspective'.[54]

The need for realigning traditional French foreign and security policy became unavoidable. During the Cold War, national independence and power projection policies were an inseparable part of the French national identity and sovereignty. Nowadays, there are trade-offs be-

---

[52] Menon, A., *France, NATO and the Limits of Independence, 1981-1997 – The Politics of Ambivalence*, p.177; Menon, A., 'From independence to co-operation: France, NATO and European Security', p.27.
[53] *Livre Blanc sur la Défense* (German language edition), (Paris: Ministère de la Défense, March 1994).
[54] 'Projet De Loi – relatif à la programmation militaire pour les années 1997 à 2002', p.3.

tween national independence and 'European' integration, with national power projection on the one hand and the European defence 'pillar' on the other; and there are spasmodic convergences between the French national identity and 'European' identity, national sovereignty for the former and European supranationalism for the latter.

(1.2.2) 'Europeanisation' versus the Concern for National Independence

De Gaulle's emphasis on national independence appeared to have become inappropriate by the 1990s. Stanley Hoffmann argued that in the post-Cold War period three main imperatives occupied the minds of French policymakers: First, 'to maintain a will to independence in French diplomacy.' Second, 'the construction of a West European entity owing to which many of the national objectives France could no longer reach by itself could be met; ... for France, Europe was "a means".' Third, 'the preservation of a sphere of French influence abroad [*Francophone*].'[55] Indeed, the second argument indicates that France having an identity crisis. Although the main political parties in France, whether left or right, have all been convinced that France, as a medium-size power in an increasingly interdependent world, can best achieve its objectives and its interests within the EU, the familiar band of anti-Europeanists – the National Front, the Communists, and some traditional Gaullists – argued that the essence of French identity and sovereignty would not only be weakened in an inflexible EU bureaucracy, but also the historically independent French nation would be subsumed under a dominant EU nation, Germany.[56] However, it is still obvious that the institutional structure of the EU is *politically* not strong enough to endanger the French national policy-making process, but there are enough good reasons why France has considered its future first

---

[55] Stanley Hoffmann 'French Dilemmas and Strategies in the New Europe' in Keohane, R. O., Nye, J. S. & Hoffmann, S., *After the Cold War – International Institutions and State Strategies in Europe, 1989-1991*, (US: Harvard University Press, 1993), pp.128-129.
[56] See McMahon, D., 'Echoes of a Recent Past: Contemporary French Anti-Americanism in Historical and Cultural Perspective.'

and foremost within the EU and appeared willing to accept the necessary compromise between 'Europeanisation' and national independence.

Firstly, since the deterioration of overall French national influence in the 1990s, due to the change of power balances in Europe and the world, French leaders understood well that the EC is the main platform to contain the reunified Germany, which suddenly emerged as a local superpower. Therefore, France deepened its already flourishing partnership with the reunified Germany, which was solidified with the signature of the Franco-German Defence and Security Council protocol on January 22, 1988, to the Elysée Treaty, through taking more cooperative initiatives in European construction: Economic (EMU), political (EPU), security (CFSP) and defence (CDP) projects. The main French idea behind these initiatives was that, if France, as the dominant power in these European projects (except in the EMU), supported the possible expansion of Germany's international responsibility, French leaders could accomplish their national objectives more easily through the robust Franco-German partnership in the EU, the WEU, and possibly in NATO and the UN. For Balladur, the Franco-German partnership is a privileged relationship necessary for the success of any European project and he declared that France would support Germany's taking on more responsibility at an international level that would open it up a 'new field for action'.[57]

Secondly, French leaders came to realise that if France's influence in European security affairs was to be enhanced, the conceptualisation of a security and defence policy in a wider European context became inevitable. Therefore, France began to revise its defence policy towards an 'autonomous' European defence capacity (a European defence 'pillar' based on the EU/WEU) on the one hand, and proposed to build a new enlarged European security order (a

---

[57] *Livre Blanc sur la Défense* (German language edition), (Paris: Ministère de la Défense, March 1994), p.34.

pan-European confederation) on the other.[58] In the beginning of the 1990s, the main concern

of Mitterand was to keep the French influence in the continent while fulfilling national objec-

tives. At this point, Mitterand's Gaullist blueprint was presented with a call for a 'pan-

European confederation', based on the EC, French nuclear power, German economic power,

and on the new democratic states of Eastern Europe. Smyser argued, with this plan Mitterand

conceived that 'Germany might have the eminent power role, but France would have the emi-

nent policy role'.[59] Mitterand's Presidency was crucial in developing a rough consensus in

France and favouring a European policy based on a tactic of combining the maximum advan-

tage of reconciling economic integration and political co-operation with the minimum disad-

vantage of supranationalism – the former provokes a confederal and the latter a federal op-

tion.[60] This is the verification of a tension at the heart of French European policy: Persistent

calls for national independence and the proclaimed need for 'Europeanisation'.

Thirdly, throughout the 1990s economic and trade rivalry between North America, Japan and

Western Europe, which has been intensified by the globalisation of international issues, com-

pelled the Europeans to pool fundamental aspects of their national sovereignty from a national

into a European domain in order to cope with hegemonic tendencies and trade competition.

As a result of increasing interdependence among European nations, French politicians came

to analyse the effects on their national independence while acting within collective European

efforts and other relevant multilateral platforms for the purpose of maintaining their influence

and steering policy outcomes at regional and global levels. This new definition of national

---

[58] Yves Boyer, 'France and the Security Order in a New Europe' in Schmidt, P. (ed.), p.22; Balladur's *cohabitation* government later put emphasis on similar points. Although he stressed that France has its ambitions to bring its defence policy into the EU, two extreme choices were not acceptable: a policy that would reject any permanent European defence coalition and an aim to have integrated army within the framework of European federation. *Livre Blanc sur la Défense*, (Paris: Ministère de la Défense, March 1994), p.33.
[59] Smyser, W. R., *Germany and America – New Identities, Fateful Rift?*, (US: Westview Press, Inc, 1993), p.113.
[60] Tiersky, R., 'Mitterand's Legacies', *Foreign Affairs*, (Vol.74, No.1, January 1995), p.115.

independence in France is expressed as a 'strategic autonomy'.[61] French President Chirac, in

his speech to the French ambassadors, said: 'To assert France's identity and defend its inter-

ests, build a united, powerful and prosperous Europe, construct a harmonious multipolar,

peaceful and safe world and control globalisation for the benefit of everyone: those are our

objectives.'[62] Hence, France's national objective is to pull the EU in line with the French

global objectives for utilising France's 'strategic autonomy'.

Fourthly, France has also been challenged by globalisation. This challenge to French national

independence has appeared in two major areas: (a) Nation-states are considerably weakened

by globalisation: Economic interdependence (free market) and civil society (individualism)

concepts are flourishing, and non-state actors are increasing their political power. (b) Even

though globalisation has been broadly considered as 'Americanisation' of cultural values, it

begun to erode the French cultural fanaticism.[63] Foreign Affairs Minister of France, Hubert

Védrine, argued that globalisation is the outcome of what he calls 'savage capitalism' and

could be confronted by the EU under the leadership of France.[64] In this struggle, France defi-

nitely needs its strategic partner, Germany, and the quality of their strategic relationship in

economic, political, and military spheres will definitely be determinant in shaping France's

overall European policy.[65] Ronald Tiersky wrote, France 'chose Europe', because 'a Franco-

---

[61] Quoted in Wyllie, James H. *European Security in the New Political Environment*, (New York: Addison Wesley Longman Limited, 1997), p.102.

[62] Speech by Jacques Chirac at the 'Meeting of the French Ambassadors' in Paris on August 26, 1998. Available at: <http://www.info-france-usa.org> (Visited on: June 04, 2000).

[63] 67% of French worry that globalisation threatens the French identity; 52% rejects the American economic model; and, 80% do not want to emulate the American lifestyle. Gordon, P. H., 'The French Position', *The National Interest*, (Fall 2000); Gordon, P. H., 'The Eternal French-American Quarrel: An Update', Conference on France and the US in a New Century, *Centre on the US and France*, (Washington, May 24, 2000).

[64] Védrine, H., Foreign Affairs Minister of France, *interview given to the 'La Revue internationale et stratégique'*, (Paris: April 11, 2001); Caldwell, C., 'Védrinism: France's Global Ambitions'. Available at: <http://www.policyreview.com/oct00/caldwell.html> (Visited on: November 17, 2000).

[65] Due to globalisation of financial markets, it is becoming unavoidable for France and Germany to combine their principle of 'shareholder value' with the 'stakeholder value'. For globalisation effect on the Franco-German social and economic relationship, see '2. Deutsch- Französischen Dialog', *Saarbrücker Erklärung*, (Saarbrücken: Mai 26/27, 2000); also see '2ᵉ Dialogue franco-allemand – La France et l'Allemagne: partenaires économiques ou rivaux en Europe et dans le monde?', *Compte rendu des débats*, (Sarrebruck: du 26 au 27 mai 2000).

German axis [in the EU] anchors French prosperity and self-confidence, and thus France's international presence and influence in the next century'.[66]

In the beginning of the 1990s, French leaders instigated the 'Europeanisation' of French foreign and security policy, in style and content, by questioning the effectiveness of their national independence policy by repositioning France's future into the EU. Each step towards greater European integration brought France closer to the point where fundamental aspects of its national independence broken up from the national level into the European one.

(1.2.3) 'Europeanisation' versus the Concern for National Power Projection

Since de Gaulle's reorganisation of French national military forces, which were fortified with nuclear weapons by making them *sine qua non* for national military self-sufficiency on the two main impulses (defence of vital national interests and securing political independence of France), there had been no significant deviation in his policies until the end of the Cold War. The end of the Cold War fundamentally changed the global security environment and marked a growing regional and international integration and interdependence that profoundly challenged French national military independence.

The post-Cold War challenges to France's national power projection policy marked the beginning of a radical change of the French security and defence policy. However, political leaders in France were uncertain about how a new French defence policy would be streamlined. In the words of Rodney Balcomb, that uncertainty was the result of 'the schizophrenic nature of official pronouncements on defence..., with nationalistic assertions of military independence mingling with calls for development of a European defence identity'.[67] Although

---

[66] Tiersky, R., 'Mitterand's Legacies', *Foreign Affairs*, (Vol.74, No.1, January 1995), p.115.
[67] Rodney Balcomb, 'Defence Policy' in Perry, S. (ed.), *Aspects of Contemporary France*, p.79.

Alain Juppé, a leading RPR member (neo-Gaullist), was inclined to deviate from the Gaullist doctrine of national military independence through favouring European defence co-operation and *rapprochement* with NATO, the socialist President Mitterand claimed the necessity of preserving the consensus on the Gaullist model, at least for an intermediate term, for examining the course of events precisely at that time. Later, he also came to realise that closer European defence co-operation was necessary in the new security environment. On the other hand, the Communist Party and the National Front were critical of any policy that would bring France closer to European defence co-operation and NATO.[68] François Léotard (from the centre-right party, UDF), the French Defence Minister in 1994, went beyond all traditional messages and claimed that European defence integration should be created through the *'mutualisation de la puissance'* (mutualisation of power) 'in the service of the defence of Europe and of a common security for the states engaged in its construction'.[69]

In theory, French security and defence policy discussions were directly related to the first circle (the French national independence, 'sanctuary', and protected by France's nuclear forces) and second circle (French foreign and security policy goals in Europe) of de Gaulle's 'three circles' doctrine. That is, for France, European defence *co-operation* would mean first and second circle divided with *less distinguishable* borders and a possible European defence *integration* would mean *no* borders between the first and the second circle. As far as the 'Europeanisation' of French power projection policy is concerned, the EU is a real challenge to French national military independence with no exact definition for such a dynamic process of 'European integrationism'. Nevertheless, sweeping changes in the European security environment have forced the French policy of power projection to embark on 'Europeanisation' for a number of reasons:

[68] Menon, A., *France, NATO and the Limits of Independence, 1981-1997*, p.177.
[69] *Livre Blanc sur la Défense*, (Paris: Ministère de la Défense, March 1994), see preamble.

Firstly, the military significance of *force de frappe*, which was justified as 'sanctuary' for France, lost one of its main *raison d'être* with the demise of the Warsaw Pact threat. In turn, as Frédéric Bozo argued, 'the nuclear club is becoming less exclusive as a result of proliferation, and being a nuclear power provides a far less indisputable international political status than before'.[70] This means that Gaullist reliance on nuclear power projection, their relevance to France's independent military power and prestigious world role once soundly emphasised, lost most of their legitimacy with the devaluation of nuclear forces in the post-Cold War era. At the same time, with the removal the of strategic nuclear war fighting approach of NATO ('flexible response' doctrine), France found it convenient to accept nuclear arms control and disarmament – once seen as an instrument of superpower control over third parties – in the new security environment.[71] Furthermore, almost thirty years after Pierre Messmer argued in 1963 that 'for Europe to exist, she will have to take responsibility for her own defence and, to that end, will require nuclear weapons. When we reach that point, it will be seen that France's possession of national nuclear weapons will become an essential element in the construction of Europe,'[72] French nuclear weapons once again came to occupy a significant place in the European integration process. In June 1990, Defence Minister Jean-Pierre Chevènement, explicitly claimed the need of 'an autonomous European defence' to replace the American defence of Europe, and Mitterand began to tantalise with the possibility of 'Europeanising' the French nuclear deterrent for building a nuclear capable 'confederal Europe' in January 1992.[73] Although 'Europeanisation' of French nuclear forces will be analysed later in the Franco-British nuclear relations section in this chapter, it has to be expressed here that there is a

---

[70] Frédéric Bozo 'France and Security in the New Europe: Between the Gaullist Legacy and the Search for a New Model' in Flynn, G., *Remarking the Hexagon – The New France in the New Europe*, p.224.
[71] France became the first nuclear power state acceding to the NPT on August 2, 1992, and came to ratify the CTBT on April 6, 1998. *Arms Control, Disarmament and Non-Proliferation: French Policy*, (Paris: La Documentation Française, April 2000).
[72] Messmer was the French Prime Minister between years 1973-1975 during Georges Pompidou's Presidency. Jolyon Howorth 'France and European Security 1944-94…' in Chafer, A. & Jenkins, B. (eds.), p.25.
[73] For their statements see, Menon, A., *France, NATO and the Limits of Independence, 1981-1997*, pp.122-123; Menon, A., 'From independence to co-operation: France, NATO and European Security', pp.22-23.

growing will among French leaders in favour of pulling the French national nuclear doctrine into the European integration process.

Secondly, as a result of France's principal nuclear power projection policy, which had long been given the utmost priority during the Cold War era, since the early 1990s a serious short-fall became evident with regard to conventional forces at a time when an enormous need for such forces began to be increasingly required in the implementation of 'soft' military mis-sions.[74] As it is officially defined in the French Defence White Paper of 1994:

> '*A true conversion must gradually be carried out in the role of conventional weapons. ...we would contribute to multinational interventions in crisis.... The principle that nuclear deterrence must by no means be banned is, of course, maintained, but it will come second to the capability of participating in the settlement of regional crisis. This means that conventional facilities will henceforth be defined first of all by **their aptitude** as such to contribute, if necessary by force, to the prevention, limitation or settlement of regional crisis or conflicts that do not involve the risk of extreme escalation'.*[75]

French political and military leaders increasingly came to recognise that national military re-sponsibilities should be replaced with a collective approach (with multilateral and multina-tional structures), not only to compensate for the national conventional military weakness, but also for minimising the burden of the defence budget on the French economy. Consequently, France, in order to remove its weaknesses in conventional forces and to maintain its military

---

[74] Although French governments in the Cold War era were also concentrated on French conventional forces, it was only thought for keeping them as compact elite force, which they could be more convenient to employ them in small-scale military interventions (mostly in *Francophone*). Therefore, France had serious shortfalls in crisis intervention operations (the Second Gulf War, Cambodia, Bosnia) in the post-Cold War era.

[75] *Livre Blanc sur la Défense* (German language edition), (Paris: Ministère de la Défense, March 1994), p.59. The original French version of this publication highlights the above words. Also see, Laird, R., 'French Security Policy in Transition – Dynamics of Continuity and Change', *McNair Paper 38*, pp.41-44.

influence in Europe and in the world, was forced to follow a more pragmatic and flexible policies in the EC and NATO.

Since the early 1990s, French politicians made their desire public by showing their willingness to take an active – if not the leading – part in making 'soft' military missions the main cornerstone for constructing a new European security and defence identity in the EC. This would provide France with a means of achieving their traditional Gaullist second circle goal (French foreign and security policy goals in Europe) by strengthening the French global role through 'community' backing.[76] On the other hand, the US NATO forces' reduction in Europe, the French conventional forces' weakness in comparison to the overwhelming 'soft' and 'hard' military capabilities of the US military forces, and the French demand of shaping policy outcomes in restructuring NATO on issues in which it was highly interested all prepared the ground for France to favour *rapprochement* with the US/NATO. This was a 'tactical' *rapprochement* for France that was bound to force the US/NATO to compromise over the creation of a European defence identity and ultimately the European 'Pillar of Defence' equal to the 'North American Pillar', and to reform NATO through 'Europeanising' its IMS. The creation of a European defence identity and the desire for building the European 'Pillar of Defence' through *rapprochement* with NATO, which were plans embarked on by Mitterand (1990-1995) and continued with Chirac's Presidency (since May 1995), also indicate a strong French intention of 'Europeanising' France's security and defence policy in more comprehensive terms than ever before.

France's foreign and security policy convergence to an ambiguous goal of 'Europeanisation' is slow, because old habits seem to reside in deeply rooted tendencies in relation to the French

---

[76] Charles Thumerelle & Philippe G. Le Prestre, 'France: The Straightjacket of New Freedom' in Le Prestre, P. G., *Role Quests in the Post-Cold War Era – Foreign Policies in Transition*, p.138.

security and defence policy and in relation to the universalist messages of the French political and strategic culture. The tension between national autonomy and pro-European rhetoric is therefore still lingering. As Dominique Moïsi argued, 'Chirac's modernised Gaullist formula for independent French action to meet the exigencies of the post-Cold War world may be irreconcilable with the constraints and demands of the European unification process'.[77] It is this tension that would, of course, force France to plunge deeper into the 'Europeanisation' process or remain mutually marginalized with the other states in a disintegrated EU in a multipolar world. However, the French military programme of 1996 is a real commitment to the former:

> *'The project of law programming has the characteristics of defence politics*
>
> *entirely framed within a European perspective... With regard to the ongoing*
>
> *political and strategic analysis of "Livre blanc sur la défense of 1994", which it so*
>
> *confirms, the new model army supports our grand options of foreign policy: a*
>
> *privileged co-operation with Germany in the area of defence and security;*
>
> *development of common actions, bilateral and multilateral, with our principal*
>
> *partners engaged in European construction...; finally, an ambition edifying of*
>
> *defence politics, which must at the same time be the expression of the European*
>
> *Union and a way of reinforcing the European pillar of Atlantic Alliance'.[78]*

This plan of Chirac's not only addressed the European perspective of French security and defence policy and the necessity of co-operative efforts, particularly with Germany, in the development of a major EU military capability, but also brings a new pragmatic and flexible dimension to the Franco-US/NATO relationship.

---

[77] Moïsi, D., 'Chirac of France – A New Leader of the West?', *Foreign Affairs*, (November/December 1995), pp.8-9.
[78] 'Projet De Loi – relatif à la programmation militaire pour les années 1997 à 2002', pp.6-7.

(2) Uneasiness in the Franco-US/NATO Relationship: 'Europeanising' NATO

(2.1) The Limited *Rapprochement*, 1990-1995

The Gaullist orthodoxy, which was crystallised during the Cold War era, involves one of the dogged French approaches towards NATO's IMS: Unless the American dominated IMS was deconstructed between the European 'Pillar of Defence' and 'North American Pillar' on the basis of equal partnership in European defence, France would continue its policy of military non-participation and political aloofness from NATO's IMS. Following the dissolution of Cold War institutional rigidities, two main strategies marked France's tactical US/NATO rapprochement in the period 1990-1995. *Firstly*, Mitterand pursued hostile policies towards NATO in the beginning of the 1990s by focusing on the creation of 'autonomous' European defence entity separate from a radically restructured NATO, reinforcing the role of the CSCE, and finalising these initiatives with a European Confederation. However, towards the mid-1990s, he realised the limits of these projects and the disadvantages of a probable US disengagement from Europe, thus he tried to defuse the Franco-American conflict by pursuing a 'tactical' *rapprochement* with NATO. *Secondly*, his dexterous determination to put the Franco-German partnership in the centre of a long-delayed European 'Pillar of Defence' project was a deliberate idea for compelling the US to consent to a stronger and 'autonomous' European defence 'pillar' in the future.

During the London Summit of July 1990 Mitterand resisted almost all NATO initiatives. He staunchly opposed US efforts to revamp NATO's function from a traditional collective defence organisation (Art.5) to a broader collective security framework, at the same time he opposed politicisation of what he believed was a purely military organisation, and its geographical enlargement, by strengthening the WEU as a rival institution in 'soft' military matters (non-Art.5) with the aim of merging it eventually into the EC's identified defence sphere for realising the European Political Union.[79] He reacted to the decision of NATO's Rapid

Reaction Force creation, which was devised for NATO's out-of-area (non-Art.5) missions

under the command of the UK in May 1991, with the Franco-German Eurocorps initiative in

October 1991. In NATO's Rome Summit of November 1991, Mitterand's dissatisfaction with

the acceptance of NATO's 'New Strategic Concept' that expanded its scope and assigned it

new political roles, led him to made a vitriolic speech in an ironic way: 'I did not know it had

a political role. I am surprised that it has a new one!'[80] Last, but not least, French foreign poli-

cymakers argued that the creation of the North Atlantic Co-operation Council (NACC) in

December 1991 was the main reason for the failure of Mitterand's European Confederation

project and sharply criticised it, saying that the NACC would leave Europe with two pan-

European security organisations along with the CSCE, but neither was robust enough for col-

lective defence.[81]

Although the real intensions of France (creation of the European defence autonomy through

the EC/WEU) and the US (expansion of NATO's political and geographical scope in Europe)

were the reasons for potential irritation and suspicion against each other at the beginning of

the 1990s, towards mid-1995 this institutional competition was suddenly replaced by France's

limited *rapprochement* with NATO for several reasons:

- The obvious military fact was that no other organisation, except NATO, could project

  serious collective defence/security power, at a time when the need for combat forces

  were growing during the Gulf War and crisis in Yugoslavia. France realised the limits

  of the strategic autonomy of Europe when the EC/WEU became befuddled and inef-

[79] For more information see, Chapter 1 - *(2.2.2) The Communitarisation of Security Policy* and the first section of Chapter 2 for the Franco-German initiative on Political Union (19 April 1990).
[80] Mitterand quoted in Menon, A., 'From independence to co-operation: France, NATO and European Security', *International Affairs*, (Vol.71, No.1, 1995), p.23. 'Alliance's Strategic Concept' reprinted in *NATO Handbook*, (Brussels: NATO Office of Information and Press, October 1995), pp.235-248; For political and military roles of NATO see 'Count Your NATOs', *The Economist*, (April 24, 1999), p.9.
[81] Gordon, P. H. (ed.), *A Certain Idea of France. French Security Policy and the Gaullist Legacy*, p.170.

fective due to the absence of political will during the Yugoslav conflict.[82] Concomitantly, French conventional forces' weakness in this type of military intervention forced France to change its politico-military position by participating in multinational force structures for the first time since 1966. This was due to the needs of command, control, and interoperability between NATO and French military forces.[83] France also grudgingly agreed in NATO's ministerial meetings that, in principle, it would support NATO collective security ('soft' military) missions on behalf of the CSCE (Oslo meeting on June 1992) and the UN (Brussels meeting on December 1992).

- Despite Franco-American competition for shaping the European security and defence structure, one of the major political goals of France was to keep the US engaged in Europe for two reasons: Firstly, uncertainties about the future of Russia and an intimidating 'strategic vacuum' in Central and Eastern Europe (CEE) require US/NATO's conventional and nuclear guarantee. Secondly, maintenance of the US's long-standing geopolitical balancing role in Europe is wittingly imperative for preventing the neutralisation or possible *Sonderweg* plans of Germany. While France wants to strengthen its relationship with Germany, it also strives to hold German power in check with the help of the US. At the same time, by limited *rapprochement* with the US/NATO, it wants to prevent an exclusive dialogue from developing between Germany and the US within a reformed NATO.[84]

- The independent status of France with regard to NATO's military organisation was well under way to generating negative effects.[85] The French military participation in

---

[82] Lellouche, P., 'France in Search of Security', *Foreign Affairs*, (Spring 1993); Kay, S., *France and the Future of European Security*, (US: Rowman & Littlefield Publishers, Inc., 1998), pp.139-145.

[83] Paris also took a step back and accepted for the first time since 1966 to allow the transfer of the Franco-German Eurocorps' operational command to NATO (see Chapter 3 - *(1.2.2) The Eurocorps Initiative*).

[84] This was also one of the reasons of Chirac's new NATO policy-style. See Frédéric Bozo 'France' in Brenner, M. (ed.), *NATO and Collective Security*, (UK: Macmillan Press Ltd., 1998), pp.59-60; Moreau-Defarges, P., 'A French Perspective on the EU's IGC', *US-CREST's Franco-American Seminar Series*, October 31, 1996. Available at: <http://www.adetocqueville.com> (Visited on: January 11, 1999).

[85] *Ibid*; Grant, C., 'France on the sidelines', *Financial Times*, (May 25, 2001), p.15.

UN-mandated peacekeeping operations together with NATO forces pushed France towards involvement in a deeper NATO military planning and decision-making processes at the expense of French independent military policy. Accordingly, although the Gaullist objective of independence seems to have been replaced with influence in the name of 'Europeanising' NATO through a growing participation in NATO decision-making processes, Mitterand's single-handed control of foreign and defence policy blocked any profound rapprochement in the first half of the 1990s.

Mitterand's limitation of the Franco-US/NATO rapprochement was based on the primary dual precondition: Reforming the IMS through strengthening political control over the military structure and 'Europeanising' NATO through developing an equivalent 'European Pillar' to the 'North Atlantic Pillar' between 'European Integrationists' and 'Atlanticists'.[86] French policymakers resolutely argued that the end of the Cold War had necessitated radical modification to the IMS through decentralising the rigid military structure of SACEUR and the Defence Planning Committee (DPC), which were militarily and politically dominated by the US, in favour of altering the permanently neglected issue of political control over military. They also emphasised that, while the IMS had been suitable for NATO's Art.5 (collective defence) in situations of full-scale war, 'soft' military missions in the post-Cold War era are subject to *diplomatic-military* or limited military operations (non-Art.5 (collective security) situations). In short, France's rapprochement with NATO was kept conditional on strengthening the strategic role of NATO's Military Committee (MC) and North Atlantic Council (NAC), where unanimity in both bodies is a rule, at the expense of SACEUR and the DPC in *diplomatic-military* operations, as well as earmarking them with a sufficient European

---

[86] Robert P. Grant devoted his article named 'France's New Relationship with NATO' on these two specific premises. See Grant, R. P., 'France's New Relationship with NATO', *Survival*, (Vol.38, No.1, Spring 1996); French Defence Minister, Charles Millon, also pointed out the importance of similar preconditions for France's moving closer to NATO in 1996. Millon, C., 'France and the Renewal of the Atlantic Alliance', *NATO Review*, (Vol.44, No.3, May 1996), pp.13-16.

'caucus' for endowing the Europeans' to act alone in non-Art.5 operations if the US chooses not to become involve.[87]

Even though socialist Mitterand was already slowly moving towards co-operation with NATO military staff particularly in the Bosnia tragedy in 1992, the defeat of socialists in the 1993 elections by the right-wing (RPR) was followed the appointment of Edouard Balladur as Prime Minister, who later fuelled France's rapprochement with NATO. In January 1993, the agreement was finalised between France, Germany, and the US upon making the Eurocorps – created primarily for the WEU non-Art.V missions – available to NATO's operational *command* in crisis and, in April 1993, the head of France's mission to the MC, General Jean-Paul Pélisson, for the first time since 1966 began to actively attend in all NATO meetings dealing with peacekeeping missions with a 'deliberative voice', instead of passive a 'consultative voice'.[88] Balladur, in a speech in May 1993, said that, 'our desire for a better balance between Europeans and Americans within the Alliance ... We have to clarify the Alliance's mission and organisation ... NATO must evolve. Within a reform, France, together with our German partners, as well as other allies in the WEU and EC, must find a defined place'.[89] A month later, the separate NATO and WEU naval task forces' combined in the Adriatic Sea under NATO command in order to monitor the Yugoslav crisis.

---

[87] Director of Policy Planning at the French Foreign Ministry, Gilles Andréani, stated that, '[NATO] will have to interact much more closely with the NAC and the political side of NATO when it comes planning, mounting and conducting operations.' Andréani, G., 'France and NATO', *US-CREST's Franco-American Seminar Series*, January 22, 1996 Available at: <http://www.adetocqueville.com> (Visited on: January 11, 1999). The principal French philosophy is that the DPC, which is managing the IMS, should not only be under the strict political control, but should also subordinate to the NAC, by leaving the NAC an 'unequivocal decision-making body of NATO' with the MC as its 'key implementing and advisory organ'. Grant bluntly put it that the absence of defence ministers in the NAC causes to two major problems: Firstly, the NAC's apparent ineffective authority to control the DPC leaves NATO with two 'coequal governing bodies (councils)'. The DPC even exercises most of the 'real power' within NATO, despite the NAC's status as the Alliance's supreme decision-making body. Secondly, the absence of 'military implementing bodies' in the NAC deprives political decision-makers of adequate technical military information. Grant, R. P., 'France's New Relationship with NATO', pp.63-71.
[88] *Ibid.*
[89] Balladur quoted in Menon, A., *France, NATO and the Limits of Independence, 1981-1997*, p.45.

Although the European defence identity assertions of France was restated three times in 1991

(NATO's Copenhagen Summit in June, Rome Summit in November, and the EC's Maastricht

Conference in December), it came into being in NATO's Brussels Summit in January 1994.

The development of a European Security and Defence Identity (ESDI) between the EU and

NATO and the establishment of a Combined Joint Tasks Force (CJTF) with two chains of

political decision (a European one and a North Atlantic one), albeit with only one military

structure (CJTF) available to both NATO and the EU/WEU for non-Art.5/V missions in sup-

port of the ESDI, became the manifestation of the French strategy of reforming NATO from

within, rather than insisting on separate formations *outside* it.[90] Evidently, the 1994 Brussels

Summit was a tactical meeting for France: While France was supporting NATO's enlarge-

ment plans of Partnership for Peace (PfP), the highly mobile, multinational, and multi-service

CJTF was conceived as a means of deconstructing the IMS by reforming it and making the

CJTF a channel to reach NATO assets for 'autonomous' EU/WEU operations where the US

might choose not to take part.[91]

The disagreement between France and the US appeared soon after the 1994 Brussels Summit.

France insisted on keeping the CJTF outside the IMS, but within the EU/WEU competency,

whereas the US pressed for bringing the CJTF under the command of IMS in order to provide

flexibility to NATO in non-Art.5 missions. The US in the end managed to draw the French

over to its own viewpoint and preserved the authority of IMS upon both Art.5 and non-Art.5

---

[90] However, until NATO's January 1994 Brussels meeting, Mitterand persistently insisted that there should be clear division of responsibilities between 'European' and 'North American Pillars'. As an indication of this, he prevented Defence Minister François Léotard's participation to NATO defence ministerial meeting at Travemünde, Germany, where PfP and CJTF proposals were initially discussed. Similarly, when the French chief of staff sought to attend the Military Committee's meeting in April 1994, Mitterand again refused. See Kay, S., *France and the Future of European Security*, (US: Rowman & Littlefield Publishers, Inc., 1998), pp.139-145; For detailed study on the CJTF, see Barry, C., 'NATO's Combined Joint Task Forces in Theory and Practice', *Survival*, (Vol.38, No.1, Spring 1996); also see, Art, R. J., 'Why Western Europe needs the US and NATO?', *Political Science Quarterly*, (Vol.111, No.1, Spring 1996).
[91] *Declaration of the Heads of State and Government Participating in the Meeting of the North Atlantic Council Held at NATO Headquarters*, (Brussels: NATO Office of Information and Press, January 10-11, 1994), see paragraphs 4, 5 and 6.

missions, but France would be likely to take more active role in latter missions (see Chapter

1). The French acceptance of this scheme, approved a month later in the *Livre Blanc sur la Défense* of 1994, was striking:

> '*NATO is taking on new duties. Without having a monopoly, it is expanding its competence for future operations to maintain peace as well; with which it can deliver powerful means that today perhaps the only organisation can provide and co-ordinate...*' [92]

In September 1994, Defence Minister François Léotard attended an *informal* meeting of NATO defence ministers in Seville, Spain, for the first time since 1966. Although French officials insisted that this would be on a case-by-case basis (not an intention for doctrinal change) for facilitating the co-ordination of diplomatic-military operations in the Balkans, this was a clear signal that the French ploy had began to be brought from outside to inside NATO to change it in the direction of greater European defence independence.

(2.2) Chirac's New Policy Style, 1995-2000

Following the election of Jacques Chirac as President of the Republic in May 1995, Mitterand's NATO policy was modified markedly in its pace and tactics by the new policy style of Chirac, so increased *rapprochement* inside NATO and in agreement with the US.[93] Shortly after he took his post in the Elysée Palace, as a result of the UN peacekeeping forces' ineffectiveness in managing the Bosnian conflict, Chirac together with his British counterpart decisively used military force to put an end to the UNPROFOR hostage crisis. This bold action of Chirac's not only sharpened France's stance among its allies and gained their praise,

[92] *Livre Blanc sur la Défense* (German language edition), (Paris: Ministère de la Défense, March 1994), p.37.
[93] Jacques Chirac, before he elected as the President of the Republic, said in February 1993, '...to play a determining role in the creation of a European defence entity.... It is clear, in effect, that the necessary rebalancing of relations within the Atlantic Alliance, relaying on existing European institutions such as the

but also, as Menon indicated, 'strengthened Chirac's hand in negotiations over the allocation

of flags and posts in the new NATO structure as such decisions partly reflected a state's mili-

tary contribution to the alliance and its activities'.[94] In September 1995, he permitted the first

NATO military exercise since 1966 to be held in France, which was simulating NATO air

strike in Bosnia.[95]

Not only Chirac, but the election of conservative (RPR) Prime Minister Alain Juppé's gov-

ernment was also well on the side of overhauling the Franco-US/NATO relationship in a

positive way. Surprisingly, on December 5, 1995, French Foreign Minister Hervé de Charette

announced in the NAC that in order to strengthen French-NATO cooperation in Bosnia and to

promote development of the European pillar of NATO, the French Defence Minister would

regularly attend NATO defence ministerial meetings; France would *fully* participate in the

MC and a number of other related bodies and would begin to improve its cooperation with

SHAPE.[96] However, de Charette said, 'France has decided to play a bigger role in all bodies

of the Atlantic Alliance in line with what we are now doing in the former Yugoslavia, but

naturally, this does not mean joining the alliance's integrated structures'.[97] Although a month

later in January 1996 Paris announced Defence Minister Charles Millon's readiness to discuss

nuclear issues in the DPC's *informal* meetings where the IMS issues are not raised, France

---

WEU, can only take place from the *inside*, not against the United States, but in *agreement* with it' (emphasis
added). Chirac quoted in Grant, R. P., 'France's New Relationship with NATO', p.63.
[94] Menon informed that this point also recognised by senior French military officials. Menon, A., *France, NATO
and the Limits of Independence, 1981-1997 – The Politics of Ambivalence*, p.117.
[95] This co-operation put French forces, for the first time since 1966, under NATO command in the IFOR
deployment at Yugoslavia in January 1996 in order to implement the Dayton Agreement.
[96] De Charette stated that participation in various bodies would also include NATO Defence College in Rome,
NATO School in Oberammergau, and NATO Situation Centre in Brussels. Grant, R. P., 'France's New
Relationship with NATO', p.62; Most commentators argued that this progress in the France-NATO relationship,
with politico-military participation but not military integration, was a long delayed reaction of France to the
collapse of the Soviet Union and German reunification, which is comparable to the 'Spanish model' that many
security analysts had suggested since the late 1980s. 'France's New Global Bid', *The Economist*, (March 2,
1996), pp.45-46; Frédéric Bozo 'France' in Brenner, M. (ed.), *NATO and Collective Security*, p.53.
[97] *Agence France Press*, 'De Charette Intends 'Bigger Role' in NATO', December 5, 1995, transcript, FBIS-
WEU-95-233; Millon also stated that the aim of that announcement was to bring 16 defence ministers into the
NAC and strengthen the role of the MC – the bodies which are not intruding the state's sovereignty. Millon, C.,
'France and the Renewal of the Atlantic Alliance', *NATO Review*, (Vol.44, No.3, May 1996), pp.13-16;

deliberately kept aloof and rejected full participation in the DPC as well as in the Nuclear Planning Group (NPG).[98]

Chirac gave the impression that he would next challenge the inherited dogmas of Gaullist legacy through the total surrender of the state's national independence and sovereignty to NATO's IMS if the US fulfilled the following set of conditions that were purposefully positioned at the heart of NATO: (a) the IMS should be radically reformed by allowing effective political control over the military structure; (b) the 'Europeanisation' of NATO should render the ESDI an effective European 'Pillar of Defence' by allocating control of NATO assets through the CJTF – permanently and even effectively in peacetime – to the EU/WEU (i.e. an EU/WEU command chain for Art.V as well as for the non-Art.V missions). De Charette put it that, France wanted a European identity that would move from 'the virtual to the tangible'.[99] Concomitantly, in March 1996, Prime Minister Juppé called for the establishment of a 'European Army' of 50,000-men capable of acting autonomously under a EU/WEU mandate.[100] These conditions, in principle, are accompanied by two concrete demands: (a) the appointment of a European Deputy-SACEUR; (b) dual-hatting NATO's Allied Forces South Europe (AFSOUTH) – dividing the two main elements of a single AFSOUTH (based in Naples, Italy) command between the US commander of Naval Forces Europe (US's Sixth Fleet) and transferring the Commander in Chief Allied Forces Southern Europe (CINCSOUTH) to a European, in fact a French, commander.[101]

---

[98] Jean de la Guérivière, an editor in *Le Monde*, argued that France's non-participation in NATO's NPG might be considered as France is hoping for creating a *European subgroup* within the NPG. Extracted from Axel Sauder, 'France's Security Policy Since the End of the Cold War' in Hodge, C. C. (ed.), p.129.

[99] 'NATO Acquires a European Identity', *The Economist*, (June 8, 1996), p.51.

[100] *Hochrangige Expertengruppe für die GASP*, 'Die Voraussetzungen für eine glaubwurdige GASP im Jahr 2000', (Brussel, den 19 Dezember 1994); also see Rees, W. G. *The Western European Union at the Crossroads*, (US: Westview Press, 1998), p.83.

[101] Within Allied Command Europe (ACE), there are two Regional Commands responsible to the SACEUR: (1) Allied Forces North Europe (AFNORTH), at Brunssum, the Netherlands, is under the command of a German or UK four-star Flag or General Officer. (2) AFSOUTH, at Naples, Italy, is under the command of a US four-star Flag or General Officer. AFSOUTH covers an area of some 4 million sq. kms. including Greece, Hungary, Italy, Spain and Turkey. It also includes the Black Sea, the Sea of Azov, the whole of the Mediterranean and the

French and American officials' protracted announcements against each other's governmental policies lasted until the June 1996 Berlin NATO Head of State and Government Summit. French claims to the Europeans' relative autonomy for circumventing the US veto during the utilisation of NATO assets in the European CJTF missions and the US claims that the EU/WEU should act only in emergency situations, so it would not need a peacetime planning and command presence in NATO, were resolved somewhat in favour of France after the Berlin NATO Summit. Whilst France conceded for unanimity – so for the US veto – in the utilisation of NATO assets for the European's CJTF missions, the US in turn, accepted that this would apply for the initial decision only and once the decision was taken the regular arrangements of the European-led mission would be under the responsibility of the countries' which had voted for the decision. This accord, mentioned in the Berlin Communiqué as 'separable but not separate military capabilities' (parag.6&7), also meant that the US would identify the European commands, headquarters in a EU/WEU-led mission and thus would allow the assigning of a European D-SACEUR in its charge.[102] As Howorth captivatingly put it, 'what France does appear to achieve is a general recognition, in NATO and WEU, that the distinction between 'Article V tasks' and 'Petersberg tasks' is a valid one, that it demands an institutional division of labour and that the most appropriate way of proceeding is via CJTFs'.[103] Moreover, one of the significant French criticisms of NATO since de Gaulle was the lack of political control over military structures that was brought somewhat into French

---

Atlantic approaches to the Strait of Gibraltar, and an area around Canary Islands and its associate airspace. See *NATO Handbook*, (Brussels: NATO Office of Information and Press, October 2001), p.261; Charillon, F., 'France and NATO: Atlanticism as the pursuit of Europe by other means?', *RUSI Journal*, (Vol.141, No.6, December 1996), pp.45-48.

[102] *Berlin North Atlantic Council Ministerial Meeting*, (Brussels: NATO Office of Information and Press, M-NAC1 (96) 63, June 3, 1996). Gilles Andréani, a senior French official in the French Foreign Ministry, said: 'I think a reasonable objective is to aim for a dual structure, allowing pre-identified elements within [NATO] – be they command headquarters, staffs, even collective means – to operate without their American counterparts in operations undertaken by the WEU'. Andréani, G., 'France and NATO', *US-CREST's Franco-American Seminar Series*, (January 22, 1996).

[103] Jolyon Howorth, 'National defence and European security integration – An illusion inside a chimera?' in Howorth, J. & Menon, A. (ed.), *The EU and National Defence Policy*, p.35; For detailed analysis of the Art.V tasks and Petersberg Tasks see Chapter 2 - *(1.2) Contours of the CDP and CD*.

lines at the Berlin Summit of June 1996. The establishment of the Policy Coordination Group (PCG) within NATO for closer coordination of diplomatic/politico-military – 'soft' – missions in the changing security environment of Europe (parag.6) and 'the effective exercise of political control by NAC through the Military Committee' (parag.7) became a watershed for the Franco-US/NATO relationship.

Whereas the Americans considered the Berlin compromise as NATO's 'Europeanisation' even more than they had previously contemplated, for the French this was just the beginning of NATO's 'Europeanistion' and 'the emancipation of the Europeans from the American tutelage'[104] that might in the end provide France with the necessary conditions to reintegrate into the NATO's IMS, if the Americans were to approve transferring the CINCSOUTH to a European general. Paris concluded that not only Art.5, 7 and 8 of the Berlin Communiqué, which refer to the identification of headquarters in support of the ESDI, as a *de facto* pledge for transferring the CINCSOUTH to a European command, but also argued that NATO's top two strategic commands (SACEUR and SACLANT) already went to a US general and, therefore, Europeans should hold the two European regional (northern and southern) commands.[105] Washington asserted that interpretation as such is due to misreading of those articles and argued that Europeans are holding already three-fourths of the most senior NATO general posts, including the European D-SACEUR.

Clinton's expression of his governments' opinion in an interview, 'the AFSOUTH Command is essentially command of the 6th Fleet of the US Navy.... if we ... divide the AFSOUTH

---

[104] 'OTAN, les Européens tentent de s'émanciper de la tutelle américaine', *Libération*, (June 4, 1996).
[105] Tiersky, R., 'French Military Reform and NATO Restructuring', *Joint Force Quarterly*, (Spring 1997), p.98; Parmentier, G., 'Madrid and Beyond: The New NATO', *US-CREST's Franco-American Seminar Series*, April 10, 1997 <http://www.adetocqueville.com> (Visited on: January 11, 1999); *Agence France Press*, 'No to NATO Military, For Now', transcript, The Tocqueville Connection, US-CREST, October 3, 1997 <http://www.ttc.org> (Visited on: May 01, 1999).

Command, it wouldn't, from our point of view, be a sensible thing to do militarily because

that's essentially the central asset of AFSOUTH',[106] was based on following reasons:

- Due to the region being both highly unstable and vital to US and European interests,
  maintaining a strong convergence of interests under the US-led AFSOUTH command,
  which is the only US-led regional command in Europe, will make the US operational
  and political support of NATO easier at a time when that command is becoming increasingly important.

- The growing need for high-tech weapons to deter possible ballistic missile proliferation threats against the AFSOUTH region still requires effective American military
  capacities and leadership.

- Detaching the command link between AFSOUTH and Sixth Fleet will increase reaction time to risks and, doing so, would certainly threaten the shared interests of all
  NATO members.

The result from these interrelated reasons indicates that the role of the Sixth Fleet in the

Mediterranean area is indispensable for both the US and Europe, and as far as the US alone is

concerned the region is a stepping-stone for its global interests from the Balkans, Aegean, and

Middle East to the Persian Gulf and Central Asia.

While Chirac recognised the vitality of the AFSOUTH command for the US, he persistently

argued that, for a healthy transatlantic relationship and a strong ESDI within NATO, regional

commands should come under the responsibility of Europeans. In a press conference on

November 5, 1996, he said:

> *'Of course there are US responsibilities in the area, but they are not more*
>
> *important than the European.... France considers that Europe's interest; Europe's*

---

[106] Clinton, B., 'Interview With European Television Journalists', *Weekly Compilation of Presidential Documents*, (Vol.33, No.27, July 3, 1997).

> *strategic interest in the Mediterranean justifies European leadership of the*
>
> *Southern command. This is a very important question for France, because one*
>
> *cannot mention Europe's defence identity if it is not translated into command of*
>
> *relevant areas'.*[107]

At Brussels NATO foreign ministers' meeting on December 10, 1996, American and French delegates became resentful of each other. Partly as a result of the Franco-German special partnership and partly as a result of Germany's interest in progressing the ESDI concept within NATO, Germany was also involved in the Franco-American dispute over AFSOUTH. Although former German Defence Minister Volker Rühe initially supported the French by offering a compromise formula that the AFSOUTH command could rotate every two-years between Americans and Europeans (most probably this was agreed secretly a day before the NATO Brussels foreign ministers' meeting at the Franco-German Common Security and Defence Council's Nuremberg meeting on December 9, 1996), he later found himself over-ruled by the Chancellor's office and Ministry of Foreign Affairs due to pressures from Washington. The US also irritably rejected an alternative French solution to the deadlock on AFSOUTH command that a European commander would take over the post after five years.[108]

French and American officials attempted to reduce the tension several times before NATO's Head of State and Government meeting in Madrid on July 8-9,1997, but no progress was made on the AFSOUTH command dispute. On January 24, 1997, Chirac's foreign policy ad-

---

[107] Chirac's press conference at the French-Spanish summit on November 5, 1996. Quoted in Yves Boyer, 'Whither Core Europe? France and the European Construction: Issues and Choices' in Lankowski, C. and Serfaty, S. 'Europeanizing Security? NATO and an Integrating Europe', *AICGS Research Report*, (US: The Johns Hopkins University, AICGS Research Report No. 9, 1999), p.31.

[108] See *Agence France Press*, 'Defence Official Outlines Position Concerning NATO Commands', January 23, 1997, transcript, FBIS-WEU-97-016; Rubinstein, A. Z., 'Germans On Their Future', *Orbis*, (Vol.43, No.1, Winter 1999), pp.127-144; Menon, A., *France, NATO and the Limits of Independence, 1981-1997*, p.57.

visor, Jean-David Levitte, flew to Washington to discuss once again the issue of restructuring

NATO's regional commands, but again the result was no progress. Due to French President

Chirac's repeated demands, American President Clinton had to say an explicit 'no' in

February 1997: 'Jacques, I must be frank about the southern command: it's no', Clinton

said.[109] On March 14, 1997, this time Clinton sought to reduce the tension by proposing the

creation of a new rapid reaction force in the south, which 'would offer considerable scope for

France and neighbouring allies to cement their links in actual operations'.[110] Meanwhile, on

April 10, 1997, final agreement came for the creation of the European D-SACEUR. Although

the tension was slightly reduced during the negotiations on May 24, 1997, by both parties

agreeing that France would not raise its claims for European command in the CINCSOUTH

to the Madrid Summit and the US, in turn, agreed to a French idea that a NATO-Russia

Security Pact would be signed in Paris on May 27,[111] the Atlanticist UK's veto for a phased

merger of the EU and WEU at the Amsterdam Council meeting in June 1997, however, poi-

soned the European Integrationists-Atlanticists relations. At the end of the Madrid Summit,

France was still refusing to reintegrate into NATO's IMS, so the authority of the ESDI, which

was the end product of French efforts, was given to a British D-SACEUR command.[112] One

of the senior NATO officials said to Menon in an interview:

> *'The French achieved a hell of a lot at Berlin. More than they could have expected*
>
> *only weeks prior to the summit. Everyone assumed that that would be the end of*
>
> *the matter. But the French find it hard to say 'yes'. They are happiest when they*

---

[109] Quoted by Menon in *Libération*, February 27, 1997, in Menon, A., *France, NATO and the Limits of Independence, 1981-1997*, p.56.
[110] Fitchett, J., 'Clinton Offers Paris Compromise on NATO', *International Herald Tribune*, (March 14, 1997).
[111] For the NATO-Russia Pact on 'The Founding Act on Mutual Relations, Co-operation and Security Between NATO and the Russia Federation' see, *Madrid Declaration of the North Atlantic Council* on 'The Partnership Between NATO and Russia', (Brussels: NATO Office of Information and Press, July 8-9, 1997).
[112] In December 1998, British and German officials agreed that the D-SACEUR would rotate among their generals. See Ehrhart, H-G., 'France and NATO: Change by Rapprochement?', *Hamburger Briträge zur Friedensforschung und Sicherheitspolitik*, (Hamburg: Institut für Friedensforschung und Sicherheitspolitik an der Universität Hamburg, No.121, January 2000), p.22.

are making a stand against the Americans. The whole CINCSOUTH episode

smacks of cutting off your nose to spite your face'.[113]

There is no doubt that the American leadership was aware of the French ploy of creating a robust European defence 'pillar' through the ESDI/CJTF, which may one day become a fully 'autonomous' European defence 'pillar' outside NATO and could be merged into the EU through the WEU. Therefore, the American leadership rejected the transfer of CINCSOUTH to a European command, because it 'involved real, not symbolic power'.[114] John R. Bolton, in his speech before the Committee on International Relations House of Representatives, pointed out: 'While these structures [ESDI/CJTF] may prove militarily feasible, and even politically constructive in the short run, overtime they will result in the fragmentation of NATO's central unifying elements, resulting in the loss of American interest in the Alliance.'[115] A retired US Army Lieutenant Colonel, Charles Barry, expressed his opinion in an interview on the US position in NATO and the American understanding of French claims to an 'equal' security and defence partnership between 'European' and 'North American' pillars strikingly: *'The Alliance is a consensus organisation. The only way you get anything done is when you have a recognised, accepted leader. So we don't envisage an Alliance of exactly equal partnership but of "more" equal partnership, with much more voice, more influence for the Europeans'* (emphasis added).[116] The idea behind this quotation is the main French concern that instead of 'Europeanisation' of NATO, the US is struggling for 'Americanisation' of the 'European Pillar'.

---

[113] Menon, A., *France, NATO and the Limits of Independence, 1981-1997*, p.138.

[114] 'Count Your NATOs', *The Economist*, (April 24, 1999), pp.9-12.

[115] Statement of John R. Bolton, Senior Vice President (American Enterprise Institute), before the Committee on International Relations House of Representatives on the 'European Common Foreign, Security and Defence Policies – Implications for the US and the Atlantic Alliance'. Available at: <http://www.house.gov/international _relations/> (Visited on: November 17, 2000).

[116] Interview with Charles Barry at Washington in 'France Sings a Different Tune in NATO', *The Tocqueville Connection, US-CREST*, (June 05, 1997). <http://www.adetocqueville.com> (Visited on: January 10, 1999).

The victory of the Socialist Party of Lionel Jospin in May 1997, which has a more traditional Gaullist profile and backs the idea of keeping France outside of NATO's IMS, not only became a decisive stumbling block in front of the possible French-US/NATO *rapprochement*, but also made the idea of French reintegration inconceivable. In addition, if the composition of Jospin's government is taken into consideration, putting the *rapprochement* aside, the cohabitation partners, the Communist Party and unwieldy Radical, Citizen and Green Group (*Radical, Citoyen, et Vert* (RCV)) even desired to see NATO dissolved.

(2.3) Overall Assessment and the Recent Franco-American Dialogue

France's unwillingness to play a passive role or subordinate itself to a US dominated NATO and, in turn, the US's reluctance to change its stance with regard to the CINCSOUTH, aggravated the hostile reactions between the French and the American policymakers. Unsurprisingly, France's traditional *grandeur* and *rank* ambitions resurfaced unequivocally in order to counter the world's remaining superpower in a unipolar world by concentrating on the advocacy of multipolarity so that France would strengthen its world leadership role in a regionally cultivated economically and politically independent Europe against the US's unilateral actions. President Chirac and Foreign Minister Hubert Védrine increasingly began to attack the US in their speeches, as they would not accept a politically unipolar, culturally uniform world, or the unilateralism of a single 'hyperpower'.[117] The French ambassador to the US, François Bujon de l'Estang, said that, 'extraterritorial sanction and unilateralism: France rejects the former as being contrary to law and advises against the latter as being inward-looking, preferring instead a multilateral, concerted approach to global problems.'[118]

---

[117] For their arguments see, Gordon, P. H., 'The French Position', *The National Interest*, Fall 2000. Available at: <http://www.brookings.edu/views/articles/Gordon/2000fall_NI.htm> (Visited on: September 13, 2000).
[118] De l'Estang, B., 'France's Diplomatic Priorities: An Agenda for 2000', *Centre on the US and France Roundtable Discussion*, (April 10, 2000).Available at:<http://www.brookings.org/fp/cusf/events/20000410.htm> (Visited on: November 11, 2000); He also made a similar speech at the Cornell University. Speech by François Bujon de l'Estang on 'France, Europe and the Transatlantic Partnership', (US: Cornell University, September 29, 1997). Available at: <http://www.info-france-usa.org/fnews.htm> (Visited on: November 11, 2000).

It became obvious in diplomatic and academic circles that serious transatlantic rifts had emerged between the Atlanticists' (the US and the UK in particular) and the European Integrationists' (France and cautious Germany). Although plenty of them are identifiable, two of them are eye-catching in the Franco-American dispute: The concept of 'rogue govern-ments' and the National Missile Defence (NMD) project.[119] The serious disagreement is not over the identification of which government is 'rogue' or not, but the application of a precise foreign and security policy against them. France conceives that international norms and insti-tutions are effective instruments for reintegrating those countries into the family of democ-ratic nations through dialogue, *diplomacy* should not be underestimated; whereas, the US who chose the strategy of containment through sanctions and periodic bombing, prefers utilising the sheer size of its *military power*. Védrine often gave Iraq as an example and questioned as, 'indefinitely, protracted sanctions has been harsh and cruel for a long time for the Iraqi people without weakening the regime. How can the emergence of a traumatized "embargo genera-tion" be good for peace and stability in the region?'[120] European Integrationists' are even more sceptical of the no-fly zones in Iraq, which 'lack the legitimacy of an international man-date beyond America and Britain,' said Antony Blinken, the former Special Assistant to the US President.[121]

However, France is not discarding the existence of a potential nuclear proliferation threat in the world, nor it is against the US's NMD project in general; but, France is concerned that the US will embrace it as an alternative to diplomacy-based solutions and thus will undermine the

---

[119] For a good account see, Daalder, I. H., 'Are the US and Europe heading for divorce?', *International Affairs*, (Vol.77, No.3, 2001), pp.531-545. In order to compare French and German politicians' similar views on these subjects see, Chapter 4 - *(2.1) Continuities and Changes within the German-US/NATO Relationship*.
[120] Védrine , H., 'French-American Dialogue in a Changing International Environment', *Centre on the US and France Roundtable Discussion*, (May 12, 2000). Available at: <http://www.brookings.org/> (Visited on: November 17, 2000); Also see similar arguments in De l'Estang, B., 'France's Diplomatic Priorities: An Agenda for 2000', *Centre on the US and France Roundtable Discussion*, (April 10, 2000).
[121] Blinken, A., 'The US, France, and Europe at the Outset of the New Administration', *US-France Analysis Paper*, (March 2001). Available at: <http://www.brookings.org/> (Visited on: March 19, 2001).

multilateral non-proliferation agreements unilaterally.[122] Védrine said that the US unilateral actions in bypassing the US-USSR ABM Treaty of 1972 would seriously damage the strategic stability that France based the unilateral reduction of its nuclear arsenal on, having put its confidence in the arms control process and its durability.[123] Chirac said in the Franco-British Summit on February 9, 2001, '... since the beginning of time ... there has been struggle between the sword and the shield. [But] no record of any world civilisation in which the shield has won'.[124] In fact, Chirac made it clear in 1995 that France's nuclear weapons must remain an instrument of deterrence rather than combat arms. He also argued that, it is impossible to develop new 'low-yield' nuclear weapons under a test ban as one of the advantages of such an agreement, because 'low-yield' nuclear weapons would be dangerous, 'one may be tempted to use them more easily' than more powerful ones and they might also provoke proliferation.[125] Thus, the French government would prefer a land-based limited NMD system with a small number of interceptors in agreement with the Russians that would not threaten the essence of mutually assured destruction and the international strategic balance.[126] As Pierre Lellouche perceptively put it, 'there is no dispute on concepts: The existence of autonomy between non-proliferation and counter-proliferation, that is to say, between a diplomacy-approach and a defence-approach. The real debate is on the optimal combination of the two approaches to reach a target between them.... In this respect, it would be illusory and destabilising for the international strategic balance if one claimed it to be possible to reach that [target] only by

---

[122] Pierre Lellouche, former diplomatic advisor to President Chirac and a member of the Defence Commission, studied broadly nuclear proliferation threats in the world. Lellouche, P., 'France in Search of Security', *Foreign Affairs*, (Spring 1993). Also see 'Rapport d'information MM Pierre Lellouche, Guy-Michel Chauveau et Aloyse Warhouver, *déposé en application de l'article 145 du Règlement par la production*, par la commission de la défense, sur la proliferation des armes de destruction massive et de leurs vecteurs', *Assemblée Nationale Rapport No.2788*, (Paris: Imprimé pour l'Assemblée nationale par la Sté Nouvelle des Librairies, December 7, 2000).
[123] Védrine , H., 'French-American Dialogue in a Changing International Environment', *Centre on the US and France Roundtable Discussion*, (May 12, 2000); Also see Chapter 2 – *Introduction*.
[124] Joint Press Conference by Jacques Chirac, Tony Blair and Lionel Jospin during the *Franco-British Summit at Cahors*, (February 9, 2001). Available at: <http://www.doc.diplomatie.fr> (Visited on: August 2, 2001).
[125] Chirac quoted in Yost, D. S., 'France's Nuclear Dilemmas', *Foreign Affairs*, (Vol.75, No.1, January/February 1996), pp.108-119.
[126] Blinken, A., 'The US, France, and Europe at the Outset of the New Administration', *US-France Analysis Paper*, (March 2001).

defence, as the US seems to be defending a similar belief; [but] it would even be inadequate for Europe to rely only on diplomacy'.[127]

French policymakers argue that a strong European partner with a balanced share of responsibilities within NATO is a key to preserving American interest and commitment to Europe and, therefore, France will push for it in NATO, join in the CJTF and NATO planning, and in the new NAC for bilateral Franco-American military co-operation.[128] This has been proven in Kosovo during NATO's Operation Allied Force. Although Chirac and Jospin accused NATO of being a US 'tool' and warned about the danger of American 'hyperpower', they were prepared to act together with the US in Kosovo to protect the common values and interests of the West.[129] This military operation was a defining moment for the CESDP in that it demonstrated the policy urgently needed strong military backing. The confirmation of its need came with the intention of creating 60,000-member European rapid reaction force by 2003, which was announced in Helsinki European Council meeting on December 10-11, 1999. As Chirac said in Strasbourg on October 19, 1999, that France envisages Europe as:

> *[It] may be able to enlarge its voice in the administration of world affairs and above all in our continent's affairs. That it may assume its responsibilities in a law-respecting world. Europe has to be able to take action in support of these goals together with its American ally when the US wants to be involved in the field. But it must also be able to operate on its own when it wishes to. This defence*

---

[127] 'Rapport d'information MM Pierre Lellouche, Guy-Michel Chauveau et Aloyse Warhouver, *déposé en application de l'article 145 du Règelement par la production*, par la commission de la défense, sur la proliferation des armes de destruction massive et de leurs vecteurs', *Assemblée Nationale Rapport No.2788*, (Paris: Imprimé pour l'Assemblée nationale par la Sté Nouvelle des Librairies, December 7, 2000), pp.247-249.
[128] Richard, A., 'French-US Relations – A View from the Defence Side', *US-CREST's Franco-American Seminar Series*, April 29, 1998 <http://www.adetocqueville.com> (Visited on: January 11, 1999);*Agence France Press*, 'No to NATO Military, For Now', transcript, The Tocqueville Connection, US-CREST, October 3, 1997.
[129] According to a survey published in 'A Survey of France: If in doubt, seek Europe', *The Economist*, (June 5, 1999) large majority of French, 68%, worried about America being the sole superpower, 61% said the American influence is too big culturally, 60% economically, and 56% militarily.

> capacity will complete the economic, humanitarian, and political instruments the EU already has at its disposal ...'[130]

French leaders also grasped well the fact that in order to claim a European military leadership role within NATO, restructuring of the French armed forces was needed to catch up with US military standards. It became apparent during Kosovo operation that although French armed forces assumed the biggest European share of NATO military activities, French forces capabilities were still lagging behind the US capabilities. French leaders knew that if NATO was to be effectively 'Europeanised' and if Europe's forthcoming 60,000-member rapid reaction forces is to be successful, then first of all France's ongoing military modernisation, which began with Chirac's announcement of a radical defence reform in May 1996 and caused France's *rapprochement* with the US/NATO, needs to be effectively 'Europeanised' for a robust CESDP.

(3) French Defence Reforms: 'Europeanisation', Modernisation, and Professionalisation of Armed Forces

The cardinal manifestation of 'defence needs a strategic vision of its future',[131] is resonated in the French Defence White Paper of 1994, *loi de programmation militaire* (LPM) 1997-2002, and in the LPM 2003-2008 that all characterize a 'Europeanised', modernised and professionalised future model of French armed forces by 2015.[132]

---

[130] Speech by French President Jacques Chirac on 'A Responsible Europe in a Renewed Atlantic Alliance' before the Assembly of Atlantic Societies on October 19, 1999, in Strasbourg/France, in *Internationale Politik*, (Vol.1, July 14, 2000). <http:// www.dgap.org/english/tip/tip2/chirac191099.html> (Visited on: July 14, 2000).
[131] This expression is the basic feature of the document called, *Thirty Years Forecasting Plan*, (Paris: Ministry of Defence, 1999), p.1.
[132] In view of the long-term review of armed forces (Model 2015), three LPMs will be informative: the LPM 1997-2002, which was published on May 20, 1996, primarily focused on the professionalisation of armed forces, so increased personnel and decreased equipment expenditure; the LPM 2003-2008, which was published on August 3, 2001, emphasised supplying high-technology equipment to the army; and, the last phase, the LPM 2009-2015 would be a study on the completion of modernisation and professionalisation of French armed forces

The White Paper of 1994 laid down the new strategic lines for France's defence policy and called for a radical reform in the force structure and organisation of the armed forces. The 'Europeanised', modernised and professionalised French armed forces envisaged in the White Paper are for facilitating French power projection in crisis prevention and ultimately military interventions with improved intelligence gathering capacities, streamlined command structures, and the enhanced strategic mobility of professional soldiers in European regional conflicts and French sovereign territories overseas (the *Départments d'Outre-Mer* and *Territories d'Outre-Mer* (DOM-TOMs)).[133] It is written in the White Paper of 1994 that, 'strategic mobility is then a determinant element of success. It depends on two factors: The aptitude of the forces to intervene in remote areas and the existence of a sufficient transport capacity.... The projection of power properly is destined to stop the outbreak of a conflict by marking an immediate impression of superiority rather than taking the risk of a long conventional war'.[134]

In addition to emphasising the enhanced mobility and flexibility of French conventional forces, it is also underlined in the White Paper that all French military actions would increasingly take place within joint (multilateral) operations, particularly within the common European defence framework.[135] It is stated that:

> *'As a European nation, [France] integrates its defence policy into a new*
> *perspective to arrive at a future "common defence", which is confirmed by the*
> *arrangement of the Treaty on European Union. [...] After all, this progressive*
> *construction leads to the verification of a political identity, which would be*

---

in connection to national (inter-service), European, and Overseas (colonial) command structures. For the Defence Budget Statistics 2000, which is worked out within the framework of the LPM 1997-2002 and defined a new model for armed forces, see *French Defence Statistics 2000* (English language edition), (Paris: Financial Services Directorate – General Secretary for the Administration and the Ministry of Defence), pp.1-16; also see 'Projet De Loi – relatif à la programmation militaire pour les années 2003 à 2008', *Assemblée Nationale No.3255*, (Paris: Imprimé pour l'Assemblée nationale par la Sté Nouvelle des Librairies, August 3, 2001).
[133] Gregory, S., 'France and *Missions de Souveraineté*', *Defense Analysis*, (Vol.16, No.3, 2000), pp.329-342.
[134] *Livre Blanc sur la Défense*, 1994, pp.75-82, quotation is on pages 81-82.
[135] *Ibid*, p.59.

incomplete if [Europe] would not express itself in the area of defence also. [...]

The role of [France] in the concert of nations is fairly dependant on the success

and failure of this [European] enterprise'.[136]

This indicates a significant French commitment to sharing its traditional aptitude and transfer-ring some of its national defence self-reliance into a multinational EU structure. However, one should also be careful in defining the threshold between the common European defence framework and the 'Europeanisation' of French security and defence policy. Like every EU country, France wishes to see a common European defence framework as French policy-makers actually conceived it to be.[137] For example, France lost its advantageous position against Germany with the devaluation of French nuclear forces; but, in the new security envi-ronment, French leaders wanted to regain that superiority by increasingly signifying France's great power status in peacekeeping and humanitarian missions, which is portrayed under the French policy of universalist responsibility.[138]

Correspondingly, France has a mechanised way of thinking. As Boucheron put it, French policymakers 'have taken care not to make any of the fundamental choices.... between allied interoperability and a more international division of labour; between concentration on Europe and on 'Overseas'; between crisis management and high intensity conflicts; between a profes-sional army and a mixture of professionals and conscripts. In new theory, the new arrange-ment will allow for all or any of these options'.[139] Although Balladur's cohabitation govern-ment during Mitterand's presidency significantly attempted to reform the French armed forces

---

[136] *Ibid*, p.28.
[137] In the preamble of the *Livre Blanc sur la Défense* of 1994, Balladur wrote: 'the primary target is to assure the independence of countries and the defence of vital interests of nations'.
[138] See Wyllie, James H., *European Security in the New Political Environment*, pp.104-105; Menon, A., *France, NATO and the Limits of Independence, 1981-1997 – The Politics of Ambivalence*, p.104.
[139] Boucheron in Jolyon Howorth, 'The Debate in France Over Military Intervention in Europe' in Freedman, L. (ed.), *Military Intervention in European Conflicts*, (UK: The Political Quarterly Publishing Ltd., 1994), p.109.

through the Defence White Paper of 1994, further reform initiatives came with the election of the Gaullist President Chirac in May 1995, who put forward his wholesale military reform plan in February 1996.

(3.1) Chirac's Military Reforms

The restructuring process of French armed forces announced by President Chirac on February 22, 1996, and the first (LPM 1997-2002) of the three transitional phases (LPM 2003-2008 and LPM 2009-2015) presented three months later on May 20, 1996, represents the most radical reform initiative since the beginning of the Fifth Republic.[140] Chirac's bold policy actions in the LPM 1997-2002 reforms initiative saw a major breakthrough for the 'Model 2015' army, which had previously been set out in the White Paper of 1994, but for legal, financial, and political reasons had its detailed implementation postponed. These major breakthroughs were to end conscription and replace it with all-professional or all-volunteer force; reorganise, modernise and cut by one-third the armed forces; to cut defence spending one-fifth; to reassess self-sufficiency in arms industry and joint ventures at the European level; and, to dismantle the land-based pre-strategic nuclear weapons.[141]

This long-delayed comprehensive reforms initiative were prompted by several factors:

- As a result of serious shortcomings in French armed forces at the time of the Gulf War and Yugoslav crisis, French policymakers felt humiliated with their poor power projection capabilities and ineffective force structures.

---

[140] 'Le Président de la République a décidé d'engager une réforme majeure de nos moyens de défense, comparable par son ampleur à celle du début des années soixante, qui, sous l'impulsion du général de Gaulle, fut à l'origine d'une modernisation de nos armées et de la réalisation des forces nucléaires françaises. 'Projet De Loi – relatif à la programmation militaire pour les années 1997 à 2002', p.1/55

[141] The pro-European former French President Valéry Giscard d'Estang (1975-1981) had proposed reforms similar to those Chirac had initiated in early 1996. Giscard argued in summer 1989 that professional army should replace the French mandatory military service and streamlined nuclear deterrence should adapt itself to this new form armed force. He also argued that this army could co-operate better with other European military forces. See Wetterqvist, F., *French Security and Defence Policy – Current Developments and Future Prospects*, (Diane Publishing Company, 1993), p.73.

- High unemployment rate and budget deficit problems, which were an obstacle to
  France's meeting the convergence criteria required for joining in the European single
  currency, led to financial cuts in defence budget and delayed previous reforms.

- As a consequence of the above reasons, Paris found itself drawn closer to its allies in
  NATO's multilateral platform (though negotiating with the US the best deal it could
  get for its *rapprochement* with NATO) for 'improvising' its defence command and
  operational capabilities, which were far from meeting NATO standard, high-
  technology and rapid reaction force capabilities.[142]

- The international responsibility (see Universalist Policy) of France in the post-Cold
  War era increased the significance of its military presence both in Europe and
  throughout the world in order to be able to manage mounting 'soft' military matters.
  This responsibility could be met by reformed armed forces, but as was often argued by
  Chirac, the structural and material means of France's defence system are 'totally un-
  suited' to the new security environment.[143]

Although the majority of French agreed that the armed forces need to be professionalised and
the conscript army needed to be brought to an end, the most sensitive equation 'national integration' versus 'military recruiting process' in France – as it is in Germany – was a basic argument for maintaining conscription.[144] Nevertheless, in order to prepare a professional and
highly mobile force, Chirac's putting an end to conscription was not only considered a daring

---

[142] It has to be noted that French Foreign Minister Hervé de Charette's announcement on December 5, 1995, in
the NAC, calling for the strengthened France-NATO cooperation in Bosnia, was the formal manifestation of
French armed forces' abandoning of the principle of self-reliance due to their inability to project power. Thus,
France participated NATO's IFOR (Implementation Force) in Bosnia under an American General's command.
[143] 'A French Projection', *The Economist*, (March 2, 1996), p.45.
[144] The abolition of the conscript army was severely criticised by members of the Communist Party and divided
the members of the Socialist Party. Menon, A., *France, NATO and the Limits of Independence, 1981-1997*,
p.179; Due to the French history of 'national integration' (the conscript being a bridge between poor and rich,
cities and countryside), 'military recruiting process' (similar to the one in Germany), and the suppression of
military putsch in Algeria by the conscript army in 1961, the conscription rule was gained appreciation in
France. Heisbourg, F. 'Trittbrettfahrer? Keine europäische Verteidigung ohne Deutschland', *Internationale
Politik*, (Nr.4, April 2000).

action against conscript supporters in the country, but was also considered an action that troubled France's partner Germany, which considers the 'citizen in uniform' concept an indisputable value of its *Innere Führung*.[145] The professionalisation and modernisation of military equipment of armed forces will not only enable effective 'projectability', but will also allow substantial flexibility in the rotation of military units in the crisis prevention and protection tasks. These tasks will be implemented in multinational and, particularly, in the 'European' domain. In fact, French defence planning has taken into account for the first time such an in-depth adaptation. It is emphasised in LPM 1997-2002:

> *'The priority assigned to our classical forces – the foundation of this projection*
>
> *capacity – will comply with the following principles: readiness is required of these*
>
> *forces, the mastering of procedures and equipment complexes, engagement in a*
>
> *frame that will often be characterised as multinational leads to the completion of*
>
> *the professionalisation of our armies; [...] if we [collectively] are not in range to*
>
> *realise projectable forces in a very short period of time, to any location and at any*
>
> *time, it is crucial to arrange an autonomous capacity for initial projection*
>
> *(territorial, aerial and maritime) in order to put the leading elements or*
>
> *reinforcements in place. As it used to be, like it is today, successful operations, will*
>
> *be [accomplished] by national means, combined means, or, a potential European*
>
> *«pool»'.[146]*

It seems that the *power projection* capacity of France, which the White Paper of 1994 and the LPM 1997-2002 sought to revamp, will have shortfalls and difficulties in deploying 15,000-

---

[145] Initially, in place of conscription, Chirac offered to those who were against the abolition of conscript army a kind of 'national civil service', like the one in Germany. See 'A French Projection', *The Economist*, (March 2, 1996), p.45; Germany in 1999 launched a major project to overhaul the entire military system in order to enable Germany to deploy professional rapid reaction forces for the EU/WEU and NATO operations. Although Germany merged the Main Defence Forces and the Crises Reaction Forces to become Readiness Forces, the Basic Military Organisation is still the backbone of the conscript army. See Chapter 4 - *(3.1) The Recent Bundeswehr Reform*, and Chapter 3 - *(2.1) Causes of the Rocky Kohl-Chirac Security and Defence Dialogue*.
[146] 'Projet De Loi – relatif à la programmation militaire pour les années 1997 à 2002', pp.9-10/55.

men for an unlimited duration and 30,000-men for up to a year in high-intensity conflicts, where all available military capacities could be needed for their utilisation, until the end of 2002. France has 30,000-men professional army and still rotates through the French colonies, where France has bilateral security agreements, to provide security and reduce regional and international instabilities. This troop is the Foreign Legion, also known as *Troupes de Marine*, *Troupes Coloniales* or *La Coloniale*, and because the majority of soldiers are career, their transition into an all-professional force would not be problematical.[147] They were the main component of French military interventions in Rwanda, Bosnia, and in Kosovo. However, according to Chirac's reform plans, an all-professional army would replace the ten-month conscript military service by 2002 and the armed forces of 1994/1995 would shrink from 395,400 (including about 50% conscripts) to a 244,500 all-professional army with a complete reorganisation of the entire new and old generation systems (see Table 5.1 below). The main goal with an all-professional army is to acquire by 2002 the capability to rapidly deploy either a combat force of 50,000-men into a major distant combat theatre within NATO's non-Art.5 framework or to project simultaneously 30,000-men into a high-intensity regional contingency and up to 5,000-men into low-intensity combat or peacekeeping operations both sustainable for up to a year through the rotation of residual 15,000-men by 2015.[148] The professionalisation of armed forces would in the end provide France with a highly mobile and flexible force operating on different missions in Europe and overseas, which they could effectively rotate between locations around the world.

---

[147] Jones, J. B., 'French Forces for the 21ˢᵗ Century', *Joint Force Quarterly*, (Summer 2000), p.35.
[148] See 'Projet De Loi – relatif à la programmation militaire pour les années 1997 à 2002', p.10/55.

Table 5.1

The Reform Phases of the French Armed Forces[149]

CATEGORY YEAR	ARMY	AIR FORCE	NAVY	TOTAL ARMED FORCES
1990/1991	288,550	93,100	65,300	446,950
1994/1995	241,400	89,800	64,200	395,400
1999/2000	178,300	76,400	62,600	317,300
Targeted Future Reform (circa.2015)	136,000	63,000	45,500	244,500

The *crisis prevention* strategy also became a priority for the professional army and the central theme of the new French security and defence policy. The preventive strategy is essentially a political move in which military measures, in particular intelligence (*renseignement*) and pre-positioning of forces (*prépositionnement de forces*), play a significant role in the identification of conflicts and preservation of international peace and security before they escalate into a potential conflict situation. 'Intelligence' would provide the necessary knowledge for the professional armed forces to prepare themselves for possible preventive missions and allow them to react accurately and early in an evolving crisis situation. 'Prepositioning of forces' would provide an immediate reaction to crisis by exploiting French standing forces located around such regions. It is also pointed out in the LPM 1997-2002 that, France, by means of a preventive strategy, would usually prefer to move together with its primary allies and friends, as this strategy has already been the main driving force behind the Balkan Stability Pact of Balladur in 1994 and the similar Franco-German initiative in 1999.[150]

---

[149] Although the *Gendarmeire* (paramilitary) is a military component, most of its missions are devoted to non-defence (inner-state security) tasks. Its functions are including administrative police and judiciary police missions, as well as maintain public order, and works almost with all ministries and state administrations. Therefore, the above figures are excluding the *Gendarmeire*, as well as the *Service Militaire Adaptée* (SMA). Data compiled from The Military Balance 1990-1991,1994-1995, and 1999-2000, (UK: IISS, Brassey's Ltd.); 'Projet De Loi – relatif à la programmation militaire pour les années 1997 à 2002', p.16/55. The mobilisation strength shall also be reduced from 577,360 to 434,000.

[150] 'La prévention doit aussi, par la renseignement, nous mettre à l'abri des surprises stratégiques, faciliter l'adaptation permanente des moyens et de l'organisation de notre défense, orienter la préparation du futur. [...] L'efficacité de la prévention repose sur les moyens de renseignement, une présence permanente à l'extérieur de nos frontières et les dispositifs de coopération avec les pays alliés ou amis. [...] Le maintien d'un dispositif de forces prépositionnées, notamment en Afrique, permettra, dans les régions concernées, l'analyse permanente des

For effective power projection, prevention, and protection, French armed forces have been

remodelled with new command, control, inter-service, and multinational interoperability for

forces' *communication interarmées*, particularly in the service of the European defence

structure. The LPM 1997-2002 explicitly stated that 'our force projection capacities are first

of all conceived for the service of European defence. The analysis of risks and threats in the

future shows that we must be capable of engaging in actions conjointly with our European

partners and allies in distant and different theatres and preserving the security of countries in

and outside of Europe. The principal measures of command, intelligence, and *communication*

interarmées of these [projectable] forces shall constitute interoperability with those of our al-

lies'.[151] Therefore, the traditional rigid division-level commands of the French army were

abandoned in favour of the four projectable force inter-service headquarters (brigade and

regimental) structure, which take as their prototype the classic NATO army corps structure.

These four projectable forces are: The heavy armoured force, the mechanised force, the ar-

moured rapid intervention force, and the infantry assault force.[152] They are largely detached

from other mobile forces, the *Force d'Action Rapide* and the *Corps Blindé Méchanisé* (based

in Lille), and their headquarters reorganised under a new command called the Land Forces

Operational Command (*Commandement Opérationnel des Forces Terrestres (COFT)*), which

was established in Lille, France, in 1998 and serves as the headquarter of these four pro-

jectable forces. There is a third mobile force, the *Eurocorps* as well as the Franco-German

Brigade. Although they were kept separate from the four projectable forces of the French

army, the LPM 1997-2002 affirmed their 'restructuration' to conform with the professionali-

---

situations, la réaction immediate… 'Projet De Loi – relatif à la programmation militaire pour les années 1997 à 2002', pp.8-9/55.

[151] *Ibid*, p.7. On page 13/55, the above argument emphasised once again: 'Dans la très grande majorité des cas, l'engagement de nos armées s'effectuera dans un contexte multinational. L'échange de renseignements, la mise en commun de moyens d'analyse et la recherche de l'interopérabilité des commandements et des forces sont donc autant de domaines à développer en priorité. La réforme entreprise donnera à nos forces la souplesse d'emploi nécessaire pour répondre aux besoins de plus en plus diversifiés de ces coopérations. Les coopérations européennes constitueront le champ privilégié de cette politique.'

[152] Loi de Finances pour 1997, 'Défense: Forces Terrestres', *Assemblée Nationale No.2993*, (Paris: Imprimé pour l'Assemblée nationale par la Sté Nouvelle des Libraires, October 10, 1996), p.19.

sation process and, according to Boyon, implies that any one of the new army's four projectable forces could be assigned to the *Eurocorps*.[153]

COFT provides a wide range of capabilities for organising and rapidly deploying forces from the national joint task force headquarters or from NATO-style inter-service division headquarters. General Jean Heinrich was nominated as the first commander of the COFT, a former second in command of the multinational force in Bosnia, who has wide experience in multilateral missions.[154] Interestingly, his office in Lille is not far away from NATO's SHAPE in Mons, Belgium. The significance of this short distance between COFT and SHAPE headquarters indicates that, in addition to the COFT's headquarter role for the French army forces, it could also easily function as a command and control organisation for the multinational corps, possibly for EU/WEU-led non-Art.V missions or the command centre for European-led CJTFs operations, where the US/NATO decides not to become involve.[155]

The successful participation of professional armed forces with the necessary power projection capabilities in multinational missions are bound to the modernisation of military equipment, which could efficiently be provided by an overhauled armament industry. The reduction in military budgets, which started with the 1994 annual investment budget under the right-wing government of Balladur, resulted in the anachronism of self-sufficiency in the defence industry area.[156] This led to the privatisation of state-owned enterprises, the pooling of resources and enhanced co-operation at the European level. It is stated in the White Paper of 1994 that

---

[153] 'La capacité opérationnelle et la disponibilité du Corps européen, de l'Eurofor et de l'Euromarfor seront accrues par la professionnalisation de nos forces. Le stationnement de nos troupes en Allemagne sera profondément modifié, à la suite de la restructuration de l'armée, à la de terre. Mais la Brigade franco-allemade sera confirmée dans ses missions et son stationnement actuels.' 'Projet De Loi – relatif à la programmation militaire pour les années 1997 à 2002', pp.13/55; Boyon quoted in Jolyon Howorth, 'France' in Howorth, J. & Menon, A. (ed.), *The EU and National Defence Policy*, (London: Routledge, 1997), p.37.
[154] Menon, A., *France, NATO and the Limits of Independence, 1981-1997 – The Politics of Ambivalence*, p.106.
[155] Jones, J. B., 'French Forces for the 21st Century', *Joint Force Quarterly*, (Summer 2000), p.34.
[156] The defence share of the GDP in France was 3.3% in 1994, 3.1% in 1995, 3.0% in 1996, 2.9% in 1997, 2.8% in 1998, and 2.8% in 1999/2000. See, *French Defence Statistics 2000*.

'... European states are showing their solidarity through the *preference for Europe*. France

has to convince its partners of the necessity for a common strategy, otherwise the European

weapons industry will be destined to collapse and the independence of Europe will be brought

into question'.[157] Nevertheless, the LPM 1997-2002 is a real commitment to the

'Europeanisation' of French defence industries:

> *'Progress in the construction of Europe has reinforced the political, economic,*
>
> *and social links between the states' interests to such an extent that their security*
>
> *interests are difficult to distinguish. France, therefore, desires to put the common*
>
> *security and defence policy ambition under the authority of the European Council.*
>
> *Even, in this spirit, France desires to constitute with its European partners a*
>
> *common European industrial and technological base, a component of the entire*
>
> *European identity in the sphere of defence'.[158]*

The stated 'European' ambitions of France are in fact serving its national ambitions by con-

structing French 'champions' big enough to overrule other defence firms and dominate the

growing European arms market, while publicly espousing a common European industrial and

technological base as one of the main components of the European defence integration proc-

ess. The competitiveness of French 'champions' with other European defence firms at the

European level would therefore not only reduce the production costs through collaborative

programmes, but would also preserve and maintain the *grandeur* and *rank* of France. This dif-

---

[157] *Livre Blanc sur la Défense* (German language edition), (Paris: Ministère de la Défense, March 1994), p.120.
On page 34, it is also stated that, 'In the area of military and armament, bilateral and multilateral co-operations
are the source of concrete rapprochement between national defence systems and promotion to a wider European
dynamism. In this regard, France will systematically co-operate with other states in every occasion that they
involve with France in European construction'.
[158] 'Projet De Loi – relatif à la programmation militaire pour les années 1997 à 2002', p.4/55. On page 5, it is
argued that, 'Notre industrie de défense doit en effet s'adapter. Depuis plusieurs années, chacun s'accorde sur un
double diagnostic: une base industrielle et technologique forte est une composante essentielle de notre politique
de défense, comme de la défense européenne; pour la préserver et lui maintenir son rang, il est indispensable de
l'adapter aux évolutions du marché et de l'environnement politique et financier de la défense. C'est pourquoi le
projet de loi de programmation repose sur une triple ambition: compétitivité des entreprises, redimensionnement
des groupes, construction européenne. La maîtrise et la réduction des coûts, la recherche d'une taille suffisante

ference between French and European defence programmes would in fact be no more than a nuance in the near future if the current rate of integration between national and European perspectives continues.[159]

The LPM 1997-2002 also endorsed the acquisition of sophisticated weapons system (satellite intelligence, strategic air lift, optics, electronics, modernisation of C3I) for meeting the technical requirements of the professional army in performing 'soft' military intervention tasks.[160] As a result of reductions in arms sales in the world market since the end of the Cold War, the subsequent increase in the rate of unemployment in the defence sector and in the whole country then ran at about 12%, instead of investing in the defence equipment needs of the professional army, the Socialist government promised more financial investment in the country's social security system and to create more jobs. The French armed forces chief of staff, General Jean-Pierre Kelche, in full agreement with General Yves Crene, put forward an unambiguous diagnosis in the National Assembly's Defence Committee: 'The anticipated inflated expenditures for pay and social security contributions are going to result in "a reduction" of available money for day-to-day living and activities in the units. They could also result in drastic cuts in the money available for equipment purchases and this translates into "accumulated delays" or postponement in armed forces modernisation'.[161]

---

pour dégager les économies d'échelle et les capacités d'investissement indispensables, le développement des alliances européennes seront constamment encouragés'.

[159] See Chapter 2, *(2.2.1) 'Big Three's' Defence Philosophies*. Also see, Menon, A., *France, NATO and the Limits of Independence, 1981-1997 – The Politics of Ambivalence*, pp.111, 140-141.

[160] For details with regard to the acquisition of new military equipments see, 'Projet De Loi – relatif à la programmation militaire pour les années 1997 à 2002', pp.36-46/55.

[161] 'In view of the rise in pay that has to be met in order to recruit career soldiers or volunteers, cuts are being made in some areas of operational expenditure and activities and current equipment maintenance, as well as credits allocated to equipment…. This budget [for the year 2001] permits only the management of routine businesses, therefore, 'the objective of professionalisation is far from having been achieved, the anomalies observed will lead to a failure of professionalisation'. In 'Budget Cuts Endanger Professionalisation', *Le Monde*, (internet version FBIS-WEU-2000-1127, November 23, 2000); 'French Chief of Stuff Finds Armed Forces 'Impoverished'', *Le Monde*, (internet version FBIS-WEU-2000-1016, October 14, 2000).

Having been initiated by Chirac in 1996, contrary to some dissidents in the political spectrum, the armed forces professionalisation and modernisation project was subsequently taken up by Lionel Jospin's government.[162] The preparations of the second transition phase of LPM 2003-2008 launched by French Defence Minister Alain Richard on October 22, 1999, and endorsed by the National Assembly on July 31, 2001, underlines the following aspects:[163]

- The dual objective of consolidating the professional army through reinforcing its operational capability and endowing it with new generation equipment (in other words, *capacités stratégiques*) tailored according to the evolutions of new missions.

- Drawing full conclusions from the Kosovo crisis with an emphasis on long-term rapid deployment, including flexible rotation, of 'projectable' professional forces.

- Adjusting 15 EU states' national military programmes to each other through a growing *rapprochement* of their operational and planning objectives. Such new formulas should progressively become visible through 'mutualisation of means' (*mutualisation des moyens*), where France would attain complementarity and interoperability of means together with its partners in order to realise the full effect of certain capacities on the horizon in the period 2010-2015.

- Constructing a plan which would give substance to French national priorities, while contributing to the force projection capacity of European defence under the ruling of the Helsinki European Council's December 10-11, 1999, decision.

For a country like France, which has pursued a national security and defence policy for almost thirty-five years without major cleavage amongst leading political parties, albeit its policy of national independence replaced by the strategy of gaining political advantage in co-operative

---

[162] According to the *French Constitution of October 4, 1958*, Prime Minister is 'responsible for national defence. He shall ensure the implementation of legislation' (Art.21), and Minister of Defence is responsible for organising and mobilising armed forces.

[163] 'Projet De Loi – relatif à la programmation militaire pour les années 2003 à 2008'; also see *Agence France Press*, 'French Premier Announces Defence Review', (October 22, 1999, transcript, FBIS-WEU-99-1022).

European and transatlantic solutions, France will find its defence policy increasingly drawn into the EU/WEU as well as into NATO multinational power projection tasks due to its diminishing national options. Thus, Chirac's main ambition for the French military reforms is not only to reorganise the army for national objectives, but also together with Germany's developing highly operational 80,000-strong all-volunteer Readiness Forces and, preferably, along with the third European partner, the UK, to be the driving force behind realising the 'Headline Goals' of the Helsinki European Council decision of creating a 50,000-60,000 strong European Rapid Reaction Corps by 2003. Before analysing radical changes in European security and defence, which are evolving in favour of French ambitions since the Anglo-French Joint Declaration on European Defence at St. Mâlo on December 4, 1998, it is imperative to examine the concept of a common European nuclear deterrent force with regard to Franco-British co-operation.

(3.2) A Common European Nuclear Deterrent?

Since de Gaulle, French politicians have regarded nuclear weapons as central to France's national independence and essential to its international status – *grandeur* and *rank*. The underlying commitment of this section is that, since the 1990s, 'Europeanisation' of French nuclear weapons has entered the EU agenda in every French defence reform attempt as a significant part of the independence versus 'Europeanisation' debate.

As a result of sweeping changes in the international security environment since the end of the Cold War era, French nuclear forces budget share not only declined, but also the production of *Pluton* missiles were banned, *Hadès* missiles were stockpiled and their further production was ceased, and Prime Minister Pierre Bérégovoy declared a moratorium in 1992 on nuclear testing in the Pacific. After more than thirty years of the unquestionable autonomy of the French nuclear deterrent force and doctrine, first President Mitterand dramatically declared his willingness in January 1992 to discuss the possibility of a 'European nuclear doctrine' that would 'be the major question of a common defence policy', and then Defence Minister Joxe evinced that France is ready to discuss the possible combination of French and British nuclear forces.[164] Under the circumstances of prevailing security risks, uncertainty of a US military (conventional and nuclear) presence in Europe, and the emerging common European defence policy, the French deterrent forces could be 'Europeanised' through one of the following four options:[165]

- *'Existential'* deterrence (*dissuasion par constat*), would be an indirect deterrent to dissuade for all of Europe simply by France's existence.

- *'Extended'* deterrence (*dissuasion par extension*), based on an explicitly agreed French deterrent encompassing the non-nuclear members' territory of the EU similar to that of the US's nuclear responsibility in NATO.

- *'Concerted'* deterrence (*dissuasion concertée*), where France would consult its European partners before it would take an action.

- *'European'* deterrence (*dissuasion européenne*), based on a Brussels-based executive politico-military authority that would steer the use of nuclear weapons.

Concomitantly, following Franco-British co-operation in the nuclear field, which flourished with the establishment of the Joint Commission on Nuclear Policy and Doctrine as a temporary measure during the NATO meeting at Gleneagles in October 1992, less than a year later in July 1993 at the first meeting of the Franco-British Joint Commission President Mitterand,

---

[164] Mitterand quoted in Gordon, P. H. (ed.), *A Certain Idea of France. French Security Policy and the Gaullist Legacy*, pp.174-175.
[165] The last option was supported by former President of the European Commission, Jacques Delors, who envisaged 'transferring of nuclear weapons to a strong [European] political authority.' *Ibid*; Also see Ehrhart, H-G., 'France and NATO: Change by Rapprochement?', *Hamburger Briträge zur Friedensforschung und Sicherheitspolitik*, pp.26-27.

Prime Minister Balladur, and British Prime Minister John Major announced that Joint Commission would be made a permanent institution.[166]

However, the most significant departure from the Gaullist nuclear orthodoxy came with the Defence White Paper of 1994. Although the nuclear forces budget was dramatically cut back from 40,446 million FFr in 1992 to 23,164 FFr in 1994 for the first time during the Fifth Republic, Defence Minister Léotard put an emphasis on the necessity of nuclear weapons for the independence of both France and Europe.[167] The White Paper of 1994 highlights that European dimension as:

> '... the European nuclear doctrine is proclaimed to be one of the major questions in the construction of a common European defence. [...] Indeed, Europe's defence autonomy is possible with nuclear weapons; without them, it is not. The dialogue with Great Britain, which has started to realise this dimension, shall go further and deepen. This is not excluding exchanges with other partners'.[168]

For France, 'with other partners' – among others – particularly means Germany. This evokes de Gaulle's tripartite partnership contemplation around which the ideal association of states in

---

[166] Stuart Croft underlined the Joint Commission's three main consultation functions: (1) While France left NATO's IMS and emphasised the utilisation of its nuclear forces independently and the UK remained committed and dependent on the US after the US-UK Nassau Accord, a great deal of concepts and issues appeared for a bilateral exchange of views on how to practice common nuclear deterrent strategies and policies on behalf of whole Europe; (2) Although France and the UK kept their nuclear arsenals out of the US-USSR arms control and disarmament negotiations in the Cold War, drawing nuclear capable states' into arms control and disarmament measures in the post-Cold War era became imperative for both countries, (3) A better collaboration on weapons procurement. Initially, discussions in the Joint Commission were focussed on replacing the UK's obsolete *WE-177* gravity bomb with the French made pre-strategic *Air-Sol Longue-Portée* (ASLP). Croft, S., 'European integration, nuclear deterrence and Franco-British nuclear co-operation', *International Affairs*, (Vol.72, No.4, 1996), pp.771-787; Stuart Croft, 'Nuclear Issues' in Howorth, J. & Menon, A. (ed.), *The EU and National Defence Policy*, (London: Routledge, 1997), pp.141-154.
[167] 'The nuclear deterrent is remaining as one of its [French defence policy] basics. France needs to count on the fact that its politics will always be criticised in this respect by others on the international level and perhaps even more and more with the cease of the Soviet threat. However, France cannot relinquish it, because it is today related to France's independence and probably tomorrow to the independence of Europe'. See 'Preface' in *Livre Blanc sur la Défense* (German language edition), (Paris: Ministère de la Défense, March 1994).
[168] *Ibid*, pp.56-57.

a 'confederation' would realise the independent European defence concept (see *policy of national independence* above). This has been written into the White Paper of 1994 as, 'the construction of European defence rests on the intentions of these three state's conception of their security interests through deepened co-operation and, if necessary, through the combination of their military means'.[169]

Moreover, in the post-Cold War era, as a result of the increasing role of conventional forces use in 'soft' military operations, one of Balladur's most striking reform initiatives had been 'inverting' the prominent role of the nuclear forces with the conventional one. This is written in the White Paper of 1994 as follows:

> '*The nuclear deterrent will guarantee that the conventional forces are not short-circuited: the role which the latter played in the Cold War is now played by nuclear forces; thus there is no rupture in strategic doctrine, but an evolution in the respective roles of nuclear and conventional means as a function of different scenarios'.*[170]

This reform initiative precisely evokes what French President Valéry Giscard d'Estang proposed at the time of the collapse of the Warsaw Pact in summer 1989: Professional army should replace French mandatory military service and streamlined nuclear deterrence should adapt itself to this new form of armed forces.[171]

Since 1989, there has been an argument in France that although 'Northern' hemisphere countries are moving gradually to a 'post-nuclear age', North-South relations may well return into

---

[169] *Ibid*, p.35.
[170] *Ibid*, pp.54-55. This translation copied from Jolyon Howorth, 'France' in Howorth, J. & Menon, A. (ed.), *The EU and National Defence Policy*, (London: Routledge, 1997), pp.32-33.
[171] Wetterqvist, F., *French Security and Defence Policy – Current Developments and Future Prospects*, p.73.

a strategic posture similar to the 1940s and 1950s – albeit no one could exactly predict how it would develop and what the conditions would look like twenty or thirty years later – when nuclear arms are increasingly coming to be conceived primarily as weapons of mass destruction.[172] This argument became the basis of division between the two main schools of thought ('more operational' and 'less operational') on how to develop a new effective deterrence strategy.[173] However, the main concern of both schools is how to 'Europeanise' the French nuclear forces for the purpose of: (a) sharing the soaring costs of nuclear forces through collaborative ventures; (b) enhancing the legitimacy of overtly devalued nuclear forces in the post-Cold War era through 'Europeanisation' in order to obtain EU-wide support; (c) making the long-lasting belief of 'without a common European nuclear deterrent, construction of 'Europe' will bound to be incomplete' a commonly accepted notion in the entire EU.

On the basis of these reasons, former Prime Minister Alain Juppé suggested the concept of *dissuasion concertée* in January 1995 that the Franco-British nuclear dialogue should be extended into a tripartite partnership by including Germany and would be kept open to other EU countries' participation or establishing a WEU Nuclear Planning Group, similar to NATO's NPG, to discuss nuclear weapon matters. By *dissuasion concertée*, Juppé meant assembling a homogenised European nuclear policy group from the EU states, which would agree tying their increasingly overlapping vital interests and future destinies to each other in a 'hybrid'

---

[172] Lellouche, P., 'France in Search of Security', *Foreign Affairs*, (Spring 1993); Howorth emphasised that the concept of 'state terrorism' exerts pressure for change on de Gaulle's classic nuclear weapons doctrine which was designed to deter the 'strong' by the 'weak' state (*la dissuasion du faible au fort*). However, the new security concept in the post-Cold War period altered this old principle to one of a nuclear deterrent of the strong (France) against the weak (e.g. Libya or Iraq). Lellouche argued that this is the nuclear capable 'strong' state's deterrent of the 'weak' (*la dissuasion du fort au faible*).

[173] Yost explained the main difference between the two schools of thought as: The 'more operational' approach put emphasis on robust and flexible nuclear weapons' deterrent (low-yield and special-effect weapons) of arcane threats, whereas the 'less operational' approach emphasise the confidence of traditional French nuclear deterrent policies, which refers to responding threats with a massive strike capability and maintaining a 'principled opposition' to limited nuclear options, and opposes developing flexible low-yield weapons. Yost also informed that the 'less operational' approach is the dominant view among French security analysts. Yost, D. S., 'France's Nuclear Dilemmas', *Foreign Affairs*, (Vol.75, No.1, January/February 1996), pp.108-119.

structure in which doctrine, deployment, and development would become a European issue, but the decisions of their actual use will be given by Paris and London,[174] instead of EU's Brussels (*dissuasion européenne*).

President Chirac on June 13, 1995, just a couple of weeks after taking his place at the Elysée Palace, as the new commander-in-chief of the armed forces (French Constitution Art.15) and solely responsible for using nuclear weapons, decisively not only broke the moratorium declared by Mitterand on nuclear testing, but also reverberated Mitterand's well known statement: '*La dissuasion, c'est moi*'.[175] The nuclear tests in the South Pacific were justified as ensuring France's national independence through nuclear capacity so that it still 'remains truly deterrent … and that the security, the safety and the effectiveness of the French nuclear arsenal are guaranteed'.[176] Although the tests were later defined as the last live tests for validating laboratory plans for providing the weapons with greater 'robustness' over a long period and perfecting simulation techniques that would make future live testing unnecessary, this did not convince ten of France's EU partners (the exceptions being the UK, Germany, Spain and Greece) and caused enormous protests in countries in the South Pacific.[177] While those ten

---

[174] Juppé did not clearly explain what he exactly meant by an ambiguous declaration '*dissuasion concertée*'. However, the LPM 1997-2002, published in May 1996 hinted not what it means, but what it should not mean: 'Cette stratégie doit prendre en compte la solidarite européenne. Aussi, l'imbrication croissante des intérêts vitaux des nations européennes et le caractère commun de bien des menaces qui les visent ont-ils conduit la France à avancer l'idée d'une dissuasion «concertée», dans le cadre d'une approche d'ensemble de la sécurité européenne et atlantique. Il ne s'agit pas d'étendre de manière unilatérale une garantie nucléaire française, ni d'imposer à nos parteneires un contrat. Le France propose une démarche pragmatique et progressive, fondée sur l'idée que la concertation renforce la dissuasion.' I interpreted and extracted what '*dissuasion concertée*' could mean from the LPM 1997-2002 and article of Stuart Croft. Croft, S., 'European integration, nuclear deterrence and Franco-British nuclear co-operation', *International Affairs*, pp.771-787; Stuart Croft, 'Nuclear Issues' in Howorth, J. & Menon, A. (ed.), *The EU and National Defence Policy*, pp.141-154.

[175] The translation of this statement to English is: '*I am the deterrent*'. This statement has historical relevance to the French citizens since it reminds them what Louis XIV once said: '*L'Etat c'est moi*', means '*I am the State!*'

[176] *Agence France Press*, 'Chirac To Propose 'Significant' Defence Reforms', (January 3, 1996, transcript, FBIS-TAC-96-001).

[177] Ten EU countries voted in favour of the UN resolution in December 1995, which condemned the French action and called for an immediate halt to nuclear tests. Moïsi stated that, while Chirac 'expected the angry and negative reactions emanating from countries of the South Pacific, he surprised by the hostility stemming not only from Western Europe but above all from France. Sixty percent of the public, according to all polls, disapproved his action'. Although government officials in Germany – particularly Kohl and Kinkel – were remained silent at that time, there was a deep resentment on the public side. Moïsi, D., 'Chirac of France – A New Leader of the West?', *Foreign Affairs*, pp.10-11. Also see, Chapter 3 - *(2.2.1) Harnessing the pre-1996 Discourses.*

EU countries argued that the French commitment to the EU's CFSP was irresponsibly mistreated, France argued that a text, which had been signed at a WEU meeting in Madrid a few days before its tests had been initiated, declaring that British and French nuclear forces contributed to European security, was enough evidence for giving collective support to tests since it is an action for the future security of the entire Europe.[178]

In September 1995, Juppé suggested once again to open the 'Europeanisation' of nuclear deterrent to a comprehensive discussion within the context of the EU's IGC in 1996 and, in October, Chirac and British Prime Minister John Major initiated a 'global partnership' with the long-term objective of co-ordinating their nuclear policies and doctrines.[179] On January 29, 1996, France announced the end of all nuclear testing and closed test facilities of the *Centre d'Expérimentation du Pacifique (CEP)* at Mururoa and Fangataufa, and signed the Raratonga South Pacific Nuclear Free Zone (NFZ) Treaty.[180] Simultaneously, France on September 24, 1996, signed the Comprehensive Test Ban Treaty (CTBT) by pursuing 'zero option', banning all nuclear tests, including low-yield ones. Later, on April 6, 1998, France and the UK became the first two nuclear-weapon states to ratify the CTBT.

French nuclear forces have also been reorganised within the framework of Chirac's defence reforms initiatives, which was announced on February 22, 1996. The removal of surface-to-surface *(sol-sol)* strategic short-range *Hadés* ballistic missiles from the *Plateau d'Albion* was authorised, which were previously stored but not dismantled during Mitterand's Presidency,

---

[178] 'France Isolated in Europe', *The Economist*, (November 25, 1995), pp.48-49; Former Defence Minister Léotard emphasised that 'the real argument over this resumption [of tests] is that, in this affair, France represents the interests of 300 million Europeans.... It is to a large extent in their name that we are undertaking this difficult exercise.' 'European Security', *Atlantic News 2745*, (31 August 1995), p.2, quoted in Croft, S., 'European integration, nuclear deterrence and Franco-British nuclear co-operation', *International Affairs*, p.772.

[179] Chirac and Major also agreed to exchange nuclear data and form a Franco-British European Air Force Group with permanent headquarters at High Wycombe, the UK.

[180] By September 1999, the personnel number was 352, who remained at *CEP* sites, but this figure will be zero by 2002. However, the French presence in *Nouvelle-Calédonie* and non-*CEP* French Polynesia largely remained unchanged. Gregory, S., 'France and *Missions de Souveraineté*', *Defense Analysis*, pp.332-333.

and the atomic plants in Marcoule (plutonium) and Pierrelatte (uranium), centres producing

fissile materials, were also closed. However, France will retain and modernise its air-to-sur-

face (*air-sol*) missiles and nuclear submarines (*sous-marines*), which were reduced from 6 to

4 between 1991 and 1996.[181] Although the LPM 1997-2002 placed less emphasis on nuclear

weapons in comparison to professionalisation of conventional forces, it not only highlighted

the four main operational functions' (deterrence, prevention, projection, protection) flexible

utilisation (or variable combinations) according to different situations,[182] but more than that

also highlighted that: 'The nuclear means will be maintained at a sufficient level to adapt to

the new environment. The renovation of ballistic (M51) and aerial (modernized ASMP) com-

ponents in the beginning of next century offers necessary guarantees and agility; reliability

and credibility of these forces are assured over the long-term'.[183] That 'sufficient level' is not

well defined, but adapting the nuclear arsenal to the new security environment through the

modernisation of submarine and air-to-surface weapons means that it has been thought they

are the most advantageous weapons in terms of versatility, mobility and precision for the sat-

isfactory deterrence of potential aggressors.

Although *dissuasion par constat* or *dissuasion concertée* are presumably better positioned

than the others in achieving a European nuclear identity, there are two main hurdles that need

to be cleared: *Firstly*, the anti-nuclear sentiments in some EU members are strong, if the

Atlanticists' view is not dominant.[184] The UK has to modify its hereditary pro-Atlantic view

---

[181] See 'Projet De Loi – relatif à la programmation militaire pour les années 1997 à 2002'; *Arms Control, Disarmament and Non-Proliferation: French Policy*, (Paris: La Documentation Française, April 2000).
[182] '... le poids respectif et l'articulation des quatre grandes fonctions opérationnelles (dissuasion, prévention, projection, protection) varieront selon les situations. Il serait périlleux de les figer dans une configuration unique et un modèle stratégique invariable.' 'Projet De Loi – relatif à la programmation militaire pour les années 1997 à 2002', p.6/55.
[183] *M51* stands for *Missile balistique stratégique embarqué sur SNLE-NG (Sous-marin nucléaire lanceur d'engines de nouvelle génération)* and *ASMP* stands for *Missile air-sol moyenne portée. Ibid*, p.13/55.
[184] Scandinavian countries and Austria, which codified an anti-nuclear clause in their constitution, demonstrates hostility to the idea of nuclear capable EU. For those countries' reactions to the French nuclear tests at the South Pacific see, Croft, S., 'European integration, nuclear deterrence and Franco-British nuclear co-operation', *International Affairs*, p.782.

into a somewhat more pro-European common defence view. France and Germany, on the other hand, have already officially agreed in December 1996, within the framework of 'Common Strategic Concept', 'to open a dialogue on the role of nuclear deterrence, in the context of a European defence policy' and a 'common position paper' on *dissuasion concertée* was discussed between Günter Verheugen (SPD) and Paul Quilès (*Parti Socialiste*) in July 1997.[185] French political analysts also argue that France's acceptance of the CTBT and discussions on non-proliferation issues with Europeans is a tactical action that France intends to draw its European partners into a concerted European nuclear doctrine via this 'back-door'.[186] However, German Foreign Minister Fischer's 'no-first-use' insistence on NATO's nuclear weapons and his party's (The Greens/Alliance'90) anti-nuclear stance would impede the development of such a nuclear capable EU.[187] *Secondly*, there are serious institutional limitations. Even if federalist thoughts – the essence of *dissuasion européenne* – were put aside, the necessary institutional structure for reaching a European nuclear identity through *dissuasion par constat* or *dissuasion concertée*, which necessitates a supranational accord to some extent, would not be an easy task.

It is clear that what exactly is meant by 'Europeanisation' of the French traditional nuclear deterrence, as suggested by Mitterand, Juppé, and later Chirac, within a broader European construction process is not yet explicable. After underlining the significance of France, the UK, and Germany's co-operation in the construction of European defence, the Defence White Paper of 1994 hinted that, a 'variable geometry' is a necessary dimension for realising 'considerable political projects'; however, the White Paper does not go further to make it particu-

---

[185] Quilès and Verheugen are in Ehrhart, H-G., 'Kontinuität oder Erneuerung?' Paris und Bonn/Berlin nach dem Machtwechseln', *Internationale Politik*, (April 1999, No.4), p.52.
[186] Bozo, Fricaud-Chagnaud, and Boniface are leading supporters of this argument. See Jolyon Howorth, 'France' in Howorth, J. & Menon, A. (ed.), *The EU and National Defence Policy*, p.31.
[187] For the Franco-German nuclear dialogue and German official stance, see Chapter 2, *(2.2.2) The Franco-German 'Common Strategic Concept'* and Chapter 3, *(2.1) Continuities and Changes within the German-US/NATO Relationship.*

larly subject to the European nuclear projects.[188] Since the Anglo-French Joint Declaration on European Defence at St. Mâlo on December 4, 1998, there have been concrete European diplomatic-military projects in relation to transferring various amounts of national conventional forces to the EU through the CESDP. The more the EU/WEU undertakes diplomatic-military responsibilities in crisis management missions, the more the question of adapting nuclear weapons to the European professional rapid reaction corps will come.

(4) The French-EU/WEU Perspective: The Ultimate Desire for a European 'Pillar of Defence'

(4.1) Harnessing the French pre-1998 European Defence Rationale

France's European 'Pillar of Defence' desire is a delicate balance, which fits somewhere in between *independence* and *co-operation*: While attempting to secure European political and defence independence from US dominated NATO, 'Europeanisation' of French security and defence policy would be realised through the medium of creating co-operative intergovernmental (habitually minimising any possible limitations to French national independence) European defence structures. The former, in general has long been an international division between France and the UK, as they are the exponents of the two polarised groups, European Integrationists and Atlanticists respectively and, the latter in particular, has long been subject to a bitter debate among the European Integrationists, notably between France's confederal and Germany's federal aspirations, with regard to the construction in the future of a medium institutional scheme for the EU.

---

[188] *Livre Blanc sur la Défense*, (Paris: Ministère de la Défense, March 1994), p.35.

Since de Gaulle, French policymakers have feverishly tried to create a discreet European 'Pillar of Defence' by reconciling European defence integration based on the WEU with the notion that 'Europe' must have *autonomy* for generating an *overall balance* in burden-sharing (in leadership and financial areas) by creating an equal pillar to the 'North American Pillar'. However, the UK and US largely conceived this equation as a *partial balance* in burden-sharing (only in the financial area with a limited leadership role) with the *autonomy* unacceptable, since it would weaken NATO rather than strengthen it. Prior to the Anglo-French Joint Declaration on European Defence at St. Mâlo on December 4, 1998, as Howorth argued, 'there have been many scenarios for the emergence of that elusive European Pillar: from the reactivation of the WEU in the 1980s, via the Platform on European Security of the Hague (October 1987), to the NAC meeting in Brussels (January 1994) and on to NATO's Berlin ministerial meeting (June 1996), which gave the green light both to a new project – ESDI – and to the military instrument underpinning it – CJTF. Yet, in large part because of the impossibility of discussing defence and even security issues *within the EU*, none of those scenarios offered any realistic prospect of recasting the underlying balance of influence and responsibilities inside the Alliance'.[189] The single main obstacle for effectively using the two tightly knitted policies (foreign (CFSP) and defence (CESDP)) in the name of the EU was the inability of France and the UK to find a medium solution.

Finding a medium solution has also been a major problem between France's confederal and Germany's federal aspirations. Except Valery Giscard d'Estaing's centre-right (UDF) party, who advocated in 1991 the creation of a West European constitution through economic, political and cultural integration in the foreseeable future, all other major political parties in France rejected relinquishing national sovereignty in a Europe integrating along federalist

---

[189] Howorth, J., 'European integration and defence: the ultimate challenge?,' *Chaillot Paper 43*, (Paris: WEU, Institute for Security Studies, November 2000), pp.3-4.

lines and supported the idea that common European defence would be the outcome of

European Political Union (EPU) in the long-term.[190] France and Germany, for the purpose of

EPU, have long tried to upgrade the WEU's posture as a 'military arm' of the EC in order to

make the WEU a major element on the road to political union and to realise the 'autonomous'

European defence structure.[191] However, the EPU is a second and complementary step to the

EMU, which in combination would lead the EU into federalism.[192] Germany, therefore,

apparently misses no opportunity to campaign for that long-term French aspiration of reach-

ing a European federation through political union. Although France at first sight seems to lean

towards German federalist aspirations, it is difficult to say if France would be willing to ex-

tensively compromise its policy of national independence for the EU. However, it is clear that

France has modified its traditional policy on national sovereignty in the interest of construct-

ing a strong and reliable common European defence structure. As Boyer argued, 'France used

the WEU as a means to deepen the debate on general principles defining what a European de-

fence posture could be and what it could require in terms of capacity and structures'.[193]

This modification of traditional French policies was reflected in the 1995 presidential

campaign as all three major political parties (UDF, RPR, and PS) came forward with pro-

European claims. Balladur vowed to revive the French economy, prepare it for the EMU, and

to work together with Germany to press for greater European defence co-operation with an

interest in merging the WEU into the EU as a 'fourth pillar' alongside the existing three

pillars structure.[194] Chirac announced that his foreign policy priority would be to

---

[190] See Yves Boyer 'France and the Security Order in a New Europe' in Schmidt, P. (ed.), *In the Midst of Change: On the Development of West European Security and Defence Co-operation*, pp.24-25.
[191] See Franco-German proposals reproduced in Rummel, R. (ed.), *Toward Political Union – Planning a CFSP in the EC*, (Germany: Baden-Baden Nomos Verlagsgesellschaft, 1992), pp.350-357; For a detailed information also see Chapter 2 – *(1.1) The Murky European 'Pillar of Defence'*.
[192] For more information on this claim see, Chapter 1 - *(2.1.2) The EU Dimension*.
[193] Yves Boyer, 'Whither Core Europe? France and the European Construction: Issues and Choices' in Lankowski, C. and Serfaty, S. 'Europeanizing Security? NATO and an Integrating Europe', p.29.
[194] Buchan, D., 'Who are you, Mr. Balladur?', *The Financial Times*, (January 19, 1995), p.11.

'Europeanise' the French nuclear forces through developing a closer dialogue with the UK and other European countries, as well as participating into the reform process of NATO for the progressive construction of a common European defence.[195] Jospin, similar to Balladur, promised to prepare the country to the European single currency, would work on social security problems, and would create a viable 'European army'.[196]

Paradoxically, with a close inspection of 'Gaullist' President Chirac's policy guidelines, one could easily find a gulf between French and German versions of common European defence that would not be easily bridged in coming years. Even though Chirac desired to create the European 'Pillar of Defence' by making the EU/WEU equal to the 'North American Pillar' within a 'Europeanised' NATO and this is in principle supported by Germany, France is pre-pared to see the EU-WEU combined and permanently based on institutionalised intergovern-mental co-operation, with elements of common European law and supranational integration articulated in a 'pioneer group' form, rather than a German style 'avant-garde group' articu-lated more along federalist lines.[197] Chirac made his view explicit in June 1996 by stating that, 'our goal must be to make the European Council [of the EU] the supreme body of orien-tation and decision in this domain [of our European policy of joint defence], particularly vis-à-vis the WEU. It is thus, and only thus, that we can make a coherent and overall plan based on what we have accomplished so far in our different projects of bilateral co-operation'.[198] On the contrary, the German policymakers always insisted for a greater involvement of the

[195] Buchan, D., 'Chirac Sets out Foreign Agenda', *The Financial Times*, (March 17, 1995), p.2.
[196] Buchan, D., 'Jospin Offers French Voters a Leftwing Election Agenda', *The Financial Times*, (March 8, 1995), p.1.
[197] This topic is studied in Chapter 1 - *(2.3.2) The Franco-German Joint Letter: 'Enhanced Co-operations'* and Chapter 2 - *(3) The Necessity for the Franco-German Tandem's Continuance: Recent Developments and Future Strategic Choices, 1998-2000.*
[198] The different projects referred to the Eurocorps, air operations co-operation between France and Great Britain, and maritime operations co-operation among France, Italy, and Spain. Chirac quoted in Cogan, Charles G., *Forced to Choose: France, the Atlantic Alliance and NATO – Then and Now*, p.136.

European Parliament and Commission for a more integrated Europe, more transparency and democracy in all policy areas.

In this respect, France and the UK – two major countries that reject pooling their national sovereignties into a federal Europe – appear closer to each other in institutional matters than France and Germany. However, the in-depth conceptualisation of this institutional analysis between France, Germany, and the UK is very delicate, since there is also a big gap between France and the UK. For France and Germany, but particularly for France, the EU is a major 'political imperative', which will be bolstered with the European 'defence arm' and the single currency, in Europe's battle against American 'hegomony', whereas the UK refrains from involvement in such an evolution. This gap between France and the UK was defined in *The Economist* as, 'where the British see Europe as a threat to their national power, the French see it as a multiplier of theirs'.[199] In his meeting with French ambassadors, Chirac echoed de Gaulle's notions by emphasising the importance of making the EU a major world player in which the German policymakers would be happier to give support to such a view than the British: 'France wants the EU to be a major player in every sphere in the twenty-first century. Because a united, democratic and peace-loving Europe must make a decisive contribution to bringing about a balanced world. Because a Europe which is making its presence felt on the stage of history is, for France, the best way to maintain its influence and promote its interests in a globalised world'.[200]

French policymakers explicitly stated that '[the French] defence policy serves to construct a credible European defence' and 'lies at the heart of a network of solidarities and interests, which are compelling Western Europe to turn into a common strategic space'.[201] Even though

---

[199] 'A Survey of France: If in doubt, seek Europe', *The Economist*, (June 5, 1999), pp.15-17.
[200] Speech by Jacques Chirac at the 'Meeting of the French Ambassadors', in Paris, on August 26, 1998.

such a concept is putting France more on the side of German integrationist ambitions, the volatile nature of the concept 'common strategic space' is a major complication in reaching an understanding that France would fully embrace integrationist ambitions during the construction of Europe. The following perceptive observation of France's institutional position came from Dominique Moïsi, the Deputy Director of the IFRI and Editor-in-Chief of *Politique Étrangère*:

> *'Like Mitterrand, Chirac is convinced that only a "Europe" can demultiply the French ambition to play a role in the world. Chirac is searching for a synthesis between the German and British views of Europe, between the integrationism of the former and the insistence on the sovereignty of national governments of the latter. ... Although France is still close to Germany on economic and monetary terms, it is closer to the UK on security and Europe's institutions'.*[202]

However, not until 1998 was it possible to pull the UK behind France's European defence rationale based on an 'autonomous' common European defence concept. France was well aware that a European defence structure would not really come into being if one of the three major European powers (France, Germany, and the UK) took no part in its construction. On December 4, 1998, France got what it wanted in the European defence matter with the UK Prime Minister Tony Blair's decision to close the existing gap by agreeing on a medium solution with Chirac at St. Mâlo.

---

[201] 'La politique de défense de la France est, en effet, au coeur d'un réseau de solidarités et d'intérêts qui tendent à faire de l'Europe occidentale un espace stratégique commun.' p.7. Also see page 4/55. 'Projet De Loi – relatif à la programmation militaire pour les années 1997 à 2002', *Assemblée Nationale No.2766*.
[202] Moïsi, D., 'Chirac of France – A New Leader of the West?', *Foreign Affairs*, (November/December 1995), p.11; Moïsi, D., 'A Union of Two Nations', *The Financial Times*, (June 20, 1995), p.18; Gloannec also observed that, 'a solution [to different versions] situated between German federalism and British abstention, an equivalent to the French version of Europe'. See Anne-Marie Le Gloannec 'Germany and Europe's Foreign and Security Policy: Embracing the "British" Vision' in 'Break Out, Break Down or Break In? Germany and the EU After Amsterdam', *AICGS Research Report*, (US: The Johns Hopkins University, Research Report No.8, 1998), p.26.

German-French Approaches to the European 'Pillar of Defence'

(4.2) The 'Big Bang': Anglo-French Initiative on European Defence

The majority of international relations analysts consider the joint Anglo-French Declaration on European Defence, which was signed at St. Mâlo on December 4, 1998, a historic breakthrough. Undeniably, the 'revolutionary' Anglo-French convergence on the creation of a CESDP with means and mechanisms to allow the EU/WEU to act 'autonomously' has drawn even more interest than that of NATO's ESDI. It was the ESDI that, due to the possible US veto, had left some European countries feeling less comfortable and thus they always continued to promote the idea of building European capabilities 'autonomous' from NATO. However, the initial euphoria felt during the joint Anglo-French Declaration, later turned into questions of how the lingering European Integrationists perception of France and the Atlanticists perception of the UK would complicate the implementation of the EU/WEU's CESDP.

(4.2.1) Ending Half-Century-Old Anglo-French Dispute on European Defence

Looking back at the end of 20th Century, most academicians will see the series of NATO military operations in the Balkans less as a victory over a dictator than a catalyst for a positive development of Anglo-French relations on European defence. The latest of those series of NATO military operations – the Kosovo military operation – became a historical watershed that marked the twelve months between the Anglo-French St. Mâlo declaration on December 4, 1998, and the Helsinki European Council declaration on December 10-11, 1999, with more constructive Anglo-French dialogues on European defence than over the past fifty years.

Although Tony Blair's decision to consent to a European defence dimension within the EU was stimulated by the former US President Clinton's policies of encouraging its European partners to undertake more global responsibilities through burden and responsibility sharing (see Chapter 1) and facilitated by the Franco-US/NATO *rapprochement* (see above), the most important leitmotiv reason was Blair's dissatisfaction with the US's Balkan policy.[203] During NATO's Kosovo military operation, the British – and also French – leaders saw once again that not only was the American leadership becoming increasingly reluctant to become involved in such diplomatic-military crisis in Europe, but also increasingly demonstrating a predilection for unilateralism.[204] Due to the unpleasant experience of Kosovo, the UK decided to eliminate the military weakness of the EU by moving into a new pragmatic policy style by enhancing European military capacity. Thus, the synchronisation of the new pragmatic British policy style with the long-desired French diplomatic-military aspirations in giving the EU a defence dimension through the WEU, brought about the Anglo-French 'Big Bang' with the creation of the CESDP at St. Mâlo and occupied the June 1999 Cologne and the December 1999 Helsinki European Council agendas.[205] After France and Germany failed to merge the EU-WEU due to the UK's impassable veto in the Amsterdam European Council meeting on June 1997, France's surprise successful co-operation with the UK at St. Mâlo in initiating the reactivation of the EU-WEU merger has been a major step to starting the realisation of the CESDP.

Although the French and British contribution to the EU/WEU's CESDP is seemingly central, the indispensable 'motor at the heart of the process [European security and defence co-operation] had two pistons' – unless there is co-operation between Paris and Berlin 'nothing of significance can really be achieved'.[206] France and the UK realised in Kosovo once again the

---

[203] For Blair's dissatisfaction from the US's Balkan policy see, Chapter 2 - *(3.1) The Road from the Joint Anglo-French St. Mâlo Declaration to the Cologne European Council Declaration.*

[204] Croft, S., Howorth, J., Terriff, T. & Webber, M., 'NATO's Triple Challenge', *International Affairs*, (Vol.76, No.3, 2000), p.505; NATO military operation in Kosovo was agreed on the basis that the US, UK, and France could 'veto' any targeted air strike as a rule of unanimity. In order to circumvent British or French veto, the US conducted part of the air strike unilaterally outside NATO framework. This led French Defence Minister, Alain Richard, to comment ironically: 'There was another country not fully integrated into the alliance – the US.' Quoted in *International Herald Tribune*, (November 11,1999), p.4 in Ehrhart, H-G., 'France and NATO: Change by Rapprochement?', *Hamburger Briträge zur Friedensforschung und Sicherheitspolitik*, p.17.

[205] The Anglo-French historic breakthrough is actually hinted by Blair's announcement at an informal EU Summit in Pörtschach/Austria (October 1998) that the UK could consent giving the EU a defence dimension.

functionality and value of their traditional intervention forces and Germany saw how *Verantwortung* (responsibility) and *Auslandseinsätzfähigkeit* (international deployment capability) are intermingled with sending armed forces in out-of-area operations as an *active multilateralist* partner (see Chapter 4). In fact, convergence between these three countries' military force structures and collaboration in the organisation of European defence projects is an essential feature for the CESDP's successful implementation.[207]

The Europeans are in the process of developing a credible crisis management capability, which will be backed by significant military force together with its new functional and effective institutions where the collective 'European security culture' could eventually be realised.[208] The full range of 'soft' military missions were defined in the Petersberg Tasks, which were at the same time made an integral part of the EU/CFSP (see Chapter 1), and are based on principles set out in the Helsinki European Council meeting (see Chapter 2). These evolutions on the way to creating a European military force were refined by the Feira European Council meeting on June 19-20, 2000, by emphasising the significance of the EU's 'soft' military and non-military missions that would effectively contribute to international peace and security in accordance with the principles of the UN Charter.[209] French Defence Minister Alain Richard defined the European military force as 'an important land force, with possible variants depending on the missions and tasks with which it may be entrusted, such as, for example, tasks

---

[206] Philip H. Gordon, 'Franco-German Security Co-operation In a Changing Context' in 'Franco-German Relations and European Integration: A Transatlantic Dialogue – Challenges for German and American Foreign Policy', *AICGS Conference Report*, (US: The Johns Hopkins University, December 16, 1999), pp.69, 78; also see Ehrhart, H-G., 'Kontinuität oder Erneuerung?' Paris und Bonn/Berlin nach dem Machtwechseln', *Internationale Politik*, (April 1999, No.4), pp.53-54.

[207] French Defence Minister, Alain Richard, said, 'the British and the French are the only countries in Europe that have readily deployable forces. With changes in the structure of its armed forces, Germany, too, might have them in 10 years.' Whitney, C. R., 'As the Battlegrounds Shift, the Draft Fades in Europe', *The New York Times*, (October 31, 1999), p.3; Also see von Bruno, R., 'Für ein transatlantisches Gleichgewicht – Frankreich, NATO und europäische Verteidigungspolitik' in Volle, A. & Weidenfeld, W. (Hrsg.), *Europäische Sicherheitspolitik in der Bewährung*, (Bielefeld: Bertelsman, 2000), pp.7-8.

[208] Howorth, J., 'European integration and defence: the ultimate challenge?,' *Chaillot Paper 43*, p.42.

[209] *Feira European Council Declaration* 'Presidency Report on Strengthening the Common European Security and Defence Policy' (June 19-20, 2000). <http:// europa.eu.int/council/> (Visited on: June 20, 2000).

with a stronger emphasis on the humanitarian angle, tasks involving the rapid evacuation of foreign nationals, or participation in peacekeeping operations far away from Europe within the framework of the UN'.[210] France declared that it would form 20% of the EU's new rapid reaction force, with 12,000 ground-troops, 75 combat planes, and 12 navy vessels, including the aircraft carrier *Charles de Gaulle*. However, Richard also emphasised that 'this is a major commitment by EU leaders', but warned that the EU is not building an 'integrated European army on an international level and that the national contingents would remain under the command of their own governments'.[211]

The US insistence on European participation in crisis management operations is considered by France as a chance to balance the global order and transatlantic partnership outside of NATO.[212] Even the UK, a fervent Atlanticist, is becoming amenable to this European Integrationists' desire. As Howorth argued, 'had the UK been convinced that NATO's future in the post-Cold War world was secure, the St. Mâlo process might never have happened'.[213] Indeed, with the Euro on the economic side and the CESDP on the defence side, the ultimate French desire of creating the European 'Pillar of Defence' became more concrete with the aim of embarking on new partnerships. The Gaullist notion of balancing transatlantic relations through the European 'Pillar of Defence' on the EU/WEU side and the 'North Atlantic Pillar' on the US side is becoming more conceivable and attainable than it ever was in the past. However, the European 'Pillar of Defence' cannot be built effectively if the US does not stop

---

[210] *Paris Radio France Internationale*, interview on 'Defence Minister Tells of EU's New Shape, Tasks' with French Defence Minister, Alain Richard, at 19:30 a.m. (GMT), translated text, September 22, 2000.

[211] British Defence Secretary Geoffrey Hoon said that Britain would initially provide 12,500 troops, 18 ships, and 72 combat aircraft. See *Agence France Press*, 'France Sets Out Contribution to EU Force' transcript, The Tocqueville Connection, US-CREST, November 23, 2000; *Agence France Press*, 'EU Members Pledge 100,000 Troops, 400 Planes to Rapid Reaction Force', transcript, The Tocqueville Connection, US-CREST, November 22, 2000. Available at: <http://www.ttc.org> (Visited on: December 27, 2000).

[212] French Defence Minister Alain Richard said that 'three things were involved – the memory of our collective failure in Bosnia, Kosovo, and finally the success of the Euro, which has demonstrated to Europeans that when political will exists, by getting together we can reshuffle the cards in the global balance of things.' Interview with Alain Richard, Minister of Defence, at the newspaper *Le Progrès* (excerpts) in Paris on March 25, 2000.

[213] Howorth, J., 'European integration and defence: the ultimate challenge?,' *Chaillot Paper 43*, p.48.

dominating NATO. It would be politically and militarily eccentric to build a European defence identity without any 'autonomous' diplomatic-military role assigned to it. European defence 'autonomy' is in fact an extremely difficult concept to define but is a major criterion in determining how close the disparity between French and British approaches has been drawn together.

(4.2.2) Resetting former differences is not yet settled: French and British Perceptions of the EU/WEU's CESDP and NATO's ESDI

Since the Kosovo conflict revealed the need for an 'autonomous' European diplomatic-military capacity and as a result of the dwindling military conviction that NATO's ESDI/CJTFs would be made available for 'autonomous' EU/WEU actions, the EU/WEU's 'autonomous' CESDP has not only materialized due to the joint Anglo-French St. Mâlo Declaration as *a military arrangement*, but is also structured as *a new political project* linked to the EU/CFSP. This is written into the Anglo-French St. Mâlo Declaration as:

> *'It will be important to achieve full and rapid implementation of the Amsterdam*
> *provisions on CFSP. This includes the responsibility of the European Council to*
> *decide on the progressive framing of a common defence policy in the framework of*
> *CFSP. [...] To this end, the Union must have the capacity for autonomous action,*
> *backed up by credible military forces, the means to decide to use them and a*
> *readiness to do so, in order to respond to international crises'.*[214]

The word 'autonomy' is at the heart of the division between France and the UK, and most commentators found themselves baffled with giving an exact definition to it, because they think in plain sense it means: The EU/WEU is simply endowed with a diplomatic-military

---

[214] *St. Mâlo Declaration*, (France: Anglo-French Summit, December 4, 1998) in Missiroli, A., 'CFSP, Defence and Flexibility', *Chaillot Paper 38*, (Paris: Institute for Security Studies, WEU, February 2000), Annexe C.

responsibility to initiate a political mission and back it up with relevant military means in order to manage 'soft' military missions without having recourse to US/NATO assets where the US is unwilling to become involve. On the whole, this definition of 'autonomy' has found approval among 15 EU states, which has long been facilitated by the Franco-US/NATO *rapprochement* on the one side and the UK-France *rapprochement* on European defence on the other, but still there are deep flaws between France and the UK regarding the 'true' definition of *European autonomy*. Despite their joint articulation of the St. Mâlo Declaration, France and the UK still continue to conceptualise the 'autonomy' of the EU/WEU's diplomatic-military action from their own traditional European Integrationists and Atlanticists lenses.

With the creation of the EU/WEU's CESDP, most unofficial political analysts initially argued that the European Integrationists would be motivated to put more emphasis on the differences and incompatibilities between the EU/WEU's CESDP project and NATO's ESDI project either by a desire to distance themselves from the Atlanticists' policies or by openly anti-Anglo-Saxon intentions. The creation of a French-led autonomous European security and defence structure had earlier attempted through a persistent struggle over control of the ESDI/CJTF and command of AFSOUTH in order to begin exercising looser political and military association with the US/NATO that would inevitably lead to meaningful European autonomy on the way to creating two equal 'European' and 'North Atlantic' pillars in NATO. As a result of the identification of the CESDP with the European 'Pillar of Defence', those analysts also argued that the CESDP being autonomous of NATO would increasingly marginalize the ESDI and thus one day NATO would collapse.[215] It is probably for these reasons, Howorth argued, that the Atlanticist UK asked for a French guarantee to not force the UK into choosing be-

---

[215] Bolton, J., 'The End of NATO?', *The World Today*, (Vol.56, No.6, June 2000), pp.12-14; also see, Statement of John R. Bolton, Senior Vice President (American Enterprise Institute), before the Committee on International Relations House of Representatives on the 'European Common Foreign, Security and Defence Policies – Implications for the US and the Atlantic Alliance'; Drozdiak, W., 'US Tepid on European Defence Plan', *The Washington Post*, (March 7, 2000).

tween the EU/WEU and US/NATO and European Integrationist France in turn asked for a

British guarantee not to force France's reintegration into NATO's IMS.[216] As a result of this

assumption, French and British officials found their European Integrationist and Atlanticist

approaches entirely compatible with the CESDP initiative; but they are still quite different on

how far to make the EU/WEU's CESDP 'autonomous' of NATO's ESDI.

In comparison to unofficial analysis, French official declarations were relatively diplomatic in

what the word 'autonomy' actually meant. French officials conceive the CESDP first and

foremost as an integral part of the 'autonomous' EU/WEU and, thus, a European element out-

side the NATO framework for fleshing out the ultimate French desire of *rebalancing* NATO

through creating two more or less equal pillars inside it. However, French officials also de-

clare that the EU/WEU would 'autonomously' be involved in diplomatic-military operations

to manage 'soft' military issues, where NATO as a whole would not engage, and it would not

operate as an alternative structure to NATO.[217] Even though, the EU/WEU 'autonomous ac-

tion' would recourse to Atlanticist means through full consultation, co-operation and trans-

parency with the US/NATO.[218] Defence Minister Richard asserted that:

> *'A European capability to intervene outside the rigid NATO framework would*
>
> *"favourably" affect the international balance. With the Kosovo crisis, the*
>
> *Americans found themselves facing a simple choice: either to condemn the*

---

[216] Howorth, J., 'European integration and defence: the ultimate challenge?,' *Chaillot Paper 43*, p.53; France has always been suspicious of American or the British initiatives, since they are bound to each other through traditional 'special relationship'. Therefore, when Blair lifted the hereditary British 'veto' and came round for the first time to the French idea of common European defence capability, 'French eyes narrowed with doubt: Was this not an Anglo-American plot to haul France back into an American dominated NATO?' 'A Survey of France: If in doubt, seek Europe', *The Economist*, (June 5, 1999).

[217] French Secretary of Defence, Jean P. Masseret, said: 'L'Europe de la défense n'est pas et ne sera pas une alternative à l'Alliance atlantique. Oui à l'autonomie de décision, mais qui n'exclut ni la concertation avec l'OTAN ni la consultation des autres Européens'. 'J. –P. Masseret: «L'Europe de la défense ne sera pas une alternative à l'OTAN»', *Le Republicain Lorrain*, (July 1, 2001); Also see his remarks in '"Knieweiche Europäer" sind nicht erwünscht', *Saarbrücker Zeitung*, (July 1, 2001).

[218] *St. Mâlo Declaration*, paragraph 7(c). The EU/WEU diplomatic-military actions will be in full consultation, co-operation and transparency with NATO. This has been explicitly stated in the paragraph 27 & 28 of the *Helsinki European Council Declaration*, (Helsinki: SN 300/99 EN, December 10-11, 1999). Available at: <http://europa.eu.int/council/off/conclu/dec99/dec99_en.pdf> (Visited on: June 20, 1999).

> *Europeans to inaction [...] or to get involved, since the Europeans were unable to*
>
> *act alone. If the Europeans were to acquire a capability to intervene militarily*
>
> *[...], this would have given the USA some freedom of choice'.*[219]

British officials on the other hand see the CESDP first and foremost as a necessary instrument to *strengthen* NATO as a primary organisation. While being fully aware of the complication of the word 'autonomy', they usually define it by a new pragmatic British policy style: There *may* be occasions that the EU's 'autonomous' diplomatic-military action is needed, but that 'autonomous action' is actually a condition for NATO's survivability, rather than an instrument for *rebalancing* NATO through creating two more or less equal pillars into it.[220] Although a solution to the French preference of the word *balancing* and the British preference of the word *strengthening* was found by adding both of them into the St. Mâlo jargon, giving the EU a diplomatic-military action capacity bound to its *direct contribution* to NATO. This was a condition of British approval for endowing the EU with the ability to act 'autonomously' and backed up by credible military forces. Paragraph 4 of the St. Mâlo Declaration stands for:

> *'We are fully convinced that, by developing our military capabilities, while*
>
> *reinforcing the EU's capacity for action, we will also contribute directly and*
>
> *substantially to the vitality of a modernised Atlantic Alliance, by making a*
>
> *stronger and more balanced partnership'.*[221]

Nevertheless, French political leaders certainly seem to believe that a more autonomous and robust CESDP will not be attained anytime soon and therefore they do not seem willing to set

---

[219] *Agence France Press*, 'France for Greater European Autonomy in Defence Issues', (November 4, 1999, transcript, FBIS-WEU-1999-1104).

[220] Croft, S., Howorth, J., Terriff, T. & Webber, M., 'NATO's Triple Challenge', *International Affairs*, p.507.

[221] *St. Mâlo Declaration*, paragraph 4.

definite short-term plans for replacing NATO guarantees completely with a 'genuine' EU/WEU one. Indeed, the most ardent French supporters of an 'autonomous' CESDP recognise that any concrete manifestation of it should be based on *long-term strategic plans* rather than on *short-term casual objectives*. As Defence Minister Richard admitted:

> *'It has taken ten years since Maastricht to progress towards a common European currency. We will need a comparable time frame to achieve the autonomous capacity for intervention that we set as a goal in Helsinki. We shall not be over-ambiguous however by setting an unrealistic short-term goal, of being able to manage crisis on the scale of Operation Allied Force in Kosovo within the next few years'.*[222]

While France was agreeing to short-term military decisions ('Headline Goal' of structuring combat forces, which are militarily self sufficient up to Corps level (50,000-60,000 men) and deploying within 60 days and sustaining for at least 1 year in 2003) and political decisions (constructing an institutional framework to set out the new political and military bodies and structures to enable the Council to run the EU-led military operations) in Cologne and Helsinki European Council meetings, its main aspiration has always been the long-term development of EU/WEU military and political capacities that would sooner or later bring into question the fundamental nature of the EU-US relationship.[223]

The British thinking is actually based on moderating long-term French objectives through extracting the best from the CESDP with short-term tactical and pragmatic plans for NATO's long-term sustainability and survivability. Both France and the UK are aware of the fact that

---

[222] Speech by Alain Richard, Defence Minister of France, on 'European Defence and the Transatlantic Link' at Georgetown University, (Washington: February 23, 2000).
[223] Howorth, J., 'Britain, France and the European Defence Initiative', *Survival*, (Vol.42, No.2, Summer 2000), pp.33-55.

the EU/WEU will not be able to exploit the 'autonomous' CESDP without assembling credible military forces supplemented by an adequately advanced military capacity. The UK is therefore not distressed that France would be able to convert the EU/WEU into a regional and global security and defence actor which would tackle a major crisis management operation with its own military assets without having recourse to US/NATO in the short-term. As the UK Secretary of State for Defence, Geoffrey Hoon, said: '[NATO] will be the organisation we would expect to use for *many crisis management operations*, certainly large and complex operations and those when Europeans and Americans wish to act together' (emphasis added).[224]

However, the most striking difference between France and the UK is that while French officials devotedly stress that in order to develop an 'autonomous' EU/WEU diplomatic-military action, particularly in the absence of explicit US/NATO support, the EU/WEU must have an intelligence capability including its own network of military intelligence satellites, British officials are indifferent to the development of an 'autonomous' EU/WEU intelligence capability. This cleavage has a historical dimension and interpretation of the following paragraph from the joint Anglo-French St. Mâlo Declaration would reveal that cleavage between French and British officials once again:

> *'In order for the EU to take decisions and approve military action where the*
> *Alliance as a whole is not engaged, the Union must be given appropriate*
> *structures and a capacity for analysis of situations, sources of intelligence and a*
> *capability for relevant strategic planning, without unnecessary duplication, taking*
> *account of the existing assets of the WEU and the evolution of its relations with the*
> *EU. In this regard, the EU will also need to have recourse to suitable military*

---

[224] Speech by the Defence Secretary of State, Mr. Geoffrey Hoon (MP), at the 'European Defence Conference', (March 28, 2000). Available at: <www.mod.uk> (Visited on: November 14, 2001).

means (European capabilities pre-designated within NATO's European pillar or

national or multinational European means outside the NATO framework)'.[225]

In terms of command, control, communication, and strategic intelligence and reconnaissance (C3I), the UK and the US are more tightly knitted to each other than any other countries in the world. Therefore, as a result of British forces' privileged access to data from US satellites, the UK's Atlanticist view is that if intelligence capability is needed in EU/WEU-led scenarios, the EU/WEU should not soon plan on developing its own 'autonomous' European satellites, because once EU-US relations are arranged around 2003 it would be possible to access NATO's planning capabilities and obtain data from US satellites through co-operation with the appropriate military intelligence mechanism. The UK's other Atlanticist criticism is that developing 'autonomous' European satellites and C3I would not only result in unnecessary duplication of the existing US/NATO satellites (in fact, US satellites under the service of NATO), but also their 'autonomous' acquisition would ratchet up the EU/WEU as an alternative to NATO. It is also stressed in the UK's *1998 Strategic Defence Review* that the EU/WEU's urgent short-term needs are transport planes, modern precision weapons, battlefield communication equipment, optical and electronic sensors for troops deployability, sustainability, flexibility, mobility, survivability and interoperability, rather than investing in costly satellites.[226] Even the development of any urgently needed short-term 'autonomous' EU/WEU military capability should be compatible with enhancing NATO's Defence Capabilities Initiative (DCI). UK Defence Secretary Hoon said on March 28, 2000, at the *European Defence Conference* that, 'we have spent fifty years developing a unique and universally effective integrated military structure within the Alliance. There is nothing to be

---

[225] See *St. Mâlo Declaration.* It is also emphasised that 'strengthened European defence capabilities need the support of a strong and competitive European defence industry and technology', paragraph 8.
[226] See *1998 Strategic Defence Review (White Paper),* (UK: British Ministry of Defence, 1998). Particularly Chapter 5 – 'The Future Shape of Our Forces'. Available at: <www.mod.uk> (Visited on: November 14, 2001).

gained, militarily, financially or politically, from duplicating what NATO can already provide'.[227]

French officials initially interpreted the paragraph quoted above from the joint Anglo-French St. Mâlo Declaration as, if the Europeans want to develop a credible 'autonomous' CESDP or a 'real' partnership with the Americans, they should have 'real' military capabilities including satellite intelligence capability 'separable' from the US/NATO in the long-term and if this requires some duplication in the field of C3I, then so be it. The major French criticism is that the Europeans cannot rely on the US as if it is a 'neutral' country that would always supply the Europeans with 'accurate' data from their spy satellites. François Heisbourg and Charles Grant argued that Europe should not rely on US satellites, 'because the American satellites may be busy dealing with crisis in another part of the world; because some of them may be faulty; or because the US may pass on *low-grade* or *misleading intelligence*' (emphasis added).[228] President Jacques Chirac's *Plan d'Action* (Action Plan), presented to his EU partners in July 1999 as a long-term plan, indicated the logic by which the EU should be able to act 'autonomously', even in the absence of US consent, and for this goal he 'called for a whole panoply of improvements, including a fully-fledged European chain of command, full multinationalisation of existing French and British Permanent Joint Headquarters (PJHQs), *autonomous* intelligence, power projection and C3 capabilities, and the establishment of a technological and industrial armaments base'.[229]

---

[227] Speech by the Defence Secretary of State, Mr. Geoffrey Hoon (MP), at the 'European Defence Conference', (March 28, 2000).
[228] They also gave the case of Iraq as an example. In September 1996, former US President Clinton launched bombing attacks against Iraq in retaliation for Iraqi troops' crossing the northern 'exclusion zone'. France claimed that imagery from its *Helios 1A* satellite showed the troop movements to be insubstantial. It therefore condemned the American air strike. Charles Grant (contributed), 'Intimate Relations: The Issue of Intelligence Sharing' in Heisbourg, F., 'European Defence: Making it Work', *Chaillot Paper 42*, (Paris: WEU, Institute for Security Studies, September 2000), pp.57-71.
[229] Quoted in Howorth, J., 'Britain, France and the European Defence Initiative', p.38.

Towards the end of 1999, French officials modified their arguments by saying that developing

EU/WEU military intervention capabilities 'autonomous' of NATO must be in line with

NATO's DCI ('win-win solution'),[230] however those 'autonomous' intervention capabilities

require 'the *convergence* of existing capabilities in the sphere of panning, command and

communications, and the exchange of data. This *common defence* means that the more deter-

mined countries should be allowed to proceed. The most effective way to progress is to grant

a degree of independence to those countries willing to build up joint capabilities' (emphasis

added), said Defence Minister Richard.[231] In the same vain, the Socialist Prime Minister,

Lionel Jospin, urged the 'development of European capacities' in defence through enhanced

capacities in 'intelligence, command and control' of operations and in 'strategic mobility'.[232]

The value of the Franco-German security and defence partnership in the development of co-

operative military programmes (Franco-German *Helios 2*, *Horus*, and *SAR* magnificent glass

radar satellite programmes) is therefore a significant indicator of progress towards an

'autonomous' EU/WEU.[233] It seems that British officials are not willing and able to match

that partnership, since playing a leading role in 'European Integrationists' desire of European

defence and keeping 'Atlanticists' links to US intelligence are two relatively incompatible

concepts. However, Charles Grant's suggestion is that, while Europeans are searching for

---

[230] Alain Richard said in Washington that, 'our efforts to give the EU a capacity of autonomous action will not be detrimental to the solidarity of the Alliance. We are not talking about a "zero-sum game" here. What we are talking about is what some in your country would call a "win-win" situation. A strong European political framework and impetus is critical to get things done within NATO. Indeed, the European effort and the NATO DCI are mutually reinforcing process, which should and will be conducted in harmony and in transparency'. Speech by Mr. Alain Richard, Defence Minister of France, 'French Defence, NATO and Europe' at Centre for Strategic and International Studies, (Washington: February 22, 2000).
[231] See *Agence France Press*, 'France for Greater European Autonomy in Defence Issues', (November 4, 1999); Also see Heisbourg, F., 'The EU needs defence convergence criteria', *Centre for European Reform Bulletin*, (No.6, June/July 1999).
[232] *Agence France Press*, 'French Premier Urges European Defence 'Capacities'', (October 22, 1999, transcript, FBIS-WEU-1999-1022).
[233] The German Defence Ministry is also complained about the quality, inadequacy and misleading of satellite imagery that the US provided during German forces on the ground in the Kosovo conflict. Charles Grant (contributed), 'Intimate Relations: The Issue of Intelligence Sharing' in Heisbourg, F., 'European Defence: Making it Work', *Chaillot Paper 42*, pp.65-66; Also see Chapter 2 - *(2.2) Defence Philosophies of France, Germany, and the UK* and Chapter 4 - *(3) Realities: The Recent Bundeswehr Reform and Kosovo Effect.*

ways of building up the EU's intelligence sharing capability, they should also search for compatible ways that would respect Britain's 'special relationship' with the US.[234] By and large, French officials believe that there is no contradiction between enhancing NATO's DCI and 'autonomy' of the EU/WEU. Since France is not fully participating in NATO's IMS, its indispensable role in an 'autonomous' EU/WEU is actually key to more *balanced* EU-US relations.

Another offshoot to French officials claims of turning the EU/WEU into a fully 'autonomous' global actor in the long-term is connected to the preservation of the collective defence guarantee of the WEU's Art.V. Contrary to the UK's wish for the WEU's dissolution by transferring its diplomatic-military function into the EU and collective defence functions into NATO, France persistently argues that when the time comes a 'Council of EU Defence Ministers' would be established and an injection of collective defence into the CESDP would be necessary.[235] The British position is that the WEU's Art.V is redundant since collective defence is at present entirely covered by NATO's Art.5 and it will still be so in the future. It has been written into the *1998 Strategic Defence Review* that, 'we must also retain the ability, at much longer notice, to rebuild a bigger force as part of NATO's collective defence should a major threat re-emerge in Europe'.[236] Furthermore, with the French desire for an 'autonomous' CESDP in mind, to insist on NATO's 'right of first refusal' (the EU/WEU could only act after US/NATO has turned down an operation), would not only deem the activation of the WEU's Art.V in some future crisis unfeasible, but would also seriously undermine the legitimacy of European 'autonomy'.

---

[234] Grant, C., 'Intimate Relations – Can Britain play a leading role in European defence – and keeps its special links to US intelligence?', *Centre for European Reform Working Paper*, (May 2000).
[235] See Speech by Jacques Chirac at the 'Meeting of the French Ambassadors', in Paris, on August 26, 1998; Also see Chapter 2 - *(3.2) The Helsinki Declaration and Beyond*.
[236] See *1998 Strategic Defence Review (White Paper)*, (UK: British Ministry of Defence, 1998), paragraph 89.

Under these circumstances, it is not a big surprise to observe that more and more commentators are becoming confused about what exactly the difference between the EU/WEU's CESDP and NATO's ESDI is, and what were the reasons for creating a CESDP in view of the existence of the ESDI. After the analysis of the reasons for cleavage between French and British perceptions of the EU/WEU's CESDP and NATO's ESDI, there are several points that needs to be clarified:

- ESDI/CJTFs had been initiated as a US-EU project within NATO at the Berlin NAC Summit in July 1996 under the Atlanticists' precondition of 'separable but not separate' NATO military assets and command positions for EU/WEU-led operations (see Chapter 1). On the other hand, CESDP has been initiated purely as a European project within the EU/CFSP at the Cologne European Council meeting in June 1999 with the European Integrationists' ambition of 'autonomous action' (see Chapter 2). 'Autonomy' is a brand new key word in questioning the compatibility between the EU/WEU's CESDP and NATO's ESDI in the overall transatlantic framework.

- The sensitive point regarding the difference between 'separable but not separate' (CJTF) and 'autonomous action' (CESDP) concepts is that whilst the former has long remained under the shadow of the US's veto threat on making military assets available for EU/WEU-led operations, the latter is basically a challenge to the vague concept of NATO's 'right of first refusal' and a bedrock for French claims of supplying the EU/WEU with defence 'convergence criteria' and 'duplicating' US/NATO assets in necessary fields. For example, EU/WEU's separate intelligence capability need.

- Meanwhile, since most assets that NATO would provide to an EU/WEU-led operation are in fact US assets, the paradox between the EU/WEU's CESDP and NATO's ESDI will be even more evident in future relations of the EU-NATO. Until the EU members put their house in order, the implementation of CESDP will be dependent on NATO's ESDI and on the goodwill of the US and non-EU members of NATO. However, transatlantic interests lie at the heart of competition between the EU/WEU and NATO, so ensuring the harmonious development of CESDP and ESDI will provide a healthier working relationship between the EU/WEU and NATO. Until the EU/WEU develops its own military capabilities, CESDP and ESDI are bound to complement each other by endowing the EU/WEU with political and military functionality.

- During the Feira European Council meeting in June 2000, four 'ad hoc working groups' were established for consultation and co-operation on issues of security, capabilities goals, modalities enabling EU access to NATO assets and capabilities, and the definition of permanent arrangements for EU-NATO consultation, in order to ease the institutional working relationship between the EU/WEU's CESDP and NATO's ESDI.[237] The involvement of non-EU NATO members or non-NATO candidates for EU accession in the 'soft' military missions, which the EU/WEU would undertake, also form one of the main themes of these working groups.

While British officials are snubbing the long-term French vision of developing 'autonomous' EU/WEU military force and prefer the short-term institutional working relationship between the EU/WEU and NATO, French officials hope that the time will come when the UK would be drawn into the long-term French vision of creating militarily as well as politically a two equal pillared structure to the Atlantic Alliance that coincides with the French ultimate desire of creating the European 'Pillar of Defence'. This could only be achieved once the EU/WEU develops its own military capabilities and then 'autonomous' – in its full sense – EU/WEU action will come to be a question of *political will* among the EU member states. At this point,

---

[237] *Feira European Council Declaration,* section D.

the intergovernmental basis of EU decisions in the CESDP would also be seriously scruti-
nised, since it makes policymaking extremely complicated.

(5) Conclusions

This chapter analysed France's new roles and desires with the difficulty of pinning down the
question of how far France has 'Europeanised' the basic conceptions of its security and defence policy. The difficulty French leaders have had in reconciling their 'Gaullist' traditions
with their growing need and will to 'Europeanise' their security and defence policies has been
apparent throughout this chapter.

On the one hand, France's tardiness, which emanates from the dilemma of *European integration* through *decentralisation* of the *French national sovereignty* (or national independence)
unavoidably causes a trade-off between French autonomy against gaining influence in the EU,
showing that the major deviation from de Gaulle's aims of national *grandeur* and *rank* is not
desired. Moreover, France is still struggling to maintain the EU's institutional structure intergovernmental, so as to use it in favour of the French national 'exceptionalism', representing
whole 'Europe' (see above Universalist Policy), and is rejecting the concept of 'European
federalism' (maximising the French influence in the EU, while minimising the chance of being absorbed by it). No one should expect that the three main classic Gaullist syntheses –
Policy of National Independence, Universalist Policy, and Policy of Power Projection –
would be abandoned any time soon in favour of 'Europeanisation' through *integration*.

On the other hand, the process of 'Europeanising' the French foreign and security policy
through *convergence* seems irreversible. It is true that France's foreign and security policy is
still characterised by universal French interests and responsibilities, but what is probably

more important than that is the need to increasingly converge France's interests with its other European partners in the EU. As a result of France's restricted resources and capacities in the sphere of crisis intervention, the French emphasis on national independence has weakened significantly in favour of multinational military co-operation in the post-Cold War era. French officials are becoming more and more willing, in fact forced, to accept much greater European as well as Atlantic military integration than ever before. Hence, each year more and more scholars are dedicating their research to the area of compatibility between French national independence and convergence towards 'Europeanisation'.

The French aspiration towards an ever greater CESDP within the EU, with the possible full merger of the WEU into it, has been the bedrock of the five-decade-old French struggle of making the EU/WEU 'autonomous' from the US defence 'hegemony' in Europe: nowadays burden and responsibility sharing under the concepts of 'hegemony' and 'autonomy' in a more or less two equal pillar structure are significantly differentiated. The manifestation of a fully 'autonomous' EU/WEU was revealed by French Defence Minister Richard as: 'I have no doubt that a combination of *political will*, economic and financial incentives (monetary union) and growing consensus will in time make a *common defence policy* a reality' (emphasis added).[238]

The EU/WEU's CESDP and US's ESDI need a flexible diplomatic-military institutional structure in order to be able to co-ordinate EU/WEU-US/NATO joint actions, but at the same time this structure should be designed to leave some viable operational area for 'autonomous' EU/WEU 'soft' military missions. It is also hoped that the combination of this flexible institutional structure with the new pragmatic British policy style would lead France into a new

---

[238] Richard, A., 'French-US Relations – A View From the Defence Side', *US-CREST's Franco-American Seminar Series*, (April 29, 1998).

Franco-US/NATO *rapprochement*. These are the areas that will no doubt continue to be explored by French officials with the aim of shaping them and attempting to create the desired two equal – 'European' and 'North American' – pillars structure in coming years.

EPILOGUE:

REASSESSMENT AND FUTURE EXPECTATIONS

'The time has come to take a qualitative leap forward and give the EU a political and

operational defence capability. The year that has seen the advent of the Euro can also be the

one that marks the start of a proper European defence. This is why we urge our governments

to rise to this historic occasion and not shirk their responsibilities'.

--WEU Assembly[1]

The painstaking bilateral efforts of Germany and France progressively transformed the EU's

trade and industrial policy (the Common Market), economic and monetary policy (the EMU,

including the Euro), and foreign and security policy (CFSP) from rhetoric to reality. However,

carrying these developments further into the worth of their meaning will not be possible

unless the EU member states integrate political and defence concepts into the EU's institu-

tional frame in order to safeguard its industrial and economic interests in a multipolar world

politically and to provide effective support for its foreign and security policy initiatives in the

new security environment militarily. The *political* impact of the EMU, with the Euro, has

been as significant as its economic and financial impact. Therefore, the emergence of the Euro

will exert more and more pressure for the development of a political Europe and press ahead

on initiatives taken at the St. Mâlo, Cologne, Helsinki, and Nice European Council meetings

upon the Common European Security and Defence Policy (CESDP). German and French

---

[1] WEU Assembly, 'Time for Defence – Plan for Action', *Document proposed by the Standing Committee*, (Paris: WEU Assembly, March 16, 1999).

policymakers are fully convinced that, after the single currency, European political and de-

fence integration processes are the next logical steps – an advance in one would lead to an

advance in the other until the European integration process is completed by integrating the

Political Union and Common Defence into the EU.

The first section of this epilogue will support the hypothesis of this dissertation by concluding

seven interrelated guiding criteria in order to determine the course of the German-French ap-

proaches to the CESDP over the medium-term. These criteria were topical and dynamic in the

last decade of the 20th Century and it seems they will remain so in the early 21st Century. The

second section will search out the impact of the Nice European Council Summit of December

11, 2000 on the CESDP, which prospects about intergovernmental or federal/pioneering

(Fischer's proposal/Chirac's proposal) future of Europe. The post-Nice Summit process

opened a new dimension to the Political Union and Common Defence that will seemingly en-

dure until the end of the first decade of the 21st Century.

(1) Seven Guiding Criteria

(a) Focus should be on 'soft' military missions for developing a clearer common strategic

   perspective.

The new security concept came into being during dramatic changes to the threat position from

an identifiable enemy to *an indefinable danger* around the early 1990s, stimulated the CFSP's

creation with the Maastricht Treaty in 1991/1992, impelled the incorporation of the WEU's

Petersberg Tasks into the CFSP with the Amsterdam Treaty in 1996/1997, and triggered the

inclusion of the defence policy, with the CESDP, by a taboo breaking initiative of the Anglo-

French Joint Declaration on European Defence at St. Mâlo, into the EU through the Cologne

and Helsinki European Council meetings and, finally, consolidated with the Treaty of Nice in

2000. This evolution undoubtedly strengthened the concept of the EU as a 'security commu-nity' in the sense that there is a commitment to mutual solidarity through security and defence assistances between the EU members based on shared common values, interests, and expecta-tions. Although the 'security community' concept in comparison to the collective defence al-liance is flimsy, it has a broader definition and therefore fits properly into the current respon-sibility of the EU in 'soft' military missions, rather than the traditional defence guarantee, which has a narrower definition.

The 'soft' military missions, well integrated into the CFSP as a credible 'stick' to the CESDP, will provide an invaluable advantage to the EU's 'carrot' – a credible security institution so that principal foreign policy, diplomatic/political and economic instruments will be fortified by quasi-military missions (or 'soft' military missions) in the military-diplomatic sphere. In between 'carrot' and 'stick', the EU has a wide range of intervention choices at its disposal and will always lean towards using the instruments that are in the scope of 'carrot', rather than using the instruments in the scope of 'stick'. However, any crisis situation that might ne-cessitate the use of 'stick' should be met by a force bigger than the sum of the conflicting forces' for stopping the deterioration of Kosovo-type ethno-nationalist conflicts (see Chapter 1). This force will operate according to international rules and under a clear legal mandate in the name of the international community,[2] but whether a clear UN mandate will always be an unbreakable condition for the EU/WEU 'soft' military mission or not remains to be seen.

In order to bring stability to those unstable regions of Europe, France and particularly Germany, due to its geopolitical situation, should shoulder European security and defence re-sponsibilities. Germany must share the leadership role of the EU in stabilising Europe to-

---

[2] Howorth, J., 'European integration and defence: the ultimate challenge?,' *Chaillot Paper 43*, (Paris: WEU, Institute for Security Studies, November 2000), p.88.

gether with France not only diplomatically and economically, but also militarily.[3] It will be painful for France to compromise its national foreign and security policy concepts in favour of 'Europeanisation' and will be that much more painful for Germany to accustom itself to the use of military force in 'soft' military operations, but both will soon fully realise their key roles in stabilising European conflicts. The 'soft' military operations, where France is more experienced, do not solve problems, but only prepare the necessary ground for post-conflict peace operations, preventive measures, stabilising projects (e.g. the Balkan Stability Pact initiative of Fischer), or re-building the disintegrated state through non-military political measures, civil-military co-operation (*Cimic*), where Germany is relatively energetic and innovative. The main prospective difficulty is on which basis human rights will be justified as a right for military intervention in a sovereign state or on which standards the European Council will make its judgement for a 'just' military operation. It seems this difficulty and the UN-mandate question will be problems for all signatory members of the EU's CESDP, but particularly this might cause serious political agitations among some political parties in Germany. This and similar problems must be solved by exhaustive interactions between politicians and military officers at the leadership level by attaching it an effective civil-military dialogue for developing a comprehensive coherent concept.

(b) The Anglo-French St. Mâlo Declaration on European Defence should be seen as a

primary opportunity for realising Franco-German security and defence projects.

The WEU was tied to the EU during the Maastricht Treaty discussions in 1991 with the Franco-German desire of making it undertake 'soft' military actions on behalf of the EU. However, the Atlanticist UK blocked such an evolution from being put into practice until the British Prime Minister Tony Blair changed the half-century-old traditional British foreign

---

[3] Lutz, D. S., 'Für eine Europäische Sicherheitsgemeinschaft – Europa zwischen "Protectorat" und Eigenständigkeit', in Volle, A. & Weidenfeld, W. (Hrsg.), *Europäische Sicherheitspolitik in der Bewährung*, (Bielefeld: Bertelsman, 2000), pp.28-29.

policy by giving the EU an 'autonomous' defence dimension at his meeting with French President Jacques Chirac in December 1998 at St. Mâlo. The three main issues this time have created more propitious conditions for realising the Franco-German desire for a European 'Pillar of Defence' from the scratch caused by the CESDP:

Firstly, the UK for the first time committed itself wholeheartedly to a credible 'autonomous' European defence creation through contributing to the diplomatic-militarily dimension of the EU. In fact, such a contribution was long considered as a necessary input for any credible European military force creation. The UK (the most Atlanticist EU member) contributed to such an intricate scratch together with France (the most European Integrationist EU member) as a co-founder of the CESDP, but might increasingly find itself one day in a tight EU frame predominantly characterised by the Franco-German axis. *Secondly*, the UK's key role in fleshing out an 'autonomous' European defence dimension to the EU/WEU initiated a histori-cal process of NATO's long-term reconfiguration. While the UK perceives this process as a condition for the survival of the Atlantic Alliance through effective contribution of the EU/WEU to missions and activities of NATO, France perceives it as an opportunity to strengthen the 'autonomous' capability of the EU/WEU for the sake of reaching the two equal 'pillars' concept – a European 'caucus' within NATO – in order to make the transatlantic se-curity relationship healthier and more balanced. *Thirdly*, a significant *political will* at the EU-15 level has created the CESDP and this gave the EU a sense of *strategie commune*. This *strategie commune*, encircle the 'security community' notion, lets the EU be seen as a 'real' Union. This 'real' Union will gain the worth of its meaning after Europe has developed its own 'defence culture' through the inclusion of the Art.V (collective defence clause) of the WEU into the EU.

Two of the Franco-German security and defence projects, the first currently being hypothetical, are waiting to be hatched in the future. *Firstly*, following the paragraph above, the Franco-German proposal of incorporating the WEU with its Art.V into the EU in three stages put forward during the Maastricht Treaty negotiations in 1991 and resonated in Art.17 of the Amsterdam Treaty in 1997. This Article, which explicitly states 'progressive framing of a common defence policy ... which might lead to a common defence', implies that the EU with a CDP and CD retains – particularly in the latter – a potential life for the incorporation of the WEU's Art.V into the EU (see Chapter 2). This option, however, seems difficult to achieve, because it is not only a serious dilemma for the Europeans themselves, but also a major factor that may trigger the US military forces' total withdrawal from Europe. The former requires a solution to the neutrals position and a clear commitment towards converging national sovereignties into the EU and, presently, neither Germany nor France would welcome the latter. NATO will remain the bedrock of European collective defence, but if the reliability of the transatlantic security relationship begins losing its value (e.g. US's unilateral actions in deploying the NMD system) then France and Germany, possibly joined by the UK, would have no other political choice, but to press for the incorporation of the WEU's Art.V into the EU.

Secondly, an informal joint study of the French and German foreign ministries concluded that the First and Second Pillar of the EU needs to be merged for developing a proactive European foreign policy (*communitarisation*) and recommended that the office of Javier Solana (High Representative of the CFSP and the Secretary-General of *the Council* and the WEU) should move from an intergovernmental to a supranational configuration by becoming the Vice-President of *the Commission* as well. Furthermore, the Policy Unit of the High Representative should operate in close co-operation with the CFSP and CESDP planning teams in the Commission in order to form the embryo of the European Foreign Ministry and to make the High Representative of the CFSP able to speak with one voice on matters of defence. This difficulty in coordination was intended to be removed by establishing a mechanism at the Council Secretariat during the Nice European Council meeting on December 11, 2000.[4] The creation of a Council of Defence Ministers, which will be responsible for military co-operation within the EU by seeking convergence in the field of defence, and to carry out a re-view of the armed forces of member states probably with a Euro-Strategic Defence Review, is another French proposal backed by Germany. Although France and the UK together put the flesh on the bones of European defence at St. Mâlo, this was a long planned Franco-German desire. Concomitantly, the above Franco-German projects verify that the Franco-German 'motor' is functioning at high speed and could draw the UK into new European defence inte-gration ventures.

(c) The EU/WEU-US/NATO relationship must clearly be redefined by institutional flexibility

on a 'two pillars' concept for a healthy future of the transatlantic relationship.

Soon after the endorsement of the ESDI/CJTF concept – a supposed European pillar within NATO – in NATO's Berlin Summit in 1996, the Europeans almost two years later found the way of circumventing the US veto possibility upon the EU/WEU 'autonomous' military ac-tion by a surprise Anglo-French St. Mâlo Declaration on the formation of the CESDP in 1998. This has been an obvious sign of the Europeans' dissatisfaction with the US post-Cold War foreign and defence policy that the Europeans – including the US's most faithful ally, the UK – will not tolerate any longer falling blindly in behind American leadership, which is in-creasingly leaning towards unilateral political and military actions. The transatlantic partner-ship is signalling that the struggling relationship needs to be restructured in fundamental ways; otherwise, the consequences of problems, which are well beyond our measurable hori-zons, could easily cause a series of unintended spin-offs.

---

[4] The Council Secretariat incorporates a military staff composed of military experts seconded by the Member States under the military direction of the Military Committee (MC).

These problems – the two most important of which are mentioned below – have gradually caused serious divergences between the Europeans and Americans over numerous security issues since the early 1990s. France and Germany, but also the UK since the US dictated its own political and military strategy in Kosovo and swept aside the British proposal of sending ground troops, have long been concerned about the US's preference for a unilateral course by ignoring multilateralism and international treaties, for example, the plan for deploying a system called the NMD thereby violating the ABM Treaty of 1972, rejecting the UN as a platform for legitimising the use of force, etc.[5] The Europeans instead prefer appeasement politics through multilateral approaches, diplomatic dialogue and negotiating forums, treaty-based normative solutions and international regimes. Given this background, the growing strain in the EU-US relationship will be tested in the future by the following dilemma: Either a compromise for collective solution would be found regarding the NMD system or the US will go it alone and push the Europeans to build their own NMD system. The Franco-British joint commission have already started collaborating on nuclear issues, but France, more than the UK, would be willing to offer the French nuclear force in the service of the whole of Europe (see Chapter 5). The US tendency for rejecting the UN mandate as an absolute necessity in NATO's future military operations will be another test case. John Bolton, Senior Vice-President at the American Enterprise Institute, argued in June 2000 that '[o]ur next President should make it clear, to NATO and to the rest of the world, that we reject Secretary General Kofi Annan's view that the UN is the world's 'sole source of legitimacy on the use of force.'[6] France and, particularly, Germany will categorically ask for a UN mandate for the EU/WEU-led military operations and this will certainly be a stumbling block for the smooth functioning of the EU/WEU-US/NATO co-operation.

---

[5] Some of other diverging points between Europeans and Americans are the US rejection of arms control measures as an essential component of security policy, refusing to sign the treaty of banning land mines, periodic interventions in Iraq and sanctions against Iran and Libya, vetoing the EU's German candidate to head the IMF...
[6] Bolton, J., 'The End of NATO?', *The World Today*, (Vol.56, No.6, June 2000), p.13.

No state, not even a superpower, can solve the pending problems of the world on its own. For that reason the terms for renewing the transatlantic partnership between the Europeans and Americans will most likely be forced towards balanced burden sharing and meaningful division of labour particularly by France and Germany until a 'realistic' autonomous European 'Pillar of Defence' within NATO – equal to the 'North American Pillar' – is constructed for maintaining the survivability of the transatlantic relationship. In fact, this has been the main target of Gaullist doctrine in France for almost fifty years. However, questioning just how much 'autonomy' from the US/NATO will ultimately grow, where its parameters are intentionally or unintentionally kept unspecified among Europeans themselves and almost left open to the French traditional desire for as much autonomy as possible, the Americans are more cautious about the progress towards a stronger European 'pillar' in NATO – a European 'pillar' was planted in NATO by the ESDI which was then inclined to grow out of NATO by the CESDP. Strobe Talbot, US Deputy Secretary of State during the Clinton Administration, warned: 'We would not want to see an ESDI that comes into being first within NATO but then grows out of NATO and finally grows away from NATO, since that would lead to an ESDI that initially duplicates NATO but that could eventually compete with NATO'.[7]

The growth of the EU/WEU autonomy from the US/NATO will inevitably cause some friction, but would not pull the transatlantic partnership apart. The main reason is that the transatlantic partnership is interwoven by a flexible institutional synergy based on multilateral institutions, which are shaped by deeply rooted democratic values that form the basis of the *new security concept*, in order to manage the international interdependence. The EU/WEU would therefore carry out 'soft' military missions through bilateral or multilateral co-operative ventures either by NATO means via the concept of the CJTF or by European means outside the

---

[7] Quoted in Sloan, S. R., 'The US and European Defence,' *Chaillot Paper 39*, (Paris: Institute for Security Studies, WEU, February 2000), p.26.

NATO framework. These multi-optional *ad hoc* EU/WEU 'soft' military missions have in general two main pistons – NATO and European-only options – and the US, for this reason, must make the EU/WEU use of the NATO piston easier if it wants to politically and militarily influence such operations or to discourage the Europeans deviations from the US/NATO course. If the US is serious about balanced burden and responsibility sharing in NATO, it should not only be more receptive to the Europeans criticisms over issues which have caused serious divergences between the EU-US in recent years, but should also support the EU/WEU's autonomous CESDP for making it a more capable partner since the French desire of maximum European autonomy will always be checked by an Atlanticist UK and moderate Germany through a flexible network of institutional interdependencies. On the other hand, if the EU/WEU does not want to harm the transatlantic partnership, it should avoid excessive rhetoric about an autonomous CESDP and should form the European 'Pillar of Defence' *within* NATO, rather than *outside* it, based on institutional flexibility, transparency, and co-operation between the EU/WEU and US/NATO.

(d) Restructuring national defence industries along European lines and spending on defence
   should be given a greater priority.

Creating a European 'Pillar of Defence' as an equal partner to the 'North American Pillar' requires real military capabilities (using latest technology weapons) similar to what the US presently possesses. The vitality of this point is hidden in two most likely scenarios: The first scenario is if US military forces engage in a theatre outside of Europe at the same time as the EU/WEU military forces have to deploy its own troops in a European theatre, then the military assets of NATO (in fact US assets), which could according to the June 1996 Berlin agreement be made available for the EU/WEU 'soft' military missions through the CJTF, will be busy in the service of the US. The second scenario is if the US does not want to launch a military operation in a theatre where the EU/WEU decided to engage but, due to the US veto over NATO assets, it could not. These two crisis scenarios are serious potential conflict situations between the EU and the US in the future since they might nullify what the EU politically gained by the 'autonomous' CESDP. In plain terms, the EU/WEU needs to produce its own armaments.

Since NATO's military operation in Kosovo and the Anglo-French St. Mâlo Declaration on European defence, which extolled the EU to act 'autonomously' and develop an appropriate military capacity without *unnecessary duplication* of US/NATO assets through a strengthened competitive European defence industry and technology, the negative effects of shrinking defence budgets, and increasing technology costs have demanded urgent restructuring of the European Defence Industrial and Technological Base (EDITB) in order to catch the post-St. Mâlo developments in the defence sphere. The good news is Europeans seem to understand well the need for acquiring the necessary military assets for power projection with at least *partial duplication* of US/NATO principal assets for 'autonomous' EU/WEU actions. Even so, the following modifications should be done: restructuring the European defence industrial base through gradual privatisation, merger, and cooperation of the national markets along European lines, systematically opening the European defence market to 'two-way street' transatlantic armaments trade, standardising weapons procurement through a European supra-national agency, gradually increasing defence budgets and spending the existing money more efficiently. The bad news is that, although the fall of the Berlin Wall is a delighted memory, persuading the European public to spend more on the defence sector instead of on the public sector will be a painful political process in Europe, particularly in Germany and neutral countries.

Although the Rome Treaty's golden rule of Art.223 excludes arms production and trade from the EU's *l'acquis communautaire*, the Commission investigates dual-use products and expands its actions gradually on defence-related issues. The EU that puts emphasis on developing an 'autonomous' CESDP, with a strengthened and more competitive European defence industry would find abolishing Art.223 inevitable in coming years in order to strengthen the EDITB and catch the rate of defence markets globalisation. Three major European agencies, launched through *enhanced co-operations*, are working towards such an end: (a) the German initiative of the Western European Armaments Organisation (WEAO), founded in November 1996, is considered as the Master Plan of the European Armaments Agency; (b) the Franco-German initiative of the Joint Armament Cooperation Structure (JACS), formally founded by France, Germany, the UK, and Italy in January 1997, is a major platform for streamlining and rationalising national armaments co-operation; (c) the European Aeronautic Defence and Space Company (EADS), came into being in July 2000, signalling a high degree of confidence among European states on the cross-border merger of national defence industries (see Chapter 2).

These three major European agencies are important platforms for converging different national interests, military doctrines, and standardising national military equipment programmes. The prospect that European integration in different spheres will increasingly make the co-operation between national defence markets easier is promising. A steady convergence between the armed forces of the major European countries is a sign of their intention to bring different defence industries closer to each other. As France and the UK did, Germany, Spain, and Italy are also embarked on professionalising and modernising their armed forces for attaining better power projection capabilities. There is no doubt that the Franco-German couple will possess a common means to evaluate 'soft' military situations and their defence industries will be restructured towards the end of 2010.

(e) The Franco-German security and defence partnership will continue to matter.

The French and German bilateral partnership has been a driving force behind every European integration process in a remarkably resilient strategic partnership in leadership form rather than a relationship simply based on some cultural and scientific agreements. While they are neighbours with a shared history, their strategic conceptions and security and defence philosophies nonetheless have differed. These differences inhibited developing a coherent common strategic perspective, but at the same time became the main reason of rapprochement between them through a historic reconciliation. The Franco-German partnership increasingly became institutionalised both bilaterally and vis-à-vis the EU integration process. The internally woven network of bilateral working relationships and the multilateral EU integration process became the source of norm setting and institution building with a growing sense of purpose. A powerful 'magnetic cycle' is thereby formed: the partnership determines an agenda in an inner Franco-German circle – it sometimes does this just for the sake of keeping the partnership robust – occasionally, but not necessarily, with the participation of other influential European powers; the partnership radiates this agenda from an inner Franco-German circle to the outer EU circle; the agenda gradually gains an institutional character by putting communal flesh on the Franco-German bones in the EU; and, finally, the agenda gains a substantial legal status in the EU chambers and turns into a community policy. This study, in the period from 1990 to 2000, clearly manifests this magnetic power cycle and focuses particularly on high-politics issues (predominantly on defence), which led by the Franco-German partnership with the participation of the UK in the fall of 2000.

The unification of Germany after the fall of the Berlin Wall has shifted the heretofore courteously accepted Franco-German centre of gravity in favour of the German side. However, what is remarkable is, instead of falling apart, France and Germany strengthened their partnership by pulling their sovereignties together in irrevocable European integration processes:

Monetary and Political Union. Germany and France put their security interests at the heart of the deepening European integration process where the Franco-German partnership is at the top of their foreign policy agendas. The former German Defence Minister, Volker Rühe, even stated that after the end of the Cold War the alliance with the US, although still necessary, is automatically ranked behind European integration.[8] One of the former high ranking officials is quoted by Rubinstein: 'Whereas Germany and the US were enemies twice in a generation, Germany and France were enemies for more than a thousand years, hence the significance of their developing friendship.'[9] However, the official German policy has never seriously deviated from its original line: France and the US wants to see Germany on their respective sides, but German policymakers, instead of making a choice between the two competing views, preferred the most intricate policy by balancing the views of France and the US against each other. France and Germany must redefine their diverse US/NATO policies unambiguously and adapt them to each other later through pragmatic and flexible institutional arrangements. In the past, the US considered the Franco-German axis as a threat to its own national interests and often tried to cause bickering between the partners. The US in the 21st Century should accept that France and Germany are the two major building blocks of the EU/WEU and encourage greater Franco-German co-operation and activism in managing European security, which would increase the political influence and the operational military flexibility of the US/NATO.

The Franco-German Common Security and Defence Concept, which was agreed in December 9, 1996, is significant evidence of the mature Franco-German alliance. It is stated in the document that, '[t]he common destiny uniting France and Germany is based, particularly, on a consensus on the basic objectives of our strategies and our societies. [...] The progress of

---

[8] Rühe's statement is extracted from Meimeth, M., 'Germany' in Brenner, M. (ed.), *NATO and Collective Security*, (UK: Macmillan Press Ltd., 1998), p.84.
[9] Rubinstein, A. Z., 'Germans On Their Future', *Orbis*, (Vol.43, No.1, Winter 1999), pp.127-144.

European integration is strengthening the political, economic, trade and social ties between our countries, to such an extent that their security interests are becoming inseparable'.[10] Following this concept and the new developments that occurred in the aftermath of the Anglo-French Joint Declaration on European Defence at St. Mâlo, the Franco-German Defence and Security Council agreed on the principles of the CESDP at Toulouse in May 1999 and enhanced the force projection capabilities of the Eurocorps in order to make it compatible with the European Rapid Reaction Corps.[11] Although the European Council has not yet articulated a strategy for the geographical range of this new European Rapid Reaction Corps, it is unlikely that the EU will deploy its military units far beyond the European periphery. As a result of their colonial past, France and the UK would look at this unit from a global perspective, but Germany would not be happy to see its army handling conflicts far beyond Europe's periphery. At this point, the essence of the Franco-German relationship would show its value with the French encouragement of the *Bundeswehr*'s crossing of the threshold of the *Realpolitik* step-by-step and taking a military role, which has hitherto been Germany's power projection in a realist mode constrained by the German political elite despite all its economic and financial power. In such a context, the *Bundeswehr* would still be checked by superior French armed forces in the Franco-German axis as well as in the EU military coalition.

The Franco-German security and defence partnership will continue to matter, because it is still a decisive power in pulling the CESDP into an 'autonomous' line, which would prepare the necessary conditions for the creation of a real and more balanced 'two equal pillars' concept in the transatlantic security relationship, while the UK is trying to restrict them. This partnership is also a determining factor in the construction of Political Union – weather fed-

---

[10] *Franco-German Common Security and Defence*, (Nuremberg: December 9, 1996, made public in Paris on January 30, 1997), Title I, parag.1.
[11] *Franco-German Summit –Defence and Security Council – Toulouse Declaration*, (Toulouse: May 29, 1999).

eral or confederal, achieving the European institutional reform or inventing a new flexible integration model for the EU will not be realised without the Franco-German coalition.

(f) Germany could do more for deepening the European security and defence integration process by moving from 'passive multilaterlaism' to 'active multilateralism' in 'soft' military missions.

Since the fall of the Berlin Wall in 1990, Germany is undoubtedly facing difficulties in developing a new internal and international consensual foreign and security policy, which is a factor affecting the 'responsibilities' of Germany in Europe at a time when the new security environment calls for a greater European role in the security and defence sphere. These difficulties originate from post-Cold War tensions so that adapting the core values of Germany's foreign and security policy – *Policy of Multilateralism, Verantwortungspolitik, Policy of 'Zivilmacht'* – into a new German role in military-diplomatic 'soft' military missions became unavoidable. Although the Federal Constitutional Court (FCC) judicially clarified in July 1994 the way for the *Bundestag*'s definition of the new German security and defence policy through exhaustive political debate, the process of defining a role for a unified sovereign Germany in European security and defence and transforming the German-American security relationship into an equal partnership in the transatlantic area have partially been made clear in the end of 2000. According to the preamble of the *Grundgesetz*, the German nation has to be conscious about its *responsibility* and Germany, as a member of and having equal rights in a united Europe, should *serve for peace* in the world.[12] The actual meaning of 'serving' demands engagement in a norm and value based foreign policy in the service of peace with the target of abolishing violence through an *active* involvement in founding international struc-

---

[12] The complete paragraph is as follows: 'Im Bewußtsein seiner Verantwortung vor Gott und den Menchen, von dem Willen beseelt, als gleichberechtigtes Glied in einem vereinten Europa dem Frieden der Welt zu dienen, hat sich das Deutsche Volk kraft seiner verfassungsgebenden Gewalt dieses Grundgesetz gegeben.' Sartorius, C., *Verfassungs- und Verwaltungsgesetze der Bundesrepublik Deutschland – Band I*, (München: C.H. Beck'sche Verlagsbuchhandlung, Februar 15, 1999), p.8.

tures for international and domestic society. Understanding the meaning of 'serving' in this way puts Germany into a pioneering role in influencing collective decision-making and collective action through realising its international and European responsibilities.

If Germany does not to want realise its military responsibility in the service of peace in Europe and in the world, this will put it in an unequal position in comparison with other member states of the EU and disrespects its own global responsibilities. In such a situation, the stability in Europe will be damaged and, as the CDU/CSU foreign policy expert Karl Lamers said in 1993, 'without Germany there will not be a CFSP and, as a result, there will not be Political Union'.[13] Hence, beside constructing Europe in economic and monetary areas, Germany has also committed itself to developing the CFSP and bringing the WEU into the EU with the ultimate aim of creating Common European Defence that will all, in the end, be complemented by Political Union. These targets gradually transferred the security and defence responsibilities' of Germany from *theory* into *practice* since it's commitments in these institutions are exposed to the new external risks and threats – 'soft' military conflict situations – in and around Europe. The putting into practice of those targets came with real military test cases and the *Bundeswehr* was deployed in various NATO out-of-area international peacekeeping and peace enforcement missions, albeit multilateralism was always kept as a condition. German policymakers have made their decisions based on a commitment to *Moralpolitik*, being responsible for peace (*Friedensverantwortung*), human rights and democratic values, in order to show solidarity with its Western allies and to keep stability and unity in Europe without deviating much from the 'civilian power' posture. Germany's participation in international peacekeeping and peace enforcement missions have always been realised in multilateral perspectives and the *Bundeswehr* has always pushed for multinational integration (see Chapter 4).

Germany, as a result of its foreign and security policy, will always prefer economic, political, and diplomatic instruments, conflict settlement, humanitarian assistance and multilateral security institutions such as the EU, WEU, the UN, or the OSCE, which are better specialised in diplomatic activities than NATO. Since the fall of the Berlin Wall, Germany has begun to lean more and more on the European integration process and press for the EU/WEU's CESDP to be largely autonomous from the US/NATO in the long term. There is a growing recognition among German policymakers that is it no longer reasonable to rely solely on the US leadership and expect it to take on the Europeans' security and defence responsibilities. This trend would presumably convince German policymakers to move from a political/diplomatic *passive multilateralism* to diplomatic/military *active multilateralism* as far as it considers this movement as an opportunity for deepening the European defence integration process. The political debate about the new role of Germany in the EU/WEU future security architecture has gained a new dimension since the Anglo-French St. Mâlo Declaration on European Defence in 1998 and after that the German foreign and security policy movement into *active multilateralism* became axiomatic with the two major developments:

- The German defence reforms, which were launched in the beginning of 1999, have largely been inspired by the St. Mâlo Declaration and subsequently legitimised by the EU's development of the CESDP. The German Defence Minister Rudolf Scharping's paper, *The Bundeswehr – Advancing Steadily into the 21ˢᵗ Century*, is making significant attributions to the St. Mâlo Declaration and the creation of the European Rapid Reaction Corps. As a result of revolutionary developments in the EU/WEU, the role of *military power*, which is complementary to any credible diplomacy in the CFSP frame, is gradually gaining legitimacy in the German foreign and security policy.

- Similar to Helsinki military decisions, the EU's Feira Summit in June 2000 concentrated particularly on Germany's preference for non-military crisis management in-

---

[13] Lamers quoted in Meimeth, M., 'Germany' in Brenner, M. (ed.), *NATO and Collective Security*, p.104.

struments. Autonomous EU/WEU missions will facilitate civil-military co-operations
(mutually reinforcing) for enforcing public order either on behalf of the UN or the
OSCE. The Feira Summit also reflected the German sensitivities on multilateralism by
developing new structural relationships between the EU/WEU and the US/NATO. It
also verified that, beside military power, Germany's non-military preferences,
diplomatic/political/economic instruments, are given significant priority.

If Germany wants to influence Europe and the world with its own vision, it should lean more
on the French view of the EU/WEU as an autonomous international power supplemented by a
prospective European 'Pillar of Defence' equal to the 'North Atlantic Pillar' rather than on the
British view of looser and more Atlanticist Europe. The pace of Germany's movement into
active multilateralism is likely to determine the fate of the French view, the precise shape of
Europe's security identity, as well as its own European and global roles.

(g) France should clearly define the relationship between its propagated strategic European

security and defence integration ambition and national independence in favour of

'Europeanisation'.

France has long been obsessed by regaining its global role and influence through classic
Gaullist imperatives of *grandeur* and *rank* among the great nations of the world through the
fundamental three French foreign and security policies (*Policy of National Independence,*
Universalist Policy, and *Policy of Power Projection*), which they contrast to the three German
traditional foreign and security policies. Since a more delicate balance of power emerged in
the centre of Europe with the end of the East-West tension, France is faced with difficulties in
adapting its foreign and security policy to the new security environment. Unlike German
policymakers, who saw the EC as an opportunity to pull Germany's sovereignty into it for
sharing national responsibilities and mitigating the difficulties of upgrading from a semi-

sovereign state to a full sovereign state posture and of becoming an economic-monetary power centre, as well as improving its political status, French policymakers saw the EC as a channel to retain France's leading position in security and defence spheres, as well as to benefit economically and financially by improving the diminished French status in Europe without giving much up from their national sovereignty and national defence autonomy. France and Germany are shaping their security and defence polices in the EU with respect to the new security demands, which have emerged in the post-Cold War new security environment. France cannot maintain its leading rank and Germany cannot fulfil its national responsibilities in the sphere of security and defence in Europe without integrating themselves into the EU.

Since the de Gaulle era, French leaders have been committed to the idea that an autonomous European security and defence entity should be created under the leadership of France for regaining a global role and achieving an influence in NATO. The EU for French leaders is more about aggregation of economic and military resources, so that it can assert European interests at the global level. This aggregation is also conceived as necessary for Political Union and kept as a central purpose to the overall European integration process. They believe that French interests could only be exercised through leading the European platform. French policymakers desire to build and steer the European platform in a multipolar world for a better balance of power between regions, for controlling and shaping the globalisation economically, financially, politically, militarily and culturally. Therefore, the EU would not only be a platform for checking and balancing powers in Europe regionally (German proclivity), but would also be a platform for nation-states to attain their interests internationally (French proclivity). Hence, there is a sort of division of labour in the Franco-German axis: While Germany is regulating the EU *regionally* through financial, economic, and political prerogatives, France will expound European thinking and lead it *internationally* through security, defence, cultural, and diplomatic prerogatives.

As far as France's US/NATO policy is concerned, although Mitterrand in the beginning of the 1990s envisaged putting the EC abruptly into a strategic entity status outside NATO, which is a driving factor behind France's European security policy since the 1960s, Chirac appeared in 1995 with his new policy style that a genuine strategic European defence entity is a long-term objective. Hence, Chirac increased France-US/NATO *rapprochement* inside NATO and in agreement with the US and also gave the impression that the creation of a European pillar *within* NATO is a more realistic option in the short-term, as opposed to that of a strictly independent European defence pillar subordinate to the EU/WEU. The main reason for this is that, Chirac thought his main European allies would be more receptive to the actual French ambitions of creating a European 'Pillar of Defence' more or less autonomous from the US/NATO in the long-term.[14] His new policy style has gained a different dimension in favour of French national ambitions since the Anglo-French St. Mâlo Declaration on European Defence, which came to formalise the creation of a Common European Security and Defence Policy (CESDP) with means and mechanisms to allow the EU to act 'autonomously' – backed by credible military forces – where NATO as a whole is not willing to engage (parag.2&3).

All NATO states, including very much the US and the UK, agree on the urgent need of the reconfiguration of transatlantic relationship in the post-Cold War era. Some sort of new balance in the long-term is unavoidable between the European Integrationists – led by France and Germany, seeking a *credible* EU/WEU *independence* while *co-operating* closely and formally with the US/NATO – and the Atlanticists – led by the UK, seeking a more US/NATO oriented EU/WEU for *strengthening* NATO as a primary organisation through the EU/WEU's *direct contribution* to the Atlantic Alliance (see Chapter 5). The following points

---

[14] This point has been neatly expressed by Frédéric Bozo in his article called 'France' in Brenner, M. (ed.), *NATO and Collective Security*, (UK: Macmillan Press Ltd., 1998), pp.60-62.

will be determinant in the long-term balance of the transatlantic security relationship in favour
of the French ambition of attaining the strategic European defence integration:

- The US and the UK are gradually accepting that NATO is a platform for balancing the
  transatlantic security relationship between the Americans and Europeans on the basis
  of equal burden and responsibility sharing since it was the original goal of the Alliance
  and sporadically affirmed by the US Presidents along these lines. Eisenhower in 1955
  said that, 'Europe must, as a whole, provide in the long run for its own defence';
  Kennedy in 1962 was the first who pledged to a variant of the 'two pillars' concept, a
  'North American Pillar' and a 'European Pillar'; and, Clinton said in 1994 that, 'we
  want Europe to be strong. That's why America supports Europe's own steps so far towards greater unity in the EU, the WEU and the development of a European security
  identity.' A militarily more self-confident EU/WEU will be more capable and willing
  to assume greater responsibility sharing in defence of Europe (see Chapter 1&2).

- The US should demonstrate its willingness for accepting equal defence burden and responsibility sharing for a balanced NATO by supporting CESDP autonomy and encouraging the EU/WEU leadership in 'soft' military missions. This would not only
  decrease the friction between France and the US, but would also draw France closer to
  NATO by considering the European 'Pillar of Defence' within NATO as more for the
  benefit of a healthy transatlantic security relationship. Additionally, the complex security dangers in the new security environment will be more justly and democratically
  evaluated through the EU/WEU-US/NATO connection, France and the US will start
  exhibiting more trust in each other's ambitions, so NATO will gain more politico-
  diplomatic credibility, prestige, international support and legitimacy.

If French policymakers desire to read the above points in favour of its long propagated strategic European security and defence integration ambition, it should first bridge the gap between

its commitment to create a genuine strategic European defence pillar and sacrosanct French national independence. France's manoeuvring between European integration and national independence has increasingly become incompatible with the permanently deepening European economic, political, and defence integration processes. French politicians avoid explicitly stating that the concept of 'Europeanisation' has slowly but already begun seriously challenging the basic tenets of the three classic Gaullist syntheses. In fact, growing European integration is testifying that France is economically, politically, and militarily accepting integration into the EU through progressive transference of French strategic European security and defence integration ambitions from the national to the EU perspective. 'Europeanisation' will be an even bigger challenge before France's national defence autonomy in coming years as the national economic and monetary policies have already been integrated into the EU and will signal the need for a major national convergence in the political sphere. The first serious challenge to the EU states' political competency came with German Foreign Minister Fischer's model of 'centre of gravity' and French President Chirac's model of 'pioneer group' towards mid-2000 and occupied the EU's agenda during the Nice European Council Summit on December 11-16, 2000, on the way to some form of European political integration.

(2) A Way Ahead: What Does the EU's Nice Summit Offer to the Future European Defence Pillar?

In years ahead, the EU states are preparing themselves to engage in a fundamental discussion about the future shape and ultimate destination of the Union, which was first coined by Lamers-Schäuble papers of 1994 and 1999 on formulating a 'quasi-constitutional document' for the EU based on the model of a 'federal state' and, later, taken up by Fischer in his speech at the Humboldt University in 2000. The EU was subsequently brought into a process of reforming its institutions radically, since the Nice European Council Summit held in the wane of the 20th Century. Similar to the EU's Amsterdam Treaty of 1997, where the Franco-German Joint Letter on 'enhanced co-operations' proposed circumventing the veto blockage of a single member state and has been variously termed as 'hard core' (by Germany), 'concentric circles' (by France), and 'à la carte' (by the UK), the Nice European Council Summit went down the same road in order to find solutions to the unresolved institutional issues through setting the agenda on: the redistribution of votes in the Council of Ministers, the reduction in the number of Commissioners, the extension of the QMV by 'enhanced co-operations' or flexibility mechanism.[15] These reforms are unavoidable for the reason that the EU enlargement to include 27 or more member states will make it no longer capable of developing a political will or mechanisms for strengthening social, industrial, monetary, foreign and security policies.

Although the last reform issue is rather complex, the divergent visions of Fischer (a sort of *supranational federalism* with a constituent EU treaty forming the 'centre of gravity') and Chirac (a sort of *hybrid intergovernmental model* with a European Constitution forming the 'pioneer group') could not only be mingled by 'enhanced co-operation', but it also offers an indispensable means for the CESDP and could ease the way for greater political integration (see Chapter 3). Fischer is fully conscious about this difficulty and argues that 'enhanced co-operation' will come first and be nothing more than 'enhanced intergovernmentalism' in view of the pressure of facts that federalism will stay as a weak concept in the medium-term. Fischer also developed the 'centre of gravity' as a 'hard core' and a step in between the 'enhanced co-operation' and the finalisation of political integration for European federation. He opposes the idea of loose European confederation on the basis that it will not be a successful

---

[15] 'Nachrichten Extra: Der EU-Reform-Gipfel von Nizza', *Frankfurter Rundschau*, (Dezember 12, 2000), pp.1-2; 'Machtkampf lähmt EU-Gipfel', *Frankfurter Rundschau*, (Dezember 11, 2000), pp.1-3.

model for the EU in a globalising era.[16] However, Chirac proposes his plan as a 'pioneer

group' in European 'concentric circles' form with a 'flexible intergovernmental co-ordination

mechanism' outside the constituent Community context.[17] Among these, even though neither

Fischer nor Chirac was specific on the institutional arrangements needed for expanding the

'enhanced co-operations' mechanism, both specifically mentioned that defence and security is

probably the most convenient area for exercising 'enhanced co-operations'. In such a view,

where does CESDP fit?

Under 'enhanced co-operations', groups of EU countries – coalitions of the willing – will be

allowed to start integrationist initiatives on their own. While this would create further dyna-

mism in the EU through 'safeguarding the values and serving the interests of the Union as a

whole by asserting its identity as a coherent force on the international scene',[18] it would also

leave the EU with a 'two-speed' Europe. In this spirit, the Commission proposed removing

the veto and setting the minimum number of member states that can establish 'enhanced co-

operations' including its possible application in the area of security and defence policy.

However, during the Treaty of Nice (ToN) negotiations, the UK – one of the two main actors

during the creation of the CESDP together with France – strongly opposed the application of

'enhanced co-operations' in the sphere of defence. The inclusion or exclusion of defence as-

pects into the 'enhanced co-operations' mechanism was a matter of dependence or independ-

ence for the EU/WEU's planned 50,000-60,000 Rapid Reaction Force vis-à-vis the

US/NATO. France and Germany pressed for an independent European military force through

the inclusion of the defence aspects into 'enhanced co-operations' on the one side, and the

---

[16] Fischer, J., *Vom Staatenverbund zur Föderation – Gedanken über die Finalität der europäischen Integration,* (Frankfurt am Main: Suhrkamp Verlag, 2000); also see 'Chevènement, Fischer Discuss EU's Future', *Le Monde,* (June 21, 2000), pp.15-17.
[17] For more information see, Schild, J., 'Über Nizza hinaus – Deutsch-französische Debatten über die Zukunft der EU', *Aktuelle Frankreich-Analysen,* (Ludwigsburg: Deutsch-Französisches Institut, August 16, 2000).
[18] Art.27(a) of the *Treaty of Nice (ToN)*, 'Amending the Treaty on European Union, the Treaties Establishing the European Communities and Certain Related Acts', *Official Journal of the European Communities,* (March 10, 2001).

UK, backed by the US, pressed for the exclusion of defence aspects from 'enhanced co-operations' on the other side. In the end, the UK succeed in convincing the French Presidency at Nice and Art.27(b) of the ToN was written as: 'Enhanced co-operation pursuant to this Title shall relate to implementation of a joint action or a common position. It shall not relate to having military or defence implications'. However, it is decided in the ToN that 'enhanced co-operations' – previously excluded during the Treaty of Amsterdam negotiations – will be applied this time to the second pillar (CFSP) with a QMV for the implementation of joint actions or common positions (see ToN Art.27(d)). Moreover, 'enhanced co-operations' also related to arms initiatives, which offers a far-reaching prospect for the realisation of a single European defence market, and security and defence initiatives *only for contributing to the acquisition of crisis management capabilities.* The minimum number of EU member states that can establish 'enhanced co-operations' is decided to be at least eight (see ToN Art.40(a) and Art.43)[19] and veto powers of member states are restricted by the ToN to the following areas: military and defence, treaty amendments, admission of a new member into the EU, and decision for transferring national competences to the EU.

In relation to the 'enhanced co-operations' model, a series of issues tackled beside defence aspects during the ToN discussions are all becoming add-ons in giving the CESDP greater substance. The clarification of transparency, legitimacy, democratic accountability, and the creation of the Charter of Fundamental Rights in the name of common European norms and values are not only necessary issues that would prepare the way for the creation of a European Constitution, but also central elements for the CESDP, since they are directly related to secu-

---

[19] The established 'enhanced co-operation' will be open to any EU member state at any time (Art.43(b)) and 'while all members of the Council shall be able to take part in the deliberation, only those representing Member States participating in enhanced co-operations shall take part in the adoption of decisions' (Art.44). 'Expenditure resulting from implementation of enhanced co-operation, other than administrative costs entailed for the institutions, shall be borne by the participating Member States, unless all members of the Council, acting unanimously after consulting the European Parliament, decide otherwise' (Art.44(a)).

rity and defence in every respect. The incorporation of these issues into Community treaties will no doubt make the German participation in future European Rapid Reaction Force's military operations easier as they will form the basis of legitimising the *Bundeswehr*'s participation into Community based multilateral missions. The main problem is that even though the application of 'enhanced co-operations' – calling to mind NATO's Berlin agreement on the CJTF concept which made the EU/WEU-led military missions possible under the leadership of the 'coalitions of the willing' – in the area of defence do not seems very problematic (except incorporation of Art.V of the WEU into the Community treaties), this would make the different groups' aggregation and meshing together a protracted process. Basing the CESDP on intergovernmentalism would not only exclude the CESDP from this protracted process, but would also impede the creation of an embryonic political integration on the way to some form of 'ever closer Union'.

The future vision of the EU is divided into three fronts: Germany favours political integration of the EU to be finalised with a sort of *supranational federalism* and the relationship to France should be based on sharing European leadership more pragmatically. The UK strictly favours an *intergovernmental model* with a clear-cut division of competencies between the EU and nation-states. France, divided between the German and British visions, favours a sort of *hybrid intergovernmental model* that would more look like a 'federation of nation-states' retaining the power of nation-states intact and reconciliation with Germany as the essence of the Franco-German axis.[20] Shaping a new model for the future of the EU came to a point that touches on basic national political cultures. The structure of state in Germany and in France is based on two different models: German federal *Bundesstaat* and French decentralised unitary state. As a result of strong correlation between federalism and integration, German policy-

---

[20] 'Fronten in der EU', *Der Spiegel*, (Nr.23, Juni 2, 2001), p.18; Vernet, D., 'Welche gemeinsame Vision? Der Grundfrage bleibt zwischen Berlin und Paris offen', *Frankfurter Rundschau*, (Februar 2, 2001), p.8.

makers find integration of their state competencies' into the EU through 'Europeanisation' compatible with their federal administrative structure. On the contrary, as a result of disparity between the decentralised unitary state and integration, French policymakers find 'Europeanisation' of unitary state competencies through various European integration proc- esses a painful diffusion to their decentralised administrative structure.[21]

France and Germany – as long as the UK stays out of the Euro – should activate the bilateral Franco-German 'motor' by combining and institutionalising the plans of the *Centre d'analyse et de prévision des Quai d'Orsay* and the *Auswärtigen Amt* as a first step to a strengthened union between themselves in various areas: Economic and monetary areas on the one hand, political and military areas on the other hand. This would provide France and Germany with the necessary platforms to converge their different national foreign and security policy con- cepts through developing common provisions without significantly diverging from their na- tional policies and would gradually give the sense that sacrificing national autonomy is worth setting conditions for and leading the group of avant-garde states. Given that the CESDP is dependent on the British military contribution, it would however be inconceivable for the Franco-German axis to form an avant-garde group without the UK. Nevertheless, once the avant-garde group began advancing under the leadership of the Franco-German tandem, the UK will find it irresistible and so will be compelled to join in.

In the light of this epilogue, in the long-term, possibly around 2010 or 2015, it seems there will be more decisive European and global developments that will gradually lead the Franco- German desire for a European 'Pillar of Defence' from rhetoric to something closer to reality. By that time, the armed forces' reform processes in Germany and France will be completed

---

[21] For detailed information see, Rill, B. (Hg.), 'Deutschland und Frankreich: Gemeinsame Zukunftsfragen', *Argumente und Materialen zum Zeitgeschehen*, (München: Hanns-Seidel-Stiftung, Nr.21, 2000).

and the complex European institutional reform dilemma – *supranational federalism* or *hybrid intergovernmentalism* – will be more or less resolved so that the future course of the EU's political integration would not only be unavoidable, but would also reinforce the EU/WEU's CESDP and ease the way for the creation of a robust European 'Pillar of Defence'. The reconfiguration of the transatlantic security relationship would not lag behind and could be elegantly adjusted by an accurate guess as to what sort of security threat conditions the Europeans might encounter and which form of European 'Pillar of Defence' would be more convenient for the defence of the EU in the future global security environment.

BIBLIOGRAPHY

Official Publications and Press Releases

Agence France Press, 'EU Members Pledge 100,000 Troops, 400 Planes to Rapid Reaction Force', transcript, The Tocqueville Connection, US-CREST, November 22, 2000 <http://www.ttc.org> (Visited on: December 27, 2000).

Agence France Press, 'France Sets Out Contribution to EU Force', transcript, The Tocqueville Connection, US-CREST, November 23, 2000 <http://www.ttc.org> (Visited on: December 27, 2000).

Agence France Press, Rosemberg, C., 'Euro-Defence Coming of Age', transcript, The Tocqueville Connection, US-CREST, December 4, 1998 <http://www.ttc.org> (Visited on: August 14, 1999).

Agence France Press, 'Calls For Common European Defence', transcript, The Tocqueville Connection, US-CREST, March 12, 1999 <http://www.ttc.org> (Visited on: August 14, 1999).

Agence France Press, 'Allies Mull Franco-German Draft Accord on EU Defence', transcript, The Tocqueville Connection, US-CREST, December 5, 1999 <http://www.ttc.org> (Visited on: August 14, 1999).

Agence France Press, 'No to NATO Military, For Now', The Tocqueville Connection, US-CREST, October 3, 1997 <http://www.ttc.org> (Visited on: May 01, 1999).

Agence France Press, 'De Charette Intends 'Bigger Role' in NATO', December 5, 1995, transcript, FBIS-WEU-95-233.

Agence France Press, 'Chirac To Propose 'Significant' Defence Reforms', January 3, 1996, transcript, FBIS-TAC-96-001.

Agence France Press, 'Defence Official Outlines Position Concerning NATO Commands',

January 23, 1997, transcript, FBIS-WEU-97-016.

Agence France Press, 'France for Greater European Autonomy in Defence Issues', November

4, 1999, transcript, FBIS-WEU-1999-1104.

Agence France Press, 'French Premier Announces Defence Review', October 22, 1999,

transcript, FBIS-WEU-99-1022.

Agence France Press, 'French Premier Urges European Defence 'Capacities'', October 22,

1999, transcript, FBIS-WEU-1999-1022.

Anglo-French Summit – Joint declaration by the British and French governments on

European defence, London: November 25, 1999 <http://www.ambafrance.org.uk/>

(Visited on: June 20, 1999).

'Antrag der Bundesregierung – Deutsche Beteiligung an der militärischen Umsetzung eines

Rambouillet-Abkommens für den Kosovo sowie an NATO-Operationen im Rahmen

der Notfalltruppe (Extraction Force). *BT-Drucksache 14/397 (22.02.1999) und 14/414*

(25.02.1999), Bonn: Deutsche Bundestag.

Arms Control, Disarmament and Non-Proliferation: French Policy, Paris: La Documentation

Française, April 2000.

Aufbruch und Erneuerung –Deutschlands Weg ins 21ˢᵗ Jahrhundert – Koalitionsvereinbarung

zwischen der Sozialdemokratischen Partei Deutschlands und Bündnis 90/Die Grünen,

Bonn: Oktober 20, 1998.

Berlin North Atlantic Council Ministerial Meeting, Brussels: NATO Office of Information

and Press, M-NAC1 (96) 63, June 3, 1996.

Bestandsaufnahme, Germany: Bundesministerium der Verteidigung, May 3, 1999.

CDU/CSU Bundestag Paper, ' Überlegungen zur europäischen Politik (Reflections on

European Policy)', Bonn: September 1, 1994.

CDU/CSU Bundestag Paper, ' Überlegungen zur europäischen Politik II (Reflections on

European Policy II) – zum Fortgang des europäischen Einigungsprozesses', Bonn:

May 3, 1999.

Cologne European Council Declaration on 'Strengthening the Common European Policy on

Security and Defence', SN 150/99 EN ANNEX, CAB 33-42, June 3&4, 1999 <http://

europa.eu.int/council/off/conclu/June99/June99_en.pdf> (Visited on: June 20, 2000).

Commission of the European Communities, COM(90) 600 final, Brussels: October 23, 1990.

Common Security and the Future of the Bundeswehr, Germany: Report of the Commission to

the Federal Government, 23 May 2000.

Communiqué, La Rochelle, Franco-German Council, France: May 22, 1992.

*Declaration of the Heads of State and Government Participating in the Meeting of the North

Atlantic Council Held at NATO Headquarters,* Brussels: NATO Office of Information

and Press, January 10-11, 1994.

Deutsche Aussenpolitik Nach Der Einheit 1990-1993 – Eine Dokumentation, Bonn:

Auswärtiges Amt, Dezember 1993.

European Council, 'Military Capabilities Commitment Declaration', *Press Release

Nr.13427/2/00*, Brussels: November 20, 2000. Available at: <http://ue.eu.int/pesc/>

(Visited on: February 24, 2000).

Feira European Council Declaration 'Presidency Report on Strengthening the Common

European Security and Defence Policy' June 19-20, 2000. Available at: <http://

europa.eu.int/council/> (Visited on: June 20, 2000).

Franco-German Common Security and Defence Council, Nuremberg: December 9, 1996,

made public in Paris on January 30, 1997.

Franco-German Potsdam Declaration, Potsdam: Franco-German Summit, December 1, 1998.

<http://www.ofaj.org/> (Visited on: June 20, 2000).

Franco-German Summit –Defence and Security Council – Toulouse Declaration, Toulouse:
    May 29, 1999 <http://www.ambafrance.org.uk/> (Visited on: June 20, 2000).

French Constitution of October 4, 1958, Paris: Assemblée nationale et Minitère des Affaires
    étrangères, September 1999. Available at: <http://www.assemble-nationale.fr>
    (Visited on: May 13, 2001).

French Defence Statistics 2000 (English language edition), Paris: Financial Services
    Directorate – General Secretary for the Administration and the Ministry of Defence.

French White Paper on the 1996 Intergovernmental Conference. <http://www.europa.eu.int/
    en/agenda/igc-home/ms-doc/state-fr/pos.htm> (Visited on: June 14, 1999).

'German Security Policy and the Bundeswehr', *Presse- und Informationsamt der
    Bundesregierung*, Berlin: November 1999.

German White Paper on the 1996 Intergovernmental Conference. <http://www.europa.eu.int/
    en/agenda/igc-home/ms-doc/state-de/pos.htm> (Visited on: June 14, 1999).

Helsinki European Council Declaration, Helsinki: SN 300/99 EN, December 10-11, 1999
    <http://europa.eu.int/council/> (Visited on: June 20, 1999).

Hochrangige Expertengruppe für die GASP, 'Die Voraussetzungen für eine glaubwurdige
    GASP im Jahr 2000', Brussel, den 19 Dezember 1994.

Joint Press Conference by Jacques Chirac, Tony Blair and Lionel Jospin during the *Franco-
    British Summit at Cahors*, (February 9, 2001) <http://www.doc.diplomatie.fr> (Visited
    on: August 2, 2001).

Livre Blanc sur la défense nationale, Paris: Documentation Française, 1972.

Livre Blanc sur la Défense (German language edition), Paris: Ministère de la Défense, March
    1994.

Loi de Finances pour 1997, 'Défense: Forces Terrestres', *Assemblée Nationale No.2993*,
    Paris: Imprimé pour l'Assemblée nationale par la Sté Nouvelle des Librairies, October
    10, 1996.

'London Declaration on Transformed North Atlantic Alliance', *North Atlantic Council Heads of State and Government Meeting*, Brussels: NATO Office of Information and Press, July 5-6, 1990.

Madrid Declaration of the North Atlantic Council on 'The Partnership Between NATO and Russia', Brussels: NATO Office of Information and Press, July 8-9, 1997.

Madrid Declaration of the North Atlantic Council on Euro-Atlantic Security and Cooperation, Official Texts Part I, Brussels: NATO Office of Information and Press, July 8-9, 1997.

NATO Handbook, Brussels: NATO Office of Information and Press, October 1995.

NATO Handbook, Brussels: NATO Office of Information and Press, October 2001.

Official Journal of the European Communities, Legislation, L367(37), Brussels: December 31, 1994.

Oslo Communiqué, North Atlantic Council, 4-5 June 1992.

Partnership for Peace (PfP) Invitation, Brussels: NATO Office of Information and Press, January 10-11, 1994.

'Projet De Loi – relatif à la programmation militaire pour les années 1997 à 2002', *Assemblée Nationale No.2766*, Paris: Imprimé pour l'Assemblée nationale par la Sté Nouvelle des Librairies, May 20, 1996.

'Projet De Loi – relatif à la programmation militaire pour les années 2003 à 2008', *Assemblée Nationale No.3255*, Paris: Imprimé pour l'Assemblée nationale par la Sté Nouvelle des Librairies, August 3, 2001.

'Rapport d'information MM Pierre Lellouche, Guy-Michel Chauveau et Aloyse Warhouver, *déposé en application de l'article 145 du Règelement par la production*, par la commission de la défense, sur la proliferation des armes de destruction massive et de leurs vecteurs', *Assemblée Nationale Rapport No.2788*, Paris: Imprimé pour l'Assemblée nationale par la Sté Nouvelle des Librairies, December 7, 2000.

'The Bundeswehr Advancing Steadily into the 21st Century', *Cornerstones of a Fundamental Renewal*, Berlin: The Federal Ministry of Defence, June 14, 2000.

The EU in a Changing World, Bruxelles: European Commission, September 19-20, 1996.

The UN Charter. Available at: <http://www.un.org>

Thirty Years Forecasting Plan, Paris: Ministry of Defence, 1999.

Treaty Between the Republic of France and the Federal Republic of Germany on French-German Co-operation, Paris: January 22, 1963 <http://info-france-usa.org/news/statmnts/germany/fglink.htm> (Visited on: August 30, 2000).

Treaty of Amsterdam (ToA), Consolidated version of the TEU is available at: <http://europa.eu.int/eur-lex/> (Visited on: July 14, 2000).

Treaty on European Union (TEU) <http://www.altairiv.demon.co.uk/maastricht/title5.html> (Visited on: September 5, 1997).

Treaty of Nice (ToN), 'Amending the Treaty on European Union, the Treaties Establishing the European Communities and Certain Related Acts', *Official Journal of the European Communities*, March 10, 2001.

Washington Summit Communiqué, April 24, 1999 <http://www.nato.int> (Visited on: September 02, 2000).

Weißbuch 1994, Bonn: Bundesministerium der Verteidigung, April 5, 1994.

WEU Assembly, *Anti-Missile Defence for Europe – Symposium 20-21 April 1993*, Rome: Second Sitting, April 20, 1993.

WEU Assembly, 'The Role and Future of Nuclear Weapons', *Document 1420*, Paris: WEU Assembly, May 19, 1994.

WEU Assembly, 'WEAG, the course to be followed', *Document 1483*, Paris: WEU Assembly, November 6, 1995.

WEU Assembly, 'Time for Defence – Plan for Action', *Document proposed by the Standing Committee*, Paris: WEU Assembly, March 16, 1999.

WEU Assembly, 'The Lisbon Initiative on "European security and defence: the parliamentary dimension"', *Press Release*, Paris: April 7, 2000.

WEU Assembly, 'WEU Assembly to agree on transformation into ESDA', *Press Release*, Paris: Plenary Session June 5-8, June 5, 2000.

WEU Assembly, 'WEU Assembly seeks common position on US missile defence', *Press Releases*, Paris: Plenary Session 5-8 June 2000, June 06, 2000.

WEU Assembly – The Interim European Security and Defence Assembly, 'WEU-ESDA urges Europe to step up policing in Kosovo', *Press Release*, Paris: Plenary Session June 8, 2000.

WEU Assembly Report, Rapporteur Sir Keith Speed, *Document 1415*, Paris: WEU Assembly, May 10, 1994.

WEU Council Declaration on 'The role of the WEU and its relations with the EU and with the Atlantic Alliance', Brussels: WEU Council, October 1997.

WEU Council of Ministers, *Noordwijk Declaration*, Noordwijk, November 14, 1994.

WEU Council of Ministers, *Ostend Declaration*, Ostend, November 19, 1996.

WEU Council of Ministers, *Porto Declaration*, Porto, May 15-16, 2000.

WEU Council Report, Rapporteur Mr. Marshall, 'European Security Policy', *Document 1370*, Brussels: WEU Council, May 24, 1993.

'WEU, Security and Defence', *European Parliament*, Brussels: Briefing No.11, March 21, 1997.

WEU Today, Brussels: Secretariat-General, March 1998.

1998 Strategic Defence Review (White Paper), (UK: British Ministry of Defence, 1998) Available at: <www.mod.uk> (Visited on: November 14, 2001).

Monographs

Aggestam, L. 'Role Conceptions and the Politics of Identity in Foreign Policy,' *ARENA WorkingPapers*, Oslo: No.8, 1999.

Bloed, A. & Wessel, R. A. (ed.), *The Changing Functions of the WEU – Introduction and BasicDocuments*, Utrecht: Martinus Nijhoff Publishers, August 1994.

Bonvincini, G., Cremasco, M., Rummel, R. & Schmidt, P. (eds.), *A Renewed Partnership for Europe –Tackling European Security Challenges by EU-NATO Interaction*, Baden-Baden: Nomos Verlagsgesellschaft, 1995/1996.

Bowen, W. N. & Dunn, D. H. *American Security Policy in the 1990s: Beyond Containment*, US: Dartmouth Publishing Company Ltd., 1996.

Brenner, M. (ed.), *NATO and Collective Security*, UK: Macmillan Press Ltd., 1998.

Bündnis 90/Die Grünen, *Grün ist der Wechsel*, Programm zur Bundestagswahl 1998.

Chafer, A. & Jenkins, B. (eds.), *France From the Cold War to the New World Order*, London: Macmillan, 1996.

Checkel, J., 'Social Construction and Integration,' *ARENA Working Papers*, Oslo: No.14, 1998.

Chuter, D., *Humanity's Soldier – France and International Security 1919-2001*, US: Berghahn Books, 1996.

Clarke, J. G., 'The Eurocorps: A Fresh Start in Europe,' *Foreign Policy Briefing No.21*, US: CATO Institute, December 28, 1992.

Clesse, A., Cooper, R. & Sakamato, Y. (eds.), *The International System After the Collapse of the East-West Order*, Dotdrecht Martinus Nifhoff, 1994.

Cogan, Charles G., *Oldest Allies, Guarded Friends – The United States and France Since 1940*, US: Praeger Publishers, 1994.

Cogan, Charles G., *Forced to Choose: France, the Atlantic Alliance and NATO – Then and Now*, US: Westport, Praeger Press, 1997.

Cox, M. *US Foreign Policy after the Cold War*, London: Royal Institute of International Affairs (RIIA), 1995.

Cremer, U. & Lutz, D. S., *Die Bundeswehr in der neuen Weltordnung*, Hamburg: VSA-Verlag, 2000.

Dehousse, R. (ed.), *Europe After Maastricht – An Ever Closer Union?*, München: C.H. Beck'sche Verlagsbuchhandlung, 1994.

Deighton, A., 'On the Cups: Britain, Maastricht and European Security,' *EUI Working Papers*, Italy: European University Institute, RSC No.97/59, October 1997.

Deutsch, K. (et. al.) *Political Community and the North Atlantic Area: International Organisation in the Light of Historical Experience,* New Jersey: Princeton University Press, 1957.

De Vestel, P., 'Defence Markets and Industries in Europe: Time for Political Decisions?,' *Chaillot Paper 21*, Paris: Institute for Security Studies, WEU, November 1995.

Drew, Nelson S., 'NATO From Berlin to Bosnia, "The Bonfire of the Certainties",' *McNair Paper 35*, US: National War College, 1995.

Duff, A., Pinder, J. & Pryce, R., (eds.), *Maastricht and Beyond: Building the EU*, London: Routledge, Federal Trust, 1994.

Duff, A., *Reforming the EU*, UK: Federal Trust, 1997.

Edinger, L. J. & Nacos, B. L., *From Bonn to Berlin – German Politics in Transition*, New York: Columbia University Press, 1998.

Ehlermann, C. D., 'Differentiation, Flexibility, Closer Cooperation: The New Provisions of the Amsterdam Treaty,' translated by Iain Fraser, *RSC Publication*, Italy: European University Institute, March 1998.

Ehrhart, H-G., 'France and NATO: Change by Rapprochement?', *Hamburger Briträge zur Friedensforschung und Sicherheitspolitik*, Hamburg: Institut für Friedensforschung und Sicherheitspolitik an der Universität Hamburg, No.121, January 2000.

Fischer, J., *Vom Staatenverbund zur Föderation – Gedanken über die Finalität der europäischen Integration*, Frankfurt am Main: Suhrkamp Verlag, 2000.

Flynn, G., *Remarking the Hexagon – The New France in the New Europe*, US: Westview Press, 1995.

Grant, C., 'Intimate Relations – Can Britain play a leading role in European defence – and keeps its special links to US intelligence?', *Centre for European Reform Working Paper*, May 2000.

Freedman, L. (ed.), *Military Intervention in European Conflicts*, UK: The Political Quarterly Publishing Co. Ltd., 1994.

Giessmann, H. J., 'The "Cocooned Giant": Germany and European Security,' *Hamburger Briträge zur Friedensforschung und Sicherheitspolitik*, Hamburg: Institut für Friedensforschung und Sicherheitspolitik an der Universität Hamburg, No.116, September 1999.

Gnesotto, N. (ed.), 'War and Peace: European Conflict Prevention,' *Challiot Paper 11*, Paris: Institute for Security Studies, WEU, October 1993.

Gordon, P. H. (ed.), *A Certain Idea of France. French Security Policy and the Gaullist Legacy*, US: Princeton University Press, 1993.

Gordon, P. H., *France, Germany, and the Western Alliance*, US: Westview Press, Inc., 1995.

Gordon, P. H. (ed.), *NATO's Transformation*, US: Rowman and Littlefield Publishers, Inc., 1997.

Grundsatzprogramm der Sozialdemokratischen Partei Deutschlands, am 20. Dezember 1989 in Berlin geändert auf dem Parteitag in Leipzig am 17.04.1998.

Guay, Terrence R., *At Arm's Length – The EU and Europe's Defence Industry*, UK:
    Macmillan Press Ltd., 1998.

Guéhenno, J-M., 'A Foreign Policy in Search of a Polity,' *EUI Working Papers*, Italy:
    European University Institute, RSC No. 97/65, December 1997.

Gutjahr, L., *German Foreign and Defence Policy after Unification*, UK: St. Martin's Press
    Inc., 1994.

Guyomarch, A., Machin, H. & Ritchie, E., *France and the EU*, US: St. Martin's Press, 1998.

Haglund, D. G., *Alliance Within the Alliance? Franco-German Military Cooperation and the
    European Pillar of Defence*, US: Westview Press, 1991.

Haglund, D., *From Euphoria to Hysteria – Western European Security After the Cold War*,
    US: Westview Press Inc., 1993.

Hampton, M. N. & Søe, C. (ed.), *Between Bonn and Berlin –German Politics Adrift?*, US:
    Rowman & Littlefield Publishers, Inc., 1999.

Hayward, K., 'Towards a European Weapons Procurement Process,' *Chaillot Paper 27*,
    Paris: Institute for Security Studies, WEU, June 1997.

Heisbourg, F., 'European Defence: Making it Work', *Chaillot Paper 42*, Paris: WEU,
    Institute for Security Studies, September 2000.

Helleiner, E., 'One Nation, One Money – Territorial Currencies and the Nation-State,'
    ARENA Working Papers, Oslo: No.17, 1997.

Heurlin, B. (ed.), *Germany in Europe in the Nineties*, UK: Macmillan Press Ltd., 1996.

Hill, C. (ed.), *The Actors in Europe's Foreign Policy*, UK: Routledge, 1996.

Hill, C., 'Convergence, Divergence & Dialectics: National Foreign Policies & the CFSP,'
    EUI Working Papers No.97/66, Italy: European University Institute, December 1997.

Hodge, C. C. (ed.), *Redefining European Security*, New York: Contemporary Issues in
    European Politics: 4, Garland, 1999.

Hoffman, A., 'Germany and the Role of the Bundeswehr: A New Consensus,' *Institute for German Studies Discussion Papers Series No. 98/9*, UK: University of Birmingham, September 1998.

Hoffmann, Hans-Viktor 'New Tasks of the Bundeswehr in Communication Processes Between Society and the Military,' *Akademie der Bundeswehr für Information und Kommunikation*, Germany: AIK-Texte, June 1999.

Howorth, J. & Menon, A. (ed.), *The EU and National Defence Policy,* London: Routledge, 1997.

Howorth, J., 'European integration and defence: the ultimate challenge?,' *Chaillot Paper 43*, Paris: WEU, Institute for Security Studies, November 2000.

Jeffrey, C. & Handl, V., 'Germany and Europe After Kohl: Between Social Democracy and Normalisation?,' *Institute for German Studies Discussion Papers Series No. 99/11*, UK: University of Birmingham, November 1999.

Jopp, M., 'The Strategic Implications of European Integration,' *Adelphi Paper 290*, London: Brassey's Publications, 1994.

Katzenstein, P. J., *Tamed Power – Germany in Europe*, US: Cornell University Press, 1997.

Kay, S., *France and the Future of European Security*, US: Rowman & Littlefield Publishers, Inc., 1998.

Keohane, R. O., Nye, J. S. & Hoffmann, S., *After the Cold War – International Institutions and State Strategies in Europe, 1989-1991*, US: Harvard University Press, 1993.

Kocs, Stephen A., *Autonomy or Power – The Franco-German Relationship and Europe's Strategic Choices, 1955-1995*, US: Praeger Publishers, 1995.

Kramer, S. P., 'France and the New Germany,' *AICGS German Issues 11*, US: The Johns Hopkins University, 1993.

Kramer, S. P., *Does France Still Count? The French Role in the New Europe*, Washington: The Centre for Strategic and International Studies, Praeger Publishers, 1994.

Krautscheid, A.(MdB), 'Contemporary German Security Policy,' *Institute for German Studies Discussion Papers Series No. 97/8*, UK: University of Birmingham, August 1997.

Kupchan, C. A., 'From the EU to the Atlantic Union,' *EUI Working Papers*, Italy: European University Institute, RSC No.97/73, December 1997.

Kümmel, G. & Prüfert, A. D. (eds.), *Military Sociology – The Richness of a Discipline*, Baden-Baden: Nomos Verlagsgesellschaft, 2000.

Laird, R., 'French Security Policy in Transition – Dynamics of Continuity and Change', *McNair Paper 38*, Washington: Institute for National Strategic Studies, National Defence University, March 1995.

Landgren, S., 'Post-Soviet Threats to Security' in *SIPRI Yearbook 1992: World Armaments and Disarmament*, Oxford: SIPRI Oxford University Press, 1992.

Lenzi, G., 'Defining the European Security Policy,' *EUI Working Papers*, Italy: European University Institute, RSC, December 1997.

Le Prestre, P.G., *Role Quests in the Post-Cold War Era – Foreign Policies in Transition*, Canada: McGrill-Queen's University Press, 1997.

Lipschutz, R. (ed.), *On Security*, New York: Columbia University Press, 1995.

Lodge, J. (ed.), *The EC and the Challenge of the Future*, London: Pinter, 1993.

Marauhn, T., *Building a European Security and Defence Identity*, Bochum: UVB – Universitätsverlag, 1996.

March, J. G. & Olsen, J. P., 'The Institutional Dynamics of International Political Order,' *ARENA Working Papers*, Oslo: No.5, 1998.

Martin, L. & Roper, J. (eds.) *Towards a Common Defence Policy*, Paris: Institute for Security Studies of WEU, 1995.

Maull, H. W., Neßhöver, C. & Stahl, B., 'Vier Monate rot-grüne Außenpolitik,' *Trierer Arbeitspapiere zur Internationalen Politik*, Lehrstuhl für Außenpolitik und Internationale Beziehungen, Universität Trier, Nr.1, März 1999.

McCarthy, P. (ed.), *France-Germany 1983-1993. The Struggle to Cooperate*, New York: Martin's Press, 1993.

McKenzie, M. M., 'Germany and the Institutions of Collective Security in Europe,' *Peace Research Institute Frankfurt*, Frankfurt: PRIF Reports No.36, November 1994.

McMahon, D., 'Echoes of a Recent Past: Contemporary French Anti-Americanism in Historical and Cultural Perspective', *Columbia International Affairs Online (Ciao) Working Papers*, US: International Security Studies, January 1995.

Menon, A., *France, NATO and the Limits of Independence, 1981-1997 – The Politics of Ambivalence*, UK: Macmillan Press Ltd., 2000.

Mertes, M., Müller, S. & Winkler, H. A. (eds.), *In Search of Germany*, US: Transactions Publications, 1996.

Missiroli, A., 'CFSP, Defence and Flexibility,' *Chaillot Paper 38*, Paris: Institute for Security Studies, WEU, February 2000.

Myers, J. A., *The WEU: Pillar of NATO or Defence Arm of the EC?*, London: Published by Brassey's for the Centre for Defence Studies, March 1993.

Pappas, S. A. & Vanhoonacker, S., *'The EU's CFSP – The Challenges of the Future,'* The Netherlands: European Institute of Public Administration, 1996.

Park, W. & Rees, W. (ed.) *Rethinking Security in Post-Cold War Europe*, New York: Addison Wesley Longman Limited, 1998.

Perry, S. (ed.), *Aspects of Contemporary France*, UK: Routledge, 1997.

Price, A. H., *The International Politics of East Central Europe*, UK: Manchester University Press, 1996.

Rees, W. G. *The Western European Union at the Crossroads*, US: Westview Press, 1998.

Rill, B. (Hg.), 'Deutschland und Frankreich: Gemeinsame Zukunftsfragen', *Argumente und Materialen zum Zeitgeschehen*, München: Hanns-Seidel-Stiftung, Nr.21, 2000.

Rummel, R. (ed.), *Toward Political Union – Planning a CFSP in the EC*, Germany: Baden-Baden Nomos Verlagsgesellschaft, 1992.

Rummel, R. & Wiedemann, J., 'Identifying Institutional Paradoxes of CFSP,' *EUI Working Papers*, Italy: European University Institute, RSC, No.97/67, December 1997.

Rühl, L., 'Conditions and options for an autonomous "Common European Policy on Security and Defence" in and by the EU in the post-Amsterdam perspective opened at Cologne in June 1999,' *Centre for European Integration Studies (ZEI)*, (Bonn: Rheinische Friedrich-Wilhelms-Universität, Discussion Paper, C54, 1999.

Sartorius, C., *Verfassungs- und Verwaltungsgesetze der Bundesrepublik Deutschland – Band I*, München: C.H. Beck'sche Verlagsbuchhandlung, Februar 15, 1999.

Sauder, A., *Souveränität und Integration – Französische und deutsche Konzeptionen europäischer Sicherheit nach dem Ende des Kalten Krieges (1990-1993)*, Germany: Nomos Verlagesellschaft, 1995.

Schild, J., 'Über Nizza hinaus – Deutsch-französische Debatten über die Zukunft der EU', *Aktuelle Frankreich-Analysen*, Ludwigsburg: Deutsch-Französisches Institut, August 16, 2000.

Schlör, W., 'German Security Policy,' *Adelphi Paper 277*, London: IISS, 1993.

Schmidt, P. (ed.), *In the Midst of Change: On the Development of West European Security and Defence Co-operation*, Baden-Baden: Nomos Verlagsgesellschaft, 1992.

Schmidt, P., 'The Special Franco-German Security Relationship in the 1990s,' *Challiot Paper 8*, Paris: Institute for Security Studies, WEU, June 1993.

Sjursen, H., 'Enlargement and the CFSP: Transforming the EU's External Policy?,' *ARENA Working Papers*, Oslo: No.18, 1998.

Sloan, S. R., 'The US and European Defence,' *Chaillot Paper 39*, Paris: Institute for Security Studies, WEU, February 2000.

Smith, G., Paterson, W. E. & Padgett, S. (eds.), *Developments in German Politics 2*, UK: Macmillan, 1996.

Smith, H., *The EU Foreign Policy and Central America*, UK: Macmillan, 1995.

Smith, K. E., 'The Instruments of EU Foreign Policy,' *EUI Working Papers*, Italy: European University Institute, RSC No.97/68, December 1997.

Smyser, W. R., *Germany and America – New Identities, Fateful Rift?*, US: Westview Press, Inc., 1993.

Sperling, J. & Kirchner, E. *Recasting the European Order*, UK: Manchester University Press, 1997.

Stares, P. B., *The New Germany and the New Europe*, US: The Brookings Institution, 1992.

Szabo, S. F. (ed.), *The Bundeswehr and Western Security*, UK: Macmillan Press Ltd., 1990.

The Military Balance 1990-1991, UK: IISS, Brassey's Ltd., 1991.

The Military Balance 1994-1995, UK: IISS, Brassey's Ltd., 1995.

The Military Balance 1999/2000, UK: IISS, Brassey's Ltd., 2000.

Van Beveren, R., 'Military Cooperation: What Structure for the Future?,' *Chaillot Paper 6*, Paris: Institute for Security Studies, WEU, January 1993.

Van Eekelen, W., *The Security Agenda for 1996 – Background and prospects*, Brussels: Centre for European Policy Studies (CEPS), Paper No. 64, 1995.

Vlachos, K., 'Safeguarding European Competitiveness – Strategies for the Future European Arms Production and Procurement,' *Occasional Papers 4*, Paris: Institute for Security Studies, WEU, January 1998.

Volle, A. & Weidenfeld, W. (Hrsg.), Europäische Sicherheitspolitik in der Bewährung, Bielefeld: Bertelsman, 2000.

Von Bredow, W., Jäger, T. & Kümmel, G., *European Security*, UK: Macmillan Press, 1997.

Von Bredow, W. & Kümmel, G., 'Das Militär und die Herausforderung globaler Sicherheit –

Der Spagat zwischen traditonalen und nicht-traditionalen Rollen', *SOWI Arbeitspapier*

Nr.119, Strausberg: September 1999.

Walker, W. & Gummett, P., 'Nationalism, Internationalism and the European Defence

Market,' *Chaillot Paper 9*, Paris: Institute for Security Studies, WEU, September 1993.

Webber, D. (ed.), *The Franco-German Relationship in the EU*, UK: Routledge, 1999.

Wetterqvist, F., *French Security and Defence Policy – Current Developments and Future*

Prospects, Diane Publishing Company, 1993.

Whitman, R. G., 'The EU's CFSP – Achievements and Prospects', *Centre for the Study of*

Democracy, London: Research Paper No.11, University of Westminster, Winter 1996.

Williams, J. A. (ed) *Reorganising Eastern Europe*, US: Dartmouth Publishing Company

Limited, 1994.

Wilson, G. (ed.), 'European Force Structures', papers presented at a seminar held in Paris on

27 & 28 May 1999, *Occasional Papers 8*, Paris: WEU Institute for Security Studies,

August 1999.

Wyllie, James H. *European Security in the New Political Environment*, New York: Addison

Wesley Longman Limited, 1997.

Zielonka, J. 'Security in Central Europe', *Adelphi Paper 272*, London: International Institute

for Strategic Studies, 1992.

Articles in Journals

Ackerman, A., 'Reconciliation as a Peace-Building Process in Post War Europe', *Peace &*

Change, Vol. 19, No.3, July 1994.

Art, R. J., 'Why Western Europe needs the US and NATO?', *Political Science Quarterly*,

Vol.111, No.1, Spring 1996.

Asmus, R. D., Kugler, R. L. & Larrabee, S. F., 'Building a New NATO', *Foreign Affairs,*
  Vol.72, No.4, September/October 1993.

Bailes, A. J. K, 'European Defence and Security – The Role of NATO, WEU and EU',
  SecurityDialogue, Vol.27, No.1, 1996.

Bailes, A., *Foreign Affairs*, Vol.76, No.1, January/February 1997.

Barrie, D., 'Launching a joint offensive', *International Management*, Vol.49, No.7,
  September 1994.

Barry, C., 'NATO's Combined Joint Task Forces in Theory and Practice', *Survival,* Vol.38,
  No.1, Spring 1996.

Baun, M. J., 'The Maastricht Treaty as High Politics: Germany, France, and European
  Integration', *Political Science Quarterly*, Vol.110, No.4, Winter 1995/1996.

Beal, C., 'Be Rational, Europe', *Jane's International Defence Review*, August 1, 1996.

Berger, T., 'Unsheathing the Sword?', *World Affairs*, Vol.158, No.4, Spring 1996.

Bishop, P., 'Strategic Change in the European Defence Industry', *European Business Review*,
  Vol.97, No.4, 1997.

Bolton, J., 'The End of NATO?', *The World Today*, Vol.56, No.6, June 2000.

Bracken, P. & Johnson, S., 'Beyond NATO: Complementary Militaries', *Orbis*, No.5, Spring
  1993.

Brenner, M., 'Multilateralism and European Security', *Survival*, Vol.35, No.2, Summer 1993.

Carchedi, B. & Carchedi, G., 'Contradictions of European Integration', *Capital & Class*,
  No.67, Spring 1999.

Chaddock, G. R., 'France Hits Snags on Path to a Euro-Defence', *Christian Science Monitor*,
  Vol.88, No.120, May 16, 1996.

Charillon, F., 'France and NATO: Atlanticism as the pursuit of Europe by other means?',
  RUSI Journal, Vol.141, No.6, December 1996.

Chilton, P., 'A European Security Regime: Integration and Cooperation in the Search for CFSP', *Journal of European Integration*, Vol.19, No.'s 2-3, Winter/Spring 1996.

Clinton, B., 'Interview With European Television Journalists', *Weekly Compilation of Presidential Documents*, Vol.33, No.27, July 3, 1997.

Conry, B., 'The WEU as NATO's Successor', *Policy Analysis*, Cato Institute: No.239, September 18, 1995.

Croft, S., 'European integration, nuclear deterrence and Franco-British nuclear co-operation', *International Affairs*, Vol.72, No.4, 1996.

Croft, S., Howorth, J., Terriff, T. & Webber, M., 'NATO's Triple Challenge', *International Affairs*, Vol.76, No.3, 2000.

Daalder, I. H., 'Are the US and Europe heading for divorce?', *International Affairs*, Vol.77, No.3, 2001.

Delors, J., 'European Integration and Security', *Survival*, Vol.33, No.2, March/April 1991.

De Puig, L. M., 'The European Sea and Defence Identity Within NATO', *NATO Review*, No.2, Summer 1998.

Deutch, J., Kanter, A. & Scowcroft, B., 'Saving NATO's Foundation', *Foreign Affairs*, Vol.78, No.6, November/December 1999.

Dorff, R. H., 'Germany and the Future of European Security,' *World Affairs*, Vol.161, No.2, Fall 1998.

Duke, S., 'The Second Death (or the Second Coming?) of the WEU', *Journal of Common Market Studies*, Vol.34, No.2, June 1996.

Ehrhart, H-G., 'Kontinuität oder Erneuerung? Paris und Bonn/Berlin nach den Machtwechseln', *Internationale Politik*, No.4, April 1999.

Fink-Hooijer, F., 'The CFSP of the EU', *European Journal of International Law*, Vol.5, No.2 <http://www.ejil.org/journal/Vol5/No2/art2.html> (Visited on: October, 20 1999).

Fox, E. & Orman, S., 'The Vital Role of Policy: Or "what happened to ballistic missile
defence?",' *The Journal of Social, Political, and Economic Studies*, Vol.21, No.3, Fall
1996.

Froehly, J-P., 'The French Perspective: France's Position Towards ESDI and ESDP',
Internationale Politik, June 2000
<http://www.dgap.org/english/text/france_esdi.html> (Visited on: September 8, 2000).

Gabriel, J. M., 'The Integration of European Security: A Functionalist Analysis',
Aussenwirtschaft, Heft I, April 1995.

Gärtner, H., 'European Security, NATO and the Transatlantic Link: Crisis Management',
Austrian Institute for International Affairs, US: International Studies Association, 40th
Annual Convention, February 16-20, 1999
<http://alhan.cc.columbia.edu/sec/dlc/ciao/isa/gah01/> (Visited on: June 12, 1999).

Gnesotto, N., 'Common European Defence and Transatlantic Relations', *Survival*, Vol.38,
No.1, Spring 1996.

Goldstein, L. & Lanzo, D., 'Negotiating New Terrain', *Harvard International Review*,
Vol.15, No.2, Winter 1993.

Gordon, P. H., 'Berlin's Difficulties. The Normalisation of German Foreign Policy', *Orbis*,
Vol.38, Spring 1994.

Gordon, P. H., 'Does the WEU Have a Role?', *Washington Quarterly*, Vol.20, No.1, Winter
1997.

Gordon, P. H., 'Europe's Uncommon Foreign Policy', *International Security*, Vol.22, No.3,
Winter 97/98.

Gordon, P. H., 'The French Position', *The National Interest*, Fall 2000. Available at:
<http://www.brookings.edu/views/articles/Gordon/2000fall_NI.htm> (Visited on:
September 13, 2000).

Goulden, J., 'The WEU's role in the new strategic environment', *NATO Review*, Vol.44,

No.3, May 1996.

Grant, R. P., 'France's New Relationship with NATO', *Survival*, Vol.38, No.1, Spring 1996.

Gregory, S., 'France and *Missions de Souveraineté*', *Defense Analysis*, Vol.16, No.3, 2000.

Guay, T. R., 'Integration and Europe's defence industry: A "reactive spillover" approach',

Policy Studies Journal, Vol.24, No.3, Autumn 1996.

Haltiner K. W., 'The Definite End of the Mass Army in Western Europe?', *Armed Forces*

and Society, Vol.25, No.1, Fall 1998.

Heathcoat-Amory, D., 'The next step for the WEU: a British view', *The World Today*, July

1994.

Heisbourg, F. 'Trittbrettfahrer? Keine europäische Verteidigung ohne Deutschland',

Internationale Politik, Nr.4, April 2000.

Heisbourg, F., 'The EU needs defence convergence criteria', *Centre for European Reform*

Bulletin, No.6, June/July 1999.

Heisbourg, F., 'European Defence Takes a Leap Forward', *NATO Review*, Vol.48, No.1,

Spring-Summer 2000.

Hibbs, M., 'Tomorrow, A Eurobomb?', *Bulletin of the Atomic Scientists*, Vol.52, No.1,

January/February 1996.

Hill, C., 'The Capability-Expectations Gap, or Conceptualising Europe's International Role',

Journal of Common Market Studies, Vol.31, No.3, September 1993.

Howorth, J., 'Britain, France and the European Defence Initiative', *Survival*, Vol.42, No.2,

Summer 2000.

Hurd, D., 'Developing the CFSP', *International Affairs*, Vol.70, No.3, 1994.

Janning, J., 'A German Europe – a European Germany? On the Debate Over Germany's

Foreign Policy', *International Affairs*, Vol.72, No.1, 1996.

Jannuzzi, G., 'The EU's CFSP and Its Contribution to Global Security', *NATO Review*, Vol.42, No.1, January 1995.

Joffe, J. 'The New Europe: Yesterday's Ghosts', *Foreign Affairs,* Vol.72, No.1, 1992.

Jones, J. B., 'French Forces for the 21st Century', *Joint Force Quarterly*, Summer 2000.

Kaiser, K., 'Forty Years of German Membership in NATO', *NATO Review*, Vol.43, No.4, July 1995.

Kaiser, K., 'Reforming NATO', *Foreign Policy*, No.103, Summer 1996.

Kelleher, M. C., 'A renewed security partnership?', *The Brookings Review*, Vol.11, No.4, Fall 1993.

Kenny, B., 'Change and Cross-Border Activity in the European Defence Industry', *European Business Review*, Vol.99, No.2, 1999.

Kinkel, K., 'Peace-keeping Missions: Germany Can Now Play Its Role', *NATO Review*, Vol.42, No.5, October 1994.

Kitfield, J. 'NATO's New Horizons', *National Journal,* Vol.28, No.37, September 14, 1996.

Kupchan, A. C., 'After Pax Americana', *International Security,* Vol.23, No.2, Fall 1998.

Lellouche, P., 'France in Search of Security', *Foreign Affairs*, Spring 1993.

Lindley-F., J., 'Time to Bite the Eurobullet', *New Statesman*, Vol.127, No.4391, June 26, 1998.

Lloyd, J., 'Prepare For a Brave New World', *New Statesman*, Vol.128, No.4432, April 19, 1999.

Longhurst, K & Roper, J., 'Forward March', *The World Today*, Vol.56, No.10, October 2000.

Ludwig, K. P. & Hess, S., 'Toward a European Space Policy', *Internationale Politik*, Vol.1, Summer Issue, July 14, 2000 <http://www.dgap.org/english/tip/tip2/eurospace.html> (Visited on: July 14, 2000).

Markusen, A., 'The Rise of World Weapons', *Foreign Policy*, No.114, Spring 1999.

Maull, H. W., 'Germany and Japan: The New Civilian Powers,' *Foreign Affairs*, Vol.69, No.5, Winter 1990/1991.

Maull, H. W., 'Zivilmacht Bundesrepublik Deutschland,' *Europa Archiv*, May 10, 1992.

Maull, H. W., 'Germany and the European Security and Defence Policy: A Time for Reflection?', *German Foreign Policy in Dialogue*, Vol.1, No.2, July 2000. Available at: <http://www.deutsche-aussenpolitik.de/> (Visited on: February 26, 2001).

Maull, H. W., 'Germany and the Use of Force: Still a 'Civilian Power'?', *Survival*, Vol.42, No.2, Summer 2000.

Maull, H. W., 'German Foreign Policy, Post-Kosovo: Still a 'Civilian Power?', *German Politics*, Vol.9, No.2, August 2000.

McAdams, J., 'Germany After Unification – Normal at Last?', *World Politics*, Vol.49, January 1997.

Menon, A., 'From independence to co-operation: France, NATO and European Security', *International Affairs*, Vol.71, No.1, 1995.

Mey, H. H., 'The Revolution in Military Affairs: A German Perspective', *Comparative Strategy*, No.17, 1998.

Millon, C., 'France and the Renewal of the Atlantic Alliance', *NATO Review*, Vol.44, No.3, May 1996.

Moïsi, D., & Mertes, M., 'Europe's map, compass, and horizon', *Foreign Affairs*, Vol.74, No.1, January 1995.

Moïsi, D., 'Chirac of France – A New Leader of the West?', *Foreign Affairs*, November/December 1995.

Monar, J., 'The EU's Foreign Affairs System after the Treaty of Amsterdam: A 'Strengthened Capacity for External Action'?,' *European Foreign Affairs Review*, Vol.2, 1997.

Morrison, D. C., 'Tattered Partnership', *National Journal*, Vol.26, No.1, January 1, 1994.

Muravchik, J. 'How to Wreck NATO', *Commentary*, Vol.107, No.4, April 1, 1999.

Nye,. Joseph S. 'Conflicts after the Cold War', *Washington Quarterly,* Vol.19, No.1 Winter 1996.

Pond, E., 'Germany in the New Europe', *Foreign Affairs,* Vol.71, No.2, Spring 1992.

Pond, E., 'Letter from Bonn: Visions of the European Dream', *Washington Quarterly,* Vol.20 No.3, Summer 1997.

Prince, K. M., 'Under Construction: The Berlin Republic,' *Washington Quarterly,* Vol.22, No.3, Summer 1999.

Rees, W. & Monar, J., 'Force for Europe', *The World Today,* June 2000.

Robertson, G., 'NATO in the New Millenium', *NATO Review,* No.4, 1999.

Rubinstein, A. Z., 'Germans On Their Future', *Orbis,* Vol.43, No.1, Winter 1999.

Santer, J., 'The EU's security and defence policy. How to avoid missing the 1996 rendezvous', *NATO Review,* Vol.43, No.6, November 1995.

Schake, K., Laine, B. A. & Grant, C., 'Building a European Defence Capability', *Survival,* Vol.41, No.1, Spring 1999.

Schmidt, P., 'ESDI: "Separable but not separate"?', *NATO Review,* Vol.48, No.1, Spring/Summer 2000.

Schwarz, B. & Layne, C. 'NATO: At 50, It's Time to Quit', *Nation,* Vol.268, No.17, October 5, 1999.

Simonis, J. B. D., 'European Integration and the Erosion of the Nation-state', *International Journal of Social Economics,* Vol.22, No.7, 1995.

Smith, C. J., 'Conflict in the Balkans and the Possibility of a EU CFSP', *International Relations,* Vol.13, No.2, August 1996.

Smith, J., 'Destination Unknown', *The World Today,* Vol.56, No.10, RIIA, October 2000.

Smith, M., 'The EU, foreign economic policy and the changing world arena', *Journal of Common Market Studies,* Vol.1, No.2, Autumn 1994.

Smyser, W. R., 'Dateline Berlin: Germany's New Vision', *Foreign Policy*, No.97, Winter 1994-95.

Solana, J., 'European Security Agenda', *NATO Review,* Vol.43, No.6, November 1995.

Stein, G., 'The Eurocorps and Future European Security Architecture', *European Security*, Vol.2, No.2, Summer 1993.

Taylor, T., 'West European security and defence cooperation: Maastricht and beyond', *International Affairs*, Vol.70, No.1, 1994.

Tiersky, R., 'France in the New Europe', *Foreign Affairs,* Vol.71, No.2, Spring 1992.

Tiersky, R., 'Mitterand's Legacies', *Foreign Affairs*, Vol.74, No.1, January 1995.

Tiersky, R., 'French Military Reform and NATO Restructuring', *Joint Force Quarterly*, Spring 1997.

Van Eekelen, W., 'WEU and the Gulf Crisis', *Survival*, Vol.32, No.6, November/December 1990.

Van Eekelen, W., 'WEU's Post-Maastricht Agenda', *NATO Review*, Vol.40, No.2, April 1992.

Vanhoonacker, S., 'CFSP: Can History be Overcome?', *European Institute of Public Administration*, Maastricht: Paper Prepared for ECSA Conference, Seattle, May 1997.

Van Mierlo, H., 'The WEU and NATO: Prospects for a more balanced relationship', *NATO Review*, No.2, March 1995.

Wallace, W., 'Foreign Policy and National Identity in the UK', *International Affairs*, Vol.67, No.1, 1991.

Wallace, W., Zielonka, J. 'Misunderstanding Europe', *Foreign Affairs,* Vol.77, No.6, November/December 1998.

Whitman, R. G., 'Creating a Foreign Policy for Europe? Implementing the CFSP from Maastricht to Amsterdam', *Australian Journal of International Affairs*, Vol.52, No.2, July 1998.

Wilds, K., 'Identity Creation and the Culture of Contrition: Recasting 'Normality' in the

Berlin Republic', *German Politics*, Vol.9, No.1, April 2000.

Yost, D., 'France and West European defence identity', *Survival*, Vol.33, No.4,

July/August 1991.

Yost, D., 'France in the New Europe', *Foreign Affairs*, Vol.69, No.5, Winter 1990/1991.

Yost, D., 'France's Nuclear Dilemmas', *Foreign Affairs*, Vol.75, No.1, January/February

1996.

Zöckler, M., 'Germany in Collective Security Systems – Anything Goes?', *European Journal

of International Law*, Vol.16, No.2, 1998.

Selected Newspapers and Magazines

European Report

European Voice

Frankfurter Rundschau

International Herald Tribune

New York Times

Le Monde

Saarbrücker Zeitung

Süddeutsche Zeitung

The Financial Times

The Los Angeles Times

The Washington Post

Washington Times

Der Spiegel

Deutschland

Europe

Focus

The Economist

Rogers, M., 'The IGC: committed to creating a common foreign capability', *Jane's Defence Weekly*, March 27, 1996.

Senk, D., 'Europäische Reaktionen auf die Rede von Joschka Fischer zur Zukunft Europas', *Welt-Report*, Bonn: Sankt Augustin, Berichte aus den Auslandsbüros der Konrad-Adenauer-Stiftung, August 2000.

'Zukunft Bundeswehr – Die Entscheidungen zur Reform der Bundeswehr' *IAP-Dienst Sicherheitspolitik – Sonderheft*, Juli 2000.

Conference, Workshop, Seminar Papers, Lectures, Reports and Interviews

An American Institute for Contemporary German Studies Seminar, 'A Discussion with Dr. Wolfgang Ischinger', Washington: July 13, 2000 <http://www.aicgs.org/events/2000/ischinger_summary.html> (Visited on: August 1, 2000).

Andréani, G., 'France and NATO', *US-CREST's Franco-American Seminar Series*, January 22, 1996 <http://www.adetocqueville.com> (Visited on: January 11, 1999).

BBC World, interview on TV with NATO Secretary-General George Robertson at 11:30 a.m. (GMT), October 10, 2000.

Blinken, A., 'The US, France, and Europe at the Outset of the New Administration', *US-France Analysis Paper*, (March 2001). Available at: <http://www.brookings.org/> (Visited on: March 19, 2001).

'Break Out, Break Down or Break In? Germany and the EU After Amsterdam', *AICGS Research Report*, US: The Johns Hopkins University, AICGS Research Report No.8, 1998.

Caldwell, C., 'Védrinism: France's Global Ambitions'. Available at:
<http://www.policyreview.com/> (Visited on: November 17, 2000).

Cameron, F., Ginsberg, R., Janning, J., 'The EU's CFSP: Central Issues ... Key Players',
Strategic Outreach Roundtable and Conference Report, summarised by Stuart
Mackintosh, US: May 10, 1995 <http://carlisle-www.army.mil/> (Visited on:
September 19, 1999).

De Areilza, Jose M., 'Enhanced Co-operations in the Treaty of Amsterdam: Some Critical
Remarks', *Conference Organised by the Copenhagen Research Project on European
Integration*, Conference on 'Rethinking Constitutionalism in the EU', Copenhagen:
March 19-20, 1998 <http://www.law.harward.edu/> (Visited on: September 16, 1999).

De l'Estang, B., 'France's Diplomatic Priorities: An Agenda for 2000', *Centre on the US and
France Roundtable Discussion*, (April 10, 2000) <http://www.brookings.org/>
(Visited on: November 11, 2000).

De l'Estang, F. B., *France, Germany and the New Europe*, remarks by François Bujon de
l'Estang, Ambassador of France to the US with German Ambassador Chrobog,
Washington: Meridian International Centre, March 16, 1999.

'Discussion with Mr. Friedbert Pflüger', *An American Institute for Contemporary German
Studies*, Washington: February 2, 2000 <http://www.aicgs.org/> (Visited on: June 20,
2000).

Fischer, J., address to the German Society for Foreign Affairs, 'The Self-Restrained of Power
Must be Maintained: Germany's Role and Objective in the Globalised World of the
21st Century', Berlin: June 8, 1998.

Fischer, J., 'Berlin's Foreign Policy', paper presented to the annual meeting of the German
Council on Foreign Relations, Frankfurt: Frankfurter Societäts, 2000.

'Franco-German Relations and European Integration: A Transatlantic Dialogue – Challenges for German and American Foreign Policy', *AICGS Conference Report*, US: The Johns Hopkins University, December 16, 1999.

'Gemeinsame Sicherheit und Zukunft der Bundeswehr', *Bericht der Komission an die Bundesregierung*, 23. Mai 2000.

Gordon, P. H., 'The Eternal French-American Quarrel: An Update', Conference on France and US in a New Century, *Centre on the US and France*, Washington, May 24, 2000. <http://www.brookings.org/fp/cusf/events> (Visited on: December 17, 2000).

Guerot, U., 'Prospects for Franco-German Relations after the German Elections: The New Look or New Deal?', US: Paul H. Nitze School for Advanced International Studies, The Johns Hopkins University <http://www.aicgs.org/After_the_1998_Election/ guerot2.htm> (Visited on: August 18, 2000).

'Guidelines adopted at the Franco-German Seminar of Ministers of Foreign Affairs', *Speeches and Statements – France/Germany/IGC/CFSP*, Freiburg im Breisgau, February 27, 1996 <http://www.info-france-usa.org/fsearch.htm> (Visited on: September 8, 1999).

Interview with Alain Richard, Minister of Defence, at the newspaper *Le Progrès* (excerpts) in Paris on March 25, 2000.

Interview with Charles Barry at Washington, 'France Sings a Different Tune in NATO', *The Tocqueville Connection, US-CREST*, June 05, 1997. Available at: <http://www.adetocqueville.com> (Visited on: January 10, 1999).

Janes, J., 'Back to the Future: The German-American Dialogue on Defence', *AICGS Issue Report*. Available at: http://www.aicgs.org/at_issue/ai_defense.shtml (Visited on: February 26, 2001).

Lankowski, C. and Serfaty, S. 'Europeanizing Security? NATO and an Integrating Europe',
    AICGS Research Report, US: The Johns Hopkins University, American Institute for
    Contemporary German Studies (AICGS) Research Report No. 9, 1999.

Le Gloannec, A. M., 'The Future of the Franco-German Relationship', *US-CREST's Franco-
    American Seminar Series*, April 16, 1998 <http://www.adetocqueville.com> (Visited
    on: January 1, 1999).

May, B., 'Domestic Political Chance and Foreign Policy: One Year "red-green" foreign
    policy in Germany' lecture at Norfolk University, USA: September 1999.

Moreau-Defarges, P., 'A French Perspective on the EU's IGC', *US-CREST's Franco-
    American Seminar Series*, October 31, 1996 <http://www.adetocqueville.com>
    (Visited on: January 11, 1999).

Parmentier, G., 'Madrid and Beyond: The New NATO', *US-CREST's Franco-American
    Seminar Series*, April 10, 1997 <http://www.adetocqueville.com> (Visited on: January
    11, 1999).

Paris Radio France Internationale, interview on 'Defence Minister Tells of EU's New Shape,
    Tasks' with the French Defence Minister, Alain Richard, at 19:30 a.m. (GMT),
    translated text, September 22, 2000.

Rede Bundeskanzler Gerhard Schröder vor dem Deutschen Bundestag (Auszug), Bonn: 5.
    Mai 1999, Presse- und Informationsamt der Bundesregierung, Nr.26, May 6, 1999.

Rede des Bundesministers der Verteidigung, Rudolf Scharping, anlässlich der 36. Münchner
    Konferenz für Sicherheitspolitik am 5. Februar 2000 in *Stichworte zur
    Sicherheitspolitik*, (Berlin: Presse- und Informationsamt der Bundesregierung, Nr.02,
    Februar 2000.

Reinhardt, K., 'Security and Stability in the Balkans: Germany's Contributions and
    Capabilities', *An AICGS Seminar*, Washington: June 21, 2000 <http://www.aicgs.org/
    events/2000/reinhardt_summary.html> (Visited on: July 3, 2000).

Richard, A., 'French-US Relations – A View from the Defence Side', *US-CREST's Franco-American Seminar Series*, April 29, 1998 <http://www.adetocqueville.com> (Visited on: January 11, 1999).

Schmidt, P., 'Germany, France and NATO', *Report presented in Stiftung Wissenschaft und Politik in Ebenhausen,* summarised by Rapporteur Maria R. Alongi, Ebenhausen: June 1994.

Speech by Mr. Alain Richard, Defence Minister of France, 'French Defence, NATO and Europe' at Centre for Strategic and International Studies, Washington: February 22, 2000.

Speech by Alain Richard, Defence Minister of France, on 'European Defence and the Transatlantic Link' at Georgetown University, Washington: February 23, 2000.

Speech by François Bujon De L'Estang, French Ambassador to the US, on 'France, Europe and the Transatlantic Partnership', US: Cornell University, September 29, 1997. <http://www.info-france-usa.org/fnews.htm> (Visited on: January 28, 2000).

Speech by François Bujon de l'Estang, French Ambassador to the US on 'The French-German Relations, Europe and the Transatlantic Partnership', Joint Conference with the French and German Ambassadors, US: University of Berkeley, February 26, 1998, and University of Stanford, February 27, 1998 <http://www.info-france-usa.org/fsearch.htm> (Visited on: August 30, 2000).

Speech by French President Jacques Chirac on 'A Responsible Europe in a Renewed Atlantic Alliance' before the Assembly of Atlantic Societies on October 19, 1999, in Strasbourg, France in *Internationale Politik*, Vol.1, July 14, 2000 <http://www.dgap.org/english/tip/tip2/chirac191099.html> (Visited on: July 14, 2000).

Speech by Jacques Chirac at the 'Meeting of the French Ambassadors' in Paris, on August 26, 1998. Available at: <http://www.info-france-usa.org> (Visited on: June 04, 2000).

Speech by Rudolf Scharping at an *American Institute for Contemporary German Studies Seminar*, Washington: September 5, 2000. <http://www.aicgs.org/events/2000/ scharping_summary.html> (Visited on: September 18, 2000).

Speech by Joschka Fischer at the general meeting of the German Society for Foreign Affairs, *German Information Centre*, Berlin: November 24, 1999.

Speech by Rudolf Scharping on 'Meeting the Challenges of the Future – Germany's Contribution to Peace and Security in and for Europe', *Centre for Strategic and International Studies*, Washington: November 23, 1998.

Speech by Secretary of Defence William S. Cohen, 'European Security and Defence Identity' at the 36th München Conference on Security Policy, 5 February 2000 in *Stichworte zur Sicherheitspolitik*, Berlin: Presse- und Informationsamt der Bundesregierung, Nr.02, Februar 2000.

Speech by the Secretary of State for Defence, Mr. Geoffrey Hoon (MP), at the 'European Defence Conference', (March 28, 2000). Available at: <www.mod.uk> (Visited on: November 14, 2001).

Speech by the Defence Secretary, Mr George Robertson, *Annual Dinner of the Society of British Aerospace Companies*, June 17, 1998. <http://www.fco.gov.uk/news/speechtext.asp?1183> (Visited on: August 1, 2000).

Statement of John R. Bolton, Senior Vice President (American Enterprise Institute), before the Committee on International Relations House of Representatives on the 'European Common Foreign, Security and Defence Policies – Implications for the US and the Atlantic Alliance', available at: <http://www.house.gov/international _relations/> (Visited on: November 17, 2000).

Szabo, S. F., 'Germany: Strategy and Defence at a Turning Point', *AICGS Academic Advisory Council Brief*, US: Johns Hopkins University. <http://aicgs.org/IssueBriefs/szabo.html> (Visited on: August 18, 2000).

Védrine, H., Foreign Affairs Minister of France, *interview given to the 'La Revue*

internationale et stratégique', Paris: April 11, 2001.

Vortrag 'Perspektiven deutscher Außen- und Sicherheitspolitik' von Staatssekretär Wolfgang

Ischinger beim 7. Aktuellen Forum zur Sicherheitspolitik der Bundesakademie für

Sicherheitspolitik für Chefredakteure am 27.01.1999, Bad Neuenahr.

'2. Deutsch-Französischen Dialog', *Saarbrücker Erklärung*, Saarbrücken: Mai 26/27, 2000.

'2ᵉ Dialogue franco-allemand – La France et l'Allemagne: partenaires économiques ou rivaux

en Europe et dans le monde?', *Compte rendu des débats*, Sarrebruck: du 26 au 27 mai

2000.

'3. Deutsch-Französischen Dialog', *Saarbrücker Erklärung*, Saarbrücken: 31 Mai-01 Juni,

2001.

'3. Deutsch-Französischen Dialog – Mit Sicherheit in die europäische Zukunft: Deutsch-

französische Perspectiven einer gemeinsamen Sicherheits – und Verteidigungspolitik',

Diskussionsbericht, Saarbrücken: 31 Mai-01 Juni, 2001.

www.ingramcontent.com/pod-product-compliance
Lightning Source LLC
Chambersburg PA
CBHW031821270326
41932CB00008B/503